Wilson's Creek . . . .

Civil War America . . . . . .

GARY W. GALLAGHER, EDITOR

William Garrett Piston
& Richard W. Hatcher III

Wilson's Creek

The Second
Battle of the
Civil War and
the Men Who
Fought It

The University of
North Carolina Press

Chapel Hill & London

Designed by April Leidig-Higgins

Set in Monotype Bulmer by Keystone Typesetting, Inc.

Manufactured in the United States of America

The paper in this book meets the guidelines for
permanence and durability of the Committee on
Production Guidelines for Book Longevity of the
Council on Library Resources.

Library of Congress Cataloging-in-Publication Data
Piston, William Garrett. Wilson's Creek: the second
battle of the Civil War and the men who fought it /
by William Garrett Piston and Richard W. Hatcher III.
p. cm.—(Civil War America)
Includes bibliographical references and index.
ISBN 0-8078-2515-8 (cloth: alk. paper)
1. Wilson's Creek, Battle of, 1861. 2. Soldiers—
United States—History—19th century. 3. United
States—History—Civil War, 1861–1865—Social
aspects. I. Hatcher, Richard W. II. Title.
III. Series.
E472.23.P57 2000   973.7'31—dc21   99-23239 CIP

A version of Chapter 18 appeared previously as
"Springfield Is a Vast Hospital," *Missouri Historical
Review* 93, no. 4 (July 1999), and is reprinted here with
permission of the journal.

04 03 02 01 00   5 4 3 2 1

For Nancy
and
For Mary and Ashton

Contents

Maps . . . .

Illustrations . . . .

In the earliest weeks of the American Civil War even the smallest military encounters, ones in which only a handful of casualties occurred, were dignified by the term "battle" in official reports and newspapers. Some of these encounters were of genuine if limited significance, such as the fight between the forces of James Longstreet and Israel B. Richardson at Blackburn's Ford on July 18, 1861, in northern Virginia. But the engagement that occurred three days later between the armies of P. G. T. Beauregard and Irvin McDowell near Manassas Junction is rightly considered the first battle of the Civil War. It marked the culmination of a major, large-scale campaign, the results of which were of great significance for both sides.

Combat occurred in Missouri prior to August 10, 1861, but, as in Virginia, the struggle that took place on that day at Wilson's Creek saw the culmination of large-scale operations. This campaign actually began before the one in Virginia, when on May 10 Union brigadier general Nathaniel Lyon captured the Missouri state militia forces at Camp Jackson in St. Louis. It ended on a blisteringly hot morning amid the oak hills and creek bottoms of southwestern Missouri when Lyon attacked the Southern forces threatening Springfield. There, at Wilson's Creek, Lyon either nobly sacrificed his life to save Missouri for the Union or paid for his crimes as the "Butcher of Camp Jackson," depending on whether one takes the Northern or Southern view. But regardless of one's perspective, the consequences of the fight (called variously the Battle of Wilson's Creek, Oak Hills, or Springfield) were of major significance for both sides. By this definition, Wilson's Creek, occurring twenty days after the fighting at Manassas, was the second battle of the Civil War.

Unlike the Eastern and Western theaters of the war, the Trans-Mississippi is terra incognita not only for most Civil War enthusiasts but for many scholars as well. Despite their significance, the battles fought west of the Mississippi have received only a fraction of the attention paid to Gettysburg, Chancellorsville, Shiloh, or Chickamauga. Wilson's Creek remains perhaps the least studied major battle of the war. The standard work is by Edwin C. Bearss, formerly chief historian for the National Park Service. Published in 1975 but never widely distributed, the 170 pages of *The Battle of Wilson's Creek* provide an excellent basic narrative of the fight but give very little context. Because his scope is deliberately limited, Bearss devotes minimal attention to either the campaign preceding it or the consequences of the battle. The most recent work on the engagement, William Riley Brooksher's misleadingly titled 1995 book, *Bloody Hill: The Civil War Battle of Wilson's Creek*, has the opposite focus. Primarily a summary of the first year of the Civil War in Missouri, this text allots only 40-odd pages of 278 to the fight itself. Indeed, Brooksher's narrative of the battle is only about half the length of Bearss's account. Moreover, both Bearss and Brooksher use only secondary sources in their studies.

Wilson's Creek is covered in a number of older but valuable works and in a group of recently published biographies. John McElroy, *The Struggle for Missouri* (1909), Jay Monaghan, *The Civil War on the Western Border, 1854–1865* (1955), Hans Christian Adamson, *Rebellion in Missouri, 1861: Nathaniel Lyon and His Army of the West* (1961), and William E. Parrish, *Turbulent Partnership: Missouri and the Union, 1861–1865* (1963), all provide excellent general accounts of the campaign and battle. Christopher Phillips, *Damned Yankee: The Life of General Nathaniel Lyon* (1990), Thomas W. Cutrer, *Ben McCulloch and the Frontier Military Tradition* (1993), and Stephen D. Engle, *Yankee Dutchman: The Life of Franz Sigel* (1993), give new insights into some of the most important figures involved in the struggle.

While we gratefully acknowledge our debt to previous students of Wilson's Creek, we choose a substantially different perspective. Much of our focus is admittedly traditional. We place the battle in the context of the larger strategic, or campaign-level, struggle that helped to determine whether Missouri would become a Confederate state or remain in the Union. We also provide a full tactical narrative of what occurred on the battlefield. In doing so, however, we include a substantial amount of primary source material not previously used in connection with the battle. Few private letters written by the soldiers survived, in part because relatively few were written to begin with. The number of troops engaged in the Battle of Wilson's Creek was not large. No one expected the conflict to be prolonged, and the military authorities consequently gave little attention to mail service until the fall of 1861. In addition, the loved ones of the soldiers of the Missouri State Guard were frequently behind enemy lines. Fortunately, the letters that did make it home, North or South, were often printed in local newspapers, as many editors maintained both official and unofficial correspondents among the soldiers. By reading each issue between April and November 1861 of every newspaper in Missouri, Texas, Louisiana, Arkansas, Iowa, and Kansas for which copies are now extant, we uncovered a substantial number of letters, most of which have never been used by historians. Because the war was new, these letters contain a wealth of detail on soldier life often absent from later writings. Combined with extant material located in archives, they paint a vivid portrait of the battle and the men who fought in it.

Our work provides a fuller social context than usually accompanies the history of a campaign or battle. To the degree that sources allow, we study the broad impact of events on the families of the soldiers and the families in whose neighborhoods these momentous events occurred. We tell the story of the common soldiers from the time they joined up through the battle and follow home many of the ninety-day troops who were discharged when their enlistments expired. This provides for a richer story and makes an important point. In his 1988 study *Soldiers Blue and Gray*, James I. Robertson Jr. states a commonly held belief, namely that although Civil War soldiers valued their individual companies, "their greatest allegiance was to their regiment."[1] Though accurate as a generalization regarding the entire course of the war, this statement needs significant modification. Our research demonstrates that among volunteers company-level identities were far stronger, and lasted much longer, than historians have previously acknowledged. Because of the manner in which troops were raised and the soldiers' determination to uphold the reputations of their hometowns, the Battle of Wilson's Creek did more than align South against North, slaveholders against abolitionists, and states' rights advocates against centralists. It also brought communities into confrontation, pitting Little Rock, Arkansas, against Olathe, Kansas. Shreveport, Louisiana, fought Mt. Pleasant, Iowa, and Rusk County, Texas, took on St. Louis, Missouri, with the honor of each self-consciously at stake. In one way or another, every village, town, city, and county that contributed troops to the struggle was affected by the experience.

We confirm the conclusions of a number of social historians, particularly Bertram Wyatt-Brown on the concept of honor, Gerald Linderman on the role of courage, and Reid Mitchell on the significance of community values. We do not disagree with the contention of Earl J. Hess and James McPherson that Civil War soldiers possessed deeply held ideological convictions that motivated and sustained them, but we argue that the soldiers' determination at the company level to uphold the honor of their hometowns deserves equal consideration as a motivating factor, at least during the first year of the war.[2]

By blending a traditional military narrative with substantial social analysis, our goal is to give the reader greater insight than would be achieved by either approach alone, to open a dual window into one of the most fascinating battles of the Civil War.

Acknowledgments . . . .

The authors have had the privilege and pleasure of working with numerous people whose generous assistance made this project possible. Existing friendships were strengthened and many new ones made. Along with these formal acknowledgments go also our warmest sentiments to family, friends, and colleagues.

The project benefited immeasurably from the support rendered by the personnel at the Wilson's Creek National Battlefield under the direction of Superintendent Malcolm Berg. Whether exploring the battlefield or utilizing the resources of the superb John K. Hulston Library, we always received a warm welcome and the kindest words of encouragement from one and all. Chief Ranger John Sutton and Seasonal Rangers Augustus "Gus" K. Klapp, Hayward Barnett, and Ken Elkins were all supportive of our efforts. Special thanks go to Ranger/Historian Jeff Patrick, who provided information and material time and time again. Former Seasonal Ranger Kip Lindberg, who is now Director of the Mine Creek State Historic Site, Pleasanton, Kansas, was an outstanding source of information on the Missouri State Guard. Former Ranger Lynn McFarland, who is currently Military History Instructor at the U.S. Army Maneuver Support Center, Fort Leonard Wood, Missouri, gave us the invaluable benefit of his many years of utilizing the history of the battle as a teaching tool.

We are grateful to Scott Price, Community Affairs Officer, Fort Riley, Kansas, and to Historian Arnold Schofield and Museum Technician Alan Chilton at Fort Scott National Historic Site, Fort Scott, Kansas. Their readiness to provide information on Kansas and the Kansas regiments was exceeded only by their enthusiasm for the project.

We thank Ranger Gary Smith, Fort Smith National Historic Site, Fort Smith, Arkansas, for providing information on the Arkansas State Troops; Cheryl Collins, Director, Riley County Historical Society, Manhattan, Kansas, for information on the Second Kansas Infantry; and Professor Earl J. Hess, Lincoln Memorial University, for supplying references to Missouri newspaper articles.

We owe a special debt to the archives, libraries, and other institutions whose resources we utilized. Robert P. Neumann, Director of the Greene County Archives, not only answered our requests but also searched through hundreds of documents on his own initiative to help us paint a picture of life in the Springfield region. Thomas P. Sweeney and Karen Sweeney, owners of "General Sweeny's: A Museum of Civil War History," near Republic, Missouri, gave us free access to their unsurpassed collection of photographs and artifacts. We are grateful for their support and permission to use material from the museum. We appreciate the help obtained from Carol J. Koenig, Rare Books Curator, Special Collections Division, U.S. Military Academy Library; Judith A. Sibley, Assistant Archivist, U.S. Military Academy Archives; William R. Erwin Jr., Senior Reference Librarian, Special Collections Library, Duke University; Douglas A. Harding, Park Ranger, Jefferson National Expansion Memorial Historic Site, St. Louis; Mary Elizabeth Sergent, Middleton, New York; Sudi Smoller, Peabody, Massachusetts; Michael E. Pilgrim, National Archives and Records Administration, Washington, D.C.; Virgil Dean, Kansas State Historical Society, Topeka; Richard J. Sommers, U.S. Army Military History Institute, Carlisle Barracks, Pennsylvania; and John Rutherford, Shepard Room, Springfield Public Library, Springfield, Missouri.

We also wish to acknowledge the assistance rendered by the staffs at the Library of Congress, Washington, D.C.; Texas State Library, Austin; Eastford Historical Society, Eastford, Connecticut; Connecticut State Library and Connecticut State Historical Society, Hartford; Hill College Research Center, Hillsboro, Texas; Missouri State Archives, Jefferson City; Arkansas History Commission, Little Rock; and Missouri Historical Society, St. Louis.

Thanks to the staffs in the special collections and archives divisions of the libraries connected with Louisiana State University, Baton Rouge; the University of North Carolina–Chapel Hill; the University of Missouri-Columbia; the University of Kansas-Lawrence; and Yale University, New Haven.

We thank Lynn Wolf Gentzler, Associate Editor of the *Missouri Historical Review*, for permission to reprint material that first appeared in the journal.

This project was facilitated in part by a sabbatical leave from Southwest Missouri State University. The steady encouragement and kind words from faculty colleagues have meant more than they can know. Special thanks to Worth Robert Miller for his friendship and countless favors over the years.

Well-wishers in Missouri and South Carolina are too numerous to mention individually, but their interest in the success of this project is deeply appreciated. Therefore a collective thanks to friends who are associated with Westminster Presbyterian Church, the Greene County Historical Society, the Civil War Round Table of the Ozarks, the Wilson's Creek National Battlefield Foundation, the National Park Service, the Sons of Union Veterans, the Sons of Confederate Veterans, the Military Order of the Stars and Bars, and the United Daughters of the Confederacy.

We gratefully acknowledge our debt to those who made working with the University of North Carolina Press a pleasure: David Perry, Editor-in-Chief; Ron Maner, Managing Editor; David VanHook, Assistant to the Editor-in-Chief; and Stevie Champion, Copyeditor. We thank Professor Gary W. Gallagher, University of Virginia, who encouraged this project from its inception and, as first reader for the Press, provided many helpful suggestions. We are equally grateful for the anonymous second reader's endorsement and constructive criticisms.

Above all others, the authors are indebted to family members whose patience and understanding made the project possible. We therefore express our love and thanks to our wives, Nancy Wall Piston and Mary Godburn Hatcher, and to daughter Amelia Ashton Hatcher.

William Garrett Piston
Springfield, Missouri

Richard W. Hatcher III
Charleston, South Carolina

Wilson's Creek . . . .

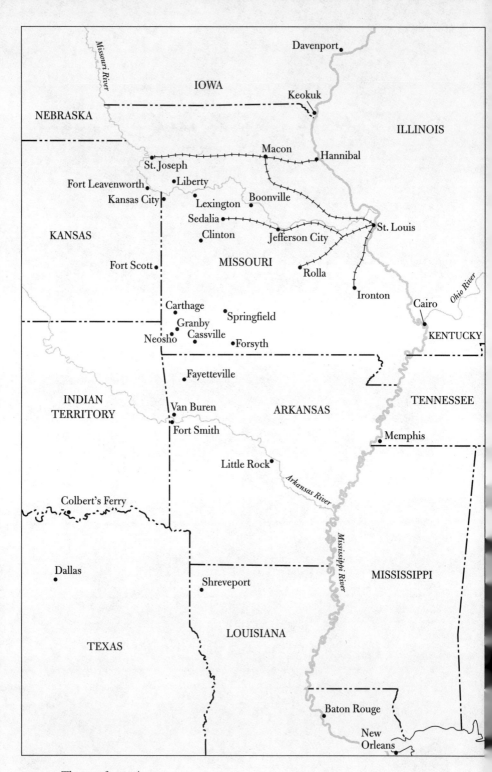

Theater of operations

Chapter 1 . . . .

Southern Rights Inviolate

illiam Watson had not come to America to fight. Born in a small village outside Glasgow, Scotland, he migrated to Louisiana in the 1850s. Thirty-five years old when secession fever swept over the Pelican State, he was a man of property and standing in Baton Rouge. Part owner in several businesses, with interests in coal, lumber, and steamboats, he had no direct stake in slavery. Thus he watched with concern as the convention meeting at the statehouse in January 1861 declared Louisiana an independent republic. The following month, Louisiana's representatives joined other Southerners in Montgomery, Alabama, to establish the Confederate States of America. Six months after that, Watson found himself staring into the muzzle of a twelve-pound howitzer as his regiment charged a Union battery at Wilson's Creek.[1]

Of the states that contributed troops to the battle, Louisiana was the first to take up arms. William Watson went to war not because he was a Louisianan, but because he was part of a Louisiana community that expected him to fight. The road he followed to war had many parallels, North as well as South. The war concerned the future of slavery in American society, but social forces also exerted extraordinary force on those confronting the crisis. These forces included community values, social expectations, and Victorian concepts of courage, honor, and masculinity. The actions of generals and the movements of troops are relatively easy to trace. But a battle can be fully understood only when one also considers both the motivations and the experiences of the common soldier. In the case of Wilson's Creek, the manner in which the troops were raised and organized, their past experiences and training (or lack thereof), their image of themselves, and their understanding of what they were doing directly influenced how the battle was fought and the soldiers' interpretation of what they accomplished by fighting it. It was the first summer of the war, and both men and values were tested.

One of the ways Watson had established himself as a bona fide member of the Baton Rouge community was by joining a company of volunteers. Replete with "tinsel and feathered hats," the Baton Rouge Volunteer Rifle Company, formed in November 1859 in response to John Brown's raid on Harpers Ferry, was typical of many such organizations that existed on the eve of the Civil War.[2] Supplementing the largely moribund militia guaranteed to the states under the Second Amendment of the Constitution, some volunteer companies were primarily social organizations, while others took military training seriously. However varied in character, they were the nuclei around which were formed the regiments that were to clash at Wilson's Creek.

The creation of those regiments is an interesting story. Studies of the coming of the Civil War naturally stress the divisions within American society, but an examination of how the opposing units came into being underscores their commonalities. The goal here is not to determine which of the Northerners who fought at Wilson's Creek were abolitionists, or how many of the Southerners who sacrificed their lives there were impelled more by states' rights than by a desire to perpetuate slavery. The goal is to understand these men in the context of their society and analyze their experiences, particularly in relation to their home communities. This is an inexact process, heavily dependent on the sources available for study, but it reveals much about the human condition.

Fort Sumter surrendered on April 14, 1861. In Washington Abraham Lincoln called for 75,000 volunteers, and from Montgomery Jefferson Davis soon made a similar appeal. But companies had been forming spontaneously throughout Louisiana since the state's secession in January. Government officials struggled to create the bureaucracy necessary to organize, arm, and sustain military forces adequate to meet the state's needs. They had at their disposal substantial captured Federal property, including the armaments from the U.S. arsenal at Baton Rouge. But while key points were quickly fortified, most of the nascent soldiers remained at home until the Fort Sumter crisis made war a reality. Thereafter, the pace of preparation accelerated.[3]

As soon as word of the bombardment at Charleston harbor reached Baton Rouge, Watson's unit commander, Captain William F. Tunnard, called his men together to consider the crisis. They voted to create a new company, the Pelican Rifles, and offer their services to either Governor Thomas O. Moore or the Confederate government, as needed. The local press reported that the Pelican Rifles were quite willing to go to "Sumter, to the d——l, or wherever the Governor might order them to go in defense of the state or the seven-stared Confederacy."[4]

Significantly, the vote was unanimous. Watson had "no sympathy with the secession movement," although he admitted irritation at the "shuffling and deceitful policy of Lincoln's cabinet." Yet he could have easily dissented, as a nonslaveholder, or abstained, as a foreigner by birth and a man past prime military age. Instead he voted to go, because, as he would recall, he sought adventure and feared that staying home would harm both his personal reputation and that of his business. As Baton Rouge had a population of less than 5,500, the positions taken by its leading citizens could not escape notice.[5]

As a Southerner by adoption, Watson may also have been influenced by the fact that the commander of the Pelican Rifles, William F. Tunnard, was a native of New Jersey. A carriage maker, Tunnard had moved to Baton Rouge with a family that included his son, William H. Tunnard. Twenty-four-year-old Willie, as the younger Tunnard was called, had also been born in New Jersey. He was educated at Kenyon College in Ohio, yet like his father he joined the local militia and supported the Confederacy. Tunnard was a sergeant in his father's company.[6]

Across the state prewar volunteer units placed advertisements in the local papers to bring their strength up to wartime levels of approximately one hundred men per company. New companies were formed as well, as plans solidified for a rendezvous of the volunteers in New Orleans. Governor Moore first issued a general appeal for men and later announced procedures for contacting the state adjutant general and enrolling for service. The public response was enthusiastic. For example, within a week of the governor's announcement, Shreveport raised two companies, one of which was Captain David Pierson's Winn Rifles. A third unit was also forming, marking a substantial contribution for a community of less than 2,200. Nearby Morehouse Parish, with only about 800 registered voters, put over 400 men in the field.[7]

Going to war was preeminently a collective experience, for it involved the entire community, not just the men who became soldiers. This can be demonstrated in Louisiana, but to an even greater extent in other states, particularly in the North, where much more historical information has survived. Throughout the 1861 campaign in Missouri, the soldiers of both sides possessed a community identity that remained as strong, if not stronger, than their allegiance to their respective regiment, state, or nation. "The soldiers of 1861," Reid Mitchell notes, "were volunteers— independent and rational citizens freely choosing to defend American ideals. In a sense, the soldiers' reputation would become the home folks' reputation as well."[8]

Watson's company required relatively little preparation. Already armed and uniformed in gray, the men lacked only camp equipage, yet the citizens competed with each other to see to their possible needs. Watson recalled that elderly men and women "furnished donations in money according to their circumstances," while "merchants and employers, whose employees and clerks would volunteer for service, made provision for their families or dependents by continuing their salaries during the time they volunteered for service." In many cases parish-level governments appropriated substantial sums of money to support both the enlistees and their families. No one expected a long war, and such encompassing community support left men of military age with few excuses for remaining at home. Women exerted direct social pressure on men to enlist. According to a young Louisiana volunteer, "The ladies will hardly recognize a young man that won't go and fight for his country. They say they are going to wait until the soldiers return to get husbands."[9]

Soldiers maintained a sense of community identity because most of them came from the same location and enlisted at the urging of some prominent member of their hometown, native village, or county of residence. One such man was Samuel M. Hyams, who despite nearly crippling arthritis raised the Pelican Rangers. A native of Charleston, South Carolina, he was a longtime resident of Louisiana, a planter and a lawyer, serving over the years as clerk of the district court at Natchitoches, register of the land office, sheriff, and deputy U.S. marshal. After the men were mustered into service, they elected Hyams captain. This was a typical pattern.[10]

Community pride ran high. The *Baton Rouge Daily Advocate* boasted that the city's Pelican Rifles was the first company raised outside of New Orleans to offer to serve anywhere in the Confederacy. When companies such as Tunnard's left for the New Orleans rendezvous, the local populace always turned out in force. Hundreds, for example, gathered at the wharf in Baton Rouge on April 29 to witness the arrival of the steamer *J. A. Cotton* to transport the city's volunteers downriver to the Crescent City. The mayor made a few patriotic remarks, and when the boat came into view at 11:00 A.M. cannons boomed, cheers rose, and a local band struck up martial tunes. With some confusion, amid tears and final hugs from loved ones pressing closely in, Tunnard's men finally got on board and the lines were cast off. Similar scenes were enacted across the state.[11]

Not surprisingly, conditions in New Orleans were chaotic and the process of mustering-in was somewhat haphazard. Watson recalled that they had no sooner docked on April 30 when Brigadier General Elisha L. Tracy boarded the vessel and without ceremony quickly swore them into Confederate service. Another soldier, however, remembered being sworn in on May 17, by a Lieutenant Pfiffer, and official records back up this date. Because Tracy at that time held only a state commission in the Louisiana militia, Watson probably confused two separate occurrences, as most troops were first sworn into state service and later mustered into the Confederacy's volunteer force, officially labeled the Provisional Army of the Confederate States.[12]

The arriving troops were quartered at Camp Walker, a training center that had been established at the Metairie Race Course, just upriver from New Orleans. As the racing season had ended on April 9, no sacrifice of entertainment was required of the local citizenry. Although placed on the highest ground in that area, the camp was surrounded by swamp and lacked both adequate shade and fresh water. The new recruits were immediately exposed to disease, the greatest killer of the Civil War. Although some 3,000 volunteers had assembled by the first week in May, only 425 tents were available. Men crowded into nearby buildings or simply sprawled in the mud, for it rained heavily. It was quite a change, wrote one volunteer, from "the comforts and luxuries of home-life."[13]

On May 11 the Pelican Rifles became part of the 1,037 men organized as the Third Louisiana Infantry. The regiment was composed of companies raised in Iberville, Morehouse, Winn, Natchitoches, Caddo, Carroll, Caldwell, and East Baton Rouge Parishes. The companies were immediately given letter designations, yet contemporary newspaper articles, wartime correspondence, and the soldiers' postwar recollections testify to the persistence of community identification. Although proud of their regiment, the men continued to think of themselves as the Iberville Grays, the Morehouse Guards, the Shreveport Rangers, or the Caldwell Guards. These designations, under which the volunteers had originally come together, were not nicknames but their primary identification, a bond with the home community. "Be assured, Mr. Editor," a soldier wrote the *Daily Advocate*, "that the Pelicans will never give Baton Rouge cause to be ashamed of her young first volunteer company." Hometown newspapers following the Third Louisiana and the other regiments, North and South, that participated in the 1861 campaign in Missouri continued to refer to "their" companies utilizing the local designations, such as Pelican Rifles, in preference to the regimental designation. They published soldiers' letters that reported rather graphically to the community the welfare and status of the hometown company, paying particular attention to the sick, listing them by name and describing their condition. When "Bob" wrote his hometown paper that "I must give the full meed of praise which is due our worthy Captain and his officers, for their kindnesses to their men," he was not engaging in idle flattery, but reassuring the homefolk of their fitness for command. "Under such officers," he continued, "the Pelicans are bound to make their mark." By extension, so would Baton Rouge.[14]

If anything, the Louisiana volunteers were overly sensitive about their reputation with the folks back home after departing for New Orleans. In May, the Pelican Rifles published statements in both the *Daily Advocate* and the *Weekly Gazette and Comet* of Baton Rouge to deny a rumor that they had been mistreated by the state authorities, were demoralized, and had threatened to desert. "We are perfectly satisfied and happy," the statement ran, "and wish no better name than that of the Pelican Rifles, which none of us will ever dishonor." Every member of the company signed the statement.[15]

Strong, if friendly, rivalries existed between the companies of the Third Louisiana, and these rivalries were based in no small part on community. George Heroman bragged about the Pelican Rifles to his mother: "When we passed through the city and whenever any visitors come here they always remark that our company is the best and the cleanest looking company on the grounds." But he was only echoing the opinion of his hometown paper. "Amid all the other companies which have formed in our State," ran one article in the *Daily Advocate*, "we will venture the assertion that this company can boast of as great a proportion of sterling worth—the real 'bone and sinew' of the country—as any other." Watson also believed that the Pelican Rifles were "the crack company of the regiment," noting that they worked to maintain their superiority over the others by proficiency in drill.[16]

Drill was important to the regiment's newly elected commander, Colonel Louis Hébert. Watson remembered Hébert as "something of a martinet," a man who "took pride in his military knowledge" and was "a stickler for military form and precision in everything." A forty-one-year-old native of Iberville Parish, Hébert had graduated from West Point in 1845 but resigned after only two years' service to help manage his family's sugar plantation.[17] Because sugar produced through slave labor resulted in great wealth for Louisiana planters, Hébert's reasons for backing secession might appear obvious. But who were the other men of the Third Louisiana and why did they enlist?

Unfortunately, detailed social studies exist for only a few Civil War regiments, and the Third is not one of them. We are left with the assessments made by the men themselves. Captain R. M. Hinson assured his wife that the Morehouse Guards—Company B—were "all high toned

Colonel Louis Hébert, Third
Louisiana Infantry (Library of
Congress)

gentlemen" whom he felt honored to lead. One hesitates to question
Hinson's laudatory appraisal, as he paid for the privilege of leading these
men by dying at Wilson's Creek. But the Morehouse Guards—indeed, all
the companies of the Third Louisiana—were probably a mixed lot. The
best description comes from Watson, who recalled that his company
contained planters and planters' sons, farmers, merchants and sons of
merchants, clerks, lawyers, engineers, carpenters, painters, compositors,
bricklayers, iron molders, gas fitters, sawmillers, gunsmiths, tailors, druggists, teachers, carriage makers, and cabinetmakers. Although most of
them were either natives of Louisiana or Southern-born, thirteen were
from Northern states; there were also men from Canada, England, Scotland, Ireland, and Germany. Watson calculated that the number "who
owned slaves, or were in any way connected with or interested in the
institution of slavery was 31; while the number who had no connection or
interest whatever in the institution of slavery was 55."[18]

The Third Louisiana went to war under a blue silk flag bearing the
state seal on one side and the words "Southern Rights Inviolate" on the
other.[19] Although the privilege of owning slaves was clearly among the
rights that Southerners were determined to defend, Watson was convinced that "very few" of the soldiers actually enlisted over "the question
of slavery." The "greatest number were motivated only by a determination

to resist Lincoln's proclamation." The Union president's call for 75,000 men—seven times the force Winfield Scott had marched into the Halls of Montezuma during the Mexican War—was seen by some as evidence of a Northern determination not merely to restore the Union but to subjugate the South entirely. A member of the Third Louisiana wrote, "The sustainers of the Lincoln Government sadly mistake the spirit, energy, and determination of the outraged and insulted people of the South if they suppose, for an instant, that we are to be intimidated by threats, or overawed by an appeal to arms." There were ardent Secessionists in the regiment, of course, such as Captain Theodore Johnson, of Iberville, the regimental quartermaster, who had been a member of Louisiana's secession convention. But there were also men like Captain David Pierson, a convention delegate who had voted against secession—one of only seventeen to do so. In a letter to his father Pierson took pains to explain why, having worked to preserve the Union, he raised a company of volunteers in Winn Parish for the Confederate army. Faced with the choice of fighting for or against the South, he chose the former. "I am not acting under any excitement whatever," Pierson wrote, "but have resolved to go after a calm and thoughtful deliberation as to the duties, responsibilities, and dangers which I am likely to encounter in the enterprise. Nor do I go to gratify an ambition as I believe some others do, but to assist as far as is in my power in the defense of our common country and homes which is [*sic*] threatened with invasion and humiliation." He was moved by a sense of community obligation as much as anything else: "I am young, ablebodied, and have a constitution that will bear me up under any hardships, and above all, there is no one left behind when I am gone to suffer for the necessities of life because of my absence. Hundreds have left their families and their infant helpless children and enlisted in their Country's service, and am I who have none of their dependents better than they?"[20]

Regardless of the volunteers' motives for enlisting, Camp Walker existed to transform them from individuals into members of disciplined military units. General Tracy established a rigorous training schedule, while Hébert, through his rigid enforcement of all rules, began to develop a reputation for exactitude, tempered by a genial manner and his obvious care for the men's welfare. Overall, the recruits responded well to instruction, although some in the Third, experiencing the "Europeanized" culture of New Orleans for the first time, could not resist its temptations. Watson recalled that men "who had always before been strictly sober in their habits were now to be seen reeling mad with drink," spouting obscenities and picking fights with their comrades.[21]

Such problems did not make Hébert's regiment different from the three thousand other volunteers at Camp Walker, and when on May 7 a military review was held on nearby Metairie Ridge, under the eyes of Governor Moore and a great crowd of the citizenry, the colonel had reason to feel proud. By now the Third was reasonably well equipped with tents, blankets, knapsacks, and canteens. Each of the regiment's separately raised companies wore uniforms manufactured by the folks in their hometowns. The cut and quality must have differed substantially, but apparently all of their uniforms were gray. Watson's company, now commanded by Captain John P. Vigilini, as Tunnard had been elected major, wore large brass belt buckles emblazoned with a Louisiana pelican. As a legacy of their prewar organization, the Pelicans of Baton Rouge carried Model 1855 Springfield rifles. Some companies of the Third carried Mexican War vintage Model 1841 "Mississippi" rifles, and the rest were issued smoothbore muskets, both percussion and flintlock.[22]

Back in camp, training continued. As each day passed the number of sick in Camp Walker increased. Governor Moore became so alarmed that he ordered Tracy to transfer all of the units except the Third Regiment to other locations. The Third was now ready for war, and most of the men eagerly anticipated orders that would dispatch them to Virginia. But those who read the New Orleans papers would have noted increasing coverage of events in Missouri. On May 16, the day before the Third was sworn into Confederate service, the *Daily Picayune* reported the massacre of civilians in St. Louis on May 10 by troops under a Union officer named Nathaniel Lyon. Succeeding articles painted a portrait of a state on the verge of civil war, as both pro- and anti-Secessionists forces rushed to arms.[23]

It thus was not a complete surprise when orders came for the Third to proceed to Fort Smith, Arkansas, to help defend the Confederacy's north-western boundary. Late in the afternoon of May 20 the regiment marched from Camp Walker to Canal Street, its progress marked by "one grand oration" from thousands of men, women, and children who lined the street, balconies, and rooftops to bid them farewell. At the river, the men crowded onto four steamers and the expedition got under way at 9:00 P.M. Progress up the Mississippi was slow, for they did not reach Baton Rouge until the following evening. Word of their coming had preceded them by telegraph, and the governor and a military band were ready to greet them. The city's own Pelican Rifles were the only troops allowed ashore, but their brief reunion with loved ones proved memorable. "The landing was packed to its utmost capacity," one soldier recalled, and "the scene that ensued beggars all description." When after half an hour of celebration the company reboarded and the vessels pulled away, fireworks shot up from the levee and burst over the river, bright flashes gleaming off the dark water. This was a final gift from "a large number of patriotic ladies who had collected for this purpose."[24]

The boats reached Vicksburg on May 23, but after a brief halt they continued north and finally turned west into the Arkansas River. Time passed slowly and the men, crowded together without proper facilities, washed their clothing by towing it behind the boats strung on fishing lines. On May 27 they reached Little Rock, where they were immediately caught up in the Confederacy's somewhat confused plans to defend Arkansas, secure the Indian Territory, and, if possible, assist Missouri.[25]

Because of the peculiar circumstances under which Arkansas left the Union, the state contributed two different types of forces to the Battle of Wilson's Creek. Some men were enlisted in the Confederate army, while others belonged to the Arkansas State Troops, the militia guaranteed to the state by the Confederate Constitution. These must not be confused with the prewar Arkansas state militia.

Although thoroughly Southern, Arkansas in 1861 was in many ways a frontier state. It possessed only a few miles of railroad, going nowhere in particular, and not until January of that year was the state capital connected with the rest of the nation by a telegraph running to Memphis, Tennessee. Governor Henry M. Rector favored secession, and he encouraged (some would even say he instigated) the unusual events that occurred at the Federal arsenal in Little Rock on February 6. These happenings involved, among others, the Totten Light Battery, Captain William E. Woodruff Jr., commanding.[26]

The Woodruff family name was "a household word all over Arkansas," thanks to the various newspaper enterprises and political activities of Woodruff's father, William Sr., who had moved to Arkansas in 1819. The younger Woodruff, born in 1831, absorbed Democratic party politics on his father's knee and culture from his father's extensive library. He graduated from Kentucky's Western Military Institute in 1852 and eventually studied law, opening a practice in Little Rock in 1859.[27]

When a volunteer artillery battery was organized at the state capital in 1860, Woodruff's social position and military training ensured his election as captain. The unit was christened the Totten Light Battery in honor of William Totten, a popular local physician. The name also honored his son, Captain James Totten, who arrived in Little Rock in November 1860 with sixty-five men of the Second U.S. Artillery to garrison the previously unmanned Federal arsenal. The captain had generously assisted the Arkansans in their artillery training.[28]

When in late January 1861 Little Rock's new telegraph line brought the news (false, as it later turned out) that reinforcements were on their way to the arsenal, prosecession volunteers poured into the capital. By the second week in February they numbered almost 5,000, and Governor Rector "intervened" by asking Totten to surrender before bloodshed occurred. Although the captain had dutifully prepared to defend the arsenal, he had no desire to harm the local populace, which contained many friends, much less fire on the battery bearing his family name. Failing to receive instructions from Washington, Totten announced that he would withdraw his forces to St. Louis.[29]

Totten had been born in Pittsburgh, Pennsylvania, but raised in Virginia, and most people assumed that if sectional differences led to war, he would side with the South. Indeed, when the captain and his men boarded a steamer for St. Louis, an almost carnival-like atmosphere prevailed. The ladies of Little Rock even presented a sword to the departing Union commander as a token of their esteem. No one could imagine that six months hence Totten would draw that same sword against the Totten Light Battery amid the hills of southwestern Missouri.[30]

More irony was in the making, as events in Arkansas soon precipitated another near clash between men who would later meet in deadly earnest at Wilson's Creek. A convention assembled in Little Rock in March to consider the state's position on secession but adjourned without taking action. After the firing on Fort Sumter in April, it reconvened and finally took Arkansas out of the Union on May 6. But even before secession occurred, Woodruff's battery and more than two hundred other volunteers were on the move to Fort Smith in the northwestern corner of the state, where a Federal garrison under Captain Samuel D. Sturgis guarded the border with the Indian Territory.[31]

Sturgis was a thirty-eight-year-old West Point graduate and native of Pennsylvania, and his garrison consisted of eighty-three men of Company E, First U.S. Cavalry. When word arrived that prosecession units were on their way upriver, he gathered as much government property as he could and decamped on the night of April 22. Although he moved west, his ultimate destination was Fort Leavenworth, Kansas. This had significant consequences for the forthcoming campaign in Missouri. It also brought Sturgis into what would be a most unhappy relationship with the Union volunteers even then organizing in Kansas.[32]

When Sturgis left, he was short one man, his erstwhile second-in-

Colonel James McQueen McIntosh, Second Arkansas Mounted Rifles (Archives and Special Collections, University of Arkansas at Little Rock)

command, Captain James M. McIntosh. A Florida native and West Point graduate now in his mid-thirties, McIntosh ended eight years of service by tendering his resignation. Having just received word of its acceptance, McIntosh was moving downriver on April 23 when he met the Totten Light Battery and the other volunteers traveling upstream on the *Lady Walton*. After advising them of conditions at the fort he departed, intending to go to Richmond to seek a Confederate commission. He did join the Confederate army, but circumstances kept him in Arkansas and eventually pitted him against Sturgis at Wilson's Creek.[33]

When the expedition found Fort Smith deserted, a garrison was established and Woodruff's men, together with most of the other volunteers, returned to Little Rock. There, after the state formally left the Union and joined the Confederacy, they became enmeshed in the general scramble to prepare for war. This was not done smoothly, as Governor Rector became involved in a bizarre struggle with the secession convention. Because of complex political rivalries in Arkansas, the convention continued to meet and attempted to keep military affairs out of the governor's hands. It set up a military board to raise forces and divided the state into two districts, assigning to command them men who were strong Unionists, barely reconciled to recent events.[34] Most prewar militia units, such as the Totten Light Battery, now joined the Arkansas State Troops.

The western district (or First Division) went to Nicholas Bartlett Pearce, a thirty-eight-year-old native of Kentucky. Nicknamed "Nota

Brigadier General Nicholas Bartlett Pearce, commander of the Arkansas State Troops (National Park Service)

Bene" Pearce by his classmates at West Point, he graduated in 1850 and served in the Seventh Infantry. He resigned in 1858 to follow business interests with his father-in-law at Osage Mills in northwestern Arkansas. As a brigadier general of Arkansas State Troops, Bart Pearce began recruiting men for the defense of the state, not the Confederacy. The state's leading Secessionists were outraged. But whatever his own views, Pearce was well aware of the shift in public opinion. Back in April he had been listening to a political speech at a pro-Union public meeting in Bentonville when a stage coach brought the news of Lincoln's call for volunteers to put down the rebellion. "The effect was wonderful—all was changed in a moment," he recalled. "What! Call on the Southern people to shoot down their neighbors . . . No, never."[35]

Pearce initially made his headquarters at Fort Smith but set up a training facility much farther north on Beatie's Prairie, a high point between Maysville and Harmony Springs. This site was christened Camp Walker. Together with Fort Smith and the state capital, it became a rallying point for volunteers, who arrived in large numbers, in varying degrees of preparation, some seeking service with the state and others eager to join the Confederate forces. Raised at the county level by community leaders following public meetings, they represented a cross section of the state. Although motivations for enlistments varied, popular sentiment can be measured by the resolutions that were adopted by the communities sponsoring the soldiers. These almost universally portrayed the Lincoln administration as "black abolitionists" and aggressors, citing the need for Arkansas to side with the other slave states in defense of liberty. The cause was personal and the crisis urgent. For example, on accepting a flag for his regiment, one colonel stated simply: "We are going to our Northern borders to battle for the rights and sacred honor of the fair and lovely daughters of our sunny South. If the enemy cross the line and invade your homes 'they will have to walk over our dead bodies.' "[36]

As in Louisiana, prewar volunteers companies in Arkansas formed a core around which larger units were organized. The Hempstead Rifles, an old militia unit commanded by John R. Gratiot, were the first to arrive at Camp Walker. Passing through Fayetteville en route, they received a flag from the local citizens. Reverend William Baxter, president of Arkansas College in Fayetteville, noted of the Hempstead Rifles that "their drill was perfect, their step and look that of veterans, their arms and uniforms all that could be desired." From Nashville in the same county came Joseph L. Neal's Davis Blues, sporting frock coats with eight rows of fancy trim and twenty-four buttons across the chest. In Van Buren, on the northern bank of the Arkansas River not far from Fort Smith, Captain H. Thomas Brown led the Frontier Guards, who represented "the flower of Van Buren chivalry." The local paper boasted that these men, "the very *elite* of the city—'gentlemen all,' " were the best drilled in the state. They were certainly among the better dressed. Raised back in January, they wore dark blue coats and sky blue pants that had been manufactured in Philadelphia. At the extreme of sartorial splendor, however, were the Centerpoint Rifles, under Captain John Arnold, a local physician. Thanks to the hard work of the ladies of Centerpoint, they wore matching checked shirts called hickory, adorned with five red stripes across the chest. Their blue trousers also had red stripes down the outside of each leg.[37]

Communities did everything they could to support "their" companies, whether they existed prior to the conflict or were newly organized. In some cases, the level of involvement was remarkable. Fort Smith, which had a population of only 1,529 in 1860, fielded five companies numbering more than eighty men each. According to the *Herald and New Elevator*, almost every adult male of military age in the community was under arms. A total of $2,000 was raised to support the men, and a subscription fund was started with the ambitious goal of supplying $1,000 per month to the families of the volunteers during their absence. Local women made uniforms for all five companies and for several other volunteer units that arrived in Fort Smith without them. The local paper noted proudly that "one widow lady, who makes her living by the needle, spent at least eight weeks in work for the soldiers, and that too, without pay."[38]

Although Unionist sentiment was strong in northwestern Arkansas, Captain Brown of Van Buren's Frontier Guards observed that defense was a great motivator. On May 2 he wrote his sister: "There is but *one voice* everywhere I have been, 'resistance till death, to the North.' There is a perfect upheaval of society; all classes are becoming aroused, and the merchant, the planter, the lawyer, and even *doctors* are enlisting." Enthusiasm was not as nearly universal as Brown indicated, but it was marked. Joining the enlistees at Camp Walker was an even older unit, Johnson County's Armstrong Cavalry, raised in October 1860. All seventy-three men in the unit were farmers, and all but one were Southern-born.[39]

The homogeneity of the Armstrong company was not unusual for units raised in rural areas. For example, the muster roll of Captain John R. Titsworth's company from Franklin County reveals many men with the same last names, suggesting that brothers and cousins frequently joined simultaneously. The oldest member in Titsworth's unit was Charles Ohaven, fifty-one, whose son Charles Jr. was at age eighteen among the youngest. In towns or villages, however, some ethnic diversity existed. Fort Smith's contributions included the Fort Smith Rifles, raised by James H. Sparks, editor of the *Herald and Times*, and Captain John G. Reid's Fort Smith Battery. But it was also home to a prewar unit, the nearly all-German Belle Pointe Guards. For dress parade they wore fancy frock coats with heavy gold epaulets and tall plumed shakos bearing the brass letters "BPG."[40] Van Buren had German enlistees too, among them a twenty-four-year-old Jewish immigrant from Baden named Baer who decided soldiering held more prospects than clerking at Alder's, a local clothing store.[41]

Woodruff's Totten Light Battery was not at Camp Walker, for it had returned to Fort Smith. Thanks to captured materiel and hard work, it was the best equipped and drilled unit of the Arkansas State Troops. Like many early war artillery units, the Tottens, as they called themselves, were fully armed with rifles and trained to fight as infantry if needed. But they soon gave their shoulder arms away in order to concentrate on their main function. The battery had two 6-pound bronze guns and two 12-pound howitzers, with caissons and full equipment.[42]

Woodruff's artillerists now sported gray jean uniforms trimmed in red, compliments of the ladies of Little Rock. These apparently replaced a prewar uniform of unknown type. The women of Little Rock sewed uniforms not only for eight companies raised locally, but for several other units stationed there as well. Such community-level support was as important for volunteers in Arkansas as it had been for those in Louisiana. General Pearce, struggling to acquire weapons and bring order out of chaos, was fully aware of the many contributions women made. "Our lovely women were as earnest, as patriotic, as any of the stronger sex," he recalled. He credited their "devotion and example" with "stimulating to exertion their dear ones, fathers, husbands, sons, and brothers." Others were also grateful for the efforts women made. The *Fort Smith Parallel* showered praise on the town's "patriotic ladies" for their "untiring perseverance" in equipping the local men for war. Some women were apparently not content with a supporting role. A soldier from Rocky Comfort boasted, "Our females are somewhat like the Spartan women, and wish to fight also in person."[43]

At the same time that Pearce was struggling to train his men at Camp Walker and the Third Louisiana was arriving in Little Rock, another portion of the forces that would fight for the South at Wilson's Creek was coming together in Texas. Texas contributed a single regiment of cavalry to the battle, but it also sent the state's most famous Texas Ranger, Ben McCulloch.

Texas had left the Union on February 1, 1861, reverting briefly to its status as an independent republic before joining the Confederacy. Because of the state's geographic position, defense against Native Americans was the most pressing concern, although in the northeastern counties along the Indian Territory, slaveholders feared a sudden descent of abolitionists from Kansas. This meant a busy spring for Ben McCulloch, who along with his brother Henry and John S. "Rip" Ford, was appointed a colonel in the Army of Texas, a force established by the secession convention to meet the state's military needs until a working government under the Confederacy was set up.[44]

McCulloch would command the Southern forces at Wilson's Creek, but were it not for a twist of fate he would have died at the Alamo. Born in Rutherford County, Tennessee, in 1811 and raised in the western portion of the state, where one of the family acquaintances was Congressman David Crockett, McCulloch had no schooling past the age of fourteen. Like his sometime mentor Crockett, Ben grew up in a frontier environment where he became a master of woods lore. He worked on the Mississippi and spent some time as a trapper, venturing as far west as Santa Fe, but did little of note before following Crockett to Texas in 1836. "Following" is the key word, for McCulloch missed an appointed rendezvous with Crockett, and although he rushed to catch up, he soon fell ill. By the time he recovered, Crockett was a martyr to the cause of Texas independence. McCulloch joined Sam Houston's army and participated

Brigadier General Ben McCulloch, commander of the Western Army (The collection of Dr. Tom and Karen Sweeney, General Sweeny's Museum, Republic, Missouri)

in the revenge at San Jacinto on April 21, displaying in this battle the bravery and aggressiveness for which he soon became famous.[45]

Whereas "Davy" Crockett's legend as a heroic frontiersman was largely created by Whig politicians and perpetuated by popular writers after his death, Ben McCulloch was the genuine article. He was the archetype of the long rider, strong and self-reliant, keeping his own counsel. One biographer described him as "a self-contradictory blend of the Victorian gentleman who drank sparingly, never indulged in the use of tobacco, treated ladies with utmost respect, and settled his personal quarrels by the rules of the *code duello*, and the southwestern brawler capable of smashing a chair over the head of an antagonist in the dining room of a Washington hotel."[46]

Following the Texas War for Independence McCulloch settled in Gonzales, working as a surveyor and serving in the legislature. More important, as a Texas Ranger he participated in a number of expeditions against Native Americans. When Texas was admitted to the Union in 1845, McCulloch was appointed a major general of the state militia, but he resigned to serve with Colonel John C. Hay's regiment in the Mexican War. He fought throughout the campaigns in northern Mexico, and General Zachary Taylor credited him with gathering vital intelligence that contributed to the American victory at Buena Vista on February 23, 1847.

Moreover, word of his exploits reached a national audience through the publication in 1850 of *The Scouting Expeditions of McCulloch's Texas Rangers*, a laudatory work by one of his subordinates.[47]

By the time this book was in press, McCulloch was in California. *"I am after money,"* he wrote frankly to his brother Henry as he departed for the gold fields, but there was more to it than that. Despite his many accomplishments, McCulloch was approaching forty and despaired of finding a wife. His features have been described as rugged and weather-beaten, but photographs suggest a man at least as handsome as his contemporaries. Yet McCulloch considered himself so *"confounded hard looking"* that without wealth he would be condemned to bachelorhood, "the last thing any sensible man would wish." Give a man money, he noted with sarcasm, and "you give him *everything*, at least it will answer all *purposes*," for it magically "renders the possessor witty or wise" in the eyes of society.[48]

But in California McCulloch found neither wealth nor wife. The state's rejection of slavery in 1850 dismayed him, for he and his family were strong supporters of that institution, and he disliked the Northerners who were flocking to the west coast. After two years as sheriff of Sacramento, he returned to Texas. For much of the next eight years he served as a Federal marshal in his adopted state. During this time he worked hard to obtain a commission as colonel of cavalry in the U.S. Army, believing that his practical experience and extensive private study of military texts outweighed the teachings of the Military Academy at West Point, an institution he despised. Yet when offered a lieutenant colonelcy in the Second Cavalry in March 1855, he refused to accept the number-two position. The episode reveals in McCulloch an inflexibility and inability to compromise that would have important consequences later on.[49]

An enthusiastic supporter of secession, McCulloch was instrumental in securing Federal property within Texas once the state left the Union, and he served as a commissioner to purchase additional arms. He was actually in New Orleans when he heard that Fort Sumter had been bombarded, and from there, too, he learned that he had been commissioned a Confederate brigadier general and assigned to a district "embracing the Indian Territory lying west of Arkansas and south of Kansas." He left immediately for Fort Smith, as that post's river communications and position made it the most logical place to gather Confederate forces. Although McCulloch's high rank certainly reflected great honor, when the old Texas Ranger arrived at Camp Walker in early May he may have wondered whether the war would be over before he could accomplish anything in such a "backwater" region.[50]

McCulloch expected troops from Texas to join him as speedily as possible, but there were delays. These were caused by logistical difficulties and the geographic distances involved, not by any lack of enthusiasm on the part of the people. In eastern Texas the key figure was Elkanah Greer, who received a Confederate colonel's commission and instructions to raise a regiment of cavalry. A native of Mississippi and a member of Jefferson Davis's regiment during the Mexican War, Greer had been a resident of Marshall, Texas, since 1851 and was now well known throughout the Lone Star State. An ardent Democrat and a fiery Secessionist, he led the Texas branch of the Knights of the Golden Circle, an organization that sought to add new slave territory to the Union. By local standards he was part of the planter elite, possessing twelve slaves and property worth $12,000. When on May 4 Governor Edward Clark called upon "every community" to raise a company "to repel the vandals of the north," prospective soldiers flocked to join Greer in Dallas.[51]

As in Louisiana and Arkansas, the companies that arrived had been raised at the community level. The *Marshall Texas Republican* reported an epidemic of "war fever" throughout the region. "It pervades all classes of society—young and old, male and female." Meetings at Marshall, the seat of Harrison County, resulted in plans to organize a unit. Two thousand dollars in public funds were appropriated for its support, while handbills were printed and distributed to drum up recruits. From his pulpit Reverend T. B. Wilson urged the young men of his congregation to enlist, proclaiming: "In the name of God I say fight for such sacred rights. Fight for the principles and institutions bequeathed to you by the blood of revolutionary sires."[52]

As the Marshall company began filling its ranks, it was joined by another raised at Jonesville in the northern portion of the county. The two units eventually merged, elected Thomas W. Winston captain, and adopted the name Texas Hunters. Courtesy of the women of Harrison County, they wore cadet gray uniforms and bore an elaborate silk banner, one side of which was emblazoned with the words "Texas Hunters" above a painted hunting scene; the other side was a version of the Confederate national flag. With Colt's revolving rifles, they were probably the best-armed unit in the state at that time.[53]

South of Marshall, across the Sabine River in Rusk County, a company was organized at Henderson. Its ranks included a young music teacher, Douglas John Cater. Although a relatively new resident of the community, he rushed to join the "leading citizens" of his adopted town in defending Texas against the "Black Republicans." Cater was appointed bugler, although he took along his violin so that he and another musician, Jim Armstrong, could entertain the men. The Rusk County Cavalry, as the recruits called themselves, went off to war nattily attired. Although their trousers were plain brown jeans, they wore matching black wool coats and vests and tall black boots. Cater added a white shirt and black silk cravat to his ensemble. "It looked well enough," he recalled, "but was very hot to wear in the summer."[54]

In all, ten companies assembled in Dallas, some in uniform and some in civilian clothes. Because Greer expected to assist McCulloch in defending the border region, he called his regiment the South Kansas–Texas Cavalry, but for the moment the men's real identity lay at the company and community level. Literally emblematic of this fact were ten flags manufactured by the ladies of Dallas, bearing not only each company's new letter designation but its "real" name as well. The Cypress Guards, Lone Star Defenders, Ed Clark Invincibles, Smith County Cavalry, Wigfall Cavalry, and Dead Shot Rangers had been raised at the villages, post offices, and county courthouses throughout eastern Texas. Local support was crucial at the beginning, and it remained so during the early part of the war. With pledges of lump sums up to $10,000, or monthly supports in the range of $200, the homefolk committed themselves to the soldiers' welfare. This was appropriate, as these men were, the *Dallas Herald* boasted, the "very flower of the land—the chivalry, 'the bone and sinew' of the country . . . engaged in the holy cause of defending their rights and liberties."[55]

Thanks to the exhaustive scholarship of Douglas Hale, more is known about the composition of Greer's regiment than any other unit that fought at Wilson's Creek. The men were overwhelmingly Southern by birth, but they were not average Southerners. "Considered as a whole," Hale writes, "the officers and men of the regiment came disproportionately from the wealthier classes in their society." The elected company captains "were men of mature years and prominent leaders in their communities." All of them owned slaves and on average possessed more than three times the wealth of the enlisted men of the regiment. Two-thirds of the enlisted men, however, also owned slaves—almost exactly the reverse of Confederate enlisted personnel nationally. With the planter and professional classes disproportionately represented in the ranks, their educational level was high. Only 14 percent of the common soldiers came from "the ranks of the poor." Their average age was twenty-three, but Private Nelson Walling was sixty-three and thirteen-year-old Walton Ector accompanied his father Matthew. The elder Ector was appointed regimental adjutant. His reasons for taking his son with him to war are unknown.[56]

Clearly the liberties these Texans gathered to defend included the right to own slaves. Indeed, they took their slaves to war with them. The record of these African American participants is almost entirely lost. Among the slaves accompanying the Texas Hunters, however, was Ned Buchanan, who not only was at Wilson's Creek but also "served" until the end of the Civil War. He owned a farm following the conflict and attended reunions of Confederate veterans.[57]

Greer's men formed many attachments with the citizens of Dallas, then a community of fewer than eight hundred people. Local merchants charged fair prices, and the women of the city gave the regiment a Confederate flag. But Greer fumed at the slow pace of organization. As his men camped in and around the town, he struggled to assemble wagon-loads of supplies and hired Mexican Americans as teamsters. Many of his men had arrived without weapons, and it seemed like a promised supply from San Antonio would never appear. Meanwhile, as May ended and June began, news of events in Missouri gradually reached Texas. From the Southern point of view, the news could hardly have been more alarming.[58]

Fan the Fire of Enthusiasm

Franz Sigel came to America to escape war. Like William Watson, Sigel fought in 1861 because he was part of a community, in this case St. Louis, Missouri. But in addition to his patriotic motivations, he hoped that his participation would win greater community acceptance for himself and other German Americans. His experiences in St. Louis marked the beginning of the campaign that culminated on August 10 at Wilson's Creek. They also reveal the significant role ethnicity played at the community level in shaping the forces that fought the battle.

Sigel was born in Baden, Germany, in 1824. A graduate of the military academy at Karlsruhe, he resigned from the German army after brief service but eventually participated in the democratic revolutions that swept his homeland beginning in 1848. He led troops in several engagements against great odds and under very difficult circumstances, proving to be a courageous but not particularly talented commander. A recent biography concludes that "Sigel's strength did not lie in a spirited and firm grasp of momentary military situations." Nevertheless, he won a considerable reputation.[1]

Sigel immigrated to the United States in 1852 and eventually settled with his family in St. Louis (where half the population was foreign-born by 1860), teaching at the Deutsches Institut. A keen intellectual who spoke five languages, he was soon appointed a district superintendent in the public school system and was widely recognized as a leader of the city's large German American population. He was also heavily involved in the local Turner Society, a fact that proved highly significant in 1861.[2]

The Turners played a crucial role at Wilson's Creek. The name was an Americanization of Turnverein, an organization founded in Berlin, in

Colonel Franz Sigel, Third Missouri Infantry (The collection of Dr. Tom and Karen Sweeney, General Sweeny's Museum, Republic, Missouri)

1811, devoted largely to physical fitness. When Germans emigrated in large numbers following the failed revolutions of 1848, they established Turnverein in metropolitan areas across America. In addition to gymnastics, a typical Turner Society included a chess club, literary study group, choir, and fencing team. The St. Louis Turnverein was established in 1850. It was not overtly political, but Germans made up the largest ethnic group in St. Louis, a city of 200,000. Although most were Democrats, a slowly increasing number supported the Republican Party following its creation in 1854.[3]

The St. Louis Turners had their own rifle company, which exercised weekly at Turner Hall on the corner of Tenth and Walnut Streets. They participated in Prussian drill competitions and target practice with Turner companies in other cities. Sigel lectured them on military tactics and in the fall of 1860 convinced them to switch to the drill manual used by the U.S. Army. In November 1860, the same week that Abraham Lincoln was elected president, the society made military training obligatory for all of its 500-odd members. A week after Lincoln's inauguration in March 1861, the Turners barricaded the doors and windows of their meeting hall with sandbags and began stockpiling arms. If the Federal government needed them to defend their adopted country, they intended to be ready.[4]

At Wilson's Creek the Turners would retain a strong community identity because, among other things, they were playing out the final scene of a community-level struggle that began in the streets of St. Louis and ended in the hills of southwestern Missouri. The city had a long history of volunteer militia companies, including the St. Louis Grays (organized in 1832), Boone Guards (1832), Native American Rangers (1841), Washington Blues (1857), Montgomery Guards (1843), and Washington Guards (1854). The two last-named companies were composed almost exclusively of Irish Americans serving with the city's volunteer fire companies. Some of these units fought in the Mexican War, and many of them were called out to restore order during ethnic riots that plagued the city during the 1850s. By the eve of the Civil War, some St. Louis units strongly identified with secession and made no secret of their anti-German sentiments. The result was "xenophobic hostility."[5] Added to this ferment, beginning in 1860, were a diverse host of "Union Clubs," some armed and uniformed, which marched and paraded in opposition to secession. Largest and best organized of these were the St. Louis Wide-Awakes, the local branch of a Republican organization that by 1860 had become overtly paramilitary in character.[6]

The ethnic tensions and political rivalries that Sigel witnessed in St. Louis occurred within a wider context. Claiborne Fox Jackson, the Democrat recently elected governor of Missouri, headed a state distinctly Southern in character but undergoing rapid changes. Slavery was largely concentrated in the Missouri River valley, and slaves made up only a little more than 10 percent of the population, but, though in the minority, white Missourians holding slaves were determined to keep them. With free states adjacent to the north and east, Missourians had waged a vicious guerrilla war with Kansans between 1854 and 1856 in an ultimately unsuccessful attempt to establish a proslavery government in the neighboring territory to the west.[7]

It was hardly surprising that secession fever ran high in the Missouri River valley, where slave-produced crops were exported downriver and economic interests combined with culture to link the local populace to the rest of the South. However, support for the Union ran strong in the more economically independent Ozarks mountain region south of the river. In urban areas such as St. Louis, Jefferson City, and Kansas City, the population was divided. But recently established railroads linked the state to neighboring Illinois and provided connections with the rest of the North. These ties were strengthened by a tremendous number of Northern-born and foreign-born people who went to Missouri during the 1850s, enough to give them parity with those of Southern birth by 1860. Missouri society was both diverse and complex.[8]

While Sigel and the Turners prepared for war, Governor Jackson schemed to take Missouri out of the Union, whether the majority of Missourians wanted to leave or not. Jackson was born in Kentucky but had resided in Missouri since his early manhood. He briefly pursued a career in business, but after his election to the state legislature in 1836 he made politics his career. A longtime advocate of the expansion of slavery, he was bitterly disappointed when in March 1861 a convention that had initially assembled at the state capital, Jefferson City, but then moved to better quarters in St. Louis, rejected secession. The convention's action reflected the people's widespread ambivalence and hope for compromise. But when Lincoln called for volunteers in April following the surrender of Fort Sumter, many Missourians of Southern heritage endorsed Governor Jackson's sharp reply, which rejected coercion of the seceded states as "illegal, unconstitutional, and revolutionary in its object, inhuman and diabolical." Missouri, Jackson asserted, would not furnish a single man "to carry on any such unholy crusade."[9]

Within days, meetings were held in cities and towns across the state, and Home Guard units organized spontaneously. For example, the citizens of Richmond, a small town near Kansas City, adopted a resolution approving and endorsing Jackson's refusal to "furnish troops for the purpose of coercing or subjugating our sister Southern States." Although they condemned secession, if "reduced to the necessity of engaging in the present war" the men of Richmond pledged to "cooperate with our sister Slave States." But citizens in the area were hardly united concerning the proper course. Many counseled neutrality. In a letter to the local paper E. M. Samuel warned that Missouri must not take sides. "To go either way, *exclusively*, is *annihilation*," he wrote.[10]

Some Missourians were genuinely neutral and only wanted to protect themselves. Such a stance was reflected in the rules adopted by the Huntsville Home Guard. These declared that the company "is intended not to make any aggression on the rights of any community or country, but is intended to secure our own homes, and the homes and firesides of our community from lawless mobs, or any insurrection or treason in our midst." Most Home Guard units, however, were conspicuously pro-Union or pro-Secession, despite claims that self-defense was their only motive for organizing. The citizens of Hardin adopted resolutions defending their "Southern Rights," whereas at Elk Horn the men who met to consider their options received a Confederate flag manufactured by the local women. But Springfield, Rolla, West Plains, Carthage, and a host of towns across the state were so divided in sentiment that competing military organizations were raised. In Johnson County, the pro- and antisecession companies actually drilled together, fully aware that if war came they might face each other in battle. "Men who were fighting for principle and what they believed to be right could do this," a participant explained.[11]

In St. Louis events soon took an extraordinary turn, bringing together within a few weeks a group of men who virtually embodied the Union cause in Missouri. Most of them would fight at Wilson's Creek. First Lieutenant John M. Schofield was on an extended leave of absence from the army, teaching natural philosophy at Washington University in St. Louis, when he received a letter from the secretary of war appointing him the mustering officer in Missouri for "the troops called out by the President's proclamation." A New York native raised in Illinois, Schofield had graduated from West Point in 1853. Twenty-nine and balding rapidly, his pudgy features gave him a somewhat jovial and cherubic appearance, despite a formidable beard. Schofield approached Governor Jackson for the men, as under the Constitution the sole way the president could raise a military force without congressional authorization was by calling the state militia into Federal service. The Missouri governor, of course, made no reply, having already spurned Lincoln's call.[12]

The need for pro-Union troops in St. Louis was acute, as the city was the site of the largest Federal arsenal in the slave states. The walls of this three-story building on the banks of the Mississippi contained "sixty thousand muskets, ninety thousand pounds of powder, one-and-a-half million ball cartridges, forty field pieces, siege guns, and machinery for the manufacture of arms." These were guarded by fewer than one hundred enlisted men, but also by one "Damned Yankee," Nathaniel Lyon, an infantry captain recently transferred from Kansas.[13]

Lyon would lead the Northern forces at Wilson's Creek, die on the field of battle, and become one of the North's first martyrs—the man who "saved Missouri for the Union." His role as savior so dominates postwar accounts, and even modern histories, that the story of Wilson's Creek has almost become subordinated to the story of Nathaniel Lyon, with little room for the other players, particularly the common soldiers. Fortunately, recent scholarship presents a balanced view, detailing the negative as well as the positive impact of this complex man on the war in Missouri.

Lyon was born in 1818 in Ashford, Connecticut, inheriting from his family a temper "that often exploded with surprising fury beyond all sense of reason." Well educated in local schools, he attended West Point, graduated in 1841, and participated in the closing stages of the Second Seminole War. He did not see combat, however, until the Mexican War, when he served with the Second U.S. Infantry under General Winfield

Scott. There his creditable conduct earned him promotion to brevet captain.[14]

Lyon's operations against Native Americans and Mexicans gave him practical experience in the conduct of war that would later prove invaluable. But his reaction to his superiors during this time is particularly revealing. He found his battleless forays against the Seminoles in the Florida swamps frustrating, as they seemed to do nothing to bring the conflict to an end. Similarly, during the Mexican War he privately criticized his superiors for not pressing their attacks with sufficient vigor and for not following up on their victories. He was livid when Scott paused for negotiations with the enemy during the American army's march on Mexico City, believing anything short of "total victory would be a travesty." In 1850 Lyon led an attack on a village of Native Americans in California. He not only defeated the warriors, he also massacred the women and children, virtually exterminating the group.[15] Complete destruction of the enemy seemed to be Lyon's only definition of victory, a fact that had significant consequences for Missouri in 1861.

Lyon had an aggressive personality that combined with an obsessive sense of duty to make him a true martinet. U.S. Army regulations sanctioned punishments that appear shocking by modern standards, but Lyon went well beyond his contemporaries in dealing with miscreants. When enforcing discipline he was a sadist. In 1842, during one of his first command assignments, a drunken sergeant protested one of his orders. Lyon lost his temper and beat the man repeatedly with the flat of his sword, drawing blood. Shortly thereafter he had the man bound and gagged for an hour. Lyon was subsequently court-martialed, and because his actions were judged to have become personal, going beyond the enforcement of discipline, he was suspended from duty for five months. He did not change his behavior, however. Following the Mexican War, while serving in Kansas, Lyon's propensity for inflicting the most severe punishments for even minor infractions won him a reputation as "the most tyrannical officer in the Army." He possessed "a nearly psychopathic appetite for inflicting pain."[16]

Given Lyon's personality and obsessions, anyone well acquainted with the new officer at the St. Louis arsenal in 1861 might have considered him particularly ill-suited to cooperate in an emergency with imperfectly disciplined Unionist volunteers, such as the Turners, to defend Federal property against Secessionists. But Lyon was not alone. He had the help of Missouri congressman Francis P. Blair Jr. The Blair family had roots in Kentucky and some of the Blairs had owned slaves, but they were prominent Unionists nevertheless. Blair's father, Frank Sr., was one of the

Brigadier General Nathaniel Lyon, commander of the Army of the West (The collection of Dr. Tom and Karen Sweeney, General Sweeny's Museum, Republic, Missouri)

founders of the Republican Party, and his brother, Montgomery, became Lincoln's postmaster general. During the 1860 presidential election, Frank Blair Jr. successfully courted many of the St. Louis Germans, including Sigel, for the Republican Party, and thereafter he assisted the Turnverein in obtaining additional firearms. In the spring of 1861 he helped establish a Committee of Public Safety and cooperated with Sigel to maintain a force of Unionists capable of responding rapidly to any crisis.[17]

Blair was a close friend to Lincoln and kept him informed of conditions in Missouri. It was due to Blair's influence that Lyon had arrived in February with reinforcements for the virtually unmanned arsenal and that Lyon soon received command of the post. Blair connived to have General William S. Harney, who commanded the army's vast Department of the West from a headquarters in St. Louis, called to Washington. Harney was a Southerner whom Blair wrongly suspected of disloyalty and wanted out of the way. Harney's temporary absence gave Blair, Lyon, and Sigel, who worked together to train Unionists throughout the city, virtually a free hand when Lincoln's call for volunteers precipitated a crisis in Missouri.[18]

On April 20 Secessionists seized the Missouri Depot, a small Federal arsenal four miles outside of Liberty, in northwestern Missouri. Usually called the Liberty Arsenal, it contained four antiquated pieces of artillery and about 1,500 small arms. Fearing that the St. Louis arsenal might be attacked next, Blair and Lyon decided to cut through red tape. Near midnight on April 21, in response to their repeated telegraphic requests to Washington, Lyon received instructions to "arm the loyal citizens, to protect the public property and execute the laws." The first enlistees were three hundred members of the Turnverein trained by Sigel.[19]

German Americans who were not members of the Turners also responded eagerly. John T. Buegel, a native of Mecklenberg who worked as a builder, felt such hostility from the pro-Secessionist elements in St. Louis that he feared for his safety. He therefore accompanied a friend to a recruitment meeting held on April 22 at the corner of Second and Elm Streets. Buegel recalled:

> Having arrived there we found to our great surprise that the large hall was full of young, sturdy Germans. Of course, a good lunch with fine beer was not lacking. Everything gratis. Since we Germans at that time were looked upon as belonging to an unworthy nation, and Americans, old and young, looked upon us with contempt and disdain, we decided, after having listened to some speeches, to sell our skins as dearly as possible. . . . Immediately five companies were formed which were to constitute a part of the Third Regiment of Missouri Volunteer Infantry to be commanded by Colonel Franz Sigel.[20]

By April 27 Lyon had 2,100 men under arms. Two weeks later more than twice that number had been supplied with weapons and sworn into Federal service by Lieutenant Schofield, who was himself elected major of the First Missouri Infantry. The president's orders to Lyon directly violated the Constitution, which reserves to Congress the right to expand the armed forces.[21] But Lincoln deliberately abstained from calling Congress into session to ask for authorization. Lyon did not care, as his thinking on the crisis was straightforward. Slavery was evil because slaveholders threatened secession. Secession was treason and treason must be punished. Moreover, Lyon saw himself as God's special instrument, chosen to inflict the severest possible punishment on Secessionists.[22]

Over the course of his life, Lyon had developed unorthodox religious views that shocked his colleagues and caused them to question his sanity. Rejecting Christianity, he came to believe that "God's will could be exerted only by those rare individuals who not only possessed the perspicacity to unfetter themselves from the obsequious tenets of their faith and to develop a true relationship with him, but who also wielded enough power among men to mete out his justice." In place of Christ, Lyon worshiped the West Point trinity of Duty, Honor, and Country. Anyone who fell short of his own extreme standards of devotion to nationalism was a target of Lyon's wrath.[23]

Lyon was a man of "strong convictions and unyielding purpose," his manner "quick and nervous, his keen eyes penetrating, at times blazing fiercely." He did not consider himself to be an abolitionist, but during his service at various posts in the Kansas Territory from 1854 to 1861 he developed such an intense hatred for slaveholders that at times he seemed to welcome a violent breakup of the Union. As a witness to "Bleeding Kansas" and the atrocities of the "border ruffians," he had reason to despise Missouri slaveholders above all others. By 1855 Lyon had concluded that "the aggressions of the pro-slavery men will not be checked till a lesson has been taught them in letters of fire and blood." Nor was he concerned with the local scene alone. That same year he wrote a friend, "I despair of living peaceably with our Southern brethren . . . I foresee ultimate sectional strife, which I do not care to delay." In 1856 he joined the Republican Party, supporting it with tremendous enthusiasm.[24]

Lyon's attitude and prior experiences directly shaped his conduct in St. Louis, setting in motion a train of events that led to Wilson's Creek. Long anticipating a national crisis, he did not hesitate to take action or assume responsibility. But at the same time Lyon was arming and organizing Unionists, Claiborne Jackson continued to work for secession. The Missouri governor, however, gave the appearance in public of staying within the boundaries of the state and national constitutions. As allowed by law, Jackson ordered the Volunteer Militia of Missouri to assemble in their respective districts for six days of training. This force, created by the Militia Act of 1858, was not the county-based militia existing under the state constitution, but, as the name suggests, a collection of volunteer companies. Most states possessed such volunteers units, and they were often more social than military in character. In Missouri, on the other hand, as a result of the border troubles with Kansas dating to 1854, many of the volunteers had significant military experience. The northeastern units of the Volunteer Militia gathered on May 6 at the outskirts of St. Louis. Two regiments of infantry, three troops of cavalry, and an artillery battery established a tent city at Lindell Grove, naming it Camp Jackson in the governor's honor.[25]

Despite regimental structures, these militiamen's primary identity lay at the company level, reflecting their community orientation. Long-established units like the St. Louis Grays and the Washington Blues, neatly uniformed in those colors, mingled with more recently raised companies in civilian garb, such as the Southern Guards and Dixie Guards. Two companies were named after Governor Jackson, and three were simply called Missouri Guards or Missouri Videttes. Captain Joseph Kelly's Washington Blues and Captain Philip Coyne's Emmett Guards were overwhelmingly Irish, traditional rivals of the city's Germans.[26]

Although the Missouri militiamen were legally assembled, the majority of them clearly favored secession. The Stars and Stripes flew over the camp, but Confederate banners were also displayed openly, for Jackson had used his patronage to commission officers and call up units sharing his sentiments. The governor and Brigadier General Daniel M. Frost, who commanded the encampment, hoped that the militia could seize the Federal arsenal. In fact, unknown to the public at that time, Jackson had already requested arms from the Confederate government. On May 8 two pieces of artillery arrived in St. Louis from Baton Rouge, disguised in packing crates marked "marble." These were brought to the camp, but they were never assembled and there was no opportunity to use them. Frost had just under nine hundred men, whereas Lyon now had nearly eight thousand and had fortified the arsenal. The *St. Louis Daily Missouri Democrat*, a staunchly pro-Union paper, assured its readers of the impotence of the state militia in the face of Lyon's thorough preparations. With nothing to do but drill until their muster period expired on May 11, Frost's men relaxed. Visitors flocked to the camp, and a carnival-like atmosphere prevailed.[27]

Lyon kept well informed of the happenings at Lindell Grove, including Frost's receipt of arms from the Confederacy. By some accounts he even passed through Camp Jackson in a carriage, disguised as Frank Blair's aged, blind mother-in-law. Although a heavy veil concealed his face and beard, Lyon took no chances, hiding a brace of revolvers beneath a lap robe. As he had already shipped all of the surplus arms from the arsenal to safety in Illinois, the real danger from Lyon's perspective was that the pro-Secessionist Missourians might disperse peaceably on May 11 before he could inflict on them the punishment that traitors deserved and that he alone was divinely sanctioned to administer. The force at his disposal to quash the Secessionists was formidable. He had five regiments of infantry and a company of artillery, enlisted for ninety days. These he declared by fiat to be the only legal militia representing the state of Missouri, and he modestly allowed the colonels he appointed to elect him brigadier general. Lincoln not only sanctioned Lyon's action, he authorized the unconstitutional creation in Missouri of a U.S. Reserve Corps, which Lyon promptly filled with five additional regiments of infantry.[28]

The majority of these men were German Americans. Although Frank Blair led the First Missouri Infantry, seven of Lyon's remaining nine infantry colonels were of German birth or ancestry, with the nativity of the

Captain Thomas William Sweeny, Second U.S. Infantry (The collection of Dr. Tom and Karen Sweeney, General Sweeny's Museum, Republic, Missouri)

enlisted men in like proportion. Many regimental and company officers were "Forty-Eighters," refugees from Europe with combat experience. Besides Sigel, who led the Third Missouri, they included Heinrich Boernstein, bespectacled Jewish editor of a St. Louis German-language newspaper, who had served for five years in the Austrian army and now commanded the Second Missouri, and Friedrich Salomon, captain in the Fifth Missouri, a native of Saxony who had held a lieutenant's commission prior to emigrating. Others, though not former soldiers, had at least some military training through the Turnverein.[29]

The Reserve Corps, also called the Home Guard, contained a somewhat larger percentage of American-born enlisted men, including many Republican Wide-Awakes, Blair's personal paramilitary force. More than a few Irish Americans were present, as the Irish of St. Louis split over the issue of secession.[30]

Lyon's Missouri Light Artillery, under Major Franz Backof, contained a mixture of experienced and amateur gunners to man its half-dozen six-pounders, but the training of its commander boded well. A forty-year-old native of Baden, Backof had been conscripted into the German military as a young man. He rose quickly to the rank of sergeant major in the artillery service and shocked his superiors by joining the revolutionary forces in 1848. He served with distinction, including a stint on Franz Sigel's staff, but was captured and sentenced to ten years in prison. Released in 1851 on the condition that he emigrate, he moved to St. Louis and renewed his friendship with Sigel. He earned his living as a contractor and served several terms on the city council.[31]

Lyon's best men were his Regulars, two companies of the Second U.S. Infantry. These were commanded by an old friend, Captain Thomas W. Sweeny, a native of Ireland who had fought in the Mexican War, losing his right arm but winning an officer's commission. If Sweeny's soldiers matched the national pattern for enlisted men in the U.S. service at the outbreak of the Civil War, two thirds of them were either German or Irish by birth.[32]

The connection between Lyon's highly ethnic force and the local community was exemplified during the first week in May, when Mrs. Josephine Weigel of the Women's Union presented a silver-starred silk flag to Sigel's Third Missouri with these words:

> It is a great honor for us to present you with this flag, made by German women and maidens, for your regiment.
>
> Germans can bear themselves with pride since men and youths stream to you as to no other to protect their adopted Fatherland against the most shameful and disgraceful treason. . . . In keeping with old German custom, we women do not wish to remain mere onlookers when our men have dedicated themselves with joyful courage to the service of the Fatherland; so far as it is in our power, we too wish to take part in the struggle for freedom and fan the fire of enthusiasm into bright flames.[33]

The Germans of St. Louis could be as racist as other white Americans. They had not flocked to arms over the issue of slavery but to preserve the Union. Most of them probably assumed that Lyon's authority was legitimate and had no idea that their enlistments were unconstitutional. Like Lincoln, they saw the conflict not in terms of the enforcement of any single law or particular portion of the Constitution, but the preservation of a system of government by majority rule. Mislabeled "Dutch" and made the butt of jokes that portrayed them as dim-witted and slow, the sons of Deutschland saw the crisis as an opportunity to gain respect through loyal service, to break down the barriers of prejudice and win acceptance in American society. Sigel felt truly American for the first time when he grasped the flag from Mrs. Weigel.[34]

Early on the morning of May 10, Sigel and Lyon led their men through the streets of St. Louis, separate columns converging on Lindell Grove. They made a remarkable pair, for they were determined, energetic men in the prime of life. Lyon was approaching his forty-third birthday, and Sigel was thirty-seven. Both were slender and nearly the same height, Lyon standing five foot five and Sigel five foot seven, but there any resemblance ended. Sigel's jet black hair, thin goatee, and piercing gaze gave him an intellectual appearance. A soldier who served under him in Europe described him as "a man of fine education and a close thinker." Sigel was neither tactful nor dashing, but trim, correct, and Prussian in appearance and conduct. Lyon had a high forehead, a florid complexion, and a large Roman nose. Some contemporaries described his wavy hair as frizzy, full beard as sandy in color, while others called it red. A newspaper reporter saw "acuteness, decision, and firmness" in Lyon's countenance but noted that he spoke slowly, hesitating often while searching for the proper words. In conversation his blue-gray eyes often lit up with a curious "moody gleam" and his expression clouded over like a thunderstorm.[35]

Word of Lyon's march soon reached Frost at Lindell Grove, but given the Unionists' overwhelming strength there was little he could do. The militia general offered no resistance when the Unionists surrounded Camp Jackson, and after protesting that Lyon had no authority for his actions he surrendered to the Connecticut Yankee. Lyon's triumph was swift and bloodless, but it left him with a dilemma. Lacking a prison camp, he had no choice but to parole the state militiamen, to make them swear allegiance to the Federal government and then let them go. But as Lyon believed that "no punishment was too great" for Secessionists, this was hardly satisfying. Therefore, as an object lesson to others of doubtful loyalty, he subjected his disarmed prisoners to a humiliating march through the main streets of the city to the arsenal.[36]

This was a tragic mistake. As word of the parade spread, men, women, and children lined the streets. Angry remarks, epithets, and ethnic slurs rose from the crowd, revealing the presence of a large number of Secessionists. They threw rocks and bottles at first, but finally someone fired on Lyon's soldiers. Other shots followed, and before Lyon could prevent it his men fired back into the crowd. By the time Lyon regained control of the situation, twenty-eight civilians had been killed and about seventy-five wounded. The dead included one woman and five teenaged children, one of whom was female. Two of Lyon's men were killed, as were three Missouri militiamen.[37]

Lyon finally herded his prisoners to the arsenal, where he held them overnight without food or water. Although he made them sign paroles in the morning, the propaganda value of his victory parade had not merely been lost, but passed to the Secessionists.[38] The "Camp Jackson Massacre" had profound repercussions. Among other things, it strengthened

Governor Jackson's influence immeasurably and led to the creation of the Missouri State Guard, a major portion of the Southern forces that would fight at Wilson's Creek.

No one can say what form the Civil War would have taken in Missouri but for the precipitous action of Nathaniel Lyon. It was a terrible war everywhere, but no state suffered as severely as Missouri, where shifting campaigns and vicious guerrilla warfare caused human misery and property damage to be more widely spread than in other Southern states. Though Lyon's actions did not create Missouri's internecine strife, they did shape and accelerate the pace of events, as they "forced Missourians to get off the fence and make immediate personal choices."[39]

The majority of state legislators opposed secession, but when news of the massacre in St. Louis reached Jefferson City, they took radical action, just short of taking the state out of the Union. Noting that a portion of the people of St. Louis were in rebellion against the laws of the state, they passed legislation making it illegal for political or social organizations, such as the Wide-Awakes or the Turnverein, to possess firearms. Next, they took steps to raise two million dollars for defense and created a new organization, the Missouri State Guard, to replace both the old county-based state militia and the volunteer militia companies. The state was divided into nine numbered geographic districts, each commanded by a brigadier general who was charged with raising therein the troops that would constitute his military division.[40]

Jackson appointed Nathaniel W. Watkins, Thomas Beverly Randolph, John Bullock Clark Sr., William Yarnel Slack, Alexander William Doniphan, Mosby Monroe Parsons, James Haggin McBride, James S. Rains, and Meriwether Lewis Clark as district/division commanders. Of these men, John Clark, Slack, Parsons, McBride, and Rains fought at Wilson's Creek.[41]

Clark, a wealthy fifty-nine-year-old native of Kentucky who owned 160 slaves, was one of the state's leading Secessionists. Described as a "born politician," he held a variety of state offices and was representing Missouri in the U.S. Congress when Jackson made him a brigadier general of the State Guard. Active in the old state militia, he had led a group of Missouri volunteers in the Black Hawk War of 1832 and thus brought significant experience to his new position as commander of the Third District in north-central Missouri. The neighboring Fourth District, just to the west, was commanded by Slack, also a Kentuckian by birth, but a resident of Missouri since childhood. A forty-five-year-old lawyer, he had been a captain in the Second Missouri Volunteers during the Mexican War. Parsons, who commanded the Sixth District in south-central Missouri, was a close political ally of the governor and had served in the state legislature, where he staunchly upheld the interests of slaveholders. Thirty-nine on his appointment as brigadier general, he was a Virginia native who had resided in Missouri since his youth. As captain of a company of Missouri volunteers with Doniphan's Expedition, he had won commendations for his gallantry at the Battle of Chihuahua during the Mexican War. The Seventh District, which shared a southern border with Arkansas, went to McBride, who had moved to Missouri from Kentucky at a young age. He eventually settled in Springfield and became a lawyer and banker. After a brief sojourn in California in the early 1850s, he returned to Missouri and served as a circuit judge. Forty-seven years old and the only division commander without even a pretense of military experience, McBride filled his staff with fellow lawyers and ran his command as if it were a courtroom. The large Eighth District encompassed most of the border with potentially volatile Kansas. Its commander, Rains, was a Tennessean by birth, but he had lived in Missouri for most of the last two decades, immersing himself in state politics. Part-time farmer, judge, and Indian agent, he cut a dashing figure, however, sporting bushy sidewhiskers in the style later popularly associated with Ambrose Burnside. He served in the Missouri state senate and house of representatives. Like many of his generation, the forty-four-year-old Rains went to California during the gold rush. Riches eluded him, but he did obtain a general's commission in the California state militia. In theory this modest service made him at least more qualified than McBride, but events would prove Rains to be the poorest commander in the Missouri State Guard.[42]

To command the State Guard, with the rank of major general, Jackson chose Sterling Price. By the time the Civil War ended in 1865, the fortunes of the state had become so closely intertwined with those of this quixotic and often ineffectual man that he came to personify the Confederacy's miniature "lost cause" in Missouri. Price turned out to be a man of very limited military ability, and this had consequences from the first. But he was the right person to lead the State Guard during the crisis summer of 1861, when Missouri's resources were severely restricted and the ability to inspire devotion was as important as expertise in strategy or tactics. The tragedy of Southern fortunes in Missouri was not that Price was initially tapped for the job, but that a more talented military leader neither later emerged nor was appointed to take the reins from his hands.

Like so many of that westering generation, Price immigrated to Missouri from the east. Born in Prince Edward County, Virginia, in 1809, he grew up the privileged son of a wealthy planter. After only one year at Hampden-Sydney College, he withdrew to study law but never practiced

Major General Sterling Price, commander of the Missouri State Guard (The collection of Dr. Tom and Karen Sweeney, General Sweeny's Museum, Republic, Missouri)

that profession. When his family decided to exchange genteel central Virginia for the frontiers of Missouri, he followed. By the early 1840s Price was married and starting a large family, residing at Keytesville in the Missouri River valley region, where he farmed tobacco with slave labor. As his wealth accumulated, he turned his attention to Democratic Party politics and rose quickly in prominence. He served as speaker of the Missouri House of Representatives and had nearly completed a term as his district's U.S. congressman when the war with Mexico erupted. Resigning from office, Price returned to Missouri and raised a regiment of mounted volunteers, which was dispatched to New Mexico to bolster the American occupation forces. Soon after his arrival in Santa Fe, Price, though only a colonel, succeeded to the top military command in the new territory. Whereupon, according to one critic, he "displayed a laxness in enforcing discipline, a tendency to quarrel with other officials, and a penchant for acting in a highly independent, almost insubordinate fashion—characteristics that were to manifest themselves in a subsequent war."[43]

Although there is much truth in this judgment, it is too harsh. After the departure of his superiors for other assignments, leaving Price with the daunting task of holding a vast expanse of land with few resources, he did tighten discipline, although not nearly enough. When a disastrous revolt occurred in January 1847, as part of the populace in Taos rose up and killed the newly arrived civilian governor, Charles Bent, Price responded quickly. Leaving Santa Fe with a force of fewer than four hundred men, he marched on Taos despite wretched weather and won several skirmishes against the "rebels" en route. On reaching the town, he attacked and defeated a well-positioned force of strength equal to, or greater than, his own.[44]

When an attorney general for the new territory arrived from Washington, he indicted two dozen "rebels" in connection with Governor Bent's death. The martyred governor's brother was allowed to serve as foreman of the grand jury, and more than two dozen New Mexicans were quickly convicted of murder and sentenced to death. When Price pardoned one of them, the attorney general protested so vigorously that Price arrested him temporarily. This sparked a lifelong political feud between the two men. The attorney general was Frank Blair Jr.[45]

Price went back to Missouri with his troops when their enlistments expired, but he was soon in action once more. Appointed a brigadier general of volunteers, he returned to Santa Fe in November 1847. Three months later he disobeyed orders by launching an invasion of the Mexican state of Chihuahua. He also ignored Mexican protests that, following Winfield Scott's victories to the south, an armistice now existed between the two nations. In March 1848 Price won a stunning, hard-fought, but pointless battle against a substantial Mexican force at Santa Cruz de Rosales. This allowed him to return home a hero and avoid any consequences for his unauthorized action.[46]

The Mexican War revealed much about Price. He was ambitious, querulous, insubordinate, and convinced of the righteousness of his own judgments and actions. His military abilities, though limited, were substantial. He knew how to motivate volunteer soldiers, and his experiences apparently led him to believe that such men, if not subjected to onerous discipline, could march rapidly with minimal supplies to attack and defeat a superior enemy.

After the war Price concentrated on business and politics. He was elected governor of Missouri in 1852, serving a four-year term. But as a strong Unionist he had little use for Claiborne Fox Jackson. After being elected president of the convention that met in the spring of 1861 to consider Missouri's place in the Union, Price supported the convention's rejection of secession. But he also endorsed a failed resolution asserting that if Lincoln attempted coercion, Missouri should stand by its sister states of the South.[47]

When Jackson appointed Price to head the State Guard in May 1861, the former governor and Mexican War hero brought to his new position a reputation for political moderation and the prestige of past military success. Portly at age fifty-two, the clean-shaven, silver-haired Price was charged with suppressing insurrection and repelling invasion. This was a formidable task. Although in theory he was supposed to defend against invasion from any direction, the borders that troubled Price were those that Missouri shared with the free states of Kansas, Iowa, and Illinois—a total of almost nine hundred miles. By comparison, in 1861 Confederate general Albert Sidney Johnston's department, running west from Cumberland Gap, on the Tennessee-Virginia line, to the Mississippi River, had a boundary only half as long. And as events turned out, Price had less time to prepare to defend Missouri, which was still in the Union, than the Confederates did to defend Tennessee or Virginia.

When General Harney returned from Washington to St. Louis on May 11, he was shocked by Lyon's actions and did what he could to keep Missouri from splitting into warring factions. In reality it was already too late. On May 21 Harney reached an agreement with Price for a truce between the Federal forces, including Lyon's illegally raised volunteers, and the legal but strongly pro-Secessionist State Guard. Ignoring this, independent Secessionist companies sprang up throughout the state. On May 30 Harney was removed from command, leaving Lyon, whom the War Department had just promoted to brigadier general, in sole control of Federal fortunes in Missouri. This was Blair's work, as he had convinced Lincoln that the situation called for a firm hand, not a pretense of neutrality.[48]

Lyon immediately began recruiting additional forces, and arming those on hand. Ironically, the arms he had shipped out of the St. Louis arsenal for safety were no longer available. Schofield, who acted unofficially as Lyon's quartermaster and was soon appointed his adjutant general, had to send all the way to Pennsylvania for equipment. The shoulder arms, cartridge boxes, belts, and bayonets that arrived were largely Mexican War surplus, although some units, such as Blair's First Missouri, got modern rifles. But even Blair, with all his influence, could not obtain uniforms for the men from the Federal government. Consequently, the women of St. Louis began sewing for their loved ones who had volunteered. There was no consistency in style or color. Blair's unit wore blue, but many of the others wore gray, apparently because a local store, Woolf's Shirt Depot, stocked hundreds of gray overshirts and sold them at discount prices. Some of the German companies were described as having "gray flannel shirts and dark-blue trousers and kepis." Sigel's Third Missouri had outfits consisting of "a gray hat, gray shirt, and gray pants, all trimmed in red." The Federal government did supply some blankets, canteens, haversacks, and knapsacks, but not enough to go around. Blair therefore appealed through the newspapers for public donations. Money came in from Wisconsin, Pennsylvania, Massachusetts, and New York. August Belmont, the well-known New York City socialite and businessman, contributed $500. By the first week in June more than $14,000 had been raised, $7,000 having come from out of state. No one did more than the citizens of Philadelphia, who donated 1,800 pairs of socks, 614 gray flannel shirts, and 900 pairs of shoes. The fact that Northern citizens from across the United States contributed to the support of Lyon's volunteers suggests a wide public recognition of Missouri's significant role in the developing crisis.[49]

Lyon now commanded almost 11,000 men, a force large enough to have been called an army in any of America's previous conflicts. On the morning of June 11, he and Blair met with Price, Jackson, and the governor's secretary, Thomas L. Snead, at the Planters' House hotel in St. Louis. The Missouri officials hoped to buy time, as they were woefully unprepared for any armed confrontation. In fact, Jackson proposed a mutual disarmament, requiring that Lyon's volunteers and Price's nascent Guardsmen disband. This was a sham, as Price had already urged the governor to seek help from the Confederacy, and Jackson's Secessionist goals were well known. Lyon responded by leaping to his feet and declaring, "Rather than concede to the State of Missouri for one single instant the right to dictate to my government in any matter however important, I would see you, and you, and you, and you, and every man, woman and child in the State, dead and buried!" He stomped out of the meeting with unequivocal parting words: "This means war."[50]

Historians have long debated whether Lyon acted wisely at the Planters' House meeting. Some argue that prolonging Missouri's pretense of neutrality would have ultimately benefited the Union cause in the state more than the Secessionist cause. But two things should be noted. First, Lyon's motives were highly personal, the result of his peculiar personality and egocentric views. "Though he couched his objections to Jackson's proposals in terms of federal authority, in truth Lyon now refused to accept any restriction of his own omnipotence. Once, he had had no power. Now, Lyon was *the* power. His duty was not—and never had been—to make peace with the Secessionists. His duty, his calling, was to punish them. No one else knew how. And now, no one could stop him. God was in him."[51] This does not mean, however, that Lyon's actions should be interpreted exclusively in terms of his mental state. Many talented, accomplished people are driven by their personal views.

The second thing to note is that Lyon was in most respects an excellent military commander, one of his country's best. Across the North in 1861 Union generals bombarded Lincoln with pessimistic assessments and unrealistic demands for men and materiel. Lyon did his own begging for reinforcements and supplies. Indeed, before the campaign ended he was almost obsessed by his shortages. But he was willing to work with what he had on hand. In June 1861 Lyon seemed to realize that the forthcoming struggle would be as much political as military, that time was the enemy of the Union and that there was no substitute for the immediate suppression of rebellion. Lyon seized the initiative. Although there would be tremendous negative consequences for his decision, in retrospect it was the greatest single factor in saving Missouri for the Union.

None of this was clear, of course, as Jackson and his party departed for Jefferson City. Lyon's declaration sent Missourians flocking to join Price, transforming the Missouri State Guard from a theoretical organization into a reality. As Price struggled to create an army, Lyon received reinforcements from out of state, bringing into the picture additional forces that eventually clashed at Wilson's Creek.

Chapter 3 . . . .

Mark Well the Spot Where They Meet

Nathaniel Lyon did not ask permission to wage war on the state of Missouri. He did not request detailed instructions from Washington or wait for orders from the War Department. Indeed, after Lyon "tasted power," he could no longer tolerate "anyone riding herd on him in Missouri." He simply informed his superiors of his overall intentions and interpreted their silence as endorsement for his course of action.[1] Although Lyon was apparently correct in his assumption of approval, the fact that he chose to operate in such a manner reveals much about his personality.

Lyon never intended to abide by any of the arrangements made between Harney and Price. A week before the Planters' House meeting at which he precipitated the crisis, he informed the War Department that he feared a dual invasion of the state by Confederate forces in northwestern Arkansas and western Tennessee. To counter this, he recommended a reinforcement of Cairo, Illinois, at the strategic junction of the Mississippi and Ohio Rivers. Then, if reinforcements were sent to him from Kansas, Iowa, and Illinois, he would undertake a movement from St. Louis "towards the southwest."[2] Whether anyone in Washington realized that this meant Lyon would drive Missouri's legally elected officials from the state capital and battle the militia guaranteed to Missouri's citizens under the Bill of Rights is unknown.

The day of the Planters' House meeting, the War Department promised Lyon 5,000 muskets and instructed him to raise as many volunteers from within Missouri as he thought necessary. Lyon now also had on hand a battery of artillery under Captain James Totten. This was Company F of the Second U.S. Artillery, but by the custom of the times it was referred to as Totten's Battery. Reinforcements were on the way, but

Lyon, characteristically, did not wait for them. He moved immediately on Jefferson City.[3]

Lyon's overall strategy was simple in concept but difficult to execute. It involved three columns operating nearly simultaneously, the first two launched from St. Louis, the third from Fort Leavenworth, Kansas. The first column from St. Louis would move up the Missouri River, capturing Jefferson City as the initial step in controlling the key railway and water connections in the central portion of the state. A second column would move by rail from St. Louis to Rolla, where the tracks ended, proceeding by road to Springfield in the southwestern corner of the state. The Leavenworth column would proceed southeast, uniting with the first column near Clinton, Missouri. Together they would move toward Springfield. Governor Jackson's Missouri State Guard would either be scattered before it could organize or be trapped between the converging columns.[4]

Although Lyon has been hailed as the man who saved Missouri for the Union politically, most historians have underrated his military achievements. When Lyon began executing the strategy outlined above, he became the first commander in the Civil War to make strategic use of steamboats and railroads. Although the forces he eventually brought into battle at Wilson's Creek were small compared to those engaged east of the Mississippi River, his theater of operations was vast. By the time Lyon's forces converged on Springfield, the main column had traveled over 260 miles. A similar advance southward by Union forces from Washington, D.C., and Louisville, Kentucky, would have reached Raleigh, North Carolina, and Decatur, Alabama, respectively.

Lyon moved quickly. Requisitioning steamboats, he reached Jefferson City on June 15, only to discover that almost every member of the state government had fled the capital. Although he soon occupied the public buildings, his protection of state property did not extend to the governor's mansion, which was systematically looted. A newspaper correspondent reported: "Sofas were overturned, carpets torn up and littered with letters and public documents. Tables, chairs, damask curtains, cigar-boxes, champaign-bottles, ink-stands, books, private letters, and family knick-knacks were scattered everywhere in chaotic confusion."[5]

Eleven years earlier Lyon had demonstrated his conviction that war should mean extermination when he not only massacred an Indian tribe but also burned its village to the ground. Jefferson City contained too many loyal citizens for Lyon to destroy it, but he had no intention of protecting the property of those he considered to be traitors, not even state governors. This time, however, his quarry got away without the thorough punishment that Lyon desired. Jackson had ordered a force of

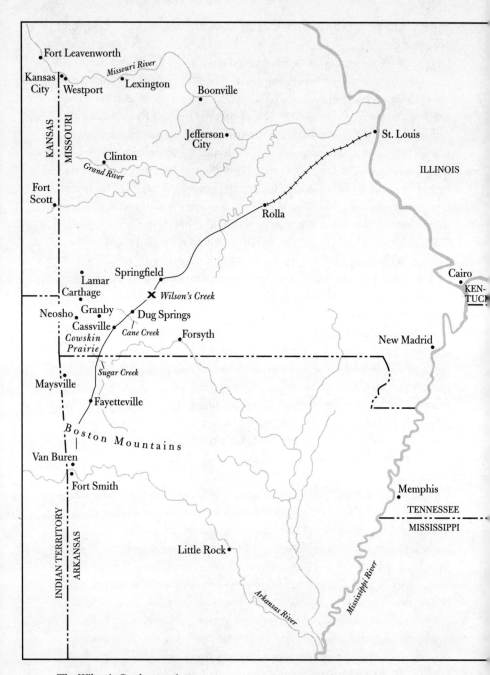

The Wilson's Creek campaign

some 450 of the Missouri State Guard, under Colonel John Sappington Marmaduke, to make a stand farther upriver at Boonville. Lyon's attack with 1,700 men routed them easily, but the governor and most of the men escaped to fight another day. Barely large enough to call a skirmish, much less a battle, the incident at Boonville nevertheless received enormous press coverage throughout the North. Lyon became a hero. Cartoons were published depicting him as a lion chasing off Jackson, who was portrayed as a jackass. If the public made too much of Lyon's exploits on the "battlefield," the strategic significance of his victory can hardly be exaggerated, as it cemented the Federals' control of the state's all-important railroad and water networks.[6] But to carry out the remainder of his plans, Lyon needed more troops than he had raised in St. Louis. Help would have to come from outside the state.

Of the reinforcements sent to Lyon, those that eventually fought at Wilson's Creek were the First and Second Kansas Infantry, the First Iowa Infantry, a twenty-one-man detachment of the Thirteenth Illinois Infantry, and several companies of infantry, cavalry, and artillery from the Regular Army. As was the case with the Northern and Southern forces previously described, the volunteers were raised at the community level. Two units, the First Iowa and the Second Kansas, were enlisted for only ninety days. As they returned home to the accolades of their loved ones after the battle, they provide an opportunity to study the full range of the soldiers' experiences in the 1861 campaign in Missouri.[7]

Granted statehood in 1846, Iowa was home to a number of largely social prewar militia companies, including the Muscatine Light Guard, the Washington Guards of Muscatine, the Mt. Pleasant Grays, and the Iowa City Dragoons. A number of relatively new units, such the Burlington Zouaves, were formed in the late 1850s in a burst of enthusiasm for volunteering that occurred after Elmer Ellsworth of New York toured the country with a colorful drill team, clad in the flashy garb of the Zouaves, Algerian soldiers serving in the French colonial armies. Leopold Matthies, a native of Bomberg, Prussia, military academy graduate, and former German army officer, put his past training and experience to work by organizing his fellow countrymen residing in Burlington into the German Rifles. Dubuque boasted the Governor's Grays, named in honor of former governor Stephen Hempstead. Davenport, home to the Davenport Rifles since their organization in February 1857, also sponsored the Davenport Guards and the Davenport Sarsfield Guards, both formed in March 1858. These volunteer companies may have enjoyed picnics more often than target practice, but they gave the state a substantial body of men who possessed at least some military training.[8]

When newspapers and telegraph lines spread the news of the bombardment of Fort Sumter in April 1861, Iowans reacted in the most American way possible. Between April 18 and 20 they met in their local communities to determine a course of action, responding to Lincoln's call for volunteers and Governor Samuel J. Kirkwood's subsequent instructions concerning Iowa's quota. In Muscatine, for example, they gathered in an abandoned dry goods store and passed resolutions to "stand by the stars and stripes wherever they float, by land or sea." Sixty-three men signed up to organize a company. During the early evening hours of April 18, concerned citizens in Iowa City nailed up hastily printed posters announcing a meeting to be held at the courthouse later that night. Despite the short notice, the crowd that gathered was too big for the facility. Men and women were forced to stand outside in the street, straining to catch the words of the patriotic addresses delivered by the mayor, local politicians, leading businessmen, and community clergy. When Captain Bradley Mahana of the Washington Guards appealed for volunteers to bring the city's peacetime militia unit up to wartime strength, forty-three men rushed forward. The meeting also secured pledges of $3,000 to support the families of the volunteers. Most of this came from two local banks. Two days later an even larger meeting was held on the grounds of the local college. Governor Kirkwood, though ill, was on hand to make a speech. The Washington Guards completed their recruiting, the subscription fund reached $8,000, and steps were taken to give land bounties to those who served their ninety days honorably. In Burlington, the citizens met on April 20 and made plans to support their prewar companies. The city council pledged $1,000 to equip the volunteers more fully, and men and women formed committees to assist the soldiers and care for their families while they were absent. In Dubuque, Mt. Pleasant, and Davenport young men competed for space in the rapidly swelling prewar companies, while brand-new companies sprang up like mushrooms across the state. Ladies everywhere began rolling bandages. Meetings were held even in the smallest communities, such as Hampton, in northern Iowa, where the local paper announced the procedures for volunteering: "In every neighborhood volunteers should form into companies of seventy-eight men each. Each company will elect a Captain and two Lieutenants, who will be commissioned by the Governor. . . . Companies as soon as organized should notify the Governor and hold themselves in readiness for orders. Regiments of ten companies each may be formed, and regimental officers elected."[9]

For the moment, at least, patriotism seemed to prevail over party politics. "War! war! is the all absorbing topic of conversation," wrote a correspondent in Davenport. "Men of all parties—ignoring former party names—are rallying under the old Flag, and keeping step to the music of the Union."[10]

During the remainder of April and the initial days of May, the ten companies that eventually formed the First Iowa completed their recruiting and prepared to gather at Keokuk, on the Mississippi River near the Missouri border. One company, the Governor's Grays under Captain Frank J. Herron, contained a large number of Irish, while three units—the Burlington Rifles, the German Volunteers of Davenport, and the Wilson Guards of Dubuque—were composed exclusively of German Americans, many of whom spoke little or no English. Proportionately, more Germans volunteered for the Union than any other group of immigrants. In Iowa, the Germans' ethnic identity was so strong that when those living in Keokuk could not raise enough men for a separate company, they went north to join the Burlington Rifles rather than merge with any of the companies native-born Americans were organizing in their city. After the First Iowa was created, the German companies tended to stick together, socializing among themselves, but they rarely encountered overt ethnic hostility. Captain Matthies of Burlington, for example, was respected throughout the regiment for his demonstrated ability, soldierly demeanor, and unfailing good humor.[11]

There were many foreign-born people living in Iowa in 1861, particularly in river cities such as Burlington, where one in every three adult males was German. As a voting bloc German Americans had won the state for the Republican Party in the recent national election. Their patriotism was widely praised in newspapers, which pointed out that many of them had military experience from the revolutions in Europe. Precisely how many of the First Iowa's Germans were veterans is unknown. Captain Augustus Wentz and Lieutenant Theodore Guelich of the Davenport company took part in the Mexican War. Another member of their unit reportedly fought in nineteen battles in Europe and America. Others were identified as having experience in the German, Austrian, and Hungarian armies.[12]

In addition to Germans and Irish, the regiment contained men born in Canada, England, Scotland, Wales, the Netherlands, Sweden, France, Switzerland, and Norway. Besides Iowa, fourteen Northern and eight Southern states, plus the District of Columbia, were represented. At the time of their enlistment all but seventeen men were residents of Iowa. The average age was twenty-one. No analysis of their occupations exists. The *Dubuque Weekly Times* claimed that the Governor's Grays was "composed largely of businessmen." John S. Clark, a twenty-year-old who withdrew from Iowa Wesleyan University to join the Mt. Pleasant Grays, recalled after the war that the regiment contained "scholars, classical students, men of high standing in all the learned professions as well as expert artisans in all lines." Franc B. Wilkie, a correspondent for the *Dubuque Herald* who accompanied the First Iowa, was more cynical or perhaps honest in his postwar reminiscence of the regiment's personnel, writing: "They were clerks on small salaries; they were lawyers with insufficient business; they were farmer's boys disgusted with the drudgery of the soil, and anxious to visit the wonderful world beyond them. To these were added husbands tired of domestic life, lovers disappointed in their affections, and ambitious elements who saw in the organization of men opportunities for command. Others, differing but little from the last named, scented political preferment, and joined the popular movement."[13]

Although the desire to advance oneself, to escape from ordinary routine, and to experience adventure were doubtless among the motives for enlistment, there is no reason to discount the Iowans' patriotism. State newspapers in April and May 1861 were filled with letters and editorials equating support of the Union with a sacred duty the people of the Hawk-Eye state owed both to the nation's Revolutionary War ancestors and to the framers of the Constitution. As Earl J. Hess and James M. McPherson note in recent studies, the language of nineteenth-century patriotism may strike modern readers as flowery and pretentious, but it asserted deeply held convictions. The *Davenport Daily Democrat & News* predicted a titanic struggle precisely because the soldiers of both the North and South were so committed: "Each army will be composed of men who are no mercenary hirelings, but whose hearts and souls are in the work," wrote the editor. "Mark well the spot where they meet. It will be known in history to the last generation of man."[14]

There is only scant information on how the men who joined the First Iowa perceived the war or why they enlisted. Their ideas were doubtless shaped in part by what they read in the letters and editorials appearing in their hometown newspapers. These made little mention of slavery, perhaps because it was unnecessary to do so. More often, they wrote of the need to punish treason and uphold national honor. The *Mt. Pleasant Home Journal* spoke of resisting the attempt by "seventy-thousand negro drivers" of the South to "compel five million white men" of the North to abandon the principles of democracy. But it also referred to honor, labeling the fall of Fort Sumter a "damming blot on our national escutcheon" that "must be wiped out." The *Burlington Daily Hawk-Eye* wrote, "Not the name of Lincoln, not the prestige of the administration, but the Stars and Stripes, has called together the thousands of free men now resolved to uphold the mighty interests represented by it." When the citizens of Iowa City presented Captain Mahana of the Washington Guards with a sword, they charged him to use it "to uphold the Constitution and the laws, and vindicate the wounded honor of the nation."[15]

When Horace Poole, who was originally from New England, joined the Governor's Grays, he wrote back to his father's newspaper in South Danvers, Massachusetts, that he sought to defend the Constitution and "our glorious Flag." In fact, the company flags the Iowans took with them, made by hometown ladies and presented in elaborate ceremonies, said something about their reasons for enlisting. Matthies's German Rifles carried a silk banner inscribed "We Defend the Flag of Our Adopted Land," while the flag of the Burlington Zouaves bore the words "The Union As Our Fathers Made It." But the best articulation of motives occurs in a set of resolutions adopted by the Washington Guards. They identified their "holy and just cause" as "the maintenance of the Constitution and Union and the enforcement of law." They fought to preserve "the wisest political arrangement possible," namely "a representative government with short terms of office, established and maintained by the will of majorities." They asserted that "the will of the minority," the South, was "entirely subversive to democratic Republicanism, and if not controlled affords us the death knell of constitutional freedom throughout the world."[16]

Eugene F. Ware, who served with the Burlington Zouaves, recalled the unpopularity of abolitionists in Iowa. Some members of his company were indeed against slavery, but only because they believed it harmful to the future of free white labor, not because they felt sympathy for the slaves themselves.[17] "Happy Land of Canaan," a song of 217 verses that was wildly popular with the First Iowa, included many overtly racist lyrics, such as the following:

> It's a funny thing to me why the nigger he should be
> The question everybody wants explaining.
> But there's not a single man for the nigger cares a damn,
> But to send him from the happy land of Canaan.[18]

Given such sentiments, it is not surprising that when the regiment was on campaign and escaped slaves sought refuge in its camp, the Iowans seized them and returned them to their masters. They did, however, use free blacks as camp servants throughout the regiment's service.[19]

While the First Iowa was in Missouri, the state's numerous newspapers printed soldiers' letters and reports from special correspondents covering almost every aspect of the unit's participation.[20] As was the case with other regiments, hometown papers focused on "their" company. The link between local communities and individual companies was particularly strong because the men expected to return home and give an account of their behavior after only three months' service. "The community," observes Reid Mitchell, "never entirely relinquished its power to oversee its men at war." Community pride helped men accept a degree of discipline that would have been anathema in civilian life. It also sustained them in battle. "A man who skulked or ran faced not just ridicule from his comrades but a soiled reputation when he returned to civilian life."[21]

Mitchell also notes the larger consequences of Civil War armies having their origins at the community level. After studying the Northern war effort he concludes: "[The] voluntary organization of small communities into a national army, the amalgamation of civic pride and national patriotism, serves as an example of how the volunteers imagined the Union should function. In 1861, a Union which went to war by creating a centralized army would have been unrecognizable to them. The local nature of the companies and regiments faithfully mirrored the body politic at large."[22]

The Iowans enjoyed intense community support from the beginning. "Everybody, old and young, vied with one another to do honor to the young volunteers," one soldier recalled. In Cedar Rapids, Dubuque, Davenport, Mt. Pleasant, Burlington, Iowa City, and Muscatine (the towns that contributed one or more companies to the regiment) committees of citizens raised thousands of dollars to help equip the soldiers and support their families. "Those who defend the hearthstones of our country should not be forgotten by those who have the ability," wrote a Davenport editor. Newspapers printed the names of relief committee members, along with those of contributors and the amount of their donations. Local physicians often pledged free medical treatment for the families of recruits.[23]

While Governor Kirkwood struggled vainly to procure uniforms for the state's troops, local men and women joined together to clothe the soldiers of their community. A Dubuque paper reported daily on the work of the Ladies Volunteer Labor Society, which supported the Wilson Guards. In Muscatine more than one hundred men and women put aside religious scruples to assemble on Sunday, sewing all day to have their men ready to leave the following day. "There is no Sunday in time of war," a newspaper reporter explained. In Iowa City professional tailors, who were presumably men, worked on coats while "generous ladies" produced trousers. Many accounts mention the use of sewing machines, often giving the brand name. As each company selected its own style and colors, the results were startling. When the regiment was formally organized, the men were found to possess overshirts, hunting shirts, jackets, and frock coats in dark and light blue, gray, bluish-gray, and even black and white tweed. Pants were gray, bluish-gray, black, and pink; coats and pants were trimmed in dark and light green, dark blue, black, red, yellow, and orange.[24]

The Iowans obviously did not blend together in the anonymity of a common uniform, but instead, through their colorful dress, retained a sense of distinctiveness that reminded each soldier of his hometown identity. During the first week in May, the companies proceeded individually to Keokuk, where on or about May 15 they were mustered into Federal service as the First Iowa. They remained at the river city for a month, until June 13, two days after the Planters' House meeting, when they were called into the field as reinforcements for Lyon. Throughout this period circumstances mitigated against their forming a bond at the regimental level strong enough to supplant their ties with their home communities.[25]

At Keokuk the companies were quartered separately in vacant buildings and only gradually, as tents became available, moved into a military camp in a grove of trees just west of the city. This process took until May 30. Although the companies drilled daily by themselves, no attempt at regimental drill appears to have been made until after arms arrived in late May. More important, thanks to the relative ease of river transportation, the companies never lost contact with home. During the rendezvous process, civilians accompanied "their" companies to Keokuk and remained for some time. As the days passed, visitors from home brought large quantities of food, ranging from staples to luxury items. These were always distributed to the community's own soldiers, never to the men of the regiment at large, even when logistical difficulties placed the First on short rations. On June 7, for example, the Mt. Pleasant Grays received individually wrapped packages containing food and a letter from a female volunteer worker. On the day before the regiment left for Missouri, a Keokuk newspaper reported that the Muscatine Grays had just received "an immense dray load of strawberries, tobacco, cakes, and other sweetmeats from the ladies of Muscatine," while the Burlington Rifles and the Wilson Guards "received hogsheads of potatoes from the Germans of Burlington."[26]

Rivalries kept community identity alive. The Burlington Zouaves persisted in following a distinctive drill and considered themselves an elite unit. They were particularly proud of being chosen the color company of the regiment. All the other companies of the First Iowa disliked the

Governor's Grays of Dubuque intensely. Jealousy was partly the cause, for the Governor's Grays arrived equipped with the modern rifles they had carried as a prewar unit, whereas the rest of the regiment was issued outdated smoothbore muskets. The Governor's Grays also initially received better quarters at Keokuk as a result of the intervention of a state supreme court judge. The soldiers in the other companies believed that the Governor's Grays looked down their noses at the rest of the regiment and accused the Grays, who wore frock coats and white gloves on dress parade, of putting on airs. A Burlington soldier reported through his hometown paper that when the Governor's Grays schemed to replace the Zouaves as the regiment's color company, "the Zouaves responded that they would have it over their dead bodies, and prepared to defend themselves." Actual violence was narrowly averted on the evening of June 4, when the Governor's Grays, assigned the duty of camp guards, chased from the parade ground at bayonet point some men who had been playing baseball or some other sport. The other companies immediately armed themselves, poured onto the field, and began threatening the Grays. The regimental commander, Colonel John Francis Bates, was forced to order everyone confined to quarters.[27]

In some ways Bates himself symbolized the divisions in the First Iowa, for the election of regimental officers on May 11 had been highly controversial. Long after the war, John Clark of Mt. Pleasant recalled that the men selected were Democratic politicians who neither possessed nor developed military talent. "I have always believed," he wrote in his memoirs, "that there was an understanding between Lincoln and the governors of the northern states that the Democrats should be favored in order to secure the loyalty of that party to the Union cause." Though Clark's suspicions were unjustified, politics played a heavy hand in the election, despite appeals that the senior officers be selected purely on the basis of military ability.[28]

Speculation about the election began even before the companies reached Keokuk. Candidates for office were numerous and interest in the election, which the state adjutant general set for May 10, ran high. Three officers and two privates were appointed judges and clerks to oversee the procedure. Rather than leave things to chance, ten company captains caucused at a local hotel and announced an "official" slate of candidates. This struck some in the regiment (probably those not selected) as undemocratic, and a rival slate appeared. Then, for reasons that are unclear, the company commanders had the election delayed until May 11, a Sunday. When the ballots were counted, Bates was declared colonel, but two "opposition" candidates had also triumphed. William H. Merritt became

country it was born in, and that of all oppressed humanity." The two hundred soldiers who were present signed a document witnessing this second, political baptism.[34]

The First Iowa left Keokuk suddenly, with little ceremony. Around 12:00 A.M. on June 13 Bates received orders to move his men by steamer to Hannibal, Missouri. He sounded reveille at 4:00 A.M., and as word spread of the regiment's destination cheers rose up from tent after tent. But breaking camp took all day, and it was 6:00 P.M. when the regiment marched down to the levee as Wunderlich's bandsmen played "Dixie." Although in light marching order, as they boarded the *Jennie Deans* their baggage included two canines, a Newfoundland named "Union" and a mongrel christened "Lize." They left behind a third mascot, an eagle that had been presented to them by the state legislature. Their only trepidation about the possibility of facing the enemy concerned their ponderous smoothbore muskets. Flintlocks manufactured in the 1820s and converted to percussion three decades later, they were the oldest type weapons that the government had held in storage. "If fire-arms had been in use at Noah's time," one soldier joked, "ours must have been the identical weapons that sentinels stood duty with over his collection of wild animals."[35]

When the First Iowa landed at Hannibal around 1:00 A.M. on June 14, they found that the Secessionists had fled and Union Home Guards were firmly in control. Although some of the Iowans referred to all Missourians as "pukes" and immediately set out souvenir hunting, others were pleased by the cordial welcome accorded them by the Union ladies of the town. The regiment was soon dispersed, some companies remaining in Hannibal to watch over government supplies, while others guarded nearby railroad bridges and depots. On the fifteenth it reassembled at Macon City, where former typographers in the regiment took over an abandoned "rebel" printing press to produce a camp newspaper, *Our Whole Union*. This was edited by Franc Wilkie, the civilian correspondent for the *Dubuque Herald*, whom some believed accompanied the regiment primarily to promote the reputation of Colonel Bates. The next day the Iowans traveled by rail to Renick, then proceeded west on foot, commandeering supplies and wagons along the way. While en route they returned six escaped slaves to their masters, as noted earlier. A soldier whose letters appeared regularly in the *Davenport Daily Democrat & News* assured his hometown folk that the First Regiment had no interest in "stealing negroes," although in a second incident they merely whipped an escaped slave out of their camp rather than turn him over to the authorities. On June 20 the Iowans joined Lyon's growing force at Boonville, taking up quarters on two steamboats docked at the bank of the Missouri River. Like all new soldiers, they found their first march fatiguing, but they were pleased to be with Lyon, whose reputation for swift, decisive action met their approval.[36]

Opinions differed sharply on the performance of the First Iowa's commander during the initial phase of the campaign, including the stay at Boonville while Lyon struggled to assemble a logistical support system. A Muscatine soldier wrote that Bates had "won praise from all quarters for his coolness, courage, and his good care of his men." Another soldier from the same city concluded that "Col. Bates has gained very much in favor with his men during this march. He evinced an anxiety for the comfort of his men which endeared him to them, and he assumes a respectful independence in the presence of his superiors which the citizen soldier likes to see." But a soldier from Iowa City reached different conclusions, perhaps because he had seen Bates join enlisted men in the looting of private property, grabbing a hat and a pair of boots from a Missouri country store. He wrote that Bates "has not a redeeming quality, and therefore not even the correspondent which he has hired to puff him can find anything to say of him. . . . As an officer he is the laughing stock of everybody, from Gen. Lyon down to the servants, and the vain fool thinks he is popular."[37]

One thing the Iowans could agree on was that their fancy uniforms, the product of so many hours of hard work by their loved ones back home, did not stand up well to the rigors of campaigning. A Davenport soldier described his company's worn-out trousers as "really indecent." One of the Burlington Zouaves stated that "foraging parties have been out for pants" as some men had "only their drawers." He joked about the prospect of using fig leaves in the near future. Wilkie informed Dubuque readers that the regiment was so shabby that it resembled "a crowd of vagabonds chased from civilization." More important from a strictly military point of view, many of the men were now barefooted, their shoes having worn out. This severely impeded their ability to perform their duties. But despite these problems, morale remained high. The Iowans' most fervent complaints concerned the constant postponements in starting after Governor Jackson and General Price.[38]

Lyon was even more eager to get at the enemy. His goal was to move overland against the Missouri State Guard with his assembled force of 2,400 men. This was not a large military body by later war standards, but the logistical aspects of Lyon's operations were highly demanding. Reserve ammunition, tents, and camp equipage had to travel by wagon. Although the soldiers marched, each man required 3 pounds of food daily; anything less would sap his strength rapidly. Moreover, Lyon's force also included more than 200 horses, many of them belonging to the artillery. Regulations specified that each horse should receive 12 pounds of grain daily (10 pounds for mules), supplemented by an additional 14 pounds of fodder or hay per day obtained by foraging. Consequently, Lyon needed to establish a continuous supply line, anchored on the Missouri River, capable of providing his men and animals with approximately 9,600 pounds of food and grain every day. In addition, to keep his horses fit he needed to collect every day from local sources en route 2,800 pounds of hay.[39]

Setting June 26 as his departure date, Lyon began purchasing or impressing wagons, horses, mules, and oxen across central Missouri. Time was of the essence, as he had already ordered Major Samuel Sturgis at Fort Leavenworth to meet him at Clinton, Missouri, with his Regulars and Kansas volunteers. It would not do for punishment to be delayed.[40]

Chapter 4 . . . .

The Boys Feel Very Proud of the Flag

While the Iowans moved west, the Union troops raised in Kansas moved east. No one had to convince Kansans that the conflict facing them was about slavery. Although both Kansans and Missourians committed atrocities during the so-called Bleeding Kansas period, which began in 1854, the free-state settlers in Kansas faced such sustained and often violent interference from proslavery Missourians that they were able to establish a government based on the principles of majority rule only after the greatest difficulties. As the struggle also became torturously enmeshed in national politics, it was ironic that the secession crisis itself largely overshadowed the entry of Kansas into the Union as a Free State on January 29, 1861.[1]

The war had real immediacy in Kansas, in part because most of the prewar Army Regulars garrisoning the west were sent east. From the Kansans' point of view, this left the state vulnerable to two types of savages: Native Americans and Missourians. Although many of the Kansans' experiences were unique, others demonstrate the strong links with community and social values that marked a commonality among the volunteer soldiers of both the North and the South.

When Lincoln called for volunteers in April 1861, Kansas had no state militia and little money. But as a result of almost six years of turmoil leading up to statehood, a high percentage of the state's adult white males had some previous military experience. Certainly the average white male Kansan was thoroughly familiar with firearms, something not true, for example, of Iowans. According to one source, most of the First Iowa had never fired a gun prior to enlisting. Regardless of their relative merits as soldiers, the enlistment fever that swept Kansas following the bombardment of Fort Sumter surpassed even that experienced in Iowa. Less than a week after Lincoln's call for volunteers, more than sixty companies had begun to organize, including the Capital Guard, composed exclusively of members of the state legislature at Topeka.[2]

Throughout the communities of Kansas men gathered to go to war, some assuming positions of leadership and others, the more humble role of private. Most had unremarkable backgrounds. Traveler Robert Schuler was so anxious to enlist that he joined the Union Rifles in Leavenworth rather than return to his hometown of Burlingame, where his father was a judge. In nearby Lawrence, Lewis T. Litchfield, L. L. Jones, and Caleb S. Pratt kissed their wives and children good-bye, joining the Oread Guards. They knew the unit well, having served in it during the troubles of the 1850s. Nicknamed "the Stubbs" because so many of the men were of short stature, the company had earned a reputation for dealing sharply with Missouri "border ruffians." Jones was a thirty-five-year-old native of New York who had earned a reputation locally as a public speaker. Pratt, a Bostonian, was an early settler in Lawrence, where he established a literacy society for young men. Now the town's leading merchant, he was also a clerk in both the city and county government. Farther south, at Emporia, Charles S. Hills left the A. G. Proctor Company to enlist in the Emporia Union Guards. His fellow soldiers there included H. H. Shuttle, who had been working in a furniture store, Michael Myers, who had a farm just outside of town, and Edward Trask, a local gunsmith.[3]

Some of the men who rushed to the colors were either politicians already or joined with an eye to political gain as a by-product of service. Samuel J. Crawford resigned from the state legislature to raise and captain the Kansas Guards in Anderson County. Ambitious John H. Halderman was from Kentucky, where his father, a physician and state senator, had known Abraham Lincoln. After teaching school and studying law, he was admitted to the bar. Moving to Kansas in 1854, he became private secretary to Andrew H. Reeder, the first territorial governor. Halderman was a stalwart free-stater despite his Southern birth and eventually settled in Lawrence, where he was twice elected mayor. When the war broke out he was a probate court judge, but he soon won a major's commission in the First Kansas. Unknown to him at the time, his older brother had just enlisted in the Confederate army as a surgeon. Atchison mayor George H. Fairchild organized the All Hazard company, which elected him captain. They met for drill in front of the office of the *Freedom's Champion*, which gave both the company and Fairchild considerable press coverage in the months to come. When Pennsylvania native Powell Clayton founded the Leavenworth Light Infantry in May 1861, he could not guess that seven years hence he would be the carpetbag governor of Arkansas. (The Southern army he faced at Wilson's Creek included four future Arkansas governors: Harris Flanagin, Thomas J. Churchill, James P. Eagle, and Daniel W. Jones.) Graduate of a small military academy in Pennsylvania, Clayton also had a degree in civil engineering and had served as city engineer in Leavenworth since 1859. Clayton was not the only man with previous military training. Camille Angiel joined the All Hazard company as a private but was elected first lieutenant. He had graduated from a military school in Lexington, Kentucky, and soon earned a reputation among his men as a strict disciplinarian but a "kind and sympathizing officer." William F. Cloud, who had been a sergeant in the Ohio militia during the Mexican War, was elected captain of the Emporia Union Guards, whereas Jack Merrick, a private in the Governor's Guards of Elwood, had served in the British army, losing an eye in the Crimean War at the Battle of Inkerman.[4]

They came from across the state, selecting and retaining throughout their service the distinctive company names signifying links with their home communities. Some chose names that described their location: Wyandotte Volunteers, Topeka Rifles, Leavenworth Fencibles, Olathe Union Guards. Others selected more dashing or imaginative names, honoring a concept or an individual: Phoenix Guards, Kansas Rangers, Union Rifles, Steuben Guards, Shield's Guards, Scott's Guards. Their organization became caught up in an ongoing political struggle between Governor Charles Robinson and the fanatical Senator James H. Lane, who desperately sought military distinction. In the end Kansas had two regiments, neither commanded by Lane. In May the governor accepted ten companies of three-month volunteers, thereby fulfilling the state's quota under Lincoln's call. As no more ninety-day units could be received, the men in ten additional companies voted to enlist for three years. But because of their dates of mustering into Federal service, the ninety-day troops became the Second Kansas while the three-year enlistees became the First Kansas.[5]

The First Kansas, which mustered in at Fort Leavenworth on June 3, was commanded by Colonel George Washington Deitzler. A Pennsylvanian who had tried his hand at harness making, medicine, and gold mining, Deitzler moved to Kansas in 1855. He prospered as a farmer and land broker, then became the mayor of Lawrence in 1860, donating his salary to the local schools. His chief interest was the antislavery movement. He had worked with Charles Robinson and the New England Emigrant Aid Society to arm free-state settlers with Sharps rifles, spending four months in jail on a trumped-up charge of treason for his efforts. A

Captain Powell Clayton, Leaven-
worth Light Infantry, First Kansas
(The collection of Dr. Tom and
Karen Sweeney, General Sweeny's
Museum, Republic, Missouri)

Republican, he served as both a senator and as speaker of the house in the
territorial legislature prior to Kansas statehood.[6] Governor Robinson's
appointment of Deitzler to command the First was a defeat for the pro-
Lane forces, and the new colonel's friendship with the governor apparently benefited the regiment. Although it took some time, Deitzler's men
received the blue fatigue blouses and trousers worn by the U.S. Regulars,
and some companies were issued modern rifles rather than outdated
smoothbore muskets.[7]

Robert Byington Mitchell, an Ohio native, became colonel of the Second Kansas, which mustered in on June 20. An officer in a volunteer
regiment in the Mexican War, he served as mayor of a small town in his
home state before moving to Kansas in 1856. There he espoused the free-
state cause as a member of the territorial legislature and was elected to the
convention that wrote a constitution for the new state. Mitchell was a
Democrat, but he opposed Lane, which is apparently what mattered to
Governor Robinson. One must wonder, however, whether there was a
connection between Mitchell's Democratic affiliation and the fact that
during its three months of service the Second Regiment received no
uniforms other than blue four-button army fatigue blouses. As was the
case in their sister regiment, some companies in the Second carried rifles
while others made do with antiquated smoothbores.[8]

Because of gaps in the records of some companies, any social analysis
of the Second Kansas must be incomplete. But a comparison of extant

Colonel George Washington Deitzler, First Kansas Infantry (The collection of Dr. Tom and Karen Sweeney, General Sweeny's Museum,
Republic, Missouri)

data suggests no significant difference between that regiment and the First Kansas, whose records have survived intact. The 110 men of Captain Job B. Stockton's Leavenworth Fencibles of the First Regiment were representative of the other Kansas companies. Twelve percent were members of the professional classes, 47 percent were skilled laborers, and the remainder were unskilled laborers or small farmers. The unit included artists, blacksmiths, carpenters, masons, printers, a cigar maker, a confectioner, a cook, a stone mason, and a college professor. The youngest enlistee was seventeen, the oldest fifty-one, while the average age was twenty-six. Officers and noncommissioned officers (sergeants and corporals) were generally older and more likely to be married.[9]

The only real surprise to emerge from a social study of the Kansas troops relates to ethnicity. Over 90 percent of the personnel of the First Kansas can be identified by nativity. Only one member of the regiment was actually born in Kansas, which is hardly surprising given the state's frontier status. But previous historians have failed to recognize the strong ethnic character of this unit. Eighteen percent of the men were German. Most of these were enlisted in Captain Gustavus Zesch's Steuben Guards of Leavenworth (named for Baron von Steuben of Revolutionary War fame) and Captain Fairchild's All Hazard company of Atchison. Twenty-five percent of the men were Irish. Most of them were in Captain William Y. Roberts's Wyandotte Volunteers, Captain Peter McFarland's Phoenix

Colonel Robert Byington Mitchell, Second Kansas Infantry. This photograph was taken after his promotion to brigadier general. (The collection of Dr. Tom and Karen Sweeney, General Sweeny's Museum, Republic, Missouri)

Guards of Leavenworth, and a second Leavenworth company, the Shield's Guards, commanded by Captain Daniel McCook. Though no other ethnic groups were represented in large numbers, the regiment also included men born in Austria, Canada, Denmark, England, France, Holland, Italy, Mexico, Norway, Poland, Scotland, Sweden, Switzerland, and Wales. In all, 48 percent of the members of the First Kansas were foreign born. The remainder of the personnel came from across the nation. Most were from the North. Connecticut, Illinois, Ohio, Massachusetts, Maine, Minnesota, New Hampshire, New Jersey, New York, Ohio, Pennsylvania, Rhode Island, Vermont, and Wisconsin were all represented. Six percent of the regiment came from the South, including every Confederate state except Mississippi.[10]

Unlike so many other volunteer troops that fought at Wilson's Creek, the Kansans were not uniformed by their home communities. The reason is unclear. No one had bothered with uniforms during the border wars of the 1850s, of course. The state had a white population of merely 106,000. There were only ten towns with more than 500 inhabitants, Leavenworth, with 5,000, being the largest. The effort of manufacturing uniforms was probably beyond the capacity of most communities. In any case, the men of the First and Second Regiments expected to receive uniforms from the Federal government at Fort Leavenworth, their designated rendezvous.[11]

But if Kansas villages and counties did not send their men off to war in the sorts of distinctive uniforms worn by the Iowans, they shared the same pride and interest in "their" companies as did other communities, North and South. Rivalries existed as well. Following Lincoln's call for volunteers, the *Freedom's Champion* counseled its readers, "Atchison should not be behind her sister towns in this matter, but should let the world know that she is true to the Government." Atchison took pride not only in the company it contributed to the First Kansas, but also in the fact that its local brass band became the regimental band. The *Fort Scott Democrat* noted that the town was "among the first to respond to the call . . . with the pride and boast of our county, our gallant young men." The *Lawrence Weekly Republican* was equally gratified, proclaiming: "We doubt whether any town has more reason to be proud of the patriotic men who have responded to their country's call."[12] Community rivalries persisted after the regiments were organized. Two days after the First Kansas mustered in at Fort Leavenworth, a soldier from Atchison assured readers of his hometown paper that "there is but one company on the ground that can in any way compete with ours, either in numbers, average weight, or height, and that is Company H, of Lawrence."[13]

Almost every Kansas company left its hometown with a flag made by the local womenfolk and presented during a public ceremony. The ladies of Emporia, for example, made a considerable effort for Captain Cloud's men. Mrs. Anna Watson Randolph recalled: "[The] flag was made of a cloth called then 'wool delaine' much like the fabric now known as challis. They either bought the red and white at a local store, or sent to Lawrence for it. They were unable to get any blue for the field, and Mrs. Edward Borton gave them enough blue cashmere from a dress pattern which her mother had sent her."[14]

On May 23, the day before their departure, the Emporia Union Guards assembled to receive their banner. Ceremonies such as this gave women a rare opportunity to speak in public to a mixed audience. By all accounts Miss Fannie Yeakly, who made the formal presentation, gave a stirring patriotic address. This was followed by a sermon from "Father" Fairchild, an aged and greatly respected Methodist minister well known on the frontier.[15]

The importance of such ceremonies in cementing community and company ties cannot be exaggerated. They reveal tremendous commonalities among the volunteers, North and South, because whether fashioned by "fair hands" in Kansas, Louisiana, Arkansas, or Iowa, company flags were the physical manifestation of a social contract between the soldiers' company and the community it represented. The citizenry pledged to support the soldiers and care for their families while they were gone. In return, the soldiers pledged to uphold the good name of their hometown. Reid Mitchell notes: "The flag, made by the women of the community, was something to be protected much as they thought their wives and mothers should be protected. If the men left their communities to protect their homes, as many of them insisted they did, they brought something of their homes with them into battle. The flag was the physical tie between the homelife they had left and fought for and the war into which they were plunged."[16]

Kansas provides clear examples of the relationship between flags and communities. A man in the Union Rifles of the Second Kansas wrote home to Leavenworth about his company's banner, "The boys feel very proud of the flag, and fully appreciate the patriotic motives of the ladies who entrusted it to their care." Every man was determined "to defend it to the last extremity and bear it off the battle field without a single stain of dishonor, or die beneath its folds." Similarly, a soldier used the Atchison newspaper to assure the women who had made the All Hazard company's flag that "it is by far the best in the camp. You may rest assured that we will never allow it to be dishonored." He was specific about the cost of this promise, for he continued, "We shall either return it with the laurels of victory, or it shall pass into the hands of the foe, dripping with the last drop of blood in our veins." Recalling this pledge twenty years later, a veteran of the same company wrote: "Right nobly were those words made good. That pledge was sacredly kept. . . . but more than one of the 'All Hazard Boys' gave his blood and his life to defend it."[17]

Texas provides an example from the other side of the conflict. A soldier from Marshall wrote home that the town's "Texas Hunters," now a part of Colonel Greer's South Kansas–Texas Cavalry assembling in Dallas, were "considered by many the finest company they have seen in the State." He continued: "We possess the handsomest, and the finest flag, and it is admired by all. Every 'Texas Hunter' looks upon it as a treasure, for it brings to mind many recollections of the past—of the fair donors, whose hands assisted in making it, and whose hands we grasped with affectionate 'good-bye' when we left home. . . . When we forsake and dishonor this banner, then we may despair of an incentive to arouse the spirit of a 'Texas Hunter.' "[18]

Soldiers spoke and wrote of upholding the honor of their flags because honor was at the core of the relationship between the soldiers of individual companies and the communities they represented. In his study of honor in the prewar South, Bertram Wyatt-Brown begins by emphasizing the importance of the concept of honor in nineteenth-century American society at large. "At the heart of honor," he writes, "lies the evaluation of the public." Honor begins with an individual's conviction of self-worth and ends with "the assessment of the claim by the public, a judgement based on the behavior of the claimant. In other words, honor is reputation." Concern for reputation powerfully affected men's behavior. In a study of the cultural values that motivated and influenced the men of 1861, Gerald Linderman concludes: " 'Death Before Dishonor' might ring today in many quarters as no more than a hopelessly hackneyed line from hoary stage drama, but for Civil War soldiers it had both vivacity and pertinence."[19]

Although Linderman writes of individual honor, the process of raising, supporting, and dispatching troops demonstrates that honor was also important in a corporate sense. Honor, pledged during company departure ceremonies and constantly present as embodied in the banners they bore, bound the soldiers together, allowing them to suffer greatly for the sake of the community's reputation. Again emphasizing the individual, Linderman links the concept of honor to that of courage on the battlefield. He argues that "the single most effective prescription for maintaining others' assumption that one was a man of honor was to act courageously." The public display of courage "was thus the best guarantor of an honorable reputation."[20] This was just as true of the reputation of a company and, by extension, the community it represented. The men who survived the battle at Wilson's Creek understood and evaluated their experiences not only as individuals, but also in terms of how their behavior reflected on their company and home community.

After occupying a series of camps in the vicinity of Fort Leavenworth, the Kansans "invaded" Missouri in mid-June, taking up quarters in buildings in Kansas City. Like most new soldiers, they grumbled about their training, the weather, and army rations. Most of all, they were anxious to come to grips with the "rebels." Although Deitzler was an avowed abolitionist, it is unclear how many of his fellow Kansans would have labeled themselves such. In his own regiment Captains Francis P. Swift and Samuel Walker had taken up arms for the free-state cause in the 1850s, as had Captains Joseph Cracklin and Samuel N. Wood in the Second Regiment.[21] But the free-state movement had championed the rights of white men, not black men. As in the case of the Iowans, the Kansas soldiers wrote of the need to preserve the Union, punish traitors, and restore national honor, yet made little mention of slavery. An examination of the more than fifty extant letters written by Kansas soldiers during the 1861 campaign reveals not a single expression of sympathy for the plight of

African Americans.[22] Indeed, following the Battle of Wilson's Creek, when Stockton's Leavenworth company discovered an African American in its ranks passing for white, it successfully petitioned for his discharge. "We have no objection to endure all the privations we may be called upon to endure," their petition read, "but to have one of the company, or even one of the regiment, pointed out as a 'nigger' while on dress parade or guard, is more than we like to be called upon to bear."[23] Some of the Kansans were obviously as committed to white supremacy as the Southerners they were eager to kill.

When they moved into Missouri, the Kansans came under the command of Samuel Sturgis, who had been breveted to major for his success in escaping from Fort Smith, Arkansas. On June 17 Sturgis had been ordered to march south and join Lyon in the vicinity of Clinton, Missouri, and now that the Kansans were fully organized and armed he was ready to move. The first units of his force, which numbered about 2,200 men, left Kansas City on the twenty-fourth. In addition to the two Kansas regiments, Sturgis had a substantial number of Regulars. As the prewar army was largely a constabulary, almost none of them had fired a shot in anger, but their drill and discipline were superior to that of the volunteers. There were four companies of infantry, plus 255 enlistees who had just arrived from Carlisle Barracks, Pennsylvania. Originally meant as reinforcements for units in New Mexico, they were now assigned to Sturgis, who organized them into two companies. Although sometimes referred to as "rifle recruits," they were armed with smoothbore muskets.[24] Sturgis also had four companies of cavalry and one of dragoons, armed with efficient Sharps and Maynard carbines, and one light battery with six guns. The battery now included two officers who had escorted the recruits west, Lieutenants George Oscar Sokalski and John Van Deusen Du Bois, both of whom would render invaluable service in the days to come.[25]

From a military point of view, the march was uneventful, although difficult because of heat and heavy rain. The Kansans named one stopping point "Camp Dismal," as their tramping had churned the prairie into a muddy swamp. While breaking camp one day, they discovered and promptly appropriated a number of dragoon sabers abandoned by the Regulars. Their posturing with these became a source of amusement to the Regulars, who particularly laughed at a Kansas officer possessing "tin-foil shoulder straps sewn on with black thread." The Regulars naturally resented the volunteers' lack of discipline. Theodore Albright, a member of Company C, First U.S. Cavalry, recalled that the Kansans "kept their camp in an uproar all the time, which was a nuisance and annoyance to us." The Regulars tended to be picky in their judgments of everyone, however. When Sturgis abandoned his regulation plumed, dress headgear for a practical but "odd-looking, fuzzy, broad brimmed, unmilitary slouched hat," some of the men made fun of it for the remainder of the campaign.[26]

On July 2 Sturgis's force reached Austin, where between three hundred and four hundred Missouri Unionists joined them as a Home Guard. New Yorker James H. Wiswell, one of the Regulars' new recruits, wrote his sister that the area around Austin was "the best country that I ever saw." The local populace, "Union to the back bone," sold them eggs and butter at low prices. The few "rebels" in the area had fled, abandoning their property. When this tempted two of the Regulars to theft, Sturgis had one of them whipped and the other drummed out of camp in his underwear.[27]

After establishing camp, Sturgis rushed two companies forward to Clinton to secure the crossing of the Grand River just south of that village. The remaining force arrived at Clinton on July 4, naming the camp after George Washington. There, as one soldier put it, the troops celebrated Independence Day "as well as a lot of hungry, worn, dirty, careworn soldiers could do."[28]

But most of the Kansans were soon in no mood to celebrate, for they ran afoul of Sturgis's standards of discipline. According to one of the Regulars, once they halted at Clinton, members of the First Kansas "robbed or plundered all, or nearly so, the farmers within a circle of five miles from camp." Although that may have been an exaggeration, deprivations unquestionably occurred, despite Deitzler's attempts to prevent them. When a group of some eight to ten men from Captain Walker's Scott's Guards were caught, Sturgis held them under guard. Accounts of subsequent events differ considerably. Captain Walker, who was Deitzler's friend, stated that the colonel called a meeting of company officers at which they determined, for the sake of good discipline, to have the men punished by Sturgis rather than within the regiment. They never anticipated the severity of Sturgis's response and were startled shortly thereafter when the enlisted men rose up in near mutiny. Word spread through the camp that the miscreants were receiving fifty lashes apiece while tied across a gun carriage. By the time Deitzler could intervene with Sturgis and halt the punishment, most of the prisoners had already been whipped. According to another report, however, Deitzler sanctioned the punishment over the protests of his subordinates.[29]

Regardless of the sequence of events, the Kansas soldiers blamed Sturgis for the whippings and Deitzler for not preventing them. Such brutal punishment, which was perfectly legal under army regulations in

1861, might be fit for the Regulars, but its application to volunteers they considered an outrage. A witness reported that "the flogging was done with a large black snake whip, giving each from forty-five to seventy-five lashes, the blood flowing halfway to their knees." The Kansas volunteers understood the need for discipline, of course. A few days earlier one company punished a member who had been absent without leave by having him run naked through a gauntlet of his comrades, who whipped him with switches. But this was child's play compared to Sturgis's actions. Rumors soon floated about that the major was secretly a Secessionist, and when he visited the Kansans' camp on July 8, he was greeted with a chorus of groans. This was too much for Sturgis, who lost his temper and began cursing them. Several men started yelling "shoot him! shoot him!" and Colonel Mitchell had to step in to prevent violence. After hearing many threats against Deitzler and Sturgis, one Kansas soldier concluded, "I should not like to occupy their positions in a battle."[30]

Given the strong links between Kansas communities and "their" companies, it is not surprising that condemnation of Deitzler and Sturgis swept the state. The *Atchison Freedom's Champion* proclaimed: "Major Sturgis should be hung from the first tree, and Col. Deitzler deserves the execrations, scorn, and contempt of every man in Kansas." Of Sturgis, the *Emporia News* declared: "There are five hundred men who have sworn to shoot him the first opportunity, and we shall have no regret on hearing that they have carried their threat into execution. He and Deitzler had both better resign and leave the army." In contrast, the commander of the Second Kansas won praise. The *Lawrence Weekly Republican* reported: "Col. Mitchell is represented as having exhibited the feelings of an honorable man, though powerless, and as having rebuked the dastard with proper spirit."[31]

The enlisted men drew up petitions condemning Sturgis and forwarded them to the War Department. Indeed, some of them asserted that had Lyon not arrived with his column from Boonville, they would have refused to march any farther under Sturgis's command.[32] It is ironic that the Kansans welcomed Lyon, an actual sadist, in preference to Sturgis, who had merely applied Regular Army discipline to volunteers.

The Kansans were soon distracted by another tragedy. On July 8 Joseph N. Cole of the Leavenworth Fencibles got into an argument with a fellow soldier of the First Kansas, Michael W. Stein, and knifed him to death. By one account Cole simply stabbed Stein in the back. By another, the two agreed to settle their differences in a fistfight, but after a few moments Cole drew a knife and dispatched his opponent. Although Cole tried to run, he was easily caught and his punishment was swift. Court-martialed the next day, he was sentenced to death and shot on July 14—the first military execution of the Civil War. The proceedings were traditional. The First Kansas formed a hollow square while Cole, blindfolded, knelt by his grave. A firing squad, selected by lot from the men of the regiment, did its duty efficiently. Cole died instantly and was buried in a blanket, his grave apparently unmarked. Unfortunately, some women from the surrounding country, in camp to visit the soldiers and not understanding the ceremony, witnessed the whole thing.[33]

While the Kansans struggled to adjust to military service, the Iowans remained largely idle at Boonville, waiting for Lyon to assemble the supplies and transportation needed to march to Clinton. The regiment moved from its temporary quarters on steamboats into a tented camp, but conditions hardly improved. In his correspondence to the *Dubuque Herald*, Franc Wilkie described the heat as "almost intolerable—the country parched for want of rain—the dust deep." Heavy rains soon brought additional discomfort without dispelling the heat. But an even greater hardship was the severance of the ties that had kept the men so well supplied by their home communities. Now there was nothing to eat but hardtack and pork. Wilkie particularly detested the latter, writing "[O]h ye gods, how I do loathe that cursed pork—its unclean stench clouds one's nostrils at every hour of the day as its smoke rises from a hundred huge frying pans—its scrofulous, greasy, foul-looking slices cover every platter—it reposes in superlative nastiness in every barrel!"[34]

In his memoirs Eugene Ware of the Burlington Zouaves left a vivid record of this period of boredom. The men either labored to construct fortifications to defend Boonville or drilled incessantly. They were also issued fresh ammunition, and as ammunition was scarce, they were charged ten cents—a significant sum in 1861—for any cartridge they lost or damaged. There were numerous inspections and dress parades, but these were no substitute for active campaigning and the men filled their time with drinking or other mischief. At least some of this was innocent, as when an Iowa soldier attempted to prevent a mule from braying at night by tying a sandbag to its tail. The resulting tumult disturbed the entire camp and landed him in the guardhouse. He refused, Ware noted, to name his comrades who had tricked him into the effort.[35]

Some men failed to measure up to even this stationary soldiering. According to Ware, some of the Burlington Zouaves were so distressed by the incompetence of their captain, George F. Streaper, that they presented him with a petition calling for his resignation. When Streaper responded by vowing revenge on the signers, some of them threatened to kill him during the first battle. A few days later Streaper appeared to be drunk on parade and ran off after a hog with his sword. Although this was reported to Colonel Bates, the commander of the First Iowa took no action. Streaper was eventually ordered back to Keokuk. Ware recalled that Lyon himself intervened to cashier the captain. A neutral observer, Horace Poole of the Governor's Grays, wrote at the time simply that Streaper had been arrested and would face a court-martial.[36]

In all probability Lyon did not concern himself with the misbehavior of an Iowa captain—not that he ignored discipline. While at Boonville he published an order reminding his soldiers that proper conduct and discipline were essential. Officers were "required" to "visit offenders with vigorous punishment." Despite this notice Lyon was either too busy to take a personal interest in inflicting pain on his command or realized wisely that Regular Army standards were not well suited to volunteers. The officers in the First Missouri did gain a reputation for the severity of their discipline, but whipping was apparently confined to the Regulars. No love was lost between the professional soldiers and the volunteers. One of the Regulars recalled "a mutual feeling of unfriendliness and aversion." He believed that this "scant civility and offishness was not confined to the ranks; officers shared it to a greater degree than the soldiers, and harbored it more tenaciously." Eugene Ware claimed that the volunteers made a distinction between the professional officers based on their age and experience. "We greatly despised the young regular army officers," he remembered, as they were "snobs of the first order" who affected "jaunty and effeminate ways." On the other hand, the men much admired Captain James Totten for the style in which he directed his battery. His drill commands were invariably punctuated with profanity: "Forward that caisson, G—d d——n you, sir" and "Swing that piece into line, G—d d——n you, sir." Ware claimed that his comrades would walk half a mile just to listen to Totten for five minutes.[37]

Ware also recalled that most of the Iowans remained aloof from the largely German regiments from St. Louis, believing that Lyon treated them with overt favoritism. Because of that, Ware noted, "we did not take very kindly to him." Indeed, views of Lyon differed. A Muscatine soldier wrote home that "the General expressed the opinion that there was too much levity among us for so solemn a mission." Nevertheless, he believed that the First Iowa was "rapidly gaining favor with Gen. Lyon." In the short time since the Camp Jackson affair and the Boonville skirmish the Connecticut Yankee's reputation had skyrocketed to the point where another Iowa soldier, Horace Poole, could write to his father: "I was very much disappointed in the appearance of our famous General—as I had pictured Gen. Lyon in my mind as a second Washington or Scott; but instead of that, I see a short, thick set, sandy haired (I might say red) and whiskered man, with a long linen coat and straw hat, looking about as much like a military man as I do a Catholic priest." Poole nevertheless concluded not to judge by appearances, as he was convinced that in the forthcoming campaign Lyon would "become one of our most distinguished military men."[38]

For Lyon's column the campaign finally began on July 3, more than a week behind schedule. According to one source, the general had spent $20,000 purchasing horses and mules in the Boonville vicinity. Lyon, of course, had no legal authority to spend the government's money, issue contracts, or confiscate property, but he did all three and tried to suppress newspapers that criticized his actions. He was desperately short of wagons and finally moved with only half the transportation he deemed necessary. One observer thought that the Federals' hodge-podge baggage train, which included every sort of wheeled vehicle imaginable, resembled "the tatterdemalion recruits of Falstaff." Yet where other commanders would have been paralyzed by such difficulties, Lyon forged ahead. When the column trudged out of Boonville in the mud, citizens lined the roads to cheer them on, while little boys wearing military caps and using sticks for toy guns followed them for a mile. After leaving a garrison behind, Lyon had 2,354 men. In addition to the Iowa and Missouri volunteers, his force included Company D of the Second U.S. Infantry, Totten's Battery, and over one hundred recruits for the Regulars not yet assigned to a specific unit. He also had detachments of pioneers, more properly called "sappers and miners" in military parlance. Commanded by Captain John D. Voerster, they carried Sharps rifles in addition to their traditional shovels, picks, and axes. Lyon needed such engineering troops to assist his crossing of Missouri's rain-swollen rivers. Although Lyon continued to dress "like a farmer," he now had a bodyguard of ten men—German Americans from St. Louis—who wore turned-up gray slouch hats with white plumes. These stalwarts followed him everywhere. Riding ahead was Lyon's chief "spy and scout," a man named Wells who was originally from Chelsea, Massachusetts. Wells had apparently lived in Missouri for some time, as in the days to come he had no difficulty passing himself off among the locals as a farmer, minister, or drover.[39]

The trek was arduous. Private Daniel Matson of the Burlington Zouaves stated in his memoirs that on one occasion the temperature reached 110 degrees Fahrenheit in the shade. He may have exaggerated for dramatic effect, but there is no question that heat made the trip difficult.

Although the country they traversed appeared to be sparsely settled, as soon as the column halted for the night local farmers wandered in with produce for sale. They took advantage of the soldiers' cravings, selling pies, melons, fruit, and buttermilk at inflated prices, but occasionally the soldiers had their revenge. "One old fellow with a load of stuff refused to take Iowa State paper,—silver or no sale," Matson recalled. "On attempting to move his wagon, the wheels came off in a mysterious way. The obliging Hawkeyes rushed to the rescue, but by the time the wagon was in running order, the contents had disappeared."[40]

When Lyon's force arrived at Clinton on July 7, after hard marching on backcountry roads that avoided most towns, he received an eleven-gun salute from Lieutenant Du Bois, to whom Sturgis had given command of a section of his guns. There was indeed much reason to celebrate. The time of preparation was over, and the road ahead beckoned. No one doubted that the road would lead to battle. Many of the volunteers feared only that it might not come before their short terms of enlistment expired. A member of the Second Kansas wrote to his friends in Leavenworth that "the boys are absolutely spoiling for a fight. They are getting tired of marching all the time, and want to try their hand on a fight."[41]

Chapter 5

Nothing Was Clear Cut— It Was Simply Missouri

Some of Nathaniel Lyon's men were already on the road to battle, for his operations since the skirmish at Boonville on June 17 included major accomplishments. Although his own column stalled at the Missouri River for a considerable time, the column he dispatched from St. Louis under Captain Thomas W. Sweeny was able to move swiftly, thanks to better communications provided by the railroad as far as Rolla. In a continuation of the unorthodox events in Missouri, the forty-one-year-old Sweeny had been "elected" a brigadier general by the Missouri Union volunteers. As these regiments still had no legal standing under state or federal law, the Missourians could vote anyone whatever rank they pleased. The War Department never recognized the title, however. Even the puppet government the Federals eventually established in Jefferson City did not allow generals in the state forces to be elected.[1]

Colonel Franz Sigel led the vanguard of Sweeny's column with nine companies of his own regiment, the Third Missouri, seven companies of the Fifth Missouri under Colonel Charles E. Salomon, and two batteries of artillery, each with four guns. Sigel left St. Louis on June 13, reaching Rolla quickly by rail. From there he began moving on foot to Springfield, hoping to cut off the retreat of the Missouri State Guardsmen whom, he learned, Lyon had defeated at Boonville. The track followed by Sigel's small brigade was commonly called the Springfield Road by travelers heading west. Some veterans in their memoirs confused its name with that of the Telegraph or Wire Road (so called because the wire-strung poles lining it were a relatively unusual sight in that day and time), which linked

Springfield with Jefferson City to the north, and Fayetteville, Arkansas, to the south.[2]

Sigel reached Springfield on June 24. Although thoroughly drenched by a recent downpour, his men proudly marched into town, preceded by a brass band. Because the majority of people in Springfield favored the Union, the soldiers felt welcome, but the local citizenry could not have been impressed by the physical appearance of these representatives of the Federal government. Private John Buegel recalled the tattered condition of the Third Missouri. "The majority of our regiment was in deplorable condition," he wrote. "We resembled a rabble more than soldiers. . . . Some had no trousers any more. In place of trousers they had slipped on sacks. Others had no shoes or boots any more, and were walking on the uppers or going barefooted. Still others had no hats or caps and used flour sacks for head covering." Otto Lademann, a private in the same unit, also noted their poor condition:

> Our equipment for field service was a very poor one. We had no blankets, no knapsacks, no great coats, and barely any camp and garrison equipage. Our whole outfit consisted of an uncovered tin canteen and white sheeting haversack, rotten white belts, condemned since the Mexican War, and cartridge boxes made by contract—flat, shaped like cigar boxes, without tin racks to hold the cartridges in place. Consequently, in a week's marching you had your cartridge box full of loose powder and bullets tied to the paper cases. Each company possessed one-half dozen Sibley tents and the same number of camp kettles and mess pans.[3]

After making his headquarters at the Bailey House hotel, Sigel immediately began confiscating wagons, horses, and mules. Although such actions were essential to the success of his operations, a member of Backof's Missouri Light Artillery recalled their consequences. He wrote: "It would seem that at Springfield General Sigel either ordered or permitted his command to seize horses and other property from the Secessionists in that region for the benefit of the Government. The execution of such an order was well calculated to raise strange and confused notions of property in the minds of an ill disciplined Army of three month Volunteers. Nor were these confused notions at all cleared up or corrected by the conduct of several of the officers of these volunteers." In fact, many of the officers simply stole local horses and sold them at the expiration of their service.[4]

Troops viewing the seat of Greene County for the first time estimated its population to be between 1,500 and 2,500. Their reactions to it differed considerably. One soldier, while praising the surrounding agricultural region, wrote his family that "Springfield is yet what we term a 'one horse' town." But another Northerner, who obviously considered himself to be deep in an alien land, described it as "decidedly the most New England–like town I have seen since I left America." Thomas W. Knox, a journalist for the *New York Herald* who arrived shortly after Sigel's men marched into the town square, left a more objective, penetrating analysis in his memoirs: "Springfield is the largest town in Southwest Missouri, and has a fine situation. Before the war it was a place of considerable importance, as it controlled the trade of the large region around it. . . . Considered in a military light, Springfield was the key to that portion of the State. A large number of public roads center at that point. Their direction is such that the possession of the town by either army would control any near position of an adversary of equal or inferior strength."[5]

When Knox checked into a local hotel, he was surprised to find but one sheet on the bed. The porter who escorted him to the room explained: "People here use only one sheet. Down in St. Louis you folks want two sheets, but in this part of the country we ain't so nice." Knox was known for his sarcasm.[6] Despite his allegations of provincialism, Springfield was a substantial, prosperous community. The town boasted the Western Commercial College, which taught bookkeeping, and the Springfield Academy, a coeducational facility whose curriculum included Latin, Greek, anatomy, and physiology. Professor Charles Carlton, who headed the academy, was a native of Britain and an ordained minister. Unlike most teachers of his day, he emphasized the development of his students' analytic ability rather than rote learning. Springfield was home to several banks, including a branch of the Missouri State Bank, and a number of large mercantile establishments where patrons could buy furniture, clothing, dry goods, and general merchandise. A music store offered lessons, music books, pianos, and organs, together with all sorts of stringed instruments. There was a nursery featuring a wide variety of fruit trees, bushes, shrubbery, and flowers. Druggists, watchmakers, and cobblers competed for business. Grocers offered, among other things, mackerel, herring, oysters, and canned peaches. There were both saloons and a Temperance Hall on the town square. Springfield residents could have their photographs made, buy a plow or kitchen stove, or have a carriage built. They could also purchase slaves.[7]

Most residents of Springfield and the surrounding region were strong Unionists. Meetings were held in Greene and adjacent Christian County denouncing the creation of the Missouri State Guard and pledging resistance if conscription was attempted. The leading figure was Congress-

A drawing by Alexander Simplot of the plaza or public square in Springfield, Missouri (The collection of Dr. Tom and Karen Sweeney, General Sweeny's Museum, Republic, Missouri)

man John S. Phelps, of Springfield, who was instrumental in organizing a Home Guard. The town did have a substantial number of Secessionists, as well as many who may not have endorsed secession but denounced Lyon's overthrow of the legal state government. Professor Carlton, for example, favored disunion, and prosecession meetings were held in Springfield until mid-June. When Unionists led by S. H. "Pony" Boyd tried to break up a gathering at the courthouse on June 11, the most prominent Secessionist speaker, John W. Payne, kicked Boyd down the courthouse steps. The news of Sigel's approach, however, produced a stream of hasty departures. The Secessionists' fears were justified. For despite his lack of authority, one of Sigel's first actions was to arrest enough people on suspicion of disloyalty to fill the local jail.[8]

The day before Sigel entered Springfield, Sweeny switched his headquarters from St. Louis to Rolla, where he began building up a substantial supply depot. He continued to funnel men toward Springfield but kept some in Rolla to guard the rail head. Newly arrived troops included Colonel John B. Wyman's Thirteenth Illinois Infantry. Organized in May at Camp Dement in Dixon for three years' service, the men of the Thirteenth were clad in gray uniforms and indifferently armed. With companies raised in Dixon, Amboy, Rock Island, Sandwich, Sycamore, Morrison, Aurora, Chicago, and Naperville, they possessed the same close community identification as other volunteers. "We called ourselves 'one thousand strong,'" a regimental historian recalled. "But was it not true that one half our strength was never seen in either camp or the battlefield. It was found in the homes and hearts left behind." When Sweeny needed guards for a supply train he was sending to Springfield, Wyman drew two men from each of the regiment's ten companies and placed them under

Detail from Simplot's drawing of the Greene County Court House, used as a hospital before and after the Battle of Wilson's Creek. (The collection of Dr. Tom and Karen Sweeney, General Sweeny's Museum, Republic, Missouri)

the command of Lieutenant James Beardsley. The wagons reached Springfield in early August. The bulk of the regiment remained in Rolla, but the twenty-one men who found themselves in Springfield took part in the Battle of Wilson's Creek.[9]

Sigel, meanwhile, had moved west of Springfield, occupying the villages of Mt. Vernon, Neosho, and Sarcoxie. Having heard rumors (which proved false) of another battle between Lyon and the Missouri State Guard, he dutifully dispatched scouts northward. Before these reported back, Sigel received exciting intelligence. Sterling Price, who had preceded Missouri's fleeing governor in order to raise troops in the southwestern portion of the state, was only a few miles south of Neosho at Poole's Prairie, and he had only seven hundred to eight hundred men. The bulk of the State Guard, under Jackson's overall command, had been retreating slowly southward ever since Boonville, steadily gathering recruits. Sigel learned that it was now camped near Lamar. As Lamar was twenty miles north of Sarcoxie, this meant that Sigel's dispersed units were in between his enemies. Even though the governor's force reportedly outnumbered him substantially, Sigel decided to concentrate his men, to attack first Price and then Jackson before they could unite.[10]

Although this ambitious plan revealed in Sigel a willingness to take dangerous risks, such risks, combined with aggressive action, were arguably necessary if Lyon's grand strategy was to succeed. But events did not turn out as Sigel envisioned. He learned almost immediately that Price's force had decamped southward, heading toward the Arkansas line. Rather than follow the smaller force he decided to concentrate against Jackson, who was the greater threat. Unfortunately, he boasted of his intentions in the presence of civilians who were Southern sympathizers, and they quickly carried warning to the Missouri governor.[11]

Claiborne Jackson had discovered that it was one thing to create a Missouri State Guard by an act of the legislature but quite another to translate such plans into an effective field force. Following his meeting with Lyon at the Planters' House, the governor issued an appeal for 50,000 volunteers "to rally under the flag of the State, for the protection of their endangered homes and firesides, and for the defense of their most sacred rights and dearest liberties." But he and Sterling Price were hampered by numerous difficulties, not the least of which was Lyon's immediate seizure of Missouri's railways and central river network. This robbed them of precious time and the resources of the most prosperous and populous areas of the state.[12]

Price was not present at the Boonville skirmish, having proceeded to Lexington to organize troops to repel an expected invasion from Kansas. Lyon's occupation of Jefferson City and victory at Boonville left the newly appointed State Guard commander no choice but to abandon central Missouri and withdraw to the southwest. There he could rally the citizens loyal to the state and appeal for help to Ben McCulloch, who was known to be commanding Confederate forces in northwestern Arkansas. Price was also hampered by a recurrent illness. He therefore left Brigadier Generals William Y. Slack and James S. Rains to assemble their divisions near Lexington and move south with Governor Jackson as quickly as possible. Riding toward the southern border with his staff, Price did gather some forces along the way, and rendezvous camps were established at Houston, seventy miles east of Springfield, and Cassville, fifty miles southwest of Springfield.[13]

Because sentiment in Missouri was deeply divided, the men who joined the State Guard may not have enjoyed as high a degree of community support as the soldiers from other states did, but it was nevertheless strong. Since the Guard was organized along geographic lines, each volunteer company, whether infantry, cavalry, or artillery, was assigned to a numbered unit. But those who fought at Wilson's Creek rarely referred to themselves as members, for example, of the First Regiment, Seventh Division; they were Wingo's Regiment of McBride's Division. Moreover, like their fellow soldiers North and South, their identity lay primarily at the company level. The names they chose for themselves demonstrated links to their home communities and their leaders. Examples include Captain F. M. McKenzie's Clark Township Southern Guards, Captain John S. Marmaduke's Saline County Jackson Guards, Captain George Vaughn's Osceola Infantry, and Captain Joseph O. Shelby's Lafayette County Mounted Rifles.[14]

Yet the average Missouri State Guard company is hard to typify. Some numbered around one hundred, but many others entered the field only days after their initial organization and never recruited up to strength. Consequently, the Guard had an even greater surplus of officers than most volunteer organizations. Parsons's Division represents an extreme case. Quartermaster records indicate that between the time of its organization and the Battle of Wilson's Creek supplies were issued to thirty-five separate companies, each commanded by a captain. These included the Henry County Rangers, the Morgan Rifles, the Miami Guards, the Columbia Grays, the Osage Tigers, and Guibor's Missouri Light Artillery. Yet Parsons's "division" fielded between 523 and 601 men at Wilson's Creek. If all thirty-five companies were present at the battle, and apparently they were, each company averaged only 15 to 17 men.[15]

One of Price's first acts as commander of the State Guard had been to instruct his men to carry a blue banner, measuring four by five feet, bearing the Missouri coat of arms in gold. These flags were presumably manufactured by the women of each company's hometown. But as most units departed for service soon after their formation, the sort of public flag presentation ceremonies that cemented company and community ties for other soldiers did not occur as often for members of the State Guard. Distinctive uniforms, another important community tie, were also largely absent. When prewar units like the Independence Grays or the Washington Blues of St. Louis joined the State Guard, they retained their old militia uniforms. But if few of the newly raised companies had matching outfits it was certainly not from community indifference. In a short space of time the women of Warsaw managed to clothe two State Guard companies and sew them a flag. One company wore blue, the other gray, the colors having yet to take on any political significance. Although a full uniform was doubtless planned, one volunteer company from Bolivar had only matching pants—brown jeans with red calico stripes down the outside seams. Several companies designating themselves "Rangers" were quite fancifully uniformed. Those from Plattin wore red caps and shirts with gray pants, while the men of Moniteau sported gray shirts, gray pants, and water repellent oil-cloth caps. DeKalb County sent its mounted com-

Private Henderson Duvall, Missouri State Guard (The collection of Dr. Tom and Karen Sweeney, General Sweeny's Museum, Republic, Missouri)

pany to war in gray hunting shirts and caps, and black trousers with yellow stripes, to mark their cavalry service. The LaGrange Guards also had gray caps and shirts, but trimmed in blue, and their pants were white with black stripes. But for style none could beat the Polk County Rangers, who adopted a uniform of baggy red Zouave trousers and short gray jackets. Nevertheless, probably no more than 15 percent of the State Guard wore uniforms made by their home folk at the onset of the war. Information about them is scare and often obtuse. A typical reference, drawn from the *Glasgow Weekly Times*, states simply that most of the officers and men in companies raised in Jackson, Clay, and Carroll Counties were "handsomely uniformed," without giving further details.[16]

No social analysis of the State Guard exists. Muster rolls are incomplete and often fail to give full information about the recruits' backgrounds. It was "a delightfully informal army, which rarely bothered with paperwork. Even when it did, because of its limited resources and habit of being self-sufficient, the morning muster-rolls were likely to be used in the evening as cartridge paper."[17]

Questions about the composition and character of the State Guard cannot be answered with great precision. In 1866, however, Southern journalist and historian Edward Pollard described it thus: "It was a heterogeneous mixture of all human compounds, and represented every condition of Western life. There were the old and the young, the rich and poor, the high and low, the grave and gay, the planter and laborer, the farmer and clerk, the hunter and boatman, the merchant and woodsman."

As was the case in other states, some veterans left impressions of their comrades. James E. Payne described the volunteers from Cass, Johnson, Lafayette, and Jackson Counties in west-central Missouri as "principally farmers, though quite an important minority represented other walks in life. There was a sprinkling of merchants and merchant's clerks, mechanics, lawyers, doctors, and laborers." He also identified plainsmen, Indian fighters, Mexican War veterans, and filibusterers associated with William Walker's failed Nicaraguan ventures.[18]

As an admittedly arbitrary sample, a hospital register kept between July 5 and August 10, gives details on over one hundred patients from four of the five divisions present at Wilson's Creek. In this sample, the youngest soldier was sixteen, the oldest was fifty-three, and the average age twenty-four. Of the half that can be identified by nativity, 30 percent were born in Missouri. Alabama, Kentucky, Tennessee, and Virginia contributed 32 percent, while only 8 percent were from the North. Foreigners, all but two of them Irish, made up another 30 percent. The Irish came from Colonel Joseph M. Kelly's largely Irish prewar militia company of St. Louis. Occupations included baker, blacksmith, boatman, bookkeeper, cabinetmaker, carpenter, clerk, grocer, merchant, miner, shoemaker, stonecutter, teacher, and teamster. The largest categories, however, were farmer (45 percent of those identified) and common laborer (9 percent).[19]

The Missouri State Guard made no provisions for mail service during the first months of its existence. Because of Lyon's swift action, many of the Guard's soldiers were from locations behind enemy lines. They were unable to write letters to their home folk and hometown newspapers chronicling their trials and tribulations as newly enlisted soldiers in the same manner that soldiers from other states did. But if information comes largely from postwar reminiscences, these reveal similar experiences. One of the first and greatest challenges facing those who wanted to join the Guard was simply locating it.

Joseph A. Mudd's journey is one example of the confused conditions many of the enlistees faced. He was in St. Louis when he learned that Lyon had declared war on Missouri. To reach his home in Millwood, a village almost sixty miles to the northwest, he took a train as far as Wentzville. The same train carried two companies of German American Unionists from Colonel B. Gratz Brown's Fourth Missouri Infantry. They were heading up the rail line to act as bridge guards. Mudd examined the arms and equipment of these new enemies carefully before leaving the train. Once home, he joined a company being raised by John Q. Burbridge in the nearby village of Louisiana. Soon more than two hundred men from both infantry and cavalry companies had assembled in the area.

Many were armed with old muskets that Burbridge and other Secessionists had taken from the Missouri Depot near Liberty in April.[20]

Their march southwest to join Governor Jackson "was a triumph," Mudd recalled. Units from the counties they traversed joined the column, swelling its ranks to almost one thousand. After slipping across the Missouri River, they marched for ten days on short rations to reach a State Guard camp just south of the Osage. Continuing on, they arrived at the main rendezvous, Camp Lamar, near the village of Lamar, in early July. There Mudd's company became part of the division-in-exile being organized by Brigadier General John B. Clark Sr. The infantry companies were consolidated into a single regiment, 270 strong, which elected Burbridge colonel. The division's 273 mounted men, likewise consolidated, were led by Colonel James Patrick Major, a West Point graduate who had resigned his lieutenancy in the Second U.S. Cavalry only ten weeks earlier.[21]

Henry Guibor had an even rougher journey. A thirty-eight-year-old native of St. Louis who initially practiced the carpenter's trade, he saw military service in the Mexican War and was active in border raids against Kansans in the 1850s. He was deputy marshal for the criminal court in St. Louis when, as commander of a battery of militia artillery, he was captured at Camp Jackson. Guibor was released after swearing not to take up arms against the Federal government, but like other parolees he dismissed that oath on the grounds that it had been forced on him at gunpoint by a man who had no authority or legal basis for demanding it. Nevertheless, Guibor remained neutral, looking after his widowed mother, until friends warned him that he was about to be arrested on suspicion of treason. Obviously civil courts could offer no protection for anyone who provoked Blair or Lyon. So together with William P. Barlow, a friend and fellow artillerist who also feared arrest, Guibor fled the city on horseback on June 13, heading for Jefferson City to join Price.[22]

Avoiding Unionist Home Guards who were scouting in the area, they approached the state capital only to find it already in Lyon's hands. Told that Price was in Versailles, they rode to that village and were promptly arrested by the local "Committee of Public Safety" on suspicion of being spies working for Lyon. They eventually convinced the leader of the State Guard company being organized there that they were loyal Missourians and were released to continue their search for Price. At Warsaw they were again arrested as spies. Price was not there, but when Governor Jackson arrived with a column of troops, one of his staff officers recognized Guibor. Promptly released, he was eventually given command of a battery consisting of four Mexican War vintage six-pound guns taken from the

Missouri Depot. Officially designated the First Light Artillery Battery, Parsons's Division, like many batteries it was more often called after its commander: Guibor's Battery. Its personnel were mostly St. Louis Irishmen.[23]

Some Missourians were simply caught up in the flow of events. Daniel H. McIntyre, a senior only days short of graduation from Westminster College in Fulton, was eating lunch at the school when he and a friend received an urgent message to go to the town square. Leaving their textbooks open and their meal unfinished, they hurried out to find groups of men drilling in the streets. "When we got there we found we'd been elected officers," McIntyre recalled. "We moved on to join General Price and never returned to college."[24]

Henry M. Cheavens was a thirty-one-year-old schoolteacher in Boone County. Although born in Philadelphia, he had been raised in Missouri. Educated at Yale and Amherst, he taught in Illinois and Minnesota before returning to his adopted state. The account he wrote a few days after being wounded at Wilson's Creek gives no explanation for his decision to join the State Guard, but it details his experiences vividly. Shortly after the fight at Boonville, Cheavens joined a group of eighty horsemen trying to reach Jackson's army. His military kit consisted of a white blanket, a Mississippi rifle, and a bowie knife. He soon lost not only the blanket but his coat as well and broke his glasses. But unlike some of his comrades, he never turned back. Dodging various Unionist Home Guard patrols as they moved south, the riders brushed past the First Iowa, which was then heading west. "We received the acclamations of the people, who seemed rejoiced to see us," Cheavens wrote, but the would-be soldiers took care to obtain local guides and whenever possible stopped only at the farms of known Secessionists. Somewhere north of the Osage River they finally located the divisions of Generals Rains and Slack and accompanied them thereafter. The pace was hard and their route sometimes confused, as Cheavens wrote of a long countermarch. As rain turned the roads to muck, "men fell from their horses with fatigue." When time allowed, he worked to sew a tent for himself and his friends. Finally, on July 3, they reached Camp Lamar, where troops from Parsons's and Clark's Divisions were waiting. Cheavens's horse was so worn out that he traded it for a draft animal, but for him the trip ended on a happy note. The quartermaster issued him a new pair of pants, and a Major Bell recommended snakeroot for his diarrhea. It worked.[25]

Virginia native Edgar Asbury provides another example. Asbury moved to Missouri in 1857 and opened a law practice in Houston. A "strong secessionist," he served in the state convention and was in Jefferson City when Governor Jackson returned to the capital following the Planters' House meeting with Lyon. Jackson asked Asbury to escort three wagons loaded with gunpowder to safety in the southern part of the state and to deliver a State Guard general's commission to Judge James H. McBride in Greene County.[26]

The trip south was a nightmare. Secrecy and speed were vital, so in addition to the civilian teamsters, Asbury took only two men, Wood Rogers and W. H. H. Thomas, with him to guard the precious cargo. The powder was stored in a variety of containers in the wagons, and the "rough and stony flint roads" they traveled "bursted and broke the packages so that it was constantly streaming and leaking the powder along the road." Fearing an explosion, Rogers and Thomas deserted, but Asbury saw the mission through to its end, although, he recalled, "my hair literally stood out straight on ends."[27]

McBride appointed Asbury a lieutenant colonel and aide-de-camp on his staff and promptly gave him another assignment: to deliver State Guard commissions to loyal Missourians in Springfield. This was "a very difficult and hazardous undertaking," as Unionists were firmly in control there. Asbury again accomplished his mission—by sneaking into town at dawn. Before he could leave, he met a former acquaintance, Mordecai Oliver, who was now a major in the local Union Home Guard company. When Oliver asked about his business in town, Asbury "told him a great, big lie." Indeed, he damned Secessionists so thoroughly that Oliver invited him to dinner later that day. "He had a very pleasant family, two handsome daughters among the rest," Asbury later wrote, "but I decided it was best for me to get out of that place." Instead of keeping his appointment with Oliver, he rode to Houston, where a rendezvous camp for the men of McBride's Division had been established. After almost a month of training and organization there, they received orders to join Price at Cassville. By that time so much of southwestern Missouri was in Union hands that they crossed into Arkansas before moving west, approaching Price's camp from the south.[28]

Finally, Colonel Joseph M. Kelly's Washington Blues illustrate the connections between prewar militia units and those of the Missouri State Guard. They were formed in 1857 as an offshoot of the St. Louis Washington Guards. Although the Blues were Irish, most belonged to a local temperance organization and their leader, Captain Kelly, was a former British soldier who demanded exacting discipline. After 1858 the unit wore dark blue frock coats and sky blue trousers and carried the Model 1855 Springfield rifle. With white waist belts and cartridge box slings, and tall shakos for dress parade, they made a natty appearance.[29]

In early May, while other units of the Missouri volunteer militia trained at Camp Jackson, Kelly's unit escorted a shipment of two hundred muskets and seventy tons of powder from St. Louis to Jefferson City. There the men learned of Lyon's capture of the state militia and the subsequent "Camp Jackson Massacre." When the state legislature created the Missouri State Guard, the Blues volunteered, technically forming a new unit but retaining their name. They promptly elected Kelly their captain. Eventually combined with other companies, including men raised by John S. Marmaduke and Basil Duke, they formed the nucleus of a First Rifle Regiment in Parsons's Division.[30]

While Price continued to assemble men at Cassville, the bulk of the State Guard was camped farther north, just outside Lamar, under Jackson's overall command. Although the men were enlisted only in the service of their state, some of the Missourians displayed Confederate banners. While this was forbidden under Price's standing orders, no effort was made to remove the Confederate flags, which raises questions concerning the allegiance of the State Guard. Governor Jackson had contributed substantially to the ambiguity of their loyalty by the carefully calculated wording of his June 12 proclamation calling on Missourians to join the Guard in order to resist Lyon. Making no mention of his own negotiations with the Confederacy, Jackson focused on the unconstitutional actions of Lyon, Blair, and Lincoln. He reminded Missourians that as American citizens they were bound by the Constitution and Federal law. But their first loyalty, he argued, should be to their state, and they were "under no obligation whatever to obey the unconstitutional edicts of the military despotism which has enthroned itself at Washington."[31]

No comprehensive study of the motivations of the men who served in the State Guard exists. One historian expresses the quandary thus: "For these were STATE troops in capitals. They were not yet Confederates officially, some of them would never be. They were in many cases fighting solely for Missouri, and Missouri was in trouble. . . . nothing was clear cut—it was simply Missouri."[32]

Some 20,000 Missourians served in the State Guard from its organization in 1861 until August 1862. At that time, all but a handful of its members either entered Confederate service or went home. Thousands chose the latter course, but whether from fatigue or faint heart, or because their political convictions made Confederate service anathema, will never be known.[33] Nor can one determine with accuracy the motivations of the more than 5,000 troops of the State Guard who fought at Wilson's Creek. The range of their views can be sampled, however.

Long after the war, one veteran asserted that the State Guard had been "typical of the cause and the times" because it was raised in "a popular outburst against the tyranny of Federal power." Contemporary evidence confirms the old soldier's memory, at least in the case of some Missourians. The Polk County Rangers are an example. Organized in 1860, long before the secession crisis, they particularly prized their beautiful silk national flag, made by the ladies of Greenfield and presented to them on the Fourth of July. But in late April 1861, following Lincoln's call for volunteers, the Rangers returned this banner to the donors. In a letter to the local press, they explained that because a "narrow-souled and fanatical minority-President" had ignored "his Constitutional obligations" and the "Rights of the States as sovereignties," they could "no longer, consistent with honor and justice, *march under* or *fight for* the Northern flag." It was now "the peculiar banner of cutthroats, murderers, and Abolitionists." But although they proclaimed their loyalty to the South and sympathy for the Confederacy, these Missourians were not Secessionists. For they also pledged that "should our deplorable national difficulties ever be adjusted and the different sections of our country be again united, as God grant that it may," they would "gladly take back from your fair hands" the Stars and Stripes.[34]

The Polk County Rangers were conditional Unionists. They wanted neither war nor independence, but their political views and, equally important, their corporate sense of honor, left them no choice when events forced them to choose sides. Early in May the ladies of Greenfield made a "Southern flag" for the Rangers, which was presented at a community picnic. After the Missouri State Guard was formed, these Polk County volunteers, under Captain Ashbury C. Bradford, became part of the large cavalry brigade commanded by Colonel James Cawthorn of Rains's Division.[35]

Warner Lewis linked his State Guard service and that of fellow Vernon County residents to fears of attack by Kansas "Jayhawkers," a name given to bands of antislavery activists who had raided western Missouri frequently during the previous six years. "At the first call for volunteers," he remembered, "the men in the border counties flew to arms as one man." Though Lewis doubtless exaggerates the unanimity of sentiment in western Missouri, his explanation of motives is revealing. "These people," he claimed, "were not all rebels, nor disunionists, but believed that they were serving the lawfully constituted authorities of the State, in repelling invasion and in protecting their homes and firesides." The Federal government was "lending aid and comfort to the enemies of the State." Consequently, "it was not possible that an honorable, self-respecting and courageous people would tamely submit to its authority."[36] Although

Lewis wrote long after the war ended, his explanations indicate that a corporate sense of honor and community reputation was as strong a motivation for Missourians as it was for soldiers elsewhere.

There is no question that many Missourians fought to preserve slavery, but at the level of individuals information is frustratingly scarce. Take, for instance, James H. McNeill, a Virginian who moved with his slaves to Missouri in 1848. When the war erupted, he owned a three-hundred-acre farm in Davies County, but his real wealth was tied up in neither land nor slaves, but cattle. At age forty-six he might have sat out the conflict without incurring social ostracism, but instead he raised a company of cavalry that included all three of his sons. McNeill's decision to take up arms eventually cost not only his own life, but that of one of his sons, yet he left no record of his motives. No one was more blunt about the role of slavery in motivating Missourians than John D. Keith, who stated after the war that he had fought "to maintain the integrity of the white race." Prominent slaveholder John Taylor Hughes also placed race at the center of the question. "The Blacks and Unionists are now all one with us," he wrote a friend. "We must all share the same fate, and submit to the conquering hosts of abolition, or maintain our independence of them at the point of the sword and bayonet." Hughes was motivated by more than just a desire to protect the "peculiar institution." He took up arms, he explained, for "our ancient rights, secured to the people by the Constitution of the State, and of the United States, but now denied to us, and ruthlessly trampled under foot by tyrants and usurpers." Hughes was a Whig, but although his party had effectively ceased to exist he was a man of influence. A Kentucky native, he was a veteran of the Mexican War, a newspaperman, a school superintendent, and a former state representative. He gave numerous speeches throughout northwestern Missouri and helped raise five companies for the State Guard. When the Caldwell Minute Men, Carroll Light Infantry, Stewartville Rifles, and others were organized into one regiment as part of Slack's Division, they elected Hughes colonel. But whether they did so because they valued his military experience, endorsed his views on race, or shared his opinion of the political situation is unknown.[37]

Like most soldiers, North and South, the average Missouri State Guardsman went to war for a variety of reasons. Among them, no doubt, were both a genuine sense of community honor and a fear of the social ostracism that failure to volunteer might incur. There was a determination to protect the status quo and defend hearth and home, which included an assumption of white supremacy and deep alarm at any hint of interference with the institution of slavery. Most supported the right of a state to secede and were shocked by the manner in which Lincoln, Lyon, and Blair violated the Constitution. They were either unaware of, or unconcerned by, Governor Jackson's direct negotiations with the Confederacy.[38]

Although there was no shortage of Irish and German Americans in the Guard, one must also wonder about the role of ethnicity in the conflict. The rapid influx of immigrants between 1850 and 1860 made St. Louis one of the fastest-growing cities in the nation. The ability of Lyon, Blair, and Sigel to raise and equip German American regiments rapidly signaled a profound shift in Missouri's political and social makeup. Power was moving out of the hands of the agriculturally oriented planters of the Missouri River valley. As they spent only a few weeks a year in the rather sleepy state capital, their strength was rural and local. Their orientation, when it went beyond the state, was Southern. The German Americans who followed Sigel, and Republicans like Blair who were eager to cooperate with them, reflected the rise of urban influences. Increasingly tied together by railways, they were national rather than sectional in outlook. Lyon's actions made St. Louis the true center of political power in Missouri. The troops that marched across the countryside under his direction would help determine, by their success or failure, just what sort of state Missouri would be.

Chapter 6

Good Tents and Bad Water

Ben McCulloch was a busy man. As he watched events unfold in Missouri, he continued to gather forces in the vicinity of Fort Smith. His task was made considerably easier when late in May the Arkansas secession convention—still holding meetings and feuding with Governor Rector— passed a resolution that required the Arkansas State Troops under Bart Pearce to cooperate with the Confederate commander. Not to be outdone, Rector sent McCulloch a message giving him command of all military forces in the state.[1]

As McCulloch was charged with defending the Indian Territory, and by implication the Confederacy's boundary from Arkansas west to the Texas–New Mexico border, much of his time was taken up with Native American affairs. On May 30 he left his Fort Smith headquarters with Captain Albert Pike to meet with various tribes in the hope of securing treaties of alliance and recruiting Native American troops for the Confederacy. In the long run, this effort benefited the Confederacy considerably. The Cherokee Nation included a number of slaveholders, mostly men of mixed ancestry, whose sympathies lay with the South. Some of them began organizing immediately under Stand Watie and Joel B. Mayes, but only a small number of Cherokee would participate in the Battle of Wilson's Creek.[2]

While McCulloch was thus occupied, troops continued to join his growing western army. Some reached Fort Smith quickly, while others took considerable time. The Third Louisiana was delayed in Little Rock because the water level in the Arkansas River had dropped. Their temporary camp, at a city park near the arsenal, reminded the European-born William Watson of "a nobleman's park in the old country." A fellow

Pelican, Willie Tunnard, left a similar description. "The grounds," he recalled, "were beautifully laid out, and shaded by large and handsome oaks." The Louisianans drilled for six hours each day and in their spare time rolled cartridges for their muskets. Captain David Pierson informed his family back in Winn Parrish: "Our regiment is rapidly improving in infantry exercises. At first we were an awful green set but have improved so far that we do pretty well." The ladies of the city made frequent visits to the camp, and not a few romantic attachments were made by moonlight. The Third Louisiana also participated in the ceremonial presentation of a flag to a Little Rock company that was part of the First Arkansas Mounted Rifles. The main address, by a Miss Faulkner, was "one of peculiar force and unsurpassed eloquence," Tunnard recalled. She presented the banner as a constant reminder of the regiment's duty to protect the state and its citizens from the "ruthless marauders" of the North, proclaiming: "Let it be borne aloft into the thickest of the fight—up to the highest eminence of honor. Let the sight of it animate and encourage you; nerving you in the hour of trial to the utmost pitch of fortitude and courage!" When the speech ended, the Louisianans passed in review, each company saluting the flag as the Arkansans cheered.[3]

The First Arkansas was organized by Thomas J. Churchill, who later became governor of the state. A native of Louisville, he had served in the Mexican War with a regiment of Kentucky mounted infantry. Moving to Arkansas following his discharge, he married the daughter of a prominent politician and settled down as a planter. His estate, which he named "Blenheim," included about fifty slaves, making him one of the wealthiest men in the area. A longtime Democrat, he entered politics modestly as Little Rock postmaster in 1857, holding that appointive position until he resigned in 1861 to raise volunteers. The decision was a natural one, as he was already captain of the Pulaski Light Cavalry (also called the Pulaski Lancers), one of the county's four prewar militia units. When enough mounted companies reached Little Rock to organize a regiment, Churchill was unanimously elected colonel.[4]

Churchill's men came from ten different counties and most of their units bore names indicating their community roots. These included the Chicot Rangers, the Augusta Guards, the Yell County Rifles, the Des Arc Rangers, and the Independence Rifles. A notable exception was the Napoleon Cavalry, made up of men from both Little Rock and Fort Smith. The Napoleons contained some unlikely talent in the form of Charles Mitchell, who had attended the Western Military Academy at Nashville for a year, then transferred to St. John's College in Little Rock. When Churchill's men camped on the college grounds, Mitchell dropped out of school to enlist, although he was only three months past his fifteenth birthday. Toward the opposite end of the spectrum, in terms of age and education, was farmer John Johnson, a second lieutenant in the Pulaski Rangers. A North Carolina native and forty-eight-year-old father of six, he joined up along with his two oldest sons, Pleasant and Harrison. John and Pleasant Johnson would not survive the fight at Wilson's Creek, nor would Harrison Johnson survive the war. John wrote dutifully to his wife during his relatively brief military service, but his surviving letters leave no clue about his reasons for enlisting.[5]

Like any good regimental commander, Churchill was serious about training. A Little Rock newspaper correspondent described his regiment as "very well drilled" and noted that the men were "burning with a desire to meet the impudent cohorts of republicanism." During one parade the fifes and drums of the Third Louisiana stopped playing because they had spooked a line of Churchill's horsemen. The colonel asked the musicians to continue so the animals could become accustomed to martial noises. Later Churchill acquired several bugles for the regiment. The horses' subsequent antics can be imagined. The greatest problem in organizing the regiment was a shortage of weapons. Some companies had arrived expecting to receive arms from the captured Little Rock Arsenal. But there were not enough to go around and a few men returned home. "If we only had arms," lamented Robert Neill to his home folk. He feared that "if Lincoln's masters knew their power and our weakness and had courage they might almost devastate our state."[6]

Standardization of arms was also a problem. Churchill provoked a near mutiny when he ordered the Pulaski Rangers to exchange their pistols and sabers for flintlock muskets. The men in Lieutenant Johnson's company considered this an outrage, and Johnson himself, from a decidedly rural perspective, looked down on the "city fops" who made up much of the regiment's officer cadre. Despite such problems, Churchill was a popular commander. "Everyone that I hear express themselves is pleased with Col. Churchill," Neill wrote. "He seems a very plain man, yet has the appearance of being a thoughtful and energetic one."[7]

By the time McCulloch returned from the Indian Territory in mid-June, the same rains that were to cause headaches for Lyon in Missouri raised the level of the Arkansas River sufficiently for the Third Louisiana and First Arkansas to start for Fort Smith. The trip was miserable, due to excessive heat and cramped conditions on the boats. Some officers of the Louisiana regiment were joined by their wives, who had accompanied them this far. Where they found accommodations in Fort Smith is a

Lieutenant Dave Alexander, Napoleon Cavalry, First Arkansas Mounted Rifles (The collection of Dr. Tom and Karen Sweeney, General Sweeny's Museum, Republic, Missouri)

mystery, as the town was overcrowded. Men were camped in fields for miles around the fort. Willie Tunnard recalled that the men suffered severely from both the daily heat and an outbreak of measles that swept through the camp. A soldier in an Arkansas unit informed his wife: "We are camped about five miles south of Ft. Smith in the prairie where the sun pours her heat on us without a tree or bush to shade our heads. We have good tents & bad water to drink."[8]

Before the month ended some of the troops were shifted across the Arkansas to the town of Van Buren. Among them was the Totten Light Battery. Captain Woodruff's men camped in the Van Buren courthouse square where the fences could act as a corral for horses. Heretofore the Tottens had exercised their guns by hand, but by purchase and impressment they now acquired the dozens of horses necessary to complete their battery. The maneuvers the men and horses needed to perfect in order to move, limber, or unlimber were quite complex. Woodruff realized to his horror that this portion of artillery drill, which he had last performed nine years ago at his military school in Kentucky, had escaped his memory. He therefore found a pretext to return to Fort Smith, where a few minutes observing Captain John G. Reid's Fort Smith Light Battery at drill brought the procedures back to him.[9]

In time, the force available to McCulloch reached considerable proportions. In addition to Colonel Louis Hébert's Third Louisiana and Colonel Thomas Churchill's First Arkansas Mounted Rifles, his Confederate troops consisted of the Second Arkansas Mounted Rifles under Colonel James M. McIntosh and a battalion of infantry under Lieutenant Colonel Dandridge McRae. Together these units eventually totaled almost two thousand men, and Greer's South Kansas–Texas Cavalry, still en route, would raise the number even higher. Although the men and animals stationed around Fort Smith consumed several tons of food and fodder daily, as long as they remained near the Arkansas River supply problems were not insurmountable, at least from the commander's point of view. On June 14 John Johnson grumbled in a letter to his wife, "Our fare is very rough. Horse food scarce."[10]

McIntosh led the Second Arkansas Mounted Rifles. He had earned a degree from West Point a year after the end of the Mexican War, a conflict that had taken the life of his father, a colonel in the Regulars. Although he graduated last in his class, by 1857 he was a captain in the First U.S. Cavalry. This was an astonishingly swift rise for peacetime service, and his regiment was considered by many to be the elite of the army. McIntosh resigned his commission in May 1861, while stationed at Fort Smith. He had no way of knowing that this action would profoundly affect his younger brother. Believing that James had disgraced the family name, John Baillie McIntosh volunteered for the Union forces. John eventually rose to the rank of major general, James to brigadier general, but only the brother in blue would survive the war.[11]

The companies that formed McIntosh's unit came mostly from northwestern Arkansas. Although no statistical analysis has been made of it, names that might indicate foreign birth are conspicuously absent from its muster rolls. The information available suggests that leadership at the company level otherwise reflected a diversity common with other units. The captains included Ben T. Embry, a prosperous farmer and merchant who had organized a company at Galla Rock. Embry was forty-one, while John A. Arrington, who led a company from Bentonville, was only twenty-four. Mexican War veteran Henry K. Brown raised a company at Paraclifta, and George E. Gamble brought in a company from Hempstead. Gamble's men joined the regiment late, on August 4, less than a week before the Battle of Wilson's Creek. Whatever the cause of their delay, it allowed them time to receive a flag from the women of the county before leaving.[12]

The list of company commanders also included future Arkansas governor Harris Flanagin. Born in Rhodestown, New Jersey, he had attained only a common school education before becoming a teacher himself at the Clermont Seminary in Frankfort, Pennsylvania. In a short time he was made professor of mathematics and English. In 1838 he opened his own school in Paoli, Illinois, and the next year was admitted to the bar. Law had apparently been his ambition from the first, for he moved to Greeneville, Arkansas, in 1839 and set up a practice. Politically Flanagin was a Whig. He was a deputy sheriff for Clark County and served a term as state senator. Described as having "a mathematical turn of mind, precise and exact in all his dealings," he was "a very poor orator unless his tongue caught fire from the force of his thoughts." Although he had opposed secession, Flanagin raised a mounted company as soon as war broke out, riding into Fort Smith with eighty-eight volunteers for the Confederacy. They were armed with double-barreled shotguns and "large home-made knives ranging from twenty-five to thirty-six inches in length." Bird, Flanagin's part-Choctaw African American slave, accompanied him, as he would throughout the war.[13]

The unit commanded by Dandridge McRae had no numerical designation, being identified on muster rolls simply as McRae's Battalion, Arkansas Volunteers. McRae, who was thirty-two, grand master of his Masonic lodge, and a slaveholder, was a native of Baldwin County, Alabama, and a graduate of the College of South Carolina. He moved to Searcy, Arkansas, in 1849, read law, and was admitted to the bar in 1854. Two years later he was elected county and circuit court clerk.[14]

When his state left the Union, McRae immediately raised a company of volunteers from White County. Shortly thereafter Governor Rector made him inspector general of Arkansas State Troops. During June and July McRae also assisted McCulloch in attracting recruits for Confederate service. His battalion was not large, fielding just over two hundred men at the Battle of Wilson's Creek. Surviving records, which are incomplete, reveal that its companies were a mixed lot. Levels of training ranged from "good" to "insufficient" and discipline from "fair" to "indifferent." Arms were described as "indifferent," varying from percussion muskets to "Common hunting guns of the country." Some men had cartridge boxes, waist belts, canteens, and blankets, while others had none. Two thirds of the men were issued matching pants and blouses, apparently gray, but shoes were desperately needed.[15]

Records for the company raised by Captain C. L. Lawrence, a twenty-eight-year-old lawyer originally from Kentucky, are unusually complete. The company's youngest member was William M. Sisco, at age fifteen only five feet tall. He was listed as a farmer and an Arkansas native. The oldest soldier, forty-seven-year-old Maston K. White, was also a farmer and a native of South Carolina. Most of the men gave their occupations as farmer, but there were also teachers, carpenters, and blacksmiths, a wood chopper, a painter, and a distiller. All but eight men were born in the South. The company contained two men born in Germany, two born in Ireland, and four born in Northern states. The battalion's most interesting recruit was Mark Mars, a seventeen-year-old farmer who was listed as one-quarter African American and three-quarters Cherokee. By the social customs of the South he was considered to be a black man. Yet Mars was not a camp servant or a slave like Flanagin's Bird, but a free man and a soldier. His motives for enlisting and his relationship with the white men in his unit remain a tantalizing mystery.[16]

When the Arkansas authorities gave McCulloch control over the state troops, they doubled the effective force available to the Confederate commander. Like McCulloch, Bart Pearce had been busy organizing and training his troops, a process that was not complete until late July. Although he had troops posted at several locations, his main facility, Camp Walker, was strategically located near Maysville, a small village in the extreme northwestern corner of the state. Roads leading due south linked it with Fort Smith, while those heading southeast gave access to Bentonville and Fayetteville, which were on the Wire Road that ran north to Springfield. The camp utilized a five-hundred-acre tract of land and set of buildings recently abandoned by the Harmonial Vegetarian Society, a failed perfectionist community. This made good sense, as the commune's main building, three stories tall with ninety rooms, made an excellent barracks. But in early June, Pearce was accused of selecting the site to allow his father-in-law, Dr. John Smith, to sell the soldiers flour at inflated prices from his nearby gristmill. A board of officers conducting an investigation of the matter exonerated Pearce, but the episode was a major distraction.[17]

The force eventually assembled by Pearce consisted of two understrength cavalry units, three infantry regiments, and two artillery batteries. Colonel DeRosey Carroll led the First Arkansas Cavalry (also called the First Arkansas Mounted Volunteers). This was supplemented by a separate, smaller unit, known simply as Carroll's Arkansas Cavalry, led by Captain Charles A. Carroll. Together they numbered almost 400 men. The three infantry units, roughly equal in strength, were 1,700 strong. Colonel John Gratiot led the Third Infantry, Colonel Jonathan D. Walker the Fourth, Colonel Tom P. Dockery the Fifth. They were supplemented by Reid's Fort Smith Battery and Woodruff's battery, each with four guns. In June Woodruff's battery changed its name from the Tottens to the

A rare prebattle photograph of
Company H of the Third Arkansas
Infantry, Arkansas State Troops
(The collection of Dr. Tom and
Karen Sweeney, General Sweeny's
Museum, Republic, Missouri)

Pulaski Light Battery, as news from Missouri now made it apparent that
Captain James Totten would be a future enemy.[18]

With the exception of Woodruff's unit, even less is known about the
Arkansas State Troops than the Missouri State Guard. Some of Pearce's
men had been examined by McRae back in early May, while he was acting
as state inspector general. He described the volunteers as "the wildest
blood in the South." He meant this as a compliment, for his praise of them
was extravagant, writing: "They are however the best men in the whole
state. It makes the heart of any true friend of Arkansas thrill with pride to
see what men we are enabled to turn out. There is no drunkenness, no
noise, no confusion, and they cheerfully obey every order."[19] Although
good troops, in reality the Arkansans fell considerably short of the saint-
hood McRae was willing to bestow on them.

When McCulloch learned that Lyon had negated the so-called Price-
Harney agreement by declaring war on the state of Missouri, he immediately began shifting as many troops as possible from the Fort Smith–
Van Buren area to join Pearce at Camp Walker. Units moved individually
over a period of several weeks. Woodruff's Pulaski Battery received quite
a send-off, as "the mistaken hospitality of some of the Van Buren people
had overflowed with something stronger than water." In plain terms, some
of the men were drunk. The first day's march was a nightmare. Officers
and men lacked experience, but worse still many of the horses had never
been trained to harness. As a result the battery was soon strung out for

miles. Although discipline improved over the next few days, crossing the Boston Mountains was onerous. The overall effect of the experience was positive, however, as it illuminated the battery's defects. Once established at Camp Walker, Woodruff instituted a vigorous program of drills.[20]

The Third Louisiana was not ordered north until June 28. For reasons that are unclear, the regiment moved in two separate battalions, with a day's interval between them. Like Woodruff's artillerists, the Louisianans had logged more miles on steamboat than on foot. In fact, they had never marched with full equipment. Consequently, the movement to Camp Walker was long remembered by veterans of the Wilson's Creek campaign. The trip commenced "amid the wildest enthusiasm" but proved to be a "severe experience." Willie Tunnard recalled: "Shoulders grew sore under the burden of supporting knapsacks; limbs wearied from the painful march, and feet grew swollen and blistered as the troops marched along the dusty road. Knapsacks were recklessly thrown by the roadside or relieved of a large portion of their contents, under the intolerable agony of that first march of only nine miles." But soon a routine was established, and the men bore their hardships "with fortitude and courage, keeping up their spirits with songs and jokes as they tramped steadily forward." Because of the intense heat, reveille was usually sounded around 2:00 A.M., with a halt for the day called at noon. Crossing the Boston Mountains was so exhausting that for weeks afterward mere mention of them produced "expletives innumerable."[21]

Captain R. M. Hinson of the Moorehouse Guards described the experience as "a hard march of seven days covered with dust & blistered feet." But in a letter to his wife Mattie, he also noted traveling through "a beautiful valley from one to three hundred yards wide, with mountains on each side higher than any bluff you have seen on the Ark. river." Nor had the trip been without its pleasures. At the home of a Mrs. Foster, who was apparently kin to his wife, Hinson and a friend obtained "a ham boiled & turkey baked which lasted us several days." The captain apparently did not share this bounty with his enlisted men, but he refused an offer to stay overnight in the comforts of the Foster home, citing his command responsibilities.[22]

The battalion that included Hinson's company had just reached the Boston Mountains when word arrived from McCulloch to make a forced march for Camp Walker. Although the prospect was dismaying, the reason for McCulloch's orders brought unparalleled excitement to the Louisianans. Governor Jackson's Missouri State Guard was reportedly about to be overwhelmed by the forces directed by Lyon. In response, "Old Ben," the self-taught Texas Ranger who eschewed swords or uniforms, wore a dark civilian suit, and rode with a rifle across his saddle horn, had just initiated the first invasion of the United States by the Confederacy.[23]

McCulloch had been preoccupied with events in Missouri for some time. If Missouri joined the Confederacy, his task of defending the Indian Territory would be much easier, as thousands of Missourians could be expected to join Confederate regiments. But the present condition of affairs, a literal civil war between the legal state government and the administration in Washington, left McCulloch in a quandary. The Confederacy's legitimacy rested on an expression of the will of the people in each state. How could Confederate authorities intervene in a state that was still in the Union and might remain so?

When McCulloch received a request for assistance from Governor Jackson, his response balanced political expediency with his own duties. On June 14 he asked the War Department for permission to move north through the Indian Territory to seize Fort Scott, Kansas. The Confederate government might proclaim that the Southern states merely wanted to depart in peace, but McCulloch considered a good offense to be the best defense. He was apparently untroubled by the larger implications of his suggestion. He believed that a movement into Kansas would probably force John Ross, the principal chief of the Cherokee, to abandon his current neutrality and begin recruiting regiments for the Confederacy. This would protect the Indian Territory, which was McCulloch's primary responsibility. Moreover, the presence of his troops in Kansas would relieve pressure on the Missouri State Guard without placing a single Confederate soldier on Missouri's sensitive soil. In response, the War Department on June 26 authorized McCulloch to move into either Kansas or Missouri, as circumstances warranted. The Texan then gave orders to concentrate all available forces in the vicinity of Maysville. Any action he contemplated would have to be prompt, for as the summer progressed the water level in the Arkansas River would decrease, exacerbating his supply problems.[24]

Although Arkansas officials had placed their state's troops at McCulloch's disposal, Arkansas was not part of his military department, and his requests to Richmond for permission to use them went unanswered. In fact, late in June the War Department appointed Brigadier General William J. Hardee, who was then in Memphis, commander of Confederate forces in Arkansas. But McCulloch did not know this, and in the absence of any prohibition he not only accepted command of Pearce's troops but also issued a proclamation calling all Arkansans to rally to the defense of their state against the "Black Republicans" invading Missouri. Like Lyon, McCulloch was not a man to quibble over legalities when action seemed necessary.[25]

Soon after reaching Maysville, McCulloch met with Sterling Price, who had crossed into Arkansas to seek his help. The Missouri general provided firsthand information about the strategic position of the State Guard. Price had established a camp on Cowskin Prairie in the extreme southwestern corner of Missouri, assembling some 1,700 men. But Springfield was in Union hands and a column of troops under Sigel was reported to be near Neosho, between Price's and Jackson's forces. Should Sigel defeat Jackson, or should Jackson be caught between Sigel's men and Lyon's column, the Missouri State Guard might never be able to concentrate at one location to complete its recruiting and training. On the other hand, if Price, Pearce, and McCulloch rushed north, their combined forces and those of the Missouri governor might crush Sigel between them. Such a movement was clearly authorized under McCulloch's June 26 dispatch from the War Department. A week after those instructions were written, the secretary of war, Leroy Pope Walker, informed McCulloch that a decision to invade the north was best left to the higher authorities. Yet he acknowledged that because of the circumstances and slow nature of communications, McCulloch might have to act on his own initiative. This loophole was fortunate for McCulloch. For on July 4, the very day Walker composed his letter in far-off Virginia, McCulloch led Confederate troops across the border. Recognizing both the peril and the opportunity, he and Pearce had agreed to assist Price.[26]

McCulloch intended to move with every available man—both the Confederate forces under his direct command, which were styled McCulloch's Brigade, as well as the Arkansas State Troops, designated Pearce's Brigade. But after receiving a message on July 5 that a battle between Jackson and Sigel was imminent, he pushed ahead with a vanguard of three thousand mounted men, drawn from both brigades. He had not gone far before learning that Sigel was now near Carthage, farther north than originally reported. Although this news made it unlikely that McCulloch's troops could arrive in time to assist Jackson, he acted as aggressively as possible under the circumstances. While the main force went into camp after its hard march, he selected his freshest men and ordered them to press on to capture the small garrison Sigel had left behind at Neosho.[27]

The attacking force was led by Colonel McIntosh, who in addition to commanding the Second Arkansas Mounted Rifles held a position on McCulloch's staff and acted, unofficially, as his second-in-command. The troops came from Churchill's First Arkansas Mounted Rifles, supplemented by Carroll's Arkansas Cavalry. The men moved in two columns, one under McIntosh, the other under Churchill, approaching Neosho from the south and west. Churchill arrived first and, fearing that the enemy would escape, attacked immediately. The result was anticlimactic, as the Federals surrendered without a shot. The first military engagement of the war involving substantial numbers of Confederate troops on Northern soil was a bloodless Southern victory.[28]

In addition to capturing Captain Joseph Conrad and 137 men of the Third Missouri Infantry, McIntosh netted a company flag, one hundred rifles, and seven wagons loaded with provisions. But this was no substitute for assisting Jackson. During the evening McCulloch heard artillery fire to the north. Consequently, he remounted his men for an all-night march. They joined McIntosh at Neosho in the morning of July 6 and after a short rest continued north. Some twenty miles beyond Neosho they finally encountered Jackson's men. The Missouri governor was jubilant and rightly so. The day before the State Guard had defeated Sigel, redeeming the disgrace of Boonville and derailing Lyon's strategy in one swoop.[29]

Although too small to be dignified by the term "battle," the skirmish that began on the morning of July 5 was prolonged. Scouts had brought Jackson word on the previous evening that the Federals were camped to the south, in the vicinity of Carthage. Although one of his subordinates urged an immediate attack, the Missouri governor abandoned the element of surprise in order to choose a favorable position. On the morning of the fifth he aligned his men on the high ground above Coon Creek, several miles north of Carthage, and waited for Sigel to find him. His troops—the State Guard divisions of Rains, Clark, Slack, and Parsons—numbered over four thousand men and included two artillery batteries. But although this gave them a numerical advantage over Sigel's reported force, the State Guard was poorly armed. Many soldiers had only shotguns or hunting rifles, and ammunition was scant not only for infantry but for artillery as well.[30]

Jackson's position was not actually a trap, but it did allow Sigel to display his own rashness and ineptitude. When the Union commander discovered his enemy, he decided to attack even though he had only 950 infantry. Crossing the creek, he placed his artillery in advantageous positions. The fight began around 11:00 A.M. as an artillery duel that pitted Major Franz Backof's Missouri Light Artillery against fellow Missourians in the State Guard batteries of Captain Hiram Bledsoe and Captain

Henry Guibor. But when Sigel's infantry advanced through the open prairie, flanks exposed and numerical inferiority plain to see, Jackson's lack of military experience hardly mattered. When the State Guard began outflanking the Federals, Sigel was forced to withdraw. This pattern was repeated throughout the day, as Sigel made a fighting retreat all the way back into the streets of Carthage.[31]

To his credit, Sigel never panicked. His men fought well, allowing Sigel to extricate himself from a desperate situation with his force intact and safely take the roads that eventually led them back to Springfield. Because of the odds against them, both Sigel and his men considered the encounter a victory and their morale was not compromised. Casualties were inconsiderable—several dozen on each side—and the men gained valuable combat experience. The German Americans who made up the bulk of Sigel's force now idolized their commander, who, thanks to national coverage of their skirmish, began to make a name for himself among his fellow immigrants across America.[32]

The fight, however, revealed much about Sigel that boded ill for the Union cause. He was laudably aggressive and willing to take risks; commanders who lack those qualities cannot win wars. But he failed to grasp the tactical situation because he neglected to perform basic reconnaissance. This was a mistake he would repeat at Wilson's Creek and on other occasions throughout his career.[33]

Lyon received word of Sigel's fight on July 9, and concluded that Sigel was in danger of being destroyed. Lyon's entire column consequently began a forced march for Springfield, the freshest troops taking the lead. Eugene Ware of the First Iowa recalled: "Lyon wanted some men on the banks of the Osage river just as soon as he could get them there, and he thought the 'greyhounds' from Iowa could get there sooner than anybody. We struck up 'The Happy Land of Canaan,' and moved off, with General Lyon evidently pleased with our style, as he sat on his horse and watched us. Lyon did not smile when he was pleased—he just pulled his chin whiskers with his mouth half open."[34]

Leaving tents and other baggage behind, the men trudged through blistering heat at a killing pace on short rations. There were few halts for rest. Indeed, at one point the Federals covered fifty miles in thirty hours.[35] Ralph D. Zublin, a private in the Governor's Grays of the First Iowa, left a particularly vivid description of a portion of the ordeal in a letter to his wife:

The dust and heat were oppressive. Along the road side were strewed by scores the regulars. . . . Out of our company of 97 men, only 27 marched into camp and stacked arms. Other companies were completely broke up. Of the Iowa City company in our regiment eight men came in. A company behind us came in twenty-one strong and not an officer. But to cap the climax we were wet with the dew and completely exhausted for the want of food and sleep. We had no place to sleep but in the wet weeds of a cornfield, as our blankets were miles back on the wagons. . . . Walking in a hot sun, carrying a ten pound musket, equipment, belts, cross belts, cartridge box, with forty rounds of cartridges in it, haversack, canteen, etc., slung on is a trial of endurance, and I find that I stand it as well as any man in the regiment. It surprised me to find out how much I could do.[36]

Riding ahead, Lyon reached Springfield on July 13. The column straggled in over the next few days. The Federal concentration was now complete, with over five thousand men occupying camps encircling the town.[37] But the military situation had changed. Sigel's withdrawal at Carthage meant that Lyon's overall strategy had failed. Lyon had neither prevented Jackson and Price from raising an army to oppose him in Missouri nor trapped the Missouri State Guard forces retreating from the central portion of the state. True, Lyon had initiated the first major campaign of the war, and his operations were more complex than those that any other general, North or South, had yet attempted. But far from destroying Secessionist strength in Missouri, Lyon's actions concentrated the State Guard in a location where it was now receiving Confederate support.

Several things should be considered in evaluating Lyon's performance. In the initial movement of his own column and the one under Sweeny, Lyon had made masterful use of rivers and railways. Given the shortages of horses, mules, and wagons that he faced once all three of his columns left their river or rail connections, his operations were as swift as humanly possible. Civil War commanders rarely trapped or pinned down their enemies. In short, Jackson and Price escaped because Lyon's strategy was too ambitious, not because its execution was poor. No officer in the Union army had accomplished more than Nathaniel Lyon had during the summer 1861. His subordinates Sturgis and Sweeny had performed creditably operating on their own, and the men Lyon had assembled at Springfield made a formidable team.

By mid-July the forces that would fight the second battle of the Civil War were largely in place. The commanders faced important decisions, and the officers and men under them still had much to learn about becoming soldiers.

Chapter 7

They Take the Rags off the Bush

When Ben McCulloch learned that Governor Claiborne Jackson's force was safe and that all the available Missouri State Guardsmen could now be concentrated on Cowskin Prairie, he withdrew to Arkansas but remained near the state line. Perhaps because there was so little good news coming out of Missouri, the Southern press greatly played up McCulloch's invasion of the Union and capture of the Federals at Neosho. The *Dallas Herald*, for example, described the incident as "the most characteristic thing of Ben we have seen yet." Aggressive action indeed typified McCulloch. Because he now commanded Bart Pearce's Arkansas State Troops as well as his own Confederates, he began organizing two brigades that he balanced in strength without regard to the troops' type of service. The bulk of the Arkansas State Troops, who remained at Camp Walker near Maysville, constituted one brigade, under Pearce's command. Three miles east of the town McCulloch established Camp Jackson, where he planned to concentrate all of his Confederate forces. Some were still en route from Fort Smith, however, and Greer's South Kansas–Texas Cavalry continued its long march to the front. To flesh out this second brigade, which he commanded in person, and provide it with artillery and additional cavalry, McCulloch ordered about seven hundred Arkansas State Troops, including Reid's Fort Smith Battery, to join him at Camp Jackson.[1]

In a letter dated July 9, McCulloch explained his recent operations in Missouri to the secretary of war: "Having made the movement without authority, and having accomplished my mission, I determined to fall back to this position and organize a force with a view to future operations." As a War Department communication of June 26 had already sanctioned a

Confederate invasion of Kansas and Missouri at McCulloch's discretion, the Texan's reference to lacking authorization is puzzling. It is possible, but unlikely, that McCulloch had by this time received Secretary Walker's letter of July 4 cautioning him to violate Missouri's sovereign territory only upon the most dire necessity. The important thing is that Mc-Culloch's July 9 report envisioned offensive operations in the near future. He wrote: "The force that was marching on the governor's rear will no doubt move to Springfield, and I think there will be an urgent necessity in the course of a few days to make an attack upon that place, or we will receive an attack from their concentrated forces. Should I receive no instructions in the mean time, I think that I will, together with General Pearce and Price, make an advance upon it as soon as the different forces are sufficiently organized to take the field." McCulloch may for some reason have grown concerned about the larger implications of his movements. Nevertheless, he was clearly willing to act on his own responsibility, and his plans anticipated a speedy return to Missouri and a decisive campaign against the Federals.[2]

Like most department commanders in 1861, McCulloch complained constantly to Richmond about his acute lack of arms, ammunition, and money to pay his troops. But he was more than satisfied with his command. "The men are all healthy and in good spirits," he reported. "They are a fine body of men, and through constant drilling are becoming very efficient. I place a great deal of reliance upon them."[3] In this assessment he made no distinction between his Confederate soldiers and Pearce's Arkansas State Troops.

Two things soon changed McCulloch's optimistic outlook. The first was his logistical situation. Less than a week after his aggressive-minded July 9 communication with Secretary Walker, McCulloch abandoned Camp Jackson, withdrawing the brigade there to Bentonville. "I find it impossible to occupy any point near the State line, owing to the scarcity of water and supplies," he explained in a letter to Sterling Price. He informed the State Guard commander that he hoped to make a personal reconnaissance into Missouri as far north as Cassville and possibly move his brigades to that point. As it turned out, McCulloch advanced with only the mixed Confederate–Arkansas State Troop brigade under his own command, moving from Bentonville a scant seven miles north up the Wire Road to camp at Sugar Creek, where water was readily available. The Southern forces gathered in northwestern Arkansas now numbered almost five thousand. As these men and their horses required about 24,000 pounds of food each day, they could not live off the land for long. Within a week or two at most, McCulloch would either have to advance into Missouri or retire to his supply base at Fort Smith. A move forward meant collecting more wagons, so for the moment the Southerners went nowhere.[4]

Logistical difficulties were only one reason why McCulloch did not return immediately to Missouri. He informed the War Department that he was "anxious" to attack Nathaniel Lyon in Springfield or at least strike his rear to cut the Federals off from supplies and reinforcements. But the "condition of the Missouri troops" made a forward movement impossible. In a letter to Secretary Walker dated July 18, he explained: "[U]pon consulting with General Price . . . I find that his force of 8,000 or 9,000 men is badly organized, badly armed, and now almost entirely out of ammunition. This force was made by the concentration of different commands under their own generals. The consequence is that there is no concert of action among them, and will not be until a competent military man is put in command of the entire force."[5]

McCulloch's reference to consulting with Price is interesting, as it is unclear from surviving documents how much time he and Price had been able to spend together or how many Missouri State Guard units McCulloch had actually seen at this point. Yet his letter to Walker suggests that he had little regard for the Missouri soldiers or their leader. The question is why. McCulloch's concern for the Missourians' lack of arms and ammunition is readily understandable. Although he loaned over six hundred muskets to the State Guardsmen, they remained poorly equipped to fight a battle. A large number had no arms of any kind, and too many of those who possessed weapons had only shotguns or hunting rifles. As a result of Lyon's whirlwind campaign, which had kept constant pressure on the State Guard, few had learned more than the rudiments of drill. But if anyone were able to see the potential rather than the liabilities of hastily armed militia, it should have been McCulloch. As a veteran of the rag-tag army that won independence for Texas and as a Ranger who fought in Mexico and led many a scouting expedition against Native Americans, McCulloch would seem to have had little reason to put faith in colorful uniforms, brightly polished buttons, and close-order drill. In any case, the State Guard contained a scattered leavening of Mexican War veterans and several well-disciplined prewar militia units like the Washington Blues of St. Louis, giving it as much potential for future excellence as any gathering of volunteers across the country.

Had the year been 1846 rather than 1861, McCulloch might not have worried as much about the condition of the Missourians. But the circumstances had changed and so had Old Ben. For although he rose to fame as a leader of some of the rowdiest volunteers in American history, in the 1850s McCulloch's ambition became achieving command of a regiment of U.S. Cavalry. Such Regular soldiers routinely endured levels of discipline that would have caused Texas Rangers to mutiny, yet their world was the one McCulloch longed to join. As of July 1861 McCulloch was the only general in the Confederate army who lacked a West Point education. But when he expressed pride in the level of training of his Confederate and Arkansas State Troop units, he spoke as a man who considered himself a professional soldier, as good as any West Pointer, and in 1861 he apparently had an appreciation for discipline that had not marked his previous military exploits.

The difference in arms and military proficiency between the forces McCulloch commanded and those under Price appears significant but hardly drastic. McCulloch's concern seems understandable, yet a bit exaggerated. But when McCulloch made his assessment, he was burdened with greater responsibilities and greater uncertainties than he had ever before experienced. He faced as a potential enemy a man who appeared to be able to create troops out of thin air and move them tremendous distances at great speed. Nathaniel Lyon's name has been obscured by later heroes of the Civil War, and McCulloch left no written record of what he thought of the Connecticut Yankee. But subsequent events suggest that the former Texas Ranger may have been intimidated by his opponent—not by Lyon's West Point education, but by his performance during the summer of 1861.

It should be noted that McCulloch did not criticize the Missourians themselves, merely their lack of preparation. His statement that they would never be ready for battle "until a competent military man is put in command" was a clear indictment of Price in terms of both his service to date and his future potential.[6] The fact that McCulloch and Price did not get along is recognized by all biographers, but the reason for their mutual dislike has never been adequately explored. Up to this point the two men had spent a few hours together at most, during which time they should have commiserated on the basis of their similar plight. Like McCulloch, Price scorned West Point pedigrees, and who was better suited to comprehend Price's challenges in attempting to establish an army without proper governmental support than McCulloch, who dispatched letter after letter to an administration in Richmond that neglected the Trans-Mississippi? Given conditions in Missouri, what more could McCulloch have expected Price to have accomplished in the short time since Lyon's unilateral declaration of war? What action, or lack of action, on the part of

Price by mid-July 1861 could have suggested to McCulloch that he was unfit for command or that he would not cooperate fully and selflessly to achieve their mutual goals?

Perhaps biographers avoid these questions because they cannot be answered with any satisfaction. The two generals' surviving private correspondence, which is slight, sheds no light on the situation. But for reasons that are unclear, McCulloch formed a low opinion of Price following their first contact. Price was able to inspire extreme devotion among his soldiers, but he never won McCulloch's confidence. Interestingly, there is no contemporary evidence indicating that Price thought ill of McCulloch at this time.[7]

While pondering his next move, McCulloch continued to concentrate his available forces at either Camp Walker near Maysville or the site on Sugar Creek north of Bentonville that had been christened Camp Yancy. For the common soldier, this was a time of adjustment to military life. Captain R. M. Hinson, who commanded the Moorehouse Guards of the Third Louisiana, was proud of his command. "The boys stood the march much better than I expected," he wrote after they reached Camp Walker. Hinson's wife Mattie had accompanied him from Shreveport all the way to Van Buren, so he was now separated from her for the first time. The feelings of affection he expressed to her in a letter on July 10 were doubtless typical of many soldiers in McCulloch's army who missed their loved ones:

> My Dearest Mat, the evening I parted with you at Van Buren will never be forgotten. The feelings that I expressed that evening were almost too much for me to endure. When we meet again (which I hope will be soon) I hope we will never be separated again. I never knew how well I love you until now. I can never be happy away from you. Let me be where I may, climbing the mountains, in the Prairie on drill or even in the field of battle my thoughts will ever be centered on my dearest Mat. Not a day passed over me but I am thinking of you and looking forward to the time I will be with you to enjoy once more the pleasures of being with the one I love so dearly. The happy days I have passed with you time can never efface. I feel that the time is not far off when I will be permitted to enjoy those blissful hours again.[8]

Similar thoughts were expressed by the pen of John Johnson of the First Arkansas Mounted Rifles on July 23:

> Dear Mother I am in high hopes that we may all succeed in getting home safe and with glory and liberty overflowing in our hearts to see

the pleasures that we have seen to gether in this life and if not in this world I hope and pray to God that we all will meet in that better world above and I expect to try to do right as well as I know how. I well remember the words that entered my ears the day I left home and thank God that I feel that I left some friends at home and in the neighborhood too.[9]

Hinson was a planter and Johnson a yeoman farmer. Although their letters reveal different levels of education, their words demonstrate that much of what the soldiers experienced cut across class lines. There are parallels too in the confidence they expressed about the future and in their low opinion of the enemy. "In a few days we will probably be face to face with the black republican dutch of Missouri," Hinson wrote. "The boys are all highly delighted at the idea of getting into some excitement. As for myself, I feel like the dutchman who will kill me is still in Jerusalem." Johnson was even more blunt, informing his wife, "We still expect to go to Spring Field Missouri where we expect to have a fight and think we can whip five to one."[10]

Pride in hometown and state ran high as the prospects of combat increased. "The boys are burning for a battle," wrote a soldier from Pulaski County, Arkansas. On parade they were "regular as clock pendlams," he asserted, and, as a result, "when the Arks. boys goes by they take the rags off the bush." A civilian who accompanied the Third Louisiana as a teamster observed, "The Shreveport Rangers are looking well and will make their mark along with the balance of the Louisiana boys." The man's name is unknown. Some difficulty, perhaps a physical defect, had denied him enlistment in the regiment, yet he was determined to fight despite his civilian status. His words, written for the *Shreveport South-Western*, testify to the manner in which love of family, pride in country, and concepts of courage were inextricably intertwined for nineteenth-century Americans: "I did not come after office, I came to fight for my country, as a duty I owe to my family and country and when you hear of the 3d La. regiment on the battle-field you will hear of me being in the hottest of it. I have every opportunity of making myself a military man, I can assure you that my whole soul is in it, without fear, not forgetting my family which I left behind, which is near and dear to me."[11]

Such letters remind us that although soldiering separated men physically from their loved ones, acute anxiety on the home front made war a community experience. To her son Omer, a lieutenant in the Pulaski Light Battery, Mary E. Weaver wrote: "At times I have the blues so bad it unfits me for my duties. Should one of my boys be sacrificed for his

An unidentified private in the Pulaski Light Battery, Arkansas State Troops, showing the unit's gray jean uniform with red stripes (The collection of Dr. Tom and Karen Sweeney, General Sweeny's Museum, Republic, Missouri)

country this world would be a blank to me—but I hope and pray the 'God of battles' will shield my dear boys & our brave army."[12]

The Weavers were one of Little Rock's most prominent families. Omer Rose Weaver was born in Kentucky in 1837, but the family moved to Arkansas in 1838. Samuel M. Weaver, Omer's father, built one of Little Rock's largest and most expensive homes. It included an extensive library, and Omer had every educational advantage growing up, graduating from the University of Nashville in 1856 when only nineteen years old. Working for the U.S. surveyor general in Arkansas, he was a prominent member of Little Rock's social circle. Active in the local debating club, he spent large sums of money on clothing. A friend wrote of Weaver: "Wearing his light hair falling down his neck in folds, carefully brushed; scrupulous in the slightest detail of dress and person almost to singularity, he was yet so unpretending in his demeanor and unaffectively kind in his sympathies as to disabuse any mind misled by such an impression, so easily discovered to be unworthy of his courteous, consistent, and reliable nature." In short, Weaver was the sort of young man usually said to exemplify the best of Southern society.[13]

By all accounts Weaver was an excellent young officer. He had joined the Pulaski Light Battery in peacetime, when the men were still called the Tottens. His mother, like many people in Little Rock, seemed personally offended when Captain Totten sided with the Union. "I hope if Old Abe's *disciples* do venture on Arkansas soil, they will meet with the

Lieutenant Omer Rose Weaver, Pulaski Light Battery, Arkansas State Troops. Weaver's girlfriend believed that the photograph captured one of his "iceberg moods." (The collection of Dr. Tom and Karen Sweeney, General Sweeny's Museum, Republic, Missouri)

warmest reception the country can afford—only to think of it, Totten is in Missouri, wielding the *sword* we gave him, *against us!!*" she declared.[14]

Mary and Samuel Weaver sent at least six letters to their son during the campaign that led up to the Battle of Wilson's Creek. Some of these were mailed, others delivered by hand. Little Rock's citizens continued to support "their" military companies as best they could. Civilians constantly journeyed to the military camps, bringing food, clothing, and correspondence from home. In this manner community ties remained strong. In Omer Weaver's case, the mail service allowed him to carry on a clandestine love affair with Annie, a girl back in Little Rock. The young lady's last name is unknown. Apparently she and Omer believed that her parents would not approve of the match, as Omer's mother took great care to deliver Omer's notes to her, and receive hers to him, in secret. Omer even sent the girl his photograph, which she criticized, writing, "I don't think the picture is very good but is like you in your *Iceberg* moods."[15]

These exchanges may seem frivolous, but continued contacts with home folk such as Weaver enjoyed were important in sustaining the morale of the soldiers. Whenever a soldier received a package from home, his whole company might celebrate. Sergeant Ras Stirman of Colonel Gratiot's Third Arkansas Infantry thanked his sister profusely for "the box of nice things" she sent. "We had the best Supper last night that I ever eat," he explained. "Only one thing was lacking & that was your presence." At Camp Walker, Stirman and his friends hunted rabbits for fun, longed for "logger beer," and attended "one of the greatest hoe downs you ever saw." In their spare time they swatted flies, which seemed to outnumber the soldiers considerably. But there were occasional reminders that soldiering was by its nature dangerous work. Stirman's unit was initially camped near the Third Louisiana, but the Pelicans soon shifted to Camp Yancy. There one evening a soldier named James Howard was killed by the accidental discharge of a comrade's musket. Either because he feared punishment or was ashamed of his action, the man who caused the accident deserted.[16] Disease, of course, remained the men's greatest fear. Prior to the Battle of Wilson's Creek, fourteen members of the Third Louisiana died of disease and twenty-six were discharged for medical reasons. Other units suffered comparable losses.[17]

To the north of McCulloch's troops, the bulk of the Missouri State Guard sprawled across Cowskin Prairie. An open area formerly used as a place for slaughtering cattle, it was well positioned as a training camp. Twelve miles north of Pearce's Brigade at Camp Walker, its center lay three miles from the Arkansas line and three miles east of the Indian Territory. Price established his headquarters at the large home of a prosperous farmer named Benjamin F. Hopkinson. As more and more units arrived, the camp spread westward until some men were camped within half a mile of the Indian Territory.[18]

Whatever McCulloch's opinion of him, Price was doing everything possible to turn his men into competent soldiers. To begin with, he appointed Alexander Early Steen drillmaster for the State Guard. The son of an officer in the U.S. Army, Steen had a checkered career that suggests a love-hate relationship with the military. Born in St. Louis, he was not a West Point graduate, yet he obtained a commission in the Regulars in 1847 and fought in the Mexican War. He resigned at the close of the conflict but was recommissioned in 1852, serving at frontier posts as a lieutenant, first with the Third and then with the Sixth Infantry. Although his father remained loyal to the Union, Steen resigned once again on May 10, the day of the "Camp Jackson Massacre." On June 18 he became a brigadier general commanding the State Guard's Fifth Division, replacing Alexander Doniphan. As the Fifth Division was in the extreme northwestern corner of the state, effectively behind enemy lines, Steen was a general without a command, and Price was wise to make use of his Regular Army experience by placing him in charge of training. The soldiers initially resented his high standards but soon came to appreciate

Private Thomas Isaac Duvall and Lieutenant William Russell Duvall, Missouri State Guard. Their imaginatively trimmed shirts reflect styles that were popular among volunteers. (The collection of Dr. Tom and Karen Sweeney, General Sweeny's Museum, Republic, Missouri)

them. "The fact is General Steen follows up the old adage and does everything well," one soldier noted. "The business of camping, or striking tents and marching, is done with the precision of clock work." Soldiers also valued Steen's humor, warmth, and accessibility when off duty. A born raconteur, he persevered in his tasks despite poor health.[19]

There was plenty of room on Cowskin Prairie to exercise cavalry, infantry, and artillery, and some soldiers recorded that the daily drill sessions lasted from four to six hours. Such a schedule was hardly excessive, but there were other demands on the men besides learning the school of the soldier. The Cowskin Prairie region was sparsely settled, and the relatively few farms nearby were taken over by the military to provide corn and wheat for the men. John Bell of Clark's Division recalled that "details were sent into the surrounding country, took possession of the wheat fields, threshed the wheat, took it to the neighborhood mills, [and] had it ground into flour that supplied us with bread." Payment was presumably offered for the produce thus confiscated. The prairie grass on which the State Guard pitched its tents fed not only cavalry and baggage horses, but also a large herd of cattle that had been collected from various points. Henry Cheavens, also of Clark's Division, recorded in his diary that beef was the staple of the soldiers' diet, but they supplemented it with potatoes, milk, and honey purchased from local farmers. "It is a fine fruit and grape country," he noted, which provided additional items to whet the palate. Yet it would not take more than a few weeks for the Missourians to literally "eat out" the region. Like McCulloch, Price would have to either advance or retreat within a short time. With neither railway nor water connections to a supply base, he could not remain stationary for long.[20]

Food was only one of Price's logistical concerns. His men needed weapons, ammunition, accoutrements, clothing, and camp equipment of every kind. To take the offensive the Missouri commander not only required additional horses, he also needed wagons, harnesses, and all the tools and supplies necessary to keep horses shod and in good health. Under the circumstances, his nascent quartermaster corps did a remarkable job.

A local newspaper joked that the standard equipment for a soldier in the Missouri State Guard was "a quart of whiskey, one loaf of bread, one pocket Bible, one Barlow knife, and one fine tooth comb." The reality was even stranger than this good-natured jibe suggests. The quartermaster's records for Parsons's Division, for example, indicate that large quantities of supplies were issued between June 28 and July 12. A list of specific items distributed to the men reads like the contents of a general store, and such mercantile establishments may indeed have been the major source for the quartermaster's procurement. Among other things, the men received cords of wood, matches, candles, and lanterns; tin cups and plates, knives and spoons; tin dippers and water buckets; skillets and baking pans; coffee mills, coffee pots, tea kettles, and mess kettles; hatchets, axes, and spades; rope and nails; weighing scales and flour sifters; butcher knives; and soap, washbasins, and washboards. They were also issued canned tomatoes, tobacco, mustard, pocket handkerchiefs, playing cards, and whiskey.[21]

The State Guard may not have kept complete records, but attempts were made to facilitate such activities. The captains commanding companies in Parsons's Division were supplied with quires of paper, blank books, pencils, pens, pen holders, bottles of ink, and inkstands. Mounted companies had special needs, and some were able to receive saddles, brushes, curry combs, surcingles, bridles, halters, double-team harnesses, and salt for horses.[22]

Clothing was issued, including undershirts, drawers, flannel coats, vests, cotton shirts, and calico shirts. These were presumably civilian rather than military items. The supply of ready-made clothing was clearly inadequate, as large quantities of bulk cloth were distributed, together with clothing patterns. In his diary Cheavens noted, "Cloth was given, and most all went to work making clothes." Cheavens made himself a pair of pants while others in his company made shirts. His diary entry gives no description of the results, but if everyone used the same color of cloth it would have given his company a common appearance. Cotton trim, which was also issued, was probably used to decorate shirts and pants in a military fashion. Such endeavors may have raised the proportion of the State Guard wearing some matching items, through not necessarily complete uniforms, to nearly 30 percent. The variety of cloth issued—jeans, calico, toweling, twills, bed ticking, hickory shirting, blue and brown drill cloth, osnaburg, striped cotton cloth, lindsey, cottonade, satinet, and cassimere—worked against standardization. As the average soldier probably had little experience with needle and thread, the results must have been wonders to behold. When one considers the combination of such camp-engendered sartorial efforts, the variety of prewar militia uniforms, uniforms made hastily by home folk at the outbreak of the war, and the ordinary civilian clothing that so many of the men wore, the Missourians gathered at Cowskin Prairie presented an appearance unique in the annals of the Civil War.[23]

When not sewing, the men labored to manufacture ammunition for small arms and artillery. Thanks to Governor Jackson's efforts, a substantial supply of powder reached the camp, as did bulk lead from the nearby Granby Mines. Details of men formed musket balls by melting the lead in cast-iron skillets and pouring it into hastily fashioned wooden molds. It was crude work and a particularly unpleasant assignment beneath the blazing summer sun. The production of artillery ammunition was an even greater challenge. As there was no way to manufacture solid shot or explosive shell, it was fortunate that the State Guard batteries already had a reasonable supply of these. But there was an acute shortage of canister, an artillery round that was essentially a tin can filled with iron spheres just over one inch in diameter. Because iron could not be melted over a campfire, iron bars were simply cut into crude slugs and loaded into metal cylinders turned out by the owner of a local tin shop.[24] But even their best efforts gave Price barely enough ammunition for a single battle.

Although ammunition was precious, a practice range was established to give the men experience firing live ammunition. While there were many experienced hunters in the ranks, it is one of the great myths of American history that such skills gave men an advantage on the battlefield. The most formidable soldiers in Western civilization during the nineteenth century, common British infantrymen, rarely handled firearms before enlisting. Training, as Ben McCulloch had begun to realize, was more important than frontier traditions. Colonel John Burbridge of Clark's Division was the firing range instructor. A soldier recalled him as "a slender man of less than medium height, very erect and graceful, wearing an officer's coat and cap of the old militia." Burbridge made "a notable appearance on the field," despite the fact that he rode "a very unwarlike, under-sized bay horse." The artillery crews trained under Captain Hiram Bledsoe. Known affectionately as "Old Hi," he was said to love his guns "more than a cavalryman loves his horse or a shepherd his dog."[25]

Like the men under McCulloch, those serving with Price took pride in their service and were confident of their ability to defeat the Federals. "Our Brigade is poorly armed, but makes up for it in strong hearts," a State Guard soldier wrote in his diary. "There can be no such word as fail with such brave men." Because of the chaotic conditions, communities in Missouri were not able to follow "their" companies with the same regularity as did home folk in other states, North and South. But the little news that did reach home was greeted with pride and confidence. In early July the editor of the *Liberty Tribune* in Clay County, 185 miles north of Cowskin Prairie, could inform his readers only that the town's company was reported to be in the southwestern corner of the state. Yet he had no doubt of its performance in any future contest, writing: "We all venture to predict that if there is any fighting to be done the gallant boys of Old Clay will do their *whole duty*."[26]

Lyon faced problems similar to those that plagued his opponents. His forces were camped in an irregular semicircle stretching from positions just south of Springfield to the village of Little York, approximately ten miles to the west. Lyon issued strict orders for the protection of private property, and relatively few problems arose regarding discipline. There was considerable shifting about over the next two weeks, from mid-July until the end of the month; but in general the troops under Captain Sweeny occupied Springfield itself and camps in the south, while the men in the columns of Lyon and Sturgis who had arrived more recently camped to the west. Most of the men seemed comfortable, although some still lacked tents and were forced to lie in the open. One of the Regulars who accompanied Lyon from St. Louis recalled that they set up camp among shady trees on a hilltop. An All Hazard boy from Atchison wrote home that the Kansans were established in a pleasant natural amphitheater one mile in diameter. "[I]n the center is a cave, out of which flows an almost exhaustless stream of pure water," he noted. Artillery was posted at strategic points to guard against attack. The First Iowa, stationed at Pond Springs, three miles from Little York, was impressed by the staunch Unionist sentiments of the locals and the Home Guard company they had formed. "Although small, Little York is true as steel," a soldier informed his home folk in Muscatine.[27]

Rest was welcome, but acute clothing shortages fueled discontent among the common soldiers. Regulars and volunteers alike had worn out almost everything while en route to Springfield. The Iowans left particularly vivid accounts of their plight. A soldier in the Muscatine Grays described his fellows as having blistered feet due to dilapidated shoes and trousers repaired with bits of carpet, coffee sacks, or scrap flannel. Only their coats were in good shape, as they were accustomed to march in their shirt sleeves.[28] A correspondent to the *Dubuque Weekly Times* contrasted the natty precampaign appearance of the Governor's Grays with their current condition:

Let me describe one of us who now passes our tent, and *ex une disco omnes*. His beard and hair are long, shaggy, and untrimmed. His hat is pierced with a dozen or more holes of different sizes and shapes in the crown and sides; it has no band, is fringed roughly around the edge of the brim, and comes down over his ears. His flannel shirt is out at the elbows and torn across the back. His pants have lost half their side stripe, are out at the knees, torn and fringed around the ankles—and (may I say it to ears more polite!) he wears an apron behind that he may not actually touch the ground when he sits down. He has no socks and his feet peep through his shoes in a half dozen different places, and are only retained upon his feet by a most ingenious application of strings and strips of leather.[29]

One must allow for journalistic exaggeration, but all sources agree that Lyon's men were severely ragged, the Iowans extremely so. Ironically, while at Springfield the Governor's Grays did get a package from the ladies of Dubuque. When opened it revealed dozens of havelocks—cloths designed to drape over the men's caps and hang down behind to protect their necks from the sun. The Grays sent their thanks to "the fair manufacturers and donors," but they doubtless would have preferred receiving almost anything else.[30]

Food was an even more pressing problem. Like Price, Lyon detailed soldiers to collect corn and wheat from surrounding farms and take it to local mills. Once ground, it was carried to Springfield bakeries, where men detached from Sigel's Third Missouri and Salomon's Fifth Missouri were "turning out loaves as fast as they could." Lyon paid $1.00 per bushel for grain, a "handsome price," according to one observer. Milling and baking went on twenty-four hours a day but produced an insufficient supply of food. As shortages continued, word of the soldiers' difficulties filtered back to their hometowns. "Much complaint is made at the tardiness with which our troops are supplied with necessary stores and provisions," a Kansas paper reported.[31]

The Iowans gave their encampment at Pond Springs the derisive title "Camp Mush," as cornmeal mixed with water was their sole government ration for days.[32] The laws of supply and demand allowed farmers living near Springfield to reap exorbitant profits. According to the diary of William W. Branson of the Muscatine Volunteers, the Iowans had been on one-quarter rations for several days prior to their arrival in the Springfield vicinity. "The fare that we get now is fifty per cent below that the slaves get here or in any other state," he recorded angrily en route. As soon as they set up their tents at Pond Springs, local civilians began to take advantage of their situation. On July 22 Branson wrote, "The farmers are now making it a practice of bringing in loads of provisions, pies, biscuit, corn bread, & selling them to us soldiers for two prices, knowing that we are short of eatables." On another occasion he lamented, "No bread for supper to night, only what we procure with our own money."[33] According to Franc Wilkie, the civilian correspondent following the campaign, these deprivations threatened to compromise the men's effectiveness. "What men so clothed and fed can fight with any degree of spirit and determination?" he asked his readers.[34]

To make matters even worse, several hundred civilians dislocated by the passage of the armies fled to Springfield, where they camped in squalor, demanding government assistance. Their complaints took up so much of Lyon's time that he finally organized a wagon train and shipped many of them, along with the sick from his army, to Rolla. Unionist congressman John Phelps took charge of this exodus, which included as escort the Home Guard he had organized in Springfield. Meanwhile, Phelps's wife Mary, accompanied by her slaves, distributed food from their farm to the soldiers at Springfield on a daily basis, without charge.[35]

Rolla was Lyon's supply base, and, as the railway ran from there to St. Louis, it should have given him a much more secure logistical base than either Price or McCulloch enjoyed. But Lyon was no longer the master of events in Missouri. On July 3 the War Department had created a new Western Department, embracing Illinois and the states and territories west of the Mississippi, under the command of Major General John Charles Frémont. A Mexican War hero known as the "Pathfinder" from his days as an explorer, Frémont was in 1856 the first Republican candidate for president. He became Lyon's superior partly due to the influence of Frank Blair Jr., who had traveled to Washington, leaving his First Missouri Infantry under the command of Lieutenant Colonel George L.

Andrews. Like Lyon, Frémont was an ardent foe of slavery and a man of driving energy. Blair had every reason to expect Lyon and Frémont to work well together.[36]

Unfortunately, Frémont did not reach his St. Louis headquarters until July 25. Lyon's pleas for increased support before that date were lost in the great bureaucratic void of the War Department. Within days of reaching Springfield, he sent several communications to Washington outlining his position. He now had more than 7,000 men concentrated in southwestern Missouri, but none of them had received any pay and their clothes were disintegrating. Despite the best efforts of the officers he had left in St. Louis and Rolla to procure food and ship it to Springfield, the men he now styled members of the Army of the West were forced to endure acute shortages. As a consequence, he expected few of his ninety-day volunteers to reenlist when their terms of service expired in late July and early August. This might leave him with no more than 4,000 men to face the combined forces of Price and McCulloch, which he estimated to be 30,000 strong.[37]

Lyon requested food, clothing, and 10,000 men as reinforcements. What he received was an order detaching Captain Sweeny and many of the Regulars for service elsewhere. As Lyon was noted for his temper, his reply to this potentially devastating directive was remarkably calm. On July 17 he wrote another letter to the War Department, patiently explaining his needs and his peril once again, concluding that he would "delay" executing the order to detach Sweeny and the Regulars until the authorities in Washington had time to reconsider his requests. Lyon could not legally prevent his volunteers from leaving when their enlistments expired, but as a career Regular Army officer he knew how to deal with bureaucrats. Sweeny stayed put.[38]

Lyon had traveled far and accomplished much, but it must have seemed to him like the world was closing in. Several contemporaries commented on his fatigue and despair during this period.[39] Far from being defeated, he responded with characteristic aggression. He would attack the enemy immediately, and Sweeny, whose importance in Missouri seemed to be questioned by the desk-bound strategists in Washington, would lead the attack.

Ripe for the Sickle of War

While Lyon made plans for Sweeny, and Mc-Culloch and Price pondered strategy, the Texans under Colonel Elkanah Greer continued their efforts to reach the seat of the war. The men of the South Kansas–Texas Regiment were sworn into Confederate service on June 13 and shortly thereafter elected their company and regimental officers. Some of these, such as Lieutenant Colonel Walter P. Lane, had substantial military experience from the Texas War for Independence, the Mexican War, or service against Native Americans, but "most were as blissfully ignorant of the ruthless nature of war as the men they commanded." Nor did Greer burden his men with excessive training or discipline during the five weeks in which the regiment sat idle in Dallas, awaiting arms and equipment being shipped to them from San Antonio. A few stole from the local citizens, but overall the Texans behaved themselves and got along exceptionally well with the townsfolk. Their boredom was acute, but the handful of men who deserted and returned home faced severe consequences for having broken the social contract between the community and "its" company. A father in Rusk County informed his son that one such man was hissed at "wherever he goes," concluding, "John, I want you to go as far as the company goes & not to return till the company returns. . . . I would rather never see you again than for you to come off as he has."[1]

When the promised supply wagons finally arrived on July 6, their contents proved to be both heartening and dismaying. The Texans received spacious Sibley tents and a generous amount of camp equipage. There were so many wagons that three were assigned to each company. The arms, however, were an acute disappointment. Although three companies had arrived in Dallas with Colt's rifles and Sharps carbines, most had only shotguns or common hunting rifles. Greer's hopes of upgrading these arms with captured Federal equipment were rudely dashed, as the wagons brought only outdated, single-shot, muzzle-loading pistols. "These pistols were a useless weight on our horses, swung on the horns of our saddles," one veteran remembered. Greer was actually in such a hurry to depart that he distributed weapons and accoutrements en route, a few of the companies receiving nothing until they reached Arkansas. The resulting issue was haphazard. Some men obtained two pistols, others only one. Captain Johnson Russell's Cypress Guards never received cartridge boxes or cap pouches, while others got fewer than they needed. Captain D. M. Short's company from Shelby and St. Augustine was given old-fashioned shot bags and powder flasks. Overall, the men were actually better off with the assortment of weapons they had brought with them from home.[2]

Although frustrated, Greer had reason to believe that his long delay was worthwhile. For the shipment from San Antonio also included a complete four-gun battery of six-pounders, their caissons, and mules. He assigned these to a previously organized but weaponless artillery unit, commanded by Captain John Good, which had arrived earlier. With the First Texas Battery and the more than one thousand mounted men of his own unit, Greer led a formidable force when his men marched out of Dallas on July 9. The town gave them a good send-off, for as a result of their long stay, "many of the ardent youth of the regiment had become smitten with the charms of the Dallas fair." Although the parting was difficult, no one expected the separation to be prolonged. Confident that each man could whip five Yankees, they expected to be back before winter.[3]

Their route took them north to Colbert's Ferry, where they were to cross the Red River and enter the Choctaw Nation. This proved dangerous when on July 16 the water rose unexpectedly as a result of rains upriver. Douglas Cater of the Rusk County Cavalry recalled seeing "a wall of water eight feet high" suddenly engulf "a wagon and team about midway of the river." Although the vehicle and its mules were lost, no one drowned. The teamsters imperiled during this episode were Mexican American civilians previously employed in that capacity by the U.S. Army who had accepted service with the Confederacy. Cater had a strong dislike for one of them. "Old Mike, our company's wagon driver, knew very little about driving a team of any kind," he recalled. As a consequence, Mike "was sure to let the wagon get turned over, emptying its contents into the dirt, and sometimes making us go hungry by getting provisions too full of dirt to use." None of the other members of Cater's regiment criticized the Mexican Americans in their reminiscences, however.[4]

The march to Fort Smith was largely uneventful but tiring, as Greer set a fast pace. Although some men resented the inevitable regimentation of military service, their commander did not insist on more formality than was necessary. "Off duty, both officers and privates were associates," noted Cater. The young soldier had brought along his violin, and one of the officers, also a violinist, often joined him in playing for the men. Rank had no place in such entertainment. "We were all boys in camp," he explained.[5]

As the Texans moved across the Indian Territory, many expressed disappointment because most of the Native Americans they encountered were hardly picturesque. Their route took them through areas inhabited largely by Choctaw highly acculturated to the white people's ways, living as farmers. They were pleased to note many homes flying Confederate banners, and two Choctaw asked to join the regiment. They served honorably and apparently encountered no prejudice due to their race. In fact, on July 19 at Boggy Depot, a group of Choctaw women presented a flag to Greer's unit. The regiment treated this banner with the same respect it did other emblems of their social contract with civilians, carrying it in so many battles that it was literally shot to pieces.[6]

The same rains that simultaneously impeded Lyon's operations to the north, but helped McCulloch by raising the level of the Arkansas River, hampered Greer's movements. He did not reach Fort Smith until July 29. There he found that McCulloch had taken the offensive, leaving instructions for the Texans to abandon their baggage and all wheeled vehicles and join the main column by forced marches. It took two days to replace worn-out horses, place the sick in the fort's hospital, finish issuing arms and equipment, and distribute scant supplies of ammunition. On July 31 the South Kansas–Texas Cavalry started north along the Wire Road to join their compatriots. Good's battery remained behind. As Greer's men passed through Van Buren at the start of their trip, a brass band honored them by playing "Dixie." Hearing the tune for the first time, Sergeant Samuel Barron of the Lone Star Defenders was impressed. The Texans began to sing it almost incessantly, for it seemed to suit the occasion.[7]

Because of the distances involved, it took some time for letters written by Greer's men to reach home and appear in hometown newspapers. Meanwhile, locals kept track of events as best they could. Although some sensed a crisis approaching, most appear to have been confident. A typical article, from the *Clarksville Standard*, proclaimed: "The news by the Ft. Smith *Times* shows that the actual work has commenced near the Arkansas border. . . . Huzza! for McCulloch and his men—the men of Missouri, of Arkansas, of Kentucky, of Tennessee, and last but not least of Texas. Forward, brothers!—the field is before you, and the harvest of hirelings and knaves is ripe for the sickle of war."[8]

A few days before Greer's force reached Fort Smith, Lyon renewed his offensive operations against the Missouri State Guard. His target was Forsyth, a community of some five hundred people lying at the head of navigation on the White River. Thirty-five miles south of Springfield, it was more than fifty miles distant as measured over the rough, twisting country roads of the day. Lyon's scouts and local Unionists reported that Forsyth served as a rallying point and supply depot for men of McBride's Division who had not yet reached the encampment at Cowskin Prairie. As Lyon faced his main enemy to the southwest, the Forsyth post potentially threatened his left flank. Lyon's decision to attack it thus made strategic sense. But as so often happens in war, Lyon's information was faulty in part. Although the town was stocked with supplies, there were only a few State Guardsmen at Forsyth, and the expedition against them took a greater physical toll on Lyon's troops than it was worth.[9]

As usual, the enlisted men were the last to learn about strategic maneuvers. When the First Iowa marched from its camp outside Springfield to the center of town and stacked arms on July 20, the men expected to be sent home, as their ninety-day enlistments were about to expire. Mail was distributed, boosting spirits considerably. Eugene Ware of the Burlington Zouaves received ten dollars from his father. He celebrated by buying candy, soda water, and a new wool shirt, then taking a bath in a nearby hotel. When the bugle sounded reassembly, he and his comrades were surprised to find a portion of the First marching south rather than north. As rumors about their destination filtered through the ranks, they were cheered at the prospect of meeting the enemy before their service ended.[10]

The Iowans were also happy to be with Sweeny of the Second Infantry, who was far more popular with the troops than Lyon. Forty years old, erect and slender, Sweeny's heavy beard and drooping eyelids gave him a somewhat sleepy appearance in photographs, but he was a man of great energy. Although he later affected a rakish plumed hat, the red-faced Irishman now wore a simple cap of Mexican War vintage. His empty right sleeve, pinned to the front of his coat at the waist, testified to his sacrifices in that previous conflict. "We all liked him very much," Ware recalled. "He was a typical Irishman, full of fun, strict in discipline, and with a kind word for everybody."[11]

The expedition contained almost 1,200 men. Along with the Burlington Zouaves, Sweeny took five additional companies of the First Iowa. This battalion was commanded by Lieutenant Colonel William H. Merritt, who rode a white horse and cut a dashing if unmilitary appearance by sporting a white coat. Captain David S. Stanley, a West Point graduate and Ohio native whose Southern friends had hoped he would join the Confederate army, led Companies C and D of the First U.S. Cavalry. Stanley had considerable service on the frontier, but another officer, baby-faced Lieutenant George Sokalski, age twenty-two, was only weeks out of West Point. The son of a Polish soldier and political refugee who had served in the U.S. Army, Sokalski was allegedly the first Polish American to graduate from the U.S. Military Academy. He now commanded a section of guns detached from Totten's Battery. The Second Kansas, under Colonel Robert Mitchell, completed the force. This regiment had captured so many horses during its march to Springfield that Captain Samuel N. Wood's company, the Kansas Rangers, was now mounted.[12]

The expedition's first day's march began at noon and ended on the banks of the James River. The distance covered was only seven miles, but temperatures were so high that several men suffered heatstroke. There were not enough tents, so when it began to rain that evening over one hundred of the men took shelter in a nearby Baptist church and in the covered bridge that spanned the James. They made a late start the next morning, as the rain continued, sometimes coming down in torrents. Soon they were joined by several dozen Home Guard volunteers from Christian and Taney Counties under a Captain Galloway. One of their number, former sheriff John M. Layton, acted as the expedition's guide thereafter. Sweeny's men passed only a few homes that morning, but some of them flew the Stars and Stripes conspicuously.[13]

In the afternoon, as the rain continued, the expedition reached the village of Ozark. Here Sweeny confiscated shoes and clothing from a store allegedly belonging to a local Secessionist. These items were desperately needed to supplement the men's bedraggled outfits. The local mill provided two wagonloads of flour, and at the opposite end of the village they discovered a store that sold "rot gut" whiskey. The owner, who was apparently a Secessionist, obviously feared confiscation, for instead of attempting to sell his wares he had shifted his stock to a wagon. But his attempted escape was foiled when it sank axle deep in the mud a short distance from town. Stanley's troopers grabbed the stock with glee.

Captain Samuel N. Wood, commander of the Kansas Rangers, the mounted company of the Second Kansas Infantry. This photograph was taken after he became an officer in the Kansas State Militia in 1863. (The collection of Dr. Tom and Karen Sweeney, General Sweeny's Museum, Republic, Missouri)

Sweeny allowed his men a liberal portion of the captured liquor, but he saw that it was issued in a strictly military fashion. As the entire expedition stood in ranks, forming a line half a mile long in the continuing drizzle, the sergeants from each unit searched the town for buckets or any other containers that might hold liquid. After filling these with whiskey from the wagon, they passed them down the ranks, allowing each man to fill his tin cup. Some of the soldiers noted with horror that their sergeants had grabbed chamber pots, but no one refused the beverage. In fact, the Iowans broke ranks in their eagerness to imbibe. Sweeny rode over and joked with them until they got back into line. When one Kansas soldier wrote home that "all were in good spirits," he meant it both figuratively and literally.[14]

The march continued south into the mountains, where Sokalski's artillery encountered particularly difficult conditions. Slick with mud, the road was so rough that it ripped the shoes from many of his horses. There was no joy that evening as the men camped in an open field. The unending rain developed into a severe storm after midnight, knocking down most of the tents. The Burlington Zouaves drew picket duty, and Ware spent a miserable night at a muddy crossroads. Having seen some riders in the distance during the day, they piled fence rails into a barrier in case of a surprise attack.[15]

On the following day, July 22, a long march finally brought the expedition to the vicinity of Forsyth. While the infantry rested, Sweeny dispatched Wood's mounted company of the Second Kansas to attack an enemy outpost his scouts had located three miles from the village. The Kansans accomplished this mission without firing a shot, but unfortunately a few State Guardsmen escaped to raise the alarm. The captured Missourians, who had seen only a small portion of the Union force, stated that there were 150 State Guardsmen in Forsyth. As this information meant Sweeny would enjoy overwhelming numerical superiority, he ordered Stanley to ride ahead with his cavalry and Wood's mounted Kansans, surround the village, and prevent the enemy's escape. No sooner had the riders passed than one of the captured Missourians bragged to Sweeny that there were actually 1,000 State Guardsmen in Forsyth. Alarmed, Sweeny sent an orderly after Stanley, urging him to use caution, then rushed his infantry and artillery forward as quickly as possible.[16]

In fact, there were only seventy-five State Guardsmen in Forsyth. The unit to which they belonged is unknown. Twenty-five of them were unarmed, and the remainder had only shotguns and hunting rifles. Camped in and around the courthouse, they were commanded by a major whose name is not given in the only extant Southern report of the encounter. Present by coincidence were Lieutenant Colonel John H. Price, inspector general for the State Guard, and L. M. Dunning, a quartermaster. When word of the Federals' approach reached Forsyth, the entire civilian population began to flee, apparently fearing the vengeance of Kansans for past atrocities committed by Missouri "border ruffians."[17]

By the time Stanley's force arrived, all the women and children had evacuated the town, although a number of male civilians, still trying to escape, were mistakenly identified by the Federals as members of the State Guard. Approaching from the northwest, the cavalry captain could see before him the courthouse that dominated Forsyth, the White River running along the town's southern border, and rain-swollen Swan Creek, which wrapped around its northern and eastern boundaries. His Regulars and Kansans numbered more than 250 men, but Sweeny's messenger had warned him that the enemy might have 1,000, so he proceeded with care. Leaving the road, they used fields of corn and other natural cover to approach the town from the west, covering the final few yards dismounted.[18]

The major commanding the State Guard had already decided to abandon the town. He divided his force in two, instructing one group to take positions just to the south, on the bluffs across the river. The other group occupied a hill east of the town, across Swan Creek. Many of his men either failed to hear these orders or decided that discretion was the better part of valor and decamped precipitously. Consequently, only a few dozen Missourians were waiting as the Federals came into view. They put up a sharp though not particularly skillful fight for some thirty minutes. The group on the river bluffs opened fire at long range. Although this wounded two men and killed Stanley's horse, it gave away their position. Unruffled, Stanley had his bugler give the signal to charge. Remounting, the Federals moved through the town, across the river, and up the bluffs. After driving away the force there, they continued east to the hill, sweeping all of the high ground and putting the Missourians to flight. Newspaperman Franc Wilkie took part in the attack, as did Thomas Knox of the *New York Herald* and a St. Louis correspondent named Fish. Feeling no obligations of journalistic neutrality, Knox and Fish fired their pistols at the fleeing State Guardsmen. Apparently victorious, the Federals soon started back toward the town. But the fight was not over. Although most of the Missourians had retreated in the face of Stanley's charge, a Lieutenant Parrish rallied a few men along the river and kept up a steady fire from dense cover. On the hill near Swan Creek, which Stanley had not searched thoroughly, Colonel Price gathered seven survivors. They had ample targets, for following a brutal forced march Sweeny arrived with the infantry and artillery.[19]

Because of the thick woods beyond the town, Stanley's location and accomplishments were not immediately clear to Sweeny. The Federal commander assumed that he faced a formidable enemy still in possession of the town and chose his positions accordingly. Placing the Second Kansas astride the main road leading to Forsyth, he sent Sokalski's artillery off to his left, across Swan Creek, to high ground overlooking the town from the north. Merritt's battalion of the First Iowa accompanied the guns, forming on their left in support, blocking a country road running into the town along the creek. When Sokalski noted numerous figures milling about among the distant buildings, he opened fire. In short order three solid shot crashed into the courthouse. As it happened, Sokalski was firing on his own men, specifically Wood's Kansas Rangers, the three newspaper correspondents, and some of Galloway's Home Guardsmen who had remained in the town. No one was killed, but before the error was discovered Wilkie was wounded by flying debris.[20]

From the hill east of town, John H. Price's small band of Missourians opened fire on the Union battery. Shifting his target, Sokalski replied with canister, supported by the muskets of the Iowa battalion. After perhaps half an hour, Price withdrew. To the Union right, the Kansans fired a few long-range volleys, apparently at the Missourians under Parrish. After a brief period these State Guardsmen retired as well. In all, no more than an hour had passed from the time of Stanley's first approach until Forsyth was securely in Union hands. Although each side was certain it had killed dozens of its enemy, the casualties were actually insignificant. Two of Stanley's troopers had been wounded and four of their horses were killed. Wilkie, the civilian hit by friendly fire, was actually the most dangerously wounded man on the Union side. A single Missouri State Guardsman was wounded, and two Guardsmen were captured.[21]

It was nearly dark when Sweeny entered the town. A lieutenant from the Second Kansas rushed to the courthouse, raising the flag of the Emporia Guards from its spire. The building, which the State Guard had used as a barracks, contained not only weapons, but also large amounts of ammunition, food, blankets, camp equipage, and one thousand pounds of lead. There was also a stock of bulk cloth, military and civilian clothing, shoes, and boots. Three wagons and a number of horses and mules were captured as well. Sweeny gave the weapons to Galloway's Home Guard and distributed the clothing and footwear to his own threadbare men. Because the lead's vast weight made its transportation difficult, some of Sweeny's men threw it down the town well.[22]

The Federals remained in Forsyth during the night of July 22. What happened next foreshadowed the fate of many Missouri communities in the years to come. During the long march through the state the men of Lyon's Army of the West had commented favorably on the large number of Unionists they encountered. Perhaps because of this they had rarely destroyed private property wantonly. But they were now tired, ragged, and hungry. The brief skirmish apparently did little to satisfy their desire to punish those whom they blamed for their discomfort. Distinctions between "loyal" and "disloyal" Missourians ceased to matter as they looted Forsyth.

Vincent Osbourne, a private in the Second Kansas, described one incident: "The regulars were passing around Port wine in buckets. I found out where they got it. Went around there, found some men there, some rolling off barrels of liquor. Others were drinking very freely out of the barrel of Port wine, which had the head knocked in, and it was about two-thirds full." Although an officer eventually put a halt to the bacchanalia, other officers participated in the plundering without apology. To his hometown newspaper in Kansas, Lieutenant C. S. Hills of the Emporia Guards wrote gleefully: "That night we occupied the finest houses in town—cooked our food on their stoves, washed our faces in their wash-bowls, lounged on their sofas, invited friends into their parlors, and, in fact, had a big time generally." Eugene Ware, who drew guard duty that night and did not visit the town's ravaged stores until the next morning, lamented that everything "worth taking" was gone. But he did not go empty-handed. He appropriated a box of patent medicine, and the First Iowa's regimental chaplain, who had stolen a large quantity of silk handkerchiefs, shared a few of them.[23]

Equally ominous was the response of Forsyth's civilians who returned the next morning. Sweeny made no attempt to compensate those claiming to be loyal to the Union for their losses. They responded by striking at the only available targets, identifying over one hundred fellow citizens as "disloyal." Sweeny promptly arrested them. How many of these political prisoners were true Secessionists and how many were merely loyal to the legally elected government of the state of Missouri, which Sweeny was helping to destroy, is unknown. The pattern of civilians appealing to the military authorities, North and South, to take punitive action against other civilians soon became widespread in Missouri.[24]

Sweeny took the civilian prisoners with him when he left Forsyth at noon on July 23. A short distance outside the town the Federal column came under fire, but Sokalski's guns soon drove away the attackers, who were presumably members of the Missouri State Guard. The return to Springfield was otherwise uneventful, and with good weather it was not nearly as arduous as the trip south had been. But the food captured at Forsyth was quickly consumed and the expedition, now burdened with a herd of political prisoners, was reduced to one-quarter rations. By the time Sweeny's men reached Springfield on the afternoon of July 25, they were desperately hungry. Although the Forsyth expedition had captured supplies that the Missouri State Guard needed badly, the toll it took on Sweeny's men made the effort counterproductive.[25]

Discipline in the First Iowa broke down completely when the troops reached the outskirts of the town. One soldier related, "The boys wandered off into orchards, cornfields, potato patches and thickets, as various dishes of potatoes, corn, apples, and blackberries were soon cooked and devoured." Many of the Iowans blamed these shortages on their own company commanders and the regiment's commissary officer, but the problem went beyond any one unit. Lyon's logistical system, which had been haphazard from the beginning, was falling apart. With more than six thousand men and over one thousand horses and mules concentrated in one area, the Federals required 15.5 tons of food and grain and 6.5 tons of supplementary fodder every day. Although Lyon had given a highly competent officer the task of shuttling supplies to Springfield from Rolla, conditions were chaotic and there were maddening delays. Army agents purchased grain throughout the surrounding region, but Lyon did not confiscate the food on the shelves in Springfield stores. Merchants sold this stock to Lyon's hungry men at inflated prices. The soldiers apparently resented this exploitation, for Lyon soon had to publish orders reprimanding his men for stealing not only food but private property as well.[26]

The impact of these conditions on the morale of the Army of the West is difficult to determine. Some wartime letters and postwar reminiscences state that the situation was not acute and that the men's spirits remained high, even after learning of the Union defeat at Manassas Junction in Virginia on July 21. "General Lyon is universally popular," an Iowa soldier informed his hometown paper in Burlington. Others sources disagreed. Although there were some optimists, a large percentage of the Iowans were thoroughly dispirited. "Most of us are sick, tired, and disgusted of the 1st Regiment," a soldier reported to his friends in Davenport. He reasoned that "many and many a one who would have enlisted for three years now will not do so, and subject themselves to such mean and contemptible treatment." Another, writing to the citizens of Dubuque, recounted the soldiers' sufferings in detail, concluding, "do you wonder that we will hail with joy the day which restores us to our homes and families, and dissolves our connection with the United States Volunteer Service?" In pledging their honor and that of their community to faithful service, the volunteers had thought largely of sacrifices on the battlefield. They had not anticipated the abject physical misery that campaigning involved, and evidence that it was exacerbated by the incompetence of their own government was infuriating.[27]

No one was more upset with conditions than Lyon himself. He reported to his superiors that his men were suffering chronic diarrhea due to weeks of substandard rations and that discipline was badly compromised. When typhoid broke out, Lyon converted Springfield's unfinished courthouse into a hospital. It was soon overcrowded. Adding to morale problems was the fact that the soldiers had received no pay from the Federal government. During the last days of July about two thousand volunteers, many of them German Americans from St. Louis, marched out of Springfield in disgust. Their ninety-day terms of service had expired, and they refused to reenlist. This sparked ethnic tensions. "Damn the Dutch element in Missouri," wrote one Regular officer. "They are useful but cowardly." Such accusations were unfair. Lyon's Missouri volunteers had served honorably. The majority of them, ragged and often barefooted, remained in Springfield.[28]

Lyon faced many strategic challenges as well. Alarming reports reached him daily concerning the strength, movement, and intentions of various units of the Missouri State Guard. Most were either erroneous or wildly exaggerated, but Lyon could not ignore them. He responded by dispatching scouts and occasionally conducting a reconnaissance in force. Though none of these was on the scale of Sweeny's expedition, they contributed to the general fatigue of the Federal troops. Lyon was also distracted by wild reports of Confederate troops moving into Missouri from Arkansas, Tennessee, and Kentucky. It is hardly surprising that his headquarters, located on College Street in a two-story building belonging to Congressman John Phelps, was the scene of feverish activity, or that the burden of command extracted considerable personal cost. By habit a light sleeper and an early riser, Lyon worked to the point of exhaustion and began losing weight, which added to his generally undignified appearance. Favoring a worn captain's coat over the fancy uniform of a general, he wore his pant legs rolled halfway up his boots like a farmer and tugged his beard nervously whenever frustrated.[29]

Lyon's military accomplishments between early May and late July had been remarkable, but without substantial reinforcements and increased supplies he would have no option except retreat. His dilemma was exacerbated by the absence of strategic direction from above. Frémont, the new commander for the Western Department, did not reach St. Louis until July 25. It took Frémont some time to put things in order, and the Federal troops in Springfield were only a small part of his new responsibilities. Lyon bombarded Frémont's headquarters with letters and telegrams explaining his desperate plight. On four occasions he dispatched personal emissaries to speak directly with Frémont. But as the month of July drew to a close, he had received neither information nor instruction from St. Louis.[30]

On July 28 circumstances forced Lyon's hand. When scouts brought news that a portion of the Missouri State Guard was moving through Carthage toward Greenfield, a town northwest of Springfield, Lyon feared that his right flank might be turned. Although the troops he sent to the scene discovered nothing, he continued to anticipate an enemy movement from that direction. Even more alarming was word that Price and McCulloch were marching toward Cassville with thirty thousand men. Located fifty miles to the southwest, Cassville lay on the Wire Road, the route the enemy would likely take to attack Springfield. Finally, Lyon learned that Confederate troops under Gideon Pillow had landed at New Madrid in southeastern Missouri. He assumed, correctly, that the silent Frémont was more likely to dispatch troops in response to this threat along the Mississippi than reinforce the Ozarks. In short, he was left completely on his own to face the greatest threat to Missouri since the war began. Characteristically, he decided to attack rather than retreat, to move down the Wire Road and confront the enemy.[31]

This proved to be a major error. The Federal army was in wretched physical condition, food was scarce, and morale was fragile in many units. Most of the men simply wanted to go home. A forward movement made every problem worse. It is to Lyon's credit that he did not want to abandon the Unionists in Springfield, but a good commander must realize when to cut his losses and fight another day. Although Lyon complained to his superiors that a retrograde movement would undo everything he had accomplished, this was simply not the case. His most obvious and sensible option was a withdrawal to the railhead at Rolla. There his forces could rest and resupply. Meanwhile, he might take the train to St. Louis, trying in person to convince Frémont that southwestern Missouri should not be abandoned simply because of threats elsewhere. Given Lyon's forceful personality, he might have succeeded. His rejection of this strategy is best explained by his peculiar sense of destiny, his belief that he was God's instrument for the punishment of treason. When Lyon marched his force of 5,868 men down the Wire Road on the blisteringly hot morning of August 1, searching for an enemy rumored to have more than five times his own strength, he was not merely undertaking a military mission. He was launching the final phase of his "punitive crusade."[32]

While Lyon overestimated the size of the force moving against him, he had not exaggerated the danger. For although Ben McCulloch had qualms about Sterling Price's ability, he was anxious for a joint move against the Federals in Springfield. Both he and Price hoped that this might be coordinated with an advance on the part of the Arkansas State Troops and Confederate forces in eastern Arkansas and perhaps even Confederate troops in western Tennessee. They wrote letters recommending this strategy to commanders in those areas and to the War Department in Richmond. The replies, which took some time to reach them, were negative, and it was fortunate that they did not count heavily on such support when making their plans.[33]

On July 25, in preparation for the advance, Price began shifting the Missouri State Guard east to Cassville. Several hundred men of McBride's Division already guarded the strategic location. By July 28 more than 7,000 men were in place. The following day McCulloch arrived. His Confederate brigade and Bart Pearce's Arkansas State Troops, which reached camp the next day, brought the total of the Southern forces to approximately 13,500. A few of the Arkansas State Troops had balked at crossing into Missouri. One company commander, Captain John J. Walker, wrote to a friend that two of his men had deserted as a consequence. He continued: "There is several others in the company who stated publicly that they would go no farther than the state line, and endeavored to induce others to join them. When we got to the line they halted for a moment, but the number that stopped with them being small they fell into ranks again. I am in hopes there will be no more desertions from my Co., but there is no telling anything about white men in a campaign like this."[34] It is unclear whether many others shared the views of Walker's company.

McCulloch referred to the combined forces as the Western Army. Pearce used the label Consolidated Army, but he also called it the Army of Arkansas, the same term he had used previously for his Arkansas State Troops. In memoirs, some veterans termed it the Army of the West. Actually, no name was ever officially adopted for this unique body of soldiers. As McCulloch led them, his designation Western Army is preferred. Even the term "Southerners" cannot do justice to the diversity of backgrounds, political viewpoints, allegiances, and loyalties of the men gathered in and around Cassville. It is used in default of a better collective word.[35]

As McCulloch and Price considered themselves to be commanding forces that belonged to separate nations, the Confederate States and the United States, respectively, the question arose of who should command their combined units in the campaign against the "usurping Lincolnites." Surprisingly, Pearce raised the issue first. On the afternoon that the forces joined, he approached Price, stating that he was willing to serve under either the Missourian or McCulloch, so long as the army had a definite head. At Price's suggestion, they immediately visited McCulloch and offered him command of the joint armies. Although Price's motivation was doubtless sincere, Pearce's action in prompting the meeting was disingenuous. The state of Arkansas, under which he held his commission, had already assigned his troops to McCulloch. By negotiating in company with Price, Pearce was assuming a status of equality with the other two men that simply did not exist, for he was McCulloch's subordinate. As McCulloch had already intermixed Confederate and Arkansas State Troops to establish provisional brigades, Pearce apparently feared that he soon might be left without a command. This concern was particularly ironic, as he alone among the top Southern commanders had been educated at West Point. McCulloch accepted the offer to command and so informed the War Department.[36]

Months after the Wilson's Creek campaign ended, at a time when he and Price were at odds with one another, McCulloch wrote that when Price offered to serve under his command, he had suspected "it was done to throw the responsibility of ordering a retreat upon me if one had to be ordered for the want of supplies." The statement apparently reflects their postbattle squabbles, as there is nothing in McCulloch's surviving correspondence for July and August to suggest that he doubted the sincerity of the Missourian's offer. Supplies were indeed a critical problem, however. Even on reduced rations the men of the combined Southern host required almost 20 tons of food daily. To remain in maximum health and strength their horses, which numbered some 3,500, needed 45.5 tons of grain and hay per day. By the end of July the soldiers had stripped the regions around their camps nearly bare, making an advance on Springfield or a retreat to Fort Smith the only viable options. In addition to these worries, McCulloch had deep concerns about the arms and ammunition supply of the Missouri State Guard. Many possessed "shot-guns and common rifles" rather than military firearms. McCulloch loaned them what ammunition he could, but even with this redistribution the Western Army had barely enough munitions to contemplate battle. The day before the march began, McCulloch pleaded with the secretary of war to dispatch "a large amount of flint-lock musket cartridges, percussion musket cartridges for percussion and minie muskets, and caps, and such cannon ammunition for field pieces as can be spared."[37]

To avoid overcrowding the country roads and to collect forage along the way, the Southerners advanced piecemeal, in three "divisions," a day's march apart. Six companies of cavalry rode ahead to scout the way and prevent surprise. The structure McCulloch adopted for the advance is interesting. The First Division, for instance, contained two Confederate units, the Third Louisiana Infantry and McRae's Battalion, Arkansas Volunteers; two units from the Arkansas State Troops, the Pulaski Light Battery and the Third Arkansas Infantry; and all the infantry from Rains's Division of the Missouri State Guard. The other two divisions were equally mixed. The Texan's reason for this organization is unknown. But as he claimed to have read military history extensively, he may have been following the example of Wellington at Waterloo. There the duke had strengthened his position by interspersing his British Regulars among the less reliable units of his Dutch allies.[38]

Equally interesting is the fact that the Third Division, which marched last, contained most of the mounted troops.[39] This may have been because so many of them were poorly armed members of the Missouri State Guard. Perhaps McCulloch considered them too ill-disciplined to be of great use. But much of his previous military experience had been with mounted troops, and his dream in the 1850s had been to lead a cavalry regiment. One might have expected him to concentrate all his cavalry in the van, where they could outflank and cut off anyone they encountered. Although a minor point, it suggests that McCulloch's eagerness to advance was balanced by a strong element of caution, even uncertainty. The onetime Ranger now commanded an army, and the fate of both Missouri and the Trans-Mississippi Confederacy rested in no small part on his shoulders. It was a heavy responsibility.

There were problems from the beginning. For contrary to an understanding he had reached with McCulloch, Price allowed some two thousand unarmed men and a significant number of women to follow along from Cowskin Prairie. As camp followers, these women had rendered invaluable support services to the State Guard, acting as cooks, laundresses, and nurses. Most were the wives, daughters, or sisters of the men in the ranks and had followed their loved ones to war, representing "their" companies and home communities in a fashion similar to the men. But because supplies were strained McCulloch wanted them left behind, as the camp followers of his Confederate units and Arkansas State Troops had been. Only a few officers' wives, such as Mrs. Pearce, were allowed to remain. The unarmed soldiers were an even more useless burden. Although orders instructed them to remain a day's march behind, the situation was unsatisfactory. Price's failure to live up to the agreement boded ill for future cooperation.[40]

Nevertheless, all seemed well as the leading elements of the Western Army went into camp on August 1 at Crane Creek, which provided excellent water. Pickets were thrown out, while scouts continued up the Wire Road. The scouts soon returned with the startling news that the Union army was only seven miles away. Lyon had not remained in Springfield. A collision was now imminent.

Chapter 9 . . . .

The Lyon and the Whang-doodle

On the evening of August 1 the Army of the West camped on the same site where nine days later it would engage in battle. Although there was no reason for Nathaniel Lyon to give special attention to the area, he probably noted its obvious features. Moving southwest, the Federals first crossed the extensive property of John Ray, which the Wire Road bisected. Continuing on, they encountered a ridge running parallel to the road on its right side. Just over half a mile from the Ray farmhouse, the road dropped into the broad valley formed by Wilson Creek.* There the ridge ended abruptly. Atop its steep end was a small farmhouse or cabin recently occupied by a family named Winn (not Guinn, as given in many accounts). Nearby, the Wire Road crossed the creek at a shallow ford. On the western bank was the farm of William B. Edwards, whose flat land offered the best place to camp. As Lyon's men pitched their tents, they could see that the dominant terrain feature on the western bank was an unnamed hill that lay north of the Edwards farm, running to the edge of the creek opposite the Winn farm and Ray's cornfields farther upstream. The hill was covered with scrub oak and prairie grass, with occasional thickets and rocky bare spots. No one could anticipate that in the near future so many lives would be expended on its slopes that it would earn the name "Bloody Hill."

Because Lyon's forces had occupied an extensive semicircle of camps surrounding Springfield, some units marched farther than others to reach Wilson Creek. Eugene Ware, of the First Iowa's Burlington Zouaves, estimated that his unit actually traveled eighteen miles. The trip took

---

*Wilson Creek was usually misnamed "Wilson's Creek" by soldiers, and the mistake stuck in references to the battle. In this book, "Wilson's Creek" refers to the battle and "Wilson Creek" to the stream.

them nine hours, and they were so late reaching the camp that they simply went to sleep in ranks in the middle of the road. They enjoyed only three hours rest before the march resumed the next morning.[1]

Lyon started his column moving early on August 2. Leaving the vicinity of the Edwards farm, the Federals crossed a small tributary of Wilson Creek called Skegg's Branch. Beyond this the road rose up a steep bank, bringing them to a plateau on which sat the home of Joseph D. Sharp. From the Sharp farm the Wire Road climbed a low hill, wooded at the top, which overlooked the whole valley. As the Federals continued southwest, temperatures rose to almost 110 degrees Fahrenheit. "No water could be found and the dust covered us to such an extent that a companion could not be recognized except by his familiar voice," one Regular testified. Although they marched only seven miles, artilleryman John Du Bois noted in his journal that fully two-thirds of Lyon's men fell by the roadside from exhaustion before they reached their destination, Dug Springs, a watering hole that lay in a long, sheltered valley.[2]

Lyon's advance scouts, who had skirmished with the enemy during the night, led him to expect that just beyond Dug Springs, near a farm belonging to a man named Hayden, he would find Rains's Division of the Missouri State Guard, estimated to be three thousand strong. Believing that Price and McCulloch had not yet linked their forces, Lyon sought an opportunity to destroy them piecemeal, on ground of his own choosing, starting with individual portions of the State Guard. To ascertain the enemy's exact strength and position he therefore formed a battalion from among his Regulars, sending it ahead as an advance guard. Commanded by Captain Frederick Steele, a balding forty-two-year-old West Pointer from Connecticut who had distinguished himself in the Mexican War, this consisted of four companies of infantry, a section of guns from Totten's Battery, Captain Stanley's cavalry, and a company of unassigned recruits commanded by a sergeant.[3]

Steele's men approached Hayden's farm cautiously around 9:00 A.M. But instead of Rains's entire division, they found only a few scouts, who fled precipitously when Totten opened fire on them. Steele pursued, but his prey soon disappeared into the surrounding dense woods. When Lyon arrived shortly afterward, he ordered Steele to set up a line of defense, blocking the far end of the valley. For the rest of the day the exhausted Federals straggled into the camp at Dug Springs. Although they had eaten one full meal before leaving Springfield, they were now on half rations of everything except beef.[4]

Sometime during the afternoon, Lyon sent at least two companies from the First Iowa to join Steele. The captain had chosen his ground well. He placed his artillery on a small rise, one gun on each side of the road, his infantry farther forward on ridges off to each side, forming a crescent-shaped line calculated to trap anyone approaching the valley. The Iowans joined Steele's mounted troops, serving as a reserve. Although the Federals exchanged shots with enemy scouts throughout the day, nothing occurred until late afternoon. Around 5:00 P.M. a great cloud of dust became visible in the distance. The enemy was obviously approaching, but the size of its force could not be determined.[5]

Lyon's foe Ben McCulloch had in fact spent most of August 2 consolidating his forces at Crane Creek, but his advance guard—six companies of cavalry from Rains's Division—continued to scout the road ahead. When Steele drove a party of them away from Hayden's farm, Rains reported the contact to McCulloch. The Texan did not want to be surprised, so he deployed his forces into better defensive positions and sent his adjutant, Colonel James McIntosh, to investigate. McIntosh took 150 men with him, probably drawn from his own Second Arkansas Mounted Rifles, reaching Rains's position about 2:00 P.M. Once there he conducted his own reconnaissance and from a hilltop was just able to make out Lyon's encampment at the far end of the valley. Uncertain about what he had seen in the afternoon haze, he ordered Rains to continue to probe the enemy's position but not to bring on an engagement. As aggressive action was neither contemplated nor desired, McIntosh started back to report to McCulloch, taking his men with him.[6]

The order in which events next occurred is impossible to determine precisely, as both Rains and Steele insisted in their reports that they were reacting to movements made by the other. Apparently Rains's probing movements, designed to collect information, made Steele afraid that he was being outflanked, and in response he called up his reserves and began adjusting his lines. Seeing movement in the woods and undergrowth, Rains also feared for his flanks and consequently launched an attack with most of his force. As a result, the Missouri State Guardsmen rode straight into Steele's defensive position, where they received a withering fire into their flanks, while canister from Totten's guns poured into their front. The Federals' aim was deplorable, for none of Rains's men were killed and only six were wounded; when some of Stanley's troopers ignored orders and launched a countercharge, four of them were killed and six were wounded. Nevertheless, Rains's entire command fled back down the Wire Road in abject panic. Many soldiers did not halt even when they encountered McIntosh's men, who were still riding back toward the Western Army's camp at Crane Creek.[7]

Militarily, the skirmish near Dug Springs was insignificant, but it had a

Captain Joseph Totten, Company
F, Second U.S. Artillery (The collection of Dr. Tom and Karen
Sweeney, General Sweeny's Museum, Republic, Missouri)

major impact on the relationship between the Missouri State Guard and
the rest of the Southern forces. Honor was all-important to these men,
and "Rains's Scare," as the episode became known, reflected negatively
on all Missourians. A Shreveport newspaper printed a letter from a soldier in the Third Louisiana stating that after Dug Springs the Confederate
troops regarded the Missourians as "dastardly cowards." A member of
the Arkansas State Troops wrote home that the Missourians "ran like
Scared dogs."[8]

Previously McCulloch had expressed doubts about Sterling Price's
capabilities, but now he questioned the reliability of the whole State
Guard. When word of Rains's flight reached him, apparently by a messenger riding ahead of the returning troops, he reacted strongly. According to one witness, "McCulloch dashed up the road fairly foaming with
rage—exhausting his whole vocabulary of vituperation, and it is no mea-
ger one—in denunciation of the Missourians." Although this fit of temper
boded ill for future cooperation between McCulloch and Price, McIntosh's actions were positively astonishing. In his report to McCulloch,
written the following day, he not only stated that he had "expected" the
Missourians to retreat, he also smugly described rejecting their request
for assistance, writing, "General Rains had engaged the enemy unad-
visedly, and had sent for my small command to re-enforce him, which I

respectfully declined, having no disposition to sacrifice it in such company." McIntosh was McCulloch's most trusted subordinate. It reveals much about the relationship between the two men, and even more about their assessment of the Missourians, that McIntosh would admit to abandoning the Missouri State Guard on the field of battle and that McCulloch would not rebuke him for having done so.[9]

With his command in poor shape, Lyon had no more desire to bring on a fight late in the day than McCulloch did, and after the skirmish he ordered Steele to withdraw to the main camp. Perhaps because his troops were so tired, he made no attempt to maintain contact with Rains's retreating men or to learn more about McCulloch's location. Instead, to deny the enemy information about his own strength, he ordered that no fires be built during the night. About 2:30 A.M. on the morning of August 3, reacting to imagined movements in the darkness, the Federals sprang to arms and Totten fired shells down the road. Convinced that they had averted a dangerous situation, the Federals slept on their arms in line of battle in case the "attack" was renewed. Although no physical harm was done, Lyon's already exhausted men were robbed of a night's sleep that they sorely needed.[10]

Lyon resumed his offensive once it became light. After a three-mile march the column's lead elements reached a point where the Wire Road "descended into a deep wide valley." In the distance lay Curran Post Office, a "community" that consisted of a single house and a few adjacent rude shelters. There and in the nearby woods the Federals could see the camps of what appeared to be several hundred mounted men. Curiously, Lyon did not use his own cavalry to probe their position and estimate their numbers. Instead, he halted for about an hour for the tail end of his column to catch up. Although it was only mid-morning, the heat was intense; before the day ended, there would be several cases of sunstroke.[11]

By 11:00 A.M. Lyon had formed a portion of his infantry into successive lines of battle off to the side of the road, while Totten's Battery was positioned on a nearby hill. The First Iowa was the leading unit, and Ware recalled Totten's characteristic language as be brought his guns into position: "Take that limber to the rear, G—d d——n you, sir. Wheel that caisson around, G—d d——n you, sir." With the artillery providing cover fire, the infantry advanced cautiously. Although the Southerners in the open spaces around Curran Post Office itself fled almost immediately, it took the Federals two hours to clear the surrounding woods. Casualties were slight, but the skirmish was so heated that the Federals were occasionally pushed back, despite their massive superiority in numbers. "The 1st Iowa behaved badly & came running back," artillerist John Du Bois noted critically. But "the other regiments did as well," he added. Still, Lyon's success was complete, and the hungry victors made good use of the spoils they found in the enemy's camps. This included corn, oats, cured pork and beef, saddles, blankets, hats, shoes, socks, and miscellaneous weapons.[12]

Avoiding the previous day's mistake of losing contact with the enemy, Lyon dispatched the Second Kansas in quick pursuit, leaving the remainder of the army to follow more slowly. By late afternoon, the Army of the West was concentrated once more, two miles farther down the Wire Road at a roadside store and farm operated by a man named McCullah. This had previously been the site of Rains's headquarters. Because the hour was late and he was still uncertain of the location of the enemy's main camp, Lyon stopped operations for the day. His soldiers' sense of frustration was tempered by a belief that their two days of skirmishing constituted great victories, and they cheered their commander whenever they saw him.[13]

The men who faced the Federals on August 3 were mostly from Churchill's First Arkansas Mounted Rifles, and they had a different interpretation of what had occurred. Far from being defeated in the day's fighting, they had deliberately given ground, hoping to draw Lyon into a carefully prepared trap that McCulloch had positioned just north of Crane Creek. Significantly, McCulloch had deployed only his Confederate and Arkansas State Troops for this operation, leaving the Missouri State Guard in camp. When Churchill sent word that evening that Lyon had halted at McCullah's store, the Texan allowed his advanced force to prepare its own dinner. Just before dark, he moved the men even farther forward, to some elevated rocky ground perhaps a mile from the Union camp. There they deployed in line of battle and went to sleep on their arms. McCulloch credited his enemy with initiative and aggressive instincts, as he fully expected to be attacked during the night. To avoid confusion, each man in his Confederate units, and possibly those in the Arkansas State Troops as well, tied a band of white cloth around his left arm (many members of the Missouri State Guard already "wore a *red* badge on their shoulder" for identification).[14]

Lyon not only made no assault during the night, he had his men build extra campfires to fool the enemy into overestimating his numbers. In fact, he was in such a quandary about his next move that he called a council of his top officers. The effects of fatigue and the weight of responsibility appear to have eroded much of Lyon's self-confidence. For the first time since his initiation of war in Missouri, the self-appointed instrument of God's wrath for the punishment of traitors sought earthly advice. He had captured a number of Southerners during the day's running fight, and two deserters had entered his lines. These informed him that McCulloch's force in his front contained between 10,000 and 15,000, many of them cavalrymen who might easily slip around the Union flanks and cut the line of communications to Springfield. Lyon had left the city only lightly garrisoned, and the freely moving Southern horsemen might even strike his supply base there. Moreover, on the basis of reports from scouts sent out earlier over a wide area, he still believed that McCulloch and Price had not yet combined their total available strength, and that a considerable body of the Missouri State Guard was near Sarcoxie, potentially threatening his rear. Lyon concluded that McCulloch's cavalry had merely been making demonstrations in his front while the Southerners awaited the arrival of these reinforcements, which might bring their total number to more than 20,000.[15]

During the council of war, Lyon's officers considered all of the possibilities, openly debating the benefits of advance or withdrawal. Though all of them favored fighting a pitched battle, the Union army's critical shortage of supplies made retreat the only prudent option. Lyon accepted their advice. The common soldiers had a more direct perspective. Hearing the news, William Branson of the First Iowa wrote in his diary, "General Lyon has come to the wise conclusion that it is all foolishness to march his men any further south, as he is killing more men every day marching them through the hot sun than by bullets."[16]

The return to Springfield began on the morning of August 4. Throughout the day Southern cavalry worried Lyon's flanks and during the afternoon even attacked his rear guard. The need to take precautions against ambush combined with temperatures reaching 105 degrees made the march both slow and miserable. "Orders were now issued to lighten the wagons of every superfluous article," recalled Joseph Cracklin of the Second Kansas. "As the day advanced the heat became intense and the dust insufferable." According to journalist Thomas Knox, a number of men died from heatstroke and scores dropped behind, delirious from thirst. He wrote: "When the army reached a small farm with a spring, all discipline broke down and the soldiers fought over the limited supply of water. This included the Regulars as well as the volunteers. A soldier who obtained a canteen full of water from a hog trough was offered five dollars in gold for it by an officer. He refused. . . . To such a frenzy were the men driven by thirst that they tore up handfuls of moist earth, and swallowed the few drops of water that could be pressed out." Finally, after marching twelve miles, the Federals obtained blessed relief from their sufferings when they reached Moody's Springs. The water from the springs flowed into nearby Terrell Creek, which ran east for less than a mile before emptying into Wilson Creek.[17]

Reveille roused the camp at 4:00 A.M. the next morning, August 5. Once again Missouri's hot sun bore down on the column as temperatures soared to 110 degrees. Whenever possible the mounted units rode in the withered prairie grass parallel to the road, but the wagons were forced to continue on the road's dusty surface. Their teams and the steady tread of the infantry kicked up a thick yellow-brown haze that filled the ears, eyes, and mouths of the men and animals. It was nearly sundown as they approached Springfield. Four miles from the town Lyon stationed a covering force of about two thousand men under Major Samuel Sturgis. The rest of the troops trudged on to occupy their old camps in and around the city, but Lyon was so afraid of an immediate attack that he had all of his men sleep on their arms that night.[18]

This continued state of heightened alert prevented the rest that the Federals desperately needed. Lyon's performance as a commander was steadily deteriorating. Since reaching Springfield, most of his decisions had been bad. Although his operations in June and July had neither trapped nor crushed the Missouri State Guard, he had secured the strategic areas of northern and central Missouri. Had he then withdrawn to Rolla because of his logistical difficulties, no one would have criticized his decision, and the showers of praise being heaped on him would have continued unabated. Lyon, however, not only refused to abandon Springfield, but he also continued to advance despite the deplorable physical condition of his men, first sending Sweeny to Forsyth, then taking the entire Army of the West into the field in search of battle. The war in Missouri had become a personal vendetta that warped Lyon's judgment.

Equally disturbing was the evidence from recent events that Lyon was a poor tactician. He consistently misused his mounted troops, giving them combat roles rather than using them to locate the enemy, report its strength and position, or cut its line of communications. Following the skirmish at Dug Springs on August 2, he failed to maintain contact with Rains's retreating horsemen. Bereft of knowledge, he huddled in a fireless camp that night, calling his weary men into line of battle in reaction to false alarms. On August 3 at Curran Post Office, his cavalry sat idle while his infantry advanced over unknown ground. Worse still, he ordered Totten's guns to fire directly over the heads of these advancing troops. Because of the composition of Civil War artillery ammunition and the fact that it was prone to explode short of its target, this needlessly exposed the

Federals to the dangers of friendly fire. No one was injured, but Lyon's men resented the experience.[19] Once the skirmishing ended, Lyon had held his cavalry in camp, sending the Second Kansas to pursue the Southerners and maintain contact with them. Although this unit included a single mounted company that was doubtless put to good use, Lyon's troop dispositions reflected considerable inexperience, if not outright ineptitude.

Little improved once the Federal forces returned to Springfield. On the evening of August 5 Lyon learned from one of the emissaries he had sent to St. Louis that General John Frémont had no intention of sending him reinforcements. Although the need to retreat to Rolla was obvious, Lyon was "gripped by indecision." The day ended with the future of the Army of the West in doubt. Lyon might have slept more peacefully had he known how much favorable news coverage his recent skirmishes would receive in the national and regional press. Reported as victorious battles, they fed the hunger of a Northern populace eager for good news to balance the recent Union debacle at Manassas. For enthusiasm, frontier slang, and parody, none of these newspaper accounts outdid the *Atchison Freedom's Champion*, which proclaimed: "The news from South-West Missouri is glorious. It thrills us like the blast of a trumpet. Gen. Lyon has met the terrible-and-grand-hobgoblin of Secessia, Ben. McCulloch, and routed him! The forces of treason are in full retreat, and the Federal troops are pursuing them. . . . 'The Lyon roareth, and the Whang-doodle fleeth to the mountain of Hepsedam, where he shall gnaw a file!' "[20]

The events of August 3 further widened the rift between Ben McCulloch and Sterling Price. The following evening Captain John Wyatt, an assistant surgeon in Foster's Infantry of McBride's Division, wrote in his diary, "Today looked gloomy for a while in consequence of disagreement among the Generals. No one in particular having charge."[21] Dr. Wyatt's vantage point doubtless allowed him to pick up current rumors, but he was ignorant of the actual command situation. McCulloch was in charge. The problem was that Price tended to forget it.

A confrontation occurred between McCulloch and Price on August 4, but precisely what happened is unclear. Twenty-five years after the battle, when both McCulloch and Price were no longer living, Colonel Thomas Snead of the Missouri State Guard wrote of witnessing a highly dramatic encounter between the two generals. According to Snead, Price learned that McCulloch was considering a retreat, rode to the Texan's headquarters, and delivered an ultimatum:

I am an older man than you, General McCulloch, and I am not only your senior in rank now, but I was a brigadier-general in the Mexican War, with an independent command when you were only a captain; I have fought and won more battles than you have ever witnessed; my force is twice as great as yours; and some of my officers rank, and have seen more service than you, and we are also upon the soil of our own State; but General McCulloch, if you will consent to help us whip Lyon and to repossess Missouri, I will put myself and all my forces under your command, and we will obey you as faithfully as the humblest of your men. . . . If you refuse to accept this offer, I will move with the Missourians alone, against Lyon.[22]

Snead wrote that when faced with this challenge, McCulloch gave in and ordered the army forward. But Snead was hardly a neutral observer. He had served as an aide to Governor Jackson before becoming Price's adjutant general and chief of ordnance. Despite what Snead wrote, one cannot imagine McCulloch, who was noted for once "smashing a chair over the head of an antagonist in the dining room of a Washington hotel," sitting still for the insults Snead described, nor would a crafty politician such as Price likely use such language to a man of McCulloch's reputation. More important, Snead is contradicted not only by the accounts of McCulloch and Pearce, which have McCulloch taking command of the combined forces on July 30, but also by his own wartime correspondence as adjutant, written on July 30 and 31, which indicates that on those dates the units of the Missouri State Guard were intermingled with McCulloch's Confederates and Pearce's Arkansas State Troops to form brigades under McCulloch's command.[23]

For these reasons Snead's narrative of the meeting cannot be trusted. Historians have apparently credited it because Price published an order on August 4 announcing that henceforward the Missouri State Guard was "under the direction of General Ben. McCulloch, whose orders as commander-in-chief of the combined armies will, during such time, be obeyed by all officers and men of the Missouri forces in the field." Indeed, on hearing this Dr. Wyatt rejoiced, writing "At last Gen. McCulloch was given supreme command of all the forces and gave orders for a march." The surgeon's remark suggests that although Price had agreed to serve under McCulloch's leadership on July 30, he had made no formal announcement of the arrangement to his troops.[24]

In the context of Snead's wartime writings rather than his postwar account, Price's August 4 announcement actually reads like a capitulation to McCulloch rather than a triumph over him. For Price's order allowed

McCulloch to give commands directly to State Guard officers, bypassing Price entirely. Although no one can be certain what actually happened at the fateful meeting, the two generals probably compromised. Because Price had already agreed to serve under McCulloch, he could not have offered to do so on August 4 as Snead wrote. Apparently, the Missouri general threatened to withdraw from their previous arrangement unless McCulloch advanced the army immediately. McCulloch acquiesced but demanded unquestioned, direct authority over Price's units in return. Price therefore issued orders to that effect.

McCulloch's reluctance to move forward is understandable. He was struggling uncomfortably with the necessity of making decisions based on incomplete information and bothered by the prospect of continuing the campaign under less-than-optimum conditions. He confronted an aggressive, unified enemy erroneously thought to be superior in numbers, arms, and discipline, comprised in large part of Regulars, and firmly anchored on a bountiful supply base at nearby Springfield. By contrast, the Western Army was a conglomeration of units with extreme variety in their weaponry and discipline. Indeed, "Rains's Scare" suggested that portions of the Missouri State Guard were little better than an armed mob. The Southerners' base at distant Fort Smith had limited resources, and due to the rugged mountain roads between there and Crane Creek, supplies were more than a week in transit. Meanwhile, an overreliance on green corn foraged locally, dehydration, and the effects of prolonged extreme heat combined to debilitate both the soldiers and the army's draft animals.[25]

One biographer concludes that McCulloch probably intended to withdraw on August 4, "leaving Price to his folly." This is unlikely. Although he had failed to induce Lyon to attack him the day before, McCulloch still held excellent defensive ground and had supplies for several days. No immediate decision was necessary, and the Southern forces could easily have remained at Crane Creek for a while longer. But circumstances changed, involving more than just the confrontation with Price. McCulloch received word that General Gideon Pillow was advancing north from New Madrid with twelve thousand Confederates, a movement that might cut Lyon off from supplies and reinforcements via Rolla and St. Louis. Although Pillow would have a long, time-consuming march, it might be possible to trap Lyon between Pillow's forces and McCulloch's command if McCulloch could occupy Lyon's attention sufficiently for the next few days. Equally encouraging was the presence of Colonel Elkanah Greer, whose long-awaited South Kansas–Texas Cavalry now rode into Crane Creek, completing their forced march from Fort Smith. Greer's men were obviously weary, but the presence of these fellow Texans seems to have restored some of McCulloch's confidence.[26]

Whatever his reasons, McCulloch issued orders for the Western Army to march at midnight. His plan was simple. Colonel Louis Hébert's Third Louisiana and Captain William Woodruff's Pulaski Light Battery would act as the vanguard and "attack the enemy as soon as seen." The infantry, artillery, and mounted troops would follow. Once contact was made, the cavalry of the Missouri State Guard would move off to the left, while the Confederate and Arkansas State Troops horsemen moved to the right. The Federals would be struck from the front and both flanks simultaneously. McCulloch apparently made no attempt to locate and utilize as guides or scouts Missouri State Guardsmen who were familiar with the area. This may reflect his continuing distrust of the State Guard or perhaps an assumption that contact would be made so quickly that such an effort was unnecessary.[27]

McCulloch's orders contained admonitions to the common soldiers that appear melodramatic by today's standards. Reminding them of the recent Confederate victory at Manassas, Virginia, he wrote: "Look steadily to the front. Remember that the eyes of your gallant brothers-in-arms who have so nobly acquitted themselves in the East are upon you. They are looking for a second victory here. Let us move forward, then, with a common resolve, to a glorious victory." But these were not superfluous platitudes. These soldiers had been raised at the community level and were imbued with a high sense of honor. McCulloch's words reminded each man that as he marched to battle he carried the weight not only of his own reputation, but that of his hometown and state as well. Willie Tunnard of the Pelican Rifles remembered the anxiety felt by the men of the Third Louisiana: "Last messages were delivered to those detailed to remain with the wagons, packages for the loved ones at home made up, and the men laid down to what many deemed their final living sleep, ere the march commenced."[28]

As it turned out, the events of August 5 were a frustrating anticlimax. The Western Army had gone but a short distance when scouts reported that the Federals were in full retreat. In anticipation of battle, McCulloch had ordered all baggage left in camp and the men had only a day's rations in the haversacks. But he was now so committed to the offensive that he ordered a forced march pursuit, leaving the wagons to catch up as best they could. The chase, which lasted all day but produced nothing more than some skirmishing with the Federals' rear guard, was as tiring for the Southerners as the retreat was for Lyon's men. Artillery commander

William Woodruff recalled: "It was fearfully hot and the men were at the verge of exhaustion. The tired Third Louisiana swarmed about our guns on the road, hoping and begging to ride. Our officers were compelled to refuse—the teams had to be protected."[29]

McCulloch shifted Greer's Texans to the front to scout the way, and he sometimes joined them in taking shots at the Federals in the distance. But by the time the column reached Moody's Springs, it was obvious that Lyon had escaped. Because of the abundance of fresh water there and the exhausted state of the Southern army, McCulloch canceled the pursuit. The halt came not a moment too soon. Tunnard testified that "the men and animals made an indiscriminate rush for the water, which was fortunately abundant and fine." Woodruff recorded that his soldiers "fell where they halted, and went to sleep where they lay, supperless; and it was only by personal exertions of the officers that the teams were unharnessed and picketed."[30]

The supply wagons were still far to the rear, and Lyon had made sure that the Southerners found little forage. "The enemy is laying waste as he goes," Dr. Wyatt wrote. "Thousands on thousands of bushels of corn [are] being burned up. Oats, wheat and corn all the same." While most of the army rested, Greer continued to scout up the Wire Road. When his men reached the point where the road crossed Wilson Creek, they noted the fields of corn and other grains on the adjacent farms. As the Western Army contained just over 12,000 men and more than 4,000 horses, requiring approximately 70 tons of supplies and forage daily, these resources could not be ignored. Word went back to McCulloch, and on the morning of August 6 the Southerners set out to establish a new camp along the banks of Wilson Creek.[31]

For approximately two months units from as far away as Iowa, Texas, and Louisiana had traveled hundreds of miles by foot, horseback, steamboat, and rail to reach southwestern Missouri. Some seventeen thousand soldiers were on a collision course, taking with them their deeply held political convictions, as well as the pride, honor, and reputations of their various units and those units' home communities. A climactic battle might have erupted anywhere along the Wire Road from Crane Creek to Moody's Springs between August 2 and 5, but a combination of circumstances postponed the confrontation. The events that occurred from August 6 through 9 ultimately led Lyon and his men to confront the Southerners in their camps along Wilson Creek on the tenth.

Chapter 10 . . . .

Wilson Creek Afforded Us Water

After the forced march from Crane Creek to Moody's Springs on August 5, the remaining two-mile distance to Wilson Creek must have seemed mercifully short to the men of Ben McCulloch's Western Army when they took to the road again on August 6. Leaving the spring, they moved north out of the narrow bottom cut by Terrell Creek and onto high ground dominated by stands of scrub oak. After the Southerners marched about half a mile, they passed a road bearing to the left that led to the community of Little York. They continued along the main road, however, and after cresting a ridge they descended into the valley formed by Wilson Creek.[1]

Named after James Wilson, who had settled near the creek's mouth around 1822, Wilson Creek was not unlike any number of other streams that meandered through the Ozarks. Formed by two smaller creeks that converged on the western edge of Springfield, it ran roughly southwest for about five miles, several minor streams adding their waters to the generally shallow, narrow watercourse. Then it turned south, flowing some nine miles before spilling into the James River. About a mile upstream from that point the water of Terrell Creek joined Wilson Creek from the west, while another mile and a half upstream from there, Skegg's Branch emptied into Wilson Creek, also from the west. Even in this small region the stream underwent numerous changes. For the most part it could be crossed on foot, but steep banks restricted wheeled vehicles to specific fords. In some areas the current moved sluggishly, the water dark and deep. In other locations the creek's width narrowed and its depth diminished, increasing the current's speed and the water's clarity. At a point where conditions permitted harnessing the flow, John Gibson had constructed a mill on the eastern bank. He was one of many settlers attracted to the fertile, well-watered region.[2]

The terrain on either side of the creek alternated between high hills, ridges, plateaus, and fields of prairie grass. The ground cover was equally varied. There were post, white, and black oaks, together with other hardwoods. Some areas were overgrown by thick underbrush, but waist-high prairie grass constituted the majority of the vegetation. Narrow dirt roads, trails, and footpaths crisscrossed the landscape, linking farms to each other and providing access to both the Wire Road and the Little York Road.[3]

Many units of the Missouri State Guard had passed through this area before, but for the Confederates and Arkansas State Troops in Mc-Culloch's composite army this was unfamiliar terrain. As they crossed the high ground that lay between Moody's Springs and Wilson Creek, their view of the surrounding countryside was initially restricted. On the left, the road skirted the edge of a heavy growth of trees and dense underbrush that ran down to Skegg's Branch. But to the right, the dense cover gave way to a field of prairie grass, approximately one-half mile wide east to west, running south about a mile to Terrell Creek. Although the land sloped gradually down to Wilson Creek, a broad plateau sat in its center. Across the creek rose a high, steep, wooded ridge that afforded a commanding view of the narrow valley.[4]

Joseph D. Sharp's farm sat on the plateau. The forty-nine-year-old Sharp was the most prosperous farmer in the region. His wife Mary was fifty-one, and their three children were between the ages of thirteen and sixteen. Tax records from 1858 indicate that Joseph owned three slaves valued at $2,000; they were presumably still with the Sharps in 1861. The family's 1,272 acres were valued at over $11,000 by the 1860 Agricultural Census. Only a portion of this land was improved. Sharp's large, white two-story home sat on the southeastern side of the Wire Road. Behind it lay a barn, outbuildings, pens, and a fenced-in area of more than 100 acres. In 1861 most of this was planted in corn. The previous year the family had harvested a combined total of 2,100 bushels of Indian corn, wheat, and oats and produced Irish potatoes, sweet potatoes, butter, cheese, and molasses as well. The Sharps owned 135 animals, including horses, hogs, sheep, and oxen.[5]

Joseph Sharp's food resources, together with those of his neighbors, explain why McCulloch chose to camp where the Wire Road crossed Wilson Creek. In 1860 ten farms in the immediate vicinity yielded 11,500 bushels of Indian corn, 2,367 bushels of oats, 1,720 bushels of wheat, and 384 bushels of Irish and sweet potatoes. In addition, these farms produced over 1.5 tons of butter, 310 pounds of honey, 170 gallons of molasses, and 26 tons of hay. They also supported 248 hogs, 160 sheep, 97 head of cattle, 35 milk cows, and other livestock.[6]

Just over one hundred people dwelt on or adjacent to what would become the battlefield, but little is known about them. They seem to have been typical of others who settled in the agricultural regions of the upper South. Not surprisingly, most were Southern by birth. Over 80 percent of the adults (thirty-four out of forty-two) had been born in the South, twenty in Tennessee alone. Most of the non-Southerners were natives of New York, New Jersey, or Illinois. Three were from locations unknown and one was from Saxony. Although none of the adults were born in Missouri, fifty-six of the seventy-four children were natives. The other children were born in Tennessee, Kentucky, Illinois, Arkansas, and Iowa. Of the twenty-eight people whose occupations are known, twenty-one were farmers and one was a farm laborer. The remainder included two blacksmiths, two carders, a schoolteacher, and a wagonmaker. Details of their lives, such as their political sympathies or their reaction to the passing Federals and approaching Southerners, are unknown.[7]

Under the assumption that the August 6 order of march remained unchanged from earlier directives, McCulloch's Brigade led the Western Army as it tramped past the Sharp home toward Wilson Creek. It was followed by Bart Pearce's and Sterling Price's foot soldiers and, finally, the combined mounted units. The Wire Road dropped abruptly as it left the plateau flatland around Sharp's farm. After crossing Skegg's Branch, the Southerners entered the property of William B. Edwards, where Lyon's men had camped on their way to Dug Springs. To the left of the road a sizable hill rose gradually to the north and west, cresting at 170 feet. Dominating the surrounding countryside, this heretofore unchristened prominence would earn the name "Bloody Hill." The hill's south slope, scarred with ravines opening into Skegg's Branch, was blanketed primarily in prairie grass. Oaks and thickets of underbrush were scattered across the entire hill, but these were rarely dense. Visible to the east, immediately across Wilson Creek, a 30-foot-high plateau rose abruptly. The natural wall it formed ran for one-fourth mile between the ford across Wilson Creek and the one at Skegg's Branch.[8]

After the lead units crossed the creek, the road they followed marked the edge of a meadow on the left and started a gradual climb out of the bottom. As it rose, the road skirted a ravine that was flanked on the right by the wall-like plateau and a partially wooded ridge on the left. In 1860 the ridge top had been home to Larkin D. Winn, his wife Sofronia, and their eight children. Winn seems to have rented his land, farming the area below the ridge adjacent to Wilson Creek. His reason for leaving is unknown, but in August 1861 his dwelling stood abandoned. McCulloch made this convenient location his headquarters, stationing the Pulaski Light Battery nearby. This was a fortuitous decision, as the ridge provided a commanding view of much of the surrounding terrain.[9]

Less than a mile from the ford, the road at its highest point bisected the Ray farm, passing not more than fifty feet from the family's front porch steps. Another prominent area farmer, John A. Ray resided in a three-room sawn lumber home with his wife Roxanna, their eight children, and Julius Short. Because Ray served as postmaster for the Wilson Creek District, his already crowded home doubled as the local post office. It had also served at one time as a stop on Butterfield's Overland Stage route. Like the Sharps, John and Roxanna were slaveholders, owning a woman named Rhoda and her three daughters. The bondswomen probably slept in a small cabin behind the Ray house, beside which stood another one-room structure, perhaps a detached kitchen. Ray owned approximately 440 acres, including, apparently, the land Winn had farmed. Ray had planted corn on some eighty acres of undulating land located about 300 yards northwest of the house. Portions of the cornfield could be seen from the Ray front porch as well as from Bloody Hill, about one-half mile to the west.[10]

Between them, the Sharp, Edwards, and Ray properties marked the main campground of the Southern forces, although some units spilled onto the land adjacent to Gibson's Mill to the north and the high ground of Caleb B. Manley's farm, which was due south of the Rays. As the Western Army was not noted for its discipline, some of the Southerners probably visited other civilian homes in the vicinity, including those of Elias B. Short to the north, John Dixon to the south, T. B. Manley to the west, and Mary A. Gwinn to the southwest.

Moving a 12,000-man column all day in the August heat on the Wire Road was time-consuming. According to William Watson of the Third Louisiana, it was not until the next morning, August 7, that "all the forces were up, and the camp was put into some kind of order and position." Although some tents were erected in neat rows, many units apparently selected positions based on convenience or the happenstance of their arrival rather than any military design. About half the army eventually camped east of the creek. Colonel Louis Hébert's Third Louisiana pitched its tents across the road from McCulloch's headquarters and the Pulaski Battery, on the northern spur of the plateau above the creek. Near the Louisianans was another Confederate unit, McRae's Battalion, as well as the infantry of Pearce's Brigade of Arkansas State Troops—John Gratiot's Third Infantry, Jonathan Walker's Fourth Infantry, and Tom Dockery's Fifth Infantry. Farther south John Reid's Fort Smith Battery occupied a strategic position opposite the mouth of Skegg's Branch. Adjacent to these camps, but stretching slightly southeast to the Caleb Manley farm, were Bledsoe's Battery (three guns) and four infantry units under Colonels Thomas H. Rosser, John R. Graves, Edgar V. Hurst, and James J. Clarkson. Combined under Colonel Richard H. Weightman, they constituted Weightman's Brigade of Rains's Division of the Missouri State Guard.[11]

The forty-three-year-old Weightman was one of the most colorful figures in the Missouri army. A native of Maryland, he entered West Point but was expelled in 1837 "for cutting a cadet in the face with a knife." After service in a St. Louis artillery unit during the Mexican War, he settled in New Mexico, edited a newspaper, and was prominent in local politics. Sometime after killing a man in a barroom fight, he returned to Missouri.[12]

The State Guard's remaining infantry, totaling over 1,600 men, occupied camps west of Wilson Creek. These lay on the Edwards farm, on both sides of the Wire Road, between the fords of Wilson Creek and Skegg's Branch. The foot soldiers of Slack's Division—a regiment under Colonel John T. Hughes and a battalion under Major John C. C. Thornton—bivouacked between the road and Wilson Creek. Colonel John Q. Burbridge's regiment, the sole infantry in Clark's Division, sat at the base of Bloody Hill. Next to it camped the regiments of Colonels Edmund T. Wingo and John A. Foster, which comprised the infantry of McBride's Division. The infantrymen of Parsons's Division, commanded by Colonel Joseph M. Kelly, occupied the ground near the mouth of Skegg's Branch. Kelly had only 142 men in six companies, but these included his own disciplined and well-equipped Washington Blues and another prewar St. Louis unit, the Washington Grays. Meanwhile, Price established his headquarters in the yard adjoining Edwards's cabin. About two hundred yards south of the Wilson Creek ford, it was a logical, central location.[13]

The Western Army's horsemen, numbering over 3,400, bivouacked in separate areas. The majority camped in the corn and stubble fields belonging to Joseph Sharp. Greer's South Kansas–Texas Cavalry occupied the ground at the northern end of this fenced-in area, while the other commands spread south. Just below Greer's men were Churchill's First Arkansas Mounted Rifles and Colonel DeRosey Carroll's First Arkansas Cavalry. Two Missouri State Guard units, under Colonel Ben Brown and Lieutenant Colonel James P. Major, fixed the extreme southern end of the army's encampment. The remaining mounted Southerners, around 1,900

An 1880s photograph of Wilson Creek at the base of Bloody Hill, which is unseen to the left (The collection of Dr. Tom and Karen Sweeney, General Sweeny's Museum, Republic, Missouri)

strong, were a mixture of Confederates and Missouri State Guardsmen. McIntosh's Second Arkansas Mounted Rifles camped east of the creek, in a grassy meadow between the water and the ridge occupied by Woodruff's Pulaski Battery and McCulloch's headquarters. Their location was logical, as McIntosh also served as McCulloch's brigade adjutant. Whenever he was absent, Lieutenant Colonel Benjamin T. Embry commanded the unit.[14]

Directly across Wilson Creek to the west, Colonel Benjamin A. Rives led the 200-odd cavalrymen of Slack's Division into camp just south of the military crest of the main ridge of Bloody Hill. Beyond them, in the substantial ravine formed by the main portion of the hill and its northernmost ridge, lay the largest single mounted command in the Southern army, led by Colonel James Cawthorn. Over 1,200-men strong, Cawthorn's Brigade of Rains's Division was divided into units commanded by Colonels Robert L. Y. Peyton, James McCowan, and De Witt C. Hunter. The ravine that sheltered these men gradually opened eastward into a wide "V" of prairie grass and scrub that intersected with a line of trees along the creek's western bank. On the other side of the water sat Gibson's Mill, where Rains established his headquarters. A small number of Cawthorn's men rode across the creek and camped near the mill itself.[15]

By nightfall on August 6 the Western Army's tents and makeshift shelters stretched for approximately two miles on either side of Wilson Creek, from Rains's headquarters at Gibson's Mill to the cavalry camps at Sharp's farm. The encampment's widest point east to west measured about one-half mile across, from Weightman's camp at Caleb Manley's farm to Rives's camp on Bloody Hill. It presented an impressive sight to Private T. Jeff Jobe, of the First Arkansas Mounted Rifles, who noted in his diary on August 6, "The Southern Army being all at this camp, this whole country for a mile or two looks like one solid camp." Others took a less prosaic, more practical view. Remembering that evening, Watson of the Third Louisiana wrote: "we were rejoiced at the arrival of some waggons with provisions. . . . Rations of flour, fresh beef, salt, and a little coffee and sugar, were served out; and some cooking utensils were obtained, and cooking and eating gone into with great vigor, and we enjoyed a fair night's rest."[16]

Next to the never-ending problem of logistics, McCulloch's greatest challenge lay in obtaining accurate information on his foe. On August 7, while his army was still settling into camp, he turned to Captain A. V. Reiff, whose independent company of cavalry, raised in Fayetteville, Arkansas, had been acting as the general's bodyguard. Reiff recalled:

General McCulloch said: "I will send Frank Robinson with you. He is well acquainted about Springfield and knows just where the Federal pickets are. Go as close as you can without disturbing them and then turn him loose." When Robinson said we were within one-half mile of the pickets and two miles from Springfield, he took to the brush and I turned to the right and crossed Wilson's Creek below and south of our encampment about eight miles, passing through our entire camp to headquarters. . . . As ordered by General McCulloch, I made a map of all the forks and crossroads on this trip, which I gave the General with my report.[17]

McCulloch's attempts to ascertain Lyon's position and intentions led to further strain with Price and the Missouri State Guard. Four months after the battle, the Texan explained in his report to the War Department:

I asked of the Missourians, owing to their knowledge of the country, some reliable information of the strength and position of the enemy. This they repeatedly promised, but totally failed to furnish, though to urge them to it I then and at subsequent periods declared I would order the whole army back to Cassville rather than bring on an engagement with an unknown enemy. It had no effect, as we remained 4 days within 10 miles of Springfield, and never learned whether the streets were barricaded or if any kind of works of defense had been erected by the enemy.[18]

This was written, however, after McCulloch's complete break with Price following the battle, at a time when he tended to belittle the State Guard's contributions to the campaign. Probably as a reaction to this, Price's adjutant Thomas Snead wrote long after the war that "McCulloch would every day sling his Maynard rifle across his shoulder and reconnoitre towards Springfield, sometimes in force, and sometimes almost alone. But adventurous, daring, and skillful as he was, he could learn nothing positive as to either Lyon's strength, or as to the defenses of Springfield. He could not even ascertain whether Lyon had fortified his position at all, or not."[19]

Snead was obviously trying to shift the blame back to McCulloch. The Texan never mentioned scouting the area himself, but given his reputation Snead's tale may be at least partially true. Whatever their contradictions, these accounts suggest that McCulloch was increasingly paralyzed by the responsibilities of command. After all, he need not have relied on either the Missourians or his own observations for information. Though Greer's recently arrived Texas unit was worn out from its trip, McCulloch could have utilized the Confederate mounted riflemen commanded by McIntosh or Churchill for reconnaissance. It is significant that he did not. The commander of the Western Army had reason to be dismayed by his logistical problems, lack of information about the enemy, and questions concerning the reliability of Price and the Missouri State Guard. But his resources equaled or exceeded those possessed by many other Civil War commanders at crucial moments during campaigns. Ultimately, Old Ben seems to have lacked confidence in himself. He apparently shrank at the prospect of committing Southern fortunes in the Trans-Mississippi to the incalculable risks of battle. McCulloch's original mission was to protect the Indian Territory for the Confederacy. Although his correspondence demonstrates that he began the joint campaign with Price enthusiastically, the former Texas Ranger was now perhaps the most reluctant participant of all.

Unaware of the strain within the high command, the Southern soldiers undoubtedly enjoyed the respite from campaigning in the August heat. Henry Cheavens of Clark's Division wrote that during the march to Wilson Creek he had foraged beets, string beans, and corn out of a garden. Once settled in camp he obtained some meat and prepared "a savory mess of pottage with soup, which made our mess enjoy it wonderfully. It was my best meal so far. Here we stayed cleaning our guns [and] getting everything prepared for battle. . . . We sang, talked, went to the springs (fine ones), etc."[20]

Perhaps because the approaching battle marked the beginning of such a long struggle, some Southerners later remembered the days before it as idyllic. Peter D. Lane, a soldier in Cawthorn's Brigade, recalled:

Wilson Creek afforded us water, and the black oak trees and bushes around us with others furnished us with wood; while the surrounding hills provided grass for our horses, upon which we constantly kept them. After the night's darkness had enveloped the earth and rendered other things invisible, then the thousand fires from the adjacent hills & valley shot forth their light like so many stars in the canopy of the sky, while the hum of thousands of voices came wafted on the evening breeze and the hoarse challenge of the camp sentinel echoed through the hills and vales around.[21]

But William Watson, who wrote with such detail on so many subjects, focused in his memoirs on less pleasant aspects:

We had lately been slightly annoyed by little insects, with which the grass in the woods abounded. They were called red bugs, a small kind of spider of a red colour. They fastened on the skin, and caused a good deal of scratching; but they were nothing to the mosquitoes, the re- membrance of which made all other annoyances of that kind seem slight. In this camp these red bugs were very plentiful; and the men slept on the banks of the creek, which were steep, sloping down towards the water. The banks were covered with large round pebbles, and the itching from the bites of these insects caused the men in their sleep to roll or welter (after the fashion of a horse or mule) on their backs, and the round pebbles on which they lay, rolling, caused them to work downwards, until several of them in their unconscious state rolled into the creek, which was here about a foot deep, to the great amusement of such as had been awakened by the splashing and ex- clamations of their drenched comrades.[22]

Although the Western Army rested from August 7 through August 9, military activity did not entirely cease. Bugler A. B. Blocker of Greer's regiment remembered a large number of men from Missouri and Arkan- sas arriving at the camp at this time. "Old, gray-headed men came in, armed with their old squirrel rifles, a pouch of bullets, a string of patching already cut out, and a powder horn full of powder, to help the boys whip the yankees when the fight came off." Although Blocker may have exaggerated their numbers and character in his reminiscences, there is no doubt that some men whose names never appeared on any muster rolls joined the Southern forces just before the battle. At some point, for example, a small group of Cherokee rode in from the Indian Territory. Many sources attest to their presence, but their names and exact number remain a mystery.[23]

Responding to a report that a company of Missouri Home Guard militia was located a few miles northwest at Little York, two of Greer's companies went "on a raid." Although they captured only a handful of prisoners, the Texans secured an estimated 15,000 pounds of pig lead. As the Federals had previously garrisoned Little York in some force, their failure to protect the lead adequately or move it to Springfield is inexplicable. Greer's men soon located two wagons with teams, loaded their prize, and headed back for camp with their prisoners. One of the wagons was so overburdened that the wheels broke as soon as they started. Transferring the pigs to their horses, the column struck out again. But either because this proved unsatisfactory or because they feared that the Federals in Springfield might now be aroused and on their trail, they soon hid the lead "in a thicket of hazelnut bushes." When they finally reported with their prisoners to Greer's second-in-command, Lieutenant Colonel Walter P. Lane, he responded by exclaiming, "Turn them out of the lines and let them go. I would rather fight them than feed them." As the freed militiamen doubtless got a good look at the Southern camp, one wonders if they reported their experiences to Lyon.[24]

At least one scouting expedition by McCulloch's mounted units resulted in a direct encounter with Lyon's main forces. On the afternoon of August 9, some of Price's cavalry engaged Captain David S. Stanley's Company C of the First U.S. Cavalry and Captain Samuel N. Wood's mounted company of the Second Kansas on Grand Prairie, about five miles west of Springfield. The State Guardsmen were defeated. Two of them suffered wounds and six or eight were captured.[25]

But mostly the Western Army did nothing. Perhaps because their units were situated at the northeastern edge of camp, nearest Springfield, Captain William Woodruff and Louis Hébert grew apprehensive about the Southerners' position. On the morning of August 9, they walked over the ground and discussed how and where they might place Woodruff's Pulaski Light Battery and the Third Louisiana if the camp were attacked. No one else seems to have shared their concern.[26]

As the lower-ranking officers and common soldiers were not privy to the plans of the commanders, they were left to speculate about the army's inactivity. In his diary on August 7 surgeon John Wyatt of McBride's

Division lamented: "It is really sickening to think of only 10 miles between us and the enemy and the men all keen to advance and give him battle, and the Commanders holding back in this way. Too bad. Too bad. Ten generals, and all together would not make one good commander. I believe we are afraid to attack." On the following day his temper could no longer be contained, for he wrote: "Hell and Damnation what do they mean. Suspense is killing us all. If we do not move today something will be done. Hell to such damn one horse commanders. God's moments are flowing and I fear time has already passed for a successful movement."[27]

The doctor did not know it, but Price agreed with him entirely, and August 8 proved, in fact, to be a turning point. That day, two women described by Pearce as "loyal ladies" were allowed, inexplicably, to leave Springfield and enter the Southern lines. Taken to Price's headquarters, the women reported that Lyon "was greatly perplexed," "continually expected" the Southerners to attack, and kept his army "under arms at all times." Furthermore, he was preparing to evacuate Springfield.[28]

If this was the situation, the Southern army's failure to obtain precise details about possible defensive works in Springfield hardly mattered. Reporting the news to McCulloch, Price requested that the Texan order an immediate advance. But McCulloch still procrastinated, telling the Missouri general that he would carefully consider the matter and let him know what he had decided that evening. Sometime later McCulloch "rode once more to the front, rifle in hand, accompanied by McIntosh and a considerable force." On returning to camp late that evening, Mc-Culloch inexplicably failed to appraise Price of his decision.[29]

Up at daybreak on August 9 and out of patience with McCulloch's intransigence, Price ordered Colonel Snead to the army commander's headquarters to find out, if possible, what course of action had been selected. The colonel was soon engaged with McCulloch, but Price, unwilling to wait for Snead's report, interrupted the briefing. Overcome with impatience, the Missourian "insisted with great vehemence that McCulloch should keep the promise . . . made at Crane Creek, and lead the army out against Lyon." McCulloch responded by calling for a meeting of all general officers at Price's headquarters at noon. At this council McCulloch spoke yet again about his unwillingness to attack, but Price could no longer endure McCulloch's inaction. The Missourian declared emphatically that he would resume command of his troops and attack, regardless of the consequences. Faced with the vigorous support of Generals Clark, McBride, Parsons, Rains, and Slack, McCulloch yielded to the ultimatum by issuing orders for the army to move at 9:00 P.M. in four columns and converge on Lyon's forces at dawn, August 10.[30]

However much the soldiers had enjoyed their rest, McCulloch's orders electrified the camp. Pearce noted the quick response of his Arkansas State Troops. "The scene of preparations, immediately following the orders so long delayed and now so eagerly welcomed by the men, was picturesque and animating in the extreme," he wrote. As he explained:

The question of ammunition was one of the most important and serious, and as the Ordnance Department was imperfectly organized and poorly supplied, the men scattered about in groups to improvise, as best they could, ammunition for their inefficient arms. Here a group would be molding bullets—there, another crowd dividing percussion-caps, and, again, another group fitting new flints in their old muskets. They had little thought then of the inequalities between the discipline, arms, and accouterments of the regular United States troops they were soon to engage in battle, and their own homely movements and equipment.

The Missouri State Guard paid equal attention to its arms. Infantryman Samuel Mudd wrote: "One hundred rounds of ammunition were distributed. Our Company—B, 'Jackson Guards'—had muskets; Company A—'Callaway Guards'—had Mississippi rifles; the other companies had double-barrel shotguns, and all these muskets and shotguns were of the same bore. A few of the men in various companies had squirrel rifles." Mudd's remarks are revealing. Other Missouri State Guard units never received even half as much ammunition as Mudd's fellow soldiers of Burbridge's Regiment in Clark's Division; in fact, McCulloch later stated that the army averaged only twenty-five rounds per man. Clearly great disparity existed among the various units in terms of ammunition supply. Perhaps because of their diverse weaponry, neither McCulloch, Pearce, nor Price attempted to even things out, even within their own commands. This was a serious problem and yet circumstances soon grew worse, for that night rain began to fall.[31]

By all accounts the shower was actually slight, but conditions suggested that a major storm might be brewing. A soldier in Greer's regiment recalled that "the night was very dark and threatening." According to one Texan, "the elements were not idle; the lightning was flashing, and the thunder was crashing and roaring down the valley of Wilson Creek, and over the hills, on which our army stood, in readiness for the order to 'Fall in.'" Many men lacked leather cartridge boxes and carried their ammunition in their trouser pockets or cloth bags. McCulloch could not chance getting the powder wet, so after consulting with Price he postponed the advance. To save time the men were ordered to sleep on their arms, ready

to go at a moment's notice. Cavalry horses remained saddled, guns limbered, and mules stood in the traces of the baggage wagons.[32]

Although the decision to remain in camp made sense, it had unfore-
seen consequences. Either different orders reached individual units or
they interpreted their orders in different ways. Mudd recalled that his
company of the Missouri State Guard was told to be ready to march later
that night. S. B. Barron of the South Kansas–Texas Cavalry remembered
that the men of his company " 'stood to horse,' as it were, all night,"
awaiting orders that never came. Eventually the men became "weary with
standing and waiting, lay down at the feet of their horses, reins in hand,
and slept." Yet A. B. Blocker, also of Greer's regiment, testified: "After the
shower of rain had passed on, an order came for the men to keep their
horses saddled up, and get what sleep they could. The camp was soon
quiet, and the boys were soon stretched out on the damp ground, asleep."
The confusion that existed in the Third Louisiana was probably typical.
As soon as the rain started, Hébert ordered the company tents that had
just been struck to be repitched and the men's equipment placed in them
to stay dry. Although the weather soon cleared, no new orders arrived.
"Another postponement? The suspense was becoming unbearable," Watson wrote. "The men sought the driest place they could find to lie down.
The weather looked better, and it was supposed that we should march
forward at dawn of day."[33]

Most of the men probably thought in some fashion about the prospect
of battle. Lieutenant H. C. Dawson of the First Arkansas Mounted Rifles
was determined not to be somber, despite the seriousness of the situation.
Turning to his friend, Private John Toomer, he called out, "John, get your
fiddle and let's have a little dance and fun; it may be the last time we will
ever dance together." The impromptu stag dance doubtless went a long
way to relieve the tension.[34]

Uncertainties about the timing of the advance meant that many Southerners got little sleep, but the confusion resulted in consequences far
more serious than fatigue. Watson's comrade Tunnard explained, "The
picket guards had been recalled so as to be ready to march with their
respective commands, and in expectation of momentarily receiving
marching orders, the different regimental commanders objected to sending them out again."[35]

Having finally been moved to act, McCulloch became uncharacteristi-
cally careless. Although poised for instant action, the Western Army, that
strangest conglomeration of men, slept unguarded. Meanwhile, Lyon's
Army of the West was beset by its own problems.

Chapter 11

Red and Blistered from Head to Foot

Although the Army of the West returned safely to Springfield late in the afternoon of August 5, its fruitless trek
through the Ozark hills seems to have had a lasting
negative impact on the commander of the Federal forces. Nathaniel Lyon
had once been a man of restless energy. Possessing self-confidence bordering on megalomania, he never shared his decisions, never appeared to
doubt the wisdom of his own actions. Now he was a changed man.
Physically exhausted, his behavior suggests that he was nearing collapse
from the stress of command. Over the next few days he made decisions
only after consulting his top subordinates. But instead of making an
intelligent analysis and drawing his own conclusions after the benefit of
their advice, he tended to be swayed by the last person with whom he
talked. Caught in a dilemma of his own making, his "punitive crusade"
threatening to collapse in the face of manpower limitations and logistical
shortages, he had few good options. To make matters worse, more bad
news was soon at hand.[1]

On the evening of August 5 Captain John S. Cavender of the First
Missouri made his way through the streets of Springfield to a house on
College Street, three blocks west of the town square, where Lyon had his
headquarters. Owned by Congressman John S. Phelps, the dwelling was
apparently quite small, as Lyon maintained his personal quarters separately—at a private residence on Jefferson Street, several blocks east. Cavender joined a meeting that Lyon had called to determine the army's
course of action. In addition to his ranking officers a number of Springfield's most prominent pro-Union citizens were present, doubtless fearing
their fate should Lyon give up his position in southwestern Missouri.
Lyon shared their concern. Part of his mental anguish sprang from the

prospect of abandoning those who had remained loyal to the Federal government to the mercy of men he considered unscrupulous traitors.[2]

Cavender had just returned from an interview with John C. Frémont in St. Louis. His report was not encouraging, for his recent experience indicated that the top commander in Missouri had little interest in Lyon's operations. Indeed, Frémont had displayed "shocking indifference." Lyon had dispatched Cavender on July 15, probably hoping that the captain's verbal report would convey more effectively, than previous correspondence, the army's accomplishments and needs. Frémont granted Cavender a scant ten-minute interview, instructing him to return at 9:00 P.M. that evening. When Cavender arrived for his appointment, he found Frémont's headquarters closed for the night. Shortly afterward, he happened to encounter Frémont's adjutant, Captain John C. Kelton, who informed him that the general had ordered both reinforcements and a paymaster to Springfield, so the men might receive the back pay due to them. Cavender interpreted this as a dismissal, for instead of insisting on details or attempting to obtain a second interview with Frémont he left St. Louis the next morning.[3]

Lyon feared that Frémont had abandoned him to his fate, nor was he wrong, for although Frémont did send a request to the War Department for two months' pay for Lyon's command, neither the paymaster, the money, nor the promised reinforcements ever appeared in Springfield. Indeed, when shortly thereafter a second emissary from Lyon, Dr. Frank Porter, spoke with Frémont, the general informed him that Lyon had already been ordered to retreat and that if he chose to remain in Springfield he must accept the consequences. Because no record of such a direct order has been found, some historians have questioned Frémont's veracity. In any case, "as far as Frémont was concerned, Lyon was on his own."[4]

The additional news Cavender brought concerning the larger military picture in the West helps explain why the department commander's attention was focused elsewhere. On July 27 Brigadier General Gideon Pillow's 6,000-man Confederate "Army of Liberation" had landed at New Madrid, Missouri, where they were joined by Missouri State Guard troops under Brigadier General M. Jeff Thompson. Four days later Brigadier General William J. Hardee moved into the Missouri bootheel with Confederate forces from northeastern Arkansas. If Southerners were to capture Cairo, Illinois, located at the confluence of the Ohio and Mississippi Rivers, the war in the West would tip dramatically in favor of the Confederacy and Missouri's secession might follow. In response, on August 2 Frémont personally led reinforcements to the threatened point. In fact, compared to Cairo and the Mississippi and Ohio River valleys, southwestern Missouri held little strategic importance for the Union war effort.[5]

Everyone at Lyon's headquarters realized that the obvious course of action would be a retreat to the closest railhead, at Rolla, where support from St. Louis would be readily available. But when Lyon found his officers as loath as he was to end the campaign without a battle, he decided to stay in Springfield. Indeed, by the time the meeting ended Lyon was once again considering an attack on his enemies. His desire to punish Secessionists was probably the greatest factor in his decision. The general's adjutant, Major John Schofield, recalled in his memoirs: "Lyon's personal feeling was so strongly enlisted in the Union cause, its friends were so emphatically his personal friends and its enemies his personal enemies, that he could not take the cool, soldierly view of the situation which should control the actions of the commander of a national army."[6]

Although Lyon contemplated offensive operations, the army needed rest. A proper defense of Springfield was therefore his immediate concern. He had already taken the most important step toward security earlier that day. During the army's march back to Springfield on August 5, he established an outpost named Camp Hunter four miles down the Wire Road, southwest of Springfield, on the most likely axis of any enemy movement. Lyon gave command to Major Samuel Sturgis, the senior Regular Army officer present, entrusting him with almost a third of the army, between 2,000 and 2,500 men. The site was linked telegraphically with Lyon's headquarters, probably by using borrowed civilian equipment and telegraphers, as there is no record of Lyon having the necessary implements or personnel as part of his command. Lyon's use of the telegraph for such relatively short-distance communications indicates that he was among the first—perhaps even the first—to understand its potential at the operational level.[7]

The force at Camp Hunter included Du Bois's Battery, one of the best units in the Army of the West. It was commanded by Lieutenant John Van Deusen Du Bois, whose experiences to date reflected the improvised nature of the Union war effort in the West. A native of New York and an 1851 West Point graduate, he served with the Mounted Rifle Regiment on the frontier but was on leave in the East when the Civil War began. Ordered to Washington, he was assigned to Company I, First U.S. Artillery, then commanded by John Bankhead Magruder, a flamboyant brevet lieutenant colonel known throughout the Regular Army as "Prince John."

Major John McAllister Schofield, First Missouri Infantry (The collection of Dr. Tom and Karen Sweeney, General Sweeny's Museum, Republic, Missouri)

Within a short time, Magruder had resigned to join the Confederacy and Du Bois was sent to Carlisle Barracks, Pennsylvania. There he joined Captain Gordon Granger and Lieutenant George O. Sokalski, escorting recruits to Fort Leavenworth. They arrived on June 6, but instead of going farther west, as anticipated, Du Bois found himself commanding a hastily assembled, "rather incomplete" battery of field artillery. The horses that pulled the six guns, their limbers, and caissons were unshod and no forge was available, yet Du Bois had his unit operational in time to join Sturgis's column when it left to unite with Lyon less than three weeks later. During the march the young lieutenant was caustic and quick to judge his superiors. In both his private journal and letters to his family he poked fun at the volunteers and vented his deep prejudices against German Americans, but he was a highly competent officer, as events later demonstrated.[8]

Although Camp Hunter constituted a blocking force, Lyon also placed guards on all the roads serving Springfield, with outposts in positions ranging from the edge of town up to five miles out. By allowing anyone to enter the town but letting no one leave without a pass, he ensured that information could flow in without restriction while its outward flow would be blocked. This was an obvious precaution, but Lyon had no way of knowing just how effective it was. By denying the enemy crucial information, Lyon's security arrangements effectively paralyzed his opponents' operations from August 6 through August 9.[9]

The common soldiers remained unaware of either their commanders' decisions or their implications as they settled into their camps on the evening of August 5. Eugene Ware of the First Iowa lay down to sleep with satisfaction because he had just managed to steal a new Springfield rifle from one of the Regulars. At 2:00 A.M. on the morning of the sixth the men of his company, the Burlington Zouaves, were awakened and ordered to take up a position a mile south of town on the property of Congressman Phelps. Pickets were sent out an additional one and one-half miles. There were compensations, however, for the disturbance of the mens' sleep, as darkness gave the ragged Iowans opportunities to further their now well-developed talents for scavenging. A friend brought Ware a badly needed pair of heavy pants. "I rather imagined some secesh family had skipped out and left their stuff in charge of their slaves, but I did not find out," he recalled. The well water was excellent at the Phelps farm and a wagonload of fresh bread arrived in the morning.[10]

Ware had a full stomach because supplies reached Springfield from Rolla on the morning of August 6, allowing the men to go back on full rations for the first time in two weeks. Morale rose considerably throughout the army, for in addition to bread the wagon train carried a quantity of hats, badly needed shoes, and some clothing.[11]

The improved supply situation also increased Lyon's confidence and strengthened his determination to take the offensive. Sometime during the day civilian spies, whose names and number are unknown, brought Lyon word that some of Ben McCulloch's Confederates had reached the point where the Wire Road crossed Wilson Creek. Lyon decided to make a surprise attack on their camp that night. It is unclear how many of the enemy Lyon thought were at Wilson Creek. Indeed, few details of his plan have survived and accounts of what took place that day are sketchy and confused. Even the number of troops delegated for this night assault is uncertain, but it may have involved up to half of the Federal army. The fact that Lyon did not contemplate utilizing his entire force indicates that he believed Price's Missouri State Guard was still west of Springfield and had not made a junction with McCulloch. It also suggests that he thought only a portion of McCulloch's force was at the creek.[12]

The troops at Camp Hunter received word of Lyon's intentions via telegraph, and their order of march was determined at a conference in Du Bois's tent. The time of departure was set at 6:00 P.M. A problem developed, however, when Lyon obtained a report from Captain Job B. Stockton, commanding the Leavenworth Fencibles of the First Kansas Infantry. Stockton's company and two companies of mounted Home Guards had skirmished with some of Sterling Price's cavalry west of town on Grand Prairie. Lyon responded by dispatching two companies to reinforce Stockton. These men saw no action, as the Southerners had already withdrawn after their initial brief exchange of fire, but Lyon could not be certain that no other threat would come from Grand Prairie. There were no significant fortifications in Springfield, only barricades across the main streets. The force he was planning to leave there while he advanced against McCulloch would be terribly vulnerable should Price suddenly appear west of the town. Unable to decide whether to pursue the night attack or abandon it in favor of a concentration in Springfield, Lyon delayed the projected movement until 10:00 P.M., apparently hoping to obtain more information from his scouts. Though the change in timing meant a late start, he would still be able to assemble his attack column at Camp Hunter by midnight and reach Wilson Creek before dawn. At Camp Hunter, Sturgis completed his preparations and sent Captain Frederick Steele's battalion of Regulars and Du Bois's Battery a short distance down the Wire Road just as darkness fell. Their assignment was to locate and drive in the enemy's pickets once the attack began.[13]

The prospect of action was probably very pleasant for Eugene A. Carr, whom Lyon released from arrest and returned to duty because in the current crisis the army needed "the services of every officer of the command." Carr, a captain in the First U.S. Cavalry, was an 1850 West Point graduate with eleven years of service and an excellent record. The specifics of his case are unknown. Lyon obviously believed that he could ill afford to lose Carr's expertise, yet he made no compromise in his standards of strict discipline. The order that returned Carr to his company also stated that "the subject matter of the charge against Capt. *Carr* will be investigated at a future time."[14]

No further details of the incident are known, but Carr's troubles are not the only mystery of August 6. In fact, the events of that night have never been adequately explained. Distracted either by the details of preparation or the need to evaluate information arriving from "a stream of visitors, messengers, and communications," Lyon did not leave Springfield until midnight. He was accompanied by Major Peter J. Osterhaus's small Second Missouri battalion, elements of the Second Kansas, and eight companies of the First Kansas. When they marched into Camp Hunter at 2:00 A.M. on the morning of August 7, two hours late, a dawn attack remained possible but only if the entire force left immediately. Yet Lyon not only gave no orders, he completely lost track of the time. Though he may have hoped to hear from spies sent to scout the Confederate camp, fatigue bordering on torpor seems to have been part of the problem. When Lyon finally glanced at his watch it was 3:00 A.M. The Federals no longer had time to march the remaining six miles to Wilson Creek and deploy before dawn. Uncertain of what to do, Lyon called a council of his principal officers. On their recommendation, he abandoned Camp Hunter and started the whole force back to Springfield.[15]

Although the Federals clearly missed an opportunity, its significance is difficult to evaluate. When on August 6 Lyon had first obtained word of the enemy's presence at Wilson Creek, the only Southerners there were 800-odd men of Colonel Elkanah Greer's regiment, plus Captain Rieff's company. The rest of the Southern army was still en route. About 9,000 soldiers were only two miles away at Moody's Springs, with orders to move up to Wilson Creek on the sixth. By the end of that day, nearly all of the Southern army had established camp along the stream. One can only speculate as to the result had Lyon attacked on the night of August 6 or during the early hours of August 7. The whole Southern force might have panicked in the dark, replicating "Rains's Scare" on a giant scale. On the other hand, this time Lyon's men would have faced a united Southern command, and the Federals could have been the ones routed.[16]

Regardless of what the canceled attack might have achieved, during the return to Springfield Adjutant Schofield received a shocking insight into his commander's confused mental state. Lyon spoke of receiving "a premonition that a night attack would prove disastrous" and confessed that he had proceeded only because surprise seemed to offer their sole chance for success. Another night attack, he thought, might still be the best plan. The major's reaction can be imagined, as he had witnessed astonishing changes in Lyon during the months since their initial association in St. Louis. Then Lyon had been convinced that he was God's instrument for the punishment of traitors, but he performed his duties with extreme professionalism. Now prey to imagined portents, the once fiercely independent Connecticut Yankee had virtually abandoned command of the army. All important decisions were presently made in council, with Lyon acting merely as an executive officer and a weak one at that. Although Schofield made only muted criticism of Lyon in the memoirs he wrote long after the war, there is contemporary evidence that he was acutely aware of Lyon's shortcomings. A letter he received on August 6 from James Totten suggests that the two men had already noted and discussed the obvious weaknesses of Lyon's tactical dispositions. From Camp Hunter the artillery captain had written Schofield that the position was "certainly not very well adapted for defence against our enemy and he may push his forces in between this and town and occupy the strong position of which you spoke yesterday. We are too far from town to aid in its defence if the enemy attacks in any other direction than the line on which this force now is."[17]

Schofield may also have been aware of growing discontent in the Union ranks. The First Iowa provides examples. Although the regiment was not slated to be part of the attack force, little happened during August 6 to calm the mens' growing anxiety. In the Governor's Grays, Horace Poole noted that "from reports we are in a very tight place. The rebel force reported to be in large numbers and within a few miles of town. A hard fight and perhaps a retreat is expected." Others worried as well. "We no [*sic*] not at what moment we may be ordered to leave," wrote William Branson of the Muscatine Volunteers. "An order has been issued by General Lyon to have a roll call every two hours." The regiment shifted its position twice during the day, for reasons unclear to the men, and the soldiers remained in line of battle the whole time. Forbidden to break ranks but allowed to lie down, they suffered for hour after hour under the blazing sun. As a result, the regiment very nearly mutinied.[18]

Although the Iowans had initially held Lyon in great esteem, they now remained with the Army of the West primarily to maintain their corporate honor, for they were in the midst of a dispute over the terms of their enlistment. Dating their ninety days of service from their initial enrollment in the Iowa state militia, they believed that their term had already expired. Yet they had seen how the departure of other volunteers compromised the safety of the army, and, as action seemed imminent, the regiment voted to remain in Springfield. "We felt we should not spoil a fight if there was a show of one; we did not want to take the responsibility of a retreat and did not want to march off to the sound of booming cannon in our rear," Eugene Ware explained. They found, however, that Lyon (like other Union commanders) calculated all volunteers' enlistments from the date of their entry into Federal service, which meant that the Iowans had another week to go before they were free. They also credited a false rumor that Lyon had sworn to keep them under arms indefinitely. "Hence we did not like Lyon, and wanted to have the thing ended and over with," Ware wrote. Yet in this crisis corporate honor prevailed, as they "did not dare to go home and have any question pending as to our services, or the military propriety of our acts."[19]

Morale problems in the Army of the West should not be exaggerated, however. For despite their poor physical condition and the odds facing them, most Union soldiers appear to have been both eager for battle and assured of success. When Lieutenant Levant L. Jones of the Scott's

Guards, First Kansas, wrote to his wife Hattie in Olathe, he predicted a "great battle" on the seventh "unless the enemy backs out." Even though he estimated that the Confederates had 15,000 soldiers and the Federals only 8,000, they were "all confident of victory." Possibly to quell any fears this may have generated in Hattie, the young lieutenant added: "But ours are drilled, disciplined, and well armed, while the Rebels are, in the main, just the reverse of this. We are in a good position for defense while they must attack, and will be terribly torn up by our batteries."[20]

Jones then turned to more personal matters. If he was to die, he wanted her to have his "last words and thoughts":

> My life now belongs to my country . . . my love belongs to you, and Dearest you have it all, all the legacy, unfortunately, I can leave to you in case I should fall. I do not anticipate any fatal result, still it may come. I shall not sleep to night being just ordered to special guard duty. I shall look at the clear heavens and the bright stars which spangle the firmament as with ornaments of gold and silver, and shall think how beneficently all this glory is wrapped over your own far off home, where you lie in sweet sleep, mayhaps dreaming of your absent husband.[21]

With soldiers such as Jones to rely on, the Union cause in Missouri did not look nearly so dark. But Jones and his comrades spent August 7 in pointless activities, their combat readiness further depleted by Lyon's inability to determine the enemy's intentions or formulate a plan of his own to counter them. For if the patrols and scouts sent out by McCulloch failed to garner the information about the Federals he desired, they had the effect of keeping Lyon in the dark about the Southerners. Schofield recalled that "our troops were kept upon their arms during the day." Continual reports from area residents and local Home Guards warned that the enemy was advancing. Around noon members of a scouting party thought they saw a large column of infantry and artillery approaching via the Little York Road, west of Springfield. In response Lyon ordered a detachment of Regulars, Kansans, and two guns from Backof's Missouri Light Artillery to meet the enemy. As it turned out, the size of the Southern force "proved in the main false" and presented no threat to the Federals. The Southerners soon fled and the Union column returned to camp, having made a forced march of about nine miles in the sweltering midday heat. There was some skirmishing between mounted patrols, but no significant combat occurred. Instead, the constant state of alert and the heat of an unforgiving August sun continued to take their toll on the men.[22]

As one of the Iowans kept "in readiness to move at ten minutes warning," William Branson was in a position to witness the growing concern of Springfield's civilian population. He recorded in his diary that everything was "in an uproar." The townsfolk were "leaving their homes & moving into or near the army for protection." The civilians had reason for concern, for when Lyon called a meeting of his officers that evening the evacuation of Springfield and abandonment of southwestern Missouri was the primary topic of discussion. Lyon favored standing his ground, but most of his officers argued for retreat, either to Rolla or perhaps Fort Scott on the Kansas border. Lyon would almost certainly have given in to the majority opinion, as he had in previous meetings, were it not for Captain Thomas Sweeny. Angered by the talk of retreat, the Irishman— his "naturally florid face flushed to livid red, and waving his one arm with excitement"—began a fierce tirade, arguing against withdrawal before fighting the enemy. Retreat without battle would not only raise the morale of the enemy, it would crush the spirit of the local Union populace and leave it prey to terror, harassment, and persecution. Sweeny favored attacking the Confederates as soon as an opportunity presented itself. "Let us eat the last bit of mule flesh and fire the last cartridge before we think of retreat!" he concluded. The captain's impassioned oration swayed so many officers that at midnight the meeting ended in consensus. They would wait to see how the situation unfolded and fall back only if forced to do so by either the nearby Confederates or the still unlocated Missouri State Guard. The conference seemed to instill new confidence in Lyon, for the next day, August 8, when Major Alexis Mudd asked when the army would retreat, the general responded without hesitation, "Not until we are whipped out."[23]

For the men of First Iowa's Governor's Grays, Thursday, August 8, began with reveille at 3:30 A.M. At 5:00 A.M. they took over picket duty from the Muscatine Volunteers and Burlington Zouaves, who had spent a quiet night. Mundane routines such as this were interrupted when, about 8:00 A.M., a courier arrived at Lyon's headquarters with a message from Captain Carr. From his outpost on Grand Prairie west of town, Carr reported that an enemy force 20,000 strong was within two miles of the Union position and advancing. Immediately, the entire army was placed under arms. As a contingency, baggage wagons were loaded and moved to a central location in town. To keep them out of enemy hands, the funds of the Springfield branch of the State Bank of Missouri were also placed in a wagon. Meanwhile, groups of anxious civilians gathered nearby, preparing to evacuate to Rolla if Lyon failed to hold Springfield. Yet the day proved to be anticlimactic for the Federals. Lyon sent Sturgis with 1,500 men to reinforce Carr and orders to bring on a general engagement. But like so many other reports of the enemy's activity, this one also proved false. Skirmishing continued between mounted scouts, but the Army of the West spent another day under arms in the broiling sun, waiting for a foe that never appeared. Sturgis's column returned to town at dark.[24]

At the inevitable officers' meeting that evening Lyon outlined their present situation. Confronted by McCulloch and still uncertain of Price's location, they also faced the danger of being cut off from St. Louis by the Confederates, under Hardee, said to be advancing from southeastern Missouri. As supplies were running short and no prospect of reinforcement existed, retreat seemed the only alternative. Yet how could it be done safely? "Shall we," Lyon reportedly asked, "endeavor to retreat without giving the enemy battle beforehand and run the risk of having to fight every inch along our line of retreat? Or shall we attack him in his position and endeavor to hurt him so that he cannot follow?" Lyon favored the latter option. He proposed to leave only a small guard in Springfield, march down the Wire Road, throw the whole army against the enemy, "and endeavor to rout him before he recovers from his surprise." Colonel Franz Sigel suggested a significant modification. He recommended that the army be divided into two columns, commanded by himself and Lyon, respectively, that would strike the enemy simultaneously from different directions.[25]

Lyon's desire to attack that very night was apparently the product of his natural aggressiveness and his desire to bring traitors to account. Indeed, he "would not retire without punishing the Secessionists, and that conviction was so all-consuming that he cast to the wind all sound military judgement." But the Federal commander had not completely lost touch with the practical details of military operations. As all of the officers were opposed to Sigel's plan, Lyon rejected it. He also paid attention to objections raised by the colonels of the regiments that had marched to Grand Prairie and back in response to Carr's false alarm. Their men had trudged some sixteen miles but had yet to be fed. Lyon therefore sensibly agreed to postpone the attack for twenty-four hours. The army would march on the night of August 9.[26]

Early on the morning of Friday, August 9, a message arrived from Frémont. Dated August 6, it is the last correspondence Lyon received from his commanding officer prior to the Battle of Wilson's Creek. Regrettably, the original has been lost. This may have been the communication Frémont mentioned to Dr. Porter, but Schofield, who handled Lyon's correspondence, asserted that Lyon never received a direct order to retreat. According to Schofield, Frémont simply wrote that "if Lyon was not strong enough to maintain his position as far in advance as

Springfield, he should fall back toward Rolla until reinforcements should meet him."[27] Although Frémont did not specifically order Springfield to be abandoned, it was clear that any action that might occur there would be Lyon's responsibility and his alone.

Never moderate in his reactions, Lyon threw the communication onto his headquarters table, clapped his hands together, and exclaimed, "God damn General Frémont! He is a worse enemy to me and the Union cause than Price and McCulloch and the whole damned tribe of rebels in this part of the State!"[28] He then directed Schofield to draft a response, which included an assessment of his situation:

> I find my position extremely embarrassing, and am at present unable to determine whether I shall be able to maintain my ground or be forced to retire. I can resist any attack from the front, but if the enemy move to surround me I must retire. I shall hold my ground as long as possible and not though I fear I may without knowing how far endanger the safety of my entire force with its valuable material, being induced by the important considerations involved to hold on to take this step. The enemy yesterday made a strong force about 5 miles distant and has doubtless a full purpose of making an attack upon me.[29]

Lyon's missive was soon on its way to St. Louis by courier. Interestingly, it contained no hint that the Army of the West was planning to attack the enemy that night. Perhaps Lyon had once again lost his will. If so, Sigel restored it when he visited headquarters at 9:00 A.M. During a long private conversation Sigel proposed a substantial modification of the attack plan, arguing again for a two-column attack that would give a greater role to the volunteer regiments of German Americans from St. Louis who regarded him as their patron. Lyon acquiesced but told no one of the changes at that time.[30]

Sometime after his talk with Sigel, Lyon received a message from Captain David S. Stanley, commanding Company C, First U.S. Cavalry, reporting yet another skirmish on Grand Prairie. This one had significant consequences. Captain Samuel N. Wood's Kansas Rangers killed two Southerners and captured six, who identified themselves as members of a foraging party from the Missouri State Guard. It is likely that they also told their captors that the State Guard was now united with McCulloch's Confederates and Arkansas State Troops at Wilson Creek. For instead of sending reinforcements toward Grand Prairie, as he had in response to previous alarms, Lyon ordered a reconnaissance south along the Wire Road. The task fell to Captain G. Harry Stone's Company C of the First Missouri Infantry and fifteen troopers from Company C of the Second U.S.

Dragoons. The patrol moved down the road about four miles, probably in the vicinity of the advance guard's abandoned Camp Hunter. Here the infantry halted, while Stone and the dragoons continued for another mile. As they approached a house, they witnessed several of the enemy mount their horses and race away. From the home owner they learned that at least two of the soldiers were Texans. The patrol then returned to Springfield, and Captain Stone reported his findings to army headquarters.[31]

As a result of the Grand Prairie skirmish, Stone's reconnaissance, and (according to one source) spies planted in the Southern forces, Lyon became convinced that his enemies were united ten miles southwest of Springfield. In one way this was a relief, as he had feared that the State Guard might have moved around his right flank, cutting him off from Rolla while the Confederates attacked from the south. On the other hand, if the attack slated to begin that evening took place as scheduled, it would pit the 5,000-odd men of the Army of the West against an enemy thought to be 20,000 strong. To assess the new situation and to inform his command of the changes he had made in his plans to accommodate Sigel, Lyon called an officers' meeting for 4:00 P.M.[32]

Meanwhile, the enlisted men of the Army of the West passed the day of August 9 with minimal knowledge of the building crisis. Soldiers needing shoes had them issued from the supply train that had arrived several days earlier. A light rain fell in the morning, "but not enough to lay the dust." Then, that afternoon, a heavy thunderstorm passed through, providing at least temporary relief from the sun. As the army's tentage had been packed away in supply wagons, the majority of the men were at the mercy of the elements.[33]

Levant Jones passed the time by writing once again to his wife Hattie. The lieutenant made no reference to the planned attack; subalterns of the First Kansas were probably as curious as those in the ranks about the army's future. Jones was clearly impatient, informing Hattie that if the campaign was not over by October he would resign his commission "and come back to you, to *home* and to business." He missed his wife terribly, confessing, "I sometimes lie awake thinking of you and . . . wish I was with you instead of out here soldiering and lying all on the *bare ground*." But after two months of active campaigning Jones had not only adjusted to soldier life, he sounded like a veteran, boasting: "I have not slept in a tent for eleven nights, as we have our wagons loaded and always ready to start at once. I can now spread down my India Rubber Blanket under a tree and spreading my blanket over me sleep as sound as ever I did." Though Jones wrote that his health was excellent, he did "suffer greatly from the heat," confiding that "I am red and blistered from head to foot."[34]

As he closed, Jones's thoughts turned to duty, honor, family, God, and country:

> It may be lonesome for you Darling! but you must reflect how much better off you are than hundreds and thousands of others of the soldiers wives, whose husbands are now fighting for the grand cause of our Constitution and Country. Be a true woman Darling, and in the Hereafter I trust we may live . . . together, honorable to ourselves and more dutiful to God than we have heretofore done.[35]

Like thousands of other Americans, North and South, Jones was coming of age, beginning to perceive, if dimly, the tremendous sacrifices that his generation would be called upon to make before peace returned to the troubled land.

When Lyon opened his council of war late that afternoon, he must have shared with his subordinates the news that McCulloch and Price were definitely united. This apparently troubled no one, as there were no recommendations that the attack be called off. Lyon then gave the floor to Sigel, allowing him to repeat the proposal he had made privately that morning. The plan as it stood was to attack straight down the Wire Road and drive the enemy away from it, thus cutting its line of supply and communication. Sigel wanted instead to divide the army. He himself would lead a column of infantry, cavalry, and artillery—some 1,200 men— on a circuitous march to a position overlooking the rear of the Southerners' camp. Lyon and the remainder of the men would move by road to the west, then turn south and march across the prairie. Instead of striking the enemy along the Wire Road, where contact might be expected, Lyon's column would attack from due north. Objections were instantly voiced by the other officers at the meeting. Sigel's proposal to attack from the open prairie rather than the road had great merit, as it would increase the element of surprise which was key to Lyon's original plan. But a division of the Army of the West in the face of superior enemy forces violated accepted military axioms, whether taught at West Point or the Karlsruhe Academy. Sigel's column would be too small to be effective. The distance traveled would necessitate a long march, so the men would be fatigued on arrival. Because communication could not be maintained between the two columns, initiating simultaneous attack would be nearly impossible.[36]

Lyon overrode all objections, accepted Sigel's plan, and set the time of march for 6:00 P.M. that evening. Given his previous lassitude and reliance on consensus, such behavior seems odd and historians have debated Lyon's reasons for accepting Sigel's plan. Lieutenant Du Bois's wartime journal offers the only known clue. He wrote: "Lyon said, 'Frémont won't sustain me. Sigel has a great reputation & if I fail against his advise it will give Sigel command & ruin me. Then again, unless he can have his own way, I fear he will not carry out my plans.' The result of all this was, Sigel had his way."[37] Perhaps, pressured by Sigel's ambitions, Lyon felt that he had no choice, or perhaps he was continuing to abdicate responsibility, placing the fate of the army in another's hands.

Du Bois does not state when, where, or to whom Lyon made his rueful remarks. The lieutenant was highly prejudiced against German Americans such as Sigel, and he recorded Lyon's alleged words not on August 9 but on August 30, more than two weeks after the battle when great controversy surrounded Sigel's performance. As there is no other evidence of Sigel pressuring Lyon, or even a hint of rivalry between them, one is tempted to dismiss Du Bois's comments. After all, Lyon had launched his campaign without waiting for authorization from Washington. He had destroyed the legal government of a state that had not left the Union and was currently battling that state's legal militia, the Missouri State Guard. If Sigel tried to force his will on Lyon, as Du Bois's journal entry indicates, would not Lyon have removed Sigel from command rather than compromise his self-ordained crusade?

Schofield recalled no friction between Lyon and Sigel, writing in his memoirs that Lyon had "great confidence in Sigel's superior military ability and experience" and "seemed to have no hesitation" in accepting his ideas.[38] Why not? The original plan was designed to stun the enemy and allow the Federals to escape safely to Rolla. Sigel's plan was more ambitious. With it the enemy might actually be defeated, not merely paralyzed. By accepting a scheme that would induce maximum pain and suffering on the enemy, Lyon was returning to the real focus of his "punitive crusade."

After the meeting was adjourned, Lyon returned to his personal quarters on North Jefferson Street. He soon had two visitors, Captain Sweeny and Florence M. Cornyn, surgeon of the First Missouri Infantry. Sweeny had not been present at the officers' meeting. He and the doctor tried to persuade Lyon to revert to the original plan. Lyon considered their arguments but refused to change his mind. He then retired to catch a few moments' rest. Outside, in the dusty streets of Springfield and the sun-baked camps surrounding it, the Army of the West prepared for the most important march in its brief, tumultuous history.[39]

Chapter 12 . . . .

I Will Gladly Give Up My Life for Victory

The enlisted men in the Union army were not privy to the details of the plans discussed by their superiors, but word that a decision had been made to attack the Southerners swept through the ranks on August 9. In his diary William Branson wrote: "Great stir in camp this evening. General Lyon has issued an order that this night shall decide the fate of southern missouri. . . . We are going to march on them to night [and] are now making every preparation for moving." Branson's hope that a climax to their efforts might be near is understandable, for much had happened since the army's initial skirmish with the Missouri State Guard at Boonville in June. The hardships had been severe. Soldiers unable to withstand the rigors of campaigning "had broken down and were things of the past." When rations fell short and uniforms wore out, the soldiers had learned to forage for both food and clothing. In the Second Kansas, for example, a soldier in the Phoenix Guards recorded that while they still had their dark blue government-issued blouses, many men were barefoot. As replacements for the shirts and trousers brought from home they now had "a miscellaneous assortment of other clothing such as the country afforded," together with every type of headgear imaginable. Nor were officers exempt from privations. The soldier noted that Lieutenant John K. Rankin was "in rags like the rest."[1]

But with tribulation had come experience, and if the men were leaner they were also tougher. By early war standards, they were seasoned campaigners, having endured weeks of long, hot marches. Because the army's quartermaster and commissary departments had been unprepared to meet the demands placed on them for this, the war's first real campaign, the men had often gone hungry and they had made their camps with inadequate tentage and equipment. Yet they had acquired invaluable combat experience, having "seen the elephant," at Boonville, Carthage, Forsyth, Dug Springs, or during the recent, almost daily skirmishing on Grand Prairie west of Springfield. Although these were brief, small-scale actions, they had allowed most of the units in Lyon's army to hear the roar of artillery and the crash of muskets. These factors offered significant compensation for the enemy's reported superiority in numbers.

Lyon knew that his men were about to face their greatest challenge yet, and as the army prepared for its night march, he moved among those close by with words of advice. His actions left a particularly strong impression on Eugene Ware. When the First Iowa responded to the bugle call to fall in, they formed an irregular line because there were no tents to serve as a guide. After standing in formation for "some minutes," they observed Lyon, mounted on his dapple gray horse, riding toward the regiment. As the companies were widely spaced, he paused for about a minute before each one. Reaching the Burlington Zouaves, he said: "Men, we are going to have a fight. We will march out in a short time. Don't shoot until you get orders. Fire low—don't aim higher than their knees; wait until they get close; don't get scared; it's no part of a soldier's duty to get scared." Lyon doubtless meant his words to be encouraging, but Ware thought them "tactless and chilling," and the only feeling they seemed to convey was one of exhaustion on the general's part. Fellow private William P. Eustis simply asked, "How is a man to help being skeered when he is skeered?" Ware recalled this episode many years following the close of the war, but an Iowa soldier writing only a week after the battle also characterized Lyon as fatigued. When the general reached the Muscatine Grays, he appealed directly to their honor. He reminded them that as the army's only representatives from Iowa, the people not only in their home state but also across the nation would judge them by their conduct in the coming battle. Victory would win the Iowans the thanks of the whole country, whereas defeat would mean surrendering the entire Ozarks region to the enemy. The general ended by telling the men that if they stood firm the enemy would not stand against them. Yet even as Lyon spoke, listeners could "detect traces of deep anxiety in his countenance and voice. The latter more subdued and milder than usual." Overall, the Iowans might have been more inspired by the words reportedly spoken by Captain Thomas Sweeny to some of the cavalry: "Stay together, boys, and we'll saber hell out of them."[2]

After Lyon departed the Iowans drew ammunition, filling not only their cartridge boxes, but trouser and shirt pockets as well. Two days' rations of beef and pork were also distributed. While they were cooking the meat, a wagon appeared and its driver tossed large turtle-shelled loaves of bread onto the ground, where they "bounced around in the dirt and bushes." Because Ware had discarded his worn-out haversack, he was forced to employ inventive methods for carrying his rations. First, he took a loaf of bread and "plugged it like a watermelon and ate my supper out of the inside." After frying his beef and pork, he stuffed the meat into the loaf and "poured in all the fat and gravy." Finally, he recalled, "I took off my gun-sling and ran it through the hard lip of the loaf, hung them over my shoulder, filled my canteen, and was ready for the march."[3]

Instructed to return to Deitzler's Fourth Brigade, the Iowans marched into Springfield around 6:00 P.M. The disciplined regiments lining the streets presented a marked contrast to the civilian population. "The town was in utter confusion," according to one soldier. "Merchandise and household goods were being loaded into wagons to be ready for the worst. The storekeepers and citizens distributed food to the soldiers with lavish hospitality, and wished them good luck in tones which betrayed forebodings of disaster."[4]

Lyon's feelings as the army assembled are unknown, but he may have been comforted by the knowledge that every possible preparation had been made for the coming contest. He led the main attack force, which had been organized into two brigades, in person. Major Samuel Sturgis's First Brigade, which spearheaded the march, was the smallest in the army, with fewer than seven hundred officers and men. It was composed of Sturgis's own infantry battalion of Regulars, now led by Captain Joseph B. Plummer; Major Peter J. Osterhaus's battalion from the Second Missouri Infantry; Captain James Totten's Company F, Second U.S. Artillery; Captain Samuel N. Wood's Kansas Rangers (the mounted company of the Second Kansas Infantry); and Lieutenant Charles W. Canfield's Company D, First U.S. Cavalry.[5]

The Regulars under Plummer headed the column. These three hundred men were from Companies B, C, and D of the First U.S. Infantry, plus a "company of rifle recruits." Plummer commanded Company C, and, as senior captain, control of the battalion fell to him as well. Although an experienced officer, the forty-four-year-old Massachusetts native had seen no combat prior to the Civil War. A 1841 graduate of West Point, in the same class as Lyon and Totten, he was initially assigned to the First U.S. Infantry. After years of garrison duty he probably welcomed the Mexican War, yet he was forced to spend the first year of that conflict on sick leave. By the time he reached the field much of the action was over. As an officer with the forces garrisoning Vera Cruz and later Mexico City, he performed necessary service, but it was hardly exciting. Plummer became his regiment's quartermaster when the war ended and spent most of the years before 1861 at various posts in Texas, reaching the rank of captain in 1852.[6]

Captain Charles Champion Gilbert, who led Company B, ranked twenty-ninth in the West Point class of 1846, which in addition to Sturgis had included A. P. Hill, Thomas J. Jackson, George B. McClellan, and George E. Pickett. Assigned to the Third U.S. Infantry, the thirty-nine-year-old native of Zanesville, Ohio, had fought at Vera Cruz during the Mexican War and had served as part of the occupation garrison after it surrendered. Promoted to first lieutenant following the war, he taught geography, history, and ethics at the Military Academy. In December 1855, he was promoted to captain and sent west. The mundane nature of the army's constabulary duty was demonstrated by the fact that during six years on the Comanche frontier in Texas, he participated in only one fight.[7]

Captain Daniel Huston was in charge of Company D. Thirty-fifth in the West Point class of 1848, he began his military career in the Eighth U.S. Infantry but soon transferred to the First Regiment. Like Plummer and Gilbert, he spent most of his early career at various Texas posts. He was promoted to captain in 1856 and spent three years back east on recruiting duty. In 1859, however, he was reassigned to garrison duty in the West.[8]

Lieutenant Henry Clay Wood of Company D, First U.S. Infantry, commanded the company of recruits. Born in Winthrop, Maine, he graduated from Bowdoin College in 1854 (two years after Joshua Lawrence Chamberlain, who was destined to win fame at Gettysburg). During the next two years Wood served as the clerk in the office of the Maine secretary of state and studied law. Though admitted to the bar in 1856, he chose a military career instead and was commissioned a second lieutenant in the First Infantry that year.[9]

In all, the officers of Plummer's battalion combined sixty-five years of military service. Although only a minor portion of their service embraced actual warfare, they were veterans in the areas of discipline, training, organization, and other aspects related to the exercise of command. While forming but a small part of the Army of the West, they stood as perhaps the foremost example of the high degree of professionalism that lent disproportionate strength to Lyon's force.

Thirty-eight-year-old Major Peter J. Osterhaus marched behind Plummer. His 150-man battalion consisted of Rifle Companies A and B of the Second Missouri Infantry. The bulk of the regiment had been left to garrison Jefferson City during the opening stages of the campaign. Orig-

Major Peter J. Osterhaus, Second Missouri Infantry. This photograph was taken after his promotion to major general. (The collection of Dr. Tom and Karen Sweeney, General Sweeny's Museum, Republic, Missouri)

inally from Coblenz in Prussia, Osterhaus was a graduate of a Berlin military school and a veteran of the 1848 revolution. After emigrating to the United States he settled initially in Illinois but later moved to St. Louis, probably attracted by its large German population.[10]

Captain James Totten's Company F, Second U.S. Artillery, followed next in line. Assisting the captain with his six-gun battery was Lieutenant George O. Sokalski. In 1857 the Polish American entered West Point, one month short of his seventeenth birthday. Probably ranked among the "Immortals" as a plebe, Sokalski stood fiftieth in a class of fifty-nine cadets at the end of the first year. But he persevered and became the first Polish American to graduate from the U.S. Military Academy. Sokalski ranked fortieth out of forty-five in the class of 1861. Commissioned a second lieutenant in the Second Dragoons in May, the twenty-two-year-old Sokalski spent most of that month drilling volunteers in Washington. Ordered to join his regiment, he accompanied Captain Gordon Granger, Lieutenant John Du Bois, and other officers in escorting a group of recruits to Fort Leavenworth. Like Granger and Du Bois, he was assigned to Sturgis's column. After it joined forces with Lyon, he went to Totten's Battery.[11]

Two mounted units completed the marching order of the First Brigade. These were Samuel Wood's Kansas Rangers, about sixty effectives, and Lieutenant Charles W. Canfield's Company D, First U.S. Cavalry. Wood was born and raised in Ohio. The son of Quaker parents, he taught school and acted as a "conductor" on the Underground Railroad. He also studied law, and after admission to the bar in 1854 he moved to Kansas, quickly earning a reputation as a leading antislavery advocate. He served as a delegate to both the Republican Party's first national convention in 1856 and to the Kansas constitutional convention in Leavenworth in 1858. Twice elected to the territorial legislature, he was also chosen a state senator following the admission of Kansas to the Union in 1861. Canfield, from Morristown, New Jersey, had entered the U.S. Military Academy in 1853. He did so poorly academically that he was arrested and briefly confined to his quarters for "a general neglect of studies." He withdrew from the academy shortly thereafter, but just two weeks following the firing on Fort Sumter, he was commissioned a second lieutenant in the Second U.S. Dragoons. With the rapid expansion of the Regular Army during the crisis, men with any degree of experience were valued.[12]

The Third Brigade, which came next in Lyon's column, was over 1,100 strong. Led by the First Missouri's Lieutenant Colonel George L. Andrews, it was composed of three units: Captain Frederick Steele's battalion of Regulars (Companies B and E, Second U.S. Infantry), a company of "Regular Service Recruits," a company of "Mounted Rifles, Recruits," Lieutenant Du Bois's four-gun battery, and the First Missouri Infantry. The command structure in the brigade demonstrates how in many cases the demands of war forced soldiers to exercise command at a higher level than their peacetime rank would have warranted.[13]

Battalion commander Frederick Steele was a New Yorker, born in 1819. Entering West Point in 1839, he ranked thirtieth in the class of 1843 and was assigned to the Second U.S. Infantry. During the Mexican War he participated in at least five combat actions, receiving brevets for his "gallant and meritorious conduct" at Contreras and Chapultepec. In the years leading up to 1861 he served in numerous posts, obtaining his captaincy in 1855. For want of officers, Companies B and E were led by their first sergeants. Technically, Nathaniel Lyon commanded Company B in his capacity as a captain in the Regular Army, but his responsibilities as brigadier general of volunteers naturally absorbed all of his attention. As the company's first lieutenant, J. D. O'Connell, was absent on recruiting duty and no second lieutenant had been assigned to the unit, command fell to the senior noncommissioned officer, William Griffin. A native of Dublin, Ireland, Griffin listed his occupation as laborer when he joined Company B as a private in 1854. Army life must have suited him, for he rose to the rank of first sergeant by 1861. The captain of Company E, Frederick Steele, now commanded the battalion. The unit's first lieutenant, James P. Roy, was on detached service at Fort Leavenworth, and Second Lieutenant Joseph Conrad had been reassigned to Lyon's staff. Therefore First Sergeant George H. McLoughlin took charge. Originally from Roscommon, Ireland, he had been a clerk before joining the army the same year as Griffin. He had also adapted well to military life, rising to first sergeant in 1861. Warren L. Lothrop led the "Regular Service Recruits." A native of Leeds, Maine, he joined the Corps of Engineers as a private in 1846 and rose slowly through the ranks. In 1857 he was commissioned a second lieutenant in the Fourth U.S. Artillery. "Lance" Sergeant John Morine commanded the Mounted Rifles recruits company. A native of Dumfries, Scotland, and a coachman before joining the army in 1851, his career was most unusual. He obtained the rank of corporal but deserted in 1856. Apprehended in December 1860, he apparently escaped severe punishment, for he not only resumed his service but also within eight months had risen to the rank of sergeant.[14]

Although Steele's battalion included only Steele and Lothrop in command positions, it did not lack experience at that level. Steele was a combat veteran with seventeen years in the military. Lothrop had been in the service for fourteen years, the last four as an artillery officer. The combined service of Sergeants Griffin, McLoughlin, and Morine totaled twenty years. In all, the leaders of Steele's battalion had fifty years of experience in the Regular Army.

Lieutenant Colonel Andrews played no role in his brigade's command during the battle. The First Missouri's colonel, Frank Blair, had been ordered to remain in St. Louis, while its major, John Schofield, served as Lyon's chief of staff. This left Andrews the senior officer, and his full attention was focused on his Missourians.[15]

The final brigade in Lyon's column was commanded by Colonel George W. Deitzler. Composed of three infantry regiments—the First Kansas, Second Kansas, and First Iowa—the Fourth Brigade, with 2,300 foot soldiers, was the army's largest. Also moving with Deitzler were 200 mounted Dade County Home Guards commanded by Captains Clark Wright and Theodore A. Switzler.[16]

All told, Lyon's column numbered 4,300 effectives—3,800 infantry, 350 mounted men, and 150 cannoneers with 10 guns. Several local citizens, including Pleasant Hart and Parker Cox, volunteered to act as guides.[17]

To protect Springfield, Lyon left Captain David S. Stanley's Company C, First U.S. Cavalry, the 1,200-man strong Greene and Christian County Home Guard, and a section of Backof's Missouri Light Artillery. The Home Guards were instructed to patrol the Wire Road toward Wilson

Creek and send word to Lyon if the Southerners moved up the road against Springfield. Meanwhile, preparations commenced for the planned Union withdrawal to Rolla, dictated by the logistical crisis regardless of the outcome of the battle.[18]

The opening scene of the final act of Lyon's long campaign to punish Secessionists in Missouri began on August 9 at 5:00 P.M., when Sturgis's brigade left its camp at the Phelps farm. The men marched about a mile north to the town square, then turned west onto the Mt. Vernon–Little York Road. Captain Gilbert's Company B, First U.S. Infantry, led the advance. The Regulars had nicknamed Lyon "the Little Red Head," and the sight of him, riding at the head of the army as drums sounded and flags were unfurled, was inspiring. The First Iowa probably followed, for Lieutenant Colonel William H. Merritt recorded the time as 6:00 P.M. when his Iowans "united with the forces at Springfield and commenced to march to Wilson's Creek." As the column moved out, Lieutenant Colonel Andrews noted that his own Missouri regiment joined the line of march at 6:30 P.M.[19]

Heading west, the column initially trudged past cornfields lining both sides of the road, but the men soon emerged onto Grand Prairie, with its rolling fields of grass and scattered trees. It was not a pleasant march. Although the setting sun shone directly into the soldiers eyes for only a short time, the shuffling of hundreds of feet kicked up a cloud of thick dust, enshrouding the men in a gloom that exceeded mere darkness. To help conceal the movement, Lyon had directed that noise be kept to a minimum. The hooves of at least some of the cavalry horses were wrapped in cloth up to the fetlocks, and blankets were tied around the wheels of the artillery to muffle the rumble of the gun carriages, limbers, and caissons.[20]

The Regular Army units maintained proper silence, but discipline was not enforced in some of the volunteer units, at least during the early phases of the march. From time to time the lyrics of various camp songs broke out along the column. Perhaps the men sought to release tension, but it is just as likely that they were excited by the prospect of finally coming to grips with the enemy that had eluded them for so long. Osterhaus's Germans sang "Morchen Rote," while the First Iowa intoned one of its favorites:

So let the wide world wag as it will,
We'll be gay and happy still.
Gay and happy, gay and happy,
We'll be gay and happy still.

The Iowans sang so loudly that some feared the Southern outposts might hear them, yet the Kansans, not to be outdone, belted out "Happy Land of Canaan" at the top of their lungs.[21]

Those not singing passed the time discussing various subjects. One soldier noted that Sam Wood of the Rangers "was chewing a paper wad as usual, and talking Kansas." Colonels George Deitzler and Robert Mitchell, Lieutenant Colonel Charles Blair, and some of the company captains "were moving back and forth along the column giving orders, interchanging views, visiting, chatting with the men, and having a good time generally." Major John A. Halderman of the First Kansas "was working on a series of lurid battle cries which were received with great approval by the hilarious crowd."[22]

On a more serious note, the Iowans and Kansans also traded messages to give loved ones back home if they did not make it through the impending fight. Some gave detailed instructions on what material they wanted their coffins to be made of, while others exchanged personal items. Lieutenant Levant Jones (who had only about twelve hours to live) gave away a "beautiful bay mare" named Dolly that he had acquired during the campaign and had planned to take home to his wife. The troubled officer requested that word be sent "to all his friends in Kansas that they would find him at Wilson Creek!" When things became too serious, Charles F. Garrett, a sergeant in the Scott's Guards of the First Kansas, would remark how the most difficult items for him "to part with were his 'g-g-g-graybacks.' "[23]

After covering nearly six miles, the column moved south off the road. If any of the Federals saw the lightning or heard the thunder that indicated rain was falling on the distant Southern camps, they left no record of it. No rain fell on Lyon's column. With the change of direction and enveloping darkness, the role of the volunteer scouts took on greater importance. Now at the mercy of the guides, the Federals followed local byroads or trails leading to a point north of the Southern army's camp. As the column moved south, closer to Wilson Creek, it left the gently rolling terrain of Grand Prairie and entered rougher, hillier country of ravines and dry washes that fed into the creek from the west. A soldier from Emporia, Kansas, wrote that the men maintained "comparative cheerfulness" despite the tedious march. Ware recalled that the column moved only "short distances from 20 to 100 yards at a time, and kept halting and closing up, and making very slow progress." The moon was a slender, waxing crescent, providing little illumination, but they could still see for a short distance by starlight, even with scattered clouds.[24]

Around midnight Lyon reiterated his order for strict silence in the ranks. When the Federals halted about 1:00 A.M., they could see the glow of the enemy's campfires beyond the hills in the distance, and the sounds of braying mules occasionally drifted across the prairie. The Federals were surprised to find no outposts. They could not have known, of course, that the Southern pickets had been withdrawn early on the evening of the ninth in preparation for the attack on Springfield but had not been reestablished after rain postponed the movement. As everything had gone as planned, the Federals lay down to rest, waiting for dawn to approach so their attack could be coordinated with that of Sigel's distant column.[25]

The main body of Lyon's force rested on the farm of Milford Norman. Although this placed the leading units less than two miles from the Southern camp, the column itself was about a mile and a half long, which means that the men at its tail end still faced a considerable march. This was an inevitable element in military movements, but the difference in time it would take for the first and the last man in Lyon's column to reach the battlefield would have a profound effect on the day's events.[26]

As soon as the order to rest was given, the Regulars destroyed Norman's fences, dragging the rails down to use as pillows. The men of the Burlington Zouaves lay down on a large rock. Ware recalled that, having become chilled in the damp night air, "the radiating heat that the rock during the day had absorbed, was peculiarly comfortable." A soldier in the Second Kansas later wrote that "when we halted . . . the men lay down for a few hours rest, with all their accoutrements strapped around them, and their guns in their hands." Lyon shared a blanket with Schofield, reclining between two rows of corn, while the rest of the staff stretched out nearby. The chief of staff later remembered that Lyon seemed depressed as he reflected on the failure of their department commander, General Frémont, to understand the importance of holding southwestern Missouri. Frémont was clearly willing to abandon the region without a fight, and Lyon feared that he "was the intended victim of a deliberate sacrifice to another's ambition." Nevertheless, he determined to fight, asserting, "I will gladly give up my life for victory."[27]

South of Springfield, at Camp Frémont, Colonel Franz Sigel prepared the Second Brigade for its role in the impending battle. His command was composed of three units: eight companies of Third Missouri Infantry, nine companies of the Fifth Missouri Infantry, and the six pieces of artillery of Backof's Missouri Light Artillery.[28]

The Third Missouri was Sigel's own unit, formed initially from the Turnverein and other German Americans in St. Louis. As Sigel was responsible for the entire brigade, command of the regiment fell to Lieutenant Colonel Anselm Albert. A native of Hungary, Albert had received a military education and served as an army officer before resigning in 1845. Three years later he joined the fight for Hungarian independence. When the revolution failed, he fled to Syria. Sailing to America, Albert landed in New Orleans, moved up the Mississippi, and settled in St. Louis, where he became caught up in the outbreak of civil war. The regiment he led was not as large as it might have been. Rifle Company B had been captured at Neosho in July—a loss of 94 officers and men. Then, on the twenty-fifth of that month, the regiment lost another 400 members, who had been ordered to St. Louis for discharge due to the expiration of their ninety-day enlistments. By August 4 the regiment was down to only 700 effectives, many of whom were recent recruits still learning to drill.[29]

Colonel Charles E. Salomon, who commanded the Fifth Missouri, was, like Sigel, a native of Germany and a veteran of the fighting in 1848. He, too, had escaped to America, settling in St. Louis. The Fifth brought nine of its ten companies to southwestern Missouri, initially about 775 officers and men, but on August 4 Salomon listed regiment strength as 600. The diminution was probably caused by both the expiration of enlistments and men lost to illness. Worse still, the two regiments apparently lost an additional 300 members on the very eve of the battle (Sigel's after-action report gives their combined strength as only 900). Existing records do not indicate whether these men departed because of expired enlistments or remained in Springfield as part of the covering force there. In either case, they were not available for the upcoming fight.[30]

Conditions in the artillery were even more disturbing. Backof's Battery contained two brass 6-pound guns and four 12-pound howitzers, but most of its original gunners had departed at the expiration of their terms. Now most of its gunners were men from the Third Missouri Infantry who had had "only a few days instruction." Finally, attrition among officers had been particularly severe due to resignations, transfers, and illnesses. Overall, Sigel's brigade had only one-third as many officers as needed. Indeed, some companies had no officers at all, command falling to the senior sergeant.[31]

Between 4:00 and 5:00 P.M. Sigel received word from Lyon to be ready to begin his phase of the operation at 6:30 P.M. To provide mounted assistance, Company I, First U.S. Cavalry, and Company C, Second U.S. Dragoons, were transferred from Sturgis's First Brigade to the Second Brigade. Captain Eugene Asa Carr, who was still free from arrest thanks to the continuing crisis, led the sixty-five members of Company I, First U.S. Cavalry. A native of Erie County, New York, he entered the U.S. Military Academy at age sixteen and graduated nineteenth out of forty-four in the class of 1850. Assigned to the Regiment of Mounted Rifles, he spent a good portion of the 1850s on the frontier, saw some combat with Indians, and was wounded in 1854. Between 1856 and 1857 he was involved in the army's feeble attempts to bring peace to "Bleeding Kansas." Promoted to captain in 1858, Carr was assigned to the famous First U.S. Cavalry Regiment and participated in actions against the Kiowa and Comanche. Lieutenant Charles E. Farrand commanded the sixty troopers in Company C, Second U.S. Dragoons. A native of New York and an 1857 West Point graduate, he spent the years prior to the Civil War in the Seventh and First U.S. Infantry regiments. He was assigned to the dragoon company while stationed at Fort Leavenworth in 1861, probably as a result of the absence of the unit's officers.[32]

With the artillery, Sigel's brigade had about 1,100 officers and men: 900 infantry, 125 troopers, and 85 artillerymen. Local civilians C. B. Owen, John Steele, Andrew Adams, Sam Carthal, and L. A. D. Crenshaw volunteered to serve as guides.[33]

At 6:30 P.M. the brigade marched south out of its camp down the Yokermill Road, Carr's cavalrymen heading the column while Farrand's dragoons guarded the rear. After crossing the James River and covering about five miles, the column moved southwest, probably following the old Delaware Trace Road. As the brigade moved through woods and past farms, the drizzle that caused the Southerners to cancel their own attack fell on the tramping men. The rain did not last long, but with almost no moon and scattered clouds, it was difficult to see the way. Only "with great difficulty" did the units manage to avoid getting lost or separated. Private Otto Lademann of the Third Missouri recalled: "On we marched in dead silence, smoking was prohibited, no commands were given aloud, a subdued, undellnable clanking of our arms and the rumbling of our artillery carriages being the only sounds emanating from our column."[34]

As the lead unit, Carr's command was ordered to seize anyone along the route who might alert the enemy to the Federal advance and to place guards at houses in the area so word could not be sent to the Southern camp after the Federals passed by. Around 11:00 P.M. Sigel halted the brigade for three hours of rest. The march resumed at 2:00 A.M. As the troops neared Wilson Creek and the Southern camps around 4:30 A.M., they captured about forty Southerners who were out foraging. Sigel turned them over to Company K of the Fifth Missouri, which had been assigned the task of guarding prisoners. Farrand spoke to one of the Southerners, who told him that reinforcements from Louisiana were expected and they had assumed the approaching Federals were those troops.[35]

The civilian guides had led Sigel's command to a point close to Wilson Creek, just below where Terrell Creek joined the stream. At 5:00 A.M., around sunrise, the dragoons were ordered to the head of the column. Farrand led his company to its assigned position on the left, while Carr's troopers took the right. Sigel rode with Carr as his company moved up onto a long hill that towered above the creek's eastern side. From this high ground the two officers had a commanding view of the unsuspecting Southern cavalry camps that blanketed the fields on the Sharp farm along the creek's western side.[36]

Sigel's accomplishment was stunning. Thanks to the excellent performance of the First Cavalry, it appeared to the Federals that no word of their approach had leaked out. Despite darkness and unfamiliar terrain, Sigel had moved his force to a point where he was in a position to inflict terrible harm on the enemy. Two drawbacks remained, however. He was severely outnumbered and had no means of communicating with Lyon. If anything went wrong with the main column's attack, Sigel's supporting column faced not merely defeat but outright destruction. There was nothing for the Union soldiers to do except await the dawn.

Chapter 13 . . . .

My Boys Stood It Like Heroes

Early on the morning of August 10, General James S. Rains was in his headquarters near Gibson's Mill, discussing events of the previous night with Dr. John F. Snyder. Although a physician, Snyder was also a lieutenant colonel and the ordnance officer for Rains's Division of the Missouri State Guard.[1] As the two men conversed, a number of empty forage wagons thundered into camp. The wagoneers brought startling news, for while moving out onto the prairie north of camp they had observed a large column of the enemy. Rains immediately ordered Snyder to "ride up there and see what is the matter." Within a few minutes, Snyder had Lyon's column under observation. The Union force was actually quite small for its daring mission, but Snyder lacked military experience. He had seen very few of the Federals to date, and their numbers stunned him. He raced back and informed Rains that the enemy's infantry, cavalry, and artillery blanketed the prairie. Ordered to repeat his message to Sterling Price, the colonel spurred his horse, galloping toward the headquarters of the State Guard commander, at the Edwards farm, about a mile to the south. Rains then dispatched a second rider to warn Ben McCulloch at the Winn farm, headquarters of the Western Army, just over one-half mile south.[2]

Neither the route that the forage wagons took nor their location when they spotted the Federals is known, but they inadvertently served as substitutes for the pickets that had been withdrawn the previous evening. The wagons probably followed a farm road that began on the left bank of Wilson Creek, across from Gibson's Mill. This initially ran southwest into a ravine. Then, curving like a fish hook, it crossed the northern spur of the unnamed rise that in a few hours would earn the sobriquet "Bloody Hill." Dropping off the spur, the road ran due north, past the 280-acre farm of Elias B. Short, and continued toward the Mt. Vernon Road, which Lyon had followed when leaving Springfield. The wagoneers apparently saw Lyon's men to the northeast, at the earliest light, just after the Federals rose from their temporary rest at the Norman farm. Either chance or some undulation in terrain hindered the Federals from spotting the Southerners.

Nathaniel Lyon had resumed the advance around 4:00 A.M. To maintain the element of surprise, he avoided roads, turning his column due south to march cross-country. The prairie grass was wet with dew and there was a slight mist in the air. The Federals soon entered a long, low valley that provided some concealment, but as they expected to make contact with the enemy eventually, Lyon deployed Captain Charles Gilbert's Regulars as skirmishers, while the main body marched in column of companies. After only a short time, they ran into a group of Southerners who fired a few shots before running away. Discipline in the Southern army was so poor that dozens of men had wandered from their camps. These men were merely foragers, but the Federals assumed that they were pickets, posted to give the alarm. Lyon therefore halted the column and formed its leading units into a line of battle. Captain Joseph Plummer's battalion filed off to the left, Major Peter Osterhaus's Second Missouri battalion took the right (singing "Morchen Rote," as the need for silence was past), while Totten's Battery, supported by Lieutenant Colonel Charles Andrews's First Missouri, occupied the center. The march resumed, with the Federals maintaining a fairly rapid pace, but they encountered no more "pickets." After following the valley for more than a mile, they discovered a farmhouse off to their right.[3]

The small white house with green shutters was home to the Shorts, relative newcomers who had moved to Missouri from Tennessee around 1851. Now in their late thirties, Elias and his wife Rebecca had six children, two young teenaged girls and sons ranging in age from four to sixteen. Their lives had already been thoroughly disrupted by the presence of the Southern army camped along Wilson Creek. Elias Short was a Unionist; as soon as he heard rumors of the Southerners' approach, he moved most of his horses and cattle to a location northwest of Springfield to prevent them from falling into enemy hands. He was unable to save the honey from his fifty stands of bees, however, and his wife and daughters were frequently coerced into fixing meals for men who wandered over to their farm. Sterling Price eventually placed a guard at the house for the family's protection, but this was withdrawn when the Southern army prepared to march on Springfield.[4]

On the morning of August 10, the Shorts rose at 4:00 A.M. Rebecca

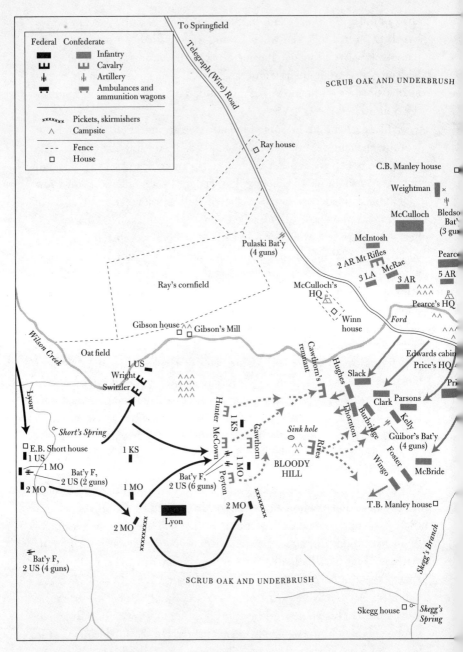

To Springfield

Federal · Confederate
▬ ▬ Infantry
⊡ ⊡ Cavalry
╪ ╪ Artillery
▭ ▭ Ambulances and
ammunition wagons

xxxxxx Pickets, skirmishers
∧ Campsite
- - - Fence
□ House

Telegraph (Wire) Road

SCRUB OAK AND UNDERBRUSH

Ray house

C.B. Manley house

Weightman

McCulloch

Bledso
Bat'y
(3 gu

McIntosh

Pulaski Bat'y
(4 guns)

2 AR Mt Rifles

McRae

Pearce

3 LA

3 AR

5 AR

Ray's cornfield

McCulloch's
HQ

Pearce's HQ

Winn
house

Ford

Gibson house

Gibson's Mill

Edwards cabin
Price's HQ

Wilson Creek

Oat field

1 US
Wright
Switzler

Cawthorn's
remnant

Hughes

Slack

Pri

Lyon

Clark

Parsons

Short's Spring

Hunter
McCown

1 KS

Cawthorn

Thornton

Kelly

Burbridge

E.B. Short house
1 US
1 MO
Bat'y F,
2 US (2 guns)
2 MO

Sink hole

BLOODY
HILL

Reves

Guibor's Bat'y
(4 guns)

1 KS

Foster

Wingo

McBride

1 MO

Peyton

1 MO

Bat'y F,
2 US (6 guns)

2 MO

T.B. Manley house

2 MO

Lyon

Bat'y F,
2 US (4 guns)

Skegg's Branch

SCRUB OAK AND UNDERBRUSH

Skegg house

Skegg's
Spring

Lyon and Sigel attack, 5:00 A.M. to 6:00 A.M.

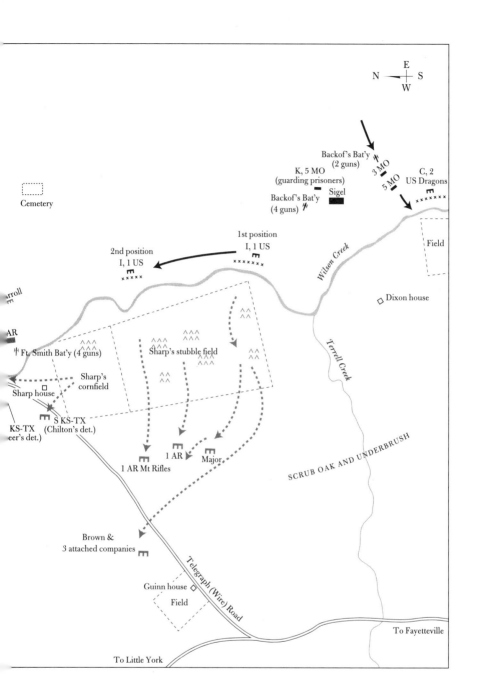

Cemetery

N
E
S
W

Backof's Bat'y
(2 guns)

3 MO

5 MO

C, 2
US Dragons

K, 5 MO
(guarding prisoners)

Sigel

Backof's Bat'y
(4 guns)

1st position
I, 1 US

2nd position
I, 1 US

Wilson Creek

Field

Dixon house

Terrell Creek

rroll

AR

Ft. Smith Bat'y (4 guns)

Sharp's stubble field

Sharp's
cornfield

Sharp house

S KS-TX
(Chilton's det.)

KS-TX
er's det.)

1 AR Mt Rifles

1 AR

Major

SCRUB OAK AND UNDERBRUSH

Brown &
3 attached companies

Telegraph (Wire) Road

Guinn house

Field

To Fayetteville

To Little York

killed a chicken—the only one they had managed to save from the hungry Southerners—and the family was eating breakfast when suddenly their yard began to fill with Union soldiers, cavalry moving at a trot and the infantry at the double. As the children ran to the door to get a better look, they saw that these men were not coming south along the road, as one might have expected, but through the back fields, from the east. Yet no sound had betrayed them. The Shorts were victims of an "acoustic shadow," a term used when people who should be able to detect noise fail to do so. It can be caused by thick woods, terrain features, wind, or "acoustic opacity" due to varying densities of air from location to location. A significant factor for the first time in the Civil War at the Battle of Wilson's Creek, this phenomenon was also reported at Seven Pines, Gaines's Mill, Perryville, and Chancellorsville. In any case, the Shorts not only failed to hear the shots fired when Lyon's men encountered the Southern foragers, they did not hear the 4,200 soldiers, ten pieces of artillery, and hundreds of horses of Lyon's column until it reached their yard. Although a battle was obviously imminent, the Shorts remained in their home. Many years later, Elias's son John, who was nine at the time of the battle, recalled that the sight of Lyon's steady ranks and the general on his gray horse "filled my heart with joy." He was certain that Price's Missouri State Guard "would be wiped off the earth."[5]

The first significant Southern response to Lyon's approach did not result from orders given by Rains, but from the initiative of Colonel James Cawthorn, who commanded the mounted brigade of Rains's Division. The foragers who fired on Lyon's column were apparently Cawthorn's men, as Cawthorn "became apprehensive and sent a patrol up the west side of Wilson Creek."[6] He was probably responding to the foragers' report of the enemy's presence, as the "patrol" he dispatched was actually a reconnaissance in force. It consisted of the 300-man regiment commanded by Colonel DeWitt C. Hunter, a thirty-one-year-old native of Illinois who had made Nevada, Missouri, his home. His unit had been raised in Vernon County, and its six companies bore names, such as Vernon Rangers and Vernon Guards, that reflected their strong community-level identification.[7]

When Hunter emerged from the ravine and onto the ridge forming the northern spur of Bloody Hill, he could see Lyon's column entering the Short farm, not quite 450 yards distant. The shock must have been considerable, as all efforts on the Southern side had been concentrated on attacking Springfield. After sending word to Cawthorn of the enemy's approach, Hunter formed his men in line atop the spur. Had the terrain been more favorable, he might have considered making a "spoiling at-

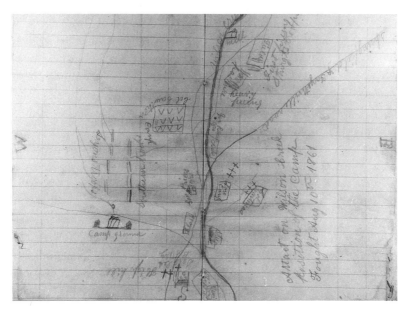

A map of the Wilson's Creek battlefield from the diary of Captain Asbury C. Bradford, Polk County Rangers, Second Cavalry, Rains's Division, Missouri State Guard, published here for the first time. The Sharp house is seen at left, Price's headquarters at the Edwards farm in the center, and Gibson's Mill at the far right. (The collection of Dr. Tom and Karen Sweeney, General Sweeny's Museum, Republic, Missouri)

tack," deliberately sacrificing his unit to throw the enemy off balance, impede its movements, and buy time. But a ravine formed by a wet weather tributary of Wilson Creek separated the two forces. The slope leading down to it from the ridge top was steep and rocky, marked by a thin growth of hardwoods, and the conditions were about the same on the ravine's northern side, where Lyon's troops were taking position. Had Hunter charged, his command would have experienced difficulty maintaining its line, while facing a superior enemy possessing artillery support. Yet his defensive action had nearly the same effect as a spoiling attack, as the line he established on the high ground forced the Federals to halt. This gave Cawthorn time to sound the alarm and organize the rest of the division's mounted troops, which were camped both in the Gibson's Mill area and on the main portion of Bloody Hill itself.[8]

Hindsight suggests that Lyon's leading elements could have easily brushed the Southern cavalry aside, but as the Union commander could not know what lay just over the ridge, he acted with understandable caution. On Lyon's orders, Totten left a section under Lieutenant George Sokalski to maintain the center, then moved his remaining four guns along a trail to a small rise at the far right end of the Union line. From there he could support the advancing infantry by delivering enfilade fire against the enemy's position atop the ridge. When Lyon gave the signal to advance, Sokalski's guns fired the opening shots of the battle. It was no later than 5:00 A.M. and perhaps even a few minutes earlier.[9]

The Shorts had never expected a battle to begin in their yard. Elias was apparently anxious to stay, but once bullets began striking the house Rebecca insisted that the family leave. They headed northwest, walking five miles to a neighbor's home, where they spent the day.[10]

As the Union formation considerably overlapped that of its opponent, the centrally positioned First Missouri met the most resistance. When word came to advance, Andrews sent Captain Theodore Yates's Company H forward as skirmishers, while the rest of the regiment followed in column of companies. Once the skirmishers came under fire, Andrews reinforced Yates with Company B, led by Captain Thomas D. Maurice, and ordered the regiment into line. To their far left, Gilbert's Regulars pushed through the rough terrain where the hillside sloped down to the creek.[11]

As the Southern horsemen were under artillery bombardment and outnumbered at least three-to-one, they gave way quickly, but not before inflicting the battle's earliest casualties. These did not all occur on the front line. Like the rest of the reserve, the First Kansas was ordered to lie down, but something caught the attention of Lieutenant John W. Dyer of the Wyandotte Guards. When he rose up to look, a "ball struck him full in the mouth." The bullet exited the back of his head, and without making a sound the officer "fell back dead." Another stray bullet killed Shelby Norman, a seventeen-year-old private in the First Iowa's Muscatine Grays.[12]

When Cawthorn heard the sound of Hunter's engagement, he formed the rest of his mounted brigade, at least six hundred strong, into position on the crest of the main portion of Bloody Hill to create a second line of defense. He apparently did this on his own initiative, without waiting for orders from Rains. Colonel Robert L. Y. Peyton placed his regiment on the left, while Lieutenant Colonel James McCown aligned his troopers on the right. They dismounted to fight on foot, as they had at Carthage in July, sheltering their horses below the crest on the slopes behind them. When Hunter's men retreated, they also found cover for their own horses, then joined Cawthorn's line, extending it to the right. The position was good, but as one soldier in four held horses, fewer than seven hundred Missouri State Guardsmen stood in line between the enemy and the unprotected Southern camps.[13]

An 1880s photograph taken in what was once John Ray's cornfield, the scene of fierce fighting. The view looks west toward Bloody Hill, which can be seen in the distance. (The collection of Dr. Tom and Karen Sweeney, General Sweeny's Museum, Republic, Missouri)

When Lyon reached the top of the northern spur of Bloody Hill, he was confident of inflicting a severe blow on his Southern enemies, remarking to Major John Schofield, "In less than an hour they'll wish they were a thousand miles away." From his position he was able to view Cawthorn's abandoned camp at the bottom of the ravine to his front and left. He could also see, to his extreme left, some of the camps of other elements of Rains's command near Gibson's Mill. A mile away to the southeast, John Ray's farmhouse stood in plain view beside the Wire Road. Because of the routes taken by Lyon's and Sigel's columns, the Southern army was now actually closer to Springfield than the attacking Federals. Therefore, before moving against Cawthorn's men in his front, Lyon took steps to secure his left flank, even though it meant dividing his small command. He directed Plummer to take his battalion of Regulars, together with the mounted Home Guards of Captains Wright and Switzler, to the east side of Wilson Creek and "carry forward the left flank of the attack."[14]

In continuing his advance, Lyon faced two challenges: the enemy immediately in his front and the remaining distance the Federals had to cross before they could accomplish their objective. After delivering supporting fire, Totten's Battery had limbered up. The gunners, together with the rest of the infantry and mounted troops, had followed close behind the battle line as it swept up the northern spur of Bloody Hill. The Union column occupied so much space that its tail still rested on the Short farm. This was significant. The troops in the front of Lyon's position would have to move about three-quarters of a mile, and those in the rear a full mile, before they could effectively deliver fire against the Southern camps. Under parade ground circumstances on flat terrain it might have taken the Federals forty minutes to move and deploy their entire force. As they faced both enemy resistance and rugged obstacles, there was not a moment to lose.

These considerations apparently influenced Lyon, for just after dispatching Plummer he decided to divide his force yet again. First, to press the attack, he called up Colonel George W. Deitzler's First Kansas to strengthen his battle line, bringing it to a total of just over 1,650 men. When Deitzler received the order, he rode past his command, speaking "a few sharp emphatic sentences" that "electrified the spirits and hopes" of the men. He punctuated these words by standing up in his stirrups and exclaiming, "Boys, we've got them, d——m them." Elated at the prospect of meeting the enemy at long last, the men from Atchison, Elwood, Lawrence, Leavenworth, and Wyandotte filed into line to the left of the First Missouri. Once they were in position, Lyon ordered the whole force forward. This time Totten's guns followed close behind rather than deploying to assist the attack. Lyon apparently judged from his first encounter that artillery fire would not be needed to defeat Cawthorn.[15]

The distance from Lyon's position on the northern spur of Bloody Hill to Cawthorn's on the main ridge was about half a mile. So instead of following the Union battle line down into the ravine, the remainder of Lyon's command moved southwest, traveling along farm roads to go around the head of the ravine. Although the distance to be traveled was over three-quarters of a mile, this maneuver made sense, as the troops would outflank Cawthorn on his left. The First Iowa, Lieutenant John Du Bois's four-gun battery, Captain Frederick Steele's battalion of Regulars, and Osterhaus's Second Missouri battalion made the trek. Colonel Robert Mitchell's Second Kansas acted as a reserve for the advancing battle line. It is not clear when the Kansans advanced, but they eventually occupied a position behind the crest of the hill, sheltered by its slopes. The horsemen of Wood's Kansas Rangers guarded the right and rear. The location of Lieutenant Charles Canfield's Company D, First U.S. Cavalry, is unknown, but the troopers probably served a similar function. The ammunition wagons and ambulances that had accompanied the column remained near the Short springhouse, located in the ravine below the house. The ambulances eventually moved to the ravine opposite Gibson's Mill.[16]

The men of the First Kansas and First Missouri moved slowly, as the steepness of the ravine made it difficult to maintain their lines. But the issue was never in doubt. After a relatively brief exchange of fire they seized the crest, pushing Cawthorn's troopers down the hill's southern slope. Indeed, the impact of their attack was disproportionate to the casualties they inflicted. Perhaps because they could see that they would soon be outflanked, the Missouri State Guardsmen raced for their horses, and in the ensuing confusion men became separated. As a result, Hunter's and Peyton's units did not rejoin Cawthorn until much later that morning.[17]

Although successful, the Union advance took time. The Kansans and Missourians did not reach the crest until around 5:30 A.M. While waiting for the rest of Lyon's column to join them, they could see a considerable portion of the Southern camps. Totten soon spotted the Pulaski Light Battery near the Winn farm, more than half a mile to the southeast. He had no way of knowing that the cannoneers in the distance were Captain William Woodruff's men, whom he had helped to train in Little Rock only a short time ago. The Federals could also see many camps of the Confederates and the Arkansas State Troops on the east side of Wilson Creek. Because Bloody Hill was so broad, they still could not view Price's headquarters or the majority of the camps of the Missouri State Guard. They did, however, notice a small group of cavalry to their right front attempting to form a line of defense. Both Totten's Battery and the First Missouri hastened to respond.[18]

The Southern high command was utterly unprepared for Lyon's attack. Around dawn Price had sent his adjutant, Captain Thomas L. Snead, to McCulloch's headquarters to be apprised of his plans for the advance on Springfield. McCulloch failed to mention to Snead that several minutes earlier he had received word from Rains of enemy activity due north or that, in response, he had ordered his most trusted horsemen, Colonel Elkanah Greer's Texans, to move from their camp at the Sharp farm to the ford of Wilson Creek on the Wire Road. He gave similar orders to Carroll's Arkansas Cavalry company. McCulloch probably found Rains's report hard to credit, as ever since "Rains's Scare" at Dug Springs the State Guard horsemen had been the laughingstock of many in the army. He apparently planned to send the two cavalry units to investigate. When Snead arrived, McCulloch decided to confer with Price in person. He left his headquarters around 5:00 A.M. His departure was unfortunate. Had he remained for only a short time, he would have been able to view, in the distance, the opening scenes of the battle on the northern spur of Bloody Hill.[19]

It took McCulloch and his adjutant, Colonel James McIntosh, only a few minutes to reach the Edwards farm. William Edwards was a man of relatively modest means, a forty-one-year-old native of Tennessee whose wife, Mary, a year younger, was from Illinois. Residents of Missouri since at least 1841, they lived with their nineteen-year-old son James in what seems to have been a relatively rude cabin. They fared well, having increased their small holdings by purchasing an additional forty acres only three years earlier. The occupation of their farm by the Western Army was obviously an intrusion of almost unimaginable magnitude. Price was just sitting down to eat in the Edwards yard when McCulloch and McIntosh arrived. At his invitation they joined him for a breakfast of cornbread, lean beef, and coffee. Within minutes, John Snyder galloped into the yard, his horse flecked with sweat. Circumstances of an unknown nature had prevented him from arriving sooner, but he announced breathlessly that the enemy was "approaching with twenty thousand men and 100 pieces of artillery."[20] This wild report was not news to McCulloch, and he had already taken what he considered to be appropriate steps. Consequently, he instructed Snyder to return to his commanding officer saying, "Tell General Rains I will come to the front myself directly." It was probably around 5:20 A.M., but the same acoustic shadow that had concealed Lyon's approach from the Short family prevented the sound of the firing on the northern spur of Bloody Hill from reaching the Edwards farm, although the distance was less than a mile. Nor did the men eating breakfast there hear the first shots fired by Franz Sigel's artillery against the Southern cavalry camped at the Sharp farm, one and one-quarter miles to the south. A few minutes later a second messenger arrived from Rains, announcing that "the main body of the enemy was upon him." This was too much to ignore. At approximately 5:30 A.M., Price set out for Gibson's Mill to confer with Rains, while McCulloch returned to his headquarters.[21]

As a result of the acoustic shadow, the 650 troopers of Benjamin A. Rives's First Cavalry Regiment of Slack's Division received a nasty surprise. Raised largely in Daviess, Carroll, Livingston, Ray, and Grundy Counties, these men had traveled more than two hundred miles from their homes north of the Missouri River under a colonel who was a physician in peacetime. Veterans of the fight at Carthage, their camp, located about three hundred yards south of the crest of Bloody Hill, marked the westernmost edge of the Southern army. For unknown reasons, the regiment's drillmaster, Captain Watson Croucher, left camp early in the morning and blundered into the fighting on the hill's northern spur. He soon returned with news that the enemy was approaching. Rives's men had not heard the firing. Nor, because of the undulations and broad expanse of Bloody Hill, had they seen Cawthorn position his men just to the northeast only minutes earlier. Although the report was difficult to believe, Rives took no chances. He dispatched a patrol of twenty men to investigate and ordered the teams hitched to the regimental wagons. One man in six, rather than the usual four, led the horses down the hill to cover, while the remainder started forming into line. But before these assignments were completed, the patrol raced back into camp, confirming the enemy's approach. Within moments, the Federals poured over the hilltop, just northeast of Rives's camp.[22]

Andrews's First Missouri, which was on the Federal right flank, shifted to face the Southerners. This created a gap of some sixty yards between it and the First Kansas, but Totten deployed his guns in between them, and both the Kansas infantry and the artillery opened fire. Rives described the incoming projectiles as "a tremendous shower of case-shot, grape, and minie-ball." Fortunately for the Southerners, the Federal aim was miserable. Lieutenant Colonel A. J. Austin and two privates were killed instantly, but the regiment suffered no further casualties when, on Rives's orders, it withdrew. In their panic to escape, Rives's men split into two parties that were not reunited until the end of the battle. The Federals may have caused few deaths, but the element of surprise allowed them to reduce the combat effectiveness of their enemy substantially. With the crest of Bloody Hill clear, Lyon needed only to wait for the arrival of the troops he had sent around the head of the ravine before advancing to a position from which he could attack the Southern camps. But, as Andrews wrote, the Federal movement "unmasked one of their batteries."[23]

Woodruff's Pulaski Light Battery was not deliberately masked or hidden. It had simply gone unnoticed by many Federals up to this time. The Arkansans were camped just northeast of the Winn farmhouse, on a lightly wooded ridge that paralleled the Wire Road between the Ray farm and Wilson Creek. The southwestern end of the ridge commanded the ford. The artillerymen had risen early that morning to prepare a breakfast of green corn gathered from nearby fields the previous day. Just as they finished, "a great commotion was observed . . . in a direction northwesterly." This was Cawthorn's retreat. As Woodruff had seen the Missouri State Guard panic before, he was "not greatly disturbed," yet as a precaution he ordered his gunners to their pieces and the drivers to their horses. No instructions came from headquarters at the Winn residence, because McCulloch had departed to meet with Price. After a short time, the Arkansans saw a battery rush into view atop Bloody Hill, more than half a mile away, unlimber, and fire. This was followed by "a second battery or section" that was soon in action not far from the first. Woodruff apparently sensed that the situation of the Southern army was critical. In fact, as he watched the Missouri State Guard being driven off Bloody Hill by the Federals, he was reminded of the Egyptians chasing the Israelites in the Book of Exodus. He had been awaiting orders, but, "satisfied the situation was grave," he acted on his own responsibility.[24]

As the caissons rumbled to the rear, the unit's two 12-pound howitzers and two 6-pound guns spun into battery. This "unmasking" activity attracted the attention of the Federal artillery, which immediately began to target them. Woodruff recalled proudly that the enemy was able to get off no more than four shots before the Pulaski Battery returned fire. Yet he knew that speed was not as important as accuracy and that artillery tended to shoot high. Because the battery had never been in action and ten of his soldiers were under the age of seventeen, he had standing instructions that in the first battle an officer would carefully direct each piece. Lieutenant Omer Weaver served Gun No. 1. Lieutenants William W. Reyburn and Lewis W. Brown were stationed at Guns No. 3 and 4, respectively, while Woodruff took Gun No. 2, to be near the center of the battery. Woodruff's gun fired first, and soon case shot and shells from the whole battery were screaming toward Bloody Hill.[25]

The willingness of junior officers to take independent action served McCulloch's army well on August 10, as it bought the Southerners badly needed time. Cawthorn had dispatched Hunter's reconnaissance in force, which delayed the Federals on the northern spur of Bloody Hill. Cawthorn's own battle line on the main ridge, together with that of Rives, further slowed them. Finally, Woodruff's counterbattery fire helped to fix the Federals in place on Bloody Hill once they finally reached it. As a consequence, Lyon began to lose the initiative. Although speed was essential, the Union commander acted cautiously. Terrain probably affected his evaluation of the situation in a major way. Totten's guns had a wealth of long-range targets. In addition to firing at the Pulaski Battery, they began striking the camps of the Confederates and the Arkansas State Troops on the far side of Wilson Creek. They also dropped a few shells onto the Missouri State Guard near the Edwards cabin. Although the range was shorter, the latter shots were fired blind, for effect, as the breadth of Bloody Hill, together with the occasional thickets dotting its slopes, prevented the Federals from seeing the enemy units closest to them clearly. Indeed, Lyon had no idea what lay directly in his front. His encounter with Rives's men, just after driving Cawthorn away, may have been particularly unnerving. For all he knew, the hill's broad expanse of folds and undulations might conceal other Southern encampments. Rather than continue forward, he began strengthening his existing battle line, feeding in troops as they arrived on his right flank and rear, via the farm roads leading around the head of the ravine.[26]

Totten's Battery formed the center of the Union line, which faced due south. Six companies of the First Kansas, under Colonel Deitzler, were posted just to its left. The men of the First Iowa, many of whom had shed their coats and haversacks, marched at the double-quick into position on their flank, forming the far left of Lyon's force. Lieutenant Colonel Merritt, who commanded in the absence of Colonel Bates, completed their multicolored appearance. Riding a white horse and wearing a white coat, he was particularly conspicuous. The remaining four companies of the First Kansas, commanded by Major John Halderman, were just to the right of Totten's Battery. The line was extended by Andrews's First Missouri and Osterhaus's small battalion of the Second Missouri. Lyon apparently became caught up in aligning the infantry, for when Du Bois reached the hilltop with his four guns, he found no one to direct his placement. Making an astute assessment of the situation, he stationed his battery eighty yards to the left and rear of Totten and targeted the Pulaski Battery, whose fire was greatly impeding the Federal deployment. Steele's small battalion of Regulars moved to support Du Bois. Lyon's line of battle soon contained ten pieces of artillery and approximately 2,800 infantry.[27]

It took the Federals until almost 6:30 A.M. to consolidate their position on Bloody Hill. Although their artillery kept up a steady shelling that panicked some of the enemy, the Southerners were beyond rifle range. Despite the Federal fire, the Southern leaders were able get most of their men out of camp and into formation. Because of the position of the Missouri State Guard camps, the task of stopping Lyon fell initially to Sterling Price. A farm road ran directly from the Edwards place up to the summit of Bloody Hill. Price presumably followed this as he "rode forward instantly towards Rains's position" on the battlefield. Haste did not cloud the Missourian's presence of mind, however. Prior to leaving his headquarters, he had dispatched messengers to Generals Slack, McBride, Clark, and Parsons, ordering them to follow with their infantry and artillery as rapidly as possible. Price's hope of reaching Gibson's Mill was quickly dashed. After riding only a few hundred yards, he reached a clearing and "came suddenly upon the main body of the enemy, commanded by General Lyon in person." Lyon was wearing a plain captain's coat rather than his general's uniform, but Price apparently had no difficulty recognizing him. Seven weeks had passed since their last meeting at the Planters' House hotel. In the interval, the Missouri State Guard had more often than not retreated in the face of the Connecticut Yankee's "punitive crusade." Whether the Missourians retreated now depended in no small part on Price, who rode back down the hill to gather his forces.[28]

Because the Federals possessed the high ground, Price began by rallying a portion of Cawthorn's command at the base of Bloody Hill, where the contours of the southern slope blocked the view of Lyon's infantry and artillery. It took some time for other units of the State Guard to join him, as each one had to form up and march to the scene. Many of the men were understandably startled to find themselves under attack. The infantry of Slack's Division was located between the Wire Road and Wilson Creek itself, a prime campsite as the trees lining the creek offered shade. Corporal Alonzo H. Shelton recalled that the men were at breakfast when they heard the boom of a cannon. This was instantly followed by a shell that "whistled along down the road close to where we were eating." Shelton was a member of Captain Gideon W. Thompson's Company B, from Platte County, which bordered the Missouri River north of Kansas City. It was one of three companies from that region organized into an Extra Battalion under Major John C. C. Thornton and assigned to Colonel John T. Hughes's First Infantry. Many of these men had no weapons, so when the firing began they were ordered to the rear with regimental wagons. Shelton noted that many refused. Staying with the command to replace casualties, they "watched their chance to get a gun, and then went into the fight."[29]

Hughes led these men into line on Cawthorn's left and acted as overall commander of the two units, which had a combined strength of 650 men. They were in good hands. A Kentucky native but Missouri resident since the age of three, Hughes was a veteran of the Mexican War, having served in the First Missouri Mounted Volunteers. Although a prosperous businessman and slaveholder, he was also a Whig, favoring gradual emancipation. But after the "Camp Jackson Massacre" he became one of the state's most vocal critics of Lyon and the Lincoln administration, whose actions he considered tyrannical and unconstitutional. Thus he brought both zeal and energy to the State Guard. "Missouri is my country," he boasted, labeling its defense the "holy cause of liberty."[30]

Colonel John Q. Burbridge's 270-man First Infantry from Clark's Division soon moved into line on Hughes's left. The regiment had camped between the Wire Road and the base of Bloody Hill. Private Joseph Mudd of the Jackson Guards recalled that it took no more than twenty minutes for his own company to move "at quick step in line of battle."

Although the remainder of Burbridge's men took a bit longer, Mudd remembered with pride that, considering their "want of drill and real discipline," the Missourians "got to the firing line in good shape." Another member of the regiment, however, was forced to scramble. Rising around dawn, Henry M. Cheavens helped some friends butcher a cow some distance from camp. On his way back he heard a rumor that the Southern army was "surrounded by Lyon's 1/2 mile distant." He refused to believe it, but on arriving in camp he saw his company being called into line. After washing his hands, he loaded his Mississippi rifle and hurried off without breakfast.[31]

Colonel Joseph M. Kelly marched the 142 soldiers of his battalion onto Burbridge's left. These few men were the only infantry in Parsons's Division, but the core of Kelly's unit was formed by his own blue-coated, well-drilled Irishmen, the Washington Blues of St. Louis. They were followed by the four 6-pound field guns of Captain Henry Guibor's First Light Artillery. Two infantry units from McBride's Division, totaling 600 men, formed the far left flank of the initial battle line. Colonel John A. Foster's men were just to the left of Guibor, while Colonel Edmond T. Wingo's soldiers held the extreme left.[32]

These units added over 1,600 State Guard infantry to Price's line. Also, Rives and about 70 of his dismounted troopers joined Hughes's Infantry, while additional elements of his command fell in with other regiments as they moved into line. By around 6:30 A.M. Price may have had as many as 2,000 infantry and dismounted cavalry in line, plus Guibor's Battery. Once these men were in position, they moved up the slopes to challenge Lyon for possession of Bloody Hill. The battle was now joined in earnest, and the level of fire soon grew so intense that it was heard as far away as Springfield.[33]

While Price established his battle line, McCulloch and Bart Pearce organized their commands on the eastern side of Wilson Creek. As was the case throughout the Southern camps, most members of the Arkansas State Troops were cooking breakfast when the battle erupted. Arising early, Pearce sent Captain Charles A. Carroll, whose forty-man Arkansas Cavalry company acted as the general's escort and bodyguard, to McCulloch's headquarters for orders. Carroll arrived just after McCulloch received his first report from Rains, and McCulloch ordered him to bring his company forward for a reconnaissance. But when Carroll returned to the Arkansans' camps, he discovered that Pearce already knew of the enemy's advance. This was another ironic example of the Southern army benefiting from its lack of discipline. In violation of orders, two of Carroll's own men had left camp before dawn, heading east up a ravine in search of a spring. They probably followed a road that led from the vicinity of Pearce's camp past the Manley farm. Both Caleb Manley, age fifty-seven, and his wife Rebecca, forty-nine, were natives of Virginia. They struggled to support three sons and a daughter, ranging in age from ten to eighteen, in very modest surroundings.[34]

It may have been close to the Manley place that Carroll's soldiers encountered an unidentified group of Federals who fired on them. The Southerners fled precipitously, and it was approximately 5:00 A.M. when they returned to camp and informed Pearce that the enemy was advancing past the flank of the Western Army. This panicky assessment was both misleading and inaccurate, as Sigel was at that point already much farther south, preparing to attack. Carroll's men had apparently encountered pickets detached by Sigel to protect the rear of his column. Pearce immediately sent the senior of the two miscreants, a Sergeant Hite, to warn McCulloch. Hite left only moments before Carroll arrived with news of the peril from the north. The Southern army was obviously in danger from at least two directions.[35]

Pearce was familiar enough with the surrounding terrain to anticipate the enemy's possible avenues of approach. The day before he and Colonel Richard H. Weightman of the Missouri State Guard had conducted a thorough reconnaissance, probably to determine alternative routes to Springfield so the entire Southern army would not have to utilize the Wire Road for its planned attack. Placed unexpectedly on the defensive, Pearce chose his ground quickly. Perhaps because he heard Woodruff's opening guns, he ordered the Pulaski Light Battery to hold its position at the Winn farm and sent Colonel John Gratiot's Third Arkansas Infantry to its support. Gratiot's regiment included a prewar militia unit, the blue-coated Van Buren Frontier Guards. They were armed with rifles and he could depend on them to be steady. Two days earlier one member of the Third, Ras Stirman, had written his sister that he expected to enter battle "with a brave heart trusting God for help." Stirman asserted that faith had entirely removed his fear, but as most of the Arkansans were facing battle for the first time, it is unlikely that many shared his composure.[36]

To meet the threat to the flank and rear, Pearce ordered Captain John Reid to place the four guns of his Fort Smith Light Battery on a slight hill a few hundred yards east of the Arkansans' camps. Colonel Tom Dockery's Fifth Arkansas Infantry remained adjacent to the artillery, while Colonel John Walker's Fourth Arkansas Infantry took up a position just north of them, in case the enemy approached from the road leading to the Manley farm. Because Walker was ill, Pearce's adjutant general, Colonel

Frank A. Rector, took his place. Finally, Pearce spread out Carroll's Arkansas Cavalry as pickets, guarding Reid's battery against surprise.[37]

Pearce's hurried dispositions demonstrate the dilemma of the Southern forces, as well as the advantage the Union gained from both the element of surprise and by attacking in two columns. Pearce prepared to defend the high ground above his camps from three directions: north, east, and south. As an immediate response, his action is understandable, but it moved the Arkansas State Troops out of supporting distance of much of McCulloch's Confederate brigade and all of Price's Missouri State Guard. Pearce also lost contact with his cavalry units camped at the Sharp farm, and he made no attempt to use Carroll's Arkansas Cavalry company for reconnaissance. Had he done so, he might have discovered that the ridge just south of his camp overlooked the farm. If the Fort Smith Light Battery had been placed on this higher ground with its better view, it might have greatly influenced the portion of the battle that soon unfolded in that area. But Pearce remained passive, making no effort to locate the Federals or understand their movements. He kept Reid in a position of limited visibility, his guns remaining silent for over an hour for lack of targets. Nor was the infantry well utilized, at least initially. While the 500 men of Third Infantry spent "some hours under a fire of shot and shell" supporting the Pulaski Light Battery, the remainder of the Arkansas infantry, some 1,200 men, stood idle in safety for at least two hours. Indeed, the 550 men of the Fourth Infantry never fired a shot in the battle and suffered no casualties. Pearce rode north to check on Woodruff, encountered McCulloch, and presumably consulted with him. Apparently, neither commander considered any immediate offensive role for the Arkansans.[38]

As Pearce was positioning his troops, to the north Plummer struggled to accomplish the mission Lyon had assigned him: to cross Wilson Creek and press the left flank of the Union attack toward the Wire Road. Instead of descending the northern spur of Bloody Hill to utilize the ford just south of Gibson's Mill, he moved east to join Gilbert's Regulars, dropping down the "rocky hillside." He overtook Gilbert "in a deep jungle" where "he had been checked by an impassible lagoon." Wilson Creek was not deep, but Gilbert had stumbled into an area of backwater between two dams built by John Gibson to provide a sufficient flow to operate his mill. "Much time was consumed in effecting the passage of this obstacle," Plummer recalled. According to one soldier, on the far bank the Federals ran into another "jungle of willows and reeds, and had to push and pull each other through, our shoes being filled with water and sand."[39]

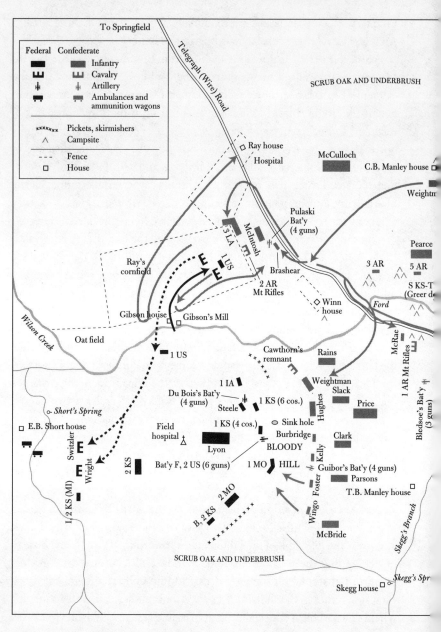

Bloody Hill, the Sharp farm, and the Ray cornfield, 6:00 A.M. to 7:00 A.M.

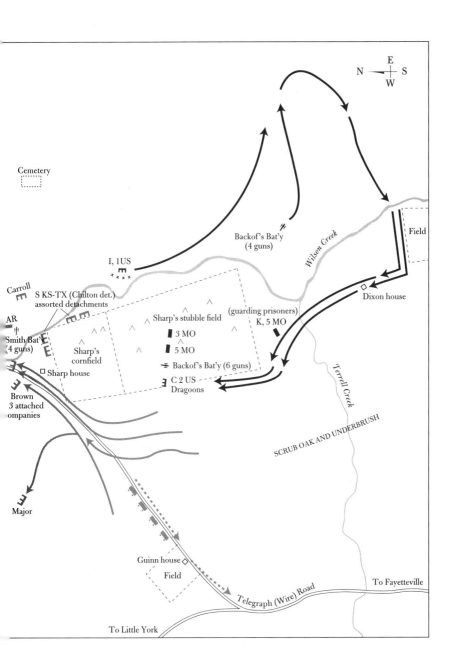

Cemetery

N E S W

Backof's Bat'y
(4 guns)

Wilson Creek

Field

I, 1US

Dixon house

Carroll

S KS-TX (Chilton det.)
assorted detachments

(guarding prisoners)
K, 5 MO

AR

Sharp's stubble field

Smith Bat'y
(4 guns)

Sharp's
cornfield

3 MO

5 MO

Backof's Bat'y (6 guns)

Sharp house

C 2 US
Dragoons

Terrell Creek

Brown
3 attached
companies

SCRUB OAK AND UNDERBRUSH

Major

Guinn house

Field

To Fayetteville

Telegraph (Wire) Road

To Little York

John Gibson may have wondered about the safety of his property as the Federals approached. A man in his fifties, he and his wife Martha were natives of Tennessee who had moved to Missouri in 1854. They arrived with their seven children (two boys and five girls), purchased eighty acres adjacent to Wilson Creek, and constructed both a mill and a substantial home. By 1861 only their youngest daughter, twenty-two-year-old Nancy, still lived with them, and they probably took in boarders. Missouri had been good to them, and their holdings, which included a few horses and cattle and a substantial field of oats, were valued at $3,000.[40]

Luckily for the Gibsons, their oats had already been harvested. Plummer's force pushed quickly through their land and, around 6:30 A.M., entered the northern end of John Ray's adjoining property. After crossing a rail fence, the Federal soldiers found themselves in a field of "Indian corn of moderate height." By this time the main column under Lyon had reached the crest of Bloody Hill and was beginning to engage the Missouri State Guardsmen advancing up the slopes toward them. Plummer consequently began moving as fast as possible to bring the overall Union attack into alignment. The ground rose steadily as the Federals advanced toward the Ray farmhouse, but both the standing corn and occasional undulations in the ground hampered their view. As the battalion advanced, it suddenly came under fire from the left. Although some of the bullets clipped ears of corn and others ricocheted from bayonets, no one was injured. These shots probably came from some of Rains's men camped on the east side of Wilson Creek who had fallen back during the opening phase of the battle. Although Plummer described this fire as "light and easily quelled," the halt he made to deal with it slowed his already tardy maneuvers still further, allowing the Southerners even more time to respond to the Union advance.[41]

As Plummer approached the center of the cornfield, he observed the Pulaski Light Battery delivering enfilade fire against the main Union line across the valley atop Bloody Hill. He responded by leading his command toward the battery "with the intention of storming it, should the opportunity offer."[42] Unfortunately for the Union officer and his command, the opportunity never materialized.

Possessing a sufficient supply of ammunition, Woodruff's gunners had maintained a steady fire since the opening of the battle. They also endured the incoming shells of the Federal guns. In a letter written the day after the battle, Woodruff stated with pride, "My boys stood it like heroes—not a man flinched, although the balls came like hail stones for all that time." Yet he added, without any apparent sense of incongruity, that only two of his men were struck while the battery was in its initial position. To the inexperienced Arkansans the counterbattery fire directed against them seemed extraordinarily heavy, as exploding shells could have a psychological impact disproportionate to their actual lethality.[43]

The first casualty in the Pulaski Light Artillery was the popular young lieutenant, Omer Weaver, who was mortally wounded by a round that struck him in the chest and nearly tore off his right arm. Weaver remained conscious for some time, and after his comrades carried him to cover he may have thought about his family and clandestine sweetheart Annie back in Little Rock. Woodruff called for a surgeon, but the artillerist had no time to spare for Weaver, as he soon sighted Plummer's approaching force, about half a mile distant. The captain sent a messenger to warn McCulloch, who had returned to the area of the Winn farm.[44]

Back at the Western Army's headquarters, McCulloch began forming his Confederate brigade. He knew that Price's Missourians were responding to the threat from Bloody Hill, and after consulting with Pearce he was assured that the Arkansas State Troops would soon be in good defensive positions. Messengers informed him, however, that chaos reigned at the Sharp farm only a short distance down the Wire Road. The enemy's attack on the Southern cavalry forces camped there had created absolute panic. McCulloch had apparently just decided to shift all of his Confederate troops to quell the danger in his rear when Woodruff's message alerted him to the more immediate peril posed by Plummer's advance. He therefore instructed his adjutant, Colonel James McIntosh, to take his own unit, the Second Arkansas Mounted Rifles, together with Lieutenant Colonel Dandridge McRae's undesignated battalion of Arkansas infantry and the Third Louisiana, to oppose Plummer. McCulloch assisted in assembling this force before returning his attention to the remaining Confederates—the First Arkansas Mounted Rifles and the South Kansas–Texas Cavalry—and the crisis at the Sharp farm.[45]

As was the case elsewhere, the men of McCulloch's Confederate brigade were calmly eating breakfast when the Union attack shattered their complacency. The Louisianans had arisen early, falling in at the sound of a bugle for roll call. They were then dismissed to prepare coffee. The peculiar acoustic shadow prevented them from hearing the opening sounds of the battle. Instead, the scurrying of couriers and the frantic movements of other troops first alerted them to impending action. When Colonel Louis Hébert ordered the Third Louisiana to reassemble, many of the men responded in such haste that they left their coats behind, changing the solid gray lines of the neatly uniformed unit to a multicolored appearance. The sense of danger combined with the thrill of finally confronting the enemy to produce tremendous emotional release among the soldiers. While ordering his own Pelican Rifles to fall in, Sergeant William Watson heard some of his men cry, "We are going to have it now, boys." The regiment's lieutenant colonel, Samuel M. Hyams, was in acute pain, suffering not only from his usual arthritis, but also from a recent kick to the knee "from a sore-backed Indian pony." Nevertheless, he "in some way got on his horse" and followed Hébert. Lieutenant O. J. Wells of the Shreveport Rangers was equally determined. He had been on the sick list for weeks, having lost thirty-five pounds due to chronic diarrhea, but once the firing began he "staggered up" to his company and "stood at his post."[46]

The 700 men of the Third Louisiana moved into position on the Wire Road. McRae's Battalion, which numbered 220, formed behind them. McRae was deeply proud of the progress his men had made since their enlistment only weeks before. Although their weapons were of inferior quality, the unit had gone from being one of the most poorly disciplined in the Southern army to one of the best. The battalion lacked tents and many of the men had no blankets, forcing them to sleep "upon the naked ground without anything to be on or cover with." Under such circumstances, some officers might have encouraged their men to scrounge what they needed from any available source. But McRae threatened to shoot "like a dog" anyone who so much as insulted a woman, much less committed theft. McRae apparently had charisma, for instead of resenting his high standards, his men developed pride in both themselves and their commander.[47]

Because McIntosh was functioning as McCulloch's adjutant and de facto second-in-command, Lieutenant Colonel Benjamin T. Embry assumed command of the four hundred men of the Second Arkansas Mounted Rifles, although McIntosh directed their initial movements in person. Leaving their camp amid "a terrible fire of grape shot and shell," they passed around Hébert's and McRae's units. Proceeding up the Wire Road toward the Ray farm, they moved just beyond the Pulaksi Light Battery and dismounted where a small patch of woods offered safety for their horses. The passage of the horsemen to the front caused some delay, which an irritated McCulloch took out on Hébert. Sergeant Willie H. Tunnard of the Pelican Rifles recalled that McCulloch galloped up to Hébert and, in a combination of excitement and rage, shouted, "Colonel, why in hell don't you lead your men out?" The inquiry was not repeated and the regiment began to move, with McRae's Battalion bringing up the rear. About the time they joined Embry's men, either McCulloch or

McIntosh ordered McRae's Battalion up onto the ridge to their left to support Woodruff's battery. The remaining two regiments, a total of some 1,100 officers and men, continued along the road.[48]

As Hébert's and McIntosh's men advanced, they passed through the impact zone of the Union counterbattery fire against Woodruff's guns. The tree cover along the road provided only limited protection for the soldiers. After moving a short distance, the column turned left onto a narrow farm road that tunneled through thick underbrush, down into a ravine, at the bottom of which sat a springhouse used by the Ray family. As the soldiers in the lead climbed to the top of the steep bank beyond, they saw immediately in their front a weed-choked rail fence that marked the southern end of John Ray's cornfield. They were shocked to discover Plummer's men just on the other side.[49]

Only two companies of the Third Louisiana had time to deploy into line before the Federals opened fire. Hébert estimated the distance to be "within fifteen paces at the most." Tunnard judged it to be less than a stone's throw, and Watson recalled it as about one hundred yards. The differences probably reflect the men's positions in line at the time. In any case, the bulk of the Confederates were still in column, and it may have taken twenty to thirty minutes for McIntosh to get all of his men into position. The rail fence was initially in between the contending soldiers, and some of the Louisianans sheltered themselves by crouching in the adjacent brush and thickets. Eventually, both the Third Louisiana and the Second Arkansas, which deployed to the left, pressed up to the fence and used it for cover. As they fought, "Sergeant," a mongrel who had attached himself to the Louisianans and become their beloved mascot, ran barking down the line. Although the men tried to call him back to safety, he was killed almost instantly, "the victim of his own fearless temerity."[50]

Although Plummer had his men kneel or lie down for protection, the Federals were at a decided disadvantage. There was considerable confusion because in places the weeds were so thick along the fence rails that the Southerners were effectively hidden. One of the Regulars remembered that "men frequently asked, 'Where are they?' 'What do you see?' We were guided mainly by the sound of musketry and the voices of men concealed in the dense thicket in front." Another Federal recalled that although his unit "lay close to the ground," four men were shot right next to him, as the Southerners "fired very low." Indeed, only the fact that the Federals caught the Confederates in mid-deployment allowed them to maintain their position for as long as they did. Plummer apparently mistrusted the ability of the mounted Home Guard companies under Switzler and Wright, for he kept them to the rear. This meant that his line of only three hundred infantrymen was outnumbered more than three to one, but most of the Union soldiers performed well. Plummer paced back and forth behind his battalion, calling out words of encouragement such as "Keep cool, my boys, you are doing well, you are mowing them down!" Although he "attracted swarms of bullets," he remained unscathed, and his courageous example had a calming effect. One of the Regulars confessed: "In the beginning we felt nervous and confused, like anyone suddenly exposed to danger; but we became warmed up with the excitement, and most of the men acted as if they had found an agreeable employment." But they soon realized that the enemy did not constitute the only danger. "Quarrels broke out among the men, for those in the front complained that their cheeks were singed by the fire of companions in the rear rank; and ramrods which had been left on the ground were taken up by others and not promptly returned." As was often the case in combat, many felt that the odds against them were even greater than they were. Private James H. Wiswell, a nineteen-year-old native of Washington County, New York, was one of the "rifle recruits" in Plummer's battalion. In a letter to his sister Mary, he wrote that the Confederates were "in some brush adjoining the cornfield and commenced playing upon us and we played back a little smarter then they did according to our number." He estimated that the Southerners to their front numbered 3,000 and thought that another three regiments were sent to turn their left flank, placing them in a "cross fire from nearly 6000 men."[51]

Actually, elements of the Third Louisiana ended up on the Federals' left flank not from any plan, but because there was not enough room. As each company deployed to the right of the previous one, they reached the eastern end of the cornfield and continued north until the Confederate line assumed the shape of an *L*. The casualties they incurred while getting into position were particularly distressing, as they could not yet retaliate. One member of the Pelican Rifles noted that his company lost a dozen men at the enemy's first volley. According to Tunnard, "Men were dropping all along the line; it was becoming uncomfortably hot." After several minutes, the smoke grew so thick that it obscured targets. Both sides ceased fire as if by mutual consent and the soldiers began to exchange taunts instead of bullets. One Federal, frustrated with his side's poor position, challenged the Confederates to come out into the open field.[52]

Concerned about the rate at which his men were suffering casualties, McIntosh ended the lull by having his troops charge. He apparently gave the order to the Third Louisiana first, as he led the Second Arkansas in person. This was brave, but he would have done better to command from the rear, where he could exercise proper control. For as a result of some

Captain Clark Wright, Dade County Union Home Guards (The collection of Dr. Tom and Karen Sweeney, General Sweeny's Museum, Republic, Missouri)

misunderstanding, only half of the Arkansans moved forward. But even with reduced numbers, the Confederate advance threatened to overwhelm Plummer, as approximately 900 cheering soldiers moved against his 300-man battalion. Despite his arthritis, Lieutenant Colonel Hyams of the Third Louisiana dismounted and followed his men on foot. The Federals did not panic, but their retreat was certainly rapid; despite the close proximity of the lines, only a few lingered long enough to participate in hand-to-hand combat. Bob Henderson, a private from Shreveport, Louisiana, was clubbed down by one Union soldier's musket, but he recovered and shot the man who struck him in the back as he ran away. When Sergeant Watson attempted to seize a small flag from a Union officer, he received a sword cut to his wrist for his pains. "I closed with him, but found the poor fellow was already sorely wounded, and he fell fainting to the ground, still holding onto the flag." Watson pressed on, following the fleeing Federals all the way into Gibson's oat field. There McIntosh, his lines disorganized by the advance, halted to close ranks and take stock of the situation. About this time McIntosh resumed direct command of the Second Arkansas from Embry. This was only temporarily, for shortly thereafter McCulloch called McIntosh away to perform other duties and Embry led the troops throughout the rest of the day.[53]

The Confederates had advanced well north of Gibson's Mill, placing them in a position to threaten the left flank and rear of Lyon's forces across Wilson Creek. They did not get an opportunity to do so. Over on Bloody Hill, Du Bois's Battery had been assisting Totten's gunners in delivering counterbattery fire. Captain Gordon Granger arrived with orders from Lyon to move the battery to the right. Du Bois was in the process of limbering the guns when he observed Plummer falling back through the cornfield. He thought that the "day seemed lost," for the small battalion of Union Regulars was facing the "overwhelming force of the enemy." Granger recognized the crisis as well, as he countermanded the move and ordered the Federal artillery to rake the exposed flank of McIntosh's Confederates. A grateful Private Wiswell noted how "our batteries . . . began to throw 'shell' among them rather thick and thereby covered us in our retreat." Plummer crossed back to the western side of Wilson Creek, taking the Home Guard horsemen with him.[54]

For the Third Louisiana, the experience of coming unexpectedly under artillery fire was psychologically devastating, even though it killed only two men out of a unit that at that point numbered more than six hundred. Watson remembered "a storm of shrapnel and grape," whereas Tunnard recalled that "shot and shell were rained upon them until it became too uncomfortable to be withstood." When Hébert ordered the regiment to fall back to the protection of some high wooded ground, the men obeyed "with zeal and alacrity." Although not a rout, the withdrawal was highly disorganized, in part because many of the dispirited Louisianans threw themselves to the ground for safety whenever they heard a Federal artillery piece discharged. As a result, the regiment split into three groups during its retreat.[55]

Hébert rallied about one hundred of his command near the southern end of Ray's cornfield, forming them into two companies. Major William F. Tunnard gathered a larger number in an open field behind the Ray house. This location was unexpectedly dangerous, as Tunnard's men were the only enemy left in view of Du Bois's gunners, who turned on the available target. Tunnard reported losing two men killed and several wounded before they moved behind the protection of a nearby hill. His command eventually rejoined Hébert, but not before a clumsy soldier in the Morehouse Fencibles accidentally discharged his musket, wounding three comrades.[56]

Firing from long distance, the Federals were unaware that the Ray home was being used as a field hospital because the Southern doctors had neglected to post the traditional yellow flag marking a medical facility. Once Tunnard's group began to draw fire, the physicians promptly remedied the error and they were no longer targeted. The Ray house itself was never struck, although a nearby chicken coop was damaged.[57]

Sergeant Major J. P. Renwick, Morehouse Guards, Third Louisiana Infantry. Killed in the Ray cornfield fight, he was the regiment's first casualty. (The collection of Dr. Tom and Karen Sweeney, General Sweeny's Museum, Republic, Missouri)

Meanwhile, Hyams gathered the largest portion of the Third Louisiana near the ford of Wilson Creek on the Wire Road. As the men rested, Watson took time to bind his wound with the strip of white cloth that the Confederate troops wore around their left arms to distinguish themselves from the enemy. The Louisianans were joined by the Second Arkansas Mounted Rifles, which had withdrawn from the fight in much better order.[58]

Because reports did not always calculate losses on individual portions of the battlefield, the number of Confederates killed and wounded in the contest between McIntosh and Plummer cannot be determined precisely. Though Du Bois wrote that "the ground was covered with their dead," he was too far away to make an accurate judgment. In all likelihood, the Southerners suffered about one hundred casualties.[59] Plummer acknowledged nineteen killed, fifty-two wounded, and nine missing, or almost 27 percent of his total force. Although Plummer himself was among the wounded, having been struck during the retreat, he retained command and eventually re-formed his battalion in the ravine opposite Gibson's Mill. There, unable to remain in the saddle, he turned command over to Captain Arch Houston. Except for part of Gilbert's Company B, First U.S. Infantry, which moved forward and joined Steele's battalion, Plummer's command remained in reserve. The Home Guard companies under Switzler and Wright took up a position to guard against possible attempts by enemy cavalry to turn the Federal right and rear.[60]

The Confederates had defeated and driven an enemy column back across Wilson Creek and secured the northeastern section of the battlefield. This was a significant accomplishment, as it allowed McCulloch to concentrate on repelling Sigel's attack from the south and assisting Price to the west. Although the fight in John Ray's cornfield had been fierce and bloody, it had been relatively brief, lasting no more than about an hour. This would not be the case for the rest of the battle, especially on Bloody Hill.

Chapter 14 . . . .

A "Stirring" Effect on the Enemy

As dawn broke, Sigel was able to assess his situation more fully. The knoll he occupied rose almost 150 feet above the southeastern edge of the Sharp farm, where many enemy cavalrymen were camped. Joseph Sharp's "large white house" stood a mile away, to the northwest, fronting the Wire Road that constituted the Southern army's logistical lifeline. Sigel could see Sharp's backyard and two large fields, roughly rectangular in shape, adjacent to the south. The fields were enclosed by split rail fencing, although some of the rails may have disappeared to feed campfires. The field farthest from Sigel, closest to the Sharp house, had been planted in corn. No doubt hungry Southerners picked it clean in short order, as a large herd of cattle belonging to the army was placed in the enclosure. The second, larger field adjoining it had been previously harvested and was now in stubble. The eastern edges of the fields paralleled Wilson Creek, the land dropping off toward the creek bottom near the fence line. A farm road ran along their western border. To the north, this road joined the Wire Road at Sharp's house, while from the southwestern corner of the stubble field it ran southeast to the John Dixon farm.[1]

The area was slightly familiar to Sigel, as the Army of the West had tramped past the Sharp farm on its way to and from Dug Springs. Some memory of it and the general topography of the place probably influenced him when he persuaded Nathaniel Lyon to divide his forces for a two-pronged attack. From his elevated position, the determined colonel could now see perhaps a quarter of the Southern army. Hundreds of men were milling about the stubble field and moving in and out of tents that lined its eastern edge. Others, including infantry and artillery, occupied camps on both sides of the creek, although Sigel could have seen only glimpses of them due to the trees along the stream. The scene was a strange mixture of order and disorder. The concentration of the enemy's baggage train on the Wire Road suggested that the Southerners were preparing to advance. Some cavalry units were mounting up, while others still had their horses picketed. Smoke rose from many dozens of campfires, and no one showed the least concern for security.[2]

After consulting with Colonel Salomon, Sigel began positioning his brigade. The civilian guides were evidently uncertain about the condition of the roads ahead, as Sigel feared he would have difficulty fording Wilson Creek with his artillery. He therefore ordered two sections (four guns) from Backof's Missouri Light Artillery to be deployed on the knoll itself. The hill made an excellent artillery platform, and the prospect of dropping shells onto the sleepy camp was irresistible, despite the long range. Sigel was unconcerned that his movements on the hilltop might be spotted by the enemy below, as he expected to hear Lyon's initial fire any moment. But once the guns opened, the battery might be vulnerable to the Southerners camped on the eastern side of the creek. As a precaution he ordered Captain Eugene Carr's company of the First Cavalry to take a position due north of the guns. Because the Fifth Missouri's Company K, commanded by Captain Samuel A. Flagg, was already detailed to guard the prisoners, Flagg's men remained with the guns on the knoll where they could provide support if necessary. To fulfill the primary mission of blocking the Wire Road in the rear of the Southern army, Sigel sent the rest of the infantry and the remaining section of artillery down the ravine toward the Dixon farm. The Second Dragoons, led by Lieutenant Charles E. Farrand, a New Yorker who had graduated from West Point in 1857, rode ahead.[3]

According to Sigel, it was 5:30 A.M. when he first heard the sound of Lyon's musketry from the north. At his signal, the largely amateur artillerymen of the Missouri Light Artillery jerked their lanyards, beginning what turned out to be, for its modest size, one of the most effective long-range bombardments of the Civil War. Sigel proudly recalled that it had "a 'stirring' effect on the enemy, who were preparing breakfast." In fact, it produced chaos. Private John T. Buegel of the Third Missouri noted gleefully, "It was a funny sight to see them running about in confusion."[4]

The Southerners who came under fire in Sharp's fields did not all respond identically. Some maintained their discipline, quickly moving out of harm's way, while others fled and took no further part in the battle. The majority rallied only after a lengthy period of confusion. Southern accounts of what took place admit to considerable disorder but tend to downplay both its duration and importance.

McCulloch, Pearce, and Price seem to have given little thought to which troops occupied the Sharp property, as units from all three components of the Western Army were there. Colonel Elkanah Greer's Confederate South Kansas–Texas Cavalry was approximately 800 strong. A company of horsemen from Arkansas, probably numbering fewer than 100 men, camped with the Texans. Led by a Captain Dalrymple, they were apparently Confederate rather than Arkansas State Troops, as McCulloch placed them under Greer's command. Colonel De Rosey Carroll's First Arkansas Cavalry, which belonged to the Arkansas State Troops, had 350 men. The Missouri State Guard was represented by two units: Colonel William B. Brown's 320 troopers from Parsons's Division and 273 horsemen from Clark's Division under Lieutenant Colonel James Patrick Major. Though relatively few of the enlisted men were experienced, two of their leaders could boast substantial accomplishments. Greer, as noted earlier, was a veteran of the Mexican War. Major, a native of Fayette, Missouri, was a West Point graduate who had served in Texas with the Second U.S. Cavalry before resigning his commission at the outbreak of the Civil War. Only twenty-five, he was heavyset, with thick eyebrows and a drooping, walrus mustache. The camp as a whole was under the command of Brigadier General Alexander Steen, who had acted as drillmaster for the Missouri State Guard since the encampment at Cowskin Prairie.[5]

The mounted units totaled over 1,500 men. It is unclear who appointed Steen to oversee them, or even why, as they were not organized into a tactical formation. True, the terrain separated them somewhat from the rest of the army, but they were hardly so isolated as to need an independent commander. Steen probably held only a figurehead position. Indeed, his real job may have been to look after the almost 2,000 unarmed State Guardsmen and a number of camp followers—slaves, women, and perhaps even children—who had accompanied the Western Army despite McCulloch's attempts to leave them behind. Most of these were apparently camped on the Sharp property, although their precise location is unknown.[6]

The northeastern corner of Sharp's cornfield ran right up to the creek. Greer's Texans, who had left most of their tents behind, camped in "a skirt of timber" that lined the stream. They had been preparing to move to the Wire Road when rain canceled the night march on August 9. Greer interpreted McCulloch's orders that the army should sleep on its arms so literally that most of his men simply stretched out on the ground, the reins of their still-saddled horses in hand. This could not have been conducive to rest, nor would the men have been happy when Greer roused them to feed their horses a full hour before sunrise, while almost everyone else in the Southern camp remained asleep. Although the colonel allowed the men to boil coffee, he restricted them to cold food, as he expected the army to march on Springfield at dawn. The Texans finished their unsatisfactory meal at first light.[7]

The acoustic shadow that prevented McCulloch and Price from discerning the opening fire on the northern spur of Bloody Hill affected those positioned at the Sharp farm in the same fashion, for they did not hear any sound from the initial engagement. Greer learned that a battle had erupted when a staff officer arrived from McCulloch, ordering the South Kansas–Texas Cavalry to take up a position at the ford where the Wire Road crossed Wilson Creek. He gave orders for his men to form up, but before word reached all of the companies Sigel's surprise bombardment alerted them to danger in their rear. Bugler Albert Blocker recalled the shock of hearing "an awful explosion" near the creek. Within moments a second shell "came crashing through the tree tops" directly over his own unit, the Texas Hunters of Harrison County. These were perhaps Greer's best men, armed with Colt's repeating rifles, and Captain Thomas W. Winston soon had them in line. The colonel wanted Winston's men to act as the anchor of the formation, the head of a column of ten companies, but it proved difficult to assemble the troopers under fire.[8]

For one thing, some of the Texans had disobeyed their commander's orders to sleep on their arms; others had strayed from camp. Douglas Cater, the music teacher who had joined the nattily dressed but miserably armed Rusk County Cavalry, was washing his face at the creek when a shell burst near him. He scurried to rejoin his company. Another soldier, Irish-born B. L. Thomas, had actually chained and padlocked his horse to a tree the night before. When the firing erupted he was unable to open the lock and fled in panic. Indeed, as one soldier recalled with unusual candor, some of the Texans "skedattled not less than three quarters of a mile before their officers could rally them." A number of these men never returned to the fight, and a few others made no attempt to join it in the first place. Stephen M. Hale, a forty-seven-year-old farmer elected captain of the Wigfall Cavalry, Company D, made a surprising discovery about two of his men once the bombardment began:

> There were two privates in Company D ... who had become notorious for their bravado on the march up from Texas, having bragged incessantly about what they would do to the Yankees when they caught them. But as their company moved out in the face of Sigel's artillery,

both men found themselves overcome by a sudden indisposition. "Captain Hale," they cried, "Where must we go? We are sick." "Go to h[ell], you d[amned] cowards!" the disgusted captain replied. "You were the only two fighting men I had until now we are in a battle, and you're both sick. I don't care [where] you go."[9]

Panic and confusion not only reduced the Texans' numerical strength, it severely weakened the unit's combat effectiveness by destroying its command structure. After only five of the regiment's companies, plus Dalrymple's Arkansans, had assembled, Greer led them up the Wire Road toward the ford in the mistaken belief that the entire regiment was following him. He soon had to move his horsemen off the road into the adjoining brush to skirt the baggage train. The remaining five companies were late in reaching the road. They were either more disrupted than the others or encountered difficulty passing through Sharp's fences. The circumstances are not clear, but arrangement of the Texans' camp probably led them to take a different exit from the cornfield than the other companies. By the time they entered the road, Greer and the others were hidden by the baggage wagons and hundreds of the unarmed members of the Missouri State Guard, attempting to get out of harm's way. With no one in charge and uncertain of which direction to take, they did nothing for some time.[10]

Major George W. Chilton finally assumed command of Companies G and H, the Deadshot Rangers and the Cypress Guards. A thirty-three-year-old native of Kentucky, Chilton was a former member of the Texas legislature as well as a delegate to the recent secession convention. Although one of the most outspoken defenders of slavery in eastern Texas, he owned only five slaves himself, far fewer than most of his fellow officers in Greer's regiment. One or more of his slaves may have accompanied him to Wilson's Creek. Historians cannot document the views of such "body servants," as they were called, but a few were seen to fight side by side with their masters and at least one was wounded. Unable to locate Greer, Chilton and his men joined a group of Missouri State Guard cavalrymen and rode toward Bloody Hill. The remaining Texans—the Kaufman County Cavalry, the Cass County Cavalry, and the Smith County Cavalry (Companies F, I, and K)—were badly disorganized. Lieutenant Colonel Walter P. Lane eventually restored order to these commands. A forty-four-year-old native of Ireland considered to be "a legend in his own time," Lane was a San Jacinto veteran, a colorful adventurer "full of blarney and bombast" who had made a fortune in mining. Not knowing where either Greer or Chilton had gone, he led the three companies into the trees along the creek for safety, where they remained idle.[11]

Once Greer reached the ford of Wilson Creek and realized that only a portion of his regiment had accompanied him, he sent his adjutant, Matthew D. Ector, back to the Sharp farm to find the errant companies. Ector was equally concerned with locating his missing thirteen-year-old son Walton, whom he had left in the care of the regimental chaplain, the Reverend Clemens. Ector could not find them (they emerged safely that afternoon), nor was he able to get any of the horsemen headed toward Greer. Because of the confusion caused by Sigel's bombardment, the South Kansas–Texas Cavalry was split into three battalions under Greer, Chilton, and Lane.[12]

Churchill's First Arkansas Mounted Rifles and Carroll's First Arkansas Cavalry were camped just south of Greer's Texans, but in the open field without any shelter. Early that morning one of Carroll's company commanders, a Captain Ramsaur of the Augusta Cavalry, left the camp for a nearby spring, perhaps seeking a cleaner source of drinking water than the creek, as his men were downstream from the rest of the army. Ramsaur's route is unknown, but at some point he spotted Sigel's column and rode back to camp to raise the alarm. Yet despite his impassioned warnings, Churchill refused to believe that the enemy could be approaching from an unexpected direction. The captain was vindicated only minutes later as the first of Sigel's shells screamed overhead. As the men's horses were unsaddled and picketed, the artillery fire reduced the two units of Arkansans to a disorganized mob within minutes. Some of the frightened soldiers abandoned their mounts and fled northwest, directly away from the enemy's fire, heading toward the Wire Road where it ran through a patch of woods on a hill overlooking the Sharp farm. They took no further part in the battle. Others who followed the same route maintained more discipline, escaping with their horses, but at least an hour passed before Churchill and Carroll were able to rally a substantial portion of their respective men. Although the Arkansans' effectiveness was greatly reduced, they finally returned to the Wire Road, moving toward the ford of the creek as their leaders searched for someone to give them orders.[13]

The Missourians camped in the southernmost stretches of Sharp's fields were also caught by surprise. Early that morning Lieutenant Colonel Richard H. Musser had approached Colonel Major with orders for the State Guard cavalry. Musser was judge advocate general for Clark's Division and volunteer aide to its commanding general. He informed Major that Clark wanted the horsemen to join him near Price's headquarters. This proved difficult, as the bombardment caught the unit just as the men were saddling up. "The horses, being untrained, became so restive under fire that I was unable to form my men in camp," Major recalled. He therefore ordered them to follow the Arkansans into the distant woods and rally there. But few of the frightened soldiers halted once they reached the trees, and a great deal of time passed before Major was able to reestablish even the beginnings of control. Meanwhile, Clark grew so anxious for cavalry support that he sent both another volunteer aide, Captain Joseph B. Finks, and his adjutant general, Colonel Casper W. Bell, to find out why Major was taking so long. Together, the three officers eventually rallied about one hundred men plus twenty-odd stragglers from other units. Most of the stalwarts were from the Windsor Guards, commanded by a Captain Burriss. As Major moved this small force toward the sounds of firing on Bloody Hill, he joined Chilton's battalion of Texans. The two remnant units acted as support for the infantry of McBride's Division rather than Clark's, apparently because they encountered these men first. Sigel's bombardment thus not only reduced Major's combat effectiveness by two-thirds, it further jumbled the organization of the Southern army.[14]

The State Guardsmen commanded by Colonel Brown were closest to Sigel's guns, yet they came under the least direct fire, as most of the shells passed over their heads. These were men from Parsons's Division in central Missouri, with company designations ranging from fanciful (the Osage Tigers) to cumbersome (the Clark Township Southern Guards). For reasons that are unclear, three additional units had been placed under Brown's command. Captain Charles L. Crews led a company of undesignated mounted infantry, while captains named Stapes and Alexander commanded cavalry battalions whose identities remain unknown. Mystery also shrouds the campsite and actions of the handful of Cherokee who had joined the army. If they were camped on Sharp's property, they probably panicked as badly as the other horsemen there. In any case, despite Brown's "gallant and desperate attempt to form his men," they fled for the timber. Hours passed before Brown was able to assemble some two hundred men from his original force and report with them to Price's headquarters at the Edwards farm. In Price's absence McCulloch placed them under Greer's command.[15]

The effects of the Union bombardment exceeded Sigel's wildest expectations. Unluckily, however, a Southern prisoner had escaped just moments before the Union guns opened fire. Details of the incident are unknown, but Sigel had to assume that the enemy would soon receive accurate information regarding his numbers and location. He considered abandoning the knoll altogether, but the artillery was having such good effect that he was loath to move it. He decided to ride after the main column to hasten its movement. One of Backof's subalterns, Lieutenant Frederick Schaeffer, remained to direct the continuing bombardment.[16]

Farrand's dragoons had meanwhile followed the road southwest to the bottom of the ravine, crossed Wilson Creek at a ford, and climbed onto a small plateau. The infantry and artillery followed without difficulty. Mixed scrub growth lay to their right, but on the left the land was cleared and fenced in. These twenty acres of fields belonged to John Dixon, whose farmhouse they reached just after the road turned sharply to the northwest.[17]

Sigel joined the column at the Dixon farm. In their passage through the property the Federals tore down some of Dixon's fences. This was a small incident on the scale of things, but emblematic of the helplessness and suffering of all the civilians living near Wilson Creek that day.[18]

Continuing up the road, the Federals discovered a small party of Southerners in the ravine through which Terrell Creek ran. These were probably foragers, but Farrand assumed that they were pickets and ordered his horsemen to charge. The enemy fled so swiftly to the southwest that it avoided either capture or casualties. Farrand was disappointed, but his men had at least driven the enemy away from the Southern camp so that no alarm could be raised.[19]

Once the Federals crossed Terrell Creek, they emerged onto the plateau farmed by the Sharp family. The southern end of the stubble field, marking the farthest extent of the Southern camp, lay less than a quarter of a mile due north. Across the intervening scrub oak and prairie grass the Federals could see that it was now almost deserted, thanks to the effective artillery bombardment. The few Southerners who remained nearby seemed not to notice as the Union soldiers continued along the road, turning north at the edge of the fence. Within moments they began capturing prisoners, men too frightened or demoralized to make any resistance.[20]

From atop the knoll, the four guns from the Missouri Light Battery continued their pounding. North of them, Captain Carr ordered his sixty-five cavalrymen to dismount. While one man in four held horses, the remainder opened fire with their carbines. Carr realized that the range was too great "to do much execution," but he wanted "to give them an idea of my being there." Not content with his passive role, and perhaps smarting from his recent arrest, Carr then pushed farther north until he was more than half a mile from the artillery he was supposed to be protecting. This was an irresponsible move, as it left him out of communication with the knoll and placed his company perilously close to the southernmost camps on the eastern side of Wilson Creek. It gave him a superb view of the enemy, however, and what he saw caused him great alarm. Looking southwest, he observed Sigel's column on the road paralleling Sharp's stubble field. The Federals appeared to be unaware that a portion of the Southerners were rallying. Some were gathering around the Sharp farm, while others were beginning to move south in the low ground along the eastern edge of the stubble field. A short march would place them squarely on Sigel's flank. Carr immediately dispatched a trooper to warn Sigel of the danger, then started his own company back toward the knoll.[21]

About the time Carr was becoming concerned, Sigel halted his column and sent a messenger back toward the knoll, instructing the detached forces to rejoin him. This action was long overdue, as almost an hour had passed since the battle opened and the brigade was dangerously dispersed. Whereas Sigel's messenger needed only five minutes to reach the knoll, the inexperienced gunners of the Missouri Light Artillery would require some ten minutes to limber their guns. Because of the ravines and the necessity of fording two creeks, the artillery would take about fifteen minutes to reach the main column. Sigel must have known, therefore, that it would take the entire brigade at least thirty minutes to assemble at his location. Yet he maintained his forces on the road in column, a highly vulnerable formation, without making any preparations for defense, even though he could see the enemy "forming across the valley" to attack him.[22]

As Sigel estimated that the troops rallying in the low land near the creek to his right were over 2,500 strong, his behavior reflected both overconfidence and tactical ineptitude. He may have been lulled into complacency by evidence that the enemy was demoralized. Throughout the deserted Southern camp breakfasts sizzled on untended campfires, wagons stood abandoned, and many horses remained picketed, their owners having fled without attempting to saddle them. Equipment of all kinds was strewn about. When Farrand's dragoons swept briefly through the southern end of the field, they discovered "a wagon load of Maynard rifles, one of regular rifled muskets, and several boxes of United States regulation sabers, all new." (Why such badly needed arms had not been issued is unknown. Perhaps they had arrived from the Southern supply base, Fort Smith, the previous evening, too late for distribution.) The Union horsemen also collected over one hundred prisoners, almost without effort. Yet remaining in column was dangerous regardless of the enemy's morale. True, even a last-minute order to go into line facing right would have given the Union infantry a usable position behind the fence lining the road in time to repel an attack from the northeast. But the angle of the line would be poor, particularly for the artillery, which would have taken longer to deploy. Moreover, Sigel ignored the possibility of a counterattack against the head or left flank of his column, from either the vicinity of the Sharp house or the wooded hill to the northwest. At the very least he should have sent scouts toward the Sharp house to investigate the condition of the enemy and deployed skirmishers on his left flank to guard against surprise. Nothing testifies to the effectiveness of the Federals' initial bombardment more than the fact that the Southern efforts to rally, observed with concern by Carr, did not result in an attack on Sigel. The colonel's column rested undisturbed on the road from approximately 6:30 to 7:00 A.M. During the lull some Union troops may have broken ranks to loot the abandoned Southern camp, although the Federal commander later hotly denied that any breach of discipline occurred.[23]

When the artillery from the knoll arrived, Sigel felt strong enough to resume the offensive. To break up the enemy rallying to the right of the head of their column, the Federals tore an opening in the fence rails lining the road and went into a line across the stubble field. Sigel placed his guns facing northeast, stationing his infantry on their left while Farrand's horsemen guarded the right. Around 7:15 A.M. the full battery opened, possibly with canister, as the closest enemy was no more than five hundred yards away. The Southerners actually numbered only some eight hundred men, and despite the protection of low ground the artillery fire unnerved them. One Union cavalryman reported that enemy officers "raved and stormed and tore their hair in trying to make their men advance." Although this was probably an exaggeration, Southern command and control had clearly evaporated. With half an hour of sustained bombardment Sigel broke up the troops facing him, driving them northeast, deeper into the woods lining Wilson Creek.[24]

Carr's cavalrymen arrived just as the Union guns fell silent for lack of targets. As the level of musketry and artillery fire indicated that Lyon must be heavily engaged to the north, Sigel ordered Carr to assume the advance while the rest of the brigade filed back onto the road. A company of the Third Missouri, deployed as skirmishers, followed closely behind the cavalry. During the bombardment the Southerners' cattle herd and a large number of stray horses apparently stampeded, collecting in the northwestern corner of Sharp's cornfield and finally breaking through the rails. Some of them blocked the road, and it took several minutes to pass through them. As Carr's horsemen neared the intersection of the farm road and the Wire Road, they saw evidence that the Southerners had been slaughtering cattle for their army at the Sharp farm. It was about 8:00 A.M. when they turned right onto the Wire Road, halting near Sharp's front yard. Sigel had every reason to feel elated. "We were now on the principal line of retreat of the enemy, and had arrived there in perfect order and discipline," he recalled with justifiable pride. "Up to this time we had made fifteen miles, had been constantly in motion, had had a successful engagement, and the troops felt encouraged by what they had accomplished."[25]

Judged strictly as a maneuver, Sigel's march from Springfield to the Wire Road was a magnificent accomplishment, equal to any similar feat of arms in previous American military history. He had moved a great distance in almost complete secrecy, opening his surprise attack at exactly the moment intended. The effect on his enemy had been devastating. In subsequent action he had broken the Southerners' attempt to rally, placing his own force squarely on their line of communications. But the ability of the Federals to exploit such remarkable success would depend on what Sigel did next.

Chapter 15 . . . .

A Perfect Hurricane of Bullets

A t the same time that Joseph Plummer was fighting in John Ray's cornfield and Franz Sigel was maneuvering toward a favorable position at the Joseph Sharp farm, events continued to unfold on Bloody Hill. It was essentially a race to determine whether Nathaniel Lyon could consolidate his forces on the crest and move forward to a position from which to assault the Southern camps before Ben McCulloch and Sterling Price could organize a counterattack.

Lyon and his subordinates had no direct knowledge of Sigel's progress. Both Major John Schofield and Major Samuel Sturgis heard artillery fire to the south, from the ridge where Sigel was to launch his attack. They also believed that Sigel's guns were being answered by two Southern batteries located on the opposite side of the valley, perpendicular to their line and at a slightly greater distance. After a discharge of ten to twelve rounds, all the guns fell silent. The Union high command therefore concluded that the Army of the West's daring two-pronged attack was working. In reality, no Southern artillery was in position to respond to Sigel's offensive. The nature of the terrain may have caused the sound of Sigel's cannon to echo off the high ground above the Southern cavalry camps on the Sharp farm, fooling Schofield and Sturgis. This misinterpretation caused no harm, as Sigel's advance was indeed going well at that moment.[1]

By 6:30 A.M. the Union battle line on the crest was about 2,800 strong. Lieutenant Colonel William Merritt's First Iowa Infantry held the far left. To its right were six companies of the First Kansas Infantry commanded by Colonel George Deitzler. Totten's Battery—the six field pieces of Company F, Second U.S. Artillery, under Captain James Totten—anchored the center. The right half of the line consisted of the remaining

four companies of the First Kansas, led by Major John Halderman, Lieu-
tenant Colonel Charles Andrews's First Missouri Infantry, and the Sec-
ond Missouri Infantry battalion under Major Peter Osterhaus. Du Bois's
Battery, with four guns, had taken a position to the left rear of Totten. Its
commander, Lieutenant John Du Bois, engaged the Southern troops in
Ray's cornfield, while Totten dueled Captain William Woodruff's Pulaski
Light Battery near the Winn farm. The Second Kansas, under Colonel
Robert Mitchell, remained in reserve.[2]

At the base of the hill south of the Federals, Price struggled to rally
Colonel James Cawthorn's horsemen, who had abandoned the crest, and
bring the infantry and artillery of the Missouri State Guard into line of
battle. This would not have been an easy task under any circumstances,
but the confusion caused by the unexpected attack and the men's lack of
experience combined to make it a difficult, time-consuming process.
Although Boonville, Carthage, and Dug Springs had exposed perhaps
four thousand State Guardsmen to combat, many present at those skirmishes had been engaged but briefly. The Mexican War veterans scattered throughout the Guard were the only ones who had experienced
anything like the challenge the Missourians faced in assaulting Lyon atop
Bloody Hill. Although the State Guard possessed well-drilled units such
as the Washington Blues from St. Louis, there were hundreds of others
whose training did not predate the camp at Cowskin Prairie. Under these
circumstances, Price achieved a minor miracle by getting some two thousand men into line by the time Lyon completed his consolidation and the
Federals renewed their attack.

Instead of sweeping forward with his entire force, Lyon initially ordered Andrews's First Missouri and the six companies of the First Kansas
led by Deitzler to advance. Together they numbered about 1,200 men.
Lyon's reason for diminishing his combat strength by moving only part of
his men forward is unknown. It is possible that he feared the enfilading
effect of the Southern artillery fire on his left flank (he ordered the infantry
there to lie prone) and sent Andrews and Deitzler forward to probe the
ground where the undulations of Bloody Hill might offer some protection. He may also have wanted to await the outcome of Captain Joseph
Plummer's activity across the creek before committing a full-scale assault
on the Southern camp.[3]

Because Lyon failed to place either Andrews or Deitzler in charge of
the movement, it was entirely uncoordinated. Andrews advanced first, in
standard linear formation, two ranks deep. To take up a position on the
Missourians' left, Deitzler ordered his men into a column of companies.
They marched at a double-quick step around the rear of Totten's Battery,

then continued toward the front in column. A tree-filled ravine sixty yards wide separated Andrews's and Deitzler's units as they proceeded. This caused them to lose contact and made mutual support impossible. The Kansans actually advanced slightly farther than the Missourians before halting to go into line of battle.[4]

When the Federals began their movement, they were perhaps eight hundred yards from the battle line Price was forming. The waist-high prairie grass, scattered scrub oaks, and occasional dense thickets prevented the opponents from seeing one another clearly. One soldier recalled: "Large black-oak trees grew all over the field, but on Bloody Hill the probable average space between them was fifty yards, with a dense undergrowth between two and three feet high, and here and there bare spots covered with flint stones." But the Southerners were warned when they heard the commands of the Federal officers and the noise made by the infantry crashing through the underbrush. Price was content to await the Federal attack. As only a portion of his command was in line, ready to fight, and ammunition was limited, he had no reason to engage Lyon's men before it was necessary. Discipline within the State Guard was far from perfect, however, and a few soldiers carrying rifles, whether military arms or hunting weapons brought from home, took long-range shots at the Federals. Once the enemy got close, the State Guard line erupted in a blaze of gunfire.[5]

For the next thirty minutes the southern slope of Bloody Hill was the scene of fighting that was continual when measured across the broad front, yet highly episodic and sometimes brief in relation to individual units. Although soldiers on both sides described the fighting as heavy, most lacked perspective or experience. Actually, the combat did not match the intense fighting of later, large battles that are the basis for most assumptions regarding "typical" combat during the Civil War. The most important factor influencing the nature of the fighting was the scarcity of ammunition among the Southern soldiers. The conflicts at the Ray and Sharp farms had been too brief for this to be significant, but it shaped the battle on Bloody Hill throughout the day. With only twenty-five rounds per man on average, the Southerners could have expended their ammunition in less than an hour had they averaged even one shot every two minutes. They did not do so because they usually waited until they were quite near the enemy, then fired in bursts, with many lulls in between. Soldiers at different locations on the field estimated that they began shooting at distances of one hundred, forty, thirty, and even as close as twenty yards. The majority of comments focus on the closeness of the combat. One Kansan stated simply, "The lines were within shotgun

An 1880s photograph taken near Joseph Sharp's farm, showing Bloody Hill in the distance (The collection of Dr. Tom and Karen Sweeney, General Sweeny's Museum, Republic, Missouri)

range." Private John Bell of the Missouri State Guard recalled, "The continual caution of our officers was 'save your ammunition; don't fire without taking steady aim.' " Bell claimed to have fired only five shots all day. More typical was Private Henry Cheavens, who fired eight times in one encounter with the enemy and considered it a major accomplishment. On several occasions the soldiers did produce a substantial volume of rapid fire, which understandably left a strong impression on those receiving it, but such episodes were never of long duration.[6]

On both the Federal and Southern sides, the relative inexperience and lack of training on the part of officers as well as men also slowed movements and added an element of caution to their operations. The soldiers' sense of the battle's ferocity probably stemmed in part from the almost constant boom of artillery. The batteries' ammunition was relatively plentiful, even among the Southerners. Lieutenant George Sokalski reported that his two guns, which formed one section of Totten's Battery, fired 240 times during the battle, an average for each gun of one shot every three minutes throughout the day. Although such statistics do not exist for other batteries, it is clear that, except for occasional brief lulls, artillery fired continuously.[7]

When directing their men, the officers on both sides tried to set the personal example expected of them. As the Federals approached, General John Clark of the Missouri State Guard ordered his men to hold their fire until they could "see the whites of their eyes, then aim at their belt buckles." He rode back and forth behind his infantry, shouting words of encouragement and cracking jokes. Yet the work was grim enough for the most sanguine hearts. When Captain Daniel McIntrye of the Calloway Guards fell wounded, the unit's first lieutenant, John Haskins, took over. Within minutes Haskins's struggle to keep the men in linear formation proved fatal. A friend recalled: "Seeing some of his men bunched behind a tree he rushed to them to scatter them, but too late. His last words were: 'Scatter, boys, you are making a target for their cannon.'" An incoming round beheaded two of the men and tore Haskins nearly in two. The adrenaline rush that accompanied participation in battle sometimes allowed soldiers to ignore frightful wounds. Robert Tanner, a teenager in the State Guard, suffered a fractured femur, but as his company sergeant carried him from the field he shouted, "Put me down! put me down! I want to kill some more Yankees!" Yet even in the midst of such fury, kindness toward the enemy's wounded was still possible. At one point the Calloway Guards encountered a badly injured Federal captain. As they had left their camp in haste without canteens, no one could respond to his pleas for water. But one soldier was able to share some whiskey and received the officer's blessing in response. Private Joseph Mudd noted the irony inherent in the Good Samaritan's actions: "The man gently placed the captain's head on the ground, stepped over him, and with us, who had stopped to watch the scene, went on to renewed murder."[8]

Because of their poor alignment, the First Missouri and the First Kansas fought separately. The Kansans reached the vicinity of Colonel Benjamin Rives's abandoned camp, near a sinkhole, before they halted. Within moments they were trading close-range volleys with a State Guard battle line that grew ever stronger as Price led additional units into position. It was a historic confrontation. Deitzler's battalion included the Scott's Guards and the Oread Guards (or "Stubbs") from Lawrence. The "Stubbs" had been founded after proslavery forces, including Missourians, sacked Lawrence in 1856. Now the Kansans faced infantry from Clark's Division, Slack's Division, and elements of Cawthorn's dismounted troopers. This force included units raised in the Missouri River valley counties where slavery was concentrated. Companies such as those from Carroll County under Captain James A. Pritchard, from Howard County under Captain H. A. Martin, and from Chariton County under Captain W. C. Maddox probably had soldiers on their rolls who had been in Lawrence. They certainly contained men who made no distinction between abolitionists and Kansans generally, seeing their presence on Missouri soil as a continuation of the earlier "Bleeding Kansas" conflict. Deitzler doubtless saw it that way, as he had barely escaped Lawrence with his life in 1856.[9]

Within minutes of the first fire, clouds of white smoke began to fill the space between the battle lines. After a short time, Lyon ordered Major Halderman and the remainder of the First Kansas to join Deitzler. He may have done this in response to a plea from Deitzler, or perhaps the volume of fire reminded him that his forward line was dangerously thin. In any case, Halderman's men were glad to change position. While supporting Totten's Battery, they had suffered a number of casualties without being able to return fire. Halderman had ordered the men to lie down for safety, but he remained mounted. Private Joseph M. Lindley of the All Hazard company was inspired by the major's coolness in the face of danger. "I looked every moment for him to be knocked off his horse," he later wrote. Lindley was not impressed, however, when Halderman assured the Kansans that any man killed in the line of duty would go directly to heaven. "I had not made up my mind that I wanted to go that day," he recalled. Whatever their individual trepidations, the men from Atchison, Leavenworth, and Wyandotte went forward with a cheer, anxious to meet the enemy at close quarters. They formed on Deitzler's left, and the reunited regiment held its position. The struggle was intense, but the men stood to their work, thanks in no small part to the leadership of their officers and their strong sense of corporate honor. Private Joseph W. Martin remembered the courage displayed by First Lieutenant Camille Angiel after he was mortally wounded: "His last words were 'give it to them, boys; remember your promise to the Atchison folks. Never disgrace your town.' Such was the feeling of us all." Also killed was Lieutenant Levant Jones. The Lawrence attorney-turned-soldier was at his post with the Scott's Guards when he suddenly turned to First Sergeant Joseph Gilford and said, "Joe, I am shot." Gilford asked him the location of the wound, and Jones replied that he had been hit in the hip. But at that moment a bullet passed close by Gilford's head and struck Jones in the chest, killing him instantly.[10]

The departure of Halderman's command left Totten's Battery without infantry support. Lyon therefore shifted Captain Frederick Steele's battalion of Regulars to replace the Kansans. Because this change, in turn, made Du Bois's Battery vulnerable, the First Iowa moved into position on the left end of Lyon's line to protect the artillery. While these maneuvers were taking place, the Federal batteries kept up a steady fire. As the contest in Ray's cornfield drew to a close, Totten and Du Bois concen-

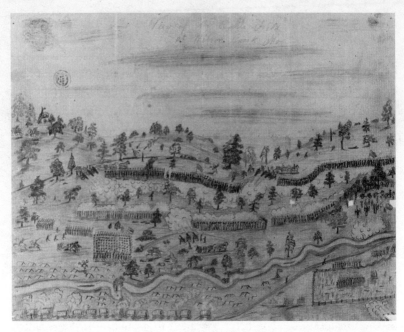

A drawing of the Battle of Wilson's Creek sent by Private Andrew Tinkham, Scott's Guards, First Kansas Infantry, to his brother David. Published here for the first time. Tinkham wrote: "I send you a picture of the battle of Wilsons C just at the time I was shot when our battery had a masking fire on the rebels the cannon on the left is Tottens battery the first reg is the 1st Kansas next is 2d Kansas next is the Missouri boys." (The collection of Dr. Tom and Karen Sweeney, General Sweeny's Museum, Republic, Missouri)

trated against Woodruff's Pulaski Light Battery across the valley. Foliage partially obscured the position of the Southern guns, but the fire and smoke from their discharges provided aiming points for counterbattery fire.[11]

This duel between Totten and his former pupil Woodruff had significant consequences, as it fixed the Federals in position. Totten's guns served as the anchor on which Lyon was gradually forming his battle line on Bloody Hill. Yet this was a poor position. Because the hill was broad, the Federals could not see its base from the crest. Lyon's deployment near the top of the hill rather than farther down the slope left a wide blind spot, a zone of relative safety that provided protection for the Missouri State Guard units struggling to get into the battle. Ironically, the opposing artillerists did almost no damage to each other. Woodruff lost only four men to Totten's fire, while the Federal gunners escaped unscathed, as both batteries consistently overshot their targets.[12]

As time passed, Totten left the artillery duel to Du Bois and reoriented his fire to support the Federal infantry's advance on the southern slope of Bloody Hill. Pressure on the Federals there was growing, due in some measure to Captain Henry Guibor's Missouri Light Artillery. This battery, which had been camped with the bulk of the Missouri State Guard at the Edwards farm, was the first Southern artillery west of Wilson Creek to go into action. Guibor deployed in a position left of the center of Price's growing battle line, where his fire struck the First Missouri. The Federals held firm for some time. In fact, Andrews was preparing to charge the Southern battery when he saw State Guard infantry moving around his right flank. He adjusted his line accordingly and began a fighting withdrawal back toward Totten's position at the crest of the hill.[13]

The infantry threatening Andrews was commanded by General James H. McBride, the circuit court judge with no military experience. His staff officers were of little assistance, as most were former country lawyers. As a result, McBride's Division was perhaps the most poorly drilled and least-disciplined element of the Missouri State Guard. Although he was described by one officer as a "clear-headed, silent, courageous man," McBride's success in confronting the Federals was largely accidental, for the maneuvers of the State Guardsmen were as poorly coordinated as those of their foe. Price's intent was clear. After ordering Slack's Division to hold the right flank, anchored on Wilson Creek, he worked to extend his front gradually to the left, by placing Clark's, Parsons's, and McBride's Divisions on line in succession. But reality did not always conform to this plan. Individual units moved out as soon as they were organized, entered the thick underbrush covering the lower slopes of Bloody Hill, and sought their appropriate place in line.[14]

McBride's command consisted of the First Infantry, 300 men under Colonel Edmond T. Wingo, and the Second Infantry, 305 men led by Colonel John Foster. Price ordered them to take a position on the left of Guibor's Missouri Light Artillery. Foster led the advance. A soldier in Clark's Division, watching them pass by on their way to the front, had both criticism and praise for McBride's men. "I remember our boys laughing at their odd appearance," he wrote. "All had deer rifles and they knew how to use them. They couldn't stand in a straight line, but all the shells that Totten's battery threw into them could not make them give back a step." Through some misunderstanding, instead of supporting Guibor's Battery, Foster marched past it, crossed a small ravine, and then moved directly up Bloody Hill. Wingo's regiment followed, and by this accidental maneuver they outflanked the Federals. McBride apparently accompanied Wingo and did not realize that anything was wrong until they came to close quarters with the enemy. Indeed, many of the officers and men were so confused about their position in relation to the Southern battle line that they feared they were being fired on by other units of the State Guard and initially hesitated to reply.[15]

McBride's situation was potentially perilous. He was isolated, his flanks were vulnerable, and there were no mounted troops nearby to scout the ground ahead. Had he been driven back, his repulse could have started a panic reverberating down the length of Price's line. Yet, in retrospect, McBride's action, causing Andrews to withdraw, marked the turning point in the struggle for Bloody Hill. Up to this point, Lyon had been on the offensive. Now the emphasis shifted. For the remainder of the battle the Federals would be on the defensive while the Southerners mounted ever larger attacks against them.

Having sent word to Totten of the enemy's advance, Andrews halted to receive the Southern assault. He positioned the right half of the First Missouri facing west, "at right angles with the line of battle." The remainder of the regiment faced south, toward Guibor's Battery, which continued to shell Andrews's men. When some of these rounds failed to explode, curious Federal soldiers examined them. Word soon swept through the ranks that the defective shells had been identified as coming from Sigel's artillery—implying that Sigel's part in the battle had gone astray. How volunteer infantrymen thought they could differentiate between Northern and Southern artillery projectiles is unclear, but according to Andrews the rumor caused "no little uneasiness." They soon had even more to worry about, as the enemy's infantry surged forward.[16]

The reports left by Price and his subordinates are so sketchy and incomplete that it is unclear how the first Southern assault on Bloody Hill began. While either Price or one of his division commanders may have given orders for a simultaneous advance, it is also possible that McBride's errant movement sparked the attack, the State Guard units to his right moving up en echelon to support. However it occurred, Missourians from the divisions commanded by Generals McBride, Parsons, and Clark pushed cautiously through the underbrush. As units advanced at different speeds according to their discipline, the terrain, and the resistance they encountered, any coordination that may have existed at the beginning of the assault soon evaporated.[17]

Henry Guibor's experience illustrates the confusion that accompanied the Southern endeavors. General Parsons ordered the commander of the Missouri Light Artillery to examine some high ground to the left as a possible position for the battery. While on this mission, Guibor became "surrounded by the enemy" and was able to escape only by riding north toward the Federal rear. This took him out of action for the rest of the battle, and command of the battery passed to Lieutenant William P. Barlow.[18]

Once the Southern assault began, the First Missouri's position on the Federal right flank was crucial. As the Southern attack pressed home, Andrews walked along the length of his line. "As I passed each company," he recalled, "I found it well up to its work, both officers and men cool and determined, using their arms with care and precision." When the color sergeant was killed, Corporal Richard Kane rescued the banner and with it the regiment's honor. Casualties mounted steadily. They were particularly heavy among the officers, eventually approaching 50 percent. Captain Nelson Cole of Company E displayed particular fortitude. Though wounded in the lower jaw and unable to speak, he continued to encourage his command through the use of body language as he was being removed from the field. The regiment's surgeon, Dr. F. M. Cornyn, exposed himself recklessly while struggling to move the wounded to safety in the rear. His behavior was unorthodox, for on several occasions he grabbed the musket of a fallen soldier and fired a round to avenge his death.[19]

The First Missouri's struggle was typical not only in its ferocity, but also in the potential for confusion that existed across the battlefield. At one point Captain Cary Gratz, commanding a company on the left flank, "discovered a body of the enemy approaching, led by a mounted officer, carrying a Union flag." The identity of this unit is a mystery, but given the Federal position, Gratz's opponents were probably either Colonel Joseph Kelly's Infantry from Parsons's Division or Colonel John Q. Burbridge's foot soldiers from Clark's Division. Because Missouri had not left the Union and the State Guardsmen were citizens of the United States, not the Confederacy, there was no reason why they should not display the Stars and Stripes. If Gratz was confused by the banner, he did not remain so for long, for he brought the officer down with a shot from his revolver. After hitting the ground, the man immediately sprang to his feet and raced back through his lines. Gratz then fired a second shot, "pitching him headlong out of sight." The opposing lines may have been only thirty or so yards apart. After the captain fired his second shot, the enemy returned fire and Gratz "fell, pierced by five shots."[20]

When Andrews reached Company G, which was in an advanced position guarding the regiment's left flank, Captain John S. Cavender reported several enemy attempts to turn his line. Shortly after this, Andrews was wounded. He was able to keep his horse and rode back toward the right end of his line, where he met Captain Theodore Yates of Company H. Andrews warned Yates that he might have to assume command. Feeling faint, he turned around, rode to the left of the First Missouri, "and obtained a stimulant." While riding back, his horse was killed. The falling animal pinned Andrews to the ground, but several members of the First Missouri were able to free him.[21]

The Southern assault that began McBride's movement against the Federal flank also brought the Missouri State Guard into a close-quarters struggle against the First Kansas, which had gone from column into line of battle. Sergeant George W. Hutt of Atchison's All Hazard company remembered "a perfect hurricane of bullets." Lieutenant Rinaldo Barker was struck three times but refused to go to the rear. With "blood streaming down his face and body," he continued "waving his sword high in the air, urging the men to deeds of valor." Nearby, in the Leavenworth Fencibles, Lieutenant James Ketner picked up a double-barreled shotgun from the battlefield. Standing calmly as if on parade, ignoring "the terrible shower of iron and lead," he used the weapon "with telling effect upon the advancing lines of the enemy, until a ball struck the rammer out of his hand and passed through his blouse in rather close proximity to his breast." With these and other acts of bravery, the Kansans maintained their position until the retreat of the First Missouri forced them to withdraw as well to avoid being outflanked. As the two units pulled back, the right flank of the Kansans and the left flank of the First Missouri briefly became entangled. This was a dangerous situation, as the Southerners continued to press forward. "For a few minutes the struggle was terrible and anxiety was exhibited on all faces," Hutt recalled. But order was soon restored, and the Federals consolidated their line on the crest.[22]

Lyon's forward movement with the First Kansas and First Missouri had ended in failure, and by 7:30 A.M. the Federals were essentially back where they had started. The First Iowa retained its position anchoring the left. The Burlington Rifles and the Burlington Zouaves were deployed as skirmishers. To the right, the line formed an arc consisting of Du Bois's Battery, the First Kansas, four of Totten's guns, and the First Missouri. Soklaski's section of Totten's Battery had been detached to support the Missourians. The Second Kansas stayed in reserve.[23]

As a result of this contraction, Deitzler's First Kansas now faced the brigaded infantry from Rains's Division, which had marched from its camps near the Caleb Manley farm. Commanded by Colonel Richard Weightman, one of the best officers in the Missouri State Guard, these men were drawn from a tier of counties either near or adjacent to the Kansas border, running from the Missouri River south to the Arkansas state line. Organized as the First, Second, and Fifth Infantry under Colonels Thomas Rosser, Jonathan Graves, and James Clarkson, respectively, the brigade included companies that wore blue uniforms and others that wore gray. Their combined ranks numbered over one thousand men. As the confusion was great and all Civil War units tended to have at least a few skulkers, it is unlikely that 100 percent of them exited their camps and reached the battle line in time for the first Southern push up Bloody Hill. But enough of them did so to cause the Federal commander the gravest possible concern.[24]

Lyon immediately ordered his reserve unit, the Second Kansas, to the front. He apparently feared that the reserves would not be able to get into line in time to avert the danger, for in a desperate move he then commanded the First Kansas to fix bayonets and charge. Deitzler promptly obeyed. Through some confusion, however, fewer than two hundred men actually made the movement. Captain Bernard Chenoweth's Elwood Guards, Captain Powell Clayton's Leavenworth Light Infantry, and a portion of the Phoenix Guards under Second Lieutenant Matthew Malone followed Deitzler down the slope, while the rest of the Kansans remained in place. The attack could easily have ended in disaster, but the movement caught the Southerners by surprise, and the units facing the Kansans fell back several hundred yards. Nevertheless, success brought danger. Deitzler was wounded and carried off the field, leaving the diminutive assault force without a commander. The Kansans' flanks were vulnerable, but thanks to the noise and smoke, and even more to the underbrush and undulating terrain, the Southern troops to their right and left failed to notice them. Recognizing the botched execution of the charge and the peril in which it left the Kansans, Lyon quickly ordered them back to the crest.[25]

The Elwood Guards and Phoenix Guards returned safely to the regiment, but the men of the Leavenworth Light Infantry experienced one of the strangest incidents of the battle. Having become separated from the others, they failed to hear Lyon's recall. After the momentum of their original charge petered out, Clayton dressed the company's ranks and continued marching south in search of the enemy. When a unit wearing gray uniforms approached perpendicular to his left flank, he assumed that it was Sigel's men breaking through the Southerners' rear. Actually, it was Clarkson's Fifth Missouri, apparently sent by Weightman to counterattack. Clarkson, in turn, took it for granted that the blue-coated Kansans were fellow members of the Missouri State Guard. When he asked Clayton the direction of the enemy, the Federal captain pointed southwest. The two opposing units then formed a single line and blithely marched off in that direction. They had not gone far before Clayton noticed that each of the gray-clad men wore a red flannel badge on his left shoulder, a distinction not used by any of the Union troops. Far from panicking, Clayton showed remarkable presence of mind. After voicing a loud complaint that his ranks were being pressed too closely, he ordered his men to march to the right oblique until a gap of thirty yards developed between the two forces. This action aroused the suspicions of Clarkson's adjutant, Captain Michael W. Buster. Riding up, he ordered the Kansans to halt and identify themselves. Clayton brought his men to a stop, but he then yanked Buster off his horse and placed a revolver to his chest, shouting, "Now, sir, God damn you, order your men not to fire on us, or you are a dead man." The adjutant fully matched Clayton in bravery and coolness. Turning, he saw that Clarkson was wheeling the Fifth Missouri to face the Kansans, having obviously realized their true identity. "There, sir, is my Colonel," Buster calmly replied—at which point the Missourians opened fire. Amazingly, Buster was unharmed by this close-range volley. He suffered only a slight wound when Clayton shot him at point-blank range and a second one from the bayonet of Sergeant Patrick Brannon, who lunged at him. The Federals were intent only on escape. Clayton yelled for his men to "run for their lives," and they did just that, rejoining the rest of the regiment in disorder. For reasons that are unclear, Clarkson did not pursue the Federals.[26]

Meanwhile, the men of the Second Kansas began to enter the fray for the first time. Their time in reserve had been uneventful, with one exception. Long after the war, John K. Rankin, who had served as a Third Lieutenant in the Olathe Union Guards, remembered how an unidentified man rode rapidly up to them from the rear. "Our boys were dressed in such a motley fashion that it was impossible for a person to tell our side, whether we were Federal or rebel," Rankin wrote. "This stranger came to the head of our line, halted to make an inquiry, saw that we were Federals, turned and tried to make away. Several of the men fired upon him unsuccessfully, until Capt. [Avra P.] Russell [of the Emporia Guards] drew his revolver, and as I have always regretted, was marksman enough to fatally wound him. He died almost immediately. We never learned the identity of the man, who was in civilian dress and rode a fine horse."[27] In all likelihood, the mystery rider was a member of one of the Missouri State Guard cavalry units dispersed at the beginning of the battle.

When Lyon's orders to advance reached Colonel Mitchell, he ordered the Kansans to their feet and marched them over the crest of Bloody Hill. After the strain of waiting, action brought tremendous emotional release. "How the blood leaped in our veins then," one soldier wrote. "Some thought of our once happy country—of the institutions we were bound to perpetuate; some thought of Kansas—of the blood of brothers spilled in

'56. During that short quick march we thought of everything but *fear* and *defeat*." Actually, optimism was hardly universal. As the Second Kansas passed behind Totten's Battery, one Irish-born gunner, standing hatless and coatless with his shirtsleeves rolled up, called out grimly, "Ah, boys, it's a devil of a hot place ye's goin' into, and it's many a one of ye kids that'll never come out o' that." The effect of such prognostication on the spirits of the men can be imagined. In one instance, the Irishman's use of the term "kid" was literally appropriate. Private Robert A. Friedrich, only fourteen years old, was rather shocked by the words of encouragement the regiment received from brigade commander, Captain Thomas Sweeny, as they went into line. "Give 'em ——, boys," the captain exclaimed, "give 'em ——. Aim at the —— scoundrels right below their belts; give em ——, I tell you." Friedrich thought Sweeny "the most hardened and reckless man I had ever known, else he would not dare to use such profanity under circumstances so serious."[28]

After taking a position on the flank of the First Missouri, the Second Kansas opened fire. Some of the companies were armed with large-bore flintlocks that had been converted to percussion. These fired "buck and ball," a cartridge containing one large musket ball and three buckshot. Although outdated by 1861, such ammunition was ideally suited for the close range combat on Bloody Hill. It gave the 600-odd Kansans devastating firepower. "There was a puff of blue smoke along the entire front of the regiment," according to Friedrich. "I have a clear recollection of the effect of that first volley on myself. I was pleased beyond measure; here was an actual 'sure enough' battle commenced, and they were going to let me be in it." His enthusiasm cooled, however, the moment he saw a fellow soldier wounded. "How cruel and heartless it seemed!"[29]

The arrival of the Second Kansas combined with the charge of its sister regiment to break the impetus of the uncoordinated Southern assault. A lull developed as Price began realigning his troops at the base of the hill. Near the crest, Lyon did the same. He might hold his position for some time, but to accomplish anything more seemed doubtful. It was about 8:00 A.M., and there had been no word from Sigel.[30]

Chapter 16 . . . .

Come On, Caddo!

The Southern army's commander was as anxious about Franz Sigel as Nathaniel Lyon was. After leaving Colonel McIntosh to handle the crisis in John Ray's cornfield, Ben McCulloch rode down the Wire Road to determine the course of events at the Sharp farm. He apparently spent at least thirty minutes, until approximately 8:15 A.M., assessing the situation. What he observed must have been discouraging, for chaos reigned on the plateau where much of the Southern cavalry had camped at the beginning of the battle. While some of the horsemen were rallying near Wilson Creek and Bart Pearce's Arkansas State Troops were well placed to challenge any crossing of Skegg's Branch, Sigel had assumed a position across the Western Army's line of communications. "Old Ben" did not require a West Point education to realize that this represented the worst possible development. He watched the Federals complete much of their maneuver before heading back up the Wire Road, searching for a way to deal with this new crisis.[1]

McCulloch had also witnessed how Sigel negated much of his previous accomplishment by deploying his force badly. The Federal commander placed the six pieces of Backof's Missouri Light Artillery in the Sharp's front yard, facing almost due north, to fire on the southern slope of Bloody Hill. The position was vulnerable, as some fifty yards to the front and right the plateau ended and the terrain dipped sharply toward Skegg's Branch, creating a substantial "dead zone" that the Federal guns could not reach.[2] Because the enemy might use this as a staging ground for a counterattack, the battery needed strong infantry support, including a heavy line of skirmishers to guard against surprise. But Sigel neglected these elemental precautions. He was apparently lulled into complacency by a steady stream of Southern stragglers who blundered into the Union lines and became prisoners. He placed only a single battalion of the Third Missouri, perhaps 250 men in all, in line to the right of the battery. Their selection was unusual, as they included some of the least experienced men in the brigade. The rest of the Third and all of the Fifth Missouri remained in reserve near the junction of the Wire Road and the farm road running along the western boundary of Sharp's fields. Company K of the Fifth continued guarding prisoners, moving even farther to the rear.[3]

Sigel dismounted Captain Eugene Carr's Company I, First U.S. Cavalry, to guard the left flank. The area it entered north of the Wire Road was wooded, and Carr repeated his error of earlier in the day by moving so deeply into the foliage that his men were beyond effective supporting distance. In fact, Carr soon lost all sense of direction. His men could no longer see, much less protect, the left flank of the battery. The other horsemen, Lieutenant Charles Farrand's Company C, Second U.S. Dragoons, filed off to the right and rear, dismounting to take up a line within Sharp's fences at or near the camp of Greer's South Kansas–Texas Cavalry. As the Texans had encountered great difficulty exiting this area expeditiously, Farrand's horsemen were not in the best position to respond quickly.[4]

The Federals in Sigel's brigade had yet to suffer casualties. Having no immediate responsibilities, Dr. Samuel H. Melcher, assistant surgeon of the Fifth Missouri, rode over to the former Southern cavalry camp spread across Sharp's fields. He discovered that some of the tents there used upended, bayoneted muskets for poles, the canvas being "caught in the flint lock." Melcher and his orderly, Private Frank Ackoff, breakfasted on "coffee, biscuit and fried green corn" abandoned by their enemy. They also noticed a number of stragglers from the Missouri infantry who "set fire to some wagons and camp equipage."[5]

Once his men were in position, Sigel ordered the artillery to shell units of the Missouri State Guard more than half a mile to the north. He assumed that they were part of the left flank of the forces facing Lyon. Despite the distance, the Southerners returned fire with both small arms and artillery. Their musket balls fell short, rattling the leaves and tree limbs above the heads of Carr's advancing troopers without causing any harm. Many Southern artillery shells burst prematurely, adding to the cavalrymen's discomfort but sparing the Federal gunners. When the enemy's fire ceased after half an hour, Sigel halted his own. Identification was difficult at any sort of distance, and he was concerned about accidentally striking Lyon's men on Bloody Hill. Whole squads of unarmed Southern soldiers approached via the Wire Road and surrendered as

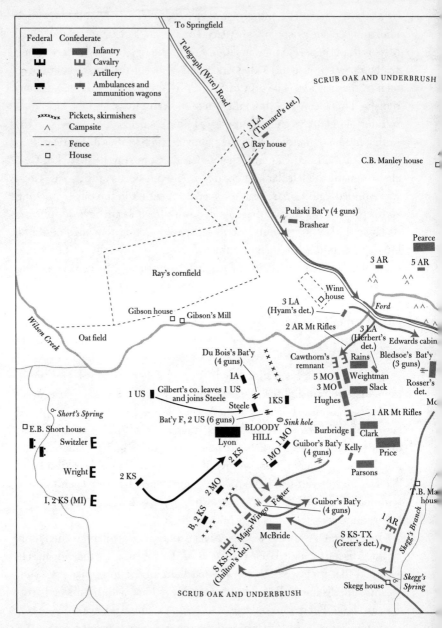

Bloody Hill and the Sharp farm, 7:30 A.M. to 8:45 A.M.

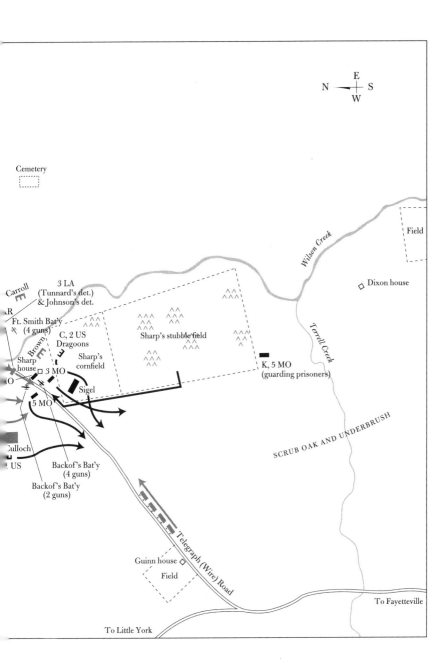

Cemetery

3 LA
(Tunnard's det.)
& Johnson's det.

Carroll

R

Ft. Smith Bat'y
(4 guns)

C, 2 US
Dragoons

Brown

Sharp
house

3 MO

O

5 MO

Sigel

Sharp's
cornfield

Sharp's stubble field

K, 5 MO
(guarding prisoners)

Dixon house

Field

Wilson Creek

Terrell Creek

SCRUB OAK AND UNDERBRUSH

Culloch

US

Backof's Bat'y
(4 guns)

Backof's Bat'y
(2 guns)

Telegraph (Wire) Road

Guinn house

Field

To Fayetteville

To Little York

N
E
W
S

soon as they reached the plateau. Sigel also thought that he detected a large number of Southerners moving south along the ridges near the Manley farm, and he assumed that Lyon was driving the bulk of Mc-Culloch's army from the field in that direction. It was nearly 8:30 A.M. Events appeared to foretell a decisive Union victory, but for safety's sake he ordered four of the artillery pieces shifted so that they faced up the Wire Road. The battery's position was thus shaped almost like an inverted *L*. The battalion of the Third Missouri remained on the right flank, south of the Wire Road. Standing in its ranks, Private John Buegel wondered why, after such initial success, the Federals suddenly went on the defensive. "It was maddening," he recalled.[6]

Despite Sigel's confidence, the Federal column at the Sharp farm was in a perilous position, as thousands of enemy soldiers stood between it and Lyon's forces stalled on Bloody Hill. Because of Sigel's poor deployment, only four of Backof's six guns and 250 infantrymen were positioned to defend against an attack coming from the Wire Road, the direction of the most likely danger. Sigel made no attempt to use his cavalry to contact Lyon, and he sent only a handful of skirmishers into the potentially dangerous blind ground to his front. He became completely passive at the very moment McCulloch was working to regain the initiative.[7]

Although more than two thousand of Pearce's Arkansas State Troops had yet to see action, McCulloch decided not to use them against Sigel. His reasons are unclear. But as the reports that reached McCulloch regarding Sigel's advance probably exaggerated the size of the Federal force, he may have wanted the Arkansans to remain on high ground, where they would have an advantage if attacked. Moreover, because Sigel had obviously moved around the Southerners' eastern flank virtually undetected, McCulloch could not discount the possibility of yet a third enemy column approaching from due east, via the road leading to the Manley farm. If he moved Pearce's men, an attack from that direction might penetrate far enough to threaten the rear of Sterling Price's Missouri State Guard as it struggled to gain Bloody Hill. In any case, Mc-Culloch made no major changes in their dispositions but went instead to check on the progress of McIntosh's force, which he had earlier sent to fight Plummer in Ray's cornfield.[8]

While moving toward his headquarters at the Winn farm, McCulloch encountered Lieutenant Colonel Hyams, who was near the Wire Road, rallying as many of the Third Louisiana as he could find. The Southerners who fought against Plummer in the Ray cornfield had become thoroughly disorganized in their flight from the Federal artillery fire. Hyams evidently informed McCulloch that, despite that retreat, the

Dr. Samuel H. Melcher, surgeon, who attended to Nathaniel Lyon's body (The collection of Dr. Tom and Karen Sweeney, General Sweeny's Museum, Republic, Missouri)

Southern right flank was secure. Free to concentrate on Sigel, and believing that there was not a moment to spare, McCulloch took command of the nearest two companies—the Pelican Rifles and the Iberville Grays—and started them across Wilson Creek. These were excellent troops. Because the Grays' commander was absent, both companies were under the Pelicans' own Captain John P. Vigilini, one of the most competent officers in the regiment. Sergeant Willie Tunnard recalled McCulloch encouraging them with the words, "Come, my brave lads, I have a battery for you to charge, and the day is ours!" Before leaving, McCulloch ordered Hyams to follow with the rest of the Louisianans as soon as possible. He also sent a messenger to McIntosh requesting all available support.[9]

Hyams meanwhile struggled to re-form the Moorehouse Guards and Moorehouse Fencibles, the Winn Rifles, the Shreveport Rangers, and the two companies bearing the name Pelican Rangers. As they were lining up, Sergeant T. G. Walcott joined them with a few men from his company, the Monticello Rifles, as did about seventy members of the Missouri State Guard under a Captain Johnson.[10] By the time they were ready to move out, McIntosh had arrived. He took charge of the column, hurrying it down the Wire Road. In retrospect, McIntosh might have done better to leave Hyams in command and remain behind to locate the missing portions of the Third Louisiana, which were still in the vicinity of the Ray farmhouse. But the wording of McCulloch's message to McIntosh apparently stressed speed rather than numbers. As a result, fewer than four hundred men made the march. Much to McIntosh's irritation, many of the Louisianans halted to fill their canteens from Wilson Creek. "The sun was now out bright and hot," Sergeant William Watson recalled, "and the dust and smoke were stifling." The men were so thirsty that they ignored the bodies of men and horses polluting the stream.[11]

When McCulloch led the two companies across Skegg's Branch, the Federal skirmishers near there retired as they approached. Returning to the plateau, they reported that "Lyon's men were coming up the road." This was a grave mistake, of course, but Dr. Melcher, who had wandered in that direction, brought apparent confirmation. "It was smoky, and objects at a distance could not be seen very distinctly," he observed. Nevertheless, when he saw "a body of men moving down the valley toward us," he rode back and informed Sigel that they appeared to be one of Lyon's regiments. He suggested that Sigel have the Stars and Stripes displayed conspicuously to avoid accidents.[12]

As both Dr. Melcher and the skirmishers withdrew from the "dead zone" in front of the Federal position without actually confirming the identity of the troops marching toward them, McCulloch was able to deploy not only his two companies but also all of the reinforcements under Hyams and McIntosh into line of battle without being observed. He was ably assisted by General Alexander Steen, drillmaster for the Missouri State Guard. Chronically ill, Steen was being "cupped" (a common medical procedure of the time) by one of the Missouri surgeons when the fighting began. Lacking a combat command, he probably spent some time reconnoitering Sigel's position, as he was able to assist McCulloch by leading the Third Louisiana into position for the attack.[13]

While deploying the troops, McCulloch probably became aware of activity on his right flank by the Missouri State Guard. In response to Sigel's fire on their rear, Lieutenant Colonel Thomas H. Rosser had assembled a force on the northern banks of Skegg's Branch. This consisted of his own First Infantry, the Fourth Infantry under Lieutenant Colonel Walter Scott O'Kane, and Captain Hiram M. Bledsoe's First Light Artillery, all of which were part of Rains's Division. Sigel failed to notice these men, who completed their alignment just as McCulloch was ready to attack.[14] McCulloch made no attempt to communicate with the Missourians or coordinate their actions with his own. Perhaps he believed that there was insufficient time to do so. In any case, he focused on positioning the Louisianans, whose assault he planned to lead in person. Like his foe Nathaniel Lyon, the former Texas Ranger forgot his responsibilities as an army commander. Caught up in the heat of battle, he concentrated on the placement of individual units. Tunnard noted McCulloch's complete coolness and intense concentration. "His actions and features were a study for the closest scrutinizer of physiognomy," the sergeant recalled. "Not a quiver on his face, not the movement of a muscle to betray anxiety or emotion. Only his grey eyes flashed forth from beneath his shaggy eyebrows a glittering, scrutinizing and penetrating glance."[15]

At the Sharp farm, Sigel took pains to avoid friendly fire casualties. He cautioned the artillerymen not to engage the troops that would soon appear in their front. Colonel Charles Salomon warned his unit, the Fifth Missouri, while Lieutenant Colonel Anslem Albert carried a similar message to both battalions of his command, the Third Missouri. As an extra precaution, one of the Union color-bearers advanced and waved the national flag. Finally, Sigel dispatched a soldier from the Third Missouri to walk down the Wire Road and challenge any approaching troops. Sigel recalled that the man was a "Corporal Tod," but records indicate he was Private Charles Todt of Company K.[16]

When Todt stepped into view, McCulloch ordered him to identify his unit. Todt obviously realized that he was facing the enemy, for after replying that he belonged to Sigel's Union forces, he aimed his musket at the Southern commander. But he was not quick enough. A bullet fired by Corporal Henry H. Gentles of the Pelican Rifles saved the general, dropping Todt "without a groan." McCulloch could hardly rebuke Gentles for firing without orders. "That was a good shot," he said simply and turned to Vigilini, who stood at his side. "Captain, take your men up and give them hell." McCulloch then moved to the left, passing the signal for the advance to the adjacent companies. When Lieutenant William A. Lacy of the Shreveport Rangers heard it, he leaped onto a log and waved his saber. "Come on, Caddo!" he shouted, his battle cry reminding his men that they represented Caddo Parish.[17]

McCulloch had apparently informed Vigilini that his men would be able to strike Sigel's exposed right flank, as the Federal line had been facing north when McCulloch last observed it. The captain exercised discretion, nevertheless. When his men neared the rim of the plateau, he halted them and moved forward with Tunnard to see what lay beyond. "I was much surprised," Vigilini recalled, "to find myself in front of and [within] about fifteen feet of the battery." Instead of a flank attack, the Louisianans faced the prospect of charging directly into the muzzles of four enemy guns. Vigilini demanded the artillerymen identify themselves. If he meant this as a ploy to buy time, Tunnard spoiled it, for the sergeant cried out, "Look at their Dutch faces." As the two Louisianans hastily withdrew, artillery fire erupted almost simultaneously from several directions.[18]

The Southern artillery actually fired first, for at this critical moment McCulloch received support from both the Arkansas State Troops and the Missouri State Guard. Throughout the early morning, Pearce had remained with Captain James Reid's Fort Smith Light Battery on a hill above the Arkansans' camps. He could not see the Sharp farm clearly, due in part to smoke drifting from the wagons burning in the fields, but he had no trouble detecting Sigel's arrival at the Wire Road. Yet he did not open fire with his own artillery, even when the Federals began shelling Bloody Hill. Indeed, for more than thirty minutes after Sigel came into view, Pearce did nothing at all. He later insisted that the distance prevented him from knowing whether the force was friend or foe, but his explanation is hardly creditable. He could have sent Carroll's Arkansas Cavalry Company to investigate, but these troops remained in a ravine. In any case, as the Southern army had neither infantry nor artillery at the Sharp farm prior to the battle, a force of such composition appearing there and firing on Bloody Hill could only be the enemy column that Southern fugitives had been reporting since shortly after dawn. Although McCulloch can be faulted for not making better use of the Arkansas State Troops, Pearce certainly did nothing to remind the army commander of their presence. He seems to have been content with a largely passive role.[19]

When Sigel's color-bearer waved the U.S. flag in front of the Union position, Pearce finally ordered the Fort Smith battery to commence firing. By coincidence, Reid's first shells exploded just as Vigilini and Tunnard scrambled back down the bank. Reid's fire actually imperiled the Louisianans, as his guns were shooting over their heads and they were only yards from the Federals. In fact, it was probably a fragment from one of the Arkansans' shells that wounded McCulloch's horse at this time. Within moments, and also by happenstance rather than by design, Bledsoe's First Light Artillery joined the fray and Rosser's Missouri State Guardsmen surged forward. As Bledsoe's three-gun battery was at an angle to McCulloch's attack, its projectiles posed less danger of accidentally harming friends. Two of the guns from Backof's Battery replied at once to the Southern onslaught.[20]

Battle having been joined, Vigilini quickly brought his two companies to the top of the plateau, where they fired into Sigel's men at almost point-blank range. The remaining companies of the Third Louisiana, together with the Missourians under Captain Johnson, arrived right afterward and fired as well. McCulloch's force was small, but he had concentrated superior power at the decisive point on the field. The Southern battle line was merely 400 yards long. But as a result of Sigel's inept troop dispositions, they faced in their immediate front only four Federal artillery pieces and 250 men of the Third Missouri, who together occupied a front of only about 300 yards. More than a third of these Federals, most of whom were poorly trained recruits, probably became casualties to Southern musketry and artillery fire at the beginning of the struggle.[21]

Because they had been cautioned not to shoot at approaching friends, many of Federals believed that they were victims of mistaken identity. Just before the firing erupted, Farrand rode over from his position on the right flank, waving an Arkansas flag discovered by his dragoons. It is unclear whether he intended to consult with Sigel or simply wanted to present a trophy to him. Some feared that the Federal artillery on Bloody Hill, seeing this enemy banner, had concluded that Sigel's men were Southerners. Melcher recalled, "The confusion was very great, many of the men saying 'It is *Totten's* battery! It is *Totten's* battery!'"[22] As neither army wore a standard color or style of uniform and Sigel's men expected to link up with Lyon's forces at some point, many also thought that the gray-clad Louisianans were members of the First Iowa, which possessed several companies wearing gray. Horrified by the apparent tragedy, Sigel lapsed into his native tongue, exclaiming "Sie haben gegen uns geschossen! Sie irrten sich!" or "They [are] firing against us; they [make] a mistake!"[23] Similar cries, expressed in English, "spread like wildfire" through the ranks. Sigel recalled that the resulting "consternation and frightful confusion" nearly defied description.[24]

Sigel did not remain mystified for long, but even after realizing that the men shooting at him were Southerners, there was little he could do to save the situation. Some Federal soldiers returned fire, but others refused, continuing to believe that they faced friends. Colonel Salomon added to the confusion by filling the air with curses in German, English, and French. Any hope of the Federals making a stand evaporated when Rosser's Missouri State Guard crested the plateau and struck their left. The Missourians had been forced to traverse rugged terrain on both sides of Skegg's Branch to reach the Sharp farm, but because of the gap Carr left between his cavalry and the Federal infantry they faced no other impediments. They were joined soon afterward by a portion of Lieutenant Colonel Dandridge McRae's undesignated battalion of Arkansas infantry. In response to McCulloch's orders, McRae had shifted his Confederates from their initial assignment, supporting Woodruff's Pulaski Light Battery, to join the assault on Sigel. During the movement a column of Southern horsemen cut across McRae's path, dividing his unit into two columns. As the larger, rearmost group was delayed, only about 75 of McRae's 220 men actually participated in the attack.[25]

Sigel exposed himself recklessly while attempting to rally his men, but the Federal brigade fell apart, despite the fact that it outnumbered its attackers three to one. The thin battle line crumbled and the survivors fled, abandoning the four guns and one of the caissons. Then this group of fugitives, led by three caissons driven at full gallop, ran into Sigel's undeployed reserves. Although more than seven hundred strong, the Fifth Missouri and the remaining battalion of the Third could not fire without hitting their comrades. They panicked, dissolving into a mob with escape as its single goal. The two guns from Backof's Battery that had been facing north barely had time to limber up and join the flight.[26]

It took the Southerners only a few minutes to gain complete control of the area around the Sharp house. The Louisianans quickly captured the four artillery pieces astride the Wire Road. One of these had been placed quite a distance to the rear of the others, perhaps so there was less of a gap between it and the two remaining guns facing north. The first Southerners to reach it were Corporal Henry H. Gentles, Corporal Thomas W. Hecox, and Private I. P. Hyams. A lone Union soldier, his name unknown, gave his life in a futile attempt to save the gun. At the same time, the left flank of the Southern line reached the northern border of Sharp's fields and began firing at the retreating enemy. It was soon joined by the companies that captured the battery. The Federals put up little resistance in their flight, although one of their parting shots mortally wounded Hecox. Unluckily, Reid's distant Fort Smith Battery mistook the rapidly advancing Louisianans for the enemy. Before the error was discovered, a shell exploded in the ranks of the Moorehouse Guards. Captain R. M. Hinson (the noblest gentleman and bravest soldier in the regiment, according to his commander) was killed as he cheered his men on. His brother-in-law, Private E. A. Whetstone, died at his side, and several others were wounded.[27]

Because of the continuing crisis on Bloody Hill, the Southerners did not make a coordinated pursuit of the Federals. When Pearce saw that a portion of the enemy was heading back toward the Dixon farm, he sent the Fourth Arkansas Infantry, commanded by Colonel Frank Rector, along the ridges overlooking Wilson Creek as a precaution. Joined by three companies from Colonel Tom Dockery's Fifth Arkansas Infantry, the force eventually occupied a position near the point where Sigel's guns had fired their first shots, but it saw no action. After the missing portion of McRae's Battalion reached the Sharp farm, its commander moved his men a short distance along the Wire Road in response to reports that the enemy had rallied. Finding no one, they returned and took no further part in the battle.[28]

Other Southern units moved more quickly, but the Federals proved hard to catch. Some simply scattered. Private Buegel and three comrades ran cross-country, making their way independently back to Springfield. But most retreated in groups. Sigel, part of the Third Missouri, one piece of artillery, and several wagons headed south on the road leading to the Dixon farm, returning the way the column had entered the battlefield. The other gun, additional wagons, and all but a handful of the remaining Federal infantry fled southwest along the Wire Road. Colonel Salomon was the highest-ranking officer among those who went in this direction. Because of their positions, the Federal horsemen on the flanks were the last to leave. While both followed the Wire Road, they did so separately.[29]

The Federals fleeing along the Wire Road fell into several groups. The first consisted of Colonel Salomon and the Fifth Infantry, which had not fired a shot and had probably suffered few casualties. These men, about four hundred strong, moved quickly out of harm's way, crossing a wooded hill and descending into a slight valley formed by an unnamed tributary of Terrell Creek. Here they encountered a Southern baggage train making its way toward the Western Army's camp in blissful ignorance of the day's events. At the sight of the Federals the wagoneers promptly wheeled about to make their escape. Fortunately for them, Salomon's infantry was not interested in pursuit. After climbing a small rise, the Federals halted at a farm owned by a family named Guinn. There they captured Dr. R. B. Smith, who identified himself as a surgeon from Rains's Division of the Missouri State Guard. His reason for being at the Guinn place is unknown, but after Dr. Melcher intervened he was released. The two physicians then rode back up the Wire Road, where they joined other doctors on the field, treating both Union and Southern casualties without regard to their affiliation. Salomon resumed his march after only the briefest pause. His group turned right onto the Little York Road and made its way to Springfield without incident.[30]

The second group departing via the Wire Road initially consisted of 150 "badly demoralized" infantry from both the Third and Fifth Missouri and one of the guns from Backof's Battery. They had not gone far before they were joined by Carr's cavalrymen. The captain had been ignorant of the disaster that had overtaken Sigel's brigade until a staff officer located him in the woods and ordered him to retreat. The dragoons lost no time in doing so, forming an impromptu rear guard for the infantry and gun. As they approached the Guinn farm, a volley tore into the column's flank from a bushy hillside on the right. This fire killed one of the wheelhorses drawing the gun and wounded another. In the ensuing confusion of tangled horses, the tongue of the limber drawing the gun broke. Carr's men returned fire, driving away the men who had ambushed them, but they decided to abandon the artillery. In their haste to get away, they passed by the junction of the Wire and Little York Roads. Instead of turning right toward Springfield, as Salomon had, they continued south.[31]

Farrand's dragoons were the final group to exit by way of the Wire Road. Dismounted behind the fences in Sharp's cornfield, they had watched helplessly as their comrades ran away. Although they were initially handicapped by their commander's absence, the real problem was their location. They were well placed to repel an attack against their front, but when danger appeared on their left they could not reposition themselves in time to affect the course of events. When Farrand returned, he ordered them to retreat. In some disorder, but ostensibly without panic, they crossed Sharp's fields and headed southwest into the woods. They went only about half a mile, just over the rise south of the Sharp farm. On the way Farrand encountered and forcibly detained A. D. Crenshaw, one of the civilians who had guided Sigel's brigade on its march to the battlefield. Farrand had no idea how to get back to Springfield in a westerly direction, and he had no desire to take chances.[32]

After gathering his horsemen and few stray Union soldiers who had also found safety in the woods, Farrand moved west until he reached the Wire Road. Almost immediately he discovered the artillery piece abandoned by Carr's group. After cutting the dead and wounded horses from the traces of the limber, Farrand moved on, taking the gun with him. In a short time, the faster-moving riders began to leave the infantry behind. Farrand apparently never considered deploying some of his dragoons as skirmishers for a rear guard. Instead, he rode ahead of the entire party, accompanied by three men. Near the Guinn farm they discovered a caisson fully stocked with ammunition. It had obviously been left behind because several of the horses were wounded. Farrand decided to salvage this as well. Removing the wounded horses proved to be a difficult task, probably because the pain-stricken animals were skittish and uncooperative. As his small party worked, the dragoons passed by and the infantry caught up. Farrand recalled that he "tried to prevail upon some of the Germans to assist us . . . but they would not stop." Perhaps they resented the fact that Farrand had done nothing to provide for their safety. In any case, Farrand eventually got the caisson under way, using "a pair of very small mules" that they probably stole from the Guinns. Soon the entire group turned right onto the Little York Road. It was almost to Springfield when some of the horses pulling the gun gave out. Farrand was forced to destroy the caisson and hitch its animals to the more valuable artillery piece. Once back in Springfield, he worked with Lieutenant Samuel Morris, an officer on Sigel's staff, to send wagons to the battlefield to remove the wounded.[33]

Sigel accompanied the members of the Third Missouri who sped down the road leading back toward the Dixon farm. This meant they passed across the rear of Farrand's dragoons while the dismounted horsemen were still in the northeastern corner of Sharp's fields. As some point, perhaps near the Dixon farm itself, Sigel halted and took stock of his situation. After organizing the remnant of his brigade, which consisted of some 250 men and one gun, into four makeshift companies, he proceeded west. The column, which also contained some wagons, apparently followed a farm road that ran in that direction from the Dixon place, meeting the Wire Road about two miles south of the Sharp farm. Here the Federals turned right, heading back toward the battlefield. They hoped to join the other, larger group of fugitives and return to Springfield via the Little York Road, which joined the Wire Road a mile ahead. After traveling only about half a mile, the Federals encountered Carr's party of men at Moody's Springs, where the Wire Road crossed Terrell Creek.[34]

When Carr stated that his group had been attacked during their flight, Sigel decided to retrace his steps. The now-enlarged column moved south, looking for a road running east that would take it to Springfield. "So we marched, or rather dragged along as fast as the exhausted men could go," Sigel later wrote. This time he took no chances with security. Carr "was instructed to remain in the advance, keeping his flankers out, and report whatever might occur in front." The artillery was positioned near the head of the infantry column, "the whole flanked on each side by skirmishers." They had gone no more than a mile and a half when good and bad fortune confronted them simultaneously. At the moment they reached the turnoff for a road back to Springfield, Carr's scouts spotted a large body of enemy cavalry farther down the Wire Road.[35]

Once the Federals turned left, safety lay in speed, yet Sigel did not redeploy Carr's cavalrymen as skirmishers at the crossroads to delay the enemy's pursuit. His reason for not doing so remains unknown. Carr not only retained the lead, he apparently concluded that the column was doomed and it would be better to save part of it than see it all die together. He refused to slow his horsemen to the pace of the tired infantry. His explanation, given in his later report, was astonishingly candid and self-centered. "Colonel Sigel asked me to march slowly, so that the infantry could keep up," Carr wrote. "I urged upon him that the enemy would try to cut us off in crossing Wilson's Creek, and that the infantry and artillery should at least march as fast as the ordinary walk of my horses. He assented, and told me to go on, which I did at a walk, and upon arriving at a creek I was much surprised and pained to find that he was not up." After watering his horses, Carr moved on. Although he paused again farther along the road, he sent no one back to investigate the fate of his comrades-in-arms. After waiting a few moments, he proceeded to Springfield.[36]

As one might imagine, Sigel was not pleased with Carr's actions. When the artillery and infantrymen finally reached the creek, they were surprised that Carr was not waiting for them. One company of infantry crossed without incident, but while the gun and caissons were in mid-passage, shots rang out from both banks. The Federals had lost the race.[37]

The Southerners' success in trapping Sigel came more from happenstance than design. When McCulloch witnessed the Federals' flight from the Sharp farm, his primary concern was for the baggage wagons that he knew were en route to the Western Army's camp. He therefore ordered Colonel Elkanah Greer to send two companies from his South Kansas–Texas Cavalry in pursuit. Greer selected Captain Hinchie P. Mabry's Deadshot Rangers and Captain Jonathan Russell's Cypress Guards. They were joined along the way by Lieutenant Colonel James Major with the Windsor Guards, a cavalry unit from Clark's Division of the Missouri State Guard. As senior officer present, Major took charge of the command, which numbered about three hundred men. They rode south along the Wire Road without incident until they saw, off in the distance, Sigel's men turning left to head back to Springfield.[38]

The Federals failed to detect Major's approach, as they were focused on the horsemen Carr had just discovered to the south. These were men from Colonel William Brown's Cavalry of Parsons's Division. It is not clear who gave them their assignment. Led by a Captain Staples, they numbered perhaps one hundred men and were divided into three groups. Staples had a cavalry battalion of his own, a Captain Alexander commanded another, and there was a battalion of mounted infantry under Captain Charles L. Crews. When the Federals first fled from the Sharp farm, Staples's force had pursued them, firing into Carr's flank and causing him to abandon his artillery piece. Instead of seizing the gun, Staples took his men through the woods, worked around Carr's flank, and finally blocked the Wire Road in his front. The Southerners naturally concluded that this action forced Sigel to detour to the east, when actually the Federals had been seeking a route in that direction all along. After the

Federals left the Wire Road, Staples's men began to ride around their flank once more, while Major's command closed on their rear. Although Carr managed to cross Wilson Creek safely near its junction with the James River, Staples reached the ford before Sigel and set up an ambush.[39]

The fight that ensued was brief but decisive. The odds were even—about 400 men on each side—but the demoralized Federals were caught by surprise for the second time that day. Staples's fire pinned them down at the ford. When Major's men arrived moments later and charged, the Federals scattered. Most fled toward Springfield, and a running fight developed that covered three miles of ground. There were many acts of individual courage, for Major himself testified that "General Sigel and his men fought with desperation." The outcome was never in doubt, however, and the Federals who escaped did so individually. Many were rounded up throughout the day, as the Southerners scoured the countryside for fugitives. Together, Major and Staples took 147 prisoners, including Lieutenant Colonel Anslem Albert. They also captured several wagons, the gun from Backof's Battery, and the colors of the Third Missouri. They reported finding 64 enemy bodies, but the actual total was probably higher. For example, 4 Union soldiers were discovered nearby at Nowlan's Mill, hiding in the space where the water rushed over the mill dam. When they refused to come out, they were blasted with shotguns. Southern losses were negligible.[40]

The Southerners last saw Sigel when he dashed into a field and disappeared among the rows of corn. At some point during the fight Sigel had decided that discretion was the better part of valor. Before galloping off, he concealed his rank by wrapping a wool blanket about his shoulders. He and another soldier were chased for six miles before they eluded their pursuers. Sigel had a good horse and he was probably the first non-wounded soldier who fought at Wilson's Creek to return to Springfield.[41]

Chapter 17 . . . .

Pandemonium Turned Loose

The lull that began following the failure of the first Southern assault on Bloody Hill lasted between thirty and forty-five minutes, until nearly 9:00 A.M. During this time Nathaniel Lyon made only one significant adjustment to his line. He moved Captain Frederick Steele's battalion of Regulars and Captain Charles Gilbert's command (Company B, First U.S. Infantry of Captain Joseph Plummer's battalion) from the vicinity of Du Bois's Battery to support Totten's guns. The remainder of Plummer's battalion, now commanded by Captain Arch Houston as Plummer had been wounded, constituted Lyon's only significant reserve, as every infantry unit was now in line of battle. Even the 21-man detachment of the Thirteenth Illinois Infantry participated, joining the Iowans at one point and fighting with them as a unit. (The earlier and later battle positions of the Illinois soldiers are unknown.) Altogether, Lyon had approximately 3,500 men and ten pieces of artillery positioned to meet the next attack. Lieutenant Colonel William Merritt's First Iowa held the left flank, with several companies deployed as skirmishers. Du Bois's Battery was to their right. A considerable space probably existed between Du Bois's position and Totten's Battery, with four guns, which was farther to the front and right. Steele's and Gilbert's Regulars guarded Totten's left. The First Kansas, with Major John Halderman substituting for the wounded Colonel George Deitzler, was just to the right of the guns. Continuing to the right were Lieutenant Colonel George Andrews's First Missouri, Colonel Robert Mitchell's Second Kansas, and Major Peter Osterhaus's Second Missouri. On the far right Lieutenant George Sokalski had two guns that had been detached from Totten's Battery to operate independently.[1]

By this point, the Federals on Bloody Hill had been engaged for a total of four hours. Individual soldiers reacted differently to the experience, of course. Private Charles Harrison of the First Kansas nervously questioned a well-educated comrade about famous battles in history, as "he wanted to know how long a battle could last as severe as this one was proving."[2] Perhaps Harrison felt some sort of premonition, as he did not survive the day. Others grew almost calm. Private Eugene Ware of the First Iowa recalled how the Southern long-range artillery fire, so disturbing initially, lost much of its terror:

> We all lay down on the ground, and for some time the shells, round shot and canister were playing closely over our heads. . . . Our company did not have much to do for a while in the way of shooting; we simply laid down on the ridge and watched the battery in front of us, or sat up or kneeled down. When we saw the puff of the artillery we dodged and went down flat, and in the course of fifteen minutes gained so much confidence that we felt no hesitation in walking around and seeing what we could see, knowing that we could dodge artillery ammunition.[3]

Ware wrote long after the war. He erred in stating that the Southerners fired canister at long range, but otherwise his memory appears to be accurate. It is confirmed by a contemporary letter from a member of the Second Kansas, who regarding long-range artillery fire noted: "Their batteries didn't do any good at all. I don't believe they killed ten men during the whole day with their batteries while ours mowed them down in scores."[4] Like many soldiers, the Kansan vastly overestimated the damage his own side did to the enemy. In actuality, both Federal and Southern batteries tended to overshoot their targets at long range.

When the Southern line of battle emerged for a second time from the cover of trees, thick brush, and prairie grass, the Federals opened fire. Combat continued with sporadic intensity for the next hour, until approximately 10:00 A.M. According to Major Samuel Sturgis, the fighting became "almost inconceivably fierce along the entire line." Some of the Southern units were in formations three or four ranks deep. Once they had closed to within range, the first rank would lie down while the second rank knelt. The third (and sometimes fourth rank) would remain standing, and all ranks would fire together. But disciplined fire usually did not exist beyond the first or second volley. A number of the Southerners opposite Totten's position were able to advance in the cover provided by a ravine, breaking into the open only thirty or forty yards from the guns. The Federal artillerymen responded valiantly, driving the enemy back by blasts of canister. It was probably at this point that the battery suffered its first casualties. Private Joseph Keyes, a twenty-eight-year-old native of Ireland who was a stonecutter before joining the army in January 1861, fell with a gunshot to his chest and buckshot in his arm. Corporal Lorenzo D. Immell and Privates James Wallace, James H. Crosby, and Cyrus H. Young were soon injured as well, two of them by buckshot. The range of combat was obviously very close.[5]

Totten's Battery continued to function as others took their places, but the Federal line remained vulnerable. Consequently, Lyon ordered the First Iowa, which was on the far left with only skirmishers engaged, to move right and support the First Kansas and First Missouri. As the "greyhounds" took up a position between the two regiments under the general's watchful eye, Colonel Andrews took the opportunity to ask Lyon if he had heard anything from Sigel. Lyon simply shook his head.[6]

Early in the fight, Lyon dismounted from his dapple-gray horse and directed the battle on foot. As he walked close to the front line a bullet grazed his right calf. Though not serious, the injury was painful and required treatment to stop the flow of blood. Shortly thereafter Lyon's mount was shot while he held its reins. The animal sank to its haunches and died. Although the August heat was intense, Lyon kept his worn captain's frock coat buttoned up to the neck. As he limped along, waving his hat and sword to encourage his troops, he suffered a second wound when a bullet brushed the right side of his head. Blood trickled down his face and matted his hair and beard. Pale and dazed, he moved to the rear, found a relatively safe spot, and sat down. An officer appeared, produced a handkerchief, and tied it around the general's head. Totten also came over and offered Lyon a swig of brandy, but he declined it. The party was soon joined by the chief of staff, John Schofield. "Major, I am afraid the day is lost," Lyon said. Schofield replied, "No, General; let us try it again." Encouraged by Schofield's enthusiasm, Lyon decided to continue the fight.[7]

Major Samuel Sturgis, who was nearby, directed one of his orderlies to dismount and offer his horse to the general. Although Lyon initially refused it, the horse remained with him and he soon mounted to deal with problems at the Federal center. In the confusion of battle, the First Missouri and the First Iowa had become misaligned, the left flank of the Missourians overlapping the right flank of the Iowans. The Iowans moved forward just as the Kansans fell back in confusion under the pressure of enemy fire. As a result, the lines became entangled and two companies of the First Iowa, the Muscatine Grays and the Mt. Pleasant Grays, became separated from their regiment. Merritt commanded the whole First Iowa to fall back, leaving a gap in the Federal line between his unit and the

Major Samuel Davis Sturgis, First U.S. Cavalry (The collection of Dr. Tom and Karen Sweeney, General Sweeny's Museum, Republic, Missouri)

Missourians. Amid the noise of battle, the Iowa companies that had become detached failed to hear the order. Merritt therefore rode over to them and was guiding them to the rear when a Southern unit approached. With an about-face and a quick volley, the Iowans sent the enemy reeling. Ordering the men to hold their position, Merritt then hastened toward the rest of the regiment, which he had left leaderless. He found it advancing, as Lyon had arrived to deal with the crisis.[8]

Followed by his aide, Lieutenant William M. Wherry, and six to eight orderlies, Lyon rode past the right end of the First Iowa's line into the recently created gap. After going a short distance, they observed a portion of the enemy's infantry to the left. A group of horsemen riding in front of this formation included two figures who appeared to be Sterling Price, commander of the Missouri State Guard, and one of his subordinates, Major Emmett McDonald. Given Lyon's obsession with punishing his enemies, nothing would have been more satisfying than personal combat. Starting toward the horsemen, he ordered his escort to "draw pistols and follow." Wherry's cooler head prevailed. He convinced Lyon that the attempt would be too dangerous and suggested instead that some troops be brought forward.[9]

During Lyon's reconnaissance Sturgis rallied the main portion of the First Iowa in Merritt's absence. When Lyon returned to his lines, the Iowans called for the general to lead them. Although his aides asked him

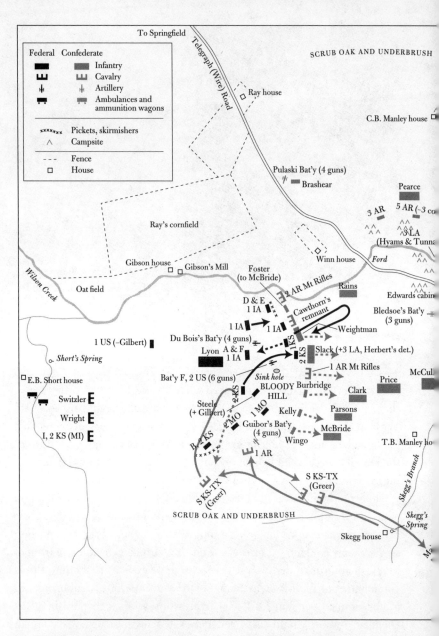

Bloody Hill, 8:45 A.M. to 10:00 A.M.

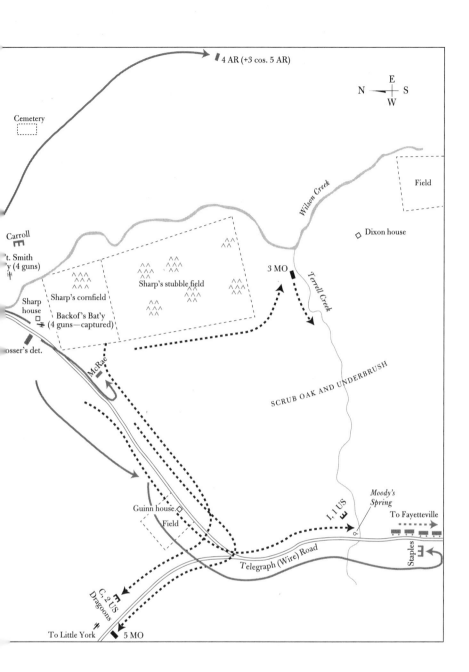

4 AR (+3 cos. 5 AR)

N E S W

Cemetery

Field

Wilson Creek

Dixon house

Carroll

t. Smith
y (4 guns)

3 MO

Terrell Creek

Sharp
house

Sharp's stubble field

Sharp's cornfield

Backof's Bat'y
(4 guns—captured)

osser's det.

McRae

SCRUB OAK AND UNDERBRUSH

Moody's
Spring

To Fayetteville

Guinn house

Field

I, 1 US

Staples

Telegraph (Wire) Road

C, 2 US
Dragoons

To Little York   5 MO

not to expose himself, Lyon replied, "I am but doing my duty." He believed that his last opportunity to win the battle was to lead a new assault. When Sweeny came up, Lyon directed him to take charge of the Iowans. He then pulled the Second Kansas out of line, moving the men in column behind the First Missouri and into the gap.[10]

Colonel Mitchell was beside Lyon as they advanced. Riding with the reins in his left hand, Lyon turned back to his right. Waving his hat in his right hand, he called out, "Come on my brave boys, I will lead you forward!" At that moment a volley exploded from the thick undergrowth to the front, striking Lyon, Mitchell, and others around them. A large-caliber bullet tore into the left side of Lyon's chest below the fourth rib, passed through both lungs and the heart, and exited just below the right shoulder blade. He attempted to dismount but began to fall from the saddle. Private Albert Lehmann, the general's personal aide, was himself able to dismount just in time to catch Lyon as he collapsed. Resting Lyon's head against his shoulder, the orderly tried to stop the rapid flow of blood. The general gasped for air, then looked at Lehmann and whispered hoarsely, "Lehmann, I am going." With these words, the first Union general officer to be killed in battle in the Civil War died.[11]

The musketry that ended Lyon's personal "punitive crusade" came so unexpectedly that some of the Kansans described it as an ambush. "It seemed as if the entire line, about three hundred yards, was fringed with a perfect blaze of fire and smoke, and the bullets rattled around us, and through out ranks, like hail," a Leavenworth soldier recalled. The lead company under Captain William Tholen fired one volley, then "broke into confusion," disordering the ranks behind them. Their panic was short lived, for the Kansans were soon fully deployed into line, standing "firm as rocks" and giving punishment as good as they had received. Captain Samuel J. Crawford, commander of the Kansas Guards from Anderson County and a future governor of the state, remembered, "We fired over Lyon's body, and three or four of Captain Tholen's men, as they lay wounded."[12]

The same volley that had cut down Lyon seriously wounded the commander of the Second Kansas. One musket ball passed through Mitchell's calf and another through his thigh, yet he remained in the saddle for some time. The combat was so close that at one point he struck a Southerner with his saber. He tried to shoot another with his pistol, but it misfired. Eventually, he was compelled to seek medical attention. After withdrawing to a field hospital behind the crest of Bloody Hill, Mitchell ordered Lieutenant Colonel Charles Blair to "take command and fight the regiment to the best of his ability." Blair assured him that he would not

Brigadier General Mosby Monroe Parsons, commander of the Sixth Division, Missouri State Guard. This photograph was taken after he was commissioned a brigadier general in the Confederate army in 1862. (The collection of Dr. Tom and Karen Sweeney, General Sweeny's Museum, Republic, Missouri)

"disgrace you or the State." Blair and the regiment's acting adjutant, Lieutenant Edward Lines, had lost their horses in the initial volley, but they found other mounts. A member of the Emporia Guards recalled how both officers "behaved with cool bravery." Although "constantly exposed to a raking fire," they "rode along the line, directing and encouraging the boys."[13]

The combat continued for some time before the Southerners on this portion of Bloody Hill broke off their attack. Their retreat allowed the two separated companies of the First Iowa to rejoin their regiment. During the lull that followed, Lieutenant Gustavus Schreyer and a detachment of men retrieved the dead and wounded. Corporal Marsh E. Spurlock and Private Andrew Kepler of the Emporia Guards carried Lyon's body to the rear, accompanied by a weeping Lehmann. Wherry arrived on the scene just as Lyon's remains were being removed. Fearing that news of the general's death might affect the men, he decided to conceal the fact for as long as possible. After quieting Lehmann, he had Lyon's body, with limbs composed and coattail pulled over the face, placed under the shade of a small blackjack oak, in a sheltered spot not far from Du Bois's guns. Someone had summoned a doctor right after Lyon was hit, but by the time Surgeon Florence M. Cornyn of the First Missouri arrived there was nothing he could do. His examination revealed that the aorta had been struck. No medical procedure could have saved the Connecticut Yankee. Meanwhile, Wherry located Schofield and informed him of Lyon's death.

Schofield realized that command would devolve upon Sturgis, as the senior Regular army officer with the forces on Bloody Hill. He therefore set out in search of Sturgis to appraise him of his new responsibility.[14]

The Southern advance that resulted in Lyon's death cost the Missouri State Guard one of its finest officers, Colonel Richard Weightman. Perhaps because of the need to skirt a thicket, he was leading his men forward in a column rather than a line when they made contact with the Federals. Struck three times, his wounds were mortal, but he took the sound of his men's cheers as they continued to advance as evidence of Southern victory. "Thank God!" he whispered and died. After carrying Weightman's body from the field, his men passed their commander's sword to Colonel John Hughes, who preserved it for Weightman's family. Such rituals were important assertions that honor had been maintained and that a man's reputation transcended his death.[15]

Weightman had not fought alone, of course. His movement was part of Price's second attempt to storm Bloody Hill, and to ensure its success "Old Pap" had sent his adjutant, Colonel Thomas Snead, in search of the Southern army's commander, Ben McCulloch. Snead found McCulloch at approximately 8:45 A.M. at the Sharp farm, where the Southerners were still jubilantly celebrating their decisive victory over the Federal column under Franz Sigel. According to one account, Snead informed McCulloch that the Missouri State Guard was "sorely pressed" and would not be able to hold without immediate assistance. The Texan promptly sent messengers to various subordinates, including Bart Pearce, commander of the Arkansas State Troops, in an effort to focus all available forces against Lyon's men. He directed Lieutenant Colonel Samuel Hyams's battalion of the Third Louisiana in person. As the fatigued Louisianans moved into column formation to advance up the Wire Road, "Old Ben" called out words of encouragement. "You have beaten the enemy's right and left wings, only their centre is left, and with all our forces concentrated upon that we will soon make short work of it," he declared.[16]

The work turned out to be anything but short, as men such as Colonel Elkanah Greer could testify. A message from McCulloch reached the commander of the South Kansas–Texas Cavalry, instructing him to turn the enemy's right flank. Greer still had only half of the regiment under his command, having never located the troops that had become separated from him during their flight from Sigel's dawn bombardment. Held in support throughout the morning, the Texans were eager to accomplish something. They were consequently enthusiastic as Greer marched the battalion, which numbered about four hundred, west on a narrow track that ran along the northern side of Skegg's Branch. As they passed behind Price's infantry, Bugler A. B. Blocker of the Texas Hunters company noted that the Missourians were firing as fast as possible. In response, the Federals "were pouring volley after volley at them, and it seemed that a perfect sheet of bullets were passing over our heads." The sixteen-year-old wrote that the "rattle and crash of the musketry" combined with the artillery, which was "bellowing forth along the entire line," reached a deafening level. It "sounded like pandemonium turned loose."[17]

Before reaching the left end of the Southern line, Greer met Colonel DeRosey Carroll and his 350-man First Arkansas Cavalry. Greer directed Carroll to join him, thereby nearly doubling the size of the striking force. Once they arrived at Skegg's Spring, the column turned into a large ravine located well beyond the Union right flank. This defile provided excellent cover. After reaching its head, Greer ordered the First Arkansas to swing right and deploy into line, while his Texans continued to probe forward. Looking east, the colonel saw that the struggle on the slopes of Bloody Hill remained a "very fierce and hotly contested." Believing that the enemy's flank and rear were vulnerable and that there was not a moment to spare, he ordered an immediate charge. This was a poor decision. Because Greer failed to notify Carroll of his intent, the Arkansas cavalry did not advance simultaneously. Worse still, Greer did not even take time to deploy his force properly or communicate with his captains. As a result, no more than three of the five companies of horsemen actually made the charge.[18]

It was a courageous effort, nevertheless. The Texans did not carry sabers, so Greer shouted, "Draw your pistols, men, and charge!" Blocker left a vivid account of what followed: "With a yell, we went toward that line of blue, like the wind. . . . On we went—pouring lead into the blue line that was standing there 50 yards in front of us, with fixed bayonets, prepared to receive cavalry. The next moment that blue line was a mass of running, stampeding soldiers trying to get out of the way of that mass of horses and men that were bearing down on them."[19]

Had Greer made a coordinated attack with 750 men rather than three companies that probably numbered no more than 240 men, his action might have posed a major threat to the Federals. As it turned out, the panic he caused was not extensive. Indeed, it is uncertain which Federal unit fled, as commanders are usually loath to mention precipitous retreats in their reports. Even so, the Federals were not as vulnerable as Greer assumed when he ordered his men forward, for they soon recovered and fought back effectively. Captain Samuel Wood's Kansas Rangers (the mounted company of the Second Kansas Infantry) and the Home Guard units of Captains Clark W. Wright and T. A. Switzler were in the rear. Some or all of these men immediately positioned themselves to fire on Greer's right flank as the Texans advanced. More important, shortly before the incident Lyon had ordered Captain James R. McClure's company of the Second Kansas deployed as skirmishers to protect the far right of the Union position. If McClure's men were the frightened fugitives Blocker described, they recovered their fortitude in short order. They sent several volleys into the Texans, causing their first losses of the battle. Worse was to come. Du Bois pivoted his entire battery to fire on the Southerners, while Totten spun several of his guns around to face the danger. Together, they drove Greer's men off "with ease." In fact, Totten later wrote contemptuously: "This was the only demonstration made by their cavalry, and it was so *effete* and ineffectual in its force and character as to deserve only appellation of child's play. Their cavalry is utterly worthless on the battle-field." The remark is harsh, but in fact Greer bungled the attack. Although the Federal rear was hardly wide open, the Texas commander squandered one of the most significant Southern opportunities of the battle. His men were lucky to suffer no more than two dozen casualties. How many they inflicted in return is unknown.[20]

Although left on its own by Greer, Carroll's First Arkansas Cavalry advanced when it saw what the Texans were doing. The cavalrymen's forward movement coincided with Totten's repositioning of guns to meet Greer. Carroll misinterpreted this development, believing that his men's fire had caused the Union artillery to abandon its position. Because the Arkansans possessed on average only eight rounds per man for their short-range weapons, they retreated after a short time. They rejoined Greer and eventually took up a position to support the left flank of the Southern line.[21]

Except for Greer's movement, the remainder of the second Southern attack was tactically straightforward, marked by courage and tenacity rather than brilliance. Price struggled valiantly to coordinate the assault, moving so close to the front that his soldiers begged him to withdraw to safety. As he was wearing a long white linen duster and a plain white felt hat, the commander of the Missouri State Guard looked more like a farmer than a military man. Several bullets struck his clothing and one finally grazed his side. Turning to an officer near him, the portly general joked calmly, "That isn't fair; if I were as slim as Lyon that fellow would have missed me entirely." Although painful the wound was not threatening, and Price did not seek medical attention until the fighting ended.[22]

Private Henry Cheavens was not as fortunate as Price. The school-teacher-turned-soldier was a member of Clark's Division, but he fell in with McBride's men after becoming separated from his own company during the confusion created by Lyon's surprise attack. While on his knees loading his Mississippi rifle, a spent ball struck his canteen, "bending it up." Then a piece of canister slammed into his right thigh, breaking his femur. Cheavens wrote that he felt no pain but "heard its *chug* as it buried itself in the flesh, felt it strike the bone, but it deadened the flesh for several inches around." A short time later his comrades fell back and left him between the lines. As bullets and artillery rounds passed close overhead, he took the strap from his canteen and ramrod from his rifle to make a tourniquet above the wound. He lay in the open for about fifteen minutes, then crawled to the safety and shade of a tree, where he remained until the battle's end.[23]

As had been the case during previous assaults, several factors negated much of the advantage the Missouri State Guard should have enjoyed from superior numbers. Due to the difficult terrain and their minimal training in the basic maneuvers of linear tactics, units rarely advanced simultaneously, despite Price's heroic attempts to preserve their alignment. Because ammunition was scarce, the Southerners had to close right up to the enemy before opening fire. As a result, this phase of combat, which lasted about an hour, was characterized not so much by a grand assault as by a series of jerky forward movements. The State Guard crept up Bloody Hill with company-sized bodies of men probing forward like tentacles of a wary octopus. Once contact was made, the Southerners almost always fell prone at the enemy's first fire. Those on the receiving end of the Federal artillery's shell or canister usually halted for good, allowing the men on their flanks to move ahead without them. One Missouri soldier described the enemy's close-range artillery fire as particularly unnerving. He wrote that some men, "unused to large reports," made a particular effort to shoot the Federal gunners, screaming with each shot "damn you, how do you like that?" It was a battle fought mainly on the company level, and few Southern companies actually fired their weapons for as long as twenty consecutive minutes before either retreating or going over to the defensive. Thus when Greer's flank attack distracted the Federals, Price used the opportunity to withdraw his troops for another reorganization.[24]

During the Southern assault, the Union forces apparently suffered little from the lack of direction caused by Lyon's death. It took Schofield about thirty minutes to find Sturgis and inform him of the situation. Sturgis was dismayed and not just because of his affection and respect for his departed commander. "The responsibility which rested upon me was duly felt and appreciated," he recalled. Fortunately, just about the time Sturgis inherited the top position, Price began withdrawing his troops. This gave the new Union commander some time to assess the situation. Although Federals had been able to drive off two assaults and still held the high ground, they were somewhat "scattered and broken" as a consequence. Moreover, Sturgis believed that the enemy possessed 20,000 men. The weary Federals had not eaten since leaving Springfield approximately fifteen hours earlier. Canteens were dry, and as the morning wore on the August sun burned hotter and hotter. Ammunition was running low, and no one knew the fate or status of Sigel's column. Consequently, Sturgis concluded that the only remaining chance of success lay in Sigel's ability to launch a substantial attack on the Confederate right flank and rear. Should this occur, the Federals on Bloody Hill might retake the offensive. Otherwise, the only recourse was retreat.[25]

Sturgis did not reach these conclusions on his own. The new commander called together as many senior officers as possible for a brief council of war. The consensus was that if Sigel did not appear soon, they must retreat, if possible. The meeting came to an abrupt conclusion when the officers observed a large column of infantry moving down a hill on the eastern side of Wilson Creek. These troops were coming from the same direction as had the cannon fire heard early that morning, believed to have been from Sigel's attack. In addition, some members of the approaching infantry wore gray uniforms similar to those in Sigel's column and they appeared to be carrying an American flag. As a consequence, spirits rose, and Sturgis issued orders for the Federals on Bloody Hill to prepare for an advance and to join forces with the approaching column.[26]

Sturgis also made several adjustments in his line of battle. Osterhaus's Second Missouri battalion marched from the right end of the line to the left, taking up a position in support of Du Bois's Battery. The First Missouri shared this assignment, but its commander, Andrews, had finally been forced by his wounds to relinquish his role. Captain Theodore Yates now led the regiment, which had been severely depleted by heavy casualties, including almost half of the officers. By this point in the battle the unit had dropped from its original strength of 775 men to perhaps 550, a testament to both the ferocity of the struggle and the soldiers' fortitude. Taken together, the two Missouri regiments and the Regular Army gunners under Du Bois formed a firm anchor for the Union left flank. To compensate for the weakness these changes made on the right flank,

Sturgis split up the First Kansas. Six companies of the regiment remained in the center, in between Totten's four guns and the First Iowa. Four companies shifted to the right. Captain Powell Clayton's Leavenworth Light Infantry formed on the left of the Second Kansas (also strengthened by the return of McClure's detached company). Captain William Roberts's Wyandotte Volunteers, Captain Samuel Walker's Scott's Guards, and Captain Gustavus Zesch's Steuben Guards took up a position adjacent to Sokalski's two guns. They now constituted the far right of the Federal battle line.[27]

While Sturgis looked to his alignment, Price, at the base of Bloody Hill, prepared for what would be the largest assault yet. The Missouri State Guard commander sent a staff officer, Captain Colton Greene, for reinforcements from Pearce's heretofore largely inactive Arkansas State Troops. Up to this point Colonel Jonathan Walker's Fourth Arkansas Infantry and Colonel Tom Dockery's Fifth Arkansas Infantry had held a position on the eastern side of Wilson Creek, on the plateau that ran opposite the mouth of Skegg's Branch, overlooking the ford of the Wire Road. These units, bolstered by Captain John Reid's Fort Smith Battery, guarded the approach on the Southern rear from the southeast. At the plateau's northern end, Colonel John Gratiot's Third Arkansas provided support for Captain William Woodruff's Pulaski Light Battery, which had shifted from its original placement near the Winn farm. The Second Infantry from Weightman's Brigade of Rains's Division, led by Major Ezra H. Brashear, also supported the artillery.[28]

After Sigel's flanking column was routed, Pearce sent the Fourth Infantry and three companies of the Fifth to occupy the same high ground from which Sigel had opened fire with his artillery at the beginning of the battle. John H. Rivers, a member of the Fifth's Centerpoint Rifles, described what these soldiers witnessed from this commanding location:

> Oh, it was pretty to see the whole of the Battle as We saw it, with the advantage of Our high position. . . . Churchills Camps were . . . on fire: Tents, and wagons, with mules tied to them . . . would pull back on the halters, and bray, and seem to beg for mercy: But the halters would have to burn into, or break, or they would have to stand there, and burn to-death: I saw mules burning, and pulling on their halters, til finally they would have to just give up, and sink to the ground, and die: Some times they would get loose, by the halters burning into, and they would start off with fire all over them.[29]

Throughout the morning Pearce remained at his command post adjacent to the Fort Smith Battery. Around 10:00 A.M. Colonel James McIntosh, McCulloch's adjutant and de facto commander of his Confederate troops, brought word that the Southern line on Bloody Hill was being hard pressed by Lyon's force and needed reinforcements. Following closely on the colonel's heels, Captain Greene raced up with a similar report. As the Southern rear was now secure, Pearce directed McIntosh to lead both the battery and the Fifth Arkansas's seven companies to the Missouri State Guard's aid. Pearce then rode to the northern end of the plateau, where the Third Arkansas, Brashear's Second Infantry, and the Pulaski Battery still guarded the Wire Road. No threat had developed in that direction since the fight in John Ray's cornfield, but he did not want to leave the road unguarded. Leaving Woodruff and Brashear in place, Pearce ordered Gratiot's regiment to join the column dispatched to help Price.[30]

Pearce led the reinforcements in person across the ford of Wilson Creek. This was the column that Sturgis and his officers had observed during their meeting and mistook for elements of Sigel's command. At a distance the Stars and Bars on the Confederate national flags carried by the Arkansas State Troops were easily mistaken for the Stars and Stripes. An eerie lull following the cessation of the second Southern assault pervaded the field as Pearce led his men toward Bloody Hill. When they approached the base, Price rode up. The Missourian welcomed their arrival. As Gratiot had served under him in the Mexican War, he asked the Third Arkansas to form on the crucial far left to extend the flank of Colonel Edmond Wingo's Infantry from McBride's Division. While leading them into place, Price offered words of encouragement. "You will soon be in a pretty tight place," he said, "but I will be near you, and I will take care of you; keep as cool as the inside of a cucumber and give them thunder." Then the general turned to Gratiot and added: "That is your position, colonel; take it and hold it whatever you do. I will see that you are not too hard-pressed. Don't yield an inch."[31]

Prior to the arrival of Pearce's soldiers, McCulloch and Price had made several adjustments to the Southern lines. As the separate battalions of the Third Louisiana were now reunited, McCulloch instructed Colonel Louis Hébert to move beyond Price's left flank, advance up Bloody Hill, turn the Federal right, and take Totten's guns. In response to a false report that enemy cavalry located beyond the Ray farm were preparing to attack down the Wire Road, the Texan had the Second Arkansas Mounted Rifles take up a position guarding the Wilson Creek ford. Since fighting in Ray's cornfield earlier that morning, the Arkansans had fallen in beside

Colonel J. A. Foster's Infantry of McBride's Division. The dismounted troopers left the struggle on Bloody Hill and spent the remainder of the battle waiting for an attack that never came.[32]

Meanwhile, Price had strengthened his position by shifting to the center both the Missouri Light Artillery (Lieutenant William Barlow substituting for the missing Henry Guibor) and the infantry of Parsons's Division that had been supporting it. They took up a position between Slack's and Clark's Divisions. Once in place, Barlow found himself within musket range of an unidentified Federal unit. Fearing for the battery's safety, he trained his guns on this force and prepared to open fire, but halted when fellow officers informed him that the troops to his front were Southerners. While Barlow held his fire, the State Guard infantry of both Clark's and Slack's Divisions began to advance. Within moments the Federal batteries on the crest opened up. Now certain that he was facing the enemy, Barlow added the weight of his four guns to the battle. The lull was over.[33]

To Barlow's left, the Third Arkansas initially advanced in column of fours, but Gratiot soon deployed them into line. Their movement ceased abruptly when they encountered enemy infantry both to their front and on their left flank. They also came under enfilade fire from artillery to their left. "So terrible was this fire," Gratiot reported, "that my regiment was obliged to lie down, and then commenced firing from that position." This fire stopped the assault. In about thirty minutes the unit suffered 110 casualties out of 571 effectives. Some of the losses came from the indiscriminate fire of Price's Missourians located to the Arkansans' rear.[34]

The unit that the Arkansans could not at first identify was the Governor's Guards of the First Kansas, which had been placed in advance of the regiment. When their commander, Captain Bernard P. Chenoweth, observed the Southerners' approach, he sent word to Totten, requesting support. In response, Totten temporarily repositioned Sokalski's section of guns to provide assistance. The young Polish American's conduct had already won Totten's admiration, who later wrote, "No officer ever behaved better under as trying circumstances as he found himself surrounded by at times during the day."[35]

Shortly after Gratiot had started his advance, McIntosh placed the seven companies of the Fifth Arkansas into line on the right of the Third, while Reid's Fort Smith Battery moved into position on the left of Barlow's Missouri Light Artillery. Overall, the Arkansas State Troops brought about one thousand fresh men into the struggle. As Gratiot's regiment advanced, the much-fatigued Missourians of the State Guard and the Confederate soldiers in Churchill's First Arkansas Mounted Ri-

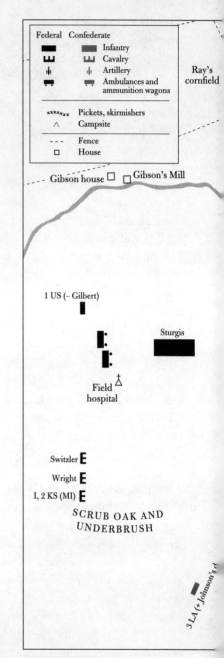

Federal   Confederate

▬▬   ▭   Infantry

⊔   ⊔   Cavalry

⊪   ⊪   Artillery

▬   ▬   Ambulances and
ammunition wagons

××××××××   Pickets, skirmishers
∧   Campsite

---   Fence
□   House

Ray's
cornfield

Gibson house □   □ Gibson's Mill

1 US (– Gilbert) ▮

Sturgis

Field ⚐
hospital

Switzler **E**

Wright **E**

I, 2 KS (MI) **E**

SCRUB OAK AND
UNDERBRUSH

3 LA (+ Johnson's d

Bloody Hill, 10:00 A.M. to 11:30 A.M.

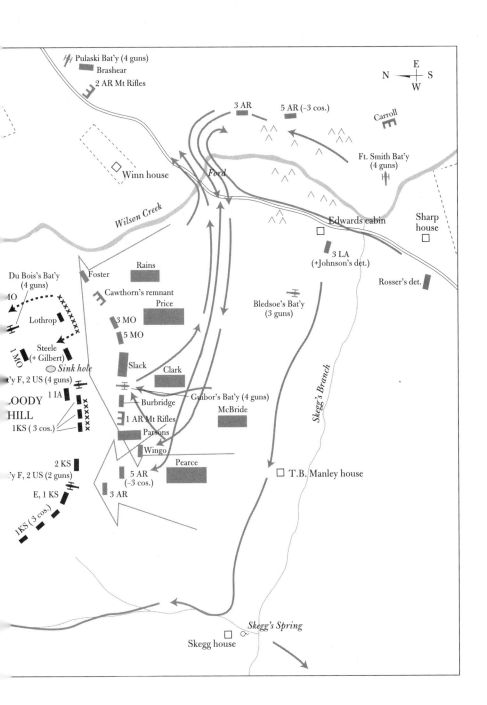

Pulaski Bat'y (4 guns)
Brashear
2 AR Mt Rifles

3 AR   5 AR (–3 cos.)   Carroll

Ft. Smith Bat'y
(4 guns)

Winn house   Ford

Wilson Creek   Edwards cabin   Sharp
house

3 LA
(+Johnson's det.)

Du Bois's Bat'y   Foster   Rains   Rosser's det.
(4 guns)
MO   Cawthorn's remnant
Price
Lothrop   Bledsoe's Bat'y
(3 guns)
3 MO
Steele   5 MO
(+ Gilbert)
Sink hole   Slack
MO   Clark
'y F, 2 US (4 guns)   Skegg's Branch
OODY   1 IA   Burbridge   Guibor's Bat'y (4 guns)
HILL   1 AR Mt Rifles
1 KS (3 cos.)   McBride
Parsons
2 KS   Wingo
'y F, 2 US (2 guns)   5 AR   Pearce
(–3 cos.)   T.B. Manley house
E, 1 KS
3 AR
1KS (3 cos.)

Skegg's Spring

Skegg house

fles began to cheer. The officers moved along their lines shouting encouragement to their men, and in a few minutes the entire Southern line began to advance. Up to three thousand Arkansas and Missouri soldiers surged toward the Federal line in a front about one thousand yards long. It was approximately 10:30 A.M.[36]

On the Union left Du Bois's Battery delivered counterbattery fire at the Missouri Light Artillery. After only a short time, the State Guard battery fell silent due to a shortage of ammunition. Barlow withdrew to replenish his ammunition chests. The Fort Smith Battery then took up the duel, but it traded rounds with the Union guns for only five minutes. McIntosh ordered the gunners to stand down, probably to protect advancing infantry from friendly fire. Yet the Southern artillery was far from discouraged. Once resupplied, the Missouri Light Artillery joined the Fourth Arkansas and the three companies of the Fifth Arkansas that had occupied the ridge where Sigel's guns first went into action. As rumors of enemy activity in that direction were inaccurate, they took no further part in the battle. Back on Bloody Hill, the reduction in fire from the Southern artillery allowed Du Bois to concentrate on the enemy infantry to his front. The lethal combination of his guns and those of the Federal infantry defeated the attack on that section of the line.[37]

The center of the Union line bore the brunt of the Southern assault. A Kansas soldier recalled that while waiting for the Southerners to renew their attack, the enlisted men "were lying flat on their faces, the line officers sitting on the ground a few paces in the rear." This was a sensible precaution. Indeed, lying prone for protection during lulls in battle was a standard procedure long before the American Civil War. Soldiers almost always fought standing up, however, because their weapons could be loaded rapidly only in that position. As ranges were relatively short and the smoke produced by black powder gave away the shooter's position, safety lay in reloading and firing as quickly as possible rather than taking cover. Though manuals such as Hardee's *Rifle and Light Infantry Tactics* included detailed instructions for loading and firing lying down, soldiers' diaries, letters, and memoirs indicate that such techniques were neither commonly taught nor frequently employed early in the Civil War. This is confirmed by Eugene Ware's memoirs. The Iowan recalled that his Burlington Zoauves was the only company that, while drilling in camp, routinely practiced how to load and fire in a prone position.[38]

At the Battle of Wilson's Creek, the waist-high prairie grass, the soldiers' relative inexperience, and, above all, the scarcity of ammunition, slowed the pace of combat. Under these conditions, a large number of men eventually ended up firing and reloading while either kneeling or lying down, despite their lack of practice in such techniques and the extra time it took them to do so. This was true for both sides throughout the battle, particularly during the fighting that broke out as the Southerners made their third assault on Bloody Hill.

As the Southerners approached, Major John Halderman of the First Kansas ordered his men "to lie down and fire from that position." A soldier in the Second Kansas recalled that they were "ordered to drop to our knees and keep close to the ground." Captain Gordon Granger of Lyon's staff moved from unit to unit across the hillcrest, instructing the soldiers to remain concealed in the grass and expose themselves only to shoot. Most obeyed. "Lying flat on their faces our men poured in their fire with telling effect," newspaperman Franc Wilkie reported. According to one Union officer, "Our men as a whole would rise enough to discharge their weapons and then lie down while loading up." One of Lyon's Regulars contrasted the reality of combat to his expectations from peacetime. He wrote: "The splendid motions we had been taught at drill and parade in anticipation of this bloody day were not practiced here. Each man assumed a position to his liking—most of them on their knees and leaning well forward." The advantages of crouching or lying down were obvious, for once the combatants came within range, the effects of their fire could be devastating even if it was not prolonged. "The bullets whistled, rattled, banged, [and] whirred over our heads," remembered one Kansan on the receiving end of a Missouri State Guard volley. "If our men had stood up, hardly a man would have been left," he concluded. Testimony on the Southern side was similar. As Private Ras Stirman of the Third Arkansas Infantry later described his encounter with the Federals: "They were lying down in the brush and grass until we were within one hundred yards of them, then they opened up on us bringing us down like Sheep but we never wavered. We did not wait for orders to fire but all of us cut loose at them like wild men, then we dropped to our knees and loaded and shot as fast as we could. We had to shoot by guess as they were upon the hill lying in the grass." Because the men kept so low to the ground, a disproportionate number of those killed or wounded were struck in the head.[39]

Artillery continued to provide essential support. As Sokalski's section was still on the right, Totten had only four guns in place at the Federal center. Although the captain's confidence in his own artillerymen increased as the fighting progressed, he felt considerable anxiety for the Federal foot soldiers. His fears were justified, for as the Southern infantry surged forward, a line of Regular Service Recruits who had been deployed as skirmishers suddenly buckled. The men streamed back up hill,

Captain Gordon Granger. This photograph was taken after his promotion to major general. (The collection of Dr. Tom and Karen Sweeney, General Sweeny's Museum, Republic, Missouri)

eventually rejoining Steele's battalion. As Southern infantry neared the crest and the fighting reached a fever pitch, Sturgis sent the left wing of the First Iowa to Totten's support. Still the Southerners advanced, some closing to within twenty feet of the artillery. Finally, the rounds of canister and musket volleys took such a terrible toll that the Southern units retreated. The Union center was safe.[40]

The firing was so intense during the Southern assault that huge clouds of gunsmoke blanketed entire sections of the Bloody Hill's southern slope. The noise reminded William Allen, a private in the Second Kansas, of "hundreds of bunches of firecrackers going off," only much louder. But after about forty-five minutes of combat all along the line, Price realized that once again his attack had failed. For a third time the Southern infantry broke off and fell back to regroup. One of the wounded left behind was Sergeant William Watson, of the Third Louisiana, who recalled, "We were pressing up the hill to get to closer quarters, when a ball took me in the pit of the stomach, and for a few minutes I remembered no more." After a short time he recovered and found himself lying downhill with his left hand, injured earlier in the Ray cornfield fight, behind his back. The only pain the sergeant experienced was from that wound, and as he moved his hand he felt a warm liquid. His first thought was that the bullet had passed through his body and out his back. Believing that he was dying, he looked at his hand but saw only a small amount of blood.

Encouraged, he rose to his feet and discovered that his heavy brass belt plate, bearing the distinctive pelican emblem worn by each member of Baton Rouge's Pelican Rifles, had deflected a bullet. He then reached for his canteen to take a drink and found a bullet hole through it. His canteen had ended up behind his back, the warm water trickling out onto his hand. Overjoyed at his narrow escape, he made his way back to the regiment.[41]

Just before the Southerners withdrew, Sturgis learned from Blair that the Second Kansas was almost out of ammunition. When another lull developed, Sturgis decided that it was time to abandon the fight. The next challenge was to disengage in the face of an enemy believed to have overwhelmingly superior numbers. It was about 11:30 A.M. and there was still no word from Sigel. The Union commander therefore ordered Blair to pull back first. The Second Kansas withdrew in good order, bringing off many of its wounded. As the regiment moved onto the northern spur of Bloody Hill, Du Bois's Battery and the Second Missouri joined it. This initial withdrawal left the Union right flank exposed. When a Southern unit, probably the Third Louisiana, began moving toward this unmanned portion of the line, Sturgis shifted Steele's infantry to the right. After "a sharp engagement" the Regulars drove the enemy back. When this action took place, Totten replaced his disabled horses, limbered up his guns, and fell back. The First Iowa, the First Kansas, the Home Guard units, and the detachment of the Thirteenth Illinois departed at the same time.[42]

As the Federals withdrew, the lead pair of horses drawing one of the caissons in Totten's Battery was killed. The crew abandoned it, lodged against a sapling. Although he was already wounded in the shoulder, Corporal Lorenzo Immell raced back on foot to rescue the valuable equipment. As bullets flew, he cut the dead horses from the traces and used an axe to chop down the sapling. While he worked a spent ball struck him painfully on the left shin, and he called to the rear guard of the First Iowa for assistance. Private Nicholas Bouquet of the Burlington Rifles helped Immell seize a horse (or possibly a mule) and harness it to the others. Riding the new animal, Immell pulled the caisson to safety while Bouquet returned to his company. For their heroic actions both soldiers later received the Congressional Medal of Honor.[43]

Steele's battalion remained on Bloody Hill to cover the column's retreat. Granger soon joined it. Observing the enemy advancing in numbers, he raced to the rear and in a matter of minutes returned with companies from the First Iowa, First Kansas, and First Missouri. Moving up on Steele's left, Granger placed his ad hoc force to enfilade the right flank of the advancing enemy. A single, devastating volley sent the South-

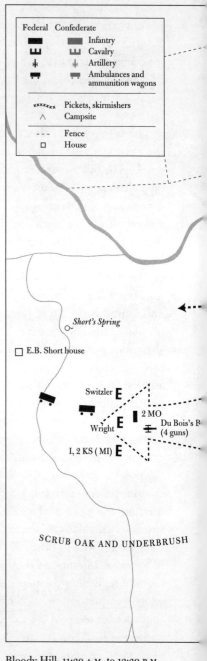

Federal	Confederate	
	Infantry
	Cavalry
	Artillery
	Ambulances and ammunition wagons
xxxxxxxx		Pickets, skirmishers
∧		Campsite
- - -		Fence
□		House

Short's Spring

□ E.B. Short house

Switzler **E**

E | 2 MO
Wright **E** | Du Bois's B (4 guns)

I, 2 KS (MI) **E**

SCRUB OAK AND UNDERBRUSH

Bloody Hill, 11:30 A.M. to 12:30 P.M.

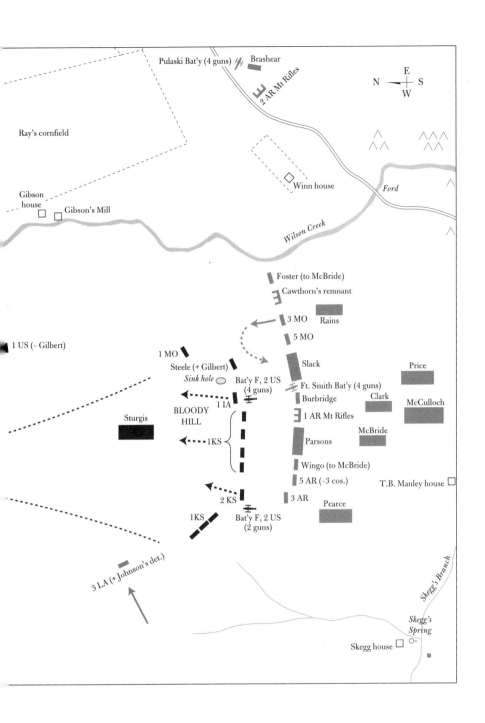

Pulaski Bat'y (4 guns)   Brashear

2 AR Mt Rifles

E
N — S
W

Ray's cornfield

Winn house   Ford

Gibson
house
Gibson's Mill

Wilson Creek

Foster (to McBride)

Cawthorn's remnant

3 MO   Rains

5 MO

1 US (– Gilbert)

1 MO   Slack

Steele (+ Gilbert)   Price

Sink hole   Bat'y F, 2 US   Ft. Smith Bat'y (4 guns)
(4 guns)   Burbridge   Clark

1 IA   McCulloch

BLOODY   1 AR Mt Rifles
HILL
McBride
Sturgis   1KS   Parsons

Wingo (to McBride)

5 AR (–3 cos.)   T.B. Manley house

2 KS   3 AR

1KS   Bat'y F, 2 US   Pearce
(2 guns)

3 LA (+ Johnson's det.)

Skegg's Branch

Skegg's
Spring

Skegg house

erners reeling down the hill. This Union rear guard held its position until the ambulances had retrieved as many wounded as possible and were safely on their way. Du Bois's Battery covered Steele's withdrawal from the spur of the northern ridge. Once the infantry had passed, Du Bois limbered up his guns and fell into column. The artillery proceeded only a short distance before one of the twelve-pound howitzers broke down. Osterhaus's Missourians stood guard while the necessary repairs were made, and the two units then rejoined the main column.[44]

After falling back about two miles Sturgis halted at Ross's Spring, allowing the exhausted soldiers to rest, drink the refreshing water, fill their canteens, and eat whatever food they had. Luckily, several wagons loaded with bread had arrived from Springfield. The soldiers "devoured" the loaves "with a relish which extreme hunger alone can give." Even after resuming the march Sturgis contemplated selecting a defensive position and awaiting news of Sigel's column. The question of the Prussian's fate was soon answered when a noncommissioned officer from the Second Brigade galloped up on a sweat-soaked horse. He reported that Sigel's column had been routed and its artillery captured; Sigel himself either had been killed or taken prisoner. There was now no reason not to return to Springfield. Just as they reached the Little York Road, Lieutenant Charles Farrand rode up with Company D, Second U.S. Dragoons, and a few fast-marching fugitives from Colonel Charles E. Salomon's Fifth Missouri Infantry. They had with them the single artillery piece that they had recovered during the retreat. The two groups continued their march together, reaching Springfield around 5:00 P.M., approximately twenty-four hours after they had first marched out to attack the Southern army.[45]

The Southerners crowded along the slopes of Bloody Hill were surprisingly slow to learn of the Union withdrawal. As a result of fatigue, acute ammunition shortages, and the inevitable breakdown in command and control caused by casualties, the Western Army was nearly "fought out." When the first units crept cautiously to the crest of the hill, their reports that the enemy had fled seemed too good to be true. After a while, McCulloch, Price, and Pearce gathered with their staff officers atop the position for which they had struggled to gain for more than five hours. In the distance to the north, they could see the Federals retreating. Woodruff's Pulaski Light Battery clattered up, unlimbered, and fired a few long-range shots that fell harmlessly. Years later Pearce recalled that at this climactic moment they felt emotional release rather than elation. "We watched the retreating enemy through our field-glasses," he wrote, "*and were glad to see him go.*"[46]

Chapter 18 . . . .

Springfield Is a Vast Hospital

Compared to later Civil War battles, the number of men engaged at Wilson's Creek and the casualties suffered there were modest. But when the casualty figures (the combination of killed, wounded, and missing) are placed in the perspective of previous American history and viewed as a percentage of the forces engaged, it is clear that Wilson's Creek was a major, costly battle. The best estimate for McCulloch's Western Army is 277 dead and 945 wounded, for a casualty rate of 12 percent. The total number of dead and wounded—1,222—was higher than the number suffered by Americans in any single battle of the Mexican War. As a percentage of the force engaged, the Southerners had a higher casualty rate than occurred in all but three of the nine major battles of the Mexican War. Lyon's Army of the West had an estimated 285 killed, 873 wounded, and 186 missing, for a casualty rate of 24.5 percent. Both in total numbers and as a percentage of the force engaged, Lyon's losses were greater than those of any battle in the Mexican War.[1]

Casualties were not distributed equally, of course. On both sides the infantry suffered more heavily than the cavalry or artillery. In the Western Army, losses were twice as high in the Confederate troops and the Missouri State Guard as in the Arkansas State Troops. Among the Missouri units, Rains's Division had the lowest casualty rate (9.7 percent), Clark's Division the highest (20 percent). Overall, the units hardest hit were the First Arkansas Mounted Rifles (32.8 percent casualties), Kelly's Infantry (34.5 percent), and Burbridge's Infantry (36.2 percent). On the Northern side, losses were particularly severe in the First Missouri Infantry (38 percent), the Second Missouri Infantry (36.6 percent), and the First Kansas Infantry (35.5 percent). Indeed, over the course of the war only six

Union regiments had a larger total number of dead and mortally wounded in a single engagement than did the First Kansas, which sacrificed 284 men at Wilson's Creek.[2]

The primitive state of medical knowledge in the nineteenth century meant that men wounded during the Civil War had a far greater chance of dying than modern combatants. Yet a statistical analysis of the casualties at Wilson's Creek does little to convey the suffering of the men who struggled there. Events during the weeks after the battle demonstrate that the tragedy that occurred on August 10 embraced an area far wider than the slopes of Bloody Hill and a much larger population than just those in uniform. For like all battles in the Civil War, Wilson's Creek was in part a community experience. Its impact on civilians, both on the battlefield itself and in Springfield, was devastating. The response of civilians to news of the battle underscores the continuing close relationship between military units and their home communities.

Few Civil War commanders prepared adequately for their men's medical needs early in the war. Shortly after his arrival in Springfield, Nathaniel Lyon had ordered Dr. E. C. Franklin to establish a military hospital. Franklin chose the unfinished courthouse building being erected on the town square. Although sometimes styled "Chief Surgeon," he was in charge of the Springfield hospital only, having previously been attached to the Fifth Missouri. Why Lyon selected Franklin, recently a civilian, over one of the three army doctors who accompanied his Regulars is unknown, but soldiers praised the hospital's cleanliness and the dedication of the doctors there. Most of Lyon's units had both surgeons and assistant surgeons attached to them, but there was no medical director for the Army of the West and no coordination among the fifteen doctors present, at least two of whom were described as incompetent by their peers. Medical supplies considered adequate by the standards of the day reached Springfield, but these were not distributed equally, and in the volunteer regiments the doctors relied on the instruments from their civilian practice, as the army had nothing to give them.[3]

Lyon's concern had been for illnesses, not battle casualties. When the Federals marched to the fray on August 9, each unit was left to look after its own wounded. Once the Federals became heavily engaged on Bloody Hill, surgeons began treating the wounded immediately behind the lines. For example, Dr. W. H. White of the First Iowa had the patients brought to him laid out in a triangle and moved back and forth among the three divisions to treat them. Eventually Major John Schofield of Lyon's staff saw that a central field hospital was set up in a ravine. This was probably the one that opened toward Gibson's Mill, although a few sources suggest that it was another one just north of Bloody Hill. No field hospital was established for the men who accompanied Colonel Franz Sigel, as they changed position frequently. Indeed, although he took along a wagon containing a quantity of medical supplies and litters for removing the wounded, these were never unpacked. As better facilities existed in Springfield, the Federal doctors did not attempt major surgery in the field. According to one report, no amputations were performed. Dr. H. M. Sprague of the Regulars admitted, "The attention shown the wounded was good, but not specially praiseworthy."[4]

The Southern forces were surprised in their camps and remained in possession of the ground. This gave them an advantage in treating their own men but left them with the burden of caring for the enemy's wounded following the Federal retreat. There were at least twenty-four surgeons assigned to the Missouri State Guard units in the field. Records are incomplete and the actual number of doctors present was probably higher. All five divisions had chief surgeons, at least three of whom were appointed prior to the battle, but coordination was absent. A soldier in Clark's Division complained that the State Guard had "no organized hospital corps, no stretchers on which to bear off the wounded."[5] Little is known about the medical personnel in the Arkansas State Troops or the Confederate units under Ben McCulloch's direct command. Nothing suggests that an effort was made above the regimental level to prepare for the inevitable consequences of battle.

The plight of the Union wounded was arguably worse than that of their foe. Fearing that the rumble of wheeled vehicles might betray his surprise march, Lyon initially ordered all ambulances to be left in Springfield. After Sturgis pleaded with him, he reluctantly allowed two ambulances to accompany the main column, but none went with Sigel. The ambulances apparently did not attempt to make round-trips to Springfield during the battle but remained until Sturgis ordered the retreat. And burdened far beyond their intended capacity, they could not have transported more than two or three dozen of the hundreds of Federal wounded from the field. Once the order to withdraw was given, wheeled vehicles of every description were confiscated from nearby farms and pressed into service. There were few in number, as almost all of the severely wounded Federal soldiers remained on the battlefield. Those with lesser injuries, the so-called walking wounded, scrambled for safety with no help from officialdom. To modern analysts such conditions are tantamount to criminal neglect, but they were hardly unusual in the initial phases of the Civil War.[6]

While community spirit helped sustain the common soldiers in battle, that same corporate sense of honor ironically weakened the armies somewhat because of the failure to prepare adequately for casualties. The men in the ranks stood literally side by side with neighbors from home, and when men fell wounded their comrades dropped out of the battle to care for them. In a newspaper letter, Joseph Martin of Atchison's All Hazard company related without apology how he left the fight to look after his friend George Keith. "I found him, took charge of him and carried him to one of the hospital wagons, dressed his wounds and placed him in a wagon to be carried to town," Martin wrote. "Many of the wagons were heaping full, every man was trying to get friends into them, but I succeeded. . . . He depended upon me to take care of him, which I did." Similarly, when Hugh J. Campbell of the Muscatine Grays captured some horses abandoned near Gibson's Mill, he gave them only to wounded fellow Iowans. Shot in the foot himself, he nevertheless managed to steal at gunpoint a horse ridden by a Northern officer's servant, giving it to his wounded friend Newton Brown. Campbell gleefully related this larceny at the expense of "a darkey" to readers of the *Muscatine Weekly Journal*. Conduct unthinkable at the beginning of the campaign became not only acceptable but also a source of humor once battle was joined.[7]

Things differed little on the Southern side, where strength was also depleted due to the lack of medical preparations. John D. Bell of Burbridge's Infantry recalled that when a man was wounded "it took from two to four of his friends to bear him to some shady nook, where he was left with a canteen of water." Although Bell contended that "in almost every case" these Good Samaritans returned to the fight, his postwar recollections are probably too forgiving. Over 900 men were wounded in the Southern army, and in all likelihood at least another 900 to 1,000 men withdrew from the fight for a significant period to care for comrades. This effectively eroded McCulloch's combat strength by as much as an additional 10 percent. On the other hand, similar behavior reduced Lyon's strength in like proportion.[8]

Several impromptu field hospitals were established along the banks of Wilson Creek, perhaps because the wounded crawled there seeking water and shade. Trees and underbrush grew thick beside the stream, and soldiers instinctively carried their wounded friends to cover. Because the battle took place amid their camps, the Southerners used their various wagons to transport the wounded to safety even during combat. This was done spontaneously, for there was no organized effort to bring in the wounded until after the battle ended, when each regiment detailed men for that purpose. The positions of the battle lines meant that no place was truly safe. Artillery and small arms fire passed constantly above the Southern hospitals, which were occasionally targeted by accident. Shortly after firing commenced Confederate surgeon William A. Cantrell set up a hospital "near the centre of the battlefield." Amazingly, he escaped injury, but a physician in Slack's Division and several wounded soldiers, both Northern and Southern, were killed at a creek bank dressing station.[9]

Cooperation in regard to medical care was one of the few humane notes amid the general carnage, as surgeons attended men without regard to political affiliation. "I have never before witnessed such a heart-rendering scene," wrote Colonel John Hughes of the Missouri State Guard. "State, Federal, and Confederate troops in one red ruin, blent on the field—enemies in life, in death friends, relieving each others' sufferings."[10] Indeed, before the last firing died away a Federal doctor risked his life to contact McCulloch, opening negotiations concerning the joint treatment of the wounded. Even so, the surgeons were overwhelmed by the task facing them. They worked incredibly long hours, but despite their best efforts suffering of the wounded was prolonged and terrible. The Federals began moving their injured to Springfield during the afternoon and evening of August 10, and the Southerners began doing the same the following day. Nevertheless, on August 12 Dr. John Wyatt wrote in his diary that "many of the wounded are lying where they fell in the blazing sun, unable to get water and any kind of aid. Blow flies swarm over the living and the dead alike. I saw men not yet dead [with] their eyes, nose & mouth full of maggots."[11]

Presumably men still lay without cover because every house, cabin, barn, or dwelling in the vicinity of the battlefield was already overflowing with wounded. The engagement was obviously an unmitigated disaster for all civilians living nearby, and for many it was probably the most memorable event in their lives. When Mary Johnson died in 1903 at the age of eighty-three, for example, her obituary mentioned that she had tended the wounded at Wilson's Creek. Living on a substantial farm just east of the Ray family, she was a widow with two children at the time of the fighting, and the disruption in their lives must have been severe. Elias Short and his family returned home to find wounded Union soldiers being transferred from their farm to Springfield. The house had not been looted or despoiled, although "the bed clothing had been torn into strips to be used in binding up the wounds of the Union men."[12]

Detailed information regarding the impact of the battle on civilians has survived only in relation to the Sharp and Ray families. Before the conflict the Sharp home was already being used as a hospital for members of Greer's South Kansas–Texas Regiment who had fallen ill. When the fighting erupted, Joseph Sharp, his wife Mary, son Robert, and daughters Margaret and Mary took shelter in the cellar, and the makeshift hospital was evacuated. Artillery projectiles began crashing through the house, devastating the interior. There was extensive damage to the barn and other outbuildings as well. What crops had not been eaten by the en-camped Southerners were probably trampled during combat. Fence rails were knocked down, and dead horses from Sigel's luckless battery lay scattered about.[13]

Three stories exist concerning the reaction of the Sharps. Writing long after the war, Private Joseph Mudd of the Missouri State Guard recalled that from a distance he saw Mary Sharp vigorously encouraging the Southerners as they drove Sigel from the field. Also writing from memory, Sergeant William Watson of the Third Louisiana described how he broke into the family's locked house and found the Sharps cowering in the cellar behind a barrel of apples. They did not object when his comrades promptly appropriated the apples, but Mary protested in a shrill voice that the morning's cannoneering had rendered Joseph deaf. "I felt like saying that, considering her gift of speech, a worse thing might have happened to the old man," Watson wrote. Mary climbed cautiously from her refuge, "but on seeing the wreck, and looking out and seeing the dead men and horses lying in the front of the house, she broke into a greater fury than ever," the sergeant noted. "Who was going to pay for all this?" she exclaimed. "Who was going to take away them dead folks and dead horses? Was she to have them lying stinking around her house?" Mary continued in this manner until Watson happily rejoined his regiment. Her comments when dozens of bleeding men with little or no control over their bodily functions were carried into her home can be imagined. Fi-nally, just a few days after the battle Colonel Elkanah Greer, in a letter to a friend in Texas, wrote: "The battle raged hottest around the house of an old gentleman named Sharp, near the centre of the battlefield. After the roar of cannon and the rattle of small arms had ceased for a short time, an old lady came out of the house with a bundle of clothes on her arm, passing over and around the dead Dutch that lay in the yard, and near the fences, to hang out clothes. Placing her spectacles high up on her nose, her right arm akimbo, she exclaimed in a singular and doleful tone, 'Well dese folks have kicked up a monstrous fuss here to-day.'"[14]

These accounts demonstrate the difficulty historians face in evaluating evidence. Can the chronicles of Mudd and Watson be reconciled? Does Greer's letter refer to Mary Sharp or (note the dialect speech) one of the household's slaves? Regardless of their differences, the stories told about the Sharps remind us that civilians were intimately involved in the battle. The families in the neighborhood of Wilson Creek lost property worth thousands of dollars without receiving a penny in compensation from either the Union or Confederate governments. If not shattered by artillery or musket fire, their homes were damaged when first beds and then every square inch of floor space was covered with the wounded. In some cases, injured soldiers remained there for weeks. Finally, dollar amounts cannot measure the psychological trauma that these residents doubtless suffered. Such things as Mrs. Sharp's fear for the safety of her teenage daughters can be assumed but not documented.

The misery endured by the Ray family was almost as great as that of the Sharps. John Ray viewed the entire fight from his front porch while the rest of the family remained in the cellar. Shortly after the engagement in Ray's cornfield ended, the house became a hospital. Although a chicken coop was hit by artillery fire and some other outbuildings were slightly damaged, the family dwelling was not struck. A large yellow hospital flag spared the site from all but accidental fire. But if the buildings were essentially unscathed, the household's ordeal was severe. For some five hours, Roxanna Ray and eight of her children, their slave Rhoda and her children, and Julius Short, who resided with the Rays, sat in a dark, cramped cellar. When they emerged, wounded men covered the floors and occupied every bed. Unlike Mary Sharp, Roxanna did not waste any time venting her feelings on the unfairness of what had happened. She, Rhoda, and perhaps some of the older children immediately began to assist in caring for the wounded, primarily by hauling water from the nearby springhouse. Some of the wounded, too badly injured to be moved to Springfield, remained in the Ray home for six weeks. John Ray's activities during the afternoon are unknown, but that evening he was forced to act as a guide for a group of prisoners being escorted to Springfield. Because all of his horses had been stolen, he had to walk. The family was very anxious for his safety, but John may have been more worried about his losses of grain and livestock. Although a Unionist, he was never compensated.[15]

The battle also had an impact on civilians living beyond its immediate confines. William Gilbert, his wife Elizabeth, and her aunt, whose name is unknown, lived about three miles from Springfield. Scouts and foragers from both the Northern and Southern forces annoyed them so frequently that they finally began sleeping in a cave for safety. Nevertheless, William formed some kind of attachment with the Kansas troops, and when they marched out on August 9 he accompanied them as an unenlisted volunteer. When Elizabeth and her aunt heard the artillery in the distance on August 10, they gathered supplies and headed toward the sound of the guns to treat the wounded. In writing about their experiences over forty years later, Elizabeth still remembered with horror the gaping wounds she

A postwar photograph of the home of John Ray (The collection of Dr. Tom and Karen Sweeney, General Sweeny's Museum, Republic, Missouri)

had seen on some of the fallen men. The scale of the suffering shocked her, and much of their labor seemed to be in vain. "We raised up the heads of many a wounded soldier and propped them up only to see them die in a few minutes," she recalled. When the cloth they had brought for bandages ran out, Elizabeth tore up her apron and her aunt her entire skirt. They did not get back to the family farm until two o'clock the next morning.[16]

Although it is impossible to estimate how many women in the neighborhood volunteered their services as nurses, the number was clearly substantial. On August 13 Dr. Wyatt wrote in his diary, "The fair sex, God bless them, are doing all they can in the way of cooking, serving, and nursing for [the] sick and wounded."[17] He may have been referring to women from Springfield as well as locals, for the town was completely caught up in the tragic aftermath of the battle.

Many Springfield citizens fled prior to August 10, heading for Rolla with one of the columns made up of Federal soldiers who were either sick or nearing their date of discharge. According to newspaperman Franc Wilkie, all who remained were awake before dawn on the fateful day, listening for the sounds that would mark the opening of the battle. "About ten minutes past five," Wilkie wrote, "the heavy boom of artillery rolled through the town like the muttering of a thunder storm upon the horizon, and sent a thrill through every heart, like a shock of electricity." Although Wilkie soon departed to view the battle firsthand, the townsfolk endured hours of anxiety before learning anything about the conflict's outcome. By mid-morning they could see smoke rising in the far distance but could not interpret its portent. Shortly after 3:00 P.M. the wounded began streaming in on foot and horseback, bringing news of Lyon's death. They were followed by ambulances, wagons, carriages, and other wheeled conveyances, all overflowing with men needing attention. The hospital in the courthouse was soon filled, so the Union authorities took over the Bailey House Hotel. When the hotel filled up, the wounded were sent to local churches and schools. But even this was insufficient, and arriving wounded soldiers had to be placed "side by side along the streets." Finally, private dwellings were requisitioned. According to one account, between thirty and forty citizens' homes were occupied by the wounded. This represented a substantial portion of the houses in Springfield. Another eyewitness stated that "nearly all the private dwellings" were taken over. A Union physician later recalled how "the women of Springfield, with their hearts full of love and tenderness for the suffering soldiers, came with prepared food, and with gentle hands assisted with every means in their power to soothe the dying soldier and relieve the pain of the suffering." The doctor could not recall the names of all who helped, but he particularly remembered the generosity of the Boyd, Graves, Jenkins, Logan, Beal, Jameston, Fairchilds, Waddle, Lindenbauer, and Crenshaw families. Their charity was not without cost. The total dollar value of damage to the town as a result of medical treatment was unquestionably large. Only a small amount of compensation was ever received, and that after the war.[18]

Most Springfield citizens were pro-Union. Once it became clear that the battle was lost and the Federal forces would retreat, many began preparing to evacuate. Left alone after the earlier departure of her husband, Congressman John Phelps, Mary Phelps sent her children and all but one of the family's seventeen slaves to Rolla in two covered wagons. She and a slave named George, who refused to leave her side, remained to tend the wounded. Some merchants, who had been charging exorbitant prices to the Union troops enduring half rations, now gave away food or dumped it into the streets rather than leave it for the enemy to confiscate. Wilkie wrote that "Springfield was the scene of great confusion—citizens anticipating an instant attack were packing up their effects and flying in crowds to all parts of the state for safety." When the Southern forces arrived, they noted that relatively few citizens, especially women, remained. Their absence made their property easy pickings for looters, despite the guards McCulloch posted to maintain order. In some cases,

A drawing of Springfield made by Private Andrew Tinkham, Scott's Guards, First Kansas Infantry, in October or November 1861, showing the camps of the Union forces that reoccupied the town. Published here for the first time. (The collection of Dr. Tom and Karen Sweeney, General Sweeny's Museum, Republic, Missouri)

Springfieldians in the Missouri State Guard may have been retaliating for damage inflicted on their own homes by the fleeing Unionists. Harris Flanagin, whose company of the Second Arkansas Mounted Rifles was detailed for guard duty, estimated that fewer than twenty women remained in the whole town. "We treat the union men much better than the Missourians do," he noted.[19]

With the state bitterly divided, it was hardly surprising that Sterling Price's men were particularly elated by the victory. Well-wishers and prospective recruits for the State Guard soon flocked to Springfield. When Dr. Wyatt first visited town to assist in shifting the wounded from the battlefield, he witnessed an important ceremony. "The flag of the Confederacy was raised amidst the wildest enthusiasm by all the people," he wrote. "Everyone seemed wild with joy except a few sad faced Dutch who had been left behind by their army."[20]

Elation soon gave way to more somber emotions amid the lingering evidence of victory's cost. "Springfield is a vast hospital," wrote Dr. William Cantrell, surgeon of the First Arkansas Mounted Rifles, to friends in Little Rock. "There is not sufficient medical aid here—a hundred doctors could be employed constantly," he lamented, estimating that four months would pass before enough soldiers recovered to alleviate the situation. Private John B. Clark, a wounded Kansan forced to stay behind, made an equally discouraging evaluation. "Springfield is the most offensive place you was ever in; the stench from the dead and dying is so offensive as to be almost intolerable in some quarters," he informed his relatives. Indeed, a Union doctor who remained with his patients recalled that days passed before the surgeons "succeeded in bringing partial order out of utter chaos." Ben McCulloch and Bart Pearce took pains to visit not only their own hospitalized men but the Union wounded as well, a fact reported favorably in Northern newspapers. But they, like Sterling Price, were too busy with strategy to give medical affairs more than scant attention.[21]

The physicians did not have to work alone for long. Help arrived rather quickly, as telegraphic communications and newspapers that copied stories from other journals spread news of the battle. The telegraph lines that ran along the Wire Road to link Fayetteville, Arkansas, and Jefferson City, Missouri, were apparently cut both north and south of Springfield, as the earliest news came out of Rolla, where the Army of the West halted its retreat. From there, word of the battle reached St. Louis. Information first published in that city's various newspapers was soon relayed west to Kansas City and throughout Kansas, north to Davenport and across Iowa, and southeast to Memphis, Tennessee, from whence it traveled to Little Rock, Arkansas, to Baton Rouge and New Orleans, Louisiana, and finally to parts of eastern Texas. Southerners thus initially heard only Northern reports of the fight. Their own side's accounts did not spread until a week or more after the battle, when hard-riding messengers reached the telegraph offices at Little Rock.

Although reports of the battle tended to be highly partisan, those printed in hometown newspapers, North and South, shared important commonalities. In previous wars civilians had waited months to learn the fate of loved ones, but the families of those who fought at Wilson's Creek obtained information quickly, often within only a few days. Newspapers printed long lists of the names of the killed and wounded in "their" company. Many of these lists were annotated, including the location of wounds and estimates of the sufferers' chances of survival. As more information became available, lists were updated, expanded, and corrected. Overall, they were remarkably accurate, which meant that while many anxieties were relieved, grief became immediate.

In addition, hometown newspapers often printed letters attesting to the fact that individual wounded soldiers had fulfilled the implicit social contract that had been formed between the community and its company when the men first volunteered. In *Embattled Courage*, Gerald Linderman notes how Victorian Americans tended to define courage in terms of fearlessness and expected wounded soldiers, even those mortally hurt, to maintain the proper spirit and decorum.[22] The soldiers who clashed in Missouri were clearly concerned about courage. In the days following the fight at Wilson's Creek the survivors reassured their home folk that those who fell in battle had suffered manfully, thereby upholding the reputation of their companies and, by extension, the good name of their hometowns.

The first two weekly editions of Little Rock's *Arkansas True Democrat* containing detailed information about the battle illustrate community interest in matters of courage and honor. Accounts of the fighting contained specific information about the behavior of the wounded. A soldier in the Fourth Arkansas Infantry wrote of his friend, "Poor Joe, as he fell, waved his hat to his men, and cried, 'onward, boys, onward.'" A member of the First Arkansas Mounted Rifles related: "When young Harper fell, they went to him, but he desired them not to stop, but to go on and whip them; and when he learned that we had taken their artillery, he pulled off his hat, gave three cheers, and said he was satisfied. Brown, of the V[an] B[uren] F[rontier] Guards, after he had received a mortal wound, cheered his brave boys to advance." Dr. Cantrell continued the story, writing that "Harper had become a favorite with the regiment and they thronged around his dying bed to see him and part with him. I could not go near him without feeling almost overcome by the spectacle of his sufferings and his magnanimous disregard for them. Poor fellow! he never murmured or complained once, but died like a soldier and a hero." Finally, Captain William Woodruff praised a fallen comrade in the Pulaski Light Battery in these terms: "Poor Omer Weaver fell like a hero, with his face to the foe, and died some two hours later, as befits a *man*. During the fight he refused to get under any shelter at all. No man ever died a more glorious death." Similar testimony appeared in newspapers throughout Louisiana, Texas, Missouri, Kansas, and Iowa.[23]

If evidence of such heroism provided solace for the bereaved, many families must have been shocked at the way newspapers reported their loved ones' deaths in gruesome detail. For example, Franc Wilkie's widely reprinted account of the engagement at Wilson's Creek related how Joseph McHenry of the First Iowa's Governor's Grays was loading his weapon when "a musket ball tore through his head, scattering his blood and brains upon his comrades on either side of him."[24] It is unlikely that any of McHenry's friends, on returning to Dubuque, would have used such language to describe his death to his family. For the McHenrys, as for other families across the warring nation, press coverage under-scored the cost of war in a far more graphic fashion than was the case in previous conflicts.

Perhaps because death had become so shockingly public, newspaper editors were quick to remind readers of the contributions that the fallen had made to their community. This might be done in an obituary, a formal eulogy, or as part of a larger article. Editors frequently mentioned how long a person had been in the community, his place of employment, civil accomplishments, and surviving relatives. In Iowa, for example, the *Mt. Pleasant Home Journal* reported the death of former law student Frank Mann, who had resided in Mt. Pleasant only briefly prior to joining the Grays. The editor noted that "in that short time he had made many warm friends. . . . He was a young man of strict morals, rare attainments and of unusual promise." Likewise, the *Atchison Freedom's Champion* in Kansas lauded Camille Angiel, who fell leading Atchison's All Hazard company. He was, the editor proclaimed, "known to our citizens as a modest, unassuming young man, faithful in the interests of his employer, cour-teous and genial in social life, industrious and active in his business and duties, and an intelligent and scholarly gentleman." The *Emporia News* remarked that Hiram Burt, the only fatality in the town's Union Guards, was the stonemason who built the local Methodist Episcopal Church. In an article entitled "Martyrs of Freedom," the *Lawrence Weekly Republican* eulogized three men of the city's Oread Guards. "Messers. Pratt and Litchfield were among the very first settlers of the town, and through all the trials and troubles of Kansas were esteemed among the truest friends of Freedom," wrote the editor. "Mr. Jones leaves a wife now with her father in Olathe, and Mr. Litchfield leaves a wife and child in this place." For patriotic fervor, none could outdo the resolutions regarding the death of John W. Wood adopted by the Lady's Sewing Society of Liberty, Missouri, and printed in the local paper. The women declared that the State Guard soldier fell "bravely fighting in defense of our sacred rights, civil and religious liberties, homes and fire-sides, and all that is dear to a free people, and doing battle against usurpation, tyranny and military despotism." They resolved that "in his death the State lost a good citizen, the neighborhood one of its brightest ornaments, and his home a faithful and affectionate son and brother."[25]

Communities recognized the need for continued support of their hometown volunteers. As soon as news of Wilson's Creek reached Law-rence, two private citizens, James C. Horton and Edward Thompson, left for Springfield to help care for the wounded. "Acts of mercy like this, having no motive but the purest philanthropy, show how deeply such men as Pratt, Jones, Deitzler, Mitchell, and others are entwined in the affections of our people," commented the *Weekly Republican*. A citizen of Des Arc, Arkansas, whose name is unknown, undertook a similar mission of mercy, as did Mrs. George Reed, of Emporia, Kansas, who joined her wounded husband in Springfield shortly after the battle. The *Fort Smith Times and Herald* urged its readers to collect supplies for the wounded: "Gather up shirts, old linen or cotton cloth, and all kinds of delicacies that are generally provided for the sick, fans, sheets, etc. Let every person in town collect all they have of these articles and send them this evening to Major George W. Clarke, the quartermaster, who will at once forward them to the front." As many residents of Missouri had only a short distance to travel, it is not surprising that they arrived in Springfield in large numbers. Nor was every moment of their time spent in nursing. One soldier recalled, "Ladies whose husbands, fathers, and brothers were in the service, some of them wounded, began to arrive and gave social life and enjoyment to the society of Springfield."[26]

Although many of the wounded probably remained in Springfield until December, those less seriously injured were discharged from the hospitals as early as the first week in September. After giving their paroles, wounded Federals traveled to Rolla. Those who had enlisted for ninety days were discharged, whereas most of the others were furloughed to complete their recovery. For weeks after the battle newspapers noted the return of wounded soldiers, lauding their sacrifices and suffering on behalf of the town. Though enlisted men were praised highly, recuperating officers understandably received disproportionate attention. Colonels Robert Mitchell and George Deitzler, for example, were cheered wherever they went in Kansas. With fewer railroads to utilize, most homeward bound Southerners faced a more difficult journey. To facilitate the evacuation of men down the Wire Road McCulloch authorized the impressment of civilian wagons in the Springfield area. Although payment was made for the wagons' use, citizens were reluctant to surrender their private property to the military. Harris Flanagin recorded the day-long efforts of Mary Phelps to prevent her family's vehicles from being pressed into service. According to Flanagin, she "would scold and rage until she got tired and then she would cry," but her protests fell on deaf ears.[27]

The families of those who lost their lives were deeply concerned with how and where their loved ones were buried. The military authorities had made even fewer preparations for the interment of the dead than they had for the medical treatment of the wounded. On the morning of August 11, soldiers were detailed from the Western Army for a process that was grim psychologically as well as physically. "Battlefields became charnel landscapes, and the hapless soldiers assigned to clean them up became under-takers of the hopes and dreams of many young men far less fortunate than they." Because of the extreme heat and the size of the job, most of the dead were laid to rest in mass graves, a few even in the sinkhole atop Bloody Hill. The Southerners began with the dead from their own side (assuming they could be identified), leaving Northern corpses for a party of Union soldiers who had remained behind to assist. "The process of burying the dead was toilsome and got on slowly," William Watson re-called. "By the early part of the forenoon the sun got intensely hot, and some of the bodies began to show signs of decomposition, and the flies became intolerable, and the men could stand it no longer." A fellow Louisianan also described how the workers quickly sickened "and were unable to finish the task."[28]

By the best estimate there were 535 bodies on the field. Each corpse had to be located, identified if possible, and then dragged or carried to a grave site. Digging the grave pits was time-consuming, fatiguing labor in the August sun, yet these difficulties and the unpleasantness of the job hardly excuse the poor performance of the burial parties. If one estimates that it took an average of three man-hours to get each fallen soldier beneath the sod, one hundred men could have completed the task in sixteen hours, the equivalent of two days' labor. No one knows how many people were assigned to the burial details, but clearly not enough, as the process took much longer than two days. Interments continued through August 12, but when the Union workers did not show up on August 13 (they had apparently departed for Rolla), the Southerners were angered at the prospect of handling the remainder of the enemy's dead as well as their own. By that time the Western Army was busy shifting to new camps in and around Springfield, so the rest of the Northern corpses were simply left to rot. Most of those thus abandoned were casualties from Sigel's routed column. A Missouri State Guardsman recalled: "I was a member of a detail of fifty men that was sent over that part of the field to gather up the arms strewn along their wild flight. The stench was awful then, and what it must have been two days later would baffle imagina-tion." When the Third Louisiana marched past the Sharp farm on August 14, a soldier reported that "the bodies of those that fell in the road near the battery had been thrown to the side of the road and were festering in worms and the advanced state of putrification; it was horrible and loath-some beyond description." Given these conditions, the Sharp family may have evacuated. A full week after the battle a large number of bodies were still reported unburied. According to one account, a captured Union officer, understandably outraged by these circumstances, finally offered civilians $500 of his own money to do the job. Inevitably, some corpses went undiscovered for a long time. Six weeks after the battle young John Short was driving a cow home when he stumbled across a dead Union soldier. The man was probably wounded in the opening phase of the battle and collapsed while attempting to reach Springfield.[29]

Not all of those who died on August 10 were buried amid the oak hills. The bodies of fallen soldiers who had been natives of Greene County and its environs may have been claimed almost immediately. Others were taken home as well. Besides geographic distance, the greatest determining factor was rank. For example, both Lieutenant Omer Weaver and Private Hugh Byler died while serving the guns of the Pulaski Light Battery. Captain Woodruff went to great lengths to obtain a zinc-lined coffin for Weaver's body, which was shipped home for a hero's funeral, one of the largest ever held in Little Rock. Byler, on the other hand, was interred on the field.[30]

As Nathaniel Lyon was the first Union general to fall in combat, it is hardly surprising that his remains were treated differently from the others, but there was great confusion in the process. Sturgis had ordered the body placed in a wagon, but the vehicle was later taken over to remove the wounded and in the haste of the retreat the general was left behind. As Lyon did not carry a sword and had worn a plain captain's coat without any insignia of rank, there was little reason for his corpse to be noticed amid so many others. His body was apparently first recognized by Colonel James McIntosh, of the Second Arkansas Mounted Rifles, who removed papers from Lyon's pockets, either as souvenirs or because they had military value. The Southerners then brought the body to Federal surgeon S. H. Melcher, who had remained on the field after Sigel's debacle to treat the wounded. Melcher took the body to the Ray home where, with proper military decorum, it occupied a bed while wounded enlisted men from both armies writhed in agony on the hard, blood-soaked floor boards. The privileges of rank went unquestioned, even in death. Nor did Melcher apparently feel any guilt in abandoning his suffering patients when, during the night, he carried the lifeless hero to Springfield under a military escort supplied by General James Rains. The body was placed in Lyon's former headquarters. There Dr. Franklin's attempts to embalm it failed because of the extensive internal damage. Since no airtight coffins were available, he ordered an ordinary one of black walnut from a Springfield cabinetmaker. A number of local women sat with the body throughout the night, a typical mourning custom of the times.[31]

Sturgis and Sigel were understandably preoccupied with organizing the Federal retreat to Rolla, and the column tramped several miles before they realized that their commander's corpse had been accidentally left behind again. Sturgis sent an armed guard back to Springfield to fetch it, but on arrival they found that other arrangements had already been made. By this time Lyon's body was decomposing badly, although Dr. Franklin concealed its smell somewhat by sprinkling it with bay rum and alcohol. It was therefore decided to store it in the icehouse at the Phelps farm nearby. The coffin was transported in an ordinary butcher's wagon, escorted by a detachment of the Missouri State Guard under the command of Captain Emmett McDonald, whom Lyon had captured at Camp Jackson back in May. During the next two days, however, soldiers who were camped in the vicinity threatened to desecrate the remains. To keep it safe Mary Phelps allowed volunteers from the State Guard to bury the coffin in a cornfield on August 13.[32]

When Lyon's kinfolk in Connecticut learned of his death, his cousin Danford Knowlton and brother-in-law John B. Hassler made haste for Springfield. General John Frémont sent Captain George P. Edgar, a member of his staff, to assist them in passing through the Southern lines. They had Lyon's body disinterred on August 23, packing it in ice and placing it in an iron coffin brought from St. Louis. Departing Springfield on August 24, the party made good time. When it reached St. Louis on August 26, Frémont had Lyon's coffin placed at his headquarters under a guard of honor.[33]

The next day witnessed the first of a series of ceremonies as the North began to mourn one of the earliest martyrs to its cause. Large crowds went to view the casket, which was transferred to a steamboat with full military honors late in the afternoon. The Adams Express Company contracted to ship the body. Once across the river the remains were placed on a train and conveyed to Cincinnati. There the coffin was on display throughout August 29, attracting many mourners. Entrained once more, the party passed through Philadelphia and New York, where flags flew at half-mast. The coffin arrived in New Haven on the last day of the month and for the next three days was on public view at City Hall. Late in the afternoon of September 3 it went by rail to Hartford, where it rested briefly at the capitol under military guard. Connecticut's fiery general lay in state, the highest honor the community could render his memory. From Hartford the casket traveled by rail to the town of Willimantic, where a four-horse hearse provided by the state government carried it to the Congregational Church in Eastford.[34]

The funeral on September 5 was well attended, the procession to the graveyard reportedly a mile and a half long. In one sense this was surprising, as Lyon's family was not especially well liked locally. His father,

Amasa, was an eccentric who had alienated many of his neighbors. Growing up in rural Connecticut Lyon himself had made relatively few friends, and he had visited his hometown but seldom during his adult years.[35] The military had been Lyon's career. Unlike the majority of the soldiers he commanded, he had not participated in the sort of joyous send-offs or emotional flag presentations that had formed tacit social contracts between the soldiers and citizens of Lawrence, Kansas, or Dubuque, Iowa, for instance. But Lyon had done his duty. He had a larger social contract with the nation, written on a West Point diploma, and the people of Connecticut turned out to honor him.

Chapter 19 . . . .

To Choose Her Own Destiny

Nathaniel Lyon's original goal had been to stun the superior enemy forces facing him, thus creating conditions that would allow the Army of the West to retreat safely to Rolla. When at the last moment he accepted Franz Sigel's suggestion to attack the Southerners from two directions, Lyon changed his goal, attempting instead to defeat his foe decisively. Lyon failed, and the question remained whether the surviving Federals could escape.

Colonel Sigel reached Springfield on August 10 about 4:30 P.M., well ahead of his men. Riding through the streets half an hour later he encountered Major John Schofield, Lyon's adjutant general and chief of staff, who told him that Lyon was dead and that Major Samuel Sturgis had just arrived at the head of the troops withdrawn from Bloody Hill. Schofield, in turn, was appraised of Sigel's disaster. Sigel recommended a council of war, and one was held that evening in Schofield's quarters. Almost all of the surviving high-ranking officers attended, and they unanimously agreed that the Army of the West should retreat to Rolla without delay. To escape an anticipated enemy attack on the town at dawn, they set the departure time at 2:00 A.M. on August 11. These decisions were hardly unexpected. Indeed, the only surprise occurred when Sturgis passed the command that had devolved upon him at Lyon's death over to Sigel. Sturgis's reasons remain a mystery, although his later career suggests that he was never really comfortable with the responsibilities of command.[1]

As Schofield was now de facto chief of staff for Sigel, he made many of the actual arrangements, including the organization of a train of 370 wagons. Tucked away amid this caravan was $250,000 in specie from the Springfield Bank. He also did everything possible for the comfort and care of the men who were too seriously wounded to be moved. Otherwise, he focused his efforts on readying Sturgis's column, which, on returning to town, had apparently camped somewhat apart from Sigel's survivors. Schofield was therefore alarmed when at 2:00 A.M. he discovered Sigel fast asleep and his men completely unprepared to move. Sigel sheepishly announced that he would get his column under way as soon as possible. The march finally began at 4:00 A.M. with Sigel's men in the lead, but the column was so long that the last Union troops did not leave Springfield until two hours later. A large number of pro-Union civilians left at the same time, fearing the wrath of the Missouri State Guard. According to one eyewitness, "immense panic existed along the route from Springfield." Had a dawn attack occurred, it would have been a disaster for the Union forces, one chargeable directly to Sigel.[2]

Forsaking the town did not mean that the Federals were safe. Lyon had feared that the Southern cavalry forces might ride ahead and envelop him during a retreat. Sigel therefore insisted that the Union column make a long march on August 11. The already exhausted soldiers suffered terribly under the blazing sun, and many blamed Sigel's late start for making things worse than they had to be. Yet Sigel moved so slowly thereafter that the force might have fallen prey to determined pursuers. He also acted as if the German American units from St. Louis were his only responsibility. Instead of rotating the order of march in the column, a standard procedure, Sigel let the Missouri volunteers lead every day. They therefore marched ahead of most of the column's horses and reached camp first at the end of the day, obtaining the best campsites, firewood, and water. On the third day out of Springfield Sigel halted for three hours while his Missourians slaughtered some cattle and cooked a meal. This delay, and the fact that the food was not shared equally, nearly provoked a mutiny. Schofield reported that "almost total anarchy reigned in the command." Sturgis had witnessed the growing debacle without interfering, but at the insistence of the other officers he finally resumed command, "giving as his reason for so doing, that, although Colonel Sigel had been for a long time acting as an officer of the army, he had no appointment from any competent authority." The hasty, unconstitutional methods used by Lyon to raise his forces had come back to haunt the Army of the West.[3]

After the column reached Rolla on August 19, responsibility for the troops passed to the department commander, General John Frémont. The ninety-day regiments were soon discharged. But for some regiments, such as the First Kansas, the war was just beginning. Whatever the different fates awaiting them, all had participated in a remarkable operation. It was the first major campaign initiated following the outbreak of the war, the second one to be completed. Eugene Ware reported that in its short service the First Iowa, which had left the railway at Renick, Missouri, proceeded on foot to Jefferson City, and after many trials and tribulations finally returned to the railhead at Rolla, had marched 620 miles.[4] Many Union units in the eastern theater did not march that far, cumulatively, during the entire four years of the war.

Although Frémont had previously denied Lyon's requests for major reinforcements, once the news of Wilson's Creek reached his St. Louis headquarters he burst into action, at least at the telegraph office. He learned of the battle on August 13 and immediately wired the secretary of war, requesting reinforcements from nearby states. The War Department concurred, and appeals went out to Illinois, Indiana, and Wisconsin. Frémont ordered several regiments already in Missouri to make haste for Rolla, but as in the past he continued to devote most of his time to planning a campaign to open up the Mississippi River. Southwestern Missouri was never his main concern. This is clear from Frémont's August 30 report to the War Department, in which he forwarded all the after-action reports from the Army of the West. Northern newspapers were busy eulogizing Lyon, but Frémont's report contained no praise whatever for the Connecticut Yankee, although it did describe him in passing as "brave." Whereas Frémont lauded the gallant services of a large number of individuals, starting with Sturgis and working down the ranks to some noncommissioned officers, he wrote nothing positive about Lyon's campaign. His silence implied that the actions of the Army of the West had been pointless, its sacrifices unnecessary.[5]

Frémont's negative assessment of Lyon's actions was understandable. The Battle of Wilson's Creek did not save Missouri for the Union. Lyon's real success lay in securing the state's river and railway communications network. His aggressive campaign disrupted Sterling Price's attempts to recruit Missouri State Guardsmen, but he also drove them almost literally into the arms of the Confederacy. Lyon's actions were not judged dispassionately, however. By coincidence, Missouri congressmen Frank Blair Jr. and John Phelps met with Abraham Lincoln at the White House in early August. They predicted disaster as a consequence of Frémont's indifference to southwestern Missouri, and Lincoln responded by asking the War Department to create a special force under Phelps's command. Missouri's largely pro-Union population gave every corner of the state a political value to Lincoln that transcended purely military considerations. When the telegraph brought news of Lyon's death, Blair and Phelps seemed tragically vindicated. Frémont's decision not to support Lyon may have had merit from a strategic point of view, but it probably contributed to Lincoln's subsequent decision to replace him.[6]

Ironically, whereas Frémont's fortunes declined before the year ended, Sigel's career was not irreparably harmed by his rout at Wilson's Creek and his mishandling of the retreat to Rolla. Across the nation the German American press trumpeted his performance and lavished praise on all those who "fought mit Sigel." Frémont may have guessed which way the political winds were blowing, for although his report did not praise Sigel above others, it did note his "gallant and meritorious conduct in the command of his brigade." In fact, Sigel was promoted to brigadier general on August 7, but he learned of it only after the battle, when many questioned his conduct. He resigned during the winter and only later returned to command. Despite Sigel's military education in Germany, many came to view him as the archetypal political general, a man appointed to command because of his ability to win votes rather than battles. "As a result of the great Missouri campaign, the German leader had made a name for himself. Unfortunately, the name had become synonymous with controversy and retreat."[7]

Controversy also marked the actions of the Western Army following Wilson's Creek. For although the common soldiers of the Missouri State Guard, Arkansas State Troops, and Confederate regiments remained caught up in the euphoria of victory, praising each other's accomplishments, their leaders were soon at odds. Their difficulties in determining a future course of action were exacerbated by their differing goals, a lack of direction from the War Department in Richmond, and the clumsy structure of the Confederate command system in the West.

Initially things went as well, as one might expect. Ben McCulloch met with Sterling Price as soon as the firing died down on August 10, and they reluctantly agreed that because of their exhausted condition and paucity of ammunition the Southern forces were in no condition to pursue the Federals. Some newspapers later criticized this position and McCulloch eventually published an angry defense of his action. Pursuit proved impossible for almost all victorious Civil War armies, however, and there is no reason to question McCulloch's decision. The Texan did make an effort to keep track of the enemy. Turning to Greer's South Kansas–Texas Cavalry, he ordered four companies under Lieutenant Colonel Walter P. Lane to Springfield at dawn on the morning of August 11. When they found only wounded Union troops in the town, the horsemen gleefully pulled the Stars and Stripes from the Court House, ripped it to shreds, and raised the regiment's Confederate banner in its place. Citizens in Springfield with Southern sympathies cheered them on. Two companies of the regiment then scouted the road to Rolla for more than a dozen miles, confirming the Federals' hasty retreat.[8]

The Southern commanders spent much of their time on August 11 and 12 shifting the men to new camps. These stretched from Springfield west to Mt. Vernon so the army might live off the surrounding countryside as much as possible. Farmers throughout the region soon responded to the opportunity the soldiers presented, offering a variety of food for sale at prices that were, at least according to one source, much lower than those charged the Federals only days earlier. Some soldiers were not content with the normal channels of commerce, and McCulloch was forced to reprimand his Confederate troops for looting. Significantly, he did so by appealing to their sense of corporate honor. "The reputation of the States that sent you here is now in your hands," he announced in an order read to the men. "If wrong is done, blame will attach to all. Let not the laurels so nobly won on the 10th instant at the battle of Oak Hills be tarnished by a single trespass upon the property of the citizens of Missouri."[9]

Despite the food coming in, the Southerners were nearly immobilized by shortages, as their logistical problems remained acute. They required tons of food daily for their own forces and now had to care for the Union wounded and prisoners as well. The latter group, which numbered less than two hundred, included a woman who had apparently served in the ranks during the battle. An officer in McBride's Division made a diary entry on August 14 reading: "Saw yesterday a specimen of the Amazonian type dressed in mens clothes. She was captured in uniform & fighting the same as the balance of them." No other reference or information regarding the woman has been found. Another State Guard officer noted that the German Americans from St. Louis among the prisoners were surprised by the humane treatment they received. Concern about their fate was understandable, not only for recent immigrants, who had historically faced prejudice, but also for the entire group. After all, what should the members of the Missouri State Guard, decidedly pro-Secessionist but still citizens of the United States, do with their fellow Americans who had enlisted in unconstitutional volunteer units and destroyed the legal state government, including its largely pro-Union legislature? Fortunately, some time would yet pass before such complex conundrums plunged the state into a savagery with few parallels in American history. Price and McCulloch decided to simply parole the prisoners. "Missouri must be allowed to choose her own destiny; no oaths binding your consciences will be administered," McCulloch announced in a public proclamation. His words and action stood in stark contrast to Lyon's recent fanaticism.[10]

The experiences of Union prisoners differed widely, of course. Officers were usually treated better than enlisted men. Lieutenant Otto Lademann of the Third Missouri witnessed striking examples of magnanimity and courtesy, but he also encountered stark hostility. On August 11 Bart Pearce invited Lademann and seven other captured officers to dine at his headquarters if they would give their word not to attempt to escape. They readily agreed and greatly enjoyed their meal, having not eaten in forty-eight hours. They spent the night in the camps of the Arkansas State Troops, met with McCulloch the next morning, and were eventually sent to Springfield. Here, their word of honor secured them the freedom of the town. They were paroled a week later and hired two wagons to transport them to Rolla. Near Lebanon the group was stopped by a dozen heavily armed men on their way to Springfield to join the Missouri State Guard. The Southerners had been drinking heavily and one of them called out, "Get out of the wagons, you d— Dutch sons of female dogs, and get in line alongside the road and then you hurrah for Jeff Davis, or you die!" The Federals lined up on the road but refused to cheer for the Confederate president. Lieutenant Gustavus Finkleberg, who had been a St. Louis attorney before enlisting in the First Missouri, argued their case as bona fide parolees, but the jury was not sympathetic. As the situation deteriorated a buggy pulled up containing Emmett McDonald. Once he grasped the situation McDonald pointed two cocked pistols at the would-be State Guardsmen and said: "Boys, I am Capt. Emmett McDonald of General Price's staff. The first one of you who touches a hair on the head of any one of these gentlemen, I will kill him like a dog. Now go to Springfield and get away from here!" The Southerners "slunk away like whipped dogs," and after thanking McDonald, Lademann and his companions continued to Rolla without further incident.[11]

Animosity between enemies was to be expected. But following the battle, ill feeling between McCulloch and Price grew stronger, in part because they assessed future prospects differently. Their divergent views surfaced during meetings held on August 11 and 12. Price argued for an immediate advance into the Missouri River valley, the strategic heartland of the state. If the army remained stationary for long, it would exhaust the rapidly dwindling food and forage available in southwestern Missouri. The city of Lexington made a tempting prize, and the process of recruiting the State Guard could accelerate. Price was not dismayed by the virtual absence of ammunition for the army or the continued presence of large numbers of unarmed men in his own force. Perhaps he remembered how, during the Mexican War, he had used speed and determination to overcome his men's numerical and logistical deficiencies, successfully suppressing the "rebellion" in New Mexico. If in retrospect Price's plans

Captain Emmett McDonald of General Price's staff, Missouri State Guard (The collection of Dr. Tom and Karen Sweeney, General Sweeny's Museum, Republic, Missouri)

were too optimistic, his desire for a swift exploitation of victory, to keep pressure on a beaten foe, was laudable. Moreover, if his chances of reestablishing control over the state were slim, they would rise but little during subsequent years of the war.[12]

McCulloch rejected Price's proposal, partly because he had just learned that the previously anticipated Confederate advance in southeastern Missouri was stalled. Were the Western Army to move north as the left flank of a coordinated Confederate sweep up the Mississippi valley, on both sides of the river, it might be possible to regain the bulk of the state. But he feared that if the army struck out on its own, the operation would degenerate into a fruitless raid. Although it might be easier to forage farther north, the army also required a secure base from which it could receive shoes, clothing, ammunition, and firearms. Price might draw recruits, but how many of them could be effectively armed? A supply line running from Fort Smith to central Missouri would be dependent on wagons, and the length involved made this impracticable. Meanwhile, the enemy could use the railway and river networks both in and adjacent to Missouri to concentrate overwhelming force against the Western Army. When the inevitable retreat occurred, Missouri State Guardsmen—especially those lacking weapons—might desert en masse and be compelled to return home to face the retribution of their Unionist neighbors. Although

McCulloch's objections suggest that he continued to think in the cautious manner that had influenced his operations up to that time, his concerns arose from a competent, professional analysis of the situation.[13]

Despite the thrill of victory, the Texan was losing patience with the Missourians. Little things added up. Prior to the battle, men from Parsons's Division had wrongly appropriated a quantity of clothing and almost one hundred tents belonging to the Third Louisiana. These were never returned, nor did either McCulloch or Pearce get back the more than six hundred muskets lent the State Guard from their resources. In fact, the Missourians refused to make an equal distribution of any of the arms and accoutrements policed from the battlefield. Most of these had been salvaged by the unarmed members of the State Guard on the afternoon of August 10. The Missourians were the first to occupy Springfield in force, and when they cleaned out the town's remaining supplies, they declined to share those either. McCulloch also blamed Price's men for failing to establish pickets, thus allowing the army to be surprised on August 10. The final straw came when Price had his report of the campaign and battle published in Springfield. Dated August 12 and evidently printed the same day, it was the first official Southern account of the fight. Price quite properly addressed his report to Governor Jackson, but it is unknown whether he submitted a copy to McCulloch simultaneously or the Texan read it for the first time in the newspapers. In either case, the account contained passages that made McCulloch livid. To begin with, Price stated that at Dug Springs "the greater portion of General Rains's command . . . behaved with great gallantry." This was hardly an accurate description of the event that the Confederates had dubbed "Rains's Scare." Next, Price wrote incorrectly that McCulloch had not exercised command over the combined forces until August 4. When describing the battle, Price naturally focused on the conduct of his own officers and men. He also praised Pearce, the Arkansas State Troops, and the Confederate regiments under Hébert and Churchill. However, other than noting that McCulloch had made "the necessary dispositions of our forces," he neither lauded his commanding officer nor gave any indication of his contribution to the victory. This omission left the impression that McCulloch's presence on the battlefield had been irrelevant. Finally, the report implied that the Missouri State Guard had been solely responsible for defeating Sigel and capturing his battery.[14]

McCulloch had given the artillery captured by the Third Louisiana to the Missourians. But after reading Price's report, he insisted on its return, explaining that the reputation of Hébert's men was at stake. Price complied but kept the Union artillery horses. Although Price was being petty,

McCulloch was not. The Louisianans had paid for those guns with their blood. They had been publicly insulted by Price's misleading report, and the restoration of their trophies was necessary for their corporate honor. McCulloch could have used his own battle report as a vehicle of revenge, but he did not. True, he omitted the despised Rains from the list of those deserving credit, but otherwise he praised the Missourians to the same degree he did others. He informed the secretary of war: "Where all were doing their duty so gallantly, it is almost unfair to discriminate. I must, however, bring to your notice the gallant conduct of the Missouri generals—McBride, Parsons, Clark, and Slack, and their officers. To General Price I am under many obligations for assistance on the battle-field. He was at the head of his force, leading them on, and sustaining them by his gallant bearing." McCulloch, it seems, would deny no man his just due, although he did take pains to indicate that he, not Price, commanded the Western Army.[15]

In his youth McCulloch might have considered challenging Price to a duel over the wording of the Missourian's battle report. Now older and presumably wiser, he seems to have been willing to work with Price under any conditions that did not involve risking his own Confederate forces. Yet it was the issue of risk that produced an impasse. Price broke it on August 14 by formally resuming command of the Missouri State Guard. He intended to move west to the Kansas border, to counter a feared "abolitionist invasion," before heading north to the Missouri River.[16]

Price's decision freed McCulloch to concentrate on his original mission: defending the Indian Territory. The challenge was formidable, as within a few days Pearce's Arkansas State Troops marched south. Those whose enlistments had expired were discharged; the remainder were transferred to Confederate service and assigned to Brigadier General William J. Hardee, as he, not McCulloch, was responsible for Confederate operations in northern Arkansas. Left with only 3,000-odd men, McCulloch soon suspected that his command rated the lowest priority in the entire Southern defense structure. He vented his frustrations in a series of letters to friends, fellow officers, and even President Jefferson Davis. On occasion he railed against the local citizenry for not taking up arms. Fewer than 1,000 Arkansans enlisted in the first weeks following the victory at Wilson's Creek. These hardly compensated for those who left when their enlistments expired, as almost all the Missourians attracted by the Western Army's victory chose to serve in the State Guard rather than the Confederate army. "I have called in vain on the people of Arkansas," McCulloch admitted in a letter to his mother, while to President Davis he complained that "little can be expected of Missouri." He made an even more negative assessment of the Missourians in a letter to Hardee on August 24, stating: "We have little to hope or expect from the people of this State. The force now in the field is undisciplined and led by men who are mere politicians; not a soldier among them to control and organize this mass of humanity. The Missouri forces are in no condition to meet an organized army, nor will they ever be whilst under their present leaders. I dare not join them in my present condition, for fear of having my men completely demoralized."[17]

Such remarks must be placed in context. Though McCulloch's judgment was harsh, he almost always separated his evaluation of Missouri's leaders from that of its common soldiers. Two months after his letter to Hardee he informed the secretary of war: "There is excellent material out of which to make an army in Missouri. They only want a military man for a general." Noting that he himself had become "very unpopular by speaking to them frequently about the necessity of order and discipline in their organizations," he suggested that should Missouri become a Confederate state, Brigadier General Braxton Bragg might be just the man to calm troubled waters. Even more important, McCulloch's subsequent correspondence with the Richmond authorities and Price himself indicates his willingness to put aside his needs or opportunities for advancement for the good of the cause. McCulloch could be feisty and critical, but he remained ready to cooperate with the Missouri State Guard in an emergency and was willing to discuss any campaign other than one aimed at a lodgment on the Missouri River. Although McCulloch's command embraced neither Missouri nor Arkansas, logistics forced him to continue drawing supplies from Fort Smith. Only a small portion of his men actually entered the Indian nations, but the recruitment of Confederate regiments from among Native Americans proceeded apace.[18]

Operations in the following months were complex, but they can be summarized to place the Wilson's Creek campaign in the context of subsequent events. Leaving Springfield on August 25, Price's Missouri State Guard defeated a Union force at Drywood Creek, near the Kansas-Missouri border, on September 2. Price reached the Missouri River on September 13 and soon after laid siege to a Federal garrison at Lexington. At times the Southerners advanced by pushing bales of hemp in front of them, making the engagement unique in the annals of Civil War combat. The Federals capitulated on September 20, and volunteers soon flocked to the cause, swelling the ranks of the State Guard to around 20,000. Yet McCulloch's dire predictions proved accurate. When Price learned that Frémont was advancing with 38,000 men, he had no choice but to withdraw, as the Missourians had neither the armaments, supplies, nor logistical support system to remain in the river valley. The retreat began on September 29, and the army dissolved steadily with every mile of the march south. By the time the State Guard crossed the Osage River on October 8, there were only 7,000 men under arms. But rather than admit to the inherent flaws in his strategy or question the commitment of his fellow Missourians, Price faulted McCulloch for not supporting him. He also criticized Jefferson Davis, believing that the president's constitutional scruples prevented Missouri from receiving the attention it deserved.[19]

The loss of Lexington finally forced Frémont's attention away from the Mississippi. Yet he advanced slowly, taking time to publish an unauthorized proclamation emancipating Missouri's slaves. Despite only moderate resistance, the Union forces did not occupy Springfield until October 27. Lincoln was not impressed. He ordered Frémont to rescind his proclamation, then relieved him of command on November 2. Major General David Hunter took over operations against the Missouri State Guard, which continued to retreat toward Pineville, near the Arkansas border.[20]

A few days before the Federals reached Springfield, Price appealed to McCulloch for help. The Texan responded favorably, partly, no doubt, from a genuine concern for Missourians' liberties, but also because the Federals now posed an even greater threat to the Indian Territory than they had in August under Lyon. Recent reinforcements brought McCulloch's force to just over 7,500 men, and he concentrated them along the Wire Road, on both sides of the Missouri-Arkansas border, in a position to move them quickly as needed. Although ready for battle, he was willing to concede all of Missouri north of Springfield to the Federals if they advanced no farther south. For whereas Price looked forward to another victory on the battlefield, followed by a march in unison to the Missouri River, McCulloch favored a more generally defensive stance to allow for continued training and recruitment. He also contemplated the use of partisan warfare and hoped that the Confederate and Missouri State Guard mounted troops might operate together, "destroying Kansas as far north as possible," as that would provide the best defense for the Indian Territory. The two men were never forced to reconcile their strategies, however, as Hunter, faced with logistical problems almost eight times larger than those Lyon had encountered, retreated after occupying Springfield for only a short time. Lincoln removed him on November 19, giving Major General Henry W. Halleck the top command in the West. In Halleck, Lincoln had a far more learned soldier than Frémont, Hunter, or Lyon, but the Union cause in Missouri never did see Lyon's equal for drive and energy. Hunter's departure allowed McCulloch to occupy Springfield, but he withdrew to northern Arkansas early in December to shorten his supply lines. Meanwhile, despite his hope for a return to the Missouri River and the strategic heart of the state, Price marched the Missouri State Guard only some fifty miles north, to a position on the Sac River near Osceola. Within weeks a want of supplies forced him south again. Christmas Day found the Missouri army back in Springfield. Across the Trans-Mississippi theater of the war soldiers began building winter quarters, while their commanders pondered options for the coming spring.[21]

Chapter 20

Never Disgrace Your Town

The Battle of Wilson's Creek was part of the complex military and political events of the first summer of the Civil War. But it also occurred within the context of the implicit social contract between the soldiers who fought there and the communities that had raised and supported them. The telegraph rapidly broadcast the news that a major battle had occurred in southwestern Missouri. Once the Union retreat began, Rolla offered the closest working telegraph office. Franc Wilkie and other pro-Union reporters reached there well ahead of Sigel, and their early accounts spread nationwide.[1] Because the Federals retreated toward their lines of communication, the news of their activities became more detailed every day. Articles appearing in St. Louis journals were quickly reprinted throughout Missouri, Iowa, and Kansas, but soon the newspapers in all of the states concerned were publishing accounts written by locals who had participated in the fight. Memphis papers picked up many of the Union articles, providing the first details of the battle for Southerners. From Memphis, word of the engagement made its way across the Confederacy. Because the Western Army remained near Springfield for some time and the telegraph lines to the south had been cut, accounts by Southern participants traveled only slowly back to Arkansas, Texas, and Louisiana. And due to the breakdown of the mail service, relatively few letters by Missouri State Guardsmen appeared in Missouri papers, regardless of whether the paper was pro-Union or pro-Missouri.

The reaction of communities in Kansas and Iowa exemplifies the response of civilians North and South. Because earlier reports had made it clear that a battle was likely, rumors were widespread in early August, and families felt understandably anxious for their loved ones in uniform. By

August 15, most major papers in Kansas had reported Lyon's death and Sigel's retreat to Rolla. Few details were available, but the news brought "sadness and painful apprehension to many a Kansas home." A widely reprinted article from the *Leavenworth Times* summed up the concern of many: "Two regiments of our brave boys were engaged in the bloody struggle, and many of them, doubtless, have fallen in defense of their country's flag. Our people will look for details of this battle with the deepest and most intense anxiety." In Lawrence, flags flew at half-mast and citizens besieged the local post office, "fathers, mothers, brothers and sisters awaiting fearfully every additional report."[2]

The first reports of the battle struck Iowa cities like an earthquake. Local newspapers used the word "anxiety" repeatedly in connection with each community's concern for its company. "At the homes of our gallant boys, the first news created an intense sensation, and many anxious hearts waited to hear the list of killed and wounded," wrote one columnist. Less than a week after the battle, detailed lists of the dead and wounded were being printed. In Iowa City, home of the Washington Guards, the *Weekly State Reporter* noted poignantly, "The parents of the two missing soldiers, who reside here, are suffering intense anxiety about the fate of their sons, and we hope that they will soon be heard from." Occasionally, there was happy news, as men who had been reported dead were discovered to be alive and well.[3]

Most Northern papers proclaimed Wilson's Creek to be a Union victory. As by traditional standards of assessment Lyon had been badly defeated, this at first appears inexplicable. Some early reports were simply based on erroneous information. A week after the battle the *Atchison Freedom's Champion* referred to "the joyous news of the brilliant victory at Springfield." A separate article claimed that Sigel had pursued the vanquished enemy until nightfall halted his chase.[4] But even after the full details became known, papers continued to refer to Wilson's Creek as a great victory. How could this be?

In his study of the ill-fated, often defeated Confederate Army of Tennessee, Larry J. Daniel notes how its soldiers evaluated their experiences selectively. Their morale did not collapse because they lauded partial triumphs, celebrating the success of local attacks or stalwart defenses. They were also sustained by a sense of their shared struggle in the face of great odds. Northern assessment of Wilson's Creek seems to have followed a similar pattern. For example, the *Davenport Daily Democrat & News* admitted that Sigel had quit the field, but claimed that he had withdrawn of his own free will, "not through compulsion on the part of the enemy." Even those papers that acknowledged that Sigel had been routed argued that Lyon's wing had accomplished its mission. Many asserted, wrongly, that the Southern baggage train had been burned, that many thousands of Southerners had been killed, and that Lyon's death alone prevented the Federals from driving the enemy from the field. They emphasized the odds that the Federals had faced, odds that, due to a lack of accurate information, they greatly exaggerated. "The victory of the Union force under Gen Lyon," wrote the editor of the *Topeka Kansas State Record*, "was brilliant and overwhelming; and accomplished under the great disadvantage of having but 8,000 of our troops to make the attack on 23,000 of the Rebels upon their chosen ground and strongly entrenched." Similarly, the *St. Louis Tri-Weekly Republican* contended that the "closer the accounts of this battle are sifted, the more certain does it appear that the Federal forces, though vastly inferior in numbers, achieved a most brilliant victory." Papers in states not directly involved in the action reached the same conclusion. The editor of an Indiana paper counseled his readers: "The battle completely upsets the gasconade heard so often that one Southerner can whip two Northerners. It was a clear triumph on the part of Gen. Lyon's men. The subsequent night retreat, without pursuit by the enemy, does not change the fact that McCulloch's army was whipped in the encounter and so the historians will record it."[5]

Southern newspapers celebrated with gusto the outcome of the battle they usually called "Oak Hills" or "Springfield." "Never has a greater victory crowned the efforts of the friends of Liberty and Equal Rights," wrote Colonel John Hughes of the Missouri State Guard in the *Liberty [Missouri] Tribune*. "The best blood of the land has been poured out to water afresh the Tree of Liberty." Another Missouri paper concluded that "as a hand to hand fight its equal is not on record." Readers of the *Shreveport Weekly News* were assured that the "Battle of Springfield is only inferior to that of its worthy predecessor, Manassas, in the number of troops engaged," while Marshall's *Texas Republican* boasted that the engagement demonstrated "the superiority of Southern soldiery." There was remarkably little criticism of the Southern generals for allowing themselves to be surprised in their camps. Instead, harmony among the allies was stressed. The battle was also seen as a vindication of the Missouri State Guard, and Missouri's eventual secession was confidently predicted.[6]

If Northern and Southern reactions to Wilson's Creek were similar, if Northerners could claim victory despite having quit the field, it was because the communities and the soldiers who represented them judged the contest largely in terms of honor. This is clear from contemporary

Colonel John Taylor Hughes,
Slack's Division, Missouri State
Guard (The collection of Dr. Tom
and Karen Sweeney, General Sweeny's Museum, Republic, Missouri)

letters and diary entries as well as postwar memoirs. It is even more
evident from newspapers, as these served as a vehicle for community self-
assessment. They acted as public report cards, first via their editorial
commentary, but even more importantly by printing letters from soldiers
in the field. In this manner each community's company was carefully
scrutinized.

Hometown newspapers were quick to proclaim that their community's
honor had been upheld. The *Olathe Mirror* bragged that the Union
Guards had "shown themselves to be worthy sons of Kansas," while the
Atchison Freedom's Champion boasted that the Kansans had erased the
disgrace of the recent Union defeat at Manassas. The editor of the *Emporia News* wrote of the hometown company, "They have done themselves honor, and we are proud of them." In Iowa, the *Dubuque Weekly
Times* stated: "The boys have done just what we could have expected
when an opportunity presented itself for them to exhibit their daring and
bravery. They have met the expectations of their friends." Pride was not
limited to towns that had contributed troops to the battle. The *Anamosa
Eureka* asserted that the First Iowa had "won the chief honors," outshin-
ing other regiments, and the *Lyons Weekly Mirror* concluded that "the
gallant First Iowa have just shown in the desperate struggle in Springfield
of what stuff her sons are made." Southern papers exhibited equal pride
in "their" companies. In Liberty, Missouri, the *Tribune* praised those

wounded in Major Thomas McCarty's company of the Missouri State Guard as "men who went into this war from *principle* and sealed it with their life's blood." The editor continued, "Whilst it causes us infinite grief to hear that some of our brave men were among the killed and wounded, it is yet a source of pleasure to know that they fought like men—like Missourians."[7]

As the men in each company knew each other and linear tactics kept them adjacent to their friends throughout the battle, no one's conduct could go unnoticed. Because the soldiers had pledged their honor in public ceremonies prior to leaving town, no one's actions went unjudged. The *Atchison Freedom's Champion* showed no hesitation in printing a letter that Private Joseph W. Martin wrote to his brother concerning the conduct of the First Kansas: "Some of the boys faltered in the first part of the fight, and three of our company, but none of your acquaintances, they all stood up like men, with but one or two exceptions. Some of the boys say that Keifer, Herman, and Jackell run, and my opinion is that they did, for I did not see them in the fight at all." Letters written to hometown editors specifically for publication were equally detailed. A civilian correspondent accompanying the First Kansas accused one officer of incompetence, writing that "Major Halderman was so excited as to be of no service in the field."[8]

There was obviously praise as well. A soldier in the Third Louisiana informed the editor of the *Baton Rouge Weekly Gazette and Comet* about the performance of the Pelican Rifles: "They fought bravely and many distinguished themselves. Bob Henderson fought like a tiger. I, myself, saw three of the enemy fall victim to the unerring aim of his trusty rifle. One of them, a U.S. officer, received a ball through the brain. Bob received a blow from a musket in the hands of one of the enemy, who immediately scampered off, but a ball from Bob's gun lodged between the fellow's shoulders and caused him to bite the earth." The writer praised several other individuals by name, concluding, "In fact the whole company, officers and men, fought with a desperation which knew no bounds and won a name for the 'Pelican Rifles' which shall not be tarnished in any future engagement."[9]

North and South, men seized pen and ink to reassure the home folk that the honor of their regiment and company, and therefore their community, had been upheld. William F. Allen of the Second Kansas wrote proudly to his parents: "Our Reg. was the last to leave the field and stands first in the good graces of the commanding officers. Maj. Sturgis made the remark that if he wanted to storm hell he would take the 2nd Kansas to do it." Joseph Martin of the First Kansas informed his brother that the last words of his company's mortally wounded lieutenant had been, "Give it to them, boys; remember your promise to the Atchison folks. Never disgrace your town." Martin concluded, "Such was the feeling of us all." A soldier from Olathe, Kansas, wrote, "The Union Guards, or Company G, acted splendidly and fully equalled, if not surpassed, the good opinion formed of them." In similar fashion, a Texan confided to his sweetheart, "Captain Comby, the other officers, and the entire company from Rusk County acted their part well, and I believe that Rusk County must feel proud that these men represent that county in the Confederate Army." Another Southerner told readers of his hometown paper in Shreveport, "we turned our faces homeward assured that our conduct as amateur soldiers would never be a source of reproach to our friends in Caddo [Parish]."[10]

Officers naturally took pride in the conduct of the men under their command. Colonel John R. Gratiot informed Arkansas readers of the *Washington Telegraph*, "Our Hempstead boys did their work nobly, and fully sustained the good name of their city, and were during the whole fight in the hottest of the fire." Louisiana captain John P. Vigilini basked in the praise that Ben McCulloch had lavished on his men, writing that "the Pelican Rifles are worthy of all honors bestowed upon them." He concluded that "Baton Rouge may well be proud of those who represent her in the great struggle in the southwest of Missouri." Lieutenant C. S. Hills of the Second Kansas asked the editor of the *Emporia News* to reassure the makers of his company's flag that "*it has not been disgraced.*" He continued: "I feel proud of our little Emporia company—of the regiment—of the State we came from. The State *shall never* be disgraced by us."[11]

Communities also took an interest in how their units appeared in the official reports, which were published within a month of the battle. Because the reputations of both men and entire communities were at stake, it is perhaps not surprising that controversies arose following Wilson's Creek. As Lyon was the first Union hero of the West and one of the war's first martyrs, associations with him were both treasured and disputed. Newspaper correspondent Thomas Knox recalled, "I know at least a dozen individuals in whose arms Lyon expired, and think there are as many more who claim that sad honor." Members of the First Iowa denounced reports by the First Kansas that Lyon had been leading that regiment at the time of his death, claiming the honor for their own unit. Members of the Second Kansas and First Missouri made like assertions. The controversy, which was picked up by the national press, continued among veterans long after the war. In a related matter, Colonel George

Deitzler of the First Kansas used the Kansas and Missouri press to denounce the official report of Lieutenant Colonel William Merritt of the First Iowa, which had appeared in the St. Louis papers, because it stated that the Kansans had retreated in confusion.[12]

Some controversies were personal. For example, the *Atchison Freedom's Champion*, which had reported the movements of the city's All Hazard company in great detail throughout the campaign, took pains to defend the reputation of its commander, Captain George H. Fairchild, who had departed Springfield on furlough on August 9. The paper's claim that Fairchild had not anticipated a battle and left merely to attend to pressing personal business affairs was hardly creditable. Perhaps to ward off any suggestion of cowardice, the paper emphasized Fairchild's intention to remain in the service for the duration of the war. Colonel John Bates, the unpopular commander of the First Iowa, also missed the battle. Although some papers attributed this to a fever, correspondent Franc Wilkie's reports implied that Bates was drunk. Bates never offered a direct public defense, but Captain George Streaper of the Burlington Zouaves turned to the pages of his hometown paper to defend his reputation. Cashiered prior to the battle, Streaper claimed that "Col. Bates and my 1st Lieut., being *determined* to detach me from my company, were the whole cause of my detachment." More than a dozen officers from nine of the regiment's companies publicly endorsed the captain's claim. In a somewhat similar case, thirteen officers of the Fifth Missouri wrote the *St. Louis Tri-Weekly Republican* to defend their commander, Colonel C. E. Salomon, against charges of cowardice that had appeared in a German-language paper.[13]

Despite his retreat, Sigel garnered as much praise as criticism for his performance at Wilson's Creek. Indeed, many Federals who had been in Lyon's column blamed Sigel's soldiers for the debacle rather than Sigel himself. Sigel's reputation among German Americans continued to climb, while Lyon's superior, department commander John C. Frémont, was frequently criticized for not sending reinforcements to Lyon. In at least one important instance the battle healed rather than provoked controversy. Papers throughout Kansas praised Deitzler's conduct during the battle, reporting that it erased the ill feelings engendered by the whipping of the volunteers en route to Springfield.[14]

Perhaps because Southerners were caught up in the afterglow of victory, there were no major controversies on their side. Although arguments later arose concerning McCulloch's decision to withdraw to Arkansas, leaving Sterling Price to fight alone at Lexington, the different elements of the Western Army generally praised each other in the days immediately following Wilson's Creek. Indeed, the conduct of the Missouri State Guard won the admiration of many who had questioned its pugnacity since the skirmish at Dug Springs. "The Missourians, who were looked upon by the Confederate army as dastardly cowards, most gallantly retrieved their characters on that day," wrote a Louisiana soldier. The Reverend Robert A. Austin, chaplin of Slack's Division, spoke for many Southerners when he observed, "The Louisiana troops, the Arkansans, the Texans and Missourians stood side by side and fought only as men can fight when fighting for their honor and their homes."[15]

All of the men who fought at Wilson's Creek received accolades from their home communities. But because they had enlisted for only ninety days, the returning survivors of the First Iowa and Second Kansas were able to participate in various public meetings, dinners, and receptions that truly validated the social contract they had established with their hometowns at the beginning of the campaign. Although the North held victory celebrations in 1865, the length and devastation of the war made that triumph bittersweet. But in August and September 1861 it was still possible to believe in a short war and even envy those who had served. Few American soldiers have ever received such profound thanks and adoration as did the Iowans and Kansans who made their way back to hearth and home.

The men of the First Iowa made a relatively speedy return, their jubilation increased by the fact that the entire regiment now wore matching gray uniforms and new shoes, which they had found waiting for them at Rolla. They were officially discharged at St. Louis on August 23, and a flotilla of steamboats brought the regiment to Burlington two days later. Twenty thousand civilians jammed the levee, many straining to identify the wounded, who disembarked first. As they had throughout their service, the companies strictly maintained their separate identities, even in the midst of celebration. Initially only the Burlington Zouaves, Mt. Pleasant Grays, and German Rifles were to have gone ashore to attend the great public feast that had been prepared. The remaining companies were invited to join the festival at the last minute. "We were honored like the return of a Roman Legion after the conquest of a new empire," one veteran recalled of the march through town. Not surprisingly, Governor Samuel Kirkwood was on hand to give a speech. He had his work cut out for him as the First Iowa's second-in-command, Lieutenant Colonel Merritt, was soon touted in the press as a potential rival for the gubernatorial chair.[16]

From Burlington, the companies traveled by rail or steamboat to their home cities, where, without exception, they received a lavish welcome. In

Iowa City, notices had been posted on August 21 for a meeting to plan a reception for the Washington Guards. In one evening over $1,800 was pledged to support the endeavor. Muscatine held an enormous parade for its two companies, with not only the soldiers, but also the men, women, and children of the town participating. At the public banquet that followed, the first toast of the evening praised the soldiers for having upheld the honor of the state. In Dubuque, ten thousand people lined the streets as the Wilson Guards and Governor's Grays marched past. Dozens of homemade banners stretched across the street bore such slogans as "Honor the Brave," "We Are Proud of You," "Welcome Brave Boys," and "Iowa First, Tried and Found True." The parade halted at the center of the city park, where rows of young girls, dressed all in white, presented each soldier with a bouquet and a wreath of oak leaves. The inevitable speeches, in both English and German, followed before the soldiers finally sat down to an outdoor dinner. The *Weekly Times*, which reported the proceedings under a subheadline reading "Honor to the Brave, and Honor to Dubuque," proclaimed that the conduct of the two companies had reflected a glory on the whole town that would be passed down for generations. When the steamer bearing Captain August Wentz and the German Volunteers came into view of Davenport, the soldiers crowded the decks, breaking into spontaneous song and dance. On landing, they found not only the levee crowded, but also every rooftop and balcony along their projected parade route filled with citizens who showered them with flowers and oak leaves. They passed through three triumphal arches. The first of these had been constructed entirely by German American women, and the second two were decorated by them. Banners welcomed home the "Pride of Iowa." The citizens inland at Mt. Pleasant had decorated in a rush, only to find the train carrying their Mt. Pleasant Grays two days late. The city's celebration was elaborate and joyous, nevertheless.[17] Meanwhile, in the *Mt. Pleasant Home Journal*, as in newspapers across the state, bad verse sprouted like dandelions as amateur poets vied to honor the gallant First.[18]

For the Kansans, celebration began when they reached St. Louis. The two regiments camped in a local park, and the men were allowed to roam the city at will. One soldier recalled, "Abundance of everything to eat was free to them, and no saloon in town would charge a cent for beer to a soldier who had 'fought mit Sigel.'" Most of all, they were anxious to return home. The men of the Second Kansas anticipated their discharge, while those in the First Kansas hoped for furlough. Most of the latter were disappointed, although a number of wounded men had been sent directly to Kansas shortly after the battle. They were universally lionized, and in this manner the First Kansas received tremendous public praise, even though the regiment remained in the field.[19]

During the last weeks of August newspapers throughout the state announced the imminent return of the Second Kansas and urged readers to make appropriate preparations for the soldiers' welcome. In Topeka, the *Kansas State Record* declared that "they must have such a public reception as will be a deserved tribute to their courage and endurance." Another paper echoed these sentiments, writing: "Shall the boys have a public reception? Every citizen will answer yes. Let us get up a meeting and take measures to give them a public and hearty reception. They deserve it at our hands."[20]

The trip home began auspiciously for the men of the Second Kansas. General Frémont gave them a personal salute in front of his St. Louis headquarters and authorized them to emblazon "Springfield" on their regimental colors in honor of their gallant service. But tragedy struck on September 2, as the train bearing the regiment to St. Joseph derailed at a bridge crossing the Platte River. Eight persons were killed, including Lucius J. Shaw, a Vermont native and Dartmouth College graduate, who had enlisted as a private in the Leavenworth Union Rifles and was subsequently elected lieutenant. Reports blamed the wreck on pro-Secessionists in the area.[21]

The Kansans remained at St. Joseph for more than a week. Then, despite fighting that raged at Lexington only a short distance away, they were ordered to Fort Leavenworth. Boarding the steamer *Omaha*, the men doubtless assumed that they were leaving danger behind them for good, yet early on the morning of September 15, near Iatan, Missouri, they sighted "a body of rebel cavalry" lining the shore. After an exchange of bloodless volleys the enemy fled, allowing the Kansans to claim their very last military action as a victory.[22]

Elaborate preparations had been made for a reception at Leavenworth honoring the entire regiment. "Although but two companies can be claimed by Leavenworth, the regiment is of Kansas, and well has it maintained the honor of our young State since it left us," explained the editor of the city's *Daily Times*. As the soldiers were expected to arrive during the evening of Sunday, September 15, there was considerable consternation when, just before 10:00 A.M., worship services were disrupted by a cannon's discharge, signifying that the *Omaha* was in sight. Soon fife and drum music could be heard from the vessel's deck, and crowds of citizens rushed to the levee to greet loved ones as the companies marched onto shore.[23]

The men and women on the celebration committees reportedly did a fine job of adapting to the changed circumstances, and everyone had a good time in spite of cloudy skies and occasional drizzle. The men of the Second waited patiently on the levee for two hours while the local militia and Home Guard companies assembled. Then a short parade, which began around noon, brought the multitude into the center of town where speeches were made from the steps of the leading hotel. In place of the public banquet that had been planned for that night, the soldiers were treated to meals at three local restaurants. By mid-afternoon tents had been unshipped, and the men were camped just outside the city in the same location they had occupied the previous June when assembling to go to war. Visitors wandered through the camp well into the night. Unlike the Iowans, the men of the Second Kansas had never received replacement uniforms, and their ragged appearance was a source of much comment. "In truth, the men looked rough," noted one observer.[24]

From Leavenworth the Second Kansas expected to go to Lawrence. That city's own Oread Guards—the "Stubbs"—were still serving in Missouri with the First Kansas. But there was a long-standing rivalry between Lawrence and Leavenworth, and the citizens of Lawrence were determined to give the Second the finest reception possible. Hundreds of posters and handbills announced the forthcoming celebration, at which "Lawrence expected to see the grandest day of her age." Farmers brought food by the cartload, while sugar and coffee were stockpiled "by the hundred weight." The women of the community labored for hours to prepare a feast worthy of heroes. Then, on the evening before the regiment was scheduled to appear, word arrived that it had been ordered to Wyandotte instead. There the regiment was broken up, the men furloughed until the expiration of their enlistments at the end of October. Disappointment in Lawrence was acute. Over the course of several days they feasted individual companies that passed through the town en route to their homes, but it was not the same.[25]

So the Kansans made their way back to Topeka, Olathe, Burlingame, and other communities, garnering even more praise from friends and relatives. The homecoming of the Union Guards was especially poignant. After an absence of 158 days, they marched down the streets of Emporia on Saturday, October 19, to "a welcome that did the very soul good." As their arrival had not been foretold, the town's reception committee postponed the official celebration until Tuesday evening. It included all of the standard elements—a parade, military music, speeches, and a public feast—but its high point was something special. The Guards had begun their military service at a public ceremony in May, receiving a banner constructed by the ladies of Emporia and being blessed by Father Fairchild, the town's leading minister. Out of the ten Second Kansas company flags so fashioned by home folk, theirs had been selected as the regimental colors, and theirs alone had actually been carried on the battlefield at Wilson's Creek. The soldier who had received the flag that day in May, pledging along with his comrades to uphold the honor of Emporia, lay buried in the soil of southwestern Missouri. Three of his comrades had also failed to return, and another seven were wounded, a casualty rate of one out of every four of the town's volunteers. As a tribute to them the flag was returned to Emporia and consecrated to their memory.[26]

The ceremony took place in the local Christian Church, with the aged Reverend Fairchild presiding, his long white locks spilling onto the collar of a shabby formal black coat. Mrs. Anna Watson Randolph, who helped to sew the flag, described the service as the Second Kansas arrived:

> Sadly they marched up the aisle. Father Fairchild, who had prayed over them and blessed them and sent them to battle such a short time ago, received them with tears rolling down his wrinkled cheeks. They placed their flag in his hands. He unfolded it. We saw it full of bullet-holes, ragged and battle-stained. He pointed to the dark stains on the staff where the blood of our brave young soldier had trickled down, and told us how even in the struggle of death he had borne it up until a comrade could take his place. . . . We sobbed and cried aloud. It was our first experience of the horrors of war.[27]

The Kansans and the Iowans had come full circle in their social contract. Sent forth from their hometowns, they had returned with their own honor as well as that of their communities intact. Honor also had been maintained by the other Northern and Southern veterans of Wilson's Creek whose enlistment kept them in the ranks. Had their hometowns been given the opportunity, doubtless they would have treated them just as grandly. But for them, as for so many other soldiers and their families across the land, the war was just beginning.

Epilogue . . . .

A Heritage of Honor

I t is hardly surprising that the accomplishments and fortunes of those who fought at Wilson's Creek differed widely following the battle. For nineteenth-century Americans these variations were evaluated in the context of honor. As Bertram Wyatt-Brown notes, honor and reputation were two sides of the same coin. Honor was linked to public perception, making what people thought of one another extremely important. Yet opinions might differ. Franz Sigel continued to display the odd combination of military talent and ineffectiveness that had brought him adroitly to a key position on the battlefield at Wilson's Creek only to fail by neglecting his security. He fought with both skill and ineptitude during the Pea Ridge campaign in 1862 and was promoted to major general. German Americans worshiped him throughout the war, even after his defeat at New Market, Virginia, in 1864 and removal from command. Sigel was a journalist for a short time after the fighting ceased but soon became heavily engaged in politics and held a number of minor positions during his remaining years. Although Samuel Sturgis became a major general of volunteers, his wartime career effectively ended in Mississippi at Brice's Cross Roads in 1864, when he proved to be no match for Nathan Bedford Forrest. In the postwar period, with his permanent Regular Army rank of colonel, Sturgis initially commanded the Sixth Cavalry and later the Seventh Cavalry. The latter assignment introduced him to a brash subordinate named George Armstrong Custer, who led the regiment on active operations while the colonel sat behind a desk. Sturgis retired in 1886. Fate forced Ben McCulloch and Sterling Price into close partnership once again, as wing commanders under Earl Van Dorn, at Pea Ridge, Arkansas. McCulloch was killed while trying to get a better view of the enemy's position. Price survived, enduring not only the Confederate defeat at Pea Ridge but also failures at Iuka and Corinth after being transferred across the Mississippi. Back in Missouri in 1864, he led the largest and longest cavalry raid in American military history. When the war ended Price initially chose exile in Mexico rather than surrender, but he returned to Missouri in 1866 and engaged in civilian pursuits. Bart Pearce exchanged his Arkansas state commission for the rank of major in the Confederate commissary department, serving in Arkansas and Texas amid accusations of graft and corruption. After the war he pursued a variety of business activities and was briefly a professor of mathematics at the University of Arkansas.[1]

Almost two dozen veterans of Wilson's Creek achieved the rank of general in either the Southern or Northern army. A few examples will illustrate the diversity of their experiences. Joseph B. Plummer became a brigadier general and served with Major General John Pope, but he died in August 1862. John M. Schofield, Lyon's chief of staff, rose to major general, commanded a corps, and won a major defensive victory at Franklin, Tennessee. He acted briefly as secretary of war under President Andrew Johnson and ended his career as the army's general-in-chief, eventually attaining the rank of lieutenant general. Gordon Granger, who had advised Union soldiers to hide in the grass and aim low, won fame as a major general at Chickamauga, Georgia, and later commanded a corps. He served in the peacetime army until his death. Francis J. Herron, onetime captain of the Governor's Grays in the First Iowa, earned a brigadier's star and much later the Congressional Medal of Honor for his heroism at Pea Ridge. When promoted to major general in 1863 at age twenty-six, he was then the youngest two-star officer of the war. Yet in peacetime he was unsuccessful in business and died in poverty. One-armed Thomas W. Sweeny, who had been unofficially elected brigadier general by the Missouri volunteers, became a brigadier in fact in 1863. A division commander during the Atlanta campaign, his poor performance led to a court-martial and despite an acquittal his career came to an end. Prior to his death in 1892, he was involved in the Fenian movement. Eugene A. Carr, whose poor performance at Wilson's Creek was mixed with a suggestion of cowardice, or at least loss of nerve, ended the war a major general. Like Herron, he won the Medal of Honor for heroism at Pea Ridge. Carr served for almost thirty years in the Far West, where his "exploits were legion." After retiring in 1893, he was active in the National Geographic Society.[2]

James Patrick Major, whose Missouri State Guard troopers had fled from Sigel's surprise bombardment, went on to fight at Vicksburg in Mississippi and at Mansfield and Pleasant Hill in Louisiana. He finished the war as a brigadier general commanding cavalry and spent the postwar years as a planter in Louisiana and Texas. John T. Hughes, the State Guard colonel who had argued that the Tree of Liberty must be watered with blood, became an acting general and died leading an attack on Independence, Missouri, in 1862. Death also claimed James M. McIntosh, who had resigned from Sturgis's command in Arkansas during the first weeks of the conflict and later directed the fight in John Ray's cornfield. Promoted to brigadier general, he was killed within minutes of succeeding to the command of McCulloch's Brigade at Pea Ridge, only a few hundred yards from the spot where his Texas chief fell. Dandridge McRae, who had assisted in organizing the Arkansas State Troops before accepting his Confederate colonel's commission, fought at Pea Ridge and won promotion to brigadier general. He served in campaigns throughout the Trans-Mississippi and practiced law after the war. Louis Hébert led the Third Louisiana at Pea Ridge, where he was captured. After being exchanged, he was promoted to brigadier general and fought in Mississippi at Iuka, Corinth, and Vicksburg. In peacetime he was a teacher and newspaper editor. Matthew Ector of the South Kansas–Texas Cavalry, who had become separated from his son Walton during the fighting in Sharp's fields, was later commissioned a brigadier general and fought at Chickamauga, but, severely wounded in the Atlanta campaign, he saw little further service. After the war Ector was a state court judge in Tyler, Texas. Others attaining the rank of general included Peter J. Osterhaus, George W. Deitzler, Robert B. Mitchell, Powell Clayton, Frederick Steele, David S. Stanley, Karl L. Matthies, Thomas P. Dockery, Elkanah Greer, Walter P. Lane, and Thomas J. Churchill.[3]

Although the Congressional Medal of Honor was instituted during the Civil War, many awards were not made until long after the conflict ended. The five men decorated for their conduct at Wilson's Creek were all honored in the final years of the nineteenth century. The first medal went to Lorenzo Immell in 1890 for his "bravery in action" with Totten's Battery. Immell received a lieutenant's commission shortly after Wilson's Creek and served in a number of artillery units. He was acting inspector of artillery for the IV Corps when the fighting ceased. In 1892 Schofield, then the army's senior officer but not yet promoted to lieutenant general, was awarded the medal for being "conspicuously gallant in leading a regiment in a successful charge against the enemy." The next year Henry Clay Wood, a native of Maine and graduate of Bowdoin College, was so honored. A first lieutenant in the Regulars at Wilson's Creek, he was cited for "distinguished gallantry." Remaining in the army until 1904, Wood retired as a brigadier general. In 1895 the medal went to William M.

Lieutenant Henry Clay Wood,
Eleventh U.S. Infantry, awarded
the Congressional Medal of Honor.
A post–Civil War photograph.
(The collection of Dr. Tom and
Karen Sweeney, General Sweeny's
Museum, Republic, Missouri)

Wherry, who as a first lieutenant in the Missouri volunteers "displayed conspicuous coolness and heroism in rallying troops that were recoiling under heavy fire." Wherry, who also fought at Atlanta, Franklin, and Nashville, was commissioned a brigadier general of volunteers during the Spanish-American War. The final medal given for exceptional service at Wilson's Creek was issued in 1895 to Nicholas Bouquet of the First Iowa's Burlington Rifles. Bouquet had risked his life assisting Immell in rescuing the caisson from Totten's Battery.[4]

Postwar medals were not available for Southerners, nor did Federal tax dollars support them in their old age. The contrast between victor and vanquished during the American Civil War may have been modest when compared to some of history's other great internecine struggles, but when viewed at the level of individuals it could be severe. For example, in the same decade that Immell, Schofield, Wood, Wherry, and Bouquet were honored, dozens of veterans of the Missouri State Guard showed up on the doorsteps of the state-run Confederate Home at Higginsville. The home's application book recorded their histories only briefly, but its testimony is poignant. Indigent veterans of Wilson's Creek included fifty-year-old T. A. J. Worsham, who as a lad of twenty had lost his left leg charging up Bloody Hill as a member of Weightman's Brigade. One-armed John F. Peers, who applied for residence at age seventy-six, had been a cavalryman in Rains's Division. Rheumatism, a term that in the nineteenth century covered a host of ills, was the reason most often cited by applicants for their inability to support themselves and their families.

Lieutenant William M. Wherry, awarded the Congressional Medal of Honor (The collection of Dr. Tom and Karen Sweeney, General Sweeny's Museum, Republic, Missouri)

One such sufferer was Albert G. Ball, fifty-six in 1891, who first saw action in the State Guard at Carthage and went on to fight in ten subsequent battles, including Wilson's Creek, Lexington, Iuka, and Corinth. He was unable to provide for his wife and three sons, the youngest of whom was fourteen. Stephen W. Hall, another veteran of Rains's Division, applied two years later because he was nearly blind at age fifty-six. A widower, he had two sons and a daughter.[5]

Individual achievement is significant and individual tragedy is moving, but the men who fought at Wilson's Creek continued to think of themselves largely in terms of their old units and what they had accomplished corporately. This was particularly true from 1881 onward. Across the nation, the twentieth anniversary of the beginning of the war was marked by a dramatic increase in veterans' activities. Because Wilson's Creek occurred so early in the conflict, it was the focus of much of the initial commemoration of the war west of the Mississippi. Organization took time, and although there was a wide variety of local activities, a joint reunion of Northern and Southern veterans was not held on the battlefield itself until 1883.[6]

The surviving participants of the war shared a heritage of honor, regardless of whether they had served in the Federal or Confederate armies, the Missouri State Guard, or the Arkansas State Troops. The best example of what the fight at Wilson's Creek meant to these men can be found in

Kansas. In 1879 veterans organized the Society of the Kansas First, and as time went on newspapers across the state printed increasing numbers of articles about their activities. But if Kansans in general were proud of their former soldiers, pride ran highest at the community level, just as it had during the war. On August 10, 1881, the *Atchison Champion* printed a brief history of the All Hazard company, which had marched from the town's dusty streets two decades earlier. Most significant of all, the article also included in large print and block letters the following names:

JAS. ERWIN, ISAAC DENTON, FRANK GERRLISH, JACOB N. KROUK, MICHAEL KATZ, ADAM MAY, WILLIAM REGAN, FRANCIS M. SHOWALTER, THOS. J. W. TARR, PHILIP WILBERGER, LUTHER MCCLENDON, JAS. MCBRIDE, WILLIAM STEWART, JNO. STRATTON.

They were identified as Atchison soldiers who had deserted the First Kansas.[7] Having broken the social contract between the community and its soldiers, having disgraced their town, their sins could never be forgiven.

Order of Battle . . . .

For the Missouri State Guard, this table shows the composite command arrangements at the time of the Battle of Wilson's Creek. For the precise organization, see Peterson et al., *Sterling Price's Lieutenants: A Guide to the Officers and Organization of the Missouri State Guard, 1861–1865.*

Numerous participants state that their units were under strength. Because reports do not list personnel unavailable due to illness or detached duty, the actual combat strength of the armies may have been more than 15 percent below the numbers given here.

Abbreviations: s = strength; k = killed; w = wounded; m = missing; t = total casualties; u = unknown.

THE WESTERN ARMY
Brigadier General Ben McCulloch, commanding

Reiff's Arkansas Cavalry Company [McCulloch's bodyguard] (Captain V. A. Reiff)
s = u; k = u; w = u; t = u

McCulloch's Confederate Brigade
Brigadier General Ben McCulloch, commanding
Colonel James M. McIntosh, de facto commander

McRae's Arkansas Infantry (Colonel Dandridge McRae)
s = 220; k = 3; w = 6; t = 9
Third Louisiana Infantry (Colonel Louis Hébert)
s = 700; k = 9; w = 48; t = 57
South Kansas–Texas Cavalry (Colonel Elkanah Greer)
s = 800; k = 4; w = 23; t = 27
First Arkansas Mounted Riflemen (Colonel Thomas J. Churchill)
s = 600; k = 42; w = 155; t = 197
Second Arkansas Mounted Riflemen (Colonel James M. McIntosh)
s = 400; k = 10; w = 44; t = 54
Brigade Total: s = 2,720; k = 68; w = 276; t = 344

Arkansas State Troops
Brigadier General Nicholas Bartlett Pearce, commanding

Third Infantry (Colonel John R. Gratiot)
s = 500; k = 25; w = 84; t = 109

Fourth Infantry (Colonel Jonathan D. Walker)

s = 550; k = 0; w = 0; t = 0

Fifth Infantry (Colonel Tom P. Dockery)

s = 650; k = 3; w = 11; t = 14

Carroll's Cavalry (Captain Charles A. Carroll)

s = 40; k = 0; w = 0; t = 0

First Cavalry (Colonel DeRosey Carroll)

s = 350; k = 5; w = 22; t = 27

Fort Smith Light Battery, 4 guns (Captain John G. Reid)

s = 73; k = 0; w = 1; t = 1

Pulaski Light Battery, 4 guns (Captain William E. Woodruff Jr.)

s = 71; k = 3; w = 0; t = 3

Brigade Total: s = 2,234; k = 36; w = 118; t = 154

Missouri State Guard

Major General Sterling Price, commanding

THIRD DIVISION (Brigadier General John B. Clark Sr.)
Burbridge's Infantry (Colonel John Q. Burbridge)

s = 270; k = 17; w = 81; t = 98

Major's Cavalry (Lieutenant Colonel James P. Major)

s = 273; k = 6; w = 5; t = 11

FOURTH DIVISION (Brigadier General William Y. Slack)
Hughes's Infantry (Colonel John T. Hughes)

s = 650; k = 36; w = 106; t = 142

Rives's Cavalry (Colonel Benjamin A. Rives)

s = 284; k = 4; w = 8; t = 12

SIXTH DIVISION (Brigadier General Mosby Monroe Parsons)
Kelly's Infantry (Colonel Joseph M. Kelly)

s = 142; k = 11; w = 38; t = 49

Brown's Cavalry (Colonel William B. Brown)

s = 320; k = 3; w = 2; t = 5

Missouri Light Artillery, 4 guns (Captain Henry Guibor)

s = 61; k = 3; w = 11; t = 14

SEVENTH DIVISION (Brigadier General James H. McBride)
Wingo's Infantry (Colonel Edmond T. Wingo)
Foster's Infantry (Colonel John A. Foster)
  Combined for Wingo and Foster:

s = 605; k = 32; w = 114; t = 146

Campbell's Cavalry (Captain [Leonidas S.?] Campbell)

s = 40; k = 0; w = 0; t = 0

EIGHTH DIVISION (Brigadier General James S. Rains)
Weightman's Infantry (Colonel Richard H. Weightman)

s = 1,316; k = 40; w = 120; t = 160

Cawthorn's Cavalry (Colonel James Cawthorn)

    s = 1,210; k = 21; w = 66; t = 87

Missouri Light Artillery, 3 guns (Captain Hiram M. Bledsoe)

    s = u; k = u; w = u; t = u

Missouri State Guard Totals:

    s = 7,171 (includes an estimated 2,000 unarmed nonparticipants); k = 173; w = 551; t = 724

Western Army Totals:

    s = 12,125 (includes an estimated 2,000 unarmed members of the Missouri State Guard); k = 277; w = 945; t = 1,222

ARMY OF THE WEST
Brigadier General Nathaniel Lyon, commanding

Lyon's Bodyguard (commander unknown)

    s = 10; k = u; w = u; m = u; t = u

Voerster's Pioneer Company (Captain John D. Voerster)

    s = u; k = u; w = u; m = u; t = u

FIRST BRIGADE (Major Samuel D. Sturgis)

Battalion of Regulars (Captain Joseph B. Plummer)

Companies B, C, and D, First U.S. Infantry, Lieutenant H. C. Wood's company of recruits

    s = 300; k = 19; w = 52; m = 9; t = 80

Second Missouri Infantry (Major Peter J. Osterhaus)

    s = 150; k = 15; w = 40; m = 0; t = 55

Kansas Rangers, mounted Company I, Second Kansas Infantry (Captain Samuel N. Wood)

Company D, First U.S. Cavalry (Lieutenant Charles W. Canfield)

    Combined for Wood and Canfield:

    s = 350; k = 0; w = 4; m = 3; t = 7

Company F, Second U.S. Artillery, 6 guns (Captain James Totten)

    s = 84; k = 0; w = 11; m = 0; t = 11

Brigade Totals:

    s = 884; k = 34; w = 107; m = 12; t = 153

SECOND BRIGADE (Colonel Franz Sigel)

Third Missouri Infantry (Lieutenant Colonel Anslem Albert)

Fifth Missouri (Colonel Charles E. Salomon)

    Combined for Albert and Salomon:

    s = 990; k = 35; w = 132; m = 126; t = 293

Company I, First U.S. Cavalry (Captain Eugene A. Carr)

    s = 65; k = 0; w = 0; m = 4; t = 4

Company C, Second U.S. Dragoons (Lieutenant Charles E. Farrand)

    s = 60; k = 0; w = 0; m = 0; t = 0

Backof's Missouri Light Artillery, 6 guns (Major Franz Backof)
  S = 85; K = 0; W = 0; M = 0; T = 0
Brigade Totals:
  S = 1,200; K = 35; W = 132; M = 130; T = 297

THIRD BRIGADE (Lieutenant Colonel George L. Andrews)
Battalion of Regulars (Captain Frederick Steele)
Companies B and E, Second U.S. Infantry, Lieutenant Warren Lothrop's company of recruits; Sergeant John Morine's company of recruits
  S = 275; K = 15; W = 44; M = 2; T = 61
First Missouri Infantry (Lieutenant Colonel George L. Andrews)
  S = 775; K = 76; W = 208; M = 11; T = 295
Du Bois's Battery, 4 guns (Lieutenant John V. Du Bois)
  S = 66; K = 0; W = 2; M = 1; T = 3
Brigade Totals:
  S = 1,116; K = 91; W = 254; M = 14; T = 359

FOURTH BRIGADE (Colonel George W. Deitzler)
First Iowa Infantry (Lieutenant Colonel William H. Merritt)
  S = 800; K = 12; W = 138; M = 4; T = 154
First Kansas Infantry (Colonel George W. Deitzler)
  S = 800; K = 77; W = 187; M = 20; T = 284
Second Kansas Infantry (Colonel Robert B. Mitchell)
  [minus Captain Wood's Kansas Rangers]
  S = 600; K = 5; W = 59; M = 6; T = 70
Thirteenth Illinois battalion (Lieutenant James Beardsley)
  S = 21; K = 0; W = 0; M = 0; T = 0
Brigade Totals:
  S = 2,221; K = 94; W = 384; M = 30; T = 508

Army of the West Totals:*
  S = 5,431; K = 258; W = 873; M = 186; T = 1,317

*Reserves remaining in Springfield
Company B, First U.S. Cavalry (commander unknown)
Company C, First U.S. Cavalry (Captain David S. Stanley)
  S = U; K = U; W = U; M = U; T = U
Greene and Christian County Home Guards (Lieutenant Colonel Marcus Boyd) (aka: Colonel John S. Phelps's Home Guard Regiment)
  S = 1,200; K = U; W = U; M = U; T = U
Backof's Missouri Light Artillery, 2 guns (commander unknown)
Reserve Totals:
  S = U; K = U; W = U; M = U; T = U

Notes . . . .

Abbreviations

AHC	Arkansas History Commission, Little Rock
CSL	Connecticut State Library, New Haven
DAB	*Dictionary of American Biography*. 20 vols., supp. New York: Charles Scribner's Sons, 1928–81.
DU	Duke University, Durham, N.C.
ENW	William S. Speer, ed. *The Encyclopedia of the New West*. Marshall, Tex.: U.S. Biographical Publishing Co., 1881.
FSNHS	Fort Smith National Historic Site, Fort Smith, Ark.
GCA	Greene County Archives, Springfield, Mo.
HL	Hulston Library, Wilson's Creek National Battlefield, Republic, Mo.
KSHS	Kansas State Historical Society, Topeka
LC	Library of Congress, Washington, D.C.
LSU	Louisiana State University, Baton Rouge
MHS	Missouri Historical Society, St. Louis
MSA	Missouri State Archives, Jefferson City
NARA	National Archives and Records Administration, Washington, D.C.
OR	U.S. War Department, *The War of the Rebellion: A Compilation of the Official Records of the Union and Confederate Armies*. 128 vols. Washington, D.C.: Government Printing Office, 1880–1901. *OR* citations take the following form: volume number: page number. Unless otherwise indicated, all citations are from series 1.
RCHS	Riley County Historical Society, Manhattan, Kans.
TSL	Texas State Library, Austin
UKL	University of Kansas at Lawrence
UMC	University of Missouri at Columbia
USAMHI	U.S. Army Military History Institute, Carlisle, Pa.
WJC	Whit Joyner Collection, New Hill, N.C.
YU	Yale University, New Haven, Conn.

Preface

1. Robertson, *Soldiers Blue and Gray*, 21.

2. See Wyatt-Brown, *Honor and Violence*; Linderman, *Embattled Courage*; Mitchell, *Civil War Soldiers*; Hess, *Liberty, Virtue, and Progress* and *Union Soldier in Battle*; McPherson, *What They Fought For* and *For Cause and Comrades*.

Chapter One

1. Watson, *Life in the Confederate Army*, 2–3; Winters, *Civil War in Louisiana*, 3.
2. Watson, *Life in the Confederate Army*, 124–25; Tunnard, *A Southern Record*, 23.
3. Winters, *Civil War in Louisiana*, 9–17.
4. "First in the Field," *Baton Rouge Daily Advocate*, Apr. 16, 1861.
5. Watson, *Life in the Confederate Army*, 121–23; Bragg, *Louisiana in the Confederacy*, 36.
6. Tunnard, *A Southern Record*, xx.
7. "Pelican Rifles," *Baton Rouge Daily Advocate*, Apr. 19, 1861; Tunnard, *A Southern Record*, 24; Odom, "The Political Career of Thomas Overton Moore," 33–34; "Our City," *Shreveport Weekly News*, Apr. 29, 1861; Perry Anderson Snyder, "Shreveport, Louisiana, during the Civil War," 33; Hardin, *Northwestern Louisiana*, 56, 59, 152; Bragg, *Louisiana in the Confederacy*, 36; William Bonner to Dear Mother, Aug. 21, 1861, Bonner Family Papers, LSU; Cutrer and Parrish, *Brothers in Gray*, 5.
8. Mitchell, *Civil War Soldiers*, 18–19.
9. Watson, *Life in the Confederate Army*, 124; Bragg, *Louisiana in the Confederacy*, 57; William Bonner to Dear Mother, Aug. 21, 1861, Bonner Family Papers, LSU.
10. Tunnard, *A Southern Record*, 29–30; "Our Friends," *Shreveport Daily News*, May 1, 1861.
11. "First in the Field" (Apr. 16, 1861) and "The Spirit of '76 Revived! Departure of the Pelican Rifles" (Apr. 30, 1861), *Baton Rouge Daily Advocate*; "Departure of the Pelicans," *Port Allen Sugar Planter*, May 4, 1861.
12. Watson, *Life in the Confederate Army*, 127; Tunnard, *A Southern Record*, 31; Allardice, *More Generals in Gray*, 224.
13. Winters, *Civil War in Louisiana*, 21–22; W. H. T. to Editor (May 3), in "Letter from Camp Walker," *Baton Rouge Daily Advocate*, May 7, 1861.
14. For a list of newspapers, see Bibliography. W. H. T. to Editor (May 3), in "Letter from Camp Walker," May 7, 1861, and Bob to Editor (May 5), in "Letter from Camp Walker," May 8, 1861, *Baton Rouge Daily Advocate*; Bergeron, *Guide to Louisiana Confederate Military Units*, 76–77.
15. "A Card," *Baton Rouge Daily Advocate*, May 9, 1861; "Rumors," *Baton Rouge Weekly Gazette and Comet*, May 11, 1861.
16. George M. Heroman to My Dear Mother, May 9, 1861, Heroman Papers, LSU; "The Spirit of '76 Revived! Departure of the Pelican Rifles," *Baton Rouge Daily Advocate*, Apr. 30, 1861; Watson, *Life in the Confederate Army*, 162.
17. Watson, *Life in the Confederate Army*, 175; Warner, *Generals in Gray*, 130–31.
18. R. M. Hinson to My Dear Mat, July 25, 1861, Hinson Papers, LSU; Watson, *Life in the Confederate Army*, 126.
19. This flag belonged to Company K; the regiment carried the first national flag of the Confederacy as well. Tunnard, *A Southern Record*, 23; Madaus and Needham, "Unit Colors of the Trans-Mississippi Confederacy," 126.
20. Watson, *Life in the Confederate Army*, 118; W. H. T. to Editor (May 12), in "Letter from Camp Walker" (May 16, 1861), and "Off to War" (May 25, 1861), *Baton Rouge Daily Advocate*; David Pierson to Dear Father, Apr. 22, 1861, Pierson Papers, LSU; Cutrer and Parrish, *Brothers in Gray*, 4–5, 13–15.
21. Tunnard, *A Southern Record*, 29; Watson, *Life in the Confederate Army*, 148, 236.
22. George M. Heroman to My Dear Mother, May 9, 1861, Heroman Papers, LSU; "The Review of the State Troops" (May 11, 1861) and W. F. Tunnard to Editor (May 21)

(May 25, 1861), *Baton Rouge Weekly Gazette and Comet*; Watson, *Life in the Confederate Army*, 124, 162, 240, 244; Harold L. Peterson to Regional Director, Dec. 4, 1969, HL.

23. Winters, *Civil War in Louisiana*, 22; Tunnard, *A Southern Record*, 32; "St. Louis Massacre" (May 16, 1861), "Another Exciting Day in St. Louis" (May 17, 1861), "The Supreme Law of the Sword" (May 19, 1861), and "Interesting from Capitol of Mo." (May 19, 1861), *New Orleans Daily Picayune*.

24. Watson's dates for the trip are erroneous. Watson, *Life in the Confederate Army*, 166; Tunnard, *A Southern Record*, 31–33.

25. Tunnard, *A Southern Record*, 33–35; A. B. P. to Editor (May 25), in "Letter from the Third Regiment (Pelican Rifle Company)," *Baton Rouge Weekly Gazette and Comet*, June 9, 1861; Cutrer and Parrish, *Brothers in Gray*, 15.

26. Harrell, *Arkansas*, 5–6; Woodruff, *With the Light Guns*, 18.

27. "Hon. W. E. Woodruff, Jr.," *ENW*, 32.

28. Woodruff, *With the Light Guns*, 9; Dougan, *Confederate Arkansas*, 41.

29. Dougan, *Confederate Arkansas*, 41–42; Woodruff, *With the Light Guns*, 12–13.

30. Woodruff states erroneously that Totten was born in Virginia. Dougan, *Confederate Arkansas*, 42; Harrell, *Arkansas*, 9–10; Woodruff, *With the Light Guns*, 13; Heitman, *Historical Register*, 1:966; "Totten, James," *Appleton's Cyclopedia of American Biography*, 6:141; "Death of General Totten," *Sedalia Daily Bazoo*, Oct. 5, 1871.

31. "Arrival of Volunteers for the Capture of Fort Smith," *Arkansas True Democrat*, May 2, 1861; Dougan, *Confederate Arkansas*, 45–47, 61, 63.

32. Dougan, *Confederate Arkansas*, 61; Warner, *Generals in Blue*, 486–87; "Arrival of U.S. Troops," *Leavenworth Daily Times*, June 1, 1861.

33. Warner, *Generals in Gray*, 202–3; Woodruff, *With the Light Guns*, 14–15.

34. Dougan, *Confederate Arkansas*, 62–65; Woodruff, *With the Light Guns*, 15–17.

35. Allardice, *More Generals in Gray*, 179; Matthews, *Pearce*, 23; "Tales of the War: Gen. N. B. Pearce Describes the Battle of Wilson's Creek," undated clipping from *St. Louis Republican*, N. Bart Pearce file, HL; Pearce, "N. B. Pearce Reminiscences," 3, Pearce Papers, AHC.

36. Geise, "Confederate Military Forces in the Trans-Mississippi," 5; Scott and Myers, "Extinct 'Grass Eaters' of Benton County," 154; "Mass Meeting" (Apr. 25, 1861), "Meeting in Hot Springs" (Apr. 25, 1861), "From Johnson County" (Apr. 25, 1861), "Public Meeting in Lawrence County" (May 2, 1861), "Meeting in Washington County" (May 2, 1861), "Public Meeting in Scott County" (May 2, 1861), "Meeting in Drew County" (May 2, 1861), "Meeting in Johnson County" (May 9, 1861), "Mass Meeting" (May 9, 1861), "Resistance Meeting—Hempstead a Unit!" (May 9, 1861), "Enthusiastic Meeting" (May 30, 1861), "Meeting in Marion County" (June 6, 1861), "From Columbia County" (June 6, 1861), "The Hempstead Rifles" (June 13, 1861), and "Officers and Members of the Invincible Guards" (June 20, 1861), *Arkansas True Democrat*; "Des Arc Rangers—Flag Presentation" (May 31, 1861), "Flag Presentation" (June 7, 1861), "To the Rector Guards" (June 22, 1861), and "Col. A. Forbes' Reply" (July 24, 1861), *Des Arc Semi-Weekly Citizen*.

37. "The Hempstead Rifles," *Arkansas True Democrat*, June 13, 1861; Montgomery, "Far from Home and Kindred," n.p.; "Davis Blues"—Company F, Fifth Arkansas State Troops and Rivers Reminiscences, n.p., Folder 5th Ark. Inf. CSA, HL; *History of Benton . . . Arkansas*, 565, 568; McCulloch, "Sketch of the Life of Clem McCulloch," 45; Roberts and Moneyhon, *Portraits of Conflict*, 59; Baxter, *Pea Ridge and Prairie Grove*, 38.

38. Weaver, "Fort Smith in the War between the States," 5, FSNHS.

39. Hugh Thomas to Dear Carrie, WJC; Muster Roll—Armstrong's Co. B, 1st Reg. Cav. Ark. Volunteers, McRae Papers, AHC.

40. The description of the Belle Pointe Guards' uniforms is based on a photograph in HL. Muster Roll—Titsworth's Co., 3d Reg., Ark. Vol. Inf., McRae Papers, AHC; *History of Benton . . . Arkansas*, 741; Weaver, "Fort Smith in the War between the States," 1–3, FSNHS.

41. Baer served throughout the war, accompanied Confederate exiles to Mexico, and finally returned to Arkansas, where he became a wealthy and highly respected citizen of Fort Smith. "Hon. B. Baer," *ENW*, 250–51.

42. Woodruff, *With the Light Guns*, 20–22.

43. The troops (including Woodruff's men) participating in the capture of Fort Smith were described as "well armed, drilled, and uniformed." The Rocky Comfort soldier wrote that "a company of young ladies will be organized Saturday next," but no confirmation of such action has been discovered. "Arrival of Volunteers for the Capture of Fort Smith" (May 2, 1861) and "The Ladies of Little Rock" (July 4, 1861), *Arkansas True Democrat*; Woodruff, *With the Light Guns*, 20; Pearce, "N. B. Pearce Reminiscences," Pearce Papers, AHC, 5; *History of Benton . . . Arkansas*, 742; Anonymous letter to Editor (June 30), in "Arkansas Correspondence," *Shreveport Weekly News*, July 15, 1861.

44. Oates, "Texas under the Secessionists," 169–70, 173–76; Geise, "Confederate Military Forces in the Trans-Mississippi," 4.

45. Cutrer, *Ben McCulloch*, 10–22; Rose, *Life and Services of Gen. Ben McCulloch*, 28, 42.

46. Cutrer, *Ben McCulloch*, 8.

47. Ibid., 65, 67–68, 103; Rose, *Life and Services of Gen. Ben McCulloch*, 55; "General Ben McCulloch," *ENW*, 296.

48. Ben McCulloch to Dear Henry, June 20, 1849, and to Dear Mother, July 28, 1851, Dibrell Collection, TSL.

49. Ben McCulloch to Dear Henry, Sept. 10, 1861, ibid.; Cutrer, *Ben McCulloch*, 124–37; "General Ben McCulloch," *ENW*, 296.

50. Cutrer, *Ben McCulloch*, 195; Josephy, *Civil War in the American West*, 24–25.

51. Hale, *Third Texas Cavalry*, 26–28; "Call for Eight Thousand Troops," *Texas Republican*, May 4, 1861; "The Rendezvous in Dallas," *Dallas Herald*, June 19, 1861.

52. "Letter from Dallas" (May 18, 1861), "The Invasion of Northern Texas" (May 18, 1861), and "A Sermon Delivered by the Rev. T. B. Wilson, D.D." (May 25, 1861), *Texas Republican*.

53. Lale, "Boy-Bugler," 73; Hale, *Third Texas Cavalry*, 28, 30; "The Invasion of Northern Texas," *Texas Republican*, May 18, 1861.

54. Cater, *As It Was*, 68, 71–73.

55. Sparks, *War between the States*, 133; Hale, *Third Texas Cavalry*, 30; "Greer's Regiment" (June 19, 1861) and "Colonel Greer's Command" (July 3, 1861), *Dallas Herald*.

56. Hale, *Third Texas Cavalry*, 39–44.

57. Johnson, *Texans Who Wore the Gray*, 407.

58. Hale, *Third Texas Cavalry*, 45–46, 48; "From the 'Texas Hunters' " (July 13, 1861), "The Ladies of Dallas . . . " (July 3, 1861), and "A Flag for the Regiment" (July 3, 1861), *Texas Republican*; Cater, *As It Was*, 77–78.

Chapter Two

1. Engle, *Yankee Dutchman*, 2–3, 6–23.
2. Ibid., 42–44; Burton, *Melting Pot Soldiers*, 39.

3. Engle, *Yankee Dutchman*, 37–38; Rombauer, *Union Cause in St. Louis*, 128, 189.

4. Rombauer, *Union Cause in St. Louis*, 128–29; Covington, "Camp Jackson Affair," 198.

5. Hopewell, "Camp Jackson," 1, 3–7, MSA; Westover, "Evolution of the Missouri Militia," 99–100, 104–5, 107–9, 114, 120; Engle, *Yankee Dutchman*, 52.

6. Political conflict in St. Louis was more complex than this brief summary can suggest. See Engle, *Yankee Dutchman*, 41–55; McElroy, *The Struggle for Missouri*, 39–45; Rombauer, *Union Cause in St. Louis*, 189.

7. Parrish, *History of Missouri*, 3:6–8; Monaghan, *Civil War on the Western Border*, 44–116.

8. Parrish, *History of Missouri*, 3:7–8.

9. Parrish, *Turbulent Partnership*, 5–14, and *History of Missouri*, 3:1; Snead, "First Year of the War in Missouri," 264; Webb, *Battles and Biographies*, 295–98; War Department, *Organization and Status of Missouri Troops*, 12.

10. "Militia Meeting" (May 3, 1861) and E. M. Samuel to Editor, in "To All Conservative Union Men" (May 3, 1861), *Richmond Weekly North-West Conservator*.

11. "Public Meeting" (May 7, 1861), W. R. Samuel to Editor (May 1) (May 16, 1861), and "Rules and Regulations" (May 16, 1861), *Randolph Citizen*; "Meeting at Hardin" (May 10, 1861), "Meeting at Elk Horn" (May 10, 1861), "Springfield, Mo., May 18" (May 24, 1861), and "Immense Union Meeting" (May 31, 1861), *Richmond Weekly North-West Conservator*; "Public Meeting," *Weekly Central City and Brunswicker*, May 4, 1861; "What Shall We Do Now?," *Glasgow Weekly Times*, Apr. 25, 1861; *History of Clay and Platte Counties*, 201; Cockrell, *History of Johnson County, Missouri*, 107.

12. Secretary of War to John M. Schofield, Apr. 15, 1861, Schofield Papers, LC; Schofield, *Forty-six Years in the Army*, 30–33; McDonough, *Schofield*, 2–14.

13. Phillips, *Damned Yankee*, 138–39; Winter, *Civil War in St. Louis*, 38–40.

14. Phillips, *Damned Yankee*, 13–14, 19, 26, 28–29, 40–58.

15. Ibid., 28, 54–55, 68–70.

16. Ibid., 33–35, 88, 90.

17. Ibid., 137; Warner, *Generals in Blue*, 35–36; Engle, *Yankee Dutchman*, 50; Parrish, *Turbulent Partnership*, 15–16.

18. No summary can do justice to the complex events in St. Louis between January and June 1861, nor do historians agree on all of the details. See Parrish, *Turbulent Partnership*, 15–32; Phillips, *Damned Yankee*, 129–69; Engle, *Yankee Dutchman*, 49–60; Reavis, *Life and Military Service of Gen. William Selby Harney*, 350–86.

19. No statistical analysis of the Federal volunteer units raised in St. Louis exists. A handful of Anglo-Saxon names like Alexander, Brown, Cook, Hayes, and Nelson appear in the records of even the most thoroughly "German" units. See Compiled Service Records for First, Second, Third, Fourth, and Fifth Infantry, NARA; Payne, "The Taking of Liberty Arsenal," 15–16; Phillips, *Damned Yankee*, 156–64; War Department, *Organization and Status of Missouri Troops*, 11–14; and *History of Clay and Platte Counties*, 195–96.

20. Bek, "Civil War Diary of John T. Buegel," 307–8.

21. War Department, *Organization and Status of Missouri Troops*, 15; L. Thomas to Nathaniel Lyon, Apr. 30, 1861, Schofield Papers, LC. The Thomas document, issued in Lincoln's name, confirmed earlier orders from the War Department.

22. For a complete discussion of Lyon's peculiarly egocentric views, see Phillips, *Damned Yankee*, 16–17, 46–49, 70–71, 85–86, 103, 106–7, 123.

23. Ibid., 71.

24. Wherry, "General Nathaniel Lyon," 68; Nathaniel Lyon to Dear Brother, June 11,

1854, Lyon Papers, CSL; Rombauer, *Union Cause in St. Louis*, 151; Phillips, *Damned Yankee*, 105–9, 117–18.

25. Parrish, *Turbulent Partnership*, 20–21; "Extra Session of Legislature—Governor's Proclamation," *St. Louis Daily Missouri Democrat*, Apr. 23, 1861; Winter, *Civil War in St. Louis*, 47.

26. For a complete list of company names, see Winter, *Civil War in St. Louis*, 49.

27. Some militia officers who supported the Union resigned rather than attend the muster. When Frost attempted to exercise his pioneer troops on the heights overlooking the arsenal, Lyon stopped him. Frost's pioneers were so few in number, however, that this was harassment rather than a real threat to the arsenal. Phillips, *Damned Yankee*, 177–79; Parrish, *Turbulent Partnership*, 21–22; "The National Guards" (Apr. 23, 1861) and "The Military Exhibition Yesterday—A Glance at the Opposing Forces" (May 7, 1861), *St. Louis Daily Missouri Democrat*.

28. War Department, *Organization and Status of Missouri Troops*, 16–17; Winter, *Civil War in St. Louis*, 45; Phillips, *Damned Yankee*, 182–84; "The Government Arsenal at St. Louis," *Kansas City Daily Western Journal of Commerce*, May 21, 1861.

29. Winter, *Civil War in St. Louis*, 43; Warner, *Generals in Blue*, 417–18; Rombauer, *Union Cause in St. Louis*, 103–4, 168.

30. "Col. Blair and Captain Lyon," *St. Louis Daily Missouri Democrat*, May 22, 1861.

31. Backof's name is frequently misspelled as "Backoff" or "Backhoff." Zucker, *The Forty-Eighters*, 209–10, 274; Franz Backof to Henry W. Halleck, Feb. 5, 1861, Compiled Service Records, Backof's Battalion, NARA.

32. War Department, *Organization and Status of Missouri Troops*, 15; Warner, *Generals in Blue*, 491–92; "Man of Resource; Active Service of Gen. T. W. Sweeny as Told in His Letters," *National Intelligencer*, Aug. 22, 1895; Winter, *Civil War in St. Louis*, 44–46; Coffman, *Old Army*, 137–38; Rombauer, *Union Cause in St. Louis*, 188.

33. Quoted in Engle, *Yankee Dutchman*, 56. Other sources give the presenter's name as Miss Josephine Wiegel; see "Presentation of a Beautiful Banner to the Third Regiment Missouri Volunteers," *St. Louis Daily Missouri Democrat*, May 4, 1861.

34. Engle, *Yankee Dutchman*, 53–57, 230; Rombauer, *Union Cause in St. Louis*, 188; Burton, *Melting Pot Soldiers*, 15–16, 36, 39–40.

35. Engle, *Yankee Dutchman*, 4, 321; "Something More about Col. Seigle," *Olathe Mirror*, Aug. 1, 1861; Phillips, *Damned Yankee*, 20; Traveller to Editor (July 8), in "War Correspondence," *Iowa City Democratic State Press*, July 31, 1861; Horace Poole to Editor (July 2), in "Army Correspondence," *South Danvers Wizard*, July 17, 1861; Wilkie, *Pen and Powder*, 28–29.

36. Phillips, *Damned Yankee*, 186–93; Wilkie, *Pen and Powder*, 29.

37. Phillips, *Damned Yankee*, 192; Winter, *Civil War in St. Louis*, 49–53.

38. "Exciting Military Demonstration," *Glasgow Weekly Times*, May 16, 1861; Covington, "Camp Jackson Affair," 211.

39. Parrish, *History of Missouri*, 3:14.

40. War Department, *Organization and Status of Missouri Troops*, 252–56; *The Laws of Missouri*, 3–57.

41. Peterson et al., *Sterling Price's Lieutenants*, 39, 81, 107, 136, 154, 172, 195, 209, 290.

42. Parsons is often erroneously credited with serving as state attorney general. Vandiver, "Reminiscences of General John B. Clark," 223, 229; Warner, *Generals in Gray*, 228–29, 278; Miller, "Missouri Secessionist," 7, 14–15, 22–23, 48, and "General Mosby M. Parsons," 34–36; Allardice, *More Generals in Gray*, 59–60, 155, 190.

43. Castel, *General Sterling Price*, 3, 5; Shalhope, *Sterling Price*, 4–8, 15–26, 30–55.

44. Shalhope, *Sterling Price*, 60–61, 64–65; Simmons, "Life of Sterling Price," 23.

45. Shalhope, *Sterling Price*, 66–67.

46. Ibid., 6–75.

47. Rea, *Sterling Price*, 28–36.

48. Monaghan, *Civil War on the Western Border*, 133–34.

49. Phillips, *Damned Yankee*, 210–11; McDonough, *Schofield*, 19; J. W. Ripley to John M. Schofield (May 28, 1861) and Requisition for Ordnance and Ordnance Stores (May 29, 1861), Schofield Papers, LC; Franc B. Wilkie to Editor (June 22), in "Army Correspondence," *Dubuque Herald*, June 26, 1861; "Attention Military" (May 2, 1861), "Supplies for the Volunteers" (May 4, 1861), "Aid to Missouri Volunteers" (May 21, 1861), and "The Missouri Volunteers Fund in New York" (June 1, 1861), *St. Louis Daily Missouri Democrat*; "Missouri Volunteer Fund—Letter from Colonel Blair" (May 27, 1861) and "Arms and Alms" (May 28, 1861), *St. Louis Republican*; Kip Lindberg, "Uniform and Equipment Descriptions of Units at Wilson's Creek," n.p., HL.

50. Snead, *Fight for Missouri*, 187–201; Castel, *General Sterling Price*, 24; Clarke, "General Lyon and the Fight for Missouri," 280–81.

51. Phillips, *Damned Yankee*, 214.

Chapter Three

1. Phillips, *Damned Yankee*, 200, 214–15.

2. *OR* 3:382.

3. Ibid., 384.

4. Ibid., 388–89, 391.

5. Parrish, *History of Missouri*, 3:24.

6. Steele and Cotrell, *Civil War in the Ozarks*, 15; Gottschalk, *In Deadly Earnest*, 21; Parrish, *History of Missouri*, 3:24; Phillips, *Damned Yankee*, 171; Rorvig, "Significant Skirmish," 127–48.

7. Surviving sources make it easier to study the Kansans and Iowans than the Union troops from Missouri. For a separate study of the Iowa troops, see Piston, "1st Iowa Volunteers."

8. Some sources give Matthies's last name as Matthiass. His first name was Charles; his middle name, by which he was generally known, was either Leopold or Leopoland. Sturdevant, "Girding for War," 107; Ware, *Lyon Campaign*, 304, 63–66; Clark, *Life in the Middle West*, 45–46, 211; Swisher, *Iowa in Times of War*, 113; Meyer, *Iowans Called to Valor*, 16; "Iowa in the Field," *Dubuque Daily Times*, Apr. 18, 1861; "Camp Ellsworth," *Keokuk Gate City*, June 6, 1861.

9. "The Volunteer Meeting" (Apr. 19, 1861) and "Patriotic Meeting at Iowa City" (Apr. 26, 1861), *Muscatine Weekly Journal*; "Immense Patriotic Meeting" (Apr. 24, 1861) and "Patriotic Meeting on Saturday" (Apr. 24, 1861), *Iowa City Weekly State Reporter*; Boeck, "Early Iowa Community," 413–14; "Iowa in the Field," *Dubuque Daily Times*, Apr. 18, 1861; "War" (Apr. 20, 1861), "Ready for Service" (Apr. 20, 1861), and "Union Meeting" (Apr. 27, 1861), *Mt. Pleasant Home Journal*; "To the Ladies," *Davenport Daily Democrat & News*, Apr. 25, 1861; Ware, *Lyon Campaign*, 70–74; "Iowa Volunteers," *Franklin Record*, Apr. 29, 1861.

10. "To Arms!" *Iowa City State Register*, Apr. 17, 1861; "War Begins" and "Grand Union Meeting," *Lyons Weekly Mirror*, Apr. 18, 1861; "Local," *Iowa Transcript*, Apr. 25, 1861; Ingersoll, *Iowa and the Rebellion*, 18–19; "The Masses Moving," *Mt. Pleasant Home Journal*, Apr. 27, 1861; Boeck, "Early Iowa Community," 414; Z. to Editor (Apr. 19), in *Muscatine Weekly Journal*, Apr. 26, 1861.

11. Michael McHenry to Editor (May 16), in "A Slander of the Adopted Citizens of the State of Iowa Refuted," *Iowa City Weekly State Reporter*, June 5, 1861; "Departure of Volunteers," *Keokuk Gate City*, April 23, 1861; "Our War Correspondence" (May 16, 1861) and Mac to Dear Dick (May 31), in "Our War Correspondence" (June 3, 1861), *Davenport Daily Democrat & News*; H. J. C. to Editor (May 27), in "Our Army Correspondence," *Muscatine Weekly Journal*, May 31, 1861; Richard D. Martin, "First Regiment Iowa Volunteers," 17; Rippley, *German-Americans*, 62.

12. The Wilson Guards were sometimes called the Jackson Guards. "To the Sons of Germany, Bohemia, and France" and "Our Volunteers," *Iowa City Weekly State Reporter*, May 1, 1861; "The Foreign Element," *Burlington Daily Hawk-Eye*, June 24, 1861; Boeck, "Early Iowa Community," 406–9; Sturdevant, "Girding for War," 94, 96, 107; "Completed" (Apr. 23, 1861), "Our War Correspondence" (May 21, 1861), "Our War Correspondence" (May 28, 1861), and Mac to Dear Dick (May 31), in "Our War Correspondence" (June 3, 1861), *Davenport Daily Democrat & News*.

13. Muster rolls, First Iowa Infantry, HL; Clark, *Life in the Middle West*, 42–43, 45, 51; "The First Iowa in the Springfield Fight," *Dubuque Weekly Times*, Aug. 22, 1861; Wilkie, *Pen and Powder*, 14.

14. McPherson, *What They Fought For*, 2–7, 27–35, and *For Cause and Comrades*, 17–26, 98–103, 105–6, 110–11, 114–16; Hess, *Liberty, Virtue, and Progress*, 8–9, 32–33, and *Union Soldier in Battle*, 97–109; "The Conflict," *Davenport Daily Democrat & News*, Apr. 20, 1861.

15. "War" (Apr. 20, 1861) and "The Cause of the War" (May 4, 1861), *Mt. Pleasant Home Journal*; "Liberty and the Union," *Burlington Daily Hawk-Eye*, May 16, 1861; "The Departure of the Washington Guards," *Iowa City Weekly State Reporter*, May 8, 1861.

16. H. P. to Editor (May 5), in "Iowa Regiment," *South Danvers Wizard*, May 15, 1861; "The Farewell to Our Volunteers," *Burlington Daily Hawk-Eye*, May 7, 1861; "To Our Kind Friends at Home," *Iowa City Democratic State Press*, May 29, 1861.

17. Ware, *Lyon Campaign*, 38, 45–46.

18. J. O. Culver to Dear Minnie, Aug. 14, 1861, Culver Papers, USAMHI; Long, "Frémont, Lyon, and Wilson's Creek," 82.

19. H. J. C. to Editor (June 21), in "Our Army Correspondence," *Muscatine Weekly Journal*, June 28, 1861; Clark, *Life in the Middle West*, 60.

20. For a list of Iowa newspapers, see Bibliography.

21. Mitchell, *The Vacant Chair*, 25, 27.

22. Ibid., 22.

23. Matson, *Life Experiences*, 59; "The Following Gentlemen . . .," *Burlington Daily Hawk-Eye*, May 16, 1861; "Aid," *Davenport Daily Democrat & News*, Apr. 25, 1861; "Patriotic Meeting on Saturday" (Apr. 24, 1861) and "Subscription to the Volunteers Fund" (May 8, 1861), *Iowa City Weekly State Reporter*; "Union Meeting," *Mt. Pleasant Home Journal*, Apr. 27, 1861; "Attention, Military!" (Apr. 26, 1861), "Fifteen Hundred Dollars for Uniforms" (Apr. 26, 1861), "Free Medical Care" (May 3, 1861), and "The Relief Committee" (June 28, 1861), *Muscatine Weekly Journal*.

24. "Ladies Volunteer Labor Society," *Dubuque Daily Times*, May 1–9, 1861; "At the Invitation of . . .," *Davenport Daily Democrat & News*, May 7, 1861; "The Generous Ladies of . . ." (May 1, 1861) and High Private of Comp'y B to Editor (May 16), in "Our Army Correspondence" (May 22, 1861), *Iowa City Weekly State Reporter*.

25. For departure ceremonies, which further strengthened ties between the companies and their home communities, see Ware, *Lyon Campaign*, 80–82; "The Farewell to Our Volunteers," *Burlington Daily Hawk-Eye*, May 7, 1861; "Departure of the Volunteers,"

Iowa City Weekly State Reporter, May 8, 1861; "Departure of the Muscatine Volunteers," *Muscatine Weekly Journal*, May 10, 1861; and "The Mt. Pleasant Grays Left . . .," *Mt. Pleasant Home Journal*, May 11, 1861. Some sources give May 13 or 14 as the date of muster, suggesting a process that took several days. See "Our War Correspondence" (May 6, 1861), Anonymous to Editor (May 14), in "Our War Correspondence" (May 16, 1861), and "Our War Correspondence" (May 21, 1861), *Davenport Daily Democrat & News*; Z. to Editor (May 15), in "Our Army Correspondence," *Muscatine Weekly Journal*, May 24, 1861; "Company B—Iowa 1st," *Iowa City Democratic State Press*, Sept. 4, 1861; and Ingersoll, *Iowa and the Rebellion*, 20.

26. Some of the troops were housed in buildings on Main Street, while others occupied quarters on Fifth Street and elsewhere. Considerable discrepancies exist concerning the dates companies moved from the city to the camp. Clark, *Life in the Middle West*, 47; "Visit to the Burlington Companies at Keokuk" (May 14, 1861) and Zouave to Editor (May 18) (May 21, 1861), *Burlington Daily Hawk-Eye*; "Our War Correspondence" (May 14, 21, 28, 1861) and Mac to Dick (May 27, 31), in "Our War Correspondence" (May 28, June 3, 1861), *Davenport Daily Democrat & News*; H. J. C. to Editor (May 7), in "Our Army Correspondence" (May 10, 1861), "Volunteers' Meeting" (May 24, 1861), H. J. C. to Editor (May 21, 27), in "Our Army Correspondence" (May 31, 1861), Z. to Dear John (May 8), in "Our Army Correspondence" (May 17, 1861), and W. F. D. to Editor (May 31), in "Our Army Correspondence" (June 7, 1861), *Muscatine Weekly Journal*; "The Muscatine Companies Had . . ." (May 18, 1861) and "Camp Ellsworth" (June 13, 1861), *Keokuk Gate City*.

27. Ware, *Lyon Campaign*, 85–86; "Resolution of the Burlington Zouaves" (May 30, 1861), "The Burlington Company" (May 30, 1861), and H. S. to Editor (June 6) (June 8, 1861), *Burlington Daily Hawk-Eye*; H. P. to Editor (May 11), in "Iowa Regiment," *South Danvers Wizard*, May 22, 1861; Mac to Dear Dick (May 27), in "Our War Correspondence," *Davenport Daily Democrat & News*, May 28, 1861; W. F. D. to Editor (June 5), in "Our Army Correspondence," *Muscatine Weekly Journal*, June 14, 1861.

28. Clark, *Life in the Middle West*, 46–47; "For the Democrat and News," *Davenport Daily Democrat & News*, May 1, 1861.

29. "At Work" (Apr. 29, 1861), Mac to Dear Dick (May 14), in "Our War Correspondence" (May 16, 1861), and Occasional to Friend Richardson (May 25), in "The Office of the First Regiment" (May 28, 1861), *Davenport Daily Democrat & News*; Z. to Dear John (May 8), in "Our Army Correspondence" (May 17, 1861), and H. J. C. to Editor (May 9), in "Our Army Correspondence" (May 17, 1861), *Muscatine Weekly Journal*; Anonymous to Editor (May 12), *Burlington Daily Hawk-Eye*, May 14, 1861.

30. Anonymous to Editor (May 12), *Burlington Daily Hawk-Eye*, May 14, 1861; Mac to Dear Dick (May 14), in "Our War Correspondence" (May 16, 1861), and Occasional to Friend Richardson (May 25), in "The Office of the First Regiment" (May 28, 1861), *Davenport Daily Democrat & News*; H. J. C. to Editor (May 12), in "Our Army Correspondence," *Muscatine Weekly Journal*, May 17, 1861.

31. "Excursion on the Pomeroy," *Davenport Daily Democrat & News*, May 15, 1861; Stuart, *Iowa Colonels and Regiments*, 22.

32. "Keokuk Items" (May 18, 1861), Mac to Dear Dick (May 27), in "Our War Correspondence" (May 28, 1861), "First Iowa Regiment" (May 29, 1861), and "Those Arms" (May 30, 1861), *Davenport Daily Democrat & News*; "We Have Some Hope . . ." (May 8, 1861), B. Z. to Editor, May 20 (May 22), and H. S. to Editor (June 6) (June 8, 1861), *Burlington Daily Hawk-Eye*; Clark, *Life in the Middle West*, 49; "Camp at Macon City," *Mt. Pleasant Home Journal*, June 22, 1861; Anonymous to Editor (May 12), in "Our Army Correspondence," *Muscatine Weekly Journal*, May 17, 1861.

33. Z. to Editor (May 15), in "Our Army Correspondence" (May 24, 1861), H. to Dear John (May 8), in "Our Army Correspondence" (May 17, 1861), and W. F. D. to Editor (May 24), in "Our Army Correspondence" (May 31, 1861), *Muscatine Weekly Journal*; Zouave to Editor (May 18), *Burlington Daily Hawk-Eye*, May 21, 1861; Occasional to Dear Dick (May 27), in "Our War Correspondence," *Davenport Daily Democrat & News*, May 28, 1861.

34. Occasional to Dear Dick, May 27, 1861, in "Our War Correspondence," *Davenport Daily Democrat & News*, May 28, 1861.

35. Ingersoll, *Iowa and the Rebellion*, 21; U. to Editor (May 18), in "Our Army Correspondence" (May 24, 1861), H. J. C. to Editor (May 21), in "Our Army Correspondence" (May 31, 1861), and W. F. D. to Editor (May 31, June 14), in "Our Army Correspondence" (June 7, 21, 1861), *Muscatine Weekly Journal*; Vici to Editor (June 15), in "Our Army Correspondence," *Iowa City Weekly State Reporter*, June 26, 1861; Ware, *Lyon Campaign*, 85, 106; Mac to Dear Dick (May 27), in "Our War Correspondence," *Davenport Daily Democrat & News*, May 28, 1861.

36. Wilkie had not been hired to promote Bates. In fact, because the *Herald* changed hands while Wilkie was in Missouri, he was never paid for his work. Mac to Dear Dick (June 16, 23), in "War Correspondence—1st Regiment," *Davenport Daily Democrat & News*, June 20, July 1, 1861; "Movement of Troops," *Hannibal Daily Messenger*, June 15, 1861; *Macon City Our Whole Union*, June 15, 1861; Wilkie, *Pen and Powder*, 9–10, 16–17; Vici to Editor (June 25), in "Our Army Correspondence," *Iowa City Weekly State Reporter*, July 10, 1861; H. to Friend Mahin (July 16), in "Our Army Correspondence," *Muscatine Weekly Journal*, Aug. 2, 1861; Traveller to Editor (July 8), *Iowa City Democratic State Press*, July 31, 1861; Franc B. Wilkie to Editor (June 22), in "Army Correspondence," *Dubuque Herald*, June 26, 1861.

37. H. J. C. to Editor (June 17), in "Our Army Correspondence," *Muscatine Weekly Journal*, June 28, 1861; H. to Editor (July 16), in "Our Army Correspondence," *Iowa City Weekly Journal*, Aug. 2, 1861; Traveller to Editor (July 8), in "War Correspondence," *Iowa City Democratic State Press*, July 31, 1861.

38. B. Z. to Editor (June 24), in *Burlington Daily Hawk-Eye*, June 29, 1861; Franc B. Wilkie to Editor (June 22), *Dubuque Herald*, June 26, 1861; "How They Went," *Davenport Daily Democrat & News*, June 15, 1861.

39. Shrader, "Field Logistics," 265–66, 269–70; Van Crevald, *Supplying War*, 34, 111; Hagerman, *American Civil War*, 44.

40. *OR* 3:388–89; Phillips, *Damned Yankee*, 222–26.

Chapter Four

1. For the relationship between prewar events in Kansas and the Civil War in the Trans-Mississippi theater, see Monaghan, *Civil War on the Western Border*.

2. Crawford, "Organization of the Kansas Troops," 3–4, 7; Richard D. Martin, "First Regiment Iowa Volunteers," 19; "We Are Informed by . . .," *Leavenworth Daily Times*, May 11, 1861.

3. Cracklin, "A War Reminiscence," n.p., Cracklin Papers, KSHS; "The Killed and Wounded," *Emporia News*, Aug. 31, 1861; "Lieut. L. L. Jones," *Olathe Mirror*, Sept. 5, 1861; "Lawrence Companies in Leavenworth" (June 6, 1861), "The Martyrs of Freedom" (Aug. 29, 1861), and "A Boston Man Killed in the Battle" (Oct. 3, 1861), *Lawrence Weekly Republican*; Caldwell, "The Stubbs," 124–25.

4. Monaghan, *Civil War on the Western Border*, 147; "Reminiscences of '61," *Boston*

Transcript, Aug. 12, 1901; "Halderman, John A." (7:556), "Eagle, James Philip" (10:191–92), and "Jones, Daniel Webster" (10:193–94), *National Cyclopedia*; "Military Companies," *Atchison Freedom's Champion*, May 18, 1861; "Gov. Thomas J. Churchill," *ENW*, 18–19; Newberry, "Harris Flanagin," 60–64; "Clayton, Powell," *DAB*, 4:187–88; "Wilson's Creek: Address by the Hon. Albert H. Horton," n.p., KSHS; "The Second Kansas," *Lawrence Weekly Republican*, Sept. 19, 1861; Webb, *Battles and Biographies*, 349–50.

5. Crawford, "Organization of the Kansas Troops," 19–20; Castel, *Frontier State at War*, 18, 21, 46–47; B. to Editor (May 29), in "News from the 'All Hazard' Boys," *Atchison Freedom's Champion*, June 1, 1861.

6. At one point Kansas had rival free-state and slave-state legislatures. Warner, *Generals in Blue*, 116–17; "Col. Deitzler Has Donated . . .," *Leavenworth Daily Times*, June 9, 1861; Monaghan, *Civil War on the Western Border*, 20, 26, 53, 56, 99, 146–47; Cordley, *History of Lawrence*, 37, 91, 97, 99, 128, 154, 179; C. M. Deitzler Reminiscences, n.p., UKL.

7. Stockton had already secured rifles for the Leavenworth Fencibles. "Gov. Robinson's Appointments," *Topeka Tribune*, June 1, 1861; "The Topeka *Tribune* of Last . . .," *Kansas State Record*, June 8, 1861; "The Leavenworth Fencibles," *Leavenworth Daily Times*, May 19, 1861; "Letter from Camp Lincoln," *Atchison Freedom's Champion*, June 22, 1861.

8. Warner, *Generals in Blue*, 328–29; Hatcher and Piston, *Kansans at Wilson's Creek*, 40; J. F. C. to Editor (July 27), in "Army Correspondence," *Kansas State Record*, Aug. 10, 1861; H. S. Moore to Dear Br. (Aug. 20), in "The Late Battle," *Lawrence Weekly Republican*, Aug. 29, 1861.

9. Hatcher and Piston, *Kansans at Wilson's Creek*, 9.

10. Ibid., 9–10.

11. Crawford, "Organization of the Kansas Troops," 4; Castel, *Frontier State at War*, 8.

12. "Military Companies" (May 18, 1861) and R. A. B. to Editor (June 12), in "Letter from Camp Lincoln" (June 22, 1861), *Atchison Freedom's Champion*; "Militia in Kansas," *Fort Scott Democrat*, June 8, 1861; "Lawrence Companies in Leavenworth," *Lawrence Weekly Republican*, June 6, 1861.

13. Captain Swift's Oread Guards of Lawrence were in Company D, not H. G. W. H. to Editor (June 5), in "News from the 'All Hazard' Boys," *Atchison Freedom's Champion*, June 8, 1861.

14. For examples, see G. W. H. to Editor (June 5), in "News from the 'All Hazard' Boys," *Atchison Freedom's Champion*, June 8, 1861; Hatcher and Piston, *Kansans at Wilson's Creek*, 39; "Wilson's Creek: Address by the Hon. Albert H. Horton," n.p., KSHS; Connelley, *Life of Preston B. Plumb*, 99.

15. Connelley, *Life of Preston B. Plumb*, 99; "On the Day Previous . . .," *Emporia News*, June 8, 1861.

16. Mitchell, *Civil War Soldiers*, 19. On the significance of flags, see also Wiley, *Life of Johnny Reb*, 20–22, and *Life of Billy Yank*, 28–30.

17. M. to Editor (June 29), in "From the Second Regiment," *Leavenworth Daily Times*, June 29, 1861; G. W. H. to Editor (June 5), in "News from the 'All Hazard' Boys," *Atchison Freedom's Champion*, June 8, 1861; "Wilson's Creek: Address by the Hon. Albert H. Horton," n.p., KSHS.

18. "From the 'Texas Hunters,'" *Texas Republican*, July 13, 1861.

19. Wyatt-Brown, *Honor and Violence*, 14; Linderman, *Embattled Courage*, 32.

20. Linderman, *Embattled Courage*, 12.

21. Monaghan, *Civil War on the Western Border*, 27, 36–37, 51, 72–78, 83–85, 92–94, 101–9; Cordley, *History of Lawrence*, 48, 91, 115–18, 130–31, 179.

22. For a list of Kansas newspapers, see Bibliography; for examples, see Hatcher and Piston, *Kansans at Wilson's Creek.*

23. Quoted in Quarles, *The Negro in the Civil War*, 32. Despite a search of the regimental records, we have been unable to establish the name of the African American or determine whether he enlisted before or after Wilson's Creek.

24. Brooksher, *Bloody Hill*, 128; *OR* 3:389; Phillips, *Damned Yankee*, 223; Hatcher and Piston, *Kansans at Wilson's Creek*, 45–46; Greene, "On the Battle of Wilson Creek," 116; Du Bois, "Journals and Letters," 349, 335–36, Du Bois Collection, YU; "In the Ranks under General Lyon," 574–75, 590.

25. On Aug. 3, 1861, the War Department renamed the existing dragoon units cavalry and altered some numerical designations among the existing cavalry regiments. As the mounted units that participated in the Wilson's Creek campaign used their pre–August 3 unit designations until long after the battle ended, we refer to the pre–August 3 unit designations throughout this study, regardless of date. William Branson Diary, July 6, 1861, UMC; Du Bois, "Journals and Letters," 337, Du Bois Collection, YU.

26. Hatcher and Piston, *Kansans at Wilson's Creek*, 43; James H. Wiswell to Dear Sister Mary, June 29, 1861, Wiswell Letters, DU; Greene, "On the Battle of Wilson Creek," 119; Sheridan, Albright, and Hudson, *Reminiscences of a Tramp Printer*, 98, 107.

27. Hatcher and Piston, *Kansans at Wilson's Creek*, 43; James H. Wiswell to Dear Sister Mary, June 29, 1861, Wiswell Letters, DU; Greene, "On the Battle of Wilson Creek," 119.

28. Hatcher and Piston, *Kansans at Wilson's Creek*, 43–46; J. W. H. to Mr. Francis (July 8), in "From Our Own Correspondent," *Olathe Mirror*, July 18, 1861.

29. Hatcher and Piston, *Kansans at Wilson's Creek*, 47; "The Whipping Affair," *Emporia News*, Sept. 21, 1861; "Whipping Volunteers under Major Sturgis," *Lawrence Weekly Republican*, July 15, 1861; "Soldiers Whipped," *Atchison Freedom's Champion*, July 15, 1861.

30. J. M. L. to Mr. Francis (July 8), in "From Our Own Correspondent" (July 18, 1861), and S. F. Hill to Dear Mildred (July 9), in "Extracts from Private Letters" (July 18, 1861), *Olathe Mirror*; "Volunteers Writing to the . . .," *Emporia News*, July 24, 1861; Hatcher and Piston, *Kansans at Wilson's Creek*, 52; Sheridan, Albright, and Hudson, *Reminiscences of a Tramp Printer*, 98.

31. "Soldiers Whipped," *Atchison Freedom's Champion*, Aug. 3, 1861; "Volunteers Writing to the . . .," *Emporia News*, July 24, 1861; "Whipping Volunteers under Major Sturgis," *Lawrence Weekly Republican*, July 18, 1861.

32. J. M. L. to Editor (July 8), in "From Our Own Correspondent," *Olathe Mirror*, July 18, 1861.

33. S. F. Hill to Dear Mildred (July 9), in "Extracts from Private Letters" (July 18, 1861), and "A Letter from the First Regiment" (July 25, 1861), *Olathe Mirror*; "News from the First Iowa Regiment," *Davenport Daily Democrat & News*, Aug. 1, 1861; Hatcher and Piston, *Kansans at Wilson's Creek*, 52–56; "In the Ranks under General Lyon," 578; General Orders No. 8, July 12, 1861, Letters Sent and General and Special Orders Issued, NARA.

34. Franc B. Wilkie to Editor (June 24), in "Army Correspondence," *Dubuque Herald*, July 2, 1861.

35. Ware, *Lyon Campaign*, 132–38.

36. Ibid., 129, 143–44; Horace Poole to Editor (July 2), in "Army Correspondence," *South Danvers Wizard*, July 17, 1861.

37. "Gen. Lyon's Movement Southward," *Mt. Pleasant Home Journal*, July 13, 1861; Ware, *Lyon Campaign*, 151–52, 155; Horace Poole to Editor (July 2), in "Army Correspon-

350 NOTES TO PAGES 69–73

dence," *South Danvers Wizard*, July 17, 1861; Greene, "On the Battle of Wilson Creek," 116–17.

38. Ware, *Lyon Campaign*, 157; W. F. D. to Editor (July 8), in "Our Army Correspondence," *Muscatine Weekly Journal*, July 26, 1861; Horace Poole to Editor (July 2), in "Army Correspondence," *South Danvers Wizard*, July 17, 1861.

39. "Soldier's Money," *Fort Scott Democrat*, July 20, 1861; Phillips, *Damned Yankee*, 225; *OR* 3:388–89; Ingersoll, *Iowa and the Rebellion*, 23; Ware, *Lyon Campaign*, 159–60; Richard D. Martin, "First Regiment Iowa Volunteers," 31; S. to Editor (June 15), in "Progress of the Army," *St. Louis Republican*, June 16, 1861; Greene, "On the Battle of Wilson Creek," 120; "In the Ranks under General Lyon," 577; Horace Poole to Editor (July 13), in "Army Correspondence," *South Danvers Wizard*, Aug. 7, 1861.

40. Matson, *Life Experiences*, 61.

41. Horace Poole to Editor (July 13), in "Army Correspondence," *South Danvers Wizard*, Aug. 7, 1861; Du Bois, "Journals and Letters," 350, Du Bois Collection, YU; Hatcher and Piston, *Kansans at Wilson's Creek*, 45.

Chapter Five

1. *OR* 3:397.

2. Ibid., 17; Engle, *Yankee Dutchman*, 62; Angus, *Down the Wire Road in the Missouri Ozarks*, 2–4.

3. Bek, "Civil War Diary of John T. Buegel," 311; Lademann, "Battle of Carthage," 131. Punctuation corrected in Lademann.

4. Charles Knibben to John C. Frémont, Sept. 21, 1861, Compiled Service Records, Backof's Battalion, NARA.

5. "News from the Southwest," *Glasgow Weekly Times*, July 11, 1861; John R. Norris to My dear Sisters, Mother, and Father, n.d., Norris Letters, LSU; J. F. C. to Editor (July 27), in "Army Correspondence," *Kansas State Record*, Aug. 10, 1861; Knox, *Camp-Fire and Cotton-Field*, 61.

6. Knox, *Camp-Fire and Cotton-Field*, 59–60; Wilkie, *Pen and Powder*, 24.

7. "Professor Charles Carlton," *ENW*, 328–29; Commercial information based on advertisements in *Springfield Advertiser* and *Springfield Equal Rights Gazette*, 1858, 1859, and 1860, and Hubble, *Personal Reminiscences*, 69.

8. "Union Meeting," *Liberty Tribune*, May 24, 1861; "The Speaking Saturday," *Springfield Mirror*, May 25, 1861; "Immense Union Meeting," *Richmond Weekly North-West Conservator*, May 31, 1861; "Payne, John W.," *ENW*, 278; Ingenthron, *Borderland Rebellion*, 42–43; "The Hegira of Secession," *Kansas City Daily Western Journal of Commerce*, July 13, 1861; Hubble, *Personal Reminiscences*, 37.

9. *OR* 3:391; Phillips, *Damned Yankee*, 227; Noble et al., *Military History and Reminiscences*, 2–6, 12–13, 20–26, 58, 62–63; Eddy, *Patriotism of Illinois*, 108, 295–96, 300–301.

10. For reasons that are unclear, Sweeny claimed credit for the plan of concentration that resulted in the fight at Carthage. *OR* 3:15–16.

11. Brooksher, *Bloody Hill*, 108; Engle, *Yankee Dutchman*, 62–63.

12. "Proclamation of Gov. Jackson," *Richmond Weekly North-West Conservator*, June 21, 1861; Kirkpatrick, "Missouri in the Early Months of the Civil War," 244.

13. Castel, *General Sterling Price*, 25–26; Snead, "First Year of the War in Missouri," 268.

14. Peterson et al., *Sterling Price's Lieutenants*, 175, 183, 235, 285.

15. Bearss, *Battle of Wilson's Creek*, 163; Knapp, *Wilson's Creek Staff Ride*, 87; CSA Missouri State Guard Quartermaster Accounts, MSA.

16. Each mounted company was to carry a white guidon with the letters "MSG" on each side. Castel, "Diary of General Henry Little," 10; *History of Clay and Platte Counties*, 202; Peterson et al., *Sterling Price's Lieutenants*, 306–7; Miles, *Bitter Ground*, 34, 53; "Troops for Jefferson," *Glasgow Weekly Times*, May 23, 1861; Brauer and Goosen, *Hier Snackt Wi Plattdütsch*, 183.

17. Peterson et al., *Sterling Price's Lieutenants*, 1.

18. Pollard, *Lost Cause*, 157; Payne, "Early Days of War in Missouri," 58.

19. Confederate Hospital Register, MSA.

20. Mudd, "What I Saw at Wilson's Creek," 89–90.

21. Ibid., 91–92; Peterson et al., *Sterling Price's Lieutenants*, 107, 110, 113; Snead, "First Year of the War in Missouri," 268.

22. "How Guibor and Barlow Ran the Gauntlet in '61," *St. Louis Post Dispatch*, Oct. 28, 1894; John C. Moore, *Missouri*, 307–8.

23. John C. Moore, *Missouri*, 307–8; "A Lively June Morning on Cowskin Prairie," *St. Louis Post Dispatch*, Nov. 11, 1894; Peterson et al., *Sterling Price's Lieutenants*, 191.

24. McIntyre was awarded his degree in absentia and became state attorney general after the war. Miles, *Bitter Ground*, 65; Conrad, *Encyclopedia of the History of Missouri*, 4:267–68.

25. Easley, "Journal of the Civil War in Missouri," 12–16.

26. According to one source, there were 12,000 kegs of powder in Jefferson City. Jackson dispersed them to hiding places in Cooper, Saline, Howard, Chariton, and Carroll Counties. Asbury, *My Experiences in the War*, 3–4, 40–43; *History of Carroll County, Missouri*, 298.

27. Asbury, *My Experiences in the War*, 4.

28. Ibid., 5–6.

29. Harding, "'Kelly's Boys': A History of the Washington Blues," 8–9, 30, HL; Peterson et al., *Sterling Price's Lieutenants*, 172n.

30. Harding, "'Kelly's Boys,'" 30, HL; Peterson et al., *Sterling Price's Lieutenants*, 181–84.

31. "General Orders No. 2, May 16, 1861," *Randolph Citizen*, May 23, 1861; Knox, *Camp-Fire and Cotton-Field*, 19; Kirkpatrick, "Missouri in the Early Months of the Civil War," 244; *OR* 53:697–98.

32. Long, "Frémont, Lyon, and Wilson's Creek," 82.

33. A handful of companies remained active after 1862. Peterson et al., *Sterling Price's Lieutenants*, 5–11.

34. W. N. M., "Battle of Wilson's Creek," 50; "Interesting Correspondence," *Boliver Weekly Courier*, May 4, 1861.

35. "Interesting Correspondence," *Boliver Weekly Courier*, May 4, 1861; Peterson et al., *Sterling Price's Lieutenants*, 251.

36. Lewis, "Civil War Reminiscences," 227–28.

37. Vandiver, "Two Forgotten Heroes," 405; Peterson et al., *Sterling Price's Lieutenants*, 139, 143–48; Keith, "John D. Keith, Confederate Soldier—'Reminiscences,'" 2, AHC; John T. Hughes to Dear Frank, May 7, 1861, *Missouri Partisan* 11, no. 2 (Summer 1995): 5; "Letter from Col. John T. Hughes," *Liberty Tribune*, Sept. 13, 1861; Allardice, *More Generals in Gray*, 132.

38. These conclusions are based on a cumulative reading of diaries, letters, memoirs, and newspaper articles and editorials relating to the topic.

Chapter Six

1. Cutrer, *Ben McCulloch*, 201.
2. *OR* 3:590–91; Cutrer, *Ben McCulloch*, 203–6; Franks, *Stand Watie and the Agony of the Cherokee Nation*, 118; Thomas F. Anderson, "Indian Territory"; Meserve, "The Mayes," 58; Josephy, *Civil War in the American West*, 324–26.
3. Watson, *Life in the Confederate Army*, 171; Tunnard, *A Southern Record*, 35–36; Cutrer and Parrish, *Brothers in Gray*, 19; "Flag Presentation," *Arkansas True Democrat*, June 6, 1861.
4. "Volunteers" (Apr. 25, 1861) and "Officers of the 1st Regiment, Arkansas Mounted Riflemen" (June 6, 1861), *Arkansas True Democrat*; "Gov. Thomas J. Churchill," *ENW*, 18–19; Haynes, "General and Mrs. Thomas J. Churchill," 2, AHC.
5. Walter, "Capsule Histories of Arkansas Military Units," 58, HL; "Hon. Charles Mitchell," *ENW*, 58–60; "Family Record," Johnson Civil War Letters, AHC.
6. Volunteer to Editor (June 30), *Arkansas True Democrat*, July 18, 1861; Watson, *Life in the Confederate Army*, 170; John Johnson to Dear Wife and Children, June 14, 1861, Johnson Civil War Letters, AHC; Warner and McGinnis, "Captain Gib's Company," 51.
7. John Johnson to Dear Wife and Children, June 21, 1861, Johnson Civil War Letters, AHC; Warner and McGinnis, "Captain Gib's Company," 50.
8. Watson, *Life in the Confederate Army*, 172; Tunnard, *A Southern Record*, 37; Geise, "Confederate Military Forces in the Trans-Mississippi," 7; John Johnson to Dear Wife and Children, June 21, 1861, Johnson Civil War Letters, AHC; Cutrer and Parrish, *Brothers in Gray*, 20.
9. Woodruff, *With the Light Guns*, 23–24.
10. Bearss, *Battle of Wilson's Creek*, 162; John Johnson to Dear Wife and Children, June 14, 1861, Johnson Civil War Letters, AHC.
11. Warner, *Generals in Gray*, 202–3, and *Generals in Blue*, 300–301.
12. Walter, "Capsule Histories of Arkansas Military Units," 72, AHC; Leeper, *Rebels Valiant*, 13–28.
13. "List of Volunteers," Flanagin Papers, AHC; Amy Jean Greene, "Governor Harris Flanagin," ibid.; Newberry, "Harris Flanagin," 59–64.
14. Strother, "Arkansas General," n.p.; Angie Lewis McRae, "Genl. D. McRae, White Co. Man," n.p., D. McRae Papers, AHC.
15. Angie Lewis McRae, "Genl. D. McRae, White Co. Man," n.p., Muster Rolls— Companies A, B, and C, McRae's Battalion, Report of Arms, Equipment, etc., Company I, Camp Walker, and Dandridge McRae, "Narrative of the Battle of Oak Hills," n.p., McRae Papers, AHC; Warner, *Generals in Gray*, 206; Bearss, *Battle of Wilson's Creek*, 220.
16. Mars is listed as a "Cherokee quarteroon," a term indicating a mixture of Native American and African American ancestry. Whites called persons of mixed white and Native American ancestry "half-breeds" or "mixed bloods." Descriptive List of Cap. Lawrence's Company in Regiment Arks. Infantry, McRae Papers, AHC.
17. Scott and Myers, "Extinct 'Grass Eaters' of Benton County," 141–42, 153–55.
18. Bearss, *Battle of Wilson's Creek*, 163; Woodruff, *With the Light Guns*, 34.
19. Dandridge McRae to Wife, May 4, 1861, McRae Papers, AHC.
20. Woodruff, *With the Light Guns*, 27–29.
21. Tunnard, *A Southern Record*, 38–39.
22. R. M. Hinson to My Dearest Mat, July 10, 1861, Hinson Papers, LSU.
23. Ibid.

24. *OR* 3:591, 594–95, 599–600.

25. Cutrer, *Ben McCulloch*, 209.

26. Ibid., 210; Castel, *General Sterling Price*, 31–32; *OR* 3:603, 606.

27. *OR* 3:606–7.

28. Ibid., 39.

29. The Federals were paroled on July 8. Conrad reported that the Southern officers were courteous, but the enlisted men were "insulting and brutal" in their manner. Ibid., 38–39, 607.

30. Britton, *Civil War on the Western Border*, 1:54.

31. John T. Hughes to R. M. Miller (July 7), in "Letter from Col. Hughes," *Richmond Weekly North-West Conservator*, July 26, 1861; Hinze and Farnham, *Battle of Carthage*, 112–201; Engle, *Yankee Dutchman*, 64–65.

32. *OR* 3:17–19; Britton, *Civil War on the Western Border*, 1:56–61; Engle, *Yankee Dutchman*, 66–67; Hinze and Farnham, *Battle of Carthage*, 163–201.

33. Engle, *Yankee Dutchman*, 66.

34. Ware, *Lyon Campaign*, 184.

35. Phillips, *Damned Yankee*, 229–30.

36. Ralph D. Zublin to Wife (July 18), in "A Letter from a G.G.," *Dubuque Weekly Times*, Aug. 8, 1861.

37. *OR* 3:394.

Chapter Seven

1. *OR* 3:607, 611; Cutrer, *Ben McCulloch*, 215; Ingenthron, *Borderland Rebellion*, 48.

2. *OR* 3:607.

3. Ibid., 612.

4. Ibid., 608, 610–11.

5. Ibid., 611.

6. Ibid., 610.

7. For standard treatments of this issue, see Cutrer, *Ben McCulloch*, 216–18, and Castel, *General Sterling Price*, 34–35.

8. R. M. Hinson to My Dearest Mat, July 10, 1861, Hinson Papers, LSU.

9. John Johnson to Dear Mother, July 23, 1861, Johnson Civil War Letters, AHC.

10. R. M. Hinson to My Dear Mat, July 25, 1861, Hinson Papers, LSU; John Johnson to Dear Wife and Children, July 22, 1861, Johnson Civil War Letters, AHC.

11. John Johnson to Dear Wife and Children, July 28, 1861, Johnson Civil War Letters, AHC; "The Following Extract of . . .," *Shreveport South-Western*, Aug. 7, 1861. The letter excerpted in this article is dated July 11, 1861.

12. Mary E. Weaver to Omer Rose Weaver, June 9, 1861, Weaver-Field Collection, AHC.

13. Harrell, "Confederate Dead," Journal of the Proceedings of the Little Rock Debating Club, Manuscripts—Omer R. Weaver's Purse Contents, AHC; Gill, "History of the Weaver Family and Home," AHC.

14. Woodruff, *With the Light Guns*, 49; Mary E. Weaver to Omer Rose Weaver, July 5, 1861, Weaver-Field Collection, AHC.

15. Mary E. Weaver to Omer Rose Weaver, June 9, 21, July 3, 5, 25, 1861, Weaver-Field Collection, AHC; Samuel Montgomery Weaver to Omer Rose Weaver, July 18, 1861, AHC. Mary Weaver's letter of July 5 encloses a letter from Omer's sweetheart, dated July 5, 1861.

16. Carr, *In Fine Spirits*, 8, 11–12, 14; Isaac Clark Diary, July 31, 1861, AHC; R. M. Hinson to My Dear Mat, July 25, 1861, Hinson Papers, LSU; "Full and Authentic Particulars of the Doings in Camp, Before and After the Battle of Oak Hills," *Shreveport Weekly News*, Sept. 2, 1861.

17. Another eighteen deserted. See muster rolls in Tunnard, *A Southern Record*, 495–566.

18. Ingenthron, *Borderland Rebellion*, 53; Easley, "Journal of the Civil War in Missouri," 20.

19. Allardice, *More Generals in Gray*, 215–16; Peterson et al., *Sterling Price's Lieutenants*, 154; A. B. C. to Editor (Aug. 27), in "Camp Correspondence," *Liberty Tribune*, Sept. 13, 1861 (spelling corrected in quotation).

20. Easley, "Journal of the Civil War in Missouri," 20; Rockwell, "A Rambling Reminiscence of Experiences," n.p., MSA; Bell, "Price's Missouri Campaign," 318; Ingenthron, *Borderland Rebellion*, 48.

21. "A Southwest Missouri Paper . . .," *Kansas City Daily Western Journal of Commerce*, June 2, 1861; CSA Missouri State Guard Quartermaster Accounts, MSA.

22. CSA Missouri State Guard Quartermaster Accounts, MSA.

23. Although there were camp followers at Cowskin Prairie, the soldiers did not turn much of the sewing over to these women. This suggests that the women were too few in number to accomplish the task. CSA Missouri State Guard Quartermaster Accounts, MSA; Easley, "Journal of the Civil War in Missouri," 20–21.

24. Webb, *Battles and Biographies*, 318; Ingenthron, *Borderland Rebellion*, 58–59.

25. Mudd, "What I Saw at Wilson's Creek," 95; Ingenthron, *Borderland Rebellion*, 59.

26. Henderson, "Confederate Diary," 2, MSA; "The State Troops," *Liberty Tribune*, July 5, 1861.

27. Extant records suggest that Lyon's punishments were swift but not unduly harsh by army standards of the time. Several soldiers accused of minor crimes were acquitted by military tribunals. Orders No. 7, 24, 44, 58, 59, Letters Sent and General and Special Orders Issued, NARA; "In the Ranks under General Lyon," 587; Anonymous to Editor (July 23), in "Letters from the 'All-Hazard' Boys," *Atchison Freedom's Champion*, Aug. 10, 1861; H. J. C. to Editor (July 27), in "Our Army Correspondence," *Muscatine Weekly Journal*, Aug. 9, 1861; Barney, *Recollections of Field Service*, 54.

28. W. F. D. to Editor (July 28), in "Our Army Correspondence," *Muscatine Weekly Journal*, Aug. 9, 1861.

29. G. to Editor (July 28), in "A Letter from Our Special Correspondent," *Dubuque Weekly Times*, Aug. 8, 1861.

30. Ware, *Lyon Campaign*, 117, 136, 156; Phillips, *Damned Yankee*, 242; *OR* 3:395, 398; G. to Editor (July 28), in "A Letter from Our Special Correspondent," *Dubuque Weekly Times*, Aug. 8, 1861.

31. Mac to Dear Dick (July 25), in "War Correspondence—1st Regiment," *Davenport Daily Democrat & News*, Aug. 8, 1861; "Affairs in Missouri," *Burlington Daily Hawk-Eye*, July 25, 1861; "From Missouri," *Olathe Mirror*, Aug. 1, 1861.

32. Barney, *Recollections of Field Service*, 53.

33. Punctuation added for clarity. William Branson Diary, July 18–23, 1861, UMC.

34. "The Iowa First," *Davenport Daily Democrat & News*, Aug. 8, 1861.

35. "Arrival of Troops from Springfield, Missouri," *Kansas State Record*, Aug. 10, 1861; Du Bois, "Journals and Letters," 345, Du Bois Collection, YU; Clark, *Life in the Middle West*, 65.

36. *OR* 3:390; Phillips, *Damned Yankee*, 227–28; Parrish, *Turbulent Partnership*, 48–49.

37. *OR* 3:390–92, 394–97.

38. Ibid., 394, 397–98.

39. Phillips, *Damned Yankee*, 231–33.

Chapter Eight

1. Hale, *Third Texas Cavalry*, 31, 47–49; Johnson, *Texans Who Wore the Gray*, 57; Barron, *Lone Star Defenders*, 22.

2. Barron, *Lone Star Defenders*, 27–28; Lale, "Boy-Bugler," 76; Cater, *As It Was*, 77; Hale, *Third Texas Cavalry*, 53.

3. Hale, *Third Texas Cavalry*, 48–49; Sparks, *War between the States*, 181.

4. Cater, *As It Was*, 77–78.

5. Ibid., 82.

6. Sparks, *War between the States*, 134–35; Barron, *Lone Star Defenders*, 32; Hale, *Third Texas Cavalry*, 51.

7. Barron, *Lone Star Defenders*, 34.

8. "The Progress of Events," *Clarksville Standard*, July 13, 1861.

9. *OR* 3:44–45.

10. Ware, *Lyon Campaign*, 228–30; G. to Editor (July 28), in "A Letter from Our Special Correspondent," *Dubuque Weekly Times*, Aug. 8, 1861.

11. Ware, *Lyon Campaign*, 231, 235; Warner, *Generals in Blue*, 493–94.

12. G. to Editor (July 28), in "A Letter from Our Special Correspondent," *Dubuque Weekly Times*, Aug. 8, 1861; H. J. C. to Editor (Aug. 25), in "Our Army Correspondence," *Muscatine Weekly Journal*, Aug. 30, 1861; Warner, *Generals in Blue*, 470–71; Sergent, *They Lie Forgotten*, 181–82; Ware, *Lyon Campaign*, 230–31; Ingenthron, *Borderland Rebellion*, 62–63.

13. Ingenthron, *Borderland Rebellion*, 62–63; Ware, *Lyon Campaign*, 231–32; G. to Editor (July 28), in "A Letter from Our Special Correspondent," *Dubuque Weekly Times*, Aug. 8, 1861; B. Z. to Editor (July 25), in "Army Correspondence," *Burlington Daily Hawk-Eye*, Aug. 5, 1861.

14. Ingenthron, *Borderland Rebellion*, 63–64; Ware, *Lyon Campaign*, 232–33; J. C. F. to Editor (July 27), in "Army Correspondence," *Kansas State Record*, Aug. 10, 1861.

15. Sokalski, "56 Fights," 6; J. C. F. to Editor (July 27), in "Army Correspondence," *Kansas State Record*, Aug. 10, 1861; Ware, *Lyon Campaign*, 233–34.

16. Ingenthron, *Borderland Rebellion*, 65; *OR* 3:44.

17. The unit cannot be identified. Price's account implies that he was not in charge; he identifies himself only as an inspector general. But as Ware describes the State Guardsmen fleeing with their horses, the men may have been part of the Second Cavalry Regiment of McBride's Division, which Price commanded temporarily. See J. H. Price and L. M. Dunning to Editor (July 29), in "Battle at Forsyth, Missouri," *Arkansas True Democrat*, Aug. 15, 1861; Ware, *Lyon Campaign*, 237–38; and Peterson et al., *Sterling Price's Lieutenants*, 198, 204.

18. Ware, *Lyon Campaign*, 238; Ingenthron, *Borderland Rebellion*, 65.

19. Ingenthron, *Borderland Rebellion*, 67; Wilkie, *Pen and Powder*, 24–25; J. H. Price and L. M. Dunning to Editor (July 29), in "Battle at Forsyth, Missouri," *Arkansas True Democrat*, Aug. 15, 1861.

20. H. L. Moore to Editor (July 27), in "Camp of the Army of the West," *Lawrence Weekly Republican*, Aug. 8, 1861; G. to Editor (July 28), in "A Letter from Our Special

Correspondent," *Dubuque Weekly Times*, Aug. 8, 1861; Ingenthron, *Borderland Rebellion*, 67–68.

21. *OR* 3:44–45; J. H. Price and L. M. Dunning to Editor (July 29), in "Battle at Forsyth, Missouri," *Arkansas True Democrat*, Aug. 15, 1861; G. to Editor (July 28), in "A Letter from Our Special Correspondent," *Dubuque Weekly Times*, Aug. 8, 1861; J. C. F. to Editor (July 27), in "Army Correspondence," *Kansas State Record*, Aug. 10, 1861.

22. *OR* 3:45; G. to Editor (July 28), in "A Letter from Our Special Correspondent," *Dubuque Weekly Times*, Aug. 8, 1861; J. C. F. to Editor (July 27), in "Army Correspondence," *Kansas State Record*, Aug. 10, 1861; B. Z. to editor (July 25), in "Army Correspondence," *Burlington Daily Hawk-Eye*, Aug. 5, 1861; Brant, *Campaign of General Lyon*, 7.

23. Osbourne, "Vincent Osbourne's Civil War Experience," 123; "Our Boys," *Emporia News*, Aug. 17, 1861; Ware, *Lyon Campaign*, 240–41.

24. Ware, *Lyon Campaign*, 242; Ingenthron, *Borderland Rebellion*, 71–72; Fellman, *Inside War*, 23–80.

25. Ingenthron, *Borderland Rebellion*, 72; G. to Editor (July 28), in "A Letter from Our Special Correspondent," *Dubuque Weekly Times*, Aug. 8, 1861; Ware, *Lyon Campaign*, 242–47.

26. Mac to Dear Dick (July 25), in "War Correspondence—1st Regiment," *Davenport Daily Democrat & News*, Aug. 8, 1861; *OR* 3:400–403, 407.

27. B. Z. to Editor (July 25), in "Army Correspondence," *Burlington Daily Hawk-Eye*, Aug. 5, 1861,; H. L. Moore to Editor (July 27), in "Camp of the Army of the West," *Lawrence Weekly Republican*, Aug. 8, 1861; Mac to Dear Dick (July 25), in "War Correspondence—1st Regiment," *Davenport Daily Democrat & News*, Aug. 8, 1861; G. to Editor (July 28), in "A Letter from Our Special Correspondent," *Dubuque Weekly Times*, Aug. 8, 1861; Ware, *Lyon Campaign*, 247–50; "In the Ranks under General Lyon," 584.

28. *OR* 3:47, 408; Du Bois, "Journals and Letters," 352, Du Bois Collection, YU; "Colonel Soloman's Regiment . . .," *Kansas City Daily Western Journal of Commerce*, Aug. 4, 1861; Davis, "Extract from a Report of His Services," 15; Brooksher, *Bloody Hill*, 146.

29. *OR* 3:409, 411–12; Phillips, *Damned Yankee*, 233–38; Clark, *Life in the Middle West*, 59; Greene, "On the Battle of Wilson Creek," 120; "Major General Lyon," *Dubuque Weekly Times*, July 11, 1861; Zogbaum, "Life of Mary Anne Phelps Montgomery," 25, Zogbaum Papers, MHS.

30. Phillips, *Damned Yankee*, 234, 236.

31. *OR* 3:47; Phillips, *Damned Yankee*, 237.

32. Phillips, *Damned Yankee*, 240.

33. *OR* 53:616–18, 622–23; Geise, "Confederate Military Forces in the Trans-Mississippi," 19–22.

34. Cutrer, *Ben McCulloch*, 220; John J. Walker to W. W. Mansfield, July 31, 1861, Mansfield Letters, AHC.

35. *OR* 53:719–20.

36. Ibid., 622–23; Cutrer, *Ben McCulloch*, 221; Pearce, "Price's Campaign of 1861," 338–39.

37. *OR* 3:622–23, 745; Cutrer, *Ben McCulloch*, 221.

38. *OR* 3:717–18.

39. Ibid., 717–18.

40. Ibid., 718; Cutrer, *Ben McCulloch*, 222; Woodruff, *With the Light Guns*, 35–36.

Chapter Nine

1. Ware, *Lyon Campaign*, 270–72.
2. Phillips, *Damned Yankee*, 240; "In the Ranks under General Lyon," 580; *OR* 3:47; Du Bois, "Journals and Letters," 353, Du Bois Collection, YU; Holcombe and Adams, *Battle of Wilson's Creek*, 12.
3. *OR* 3:49.
4. Ibid., 47; Ware, *Lyon Campaign*, 269.
5. *OR* 3:49; Ware, *Lyon Campaign*, 274.
6. *OR* 3:51–52.
7. Other sources give slightly different casualty figures. Ibid., 48–52; Du Bois, "Journals and Letters," 353–54, Du Bois Collection, YU.
8. Alf to Dear Mother (Aug. 12), in "Battle of Oak Hills, near Springfield, Mo.," *Shreveport South-Western*, Sept. 4, 1861; Carr, *In Fine Spirits*, 15.
9. "Full and Authentic Particulars of the Doings in Camp, Before & After the Battle of Oak Hills," *Shreveport Weekly News*, Sept. 2, 1861; *OR* 3:52.
10. Du Bois, "Journals and Letters," 354, Du Bois Collection, YU; Horace Poole Diary, Aug. 3, 1861, HL.
11. *OR* 3:58; Ware, *Lyon Campaign*, 279; "In the Ranks under General Lyon," 581; Horace Poole Diary, Aug. 3, 1861, HL.
12. Ware's postwar claim that he saw the graves of twenty-five Southerners at Curran's Post Office is difficult to credit. If so, they were victims of disease who had died earlier, not combat casualties. Ware, *Lyon Campaign*, 278–79, 281; Du Bois, "Journals and Letters," 355, Du Bois Collection, YU; Wilkie, *The Iowa First*, 100–103.
13. Lyon's report refers to "McCulla's Farm," but extant sources include many variations on the spelling of the name. *OR* 3:47, 58–59; Ingenthron, *Borderland Rebellion*, 79; Phillips, *Damned Yankee*, 241; "In the Ranks under General Lyon," 579.
14. "Full and Authentic Particulars of the Doings in Camp"; Alf to Dear Mother (Aug. 12), in "The Battle of Oak Hills, near Springfield, Mo.," *Shreveport Weekly News*, Sept. 4, 1861; Tunnard, *A Southern Record*, 45; Watson, *Life in the Confederate Army*, 195–97.
15. Ware, *Lyon Campaign*, 284; *OR* 3:59; Wilkie, *The Iowa First*, 100–103; Holcombe and Adams, *Battle of Wilson's Creek*, 12–13.
16. William Branson Diary, Aug. 4, 1861, UMC. Spelling corrected.
17. Ibid.; Cracklin, "A War Reminiscence, By Old Cap," n.p., Cracklin Papers, KSHS; Knox, *Camp-Fire and Cotton-Field*, 62–66.
18. Phillips, *Damned Yankee*, 244; Ware, *Lyon Campaign*, 291–93; Holcombe and Adams, *Battle of Wilson's Creek*, 13; Bearss, *Battle of Wilson's Creek*, 29; Horace Poole Diary, Aug. 4–5, 1861, HL.
19. Ware, *Lyon Campaign*, 280.
20. Phillips, *Damned Yankee*, 244; "The Lyon Roareth," *Atchison Freedom's Champion*, Aug. 10, 1861.
21. Henderson, "Confederate Diary," 3, MSA. Despite the editor's title, this diary's contents reveal the author to have been an assistant regimental surgeon in Colonel John A. Foster's Second Infantry Regiment, McBride's Division, Missouri State Guard, not the Confederate army. Although the author is not identified, Peterson et al. (*Sterling Price's Lieutenants*, 203) convinces us that he was Dr. John Wyatt.
22. Snead, *Fight for Missouri*, 254.
23. Castel, *General Sterling Price*, 24–25, 28; Cutrer, *Ben McCulloch*, 8; *OR* 3:717–18.
24. *OR* 3:720; Henderson, "Confederate Diary," 4, MSA.

25. *OR* 3:745.

26. Pillow's movement never materialized. *OR* 3:745; Cutrer, *Ben McCulloch*, 225; Hale, *Third Texas Cavalry*, 57.

27. McCulloch's orders placed all but one unit of the Missouri State Guard to the rear of his other infantry. This was infantry from Rains's Division, which had been consolidated into a 1,300-man brigade under Colonel Richard H. Weightman. *OR* 3:720–21; Peterson et al., *Sterling Price's Lieutenants*, 212.

28. *OR* 3:721; Tunnard, *A Southern Record*, 47.

29. Woodruff, *With the Light Guns*, 37.

30. Cutrer, *Ben McCulloch*, 226–27; Tunnard, *A Southern Record*, 48; Woodruff, *With the Light Guns*, 37.

31. Henderson, "Confederate Diary," 4, MSA; Lale, "Boy-Bugler," 79.

Chapter Ten

1. Bearss, *Battle of Wilson's Creek*, 33–34.

2. *History of Greene County*, 131.

3. Historic Base and Ground Cover Map, HL.

4. Ibid.

5. The Sharp farm lay in the southern portion of Greene County that was detached in 1860 to form Christian County. The absence of a slave schedule for Christian County in 1860 makes it impossible to determine precisely how many slaves Sharp owned at the time of the battle. Barron, *Lone Star Defenders*, 40–41; *Greene County, Missouri, Federal Census of 1860*, 101–18; Abstracts of Park Research Funded by the Midwest Regional Office, National Park Service, pp. 117–18, HL.

6. *Greene County, Missouri, Federal Census of 1860*, 101–18. The ten farms surveyed belonged to John Dixon, Samuel Dixon, William B. Edwards, John M. Gibson, Mary A. Gwinn, Mercer Moody, Joseph D. Sharp, Elias B. Short, Samuel Short, and John A. Ray.

7. Ibid.

8. Historic Base and Ground Cover Map, HL.

9. Previous accounts place the Pulaski Battery at the "Guinn farm" without further identification. Records in the Greene County Archives indicate that individuals with names spelled Guynne, Guinn, and Gwin owned land near the battlefield, but none place them on the site in question. Larkin Winn apparently rented from John Ray, as his name does not appear as a property owner. Winston Winn, great-great grandson of Larkin, indicates that the Winn family lived at the hilltop farm but had abandoned the property prior to the battle. Winston Winn to Richard W. Hatcher III, Feb. 24, 1989, HL; *Greene County, Missouri, Federal Census of 1860*, 68; Woodruff, *With the Light Guns*, 38; Bearss, *Battle of Wilson's Creek*, 36.

10. Bearss, "Ray House Report," HL.

11. Watson, *Life in the Confederate Army*, 209; Rivers Reminiscences, n.p., HL; Peterson et al., *Sterling Price's Lieutenants*, 212n.

12. Peterson et al., *Sterling Price's Lieutenants*, 14–15, 212n; "General Weightman," *Liberty Tribune*, Sept. 6, 1861. According to the newspaper, Weightman was born in England but immigrated to the United States at an early age.

13. *OR* 3:3, 128, 53:434–35; Mudd, "What I Saw at Wilson's Creek," 93; Bearss, *Battle of Wilson's Creek*, 34–37, 149; Snead, *Fight for Missouri*, 258–61, 315.

14. Bearss, *Battle of Wilson's Creek*, 34–37, 260–61.

15. Ibid.

16. Allen, *First Arkansas Confederate Mounted Rifles*, 33; Watson, *Life in the Confederate Army*, 209.

17. Reiff, "History of 'Spy' Company," 169–70.

18. *OR* 3:745.

19. Snead, *Fight for Missouri*, 261.

20. Easley, "Journal of the Civil War in Missouri," 12–25; Watson, *Life in the Confederate Army*, 210.

21. Lane, "Recollections of a Volunteer," Lane Papers, MHS. Punctuation corrected.

22. Watson, *Life in the Confederate Army*, 209.

23. These men apparently later enlisted in a company commanded by Joel B. Mayes, who may himself have been present at the battle. Some accounts state that William Clarke Quantrill accompanied the group. Trickett, "Civil War in the Indian Territory," 146; Mabel Washbourne Anderson, *Life of General Stand Watie*, 15; Thomas F. Anderson, "Indian Territory," 85–87; Fischer and Rampp, "Quantrill's Civil War Operations," 158; Connelley, *Quantrill and the Border Wars*, 198; Lale, "Boy-Bugler," 79; Fischer and Gill, *Confederate Indian Forces Outside of Indian Territory*, 3.

24. Barron, *Lone Star Defenders*, 41–42.

25. Bearss, *Battle of Wilson's Creek*, 45.

26. Woodruff, *With the Light Guns*, 38.

27. Henderson, "Confederate Diary," 5–6, MSA.

28. Pearce, "Arkansas Troops," 299; Snead, *Fight for Missouri*, 261.

29. Snead, *Fight for Missouri*, 261.

30. Ibid., 262–63.

31. Pearce, "Arkansas Troops," 299; Mudd, "What I Saw at Wilson's Creek," 93–94.

32. Barron, *Lone Star Defenders*, 42; Lale, "Boy-Bugler," 14–15; *OR* 3:746.

33. Mudd, "What I Saw at Wilson's Creek," 93–94; Barron, *Lone Star Defenders*, 42; Lale, "Boy-Bugler," 14–15; Watson, *Life in the Confederate Army*, 211.

34. Dawson, Toomer, and forty other members of the unit were killed during the battle. Dacus, *Reminiscences of Company "H,"* 2.

35. Tunnard, *A Southern Record*, 50.

Chapter Eleven

1. Phillips, *Damned Yankee*, 244–45.

2. Holcombe and Adams, *Battle of Wilson's Creek*, 17–18; Phillips, *Damned Yankee*, 245.

3. Phillips, *Damned Yankee*, 237–38.

4. Ibid., 238–39.

5. Ibid., 234–39; Snead, *Fight for Missouri*, 244–47.

6. Schofield, *Forty-six Years in the Army*, 39; *OR* 3:59; Lobdell, "Civil War Journal and Letters," pt. 2, 23.

7. *OR* 3:59; Holcombe and Adams, *Battle of Wilson's Creek*, 19.

8. Lobdell, "Civil War Journal and Letters," pt. 1, 441–47; Haskin, *History of the First Regiment of Artillery*, 620; Du Bois, "Journals and Letters," 342, 347–48, 352, Du Bois Collection, YU.

9. Bearss, *Battle of Wilson's Creek*, 41; Phillips, *Damned Yankee*, 244.

10. Bearss, *Battle of Wilson's Creek*, 41; Phillips, *Damned Yankee*, 244; Horace Poole

Diary, Aug. 5, 1861, HL; Holcombe and Adams, *Battle of Wilson's Creek*, 17; Ware, *Lyon Campaign*, 293–94.

11. Lobdell, "Civil War Journal and Letters," pt. 2, 23; Phillips, *Damned Yankee*, 244–45; Ware, *Lyon Campaign*, 249.

12. Holcombe and Adams, *Battle of Wilson's Creek*, 19; Phillips, *Damned Yankee*, 245.

13. Holcombe and Adams, *Battle of Wilson's Creek*, 20; Lobdell, "Civil War Journal and Letters," pt. 2, 23–24.

14. Warner, *Generals in Blue*, 70–71; Bearss, *Battle of Wilson's Creek*, 43; *OR* 3:59; Heitman, *Historical Register*, 2:285; William Branson Diary, Aug. 7, 1861, UMC; Horace Poole Diary, Aug. 7, 1861, HL.

15. *OR* 3:59; Phillips, *Damned Yankee*, 246.

16. *OR* 3:98–99.

17. Holcombe and Adams, *Battle of Wilson's Creek*, 20; James Totten to My dear Major, Aug. 6, 1861, Schofield Papers, LC.

18. Horace Poole Diary, Aug. 6, 1861, HL; William Branson Diary, Aug. 6, 1861, UMC; Ware, *Lyon Campaign*, 295.

19. Ware, *Lyon Campaign*, 296.

20. Levant L. Jones to Wife, Aug. 8, 1861, Jones Papers, MHS. Jones's letter was actually written on August 6 but misdated.

21. Ibid.

22. *OR* 3:59.

23. Mary Anne Montgomery asserts that on the night of August 7 she heard Lyon predict his own death and request her mother to care for his body; this account is almost certainly spurious. Zogbaum, "Life of Mary Anne Phelps Montgomery," 25, Zogbaum Papers, MHS; Holcombe and Adams, *Battle of Wilson's Creek*, 21–22; *OR* 3:59; Phillips, *Damned Yankee*, 246–47; William Branson Diary, Aug. 8, 1861, UMC.

24. Four Northerners and thirteen Southerners were lost during the skirmishing. *OR* 3:96; Horace Poole Diary, Aug. 8. 1861, HL; Bearss, *Battle of Wilson's Creek*, 43; Ware, *Lyon Campaign*, 298; Lobdell, "Civil War Journal and Letters," pt. 2, 25.

25. *OR* 3:60, 65, 94; Ware, *Lyon Campaign*, 303–4; Bearss, *Battle of Wilson's Creek*, 47–49.

26. Schofield believed that Lyon abandoned rather than postponed the attack. Du Bois, who was apparently present at the meeting, simply states, "Gen. Lyon changed his plan." Schofield's report is potentially misleading, as the wording implies that the Federals returned to Springfield on August 6 rather than August 5. *OR* 3:94; Phillips, *Damned Yankee*, 248; Bearss, *Battle of Wilson's Creek*, 44–49; Holcombe and Adams, *Battle of Wilson's Creek*, 22; Du Bois, "Journals and Letters," 362, Du Bois Collection, YU; *OR* 3:61–62.

27. Original in italics. Schofield, *Forty-six Years in the Army*, 18.

28. Punctuation and elisions corrected; quoted in Holcombe and Adams, *Battle of Wilson's Creek*, 19.

29. Order No. 16, Army of the West Order Book, Letters Sent and General and Special Orders Issued, NARA. There are three other versions of this order, differing slightly but without consequence in their wording. See *OR* 3:57; Schofield, *Forty-six Years in the Army*, 41; Nathaniel Lyon to John C. Frémont, Aug. 9, 1961, Schofield Papers, LC.

30. *OR* 3:94–95; Engle, *Yankee Dutchman*, 70; Schofield, *Forty-six Years in the Army*, 43–44.

31. Bearss, *Battle of Wilson's Creek*, 45.

32. Phillips, *Damned Yankee*, 250; Holcombe and Adams, *Battle of Wilson's Creek*, 26–27.

33. *OR* 3:59–60.

34. *OR* 3:59; William Branson Diary, Aug. 9, 1861, UMC; Ware, *Lyon Campaign*, 310; Levant L. Jones file, HL.

35. Levant L. Jones file, HL.

36. Sigel, "Flanking Column at Wilson's Creek," 304; Du Bois, "Journals and Letters," 361–63, Du Bois Collection, YU; Phillips, *Damned Yankee*, 249–50; Engle, *Yankee Dutchman*, 70–71.

37. Spelling corrected. Du Bois, "Journals and Letters," 363, Du Bois Collection, YU.

38. Schofield, *Forty-six Years in the Army*, 43.

39. Phillips, *Damned Yankee*, 250.

Chapter Twelve

1. William Branson Diary, Aug. 8–9, 1861, UMC; Ware, *Lyon Campaign*, 314; Greene, "On the Battle of Wilson Creek," 119.

2. H. J. C. to Editor (Aug. 18), in "The Battle of Springfield," *Muscatine Weekly Journal*, Aug. 30, 1861. H. J. C. was probably First Sergeant Hugh J. Campbell of the Muscatine Grays, a resident of Muscatine wounded in the battle. See also *Roster and Record of Iowa Soldiers*, 20, and Ware, *Lyon Campaign*, 310.

3. Ware, *Lyon Campaign*, 313.

4. Ibid., 314; *OR* 3:81; Greene, "On the Battle of Wilson Creek," 118.

5. *OR* 3:3, 65; Bearss, *Battle of Wilson's Creek*, 161. Bearss lists the First Brigade as 884 strong, a figure that apparently includes the mounted company of the Second Kansas, Company D, First U.S. Cavalry, and around 200 mounted Dade County Home Guards under Captains Clark Wright and T. A. Switzler. Actually, Sturgis placed the Home Guards with the Third Brigade.

6. Company C of the First U.S. Infantry had no first lieutenant assigned to it at the time of the Wilson's Creek campaign. The unit's second lieutenant, Texan William E. Burnet, resigned in July 1861 to join the Confederate army. Cullum, *Biographical Register*, 18; Heitman, *Historical Register*, 2:264.

7. The first lieutenant of Company B of the First U.S. Infantry, Samuel Holibird, was on detached service at West Point. Second Lieutenant Charles E. Farrand was attached temporarily to Company C of the Second U.S. Dragoons. Warner, *Generals in Blue*, 173; Cullum, *Biographical Register*, 153–54.

8. George A. Williams, the first lieutenant of Company D of the First U.S. Infantry, was assigned to West Point. Second Lieutenant H. C. Wood had been detached to command dragoon and rifle recruits. Cullum, *Biographical Register*, 224; Heitman, *Historical Register*, 2:559.

9. Heitman, *Historical Register*, 2:1054; Cleaveland, *History of Bowdoin College*, 693.

10. Each of the Missouri volunteer regiments raised in St. Louis initially contained both regular companies, presumably armed with smoothbores, and two companies armed with rifles. Thus the same regiment would possess both Companies A and B and Rifle Companies A and B. Warner, *Generals in Blue*, 352–53; Rombauer, *Union Cause in St. Louis*, 367; Sergent, *They Lie Forgotten*, 180–82.

11. "Recent Deaths," *Army and Navy Journal* 56 (September 1918): 14.

12. Heitman, *Historical Register*, 2:280; *OR* 3:65; Elliot, "Events of 1856," 526–27.

13. Cullum, *Biographical Register*, 92; "Steele, Frederick," *DAB*, 17:555–56.

14. *Official Register*, U.S. Military Academy; Heitman, *Historical Register*, 2:479, 642, 676; *OR* 3:78–79; Special Orders No. 4, Headquarters, Department of the West, June 1, 1861, Gundlach Collection, MHS.

15. *OR* 3:65; Holcombe and Adams, *Battle of Wilson's Creek*, 28.

16. *OR* 3:65.

17. Bearss, *Battle of Wilson's Creek*, 161–62; Holcombe and Adams, *Battle of Wilson's Creek*, 29.

18. *OR* 3:65, 75, 81; James H. Wiswell to Dear Sister, Aug. 31, 1861, Wiswell Letters, DU.

19. Bearss, *Battle of Wilson's Creek*, 51–52; Ware, *Lyon Campaign*, 314–15; Holcombe and Adams, *Battle of Wilson's Creek*, 28–29.

20. Ware, *Lyon Campaign*, 314–15; Holcombe and Adams, *Battle of Wilson's Creek*, 28–29. Thomas (*Old Farmer's Almanac*, 20) gives sunrise at 5:02 A.M. and sunset at 7:08 P.M. on Aug. 10, 1861. For the same date the U.S. Naval Observatory gives the following data: civil twilight, 4:57 A.M.; sunrise, 5:24 A.M.; sunset, 7:11 P.M.; end of civil twilight, 7:39 P.M.

21. Greene, "On the Battle of Wilson Creek," 118–19; Holcombe and Adams, *Battle of Wilson's Creek*, 28–29.

22. Levant L. Jones to My Own Hattie, July 22, 1861, Jones Papers, MHS; Ware, *Lyon Campaign*, 314; Greene, "On the Battle of Wilson Creek," 119.

23. Hatcher and Piston, *Kansans at Wilson's Creek*, 66–67; Ware, *Lyon Campaign*, 315.

24. *OR* 3:65; Ware, *Lyon Campaign*, 315; Tunnard, *A Southern Record*, 50; *History of Greene County*, 312; "In the Ranks under General Lyon," 587.

25. *OR* 3:65; Bearss, *Battle of Wilson's Creek*, 53.

26. Bearss, *Battle of Wilson's Creek*, 53.

27. "In the Ranks with the Regulars," 587; *OR* 3:73; Horace Poole Diary, Aug. 10, 1861, HL; William Branson Diary, Aug. 9, 1861, UMC; Hatcher and Piston, *Kansans at Wilson's Creek*, 67; Ware, *Lyon Campaign*, 315; Schofield, *Forty-six Years in the Army*, 42–43; Phillips, *Damned Yankee*, 252.

28. *OR* 3:86–87.

29. Ibid., 38, 48, 88.

30. *OR* 3:86–88; Cullum, *Biographical Register*, 264; Warner, *Generals in Blue*, 70.

31. *OR* 3:88.

32. *OR* 3:86, 88–89; Cullum, *Biographical Register*, 466; Holcombe and Adams, *Battle of Wilson's Creek*, 29–30; Sigel, "Flanking Column at Wilson's Creek," 304; Bearss, *Battle of Wilson's Creek*, 54.

33. *OR* 3:86; Holcombe and Adams, *Battle of Wilson's Creek*, 29–30.

34. *OR* 3:86, 89; Sigel, "Flanking Column at Wilson's Creek," 304; "Tales of the War: Otto C. Lademann's Reminiscences of Wilson's Creek," *St. Louis Republican*, Apr. 2, 1861.

35. *OR* 3:86, 89–91; Sigel, "Flanking Column at Wilson's Creek," 304; "Tales of the War: Otto C. Lademann's Reminiscences."

36. *OR* 3:86, 89–91; Sigel, "Flanking Column at Wilson's Creek," 304.

Chapter Thirteen

1. During his relatively brief service Snyder was also the division's chaplain, inspector general, provost marshal general, chief of transportation, and assistant surgeon general. Peterson et al., *Sterling Price's Lieutenants*, 28, 211.

2. Rains's report is misleading, as it refers to the forage wagons, Snyder's scout, and the

subsequent movement of DeWitt Hunter's cavalry as "the pickets which I had sent out at daybreak." *OR* 3:127; J. F. Snyder, "A Few Points about the Battle," 5–7.

3. *OR* 3:60, 65; Bearss, *Battle of Wilson's Creek*, 56; "In the Ranks under General Lyon," 588; Greene, "On the Battle of Wilson Creek," 118.

4. "A Boy's Experiences," 2.

5. Boatner, *Civil War Dictionary*, 2; Bearss, *Battle of Wilson's Creek*, 56; "In the Ranks under General Lyon," 588; Extracts from Greene County Tax Records, HL; *Greene County, Missouri, Federal Census of 1860*, 71; "A Boy's Experiences," 3.

6. Rains attempted to take credit for this in his report, claiming that he sent out pickets at daybreak. But, as the army was slated to advance on Springfield, Rains had no reason to dispatch pickets to the north. *OR* 3:27; Bearss, *Battle of Wilson's Creek*, 57.

7. Bartels, *Forgotten Men*, 180; Peterson et al., *Sterling Price's Lieutenants*, 267–69.

8. Snead, *Fight for Missouri*, 269; Bearss, *Battle of Wilson's Creek*, 57; Historic Base and Ground Cover Map, HL.

9. As Sokalski moved into position, Irish-born Corporal Stephen Nolan became perhaps the battle's first "casualty" when he was struck in the right eye by a low-hanging limb. Nolan remained at his post despite the injury. He served until his enlistment expired in 1863 and after the war claimed compensation for a permanent loss of vision. Ingrisano, *Artilleryman's War*, 70; *OR* 3:60, 73.

10. "A Boy's Experiences," 4.

11. *OR* 3:72, 76.

12. Hatcher and Piston, *Kansans at Wilson's Creek*, 84; Throne, "First Battle—Wilson's Creek," 377.

13. *OR* 3:27–28; Peterson et al., *Sterling Price's Lieutenants*, 252; Hatcher and Piston, *Kansans at Wilson's Creek*, 84; Snead, *Fight for Missouri*, 269.

14. "In the Ranks under General Lyon," 588; *OR* 3:60, 72.

15. *OR* 3:66; Burke, *Official Military History*, 6.

16. *OR* 3:66; Burke, *Official Military History*, 6.

17. Bearss, *Battle of Wilson's Creek*, 58.

18. Totten's official report compresses events; it also contains errors concerning the direction and number of Southern troops he could have seen when he first reached the crest. *OR* 3:73–74.

19. *OR* 3:104–5, 118, 126–27; Snead, *Fight for Missouri*, 263.

20. How McCulloch could have arrived at Price's headquarters before Snyder remains a mystery; the time sequence Snyder presents in his memoirs is not creditable. J. F. Snyder, "A Few Points about the Battle," 5–7; *Greene County, Missouri, Federal Census of 1860*, 69; Deed of Records Book J, 152–53, GCA; Snead, *Fight for Missouri*, 263.

21. Bearss (*Battle of Wilson's Creek*, 62) and Brooksher (*Bloody Hill*, 182–83) accept uncritically the 1883 account by Holcombe and Adams, who were biased against the Southerners, and the 1886 account by Snead, who was biased against McCulloch. Holcombe and Adams (*Battle of Wilson's Creek*, 53), without giving a source, have McCulloch pompously dismiss two messengers from Rains; moments later Rains's fugitives appear and Lyon's and Sigel's artilleries are heard. Snead was an eyewitness, but he wrote after both Price and McCulloch were dead. In *The Fight for Missouri*, 271–72, he follows McCulloch's rebuffing of Snyder with a vivid passage underscoring "Old Ben's" alleged foolishness: "Looking up, we could, ourselves, see a great crowd of men on horseback, some armed, and others unarmed, mixed in with wagons and teams and led horses, all in dreadful confusion, scampering over the hill, and rushing down toward us—a panic-stricken drove. In another instant, we saw the flash and heard the report of Totten's guns, which had gone into battery on the top of the hill, not more than a thousand yards away,

and were throwing shot into the flying crowd. And then, in quick response, came the sound of Sigel's guns, as they opened." In fact, Snead could not have seen any of the Federal artillery on the crest of Bloody Hill from Price's headquarters. Price's August 12 battle report disproves any procrastination on McCulloch's part: "General McCulloch was with me when these messengers came, and left at once for his own headquarters to make the necessary disposition of our forces." Neither Price nor McCulloch mention seeing any fugitives; it is unlikely that they saw a large number before taking action. Price states that Lyon's attack began at 6:00 A.M., but a multitude of Northern and Southern sources place it much earlier. McCulloch gives the time as 5:30 A.M., but he and Price may actually have left the Edwards farm as early as 5:20 A.M. See *OR* 3:98–105.

22. *OR* 53:427–28; Peterson et al., *Sterling Price's Lieutenants*, 136–41.

23. *OR* 3:60, 76, 427–28, 53:428.

24. Woodruff, *With the Light Guns*, 39–40.

25. Ibid., 39–40, 44.

26. *OR* 3:111, 53:429.

27. *OR* 3:60, 66, 78; H. J. C. to Editor (Aug. 18), in "The Battle of Springfield: All about the Muscatine Boys," *Muscatine Weekly Journal*, Aug. 30, 1861.

28. *OR* 3:100; Holcombe and Adams, *Battle of Wilson's Creek*, 98.

29. According to one source, Shelton's men were part of a different unit. *OR* 3:100; Snead, *Fight for Missouri*, 273; Peterson et al., *Sterling Price's Lieutenants*, 167–68; Shelton, *Memoir of a Confederate Veteran*, 4, 6, 10; Connelley, *With Mexico, 1846–1847*, 46–54.

30. John T. Hughes to R. H. Miller (Aug. 29), in "Letter from Col. John T. Hughes," *Liberty Tribune*, Sept. 13, 1861; Allardice, *More Generals in Gray*, 132–33.

31. Mudd, "What I Saw at Wilson's Creek," 94–95; Easley, "Journal of the Civil War in Missouri," 22.

32. Snead, *Fight for Missouri*, 273; Bearss, *Battle of Wilson's Creek*, 163–64.

33. *OR* 3:100; Holcombe and Adams, *Battle of Wilson's Creek*, 67.

34. *Greene County, Missouri, Federal Census of 1860*, 69.

35. No record exists of Sergeant Hite contacting McCulloch, but he may have given the Texan the first word that the Southern army faced an enemy from two directions. *OR* 3:121, 126–27; Pearce, "Arkansas Troops," 299–300.

36. *OR* 3:121; Pearce, "Arkansas Troops," 300; Carr, *In Fine Spirits*, 16; McCulloch, "Sketch of the Life of Clem McCulloch," 45.

37. The compass and facing directions found in the after-action reports of Pearce, Reid, Gratiot, and Dockery are misleading, perhaps from a mistaken impression that the Wire Road ran due north toward Springfield, when it actually ran northeast. Probably for that reason, Woodruff's and Reid's batteries are mislocated on Cowles, *Atlas to Accompany the Official Records*, plate CXXV, map 1. See *OR* 3:120–21, 123–25, 127; Pearce, "Arkansas Troops," 300; Bearss, *Battle of Wilson's Creek*, 75; Frank A. Rector to Mrs. C. B. Johnson (n.d.), in "Latest from Missouri," *Arkansas True Democrat*, Aug. 22, 1861.

38. *OR* 3:120–25; Woodruff, *With the Light Guns*, 40–41.

39. *OR* 3:72; "In the Ranks under General Lyon," 589–90; Historic Base and Ground Cover Map, HL.

40. *Greene County, Missouri, Federal Census of 1860*, 69; Extracts from Greene County Tax Records, HL; "Parents' Record," HL; Charles T. Meier, Management Assistant, to Superintendent, GWCA, HL.

41. "In the Ranks under General Lyon," 59, 90; *OR* 3:72; Bearss, *Battle of Wilson's Creek*, 82.

42. *OR* 3:72.

43. William E. Woodruff Jr. to Dear Father (Aug. 11), in "Latest from Missouri," *Arkansas True Democrat*, Aug. 22, 1861.

44. John H. Newbern to Messrs. Ed. True Dem. (Aug. 11), in "Latest from Missouri," *Arkansas True Democrat*, Aug. 22, 1861; "Extracts from a Letter Written at Springfield, Mo., by Dr. W. A. Cantrell," ibid., Aug. 29, 1861; Woodruff, *With the Light Guns*, 44–45.

45. Bearss errs in stating that McCulloch ordered the Third Arkansas to support the Pulaski Light Battery as a consequence of Plummer's threat; Pearce had already directed the regiment to support Woodruff. Sources do not indicate how detailed McCulloch's knowledge of conditions at the Sharp farm were at this time. *OR* 3:110–11, 117, 121; Bearss, *Battle of Wilson's Creek*, 75.

46. Watson's account of seeing McCulloch emerge from his tent is not creditable, as McCulloch had already gone to Price's headquarters. As Watson was writing long after the war, he may have confused McCulloch with Hébert in regard to the incident. For the same reason, we discount the story of William Brown related by Cutrer. Watson, *Life in the Confederate Army*, 213; Tunnard, *A Southern Record*, 50–51; Cutrer, *Ben McCulloch*, 229; "Further Interesting Particulars about the Doings at the Battle of Oak Hills," *Shreveport Weekly News*, Sept. 2, 1861.

47. Dandridge McRae to Wife, Aug. 6, 1861, McRae Papers, AHC; McRae, "Narrative of the Battle of Oak Hills," n.p., ibid.

48. A discrepancy exists between the reports of McIntosh and Embry. McIntosh writes that he led the unit from the first, whereas Embry states that McIntosh joined them after they dismounted. As Embry errs by asserting that the movement was made to protect the Pulaski Light Battery, we consider McIntosh's account more creditable overall. *OR* 3:110–12; Bearss, *Battle of Wilson's Creek*, 75; Watson, *Life in the Confederate Army*, 213; Tunnard, *A Southern Record*, 51.

49. *OR* 3:72, 113.

50. Southern sources indicating that the Federals used the fence for cover appear to be in error. *OR* 3:113; Tunnard, *A Southern Record*, 51, 67; Watson, *Life in the Confederate Army*, 215; A. to Editor (Sept. 17), in "Letter from the Third Regiment," *Baton Rouge Weekly Gazette and Comet*, Oct. 5, 1861.

51. *OR* 3:72; Watson, *Life in the Confederate Army*, 215; "In the Ranks under General Lyon," 590; James H. Wiswell to Mary and Wiswell to Dear Sister, Aug. 31, 1861, Wiswell Letters, DU.

52. Alf to Dear Mother (Aug. 12), in "The Battle of Oak Hills, near Springfield, Mo.," *Shreveport South-Western*, Sept. 4, 1861; Tunnard, *A Southern Record*, 51; Watson, *Life in the Confederate Army*, 216–17.

53. *OR* 3:110–16; Watson, *Life in the Confederate Army*, 217–18; A. to Editor (Sept. 17), in "Letter from the Third Regiment," *Baton Rouge Weekly Gazette and Comet*, Oct. 5, 1861; Sam. Hyams to Reuben White (Aug. 13), in "The Battle of Oak Hills, near Springfield, Mo.," *Shreveport South-Western*, Aug. 28, 1861; Bearss, *Battle of Wilson's Creek*, 86.

54. James H. Wiswell to Dear Sister, Aug. 31, 1861, Wiswell Letters, DU; Lobdell, "Civil War Journal and Letters," pt. 2, 30; *OR* 3:80.

55. Du Bois's guns probably fired spherical case shot, not shell. Participants on both sides also erred by frequently referring to canister as grape shot. James H. Wiswell to Dear Sister, Aug. 31, 1861, Wiswell Letters, DU; Tunnard, *A Southern Record*, 52; Watson, *Life in the Confederate Army*, 217; Lobdell, "Civil War Journal and Letters," pt. 2, 30; *OR* 3:113, 115.

56. *OR* 3:117.

57. *OR* 3:116; Bearss, *Battle of Wilson's Creek*, 86.

58. Watson, *Life in the Confederate Army*, 217–18.

59. This estimate assumes that most of the casualties suffered by the Third Louisiana and the Second Arkansas Mounted Rifles during the battle occurred in the cornfield fight. See Bearss, *Battle of Wilson's Creek*, 162.

60. James H. Wiswell to Dear Sister, Aug. 31, 1861, Wiswell Letters, DU; *OR* 3:72–73; Holcombe and Adams, *Battle of Wilson's Creek*, 96; Lobdell, "Civil War Journal and Letters," pt. 2, 30.

Chapter Fourteen

1. Because of the need to accommodate the tour road, the reconstructed fences at Wilson's Creek National Battlefield enclose a smaller area than the original fields. As Sigel mentions moving through "a number of cattle near Sharp's house," they must have been in the northernmost fenced area. Because some were still present to block the road after Sigel's first and second bombardments ended, they probably did not break through the fences until just moments before Sigel's final advance toward the Sharp house. Sigel, "Flanking Column at Wilson's Creek," 304; *OR* 3:86, 116; Cowles, *Atlas to Accompany the Official Records*, plate CXXXV-1, map 1.

2. *OR* 3:86–87; Engle, *Yankee Dutchman*, 73; Sigel, "Flanking Column at Wilson's Creek," 304; Holcombe and Adams, *Battle of Wilson's Creek*, 29– 30; Knox, *Camp-Fire and Cotton-Field*, 70.

3. *OR* 3:86–87; Engle, *Yankee Dutchman*, 73; Sigel, "Flanking Column at Wilson's Creek," 304; Holcombe and Adams, *Battle of Wilson's Creek*, 29–30, 46; Eugene A. Carr to Dear Father, Aug. 16, 1861, Carr Papers, USAMHI; Heitman, *Historical Register*, 1:414.

4. Sigel, "Flanking Column at Wilson's Creek," 304; Bek, "Civil War Diary of John T. Buegel," 312.

5. *OR* 3:119; Bearss, *Battle of Wilson's Creek*, 34–36, 162–63; Peterson et al., *Sterling Price's Lieutenants*, 174; Warner, *Generals in Gray*, 209–10.

6. *OR* 3:89. The camps of the unarmed Missourians cannot be precisely identified. As they marched at the rear of the Southern army and reached Wilson Creek last, many probably camped in Sharp's stubble field or along the western edge of the creek itself. Carr apparently saw them moving through Sharp's property in an attempt to escape the battlefield. Sigel's gross overestimate of the troops that rallied to face him would be easier to understand if he accidentally had included in that number the unarmed Missourians leaving the field. Such a mistake would have been easy to make.

7. "Reliable Letter from Springfield," *Texas Republican*, Aug. 24, 1861; Lale, "Boy-Bugler," 80.

8. *OR* 3:118; Hale, *Third Texas Cavalry*, 29; Lale, "Boy-Bugler," 80.

9. Hale, *Third Texas Cavalry*, 61–62; Cater, *As It Was*, 87.

10. *OR* 3:118–19; Sparks, *War between the States*, 139; Barron, *Lone Star Defenders*, 44–45.

11. Du Bois wrote his father that "negroes (servants) got arms & followed their masters, some of them behaving very well." Du Bois, "Journals and Letters," 361, Du Bois Collection, YU; *Confederate Women of Arkansas*, 83; Hale, *Third Texas Cavalry*, 47, 62–64.

12. The chaplain's full name is unknown. "Reliable Letter from Springfield," *Texas Republican*, Aug. 24, 1861; Hale, *Third Texas Cavalry*, 31, 63–64.

13. "The Little Rock True Democrat . . .," *Des Arc Semi-Weekly Citizen*, Sept. 18, 1861; *OR* 3:109; Bearss, *Battle of Wilson's Creek*, 69.

14. Burriss is listed in some sources as Burress; his full name is unknown. *OR* 53:425;

Peterson et al., *Sterling Price's Lieutenants*, 108; Bearss, *Battle of Wilson's Creek*, 67; Bartels, *Forgotten Men*, 42.

15. A Mexican War veteran named Thomas E. Staples was wounded at Wilson's Creek, but he was a sergeant in Clark's Division. Alexander was probably Captain Robert L. Alexander, who in September 1861 was appointed regimental quartermaster of a cavalry unit in Rains's Division. Peterson et al., *Sterling Price's Lieutenants*, 177–78, 190, 253; *OR* 3:432–33.

16. Some sources refer to the lieutenant commanding the section of guns on the hilltop as Lieutenant Gustavus Adolphis Schaefer. Sigel, "Flanking Column at Wilson's Creek," 304; Eugene A. Carr to My Dear Father, Aug. 16, 1861, Carr Papers, USAMHI; "Tales of the War: Otto C. Lademann's Reminiscences of Wilson's Creek," *St. Louis Republican*, Apr. 2, 1887.

17. Deed of Records Book J, 122, GCA.

18. Sigel, "Flanking Column at Wilson's Creek," 304.

19. In his postwar article, Sigel confused Farrand's encounter with the pickets and the earlier escape of the Southern prisoner. Bearss is misled by this. Farrand states that after he crossed the ravine the Southern camp was in plain sight. This could only have been the Terrell Creek ravine. *OR* 3:91; Sigel, "Flanking Column at Wilson's Creek," 304; Eugene A. Carr to My Dear Father, Aug. 16, 1861, Carr Papers, USAMHI; Bearss, *Battle of Wilson's Creek*, 69.

20. *OR* 3:87, 91.

21. Sigel's report states: "As the enemy made his rally in large numbers before us, about 3,000 strong, consisting of infantry and cavalry, I ordered the artillery to be brought forward from the hill, and formed them in battery across the valley." But in a postbattle letter to his father, Carr writes: "I immediately sent him [Sigel] word and commenced to retire towards him as they were getting between me and him." The alignment Carr describes means that he was farther north than previous accounts indicate, and that the threat to Sigel was not so much against his front, as many accounts assume from the language of Sigel's report, but to his right flank. *OR* 3:87; Eugene A. Carr to My Dear Father, Aug. 16, 1861, Carr Papers, USAMHI.

22. *OR* 3:87; Sigel, "Flanking Column at Wilson's Creek," 304.

23. *OR* 3:87, 91; Eugene A. Carr to My Dear Father, Aug. 16, 1861, Carr Papers, USAMHI; Sigel, "Flanking Column at Wilson's Creek," 304–5.

24. *OR* 3:87, 89; Sigel, "Flanking Column at Wilson's Creek," 304.

25. Sigel does not give a detailed description of his deployment, but a standard battery front for six guns was 240 feet and his infantry, in double ranks, would have occupied 990 feet. If the cavalry dismounted, every fourth man holding a horse, it would have occupied a minimum of 64 feet and two or three times that if it was in skirmish formation. Sigel, "Flanking Column at Wilson's Creek," 304; *OR* 3:87; "Tales of the War: Otto C. Lademann's Reminiscences of Wilson's Creek," *St. Louis Republican*, Apr. 2, 1887. According to Lademann, the Federals fired on a herd of cattle and its drivers near the southern end of Sharp's fields. No other sources substantiate this, however.

Chapter Fifteen

1. *OR* 3:61, 66.

2. *OR* 3:60, 66, 78.

3. Bearss places the advance of the First Missouri and First Kansas, in response to the Southerners' second assault on Bloody Hill, much later in the battle. But Sturgis's report

states that as soon as the Federals reached the crest of the main ridge of Bloody Hill, the "First Missouri and First Kansas moved at once to the front, supported by Totten's battery; the First Iowa Regiment, Du Bois's battery, Steele's battalion, and the Second Kansas were held in reserve." *OR* 66, 82–83; Bearss, *Battle of Wilson's Creek*, 107–8; Geo. W. Hutt to Dear Champion, Aug. 19, 1861, in "Our Boys at Springfield," *Atchison Freedom's Champion*, Aug. 24, 1861; Ware, *Lyon Campaign*, 317.

4. Because he was wounded in the battle, Andrews did not submit his report until August 28. He conflates and confuses the Federal attack on the northern spur of Bloody Hill with the movements to and beyond the main ridge. As a consequence, the position of the First Missouri cannot always be established with accuracy. *OR* 3:75–76, 82–83; Bearss, *Battle of Wilson's Creek*, 79–80.

5. *OR* 3:100; Snead, *Fight for Missouri*, 274–75; Bearss, *Battle of Wilson's Creek*, 78–79.

6. Mudd, "What I Saw at Wilson's Creek," 96; *OR* 3:100; Snead, *Fight for Missouri*, 274–75; Bearss, *Battle of Wilson's Creek*, 78–79; Greene, "On the Battle of Wilson Creek," 125; Lobdell, "Civil War Journal and Letters," pt. 2, 30; Alf to Dear Mother, Aug. 12, 1861, in "The Battle of Oak Hills, near Springfield, Mo.," *Shreveport South-Western*, Sept. 4, 1861; Jos. W. Martin to Geo. Martin, Aug. 20, 1861, in "The Battle of Springfield," *Atchison Freedom's Champion*, Aug. 31, 1861; Carr, *In Fine Spirits*, 18–19; Bell, "Price's Missouri Campaign," 319; Easley, "Journal of the Civil War in Missouri," 25.

7. Sokalski, "56 Fights," 6.

8. Mudd, "What I Saw at Wilson's Creek," 96, 98, 100; Bell, "Price's Missouri Campaign," 318.

9. This first sacking of Lawrence, which caused only property damage, should not be confused with Quantrill's bloody raid in 1863. One Kansas newspaper subtitled its first detailed report of the Battle of Wilson's Creek, "Bravery of the Kansas Boys: They Settle an Old Score." Peterson et al., *Sterling Price's Lieutenants*, 116–17; Monaghan, *Civil War on the Western Border*, 52–55; "Our Boys at Springfield," *Atchison Freedom's Champion*, Aug. 24, 1861.

10. "Wilson's Creek," *National Tribune*, Nov. 10, 1892; *OR* 3:83; Geo. W. Hutt to Dear Champion (Aug. 19), in "Our Boys at Springfield" (Aug. 24, 1861), and Geo. J. Martin to Jos. W. Martin (Aug. 20), in "The Battle of Springfield" (Aug. 31, 1861), *Atchison Freedom's Champion*; Bearss, *Battle of Wilson's Creek*, 80; Jones file, HL.

11. *OR* 3:73–74, 78, 81; Bearss, *Battle of Wilson's Creek*, 81.

12. Woodruff was distressed at the thought of firing on Totten. On August 15 he wrote his father: "Information has just been received from Springfield, to the effect that Capt. Totten was not in the fight—that he had peremptorily refused to take up arms against Arkansas, and that consequently he had been sent to St. Louis in disgrace. I hope, for my 'ancient love' for Capt. T., that this is true. But I doubt it. I was told, on the battlefield, by a prisoner brought to my battery, without leading question, that he was there. And, afterwards, was told by a second prisoner, the same thing. Lt. Col. Provine, of the 3d regiment, reported a conversation had by him, with one of Totten's wounded men, in which he said that 'Capt. T. had said he was mad with himself for having drilled us.' There is no doubt in the world that Totten's battery was the one we played against. . . . It would be a pleasure to me to believe that he was *not* there." William E. Woodruff Jr. to Dear Pa (Aug. 15), in "Extract of a Letter from Capt. Wm. E. Woodruff, jr.," *Arkansas True Democrat*, Sept. 5, 1861; *OR* 3:73–75, 80; Woodruff, *With the Light Guns*, 40–41; "Wilkie's Description of the Battle of Springfield," *Davenport Daily Democrat & News*, Aug. 21, 1861.

13. *OR* 3:76–77.

14. *OR* 3:100; Snead, *Fight for Missouri*, 273–74; Allardice, *More Generals in Gray*, 155; Colton Greene to Thomas L. Snead, May 29, 1882, Snead Papers, MHS.

15. McBride's battle report is so poorly worded that it is impossible to determine accurately his decisions, actions, or even his physical location at critical points. He writes: "From our camp we marched toward the high ground to the northwest and formed on the left of General Parson's battery [Guibor's Battery]. Some confusion occurred here by [Foster's] Second Regiment advancing too far west, breaking the connection between our line and the battery. The command [both Wingo and Foster?] preceded west, crossing a small ravine . . . and then moved north, in which direction the enemy was supposed to be." *OR* 53:434–35; Mudd, "What I Saw at Wilson's Creek," 96.

16. *OR* 3:76.

17. Bearss, *Battle of Wilson's Creek*, 79.

18. *OR* 53:431, 434.

19. *OR* 53:76.

20. Although the State Guardsmen may have been displaying a trophy captured from one of Sigel's units, the time and location involved make this unlikely. Gratz's stepbrother and cousin, Joseph O. Shelby, fought opposite him in the Missouri State Guard. Ibid.; O'Flaherty, *General Jo Shelby*, 12–15.

21. *OR* 3:76–77; Bearss, *Battle of Wilson's Creek*, 18.

22. Hatcher and Piston, *Kansans at Wilson's Creek*, 82; Geo. W. Hutt to Dear Champion (Aug. 19), in "Our Boys at Springfield," *Atchison Freedom's Champion*, Aug. 24, 1861; *OR* 3:82–83.

23. *OR* 3:66–67, 76–77, 80–81, 83–84.

24. *OR* 3:83; Peterson et al., *Sterling Price's Lieutenants*, 209–26, 236–39.

25. The only detailed description of the charge suggests that Lyon accompanied it. Azel W. Spaulding to Editor (Aug. 20), in "First Kansas Regiment at Wilson's Creek," *Atchison Freedom's Champion*, Aug. 24, 1861.

26. The style of the shoulder badge worn by the Fifth Missouri is unknown. The incident provides a classic example of how events are misreported and exaggerated. Writing just after the battle, Azel Spaulding of the First Kansas reported that Clayton "shot the Adjutant [Buster] and Sergeant Brennan [*sic*] rushed forward as he fell and pinned him to the earth with his bayonet, leaving the gun sticking upright in his body and the ground." The story lost nothing in the telling after the war. Writing in 1870, W. S. Burke claimed that Clayton first realized that the troops next to him were Southerners when at a distance he recognized Clarkson as "an ex-postmaster of Leavenworth" and a border ruffian. Adjutant Buster was unimpeded by his fictional impalement. He later entered the Confederate army, rose to the rank of lieutenant colonel, and served with the First Indian Brigade. Azel W. Spaulding to Editor (Aug. 20), in "First Kansas at Wilson's Creek," *Atchison Freedom's Champion*, Aug. 24, 1861; Peterson et al., *Sterling Price's Lieutenants*, 236; Burke, *Official Military History*, 12; Bearss, *Battle of Wilson's Creek*, 107–8.

27. John K. Rankin to My Dear Greene, May 16, 1906, Rankin File, KSHS; *Report of the Adjutant General of the State of Kansas*, 1:69, 74.

28. H. S. Moore to Dear Br. (Aug. 20), in "The Late Battle," *Lawrence Weekly Republican*, Aug. 29, 1861; "Fighting Them Over: Reminiscences of Wilson's Creek," newspaper clipping from *The Commonwealth*, Jan. 24, 1884, in *Kansas in the Civil War*, KSHS.

29. "Fighting Them Over: Reminiscences of Wilson's Creek."

30. *OR* 3:61.

Chapter Sixteen

1. Bearss, *Battle of Wilson's Creek*, 86.

2. Sigel does not describe the direction in which his guns initially pointed in any of his writings, but as he exchanged shots with Rosser's First Infantry of Rains's Division of the Missouri State Guard, they must have initially faced almost due north. Although the hill southwest of the Sharp farm in Sigel's rear offered greater elevation, the vegetation there apparently precluded the effective deployment of the battery, which with standard spacing would have occupied an 82-yard front. Though extant sources do not describe the precise terrain conditions at the rim of the plateau, none suggest that Sigel could not have stationed his guns farther forward, thereby commanding a more effective field of fire directly to either his front or right. Had he done so, however, his position (and perhaps a line of trees) might have reduced his ability to fire on Bloody Hill. In addition, the drop-off at the edge of the plateau may have been so great that the muzzles of the artillery pieces could not have been depressed sufficiently to eliminate the "dead zone." *OR* 3:87; Sigel, "Flanking Column at Wilson's Creek," 305.

3. Sigel never described the placement of his infantry in detail. Our conclusions are based on Holcombe and Adams, *Battle of Wilson's Creek*, 46, and the map drawn by Captain William Hoelcke, chief engineer of the Department of the Missouri, in 1865, which is printed in Cowles, *Atlas to Accompany the Official Records*, plate CXXXV, map 1. "Tales of the War: Otto C. Lademann's Reminiscences of Wilson's Creek" (*St. Louis Republican*, Apr. 2, 1887) states that initially Sigel "formed his two infantry battalions in column closed in mass across the telegraph road in front of Sharp's house." Writing from memory long after the battle, Lademann admits that he was at the rear of the column, where his view was restricted. In any case, Lademann confirms that Sigel's force was not deployed in the standard linear formation that would have allowed him to use all of his firepower for defense.

4. Carr's report suggests he did not even realize that the Federal position at the Sharp farm was on the Wire Road (which he refers to as the Fayetteville Road). *OR* 3:89–91.

5. Holcombe and Adams, *Battle of Wilson's Creek*, 46.

6. *OR* 3:87, 89, 128; Sigel, "Flanking Column at Wilson's Creek," 305; Bek, "Civil War Diary of John T. Buegel," 313; "Tales of the War: Otto C. Lademann's Reminiscences of Wilson's Creek." Lademann claims that Sigel ordered Lieutenant Schaeffer to shift a section of guns far to the right, into Sharp's cornfield, to draw the enemy's fire away from the Federal infantry. Only fifteen minutes later, having forgotten his own orders, Sigel chastised Schaeffer for undertaking the movement. The guns returned to their original positions. Lademann's overall hostility toward Sigel casts doubt on the story.

7. In his report Sigel states, "This was the state of affairs at 8:30 o'clock in the morning, when it was reported to me by Dr. Melchior [*sic*] and some of our skirmishers that Lyon's men were coming up the road." This is the only known reference to skirmishers. Neither Dr. Melcher nor any Southern source mentions them. *OR* 3:87.

8. Bearss, *Battle of Wilson's Creek*, 86–87.

9. *OR* 3:105; Tunnard, *A Southern Record*, 52.

10. The Missourians were members of either J. Johnson's Cedar County Company, attached to the First Cavalry, Rains's Division; Thomas B. Johnson's Company C, Second Cavalry, Rains's Division; or James Johnson's Osage Tigers, Company A, First Cavalry, Parsons's Division. *OR* 3:113; Peterson et al., *Sterling Price's Lieutenants*, 175, 247, 249.

11. Watson's chronology is confused, as he incorrectly has Major Tunnard rejoin Hyams's portion of the regiment at the ford. Watson, *Life in the Confederate Army*, 218–19.

12. *OR* 3:87; Holcombe and Adams, *Battle of Wilson's Creek*, 46–47.

13. The sequence of events regarding skirmishers is implied by Sigel's report, which is the only source that mentions them. As he was writing after the battle to explain away a great disaster, the possibility that he actually had no skirmishers in his front cannot be dismissed. If one accepts Sigel's account at face value, he is guilty at the very least of failing to confirm the skirmishers' report. *OR* 3:87, 105; A. B. C. to Dear Tribune (Aug. 27), in "Camp Correspondence," *Liberty Tribune*, Sept. 13, 1861.

14. Rosser probably received his assignment from Rains, although this is not clear from the wording of Rains's report. Nor is it certain that all companies in the First and Fourth Infantries took part in the operation. *OR* 3:127; Bearss, *Battle of Wilson's Creek*, 72, 87; Snead, *Fight for Missouri*, 279–80; Peterson et al., *Sterling Price's Lieutenants*, 214, 232, 287.

15. Tunnard, *A Southern Record*, 52; Cutrer, *Ben McCulloch*, 234.

16. Sigel, "Flanking Column at Wilson's Creek," 30; Holcombe and Adams, *Battle of Wilson's Creek*, 47; Rombauer, *Union Cause in St. Louis*, 393; "Tales of the War: Otto C. Lademann's Reminiscences of Wilson's Creek," *St. Louis Republican*, Apr. 2, 1887. Although Lademann also uses the spelling "Tod," he identifies the individual as a member of Company K. Todt may have been an acting corporal.

17. Gentles rose to the rank of captain and served until the end of the war, but he had the unfortunate experience of being captured three times. Lacy's name is also given as Lacey. *OR* 3:115, 117; Tunnard, *A Southern Record*, 53, 520, 533; Watson, *Life in the Confederate Army*, 220.

18. Many accounts, including the histories written by Bearss and Holcombe and Adams, imply that the Southern infantry sent at least one volley into the Union troops before Backof's Battery opened fire. But Vigilini, whose troops were leading the Southern assault, states that the Union artillery fired before the Louisianans. Sigel reported his men's belief that Lyon's troops were firing on them, but this could be a reference to incoming Southern artillery fire. Although the evidence is confused, we conclude that Reid's Fort Smith Battery fired first, followed by Bledsoe's Missouri Light Artillery. At least two of Sigel's guns replied instantly, and only after that did the Louisianans fire. *OR* 3:87, 105, 115–18; Bearss, *Battle of Wilson's Creek*, 88–89; Holcombe and Adams, *Battle of Wilson's Creek*, 46–47; Tunnard, *A Southern Record*, 52–53.

19. *OR* 3:121–22; Pearce, "Arkansas Troops," 300–301.

20. Hyams reported that McCulloch's horse was wounded by the first fire from Sigel's guns, but it is much more likely that the injury was caused accidentally by Reid's battery. *OR* 3:87, 105, 117, 121.

21. Separate casualty figures do not exist for the Third and Fifth Infantries. No casualty figures exist for Backof's Battery. Bearss, *Battle of Wilson's Creek*, 162.

22. Holcombe and Adams, *Battle of Wilson's Creek*, 47.

23. Quotation and translation from Engle, *Yankee Dutchman*, 77.

24. *OR* 3:87.

25. McRae had a poor sense of direction and terrain. From his sketchy and inaccurate report, it is impossible to determine his precise route or position on the field. The time elements involved suggest that he was between Rosser's Missourians and Hyams's Louisianans. *OR* 3:87, 91, 112–13; Sigel, "Flanking Column at Wilson's Creek," 305; Holcombe and Adams, *Battle of Wilson's Creek*, 47–48; Engle, *Yankee Dutchman*, 77; Bearss, *Battle of Wilson's Creek*, 88–91.

26. *OR* 3:113–18; Sigel, "Flanking Column at Wilson's Creek," 305; Engle, *Yankee Dutchman*, 76–77.

27. In Hyams's battle report, Hecox's name is misspelled as "Hicock." *OR* 3:114, 116–18; Tunnard, *A Southern Record*, 53, 520, 525.

28. *OR* 3:113, 121, 124; Pearce, "Arkansas Troops," 301; Bearss, *Battle of Wilson's Creek*, 92.

29. *OR* 3:87, 91; Bek, "Civil War Diary of John T. Buegel," 313; Sigel, "Flanking Column at Wilson's Creek," 305; Holcombe and Adams, *Battle of Wilson's Creek*, 47–48; Engle, *Yankee Dutchman*, 77; Bearss, *Battle of Wilson's Creek*, 88–90.

30. Smith did not actually receive his commission until November. Made a captain, he was assigned to the Sixth Cavalry. Holcombe and Adams, *Battle of Wilson's Creek*, 48; Peterson et al., *Sterling Price's Lieutenants*, 264.

31. *OR* 3:90–91; Bearss, *Battle of Wilson's Creek*, 95.

32. *OR* 3:91–92; Bearss, *Battle of Wilson's Creek*, 94.

33. Bearss errs when stating that Farrand's troops were already ahead of him when he discovered the caisson. *OR* 3:92; Bearss, *Battle of Wilson's Creek*, 94.

34. Sources do not describe Sigel's route precisely. It is unlikely that he moved across country. The road leading from the Dixon farm to the Wire Road was the only route suitable for the artillery that accompanied the Federals. *OR* 3:90; Sigel, "Flanking Column at Wilson's Creek," 305; Bearss, *Battle of Wilson's Creek*, 95.

35. Neither the name nor the precise location of the road onto which Sigel's column turned is known. *OR* 3:90; Sigel, "Flanking Column at Wilson's Creek," 305.

36. Carr's report concluded: "It turned out that the colonel was ambuscaded, as I anticipated, his whole party broken up, and that he himself narrowly escaped. It is a subject of regret with me to have left him behind, but I supposed all the time that he was close behind me till I got to the creek, and it would have done no good for my company to have been cut to pieces also. As it was, four of my men were lost who had been placed in rear of his infantry." Without giving their source, Holcombe and Adams attribute an even more astonishing passage to Carr: " 'To use a Westernism,' say Gen. Carr, 'there was no time for fooling then, and as I had waited long enough for the slow-moving infantry . . . I lit out for a place of safety which I soon reached, and after waiting another while for Sigel, I went on to Springfield.' " *OR* 3:90; Holcombe and Adams, *Battle of Wilson's Creek*, 49–50.

37. Sigel, "Flanking Column at Wilson's Creek," 305.

38. *OR* 53:425, 433; Bearss, *Battle of Wilson's Creek*, 96–97.

39. *OR* 53:425, 433; Bearss, *Battle of Wilson's Creek*, 97.

40. *OR* 53:425–26, 433; Bearss, *Battle of Wilson's Creek*, 97.

41. Sigel, "Flanking Column at Wilson's Creek," 305; Engle, *Yankee Dutchman*, 236.

Chapter Seventeen

1. Because reports are sketchy and rarely give precise times for movements, it is difficult to reconstruct the Federal alignment at this point. As Deitzler and Hutt state that after retiring the First Kansas took up a position on Totten's right, Steele and Gilbert were almost certainly on Totten's left, filling the gap between his guns and those of Du Bois. *OR* 3:60–61, 72–73, 77–82; Bearss, *Battle of Wilson's Creek*, 106; Geo. W. Hutt to Dear Champion (Aug. 19), in "Our Boys at Springfield," and George W. Deitzler to W. H. Merritt (Aug. 20), in "Col. Geo. W. Deitzler," *Atchison Freedom's Champion*, Aug. 24, 1861.

2. "Incidents of the Battle at Springfield," *Leavenworth Daily Times*, Sept. 6, 1861.

3. Ware, *Lyon Campaign*, 317.

4. "Battle Accounts," *Olathe Mirror*, Aug. 29, 1861.

5. Keyes lay for three days on the battlefield before being removed to a hospital in Springfield. Although numbered in Totten's report among those killed, all five recovered from their wounds, served throughout the rest of the war, and lived into the twentieth century. *OR* 3:67, 77, 81; Bearss, *Battle of Wilson's Creek*, 106–7; Ingrisano, *Artilleryman's War*, 211, 223–24, 246, 248.

6. *OR* 3:67, 77, 81; Bearss, *Battle of Wilson's Creek*, 106–7.

7. Holcombe and Adams attribute to Lyon a prediction of failure: "It is as I expected; I am afraid the day is lost." But this appears to be an embellishment of Schofield's battle report by the authors, unsubstantiated by any other source. *OR* 3:62, 74; Schofield, *Forty-six Years in the Army*, 44; Holcombe and Adams, *Battle of Wilson's Creek*, 36; Phillips, *Damned Yankee*, 254.

8. In his report Merritt confused his left and right flanks, misidentifying the troops on his right as the First Kansas. Using Merritt's report as the basis for theirs, Sturgis and Schofield repeat the error. This sparked a brief postbattle newspaper controversy. *OR* 3:81; Geo. W. Hutt to Dear Champion (Aug. 19), in "Our Boys at Springfield," and George W. Deitzler to W. H. Merritt (Aug. 20), in "Col. Geo. W. Deitzler," *Atchison Freedom's Champion*, Aug. 24, 1861.

9. *OR* 3:81, 85; Phillips, *Damned Yankee*, 254–55; Wherry, "Wilson's Creek," 15.

10. The precise sequence of events is difficult to reconstruct as battle reports are imprecise in relation to the timing of movements. Because Colonel Mitchell was wounded, Lieutenant Colonel Blair wrote the report for the Second Kansas. Blair erroneously states that the regiment was held in reserve until this point. Both Schofield and Sturgis assert that Lyon brought the Second Kansas to the front earlier to save the imperiled First Missouri toward the very end of the fighting caused by the first Southern attack. *OR* 3:61–62, 67, 74, 84; Schofield, *Forty-six Years in the Army*, 44; Phillips, *Damned Yankee*, 254–55.

11. Phillips, *Damned Yankee*, 255–56; Bearss, *Battle of Wilson's Creek*, 115–16; Wherry, "Wilson's Creek," 15.

12. Bearss, *Battle of Wilson's Creek*, 117; *OR* 3:70; "Colonel Mitchell," *Kansas State Record*, Sept. 21, 1861; Hatcher and Piston, *Kansans at Wilson's Creek*, 72.

13. Bearss, *Battle of Wilson's Creek*, 117; *OR* 3:70; "Colonel Mitchell," *Kansas State Record*, Sept. 21, 1861.

14. Crawford, *Kansas in the Sixties*, 33; Hatcher and Piston, *Kansans at Wilson's Creek*, 73; Phillips, *Damned Yankee*, 256; Bearss, *Battle of Wilson's Creek*, 116.

15. In a letter written for newspaper publication, Hughes affirmed that Weightman's sword had not fallen into enemy hands. J. T. Hughes to editor (n.d.), in "Further from the Battle of Oak Hill," *Arkansas True Democrat*, Sept. 5, 1861; *OR* 3:101; Snead, *Fight for Missouri*, 289.

16. Cutrer, *Ben McCulloch*, 236; Watson, *Life in the Confederate Army*, 223.

17. *OR* 3:118–19; Lale, "Boy-Bugler," 81.

18. According to R. Q. Mills, only one full company and portions of others made the charge. *OR* 3:118–19; "Reliable Letter from Springfield," *Texas Republican*, Aug. 24, 1861; R. Q. Mills to C. R. Pryor (Aug. 22), in "A Texan's Description of the Battle of Oak Hill," *Texas Republican*, Sept. 7, 1861.

19. Lale, "Boy-Bugler," 81.

20. Blocker wrote, "The slaughter of the enemy was terrible—we took no prisoners, did not have time." Such exaggeration is common in soldiers' accounts, however. Federal

casualties probably did not exceed a dozen. *OR* 3:74; Lale, "Boy-Bugler," 81–82; Bearss, *Battle of Wilson's Creek*, 117.

21. *OR* 3:118–19, 126; Bearss, *Battle of Wilson's Creek*, 118–19.

22. Snead, *Fight for Missouri*, 286.

23. Easley, "Journal of the Civil War in Missouri," 23–24.

24. Ibid., 275–76, 286; *OR* 3:98–102, 127–30; Holcombe and Adams, *Battle of Wilson's Creek*, 56; Typo to Dear Oliver (Aug. 12), in *St. Genevieve Plain Dealer*, Aug. 30, 1861.

25. *OR* 3:67–68.

26. *OR* 3:62, 67–68.

27. *OR* 3:68, 77; Bearss, *Battle of Wilson's Creek*, 121–24, 161.

28. Bearss, *Battle of Wilson's Creek*, 125–26; *OR* 3:121.

29. Rivers Reminiscences, HL.

30. *OR* 3:121; Bearss, *Battle of Wilson's Creek*, 126–27.

31. Snead, *Fight for Missouri*, 283; Bearss, *Battle of Wilson's Creek*, 127.

32. Bearss, *Battle of Wilson's Creek*, 124.

33. Ibid., 125.

34. *OR* 3:123.

35. *OR* 3:75, 84.

36. Bearss, *Battle of Wilson's Creek*, 128.

37. Ibid., 128–29.

38. Greene, "On the Battle of Wilson Creek," 124; Ware, *Lyon Campaign*, 123, 325; Hardee, *Rifle and Light Infantry Tactics*, 58–59.

39. Punctuation and spelling corrected in quotations. "The Kansas Regiments at Wilson's Creek," *Emporia News*, Aug. 31, 1861; William F. Allen to Dear Parents, Aug. 19, 1861, Allen Letters, RCHS; "Wilkie's Description of the Battle of Springfield," *Davenport Daily Democrat & News*, Aug. 21, 1861; "Reports of Our Regiments," *Atchison Freedom's Champion*, Aug. 31, 1861; Carr, *In Fine Spirits*, 18–19; Knox, *Camp-Fire and Cotton-Field*, 78; "Reminiscences of '61," *Boston Transcript*, Aug. 12, 1901; "In the Ranks under General Lyon," 590; Brant, *Campaign of General Lyon*, 10.

40. *OR* 3:68, 74–75.

41. *OR* 3:100; William F. Allen to Dear Parents, Aug. 19, 1861, Allen Letters, RCHS; Watson, *Life in the Confederate Army*, 224.

42. *OR* 3:68–69; Bearss, *Battle of Wilson's Creek*, 129–30.

43. Ingrisano, *Artilleryman's War*, 72, 222; Medal of Honor files, HL.

44. *OR* 3:79, 80.

45. *OR* 3:69; Bearss, *Battle of Wilson's Creek*, 131.

46. Pearce, "Arkansas Troops," 303.

Chapter Eighteen

1. Comparisons are based on the figures given in Bearss, *Battle of Wilson's Creek*, 161–64, and Eggenberger, *Dictionary of Battles*, 63–64, 88–89, 104, 280, 321, 359, 458. Buena Vista (15.1%), Churubusco (14%), and Molino del Rey (22.8%) exceeded the Southern casualty rate.

2. Bearss, *Battle of Wilson's Creek*, 161–64; Long, *Civil War Day by Day*, 717.

3. B. to Editor (July 22), in "From Springfield," *Kansas City Daily Western Journal of Commerce*, Aug. 6, 1861; Barnes, *Medical and Surgical History*, 16–17; Phillips, *Damned Yankee*, 258.

4. Sigel's medical supplies were captured by Greer's Texans. E. Greer to Editor (n.d.), *Texas Republican*, Sept. 28, 1861; Barnes, *Medical and Surgical History*, 15–18.

5. Bell, "Price's Missouri Campaign," 416. For personnel, see Peterson et al., *Sterling Price's Lieutenants*, 35, 108, 114, 137–38, 143, 173, 175, 196, 203, 211, 215, 222, 232, 245, 248, 253, 257, 260, 267.

6. Barnes, *Medical and Surgical History*, 16; Bearss, *Battle of Wilson's Creek*, 162.

7. Jos. W. Martin to Geo. J. Martin (Aug. 20), in "The Battle of Springfield," *Atchison Freedom's Champion*, Aug. 31, 1861; H. J. C. to Editor (Aug. 18), *Muscatine Weekly Journal*, Aug. 30, 1861; Ware, *Lyon Campaign*, 358.

8. Bell, "Price's Missouri Campaign," 416; Bearss, *Battle of Wilson's Creek*, 164.

9. Austin, "Battle of Wilson's Creek," 48; Wm. A. Cantrell to Editor (Aug. 17), in "Extracts from a Letter Written at Springfield, Mo., by Dr. W. A. Cantrell," *Arkansas True Democrat*, Aug. 29, 1861; Watson, *Life in the Confederate Army*, 225; "Reliable Letter from Springfield," *Texas Republican*, Aug. 24, 1861.

10. Punctuation and capitalization corrected. Hughes was hardly forgiving, however, for he continued, "President Lincoln ought to suffer death for this awful ruin, brought upon a once happy country." "Further from the Battle of Oak Hill," *Arkansas True Democrat*, Sept. 5, 1861, reprinting an undated letter from Hughes originally published in the *Western Missouri Argus Extra*, date unknown and no longer extant.

11. Punctuation added. Henderson, "Confederate Diary," 9–10, MSA; Watson, *Life in the Confederate Army*, 221–22.

12. Hall, *Springfield . . . Newspaper Abstracts*, 8; *Greene County, Missouri, Federal Census of 1860*, 69; "A Boy's Experiences," 4.

13. "The Great Missouri Fight," *Bellview Countryman*, September 11, 1861; Watson, *Life in the Confederate Army*, 222.

14. Mudd, *With Porter in North Missouri*, 124; Watson, *Life in the Confederate Army*, 222–23; E. Greer to R. W. Loughery (n.d.), in *Texas Republican*, Sept. 28, 1861.

15. "Mrs. Ollie Burton Recalls Wilson Creek Battle," Springfield Press, April 5, 19—, Eyewitness Accounts file, HL.

16. "An Eye Witness Account of the Battle of Wilson's Creek," n.p., ibid.

17. Henderson, "Confederate Diary," 11, MSA.

18. "The Battle near Springfield," *Burlington Daily Hawk-Eye*, Aug. 21, 1861; Zogbaum, "The Life of Mary Anne Phelps Montgomery," 26, Zogbaum Papers, MHS; Barnes, *Medical and Surgical History*, 15–16; "Army Correspondence," *Dubuque Herald*, Aug. 18, 1861; Harris Flanagin to M. E. Flanagin, Aug. 24, 1861, Flanagin Papers, AHC; "Dr. Melcher Remembers," n.p.

19. Zogbaum, "The Life of Mary Anne Phelps Montgomery," 26, Zogbaum Papers, MHS; Ware, *Lyon Campaign*, 341; "Army Correspondence," *Dubuque Herald*, Aug. 18, 1861; Harris Flanagin to M. E. Flanagin, Aug. 24, 1861, Flanagin Papers, AHC; "Latest from Missouri," *Emporia News*, Aug. 31, 1861; "Further Interesting News about the Doings at the Battle of Oak Hills," *Shreveport Weekly News*, Sept. 2, 1861.

20. Henderson, "Confederate Diary," 10, MSA; Musser, "The War in Missouri," 684.

21. Wm. A. Cantrell to Editor (Aug. 17), in "Extracts from a Letter Written at Springfield, Mo., by Dr. W. A. Cantrell," *Arkansas True Democrat*, Aug. 29, 1861; "Latest from Missouri," *Emporia News*, Aug. 31, 1861; Barnes, *Medical and Surgical History*, 16; "From Springfield, Mo.," *Olathe Mirror*, Oct. 24, 1861.

22. Linderman, *Embattled Courage*, 17–33.

23. "Latest from Missouri" (Aug. 22, 1861) and Wm A. Cantrell to Editor (Aug. 17), in "Extracts from a Letter Written at Springfield, Mo., by Dr. W. A. Cantrell" (Aug. 29, 1861), *Arkansas True Democrat*.

24. "Full Particulars of the Battle of Springfield," *Clinton Herald*, August 24, 1861.

25. "The Noble Dead," *Mt. Pleasant Home Journal*, Aug. 24, 1861; "Killed," *Atchison Freedom's Champion*, Aug. 24, 1861; "Latest from Our Army in Missouri," *Emporia News*, Aug. 24, 1861; "The Martyrs of Freedom," *Lawrence Weekly Republican*, Aug. 29, 1861; "Ladies Public Meeting," *Liberty Tribune*, Aug. 30, 1861.

26. "For the Battlefield," *Lawrence Weekly Republican*, Aug. 22, 1861; "The Late Battle Near Springfield," *Des Arc Semi-Weekly Citizen*, Sept. 4, 1861; "Letter from Lieut. Hills," *Emporia News*, Aug. 31, 1861; Musser, "The War in Missouri," 684; Weaver, "Fort Smith in the War between the States," 9, FSNHS.

27. "From Springfield," *Emporia News*, Sept. 21, 1861; "The Reception of Colonel Mitchell" (Sept. 19, 1861) and "Arrival of Colonel Deitzler" (Sept. 26, 1861), *Leavenworth Weekly Conservative*; Harris Flanagin to M. E. Flanagin, Sept. 6, 1861, Flanagin Papers, AHC.

28. Hess, *Union Soldier in Battle*, 37; Watson, *Life in the Confederate Army*, 229; "Full and Authentic Particulars of the Doings in Camp, Before & After the Battle of Oak Hills," *Shreveport Weekly News*, Sept. 2, 1861.

29. Rockwell, "A Rambling Reminiscence," n.p., MSA; "From Springfield, Mo.," *Olathe Mirror*, Oct. 24, 1861; "Full and Authentic Particulars of the Doings in Camp"; William E. Woodruff to Dear Pa (Aug. 15), in "Extract of a Letter from Capt. William E. Woodruff, jr." (Sept. 5, 1861), and Wm. A. Cantrell to Editor (Aug. 17), in "Extracts from a Letter Written at Springfield, Mo., by Dr. W. A. Cantrell" (Aug. 29, 1861), *Arkansas True Democrat*; "A Boy's Experiences," 4.

30. Woodruff, *With the Light Guns*, 42; William E. Woodruff to Dear Pa (Aug. 15), in "Extract of a Letter from Capt. William E. Woodruff, jr.," *Arkansas True Democrat*, Sept. 5, 1861.

31. According to two accounts, Southerners cut up Lyon's coat for souvenirs, but this is refuted by the report of Dr. S. H. Melcher, the Federal surgeon who took charge of the body. Likewise, two accounts say that the body was bayoneted. One states that this occurred in the heat of the battle, just moments after Lyon's death; the other maintained that it took place long after the fighting ended. Melcher reported no bayonet wounds on the body. Apparently another corpse was mistaken for Lyon's and despoiled. Holcombe and Adams, *Battle of Wilson's Creek*, 98–102; Knox, *Camp-Fire and Cotton-Field*, 79; "Further Interesting Particulars about the Doings at the Battle of Oak Hills," *Shreveport Weekly News*, Sept. 2, 1861; Alf to Dear Mother (Aug. 12), in "The Battle of Oak Hills, near Springfield, Mo.," *Shreveport South-Western*, Sept. 4, 1861; Hubble, *Personal Reminiscences*, 93; R. A. W. Jr. to Father (Aug. 11), in "Latest from Missouri," *Arkansas True Democrat*, Aug. 22, 1861.

32. By another account, the body was first placed in a "sod-covered apple house," then buried in the Phelps family graveyard. Zogbaum, "The Life of Mary Anne Phelps Montgomery," 28, Zogbaum Papers, MHS; Phillips, *Damned Yankee*, 258–59; Hubble, *Personal Reminiscences*, 90–96; Holcombe and Adams, *Battle of Wilson's Creek*, 98–104.

33. Phillips, *Damned Yankee*, 259–60; "Gen. Lyon's Body," *St. Genevieve Plain Dealer*, Aug. 30, 1861.

34. J. C. Frémont to John M. Schofield, Aug. 27, 1861, Schofield Papers, LC; "Remains of Gen. Lyon," *Burlington Daily Hawk-Eye*, Aug. 29, 1861; Phillips, *Damned Yankee*, 260–61; Receipt from State of Connecticut to Trustees, Hartford, Providence & Fishkill Railroad, September 6, 1861, Nathaniel Lyon Letters, CSL.

35. Phillips, *Damned Yankee*, 7–18.

Chapter Nineteen

1. *OR* 3:63; Sigel, "Flanking Column at Wilson's Creek," 306.

2. *OR* 3:64; "A Captain in Siegel's command . . .," *Kansas State Record*, August 24, 1861.

3. *OR* 3:64. In July Congress had retroactively approved Lincoln's unconstitutional creation of a volunteer army. Sturgis apparently argued that the volunteers enlisted illegally in April would have to be reenlisted to conform to the July legislation. In actual practice, the volunteers who had enlisted prior to July were simply assumed to be legal.

4. Ware, *Lyon Campaign*, 344.

5. *OR* 3:54–57, 425, 431, 439–40.

6. Ibid., 429–30.

7. Ibid., 71; Engle, *Yankee Dutchman*, 86, 97–101.

8. "A Card from Brig. Gen. McCulloch," *Texas Republican*, Feb. 1, 1862; Alf to Dear Mother (Aug. 12), in "The Battle of Oak Hills, near Springfield, Mo.," *Shreveport South-Western*, Sept. 4, 1861; Lale, "Boy-Bugler," 83.

9. Watson, *Life in the Confederate Army*, 232–34; *OR* 3:653.

10. Henderson, "Confederate Diary," 12, MSA; John T. Hughes to R. H. Miller, Aug. 29, 1861, Parson Papers, DU; *OR* 3:109.

11. Lademann, "Prisoner of War," 439–43.

12. Castel, *General Sterling Price*, 48–49.

13. Cutrer, *Ben McCulloch*, 246–47.

14. Ibid., 252; *OR* 3:98–102, 746–47; Castel, *General Sterling Price*, 48–49.

15. *OR* 3:106, 746–47.

16. Cutrer, *Ben McCulloch*, 251; Castel, *General Sterling Price*, 49.

17. *OR* 3:672, 689; Ben McCulloch to My Dear Mother, Nov. 8, 1861, Dibrell Collection, TSL.

18. *OR* 3:700, 718–19, 733–34, 736–38, 748–49.

19. Castel, *General Sterling Price*, 57–58.

20. Monaghan, *Civil War on the Western Border*, 198–205; Parrish, *History of Missouri*, 3:36–37.

21. *OR* 3:718–19, 721–22, 730; Castel, *General Sterling Price*, 59; Cutrer, *Ben McCulloch*, 267; Monaghan, *Civil War on the Western Border*, 207; Geise, "Confederate Military Forces in the Trans-Mississippi," 37–39.

Chapter Twenty

1. Wilkie, *Pen and Powder*, 32–37.

2. "Wilson's Creek: Address by the Hon. Albert H. Horton," n.p., KSHS; "Startling News!" (Aug. 15, 1861) and "For the Battlefield" (Aug. 22, 1861), *Lawrence Weekly Republican*; "St. Louis News," *Olathe Mirror*, Aug. 15, 1861.

3. Wilkie, *Pen and Powder*, 32–37; "The Great Battle," *Iowa City Weekly State Reporter*, Aug. 21, 1861; "The Dead Alive," *Lawrence Weekly Republican*, Oct. 10, 1861.

4. "The Stars and Stripes" and "Great Battle at Springfield, Mo.," *Atchison Freedom's Champion*, Aug. 17, 1861.

5. Daniel, *Soldiering in the Army of Tennessee*, 149–50; "The News from Missouri," *Davenport Daily Democrat & News*, Aug. 14, 1861; "Great Battle in South-West Missouri—Death of Gen. Lyon," *Kansas State Record*, Aug. 17, 1861; "The Battle Near

Springfield," *St. Louis Tri-Weekly Republican*, Aug. 19, 1861; "Wilson's Creek and Buena Vista," *Mishawaka Enterprise*, Aug. 30, 1861.

6. John T. Hughes to R. H. Miller (Aug. 12), in "Battle of Springfield," and "The Late Battle of Springfield," *Liberty Tribune*, Aug. 23, 1861; Untitled editorial, *St. Genevieve Plain Dealer*, Aug. 29, 1861; "New Orleans Correspondence" (Aug. 26, 1861) and "Full and Authentic Particulars of the Doings in Camp, Before & After the Battle of Oak Hills" (Sept. 2, 1861), *Shreveport Weekly News*; "The Victory in Missouri," *Texas Republican*, Aug. 24, 1861; Dirck, " 'We Have Whipped Them Beautifully,' " 291–92.

7. "The Kansas Boys," *Olathe Mirror*, Aug. 22, 1861; "The Battle of Springfield," *Atchison's Freedom's Champion*, Aug. 17, 1861; "Kansas Second—Reception," *Emporia News*, Sept. 7, 1861; "The First Iowa in the Springfield Fight," *Dubuque Weekly Times*, Aug. 22, 1861; "In the Late Battle . . .," *Anamosa Eureka*, Aug. 23, 1861; "War! War!," *Lyons Weekly Mirror*, Aug. 22, 1861; "The Late Battle at Springfield," *Liberty Tribune*, Aug. 23, 1861.

8. Jos. W. Martin to Geo. Martin (Aug. 20), in "The Battle of Springfield," *Atchison Freedom's Champion*, Aug. 21, 1861; Hatcher and Piston, *Kansans at Wilson's Creek*, 82.

9. A. to Editor (Sept. 17), in "Letter from the Third Regiment," *Baton Rouge Weekly Gazette and Comet*, Oct. 5, 1861.

10. William F. Allen to Dear Parents, Aug. 19, 1861, Allen Letters, RCHS; Jos. W. Martin to George K. Martin (Aug. 20), in "The Battle of Springfield," *Atchison Freedom's Champion*, Aug. 31, 1861; "Battle Accounts," *Olathe Mirror*, Aug. 29, 1861; Cater, *As It Was*, 94; "Full and Authentic Particulars of the Doings in Camp."

11. John R. Gratiot to Editor (n.d.), *Washington Telegraph*, Aug. 12, 1861; OR 3:118; C. S. Hills to Editor (Aug. 22), in "Letter from Lieut. Hills," *Emporia News*, Aug. 31, 1861.

12. "It Will No Doubt . . .," *Kansas State Record*, Sept. 14, 1861; Knox, *Camp-Fire and Cotton-Field*, 79; "Correspondence N.Y. Herald," *Kansas State Record*, Sept. 14, 1861; J. K. C. to Editor (Aug. 19), in "Correspondence to the Hawk-Eye," *Burlington Daily Hawk-Eye*, Aug. 23, 1861; "The Iowa Boys," *Iowa City Weekly State Reporter*, Apr. 21, 1861; "Honor to Whom Honor Is Due," *Lawrence Weekly Republican*, Aug. 22, 1861; Ware, *Lyon Campaign*, 332–33; George W. Deitzler to W. H. Merritt (Aug. 20), in "Col. Geo. W. Deitzler," *Atchison Freedom's Champion*, Aug. 24, 1861.

13. "Captain Geo. H. Fairchild" and "The Battle of Springfield," *Atchison Freedom's Champion*, Aug. 17, 1861; "The Iowa Boys," *Iowa City Weekly State Reporter*, Apr. 21, 1861; "The Battle near Springfield" (Aug. 21, 1861) and George F. Streaper to Editor (n.d.), in "To the Editor of the Hawk-Eye" (Aug. 24, 1861), *Burlington Daily Hawk-Eye*; "Editor of the Missouri Republican," *St. Louis Tri-Weekly Republican*, Aug. 22, 1861.

14. "The Northwest in Motion" (Aug. 24, 1861), "The Springfield Battle Again" (Aug. 24, 1861), "The West Neglected" (Aug. 2, 1861), and "Army Correspondence of the State Record" (Sept. 28, 1861), *Kansas State Record*; "General Sigel" and "Our Officers," *Emporia News*, Sept. 7, 1861; "The Battle of Springfield, Mo.," *Independence Civilian*, Aug. 20, 1861; "The Death of Gen. Lyon" (Aug. 14, 1861) and "The War Crisis" (Aug. 22, 1861), *Burlington Daily Hawk-Eye*; "Whose Fault Was It?" (Aug. 17, 1861) and "Col. Geo. W. Deitzler" (Aug. 24, 1861), *Atchison Freedom's Champion*; "Secession in Missouri," *Sioux City Register*, Sept. 7, 1861; S. to Editor (Aug. 20), in "From Rolla," *St. Louis Tri-Weekly Republican*, Aug. 22, 1861; Phillips, *Damned Yankee*, 257; Engle, *Yankee Dutchman*, 78–79; "Battle Accounts," *Olathe Mirror*, Aug. 29, 1861.

15. Alf to Dear Mother (Aug. 12), in "The Battle of Oak Hills, near Springfield, Mo.," *Shreveport South-Western*, Sept. 4, 1861; Austin, "Battle of Wilson's Creek," 47.

16. The total cost to Iowa taxpayers for feeding, clothing, transporting, and paying the

First Iowa was $39,230. Meyer, *Iowans Called to Valor*, 30–31; Clark, *Life in the Middle West*, 72–73; "Another Welcome to the Volunteers," *Burlington Daily Hawk-Eye*, Aug. 27, 1861.

17. "Reception Meeting" and "Reception of the Returned Volunteers," *Iowa City Weekly State Reporter*, Aug. 21, 1861; "Reception of the Returned Volunteers," *Dubuque Weekly Times*, Aug. 29, 1861; "Return Home of the Gallant Iowa First!," *Davenport Daily Democrat & News*, Aug. 27, 1861; "Return of Company F," *Mt. Pleasant Home Journal*, Aug. 31, 1861.

18. Particularly execrable examples include "Frank Mann," "Lines for the 1st Iowa Regiment," and "Welcome to Company F, First Iowa Regiment," *Mt. Pleasant Home Journal*, Aug. 31, 1861.

19. "St. Louis Hospitality: Reminiscences of Wilson's Creek and the Entertainment Provided for Sigel's Men," *National Tribune*, May 15, 1902; "Returned," *Emporia News*, Sept. 7, 1861; "Sword Presentation," *Atchison Freedom's Champion*, Oct. 19, 1861.

20. "Give Them a Cordial Welcome," *Kansas State Record*, Aug. 24, 1861; "Kansas Second—Reception," *Emporia News*, Sept. 7, 1861.

21. "Kansas Second—Reception," *Emporia News*, Sept. 7, 1861; "The Railroad Murder," *Lawrence Weekly Republican*, Sept. 2, 1861; "Funeral of Lieut. Shaw," *Emporia News*, Sept. 21, 1861.

22. "The Omaha Fired into at Iatan," *Leavenworth Daily Times*, Sept. 17, 1861; "An Enthusiastic Reception Was . . .," *Kansas State Record*, Sept. 21, 1861.

23. "Return of the Kansas Second," *Leavenworth Daily Times*, Sept. 17, 1861.

24. Ibid.; "Arrival of the Second Kansas" and "The Reception of the Second," *Leavenworth Weekly Conservative*, Sept. 19, 1861.

25. "When the Second Regiment . . .," *Olathe Mirror*, Oct. 24, 1861.

26. Early in the war when companies retained individual flags, it was common practice to allow only one to be flown during combat to avoid confusion. "Return of the Emporia Boys," *Emporia News*, Oct. 12, 1861; Connelley, *Life of Preston B. Plumb*, 98–100.

27. Connelley, *Life of Preston B. Plumb*, 99–100.

Epilogue

1. Warner, *Generals in Blue*, 447–48, 486–87; Engle, *Yankee Dutchman*, 229–33; Warner, *Generals in Gray*, 200–201, 246–47; Castel, *General Sterling Price*, 273–85; Cutrer, *Ben McCulloch*, 302–4; Allardice, *More Generals in Gray*, 179–80.

2. Warner, *Generals in Blue*, 70–71, 181, 486–87, 425–26, 491–92; Cullum, *Biographical Register*, 18; Heitman, *Historical Register*, 2:264.

3. Warner, *Generals in Gray*, 81, 131, 202–3, 205–6, 209–10; Allardice, *More Generals in Gray*, 132–33.

4. Committee on Veterans Affairs, U.S. Senate, *Medal of Honor Recipients, 1863–1978*, 36, 126, 211, 254, 262.

5. Confederate Home Applications, 11, 21, 61, 69, MSA.

6. "Bitterness Buried," *Kansas City Times*, Aug. 8, 1883, clipping in *Kansas in the Civil War*, vol. 2, *Wilson's Creek*, n.p., KSHS.

7. "August 10, 1861," *Atchison Freedom's Champion*, clipping in ibid.

Bibliography

Manuscripts

Austin, Tex.
Texas State Library and Archives Commission
Garnet A. Dibrell Collection of the Papers of Ben and Henry Eustace McCulloch
Governor's Papers
Baton Rouge, Louisiana
Louisiana and Lower Mississippi Valley Collections, LSU Libraries, Louisiana State
University
Samuel C. Bonner Family Papers
George M. Heroman Papers
R. M. Hinson Papers
John R. Norris Letters
William Pierson Papers
George D. Waddill Papers
Bellview, Ill.
Bellview Public Library
Peter J. Osterhaus, "What I Saw of the War"
Carlisle, Pa.
U.S. Army Military History Institute
Eugene A. Carr Papers
J. O. Culver Papers
Alexander A. Russell Letters
Columbia, Mo.
University of Missouri at Columbia
Western Historical Manuscript Collection
William W. Branson Diary
Durham, N.C.
Rare Book, Manuscript, and Special Collections Library, Duke University
Sarah Horton Cockrell Papers
Confederate Veteran Papers
J. M. Bailey, "1861"
Mosby Monroe Parson Papers
James H. Wiswell Letters
Eastford, Conn.
Eastford Historical Society
Nathaniel Lyon Papers
Fort Smith, Ark.
Fort Smith National Historic Site
J. F. Weaver, "Fort Smith in the War between the States"

Hartford, Conn.
  Connecticut Historical Society
    Nathaniel Lyon Papers
  Connecticut State Library
    Nathaniel Lyon Papers
Hillsboro, Tex.
  Hill College Research Center
    Theodrick Jones Logwood Diary
    Allen T. Pettus Papers
    Third Texas Cavalry Letters
Jefferson City, Mo.
  Missouri State Archives
    Confederate Home Applications
    Confederate Hospital Register, 1861–62
    CSA Missouri State Guard Quartermaster Accounts, 1861
    Orval Henderson Jr., ed., "A Confederate Diary Maintained by a Surgeon of the
      Missouri State Guard, 1 August 1861–9 January 1862"
    M. Hopewell, "Camp Jackson: History of Missouri Volunteer Militia of St. Louis"
    J. H. Rockwell, "A Rambling Reminiscence of Experiences during the Great War
      between the States"
Lawrence, Kans.
  University of Kansas at Lawrence
    C. M. Deitzler Reminiscences
Little Rock, Ark.
  Arkansas History Commission
    Isaac Clark Diary
    Harris Flanagin Papers
      Amy Jean Greene, "Governor Harris Flanagin"
      List of Volunteers
    Genevieve Tapscott Gill, "History of the Weaver Family and Home"
    W. H. Haynes, "General and Mrs. Thomas J. Churchill"
    John Johnson Civil War Letters
      "Family Record"
    John D. Keith, "John D. Keith, Confederate Soldier—'Reminiscences': 1912"
    Dandridge McRae Papers
      Descriptive List of Cap. Lawrence's Co. in Regiments Ark. Infantry
      Angie Lewis McRae, "Genl. D. McRae, White Co. Man"
      Dandridge McRae, "Narrative of the Battle of Oak Hills"
      Muster Roll—Armstrong's Co. B, 1st Reg. Cav. Ark. Volunteers
      Muster Rolls—Companies A, B, C, McRae's Battalion, Ark. Volunteers
      Muster Roll—Titsworth's Co. B, 3d Reg., Ark. Vol. Inf.
      Report of Arms, Equipment, etc., Co. I, Camp Walker, 2-1-1861
    W. W. Mansfield Letters
    Nicholas Bartlett Pearce Papers
      "N. B. Pearce Reminiscences"
    Weaver-Field Collection
      J. M. Harrell, "Confederate Dead: Omer Rose Weaver"
      Journal of the Proceedings of the Little Rock Debating Club
      Manuscripts—Omer R. Weaver's Purse Contents

Manhattan, Kans.
  Riley County Historical Society
    William F. Allen Letters
New Haven, Conn.
  Yale Collection of Western Americana, Beinecke Rare Book and Manuscript Library,
    Yale University
    John Van Deusen Du Bois Collection
      John Van Deusen Du Bois, "The Journals and Letters of Col. John Van D. Du
        Bois Embracing His Campaigns in the West, 1850–1861"
    Nathaniel Lyon Papers
    Henry Miles Moore Journals
New Hill, N.C.
  Whit Joyner Collection
Republic, Mo.
  John K. Hulston Library, Wilson's Creek National Battlefield
    Abstracts of Park Research Funded by the Midwest Regional Office, National Park
      Service, 1973–82, Research/Resources Management Report MWR-1, App. B,
      Persons Living on or near the Battlefield in 1860
    Edwin C. Bearss, "Ray House Report"
    Eyewitness Accounts file
      "An Eye Witness Account of the Battle of Wilson's Creek"
    Folder 5th Ark. Inf. CSA
      "Davis Blues"—Company F, Fifth Arkansas State Troops
      "Hempstead Cavalry"—Company H, Second Arkansas Mounted Rifles
    James Henry Hopson Memoirs
    John H. Rivers Reminiscences
    John F. Walter, "Capsule Histories of Arkansas Military Units"
    Gibson Mill, House and Family file
      Charles T. Meier, Management Assistant, to Superintendent, GWCA, Nov. 3,
        1961
      "Parents' Record"
    Douglas A. Harding, " 'Kelly's Boys': A History of the Washington Blues"
    Historic Base and Ground Cover Map—December 1978
    Levant L. Jones file
    Kip Lindberg, "Uniform and Equipment Descriptions of Units at Wilson's Creek"
    Local Families file folder
      Extracts from Greene County Tax Records
    Medal of Honor files
    Muster Rolls, First Iowa Infantry
    N. Bart Pearce file
    Harold Peterson to Regional Director, Dec. 4, 1969
    Horace Poole Diary
    Winston Winn to Richard W. Hatcher III, Feb. 24, 1989
St. Louis, Mo.
  Missouri Historical Society
    William C. Breckenridge Collection
    John H. Gundlach Collection
    Levant L. Jones Papers
    Peter D. Lane Papers
      Peter D. Lane, "Recollections of a Volunteer"

Peter J. Osterhaus Papers

M. M. Parsons Papers

J. C. McNamara, "Historical Sketch of the Sixth Division of the Missouri State Guard"

Thomas L. Snead Papers

Margaret Montgomery Zogbaum Papers

Margaret Montgomery Zogbaum, "The Life of Mary Anne Phelps Montgomery, 1846–1942"

Springfield, Mo.

Greene County Archives

Deed of Records Books

Topeka, Kans.

Kansas State Historical Society

Joseph Cracklin Papers

Joseph Cracklin, "A War Reminiscence, by Old Cap"

David O. Crane Papers

Robert A. Friedrich, "Fighting Them Over: Reminiscences of Wilson's Creek," in *Kansas in the Civil War*, vol. 2, *Wilson's Creek*

Kansas Scrapbook

James A. McGonigle, "First Kansas Infantry in the Battle of Wilson's Creek, Missouri, Tenth Day of August, 1861"

John W. Rankin File

"Wilson's Creek: Address by the Hon. Albert H. Horton at 20th Anniversary, Aug. 10 [1881]," *The Patriot*, n.d., clipping in *Kansas in the Civil War*, vol. 2, *Wilson's Creek*

Washington, D.C.

Library of Congress

C. C. Gilbert Papers

John M. Schofield Papers

National Archives and Records Administration

Compiled Service Records of Volunteer Soldiers Who Served in Organizations from the State of Missouri

Backof's Battalion, Artillery (3 months, 1861)

First Infantry (3 months, 1861)

Second Infantry (3 months, 1861)

Third Infantry (3 months, 1861)

Fourth Infantry (3 months, 1861)

Fifth Infantry (3 months, 1861)

Letters Sent and General and Special Orders Issued by the Army of the West, June–August 1861

West Point, N.Y.

U.S. Military Academy

Official Register

Newspapers

Arkansas True Democrat (Little Rock)

Atchison (Kans.) Freedom's Champion

Baton Rouge Daily Advocate

Baton Rouge Weekly Gazette and Comet
Bellview (Tex.) Countryman
Boliver (Mo.) Weekly Courier
Boston Transcript
Burlington (Iowa) Daily Hawk-Eye
Clarksville (Tex.) Standard
Dallas Herald
Davenport Daily Democrat & News
Des Arc (Ark.) Semi-Weekly Citizen
Dubuque Daily Times
Dubuque Herald
Dubuque Weekly Times
Emporia (Kans.) News
Fort Scott (Kans.) Democrat
Franklin Record (Hampton, Iowa)
Glasgow (Mo.) Weekly Times
Hannibal (Mo.) Daily Messenger
Independence (Iowa) Civilian
Iowa City Democratic State Press
Iowa City State Register
Iowa City Weekly State Reporter
Iowa Transcript (Toledo)
Kansas City (Mo.) Daily Western Journal of Commerce
Kansas State Record (Topeka)
Keokuk (Iowa) Gate City
Lawrence (Kans.) Weekly Republican
Leavenworth (Kans.) Daily Times
Leavenworth (Kans.) Weekly Conservative
Liberty (Mo.) Tribune
Lyons (Iowa) Weekly Mirror
Macon City (Mo.) Our Whole Union
Mishawaka (Ind.) Enterprise
Mt. Pleasant (Iowa) Home Journal
Muscatine (Iowa) Weekly Journal
National Intelligencer (Washington, D.C.)
National Tribune (Washington, D.C.)
New Orleans Daily Picayune
Olathe (Kans.) Mirror
Port Allen (La.) Sugar Planter
Randolph Citizen (Huntsville, Mo.)
Richmond (Mo.) Weekly North-West Conservator
St. Genevieve (Mo.) Plain Dealer
St. Louis Daily Missouri Democrat
St. Louis Post Dispatch
St. Louis Republican
St. Louis Tri-Weekly Republican
Sedalia (Mo.) Daily Bazoo
Shreveport (La.) Daily News
Shreveport (La.) South-Western
Shreveport (La.) Weekly News

South Danvers (Mass.) Wizard
Springfield (Mo.) Advertiser
Springfield (Mo.) Equal Rights Gazette
Springfield (Mo.) Mirror
Texas Republican (Marshall)
Topeka Tribune
Washington (D.C.) Telegraph
Weekly Central City (Mo.) and Brunswicker

Printed Primary Sources

Books

Asbury, Ai Edgar. *My Experiences in the War, 1861 to 1865: A Little Autobiography.* Kansas City: Berkowitz and Co., 1894.
Barney, Capt. C. *Recollections of Field Service with the Twentieth Iowa Volunteers.* Davenport: By the author, 1865.
Barron, S. B. *The Lone Star Defenders: A Chronicle of the Third Texas Cavalry, Ross' Brigade.* New York: Neale Publishing Co., 1908.
Bevier, R. S. *History of the First and Second Missouri Confederate Brigades, 1861–1865; and From Wakarusa to Appomattox: A Military Anagraph.* St. Louis: Bryan, Brand and Co., 1879.
Brant, Randolph C. *Campaign of General Lyon in Missouri: Its Value to the Union Cause.* Portland, Oreg.: Schwab Bros. Printing and Litho. Co., 1895.
Britton, Wiley. *The Civil War on the Western Border.* 2 vols. New York: G. P. Putnam, 1899.
Carr, Pat, ed. *In Fine Spirits: The Civil War Letters of Ras Stirman.* Fayetteville, Ark.: Washington County Historical Society, 1986.
Cater, Douglas John. *As It Was: Reminiscences of a Soldier of the Third Texas Cavalry and the Nineteenth Louisiana Infantry.* Austin: State House Press, 1990.
Clark, John S. *Life in the Middle West: Reminiscences of J. S. Clark.* Chicago: Advance Publishing Company, n.d.
Crittenden, Henry Houston. *The Crittenden Memoirs.* New York: G. P. Putnam, 1936.
Cutrer, Thomas, and T. Michael Parrish, eds. *Brothers in Gray: The Civil War Letters of the Pierson Family.* Baton Rouge: Louisiana State University Press, 1997.
Dacus, Robert H. *Reminiscences of Company "H," First Arkansas Mounted Rifles.* Daniel, Ark.: By the author, 1897.
Haskin, William L. *The History of the First Regiment of Artillery.* Portland, Maine: B. Thurston and Co., 1879.
Hatcher, Richard W., III, and William Garrett Piston. *Kansans at Wilson's Creek: Soldiers' Letters from the Campaign for Southwest Missouri.* Springfield, Mo.: Wilson's Creek National Battlefield Foundation, 1993.
Hubble, Martin J., comp. *Personal Reminiscences and Fragments of the Early History of Springfield, Greene County, Missouri.* Springfield: Museum of the Ozarks, 1979.
Knox, Thomas W. *Camp-Fire and Cotton-Field: Southern Adventure in Time of War.* New York: Blelock and Co., 1865.
Matson, Daniel. *Life Experiences of Daniel Matson.* N.p., ca. 1924.
Mudd, Joseph A. *With Porter in North Missouri: A Chapter in the History of the War between the States.* Washington, D.C.: National Publishing Co., 1909.

Pomeroy, Dixon, and Foster. *Obituary Addresses of Messrs. Pomeroy, Dixon, and Foster on the Death of Brigadier General Lyon: Delivered in the Senate of the United States, December 20, 1861*. Washington, D.C.: Congressional Globe Office, 1861.

Schofield, John M. *Forty-six Years in the Army*. New York: Century Co., 1897.

Shelton, Alonzo H. *Memoir of a Confederate Veteran: Alonzo H. Shelton, 1839–1930*. Clay County, Mo.: Clay County Historical Museum, 1974.

Sheridan, Mary, T. Ed. Albright III, and Charles Hudson, comps. *Reminiscences of a Tramp Printer: Theodore Cline Albright*. N.p.: By the compilers, 1998.

Snead, Thomas L. *The Fight for Missouri from the Election of Lincoln to the Death of Lyon*. New York: Charles Scribner's Sons, 1886.

Sparks, A. W. *The War between the States, As I Saw It: Reminiscent, Historical and Personal*. Tyler, Tex.: Lee and Burnett, Printers, 1901.

Stanley, D. S. *Personal Memorial of Major-General D. S. Stanley, U.S.A.* Cambridge: Harvard University Press, 1917.

Tunnard, W. H. *A Southern Record: The History of the Third Regiment of Louisiana Infantry*. Baton Rouge: By the author, 1866. Reprint, Fayetteville: University of Arkansas Press, 1997.

U.S. War Department. *The War of the Rebellion: A Compilation of the Official Records of the Union and Confederate Armies*. 128 vols. Washington, D.C.: Government Printing Office, 1880–1901.

Ware, E. F. *The Lyon Campaign in Missouri: Being a History of the First Iowa Infantry*. Topeka: Crane and Co., 1907.

Watson, William. *Life in the Confederate Army*. 1887. Reprint, Baton Rouge: Louisiana State University Press, 1995.

Wilkie, Franc B. *The Iowa First: Letters from the War*. Dubuque: Herald Book and Job Establishment, 1861.

———. *Pen and Powder*. Boston: Ticknor and Co., 1888.

Woodruff, W. E. *With the Light Guns in '61–'65: Reminiscences of Eleven Arkansas, Missouri, and Texas Light Batteries in the Civil War*. Little Rock: Central Printing Co., 1903.

Articles

Bek, William G. "The Civil War Diary of John T. Buegel, Union Soldier." Part 1 (April 1946): 307–29 and Part 2 (July 1946): 503–30, *Missouri Historical Review* 40.

Bell, John D. "Price's Missouri Campaign, 1861." *Confederate Veteran* 22 (June 1914): 271–72; 22 (July 1914): 318–19; 22 (September 1914): 416.

"A Boy's Experiences at the Battle of Wilson's Creek." *Volunteer Wire* 18 (September 1998): 2–4.

Childress, R. G. "Battle of Oak Hill." *Confederate Veteran* 7 (April 1899): 169.

Clarke, J. C. "General Lyon and the Fight for Missouri." In *War Sketches and Incidents as Related to the Campaigns of the Iowa Commandery, Military Order of the Loyal Legion of the United States*, 2:274–92. Des Moines: Kenyon Press, 1898.

Davis, Philip C. "Extract from a Report of His Services from June 1st, 1861, to June 19, 1863, Relative to the Battle of Wilson's Creek." In *The Medical and Surgical History of the War of the Rebellion, 1861–1865*, edited by Joseph K. Barnes, 145–47. Washington, D.C.: Government Printing Office, 1870.

"Dr. Melcher Remembers." *Volunteer Wire* 17 (November 1998): n.p.

Easley, Virginia, ed. "Journal of the Civil War in Missouri, 1861: Henry Martyn Cheavens." *Missouri Historical Review* 62 (October 1961): 12–25.

Elliott, R. G. "The Events of 1856: Papers Read before the Meeting of the '56ers at Lawrence, Oct. 26, 1901." In *Transactions of the Kansas State Historical Society, 1901–1902*, 526–37. Topeka: Kansas State Historical Society, 1902.

Frémont, John C. "In Command in Missouri." In *Battles and Leaders of the Civil War*, 4 vols., edited by Robert U. Johnson and C. C. Buel, 1:278–88. New York: Century, 1887–88.

Greene, Albert R. "On the Battle of Wilson Creek." In *Transactions of the Kansas State Historical Society, 1889–1896*, edited by F. G. Adams, 5:16–27. Topeka: Press of the Kansas State Printing Co., 1896.

"In the Ranks under General Lyon in Missouri—1861: The Observations of a Private Soldier." *Blue and Gray* 4 (1894): 142–47, 574–91; 5 (1895): 66–70, 141–47, 198–203.

King, W. H. "Early Experiences in Missouri." *Confederate Veteran* 17 (October 1909): 502–3.

Lademann, Otto C. B. "The Battle of Carthage, Mo." In *War Papers Read before the Commandery of the State of Wisconsin, Military Order of the Loyal Legion of the United States*, 4:131–39. Milwaukee: Burdick and Allen, 1914.

——. "The Battle of Wilson's Creek, August 10, 1861." In *War Papers Read before the Commandery of the State of Wisconsin, Military Order of the Loyal Legion of the United States*, 4:433–39. Milwaukee: Burdick and Allen, 1914.

——. "A Prisoner of War: A Sequel to the Battle of Wilson's Creek." In *War Papers Read before the Commandery of the State of Wisconsin, Military Order of the Loyal Legion of the United States*, 4:439–43. Milwaukee: Burdick and Allen, 1914.

Lale, Max S., ed. "The Boy-Bugler of the Third Texas Cavalry: The A. B. Blocker Narrative." *Military History of the Southwest* 14 (1978) no. 2: 71–92; no. 3: 147–67.

Lewis, Warner. "Civil War Reminiscences." *Missouri Historical Review* 2 (April 1908): 221–37.

Lobdell, Jared C., ed. "The Civil War Journal and Letters of Colonel John Van Deusen Du Bois, April 12, 1861 to October 16, 1861." Part 1, 60 (July 1966): 430–59; Part 2, 61 (October 1966): 22–50, *Missouri Historical Review*.

McCulloch, Clem. "A Sketch of the Life of Clem McCulloch: In the Confederate Army, 1861–1865." In *The Battle of Prairie Grove: Records with Mementoes of December 7, 1862*, 45–46. Fayetteville, Ark.: Washington County Historical Society, 1992.

Mudd, Joseph A. "What I Saw at Wilson's Creek." *Missouri Historical Review* 8 (January 1914): 89–105.

Musser, Richard H. "The War in Missouri: From Springfield to Neosho." *Southern Bivouac* 4 (April 1886): 678–85.

Payne, James E. "Early Days of War in Missouri." *Confederate Veteran* 39 (February 1931): 58–60.

——. "The Taking of Liberty Arsenal." *Confederate Veteran* 37 (January 1930): 15–16.

Pearce, Nicholas Bartlett. "Arkansas Troops in the Battle of Wilson's Creek." In *Battles and Leaders of the Civil War*, 4 vols., edited by Robert U. Johnson and C. C. Buel, 1:298–303. New York: Century, 1887–88.

——. "Price's Campaign of 1861." *Publications of the Arkansas Historical Association* 4 (1917): 332–51.

Reiff, A. V. "History of 'Spy' Company, Raised at Fayetteville, Ark." In *The War of the 'Sixties*, compiled by E. R. Hutchins, 164–76. New York: Neale Publishing Co., 1912.

Sigel, Franz. "The Flanking Column at Wilson's Creek." In *Battles and Leaders of the Civil War*, 4 vols., edited by Robert U. Johnson and C. C. Buel, 1:304–6. New York: Century, 1887–88.

Snead, Thomas L. "The First Year of the War in Missouri." In *Battles and Leaders of the*

Civil War, 4 vols., edited by Robert U. Johnson and C. C. Buel, 1:262–776. New York: Century, 1887–88.

Snyder, J. F. "A Few Points about the Battle of Wilson Creek, by Dr. J. F. Snyder, the Messenger Who Informed Gen'l. Price of the Federal Surprise." *Missouri Republican*, October 1, 1886, 5–7.

Sokalski, George Oscar. "56 Fights Including Eighteen Pitched Battles." Edited by Charles G. Stevenson. *American Polonia Reporter* 10 (Summer–Autumn 1965): 6–9.

Wherry, William M. "General Nathaniel Lyon and His Campaign in Missouri in 1861." In *Sketches of War History, 1861–1865: Papers Prepared for the Ohio Commandery of the Military Order of the Loyal Legion of the United States, 1890–1896*, edited by W. H. Chamberlin, 4:68–74. Cincinnati: Robert Clarke Co., 1896.

——. "Wilson's Creek, and the Death of Lyon." In *Battles and Leaders of the Civil War*, edited by Robert U. Johnson and C. C. Buel, 1:289–97. New York: Century, 1887–88.

——. "Wilson's Creek, and the Death of Lyon, by William M. Wherry, Sixth U.S. Infantry, Brevet Brigadier-General, U.S.V. at Wilson's Creek, Aide-de-Camp to General Lyon." *Grand Military Festival in Commemoration of the Battle of Wilson's Creek, Given by Frank P. Blair Post No. 1, Department of Missouri, G.A.R. Corcordia Park, Sunday, August 5, 1884*. St. Louis: Nixon-Jones Ptg. Co., n.d.

W. N. M. "Battle of Wilson's Creek." *Southern Bivouac* 3 (October 1884): 49–54.

Secondary Sources

Books

Adamson, Hans Christian. *Rebellion in Missouri, 1861: Nathaniel Lyon and His Army of the West*. New York: Chilton Co., 1961.

Allardice, Bruce S. *More Generals in Gray*. Baton Rouge: Louisiana State University Press, 1995.

Allen, Desmond Wall, comp. *First Arkansas Mounted Rifles*. Conway, Ark.: By the author, 1988.

——. *Index to Arkansas Confederate Soldiers*. 3 vols. Conway, Ark.: Arkansas Research, 1990.

Anderson, Mabel Washbourne. *Life of General Stand Watie*. Pryor, Okla.: By the author, ca. 1915.

Angus, Fern. *Down the War Road in the Missouri Ozarks*. Marionville, Mo.: By the author, ca. 1992.

Barnes, Joseph K., ed. *The Medical and Surgical History of the War of the Rebellion, 1861–1865*. Washington, D.C.: Government Printing Office, 1870.

Bartels, Carolyn M. *The Forgotten Men: Missouri State Guard*. Shawnee Mission, Kans.: Two Trails Publishing, 1995.

Baxter, William. *Pea Ridge and Prairie Grove*. 1864. Reprint, Van Buren, Ark.: Press-Argus, 1957.

Bearss, Edwin C. *The Battle of Wilson's Creek*. Bozeman, Mont.: Artcraft Printing, 1975.

Bergeron, Arthur W., Jr. *Guide to Louisiana Confederate Military Units, 1861–1865*. Baton Rouge: Louisiana State University Press, ca. 1989.

Boatner, Mark M., III. *The Civil War Dictionary*. New York: David McKay Co., Inc., 1959.

Bragg, Jefferson Davis. *Louisiana in the Confederacy*. Baton Rouge: Louisiana State University Press, 1941.

Brauer, Leonard, and Evelyn Goosen, eds. *Hier Snackt Wi Plattdütsch: Here We Speak Low German*. Camp Cole, Mo.: City of Camp Cole, 1989.

Brooksher, William Riley. *Bloody Hill: The Civil War Battle of Wilson's Creek*. Washington, D.C.: Brassey's, 1995.

Burke, W. S. *Official Military History of Kansas Regiments during the War for the Suppression of the Great Rebellion*. Leavenworth, Kans.: N.p., 1870.

Burton, William L. *Melting Pot Soldiers: The Union's Ethnic Regiments*. Ames: Iowa State University Press, 1988.

Castel, Albert. *A Frontier State at War: Kansas, 1861–1865*. Lawrence: Kansas Heritage Press, 1992.

———. *General Sterling Price and the Civil War in the West*. Baton Rouge: Louisiana State University Press, 1968.

Cleaveland, Nehemiah. *History of Bowdoin College with Biographical Sketches of the Graduates from 1806 to 1870, Inclusive*. Boston: James Ripley Osgood and Co., 1882.

Cockrell, Ewing. *History of Johnson County, Missouri*. Topeka: Historical Publishing Co., 1918.

Coffman, Edward M. *The Old Army: A Portrait of the American Army in Peacetime, 1784–1898*. New York: Oxford University Press, 1986.

Committee on Veterans Affairs, U.S. Senate. *Medal of Honor Recipients, 1863–1978*. Washington, D.C.: Government Printing Office, 1979.

Confederate Women of Arkansas, 1861–1865: Memorial Reminiscences. Little Rock: H. G. Publishing Co., 1907.

Connelley, William Elsey. *The Life of Preston B. Plumb, 1837–1891*. Chicago: Browne and Howell, 1913.

———. *Quantrill and the Border Wars*. New York: Pageant Book Co., 1956.

———. *With Mexico, 1846–1847: Doniphan's Expedition and the Conquest of New Mexico and California*. Kansas City, Mo.: Bryant and Douglas Book and Stationery Co., 1907.

Conrad, Howard L., ed. *Encyclopedia of the History of Missouri*. 6 vols. New York: Southern History Co., 1901.

Cordley, Richard. *A History of Lawrence, Kansas, from the First Settlement to the Close of the Rebellion*. Lawrence: Lawrence Journal Press, 1895.

———. *Pioneer Days in Kansas*. Boston: Pilgrim Press, n.d.

Cotrell, Steve. *The Battle of Carthage and Carthage in the Civil War*. N.p.: By the author, 1990.

Cowles, Calvin D., comp. *Atlas to Accompany the Official Records of the Union and Confederate Armies*. Washington, D.C.: Government Printing Office, 1881–85.

Crawford, Samuel J. *Kansas in the Sixties*. Chicago: A. C. McClurg and Co., 1911.

Cullum, George W. *Biographical Register of the Officers and Graduates of the U.S. Military Academy at West Point, New York, since Its Establishment in 1807*. Cambridge, Mass.: Riverside Press, 1901.

Cutrer, Thomas. *Ben McCulloch and the Frontier Military Tradition*. Chapel Hill: University of North Carolina Press, 1993.

Daniel, Larry J. *Soldiering in the Army of Tennessee: A Portrait of Life in a Confederate Army*. Chapel Hill: University of North Carolina Press, 1991.

Dictionary of American Biography. 20 vols., supp. New York: Charles Scribner's Sons, 1928–81.

Dougan, Michael B. *Confederate Arkansas: The People and Policies of a Frontier State in Wartime*. University, Ala.: University of Alabama Press, 1976.

Eddy, T. H. *Patriotism of Illinois: A Record of the Civil and Military History of the State in the War for the Union.* Chicago: Clarke and Co., 1865.

Eggenberger, David. *A Dictionary of Battles.* New York: Thomas Y. Crowell Co., 1967.

Engle, Stephen. *Yankee Dutchman: The Life of Franz Sigel.* Fayetteville: University of Arkansas Press, 1993.

Fellman, Michael. *Inside War: The Guerrilla Conflict in Missouri during the American Civil War.* New York: Oxford University Press, 1989.

Fischer, LeRoy H., and Jerry Gill. *Confederate Indian Forces Outside of Indian Territory.* Oklahoma City: Oklahoma Historical Society, 1969.

Franks, Kenny A. *Stand Watie and the Agony of the Cherokee Nation.* Memphis: Memphis State University Press, 1979.

Gottschalk, Phil. *In Deadly Earnest: The History of the First Missouri Confederate Brigade.* Columbia: Missouri River Press, Inc., 1991.

Greene County, Missouri, Federal Census of 1860. Springfield: Ozarks Genealogical Society, 1984.

Hagerman, Edward. *The American Civil War and the Origins of Modern Warfare: Ideas, Organization, and Field Command.* Bloomington: Indiana University Press, 1988.

Hale, Douglas. *The Third Texas Cavalry in the Civil War.* Norman: University of Oklahoma Press, 1993.

Hall, William Kearney. *Springfield, Greene County, Missouri, Newspaper Abstracts, 1903.* Springfield: Ozarks Genealogical Society, 1987.

Hardee, William Joseph. *Rifle and Light Infantry Tactics.* New York: J. O. Kane, 1862.

Hardin, J. Fair. *Northwestern Louisiana: A History of the Wasteland of the Red River, 1714–1937.* 3 vols. Louisville and Shreveport: Historical Record Association, n.d.

Harrell, John M. *Arkansas.* Vol. 10 of *Confederate Military History,* edited by Clement A. Evans. 1899. Reprint, Wilmington, N.C.: Broadfoot Publishing Co., 1987.

Heitman, Francis B. *Historical Register and Dictionary of the United States Army, from Its Organization, September 29, 1789, to March 2, 1903.* 2 vols. Washington, D.C.: Government Printing Office, 1903.

Henderson, Harry McCorry. *Texas in the Confederacy.* San Antonio: Naylor Co., 1955.

Hess, Earl J. *Liberty, Virtue, and Progress: Northerners and Their War for the Union.* New York: New York University Press, 1988.

———. *The Union Soldier in Battle: Enduring the Ordeal of Combat.* Lawrence: University of Kansas Press, 1997.

Hinze, David C., and Karen Farnham. *The Battle of Carthage: Border War in Southwest Missouri, July 5, 1861.* Campbell, Calif.: Savas Publishing Co., 1997.

History of Benton, Washington, Carroll, Madison, Crawford, Franklin, and Sebastian Counties, Arkansas. Chicago: Goodspeed Publishing Co., 1889.

History of Carroll County, Missouri. St. Louis: National Historical Co., 1884.

History of Clay and Platte Counties, Missouri. St. Louis: National Historical Co., 1885.

History of Greene County, Missouri. St. Louis: Western Historical Co., 1883.

History of Lafayette County, Mo. St. Louis: Missouri Historical Co., 1881.

Holcombe, Return I., and W. S. Adams. *An Account of the Battle of Wilson's Creek, of Oak Hills.* Springfield, Mo.: Dow and Adams, 1883.

Hyde, William, and Howard L. Conrad, eds. *Encyclopedia of the History of St. Louis: A Compendium of History and Biography for Ready Reference.* New York: Southern Heritage Co., 1899.

Ingenthron, Elmo. *Borderland Rebellion: A History of the Civil War on the Missouri-Arkansas Border.* Branson, Mo.: Ozarks Mountaineer, ca. 1980.

Ingersoll, Lurton Dunham. *Iowa and the Rebellion*. Philadelphia: J. P. Lippincott and Co., 1866.

Ingrisano, Michael N., Jr. *An Artilleryman's War: Gus Dey and the 2nd United States Artillery*. Shippensburg, Pa.: White Mane Publishing Co., Inc., 1998.

Iowa State Almanac and Statistical Register. N.p.: Publishing House of Luse, Lane and Co., 1860.

Johnson, Sid S. *Texans Who Wore the Gray*. N.p., n.d.

Josephy, Alvin M., Jr. *The Civil War in the American West*. New York: Alfred A. Knopf, 1991.

Knapp, George E. *The Wilson's Creek Staff Ride and Battlefield Tour*. Fort Leavenworth, Kans.: Combat Studies Institute, n.d.

Lankford, Ella Malloy. *The History of Johnson County, Arkansas—The First Hundred Years*. N.p., 1921.

The Laws of the State of Missouri Passed at the Called Session of the Twenty-first General Assembly. Jefferson City: J. P. Ament, Public Printer, 1861.

Leeper, Wesley Thurman. *Rebels Valiant: Second Arkansas Mounted Rifles (Dismounted)*. Little Rock: Pioneer Press, ca. 1964.

Linderman, Gerald. *Embattled Courage: The Experience of Combat in the American Civil War*. New York: Free Press, 1987.

Long, E. B., with Barbara Long. *The Civil War Day by Day: An Almanac, 1861–1865*. Garden City, N.Y.: Doubleday, 1971.

McDonough, James L. *Schofield: Union General in the Civil War and Reconstruction*. Tallahassee: Florida State University Press, 1972.

McElroy, John. *The Struggle for Missouri*. Washington, D.C.: National Tribune Co., 1909.

McPherson, James. *For Cause and Comrades: Why Men Fought in the Civil War*. New York: Oxford University Press, 1997.

———. *What They Fought For, 1861–1865*. Baton Rouge: Louisiana State University Press, 1994.

Matthews, James Alonzo, Jr. *Pearce, Bartlett, Matthews, Smart and Allied Families*. Midlands, Tex.: By the author, n.d.

Melville, Herman. *Battle-Pieces and Aspects of the War*. New York: Harper and Brothers, 1866.

Meyer, Steve. *Iowans Called to Valor*. Garrison, Iowa: Meyer Publishing, 1993.

Miles, Kathleen. *Bitter Ground: The Civil War in Missouri's Golden Valley: Benton, Henry, and St. Clair Counties*. Warsaw, Mo.: Printery, 1971.

Mitchell, Reid. *Civil War Soldiers*. New York: Viking, 1988.

———. *The Vacant Chair: The Northern Soldier Leaves Home*. New York: Oxford University Press, 1993.

Monaghan, Jay. *The Civil War on the Western Border, 1854–1865*. Boston: Little, Brown, 1955.

Monks, William. *A History of Southern Missouri and Northern Arkansas*. West Plains, Mo.: West Plains Journal Co., 1907.

Moore, Frank, ed. *The Rebellion Record: A Diary of American Events, with Documents, Narratives, Illustrative Incidents, Poetry, etc.* 12 vols. New York: G. P. Putnam, 1861–68.

Moore, John C. *Missouri*. Vol. 12 of *Confederate Military History*, edited by Clement A. Evans. Reprint, Wilmington, N.C.: Broadfoot Publishing Co., 1987.

Neumann, Robert P. *An Illustrated History of the Civil War in Springfield, Mo., 1861–1865*. Springfield: By the author, 1975.

Noble, H. T., et al. *Military History and Reminiscences of the Thirteenth Regiment of Illinois Volunteer Infantry in the Civil War in the United States, 1861–1865: Prepared by a Committee of the Regiment, 1891.* Chicago: Women's Temperance Publishing Association, 1892.

Nofi, Albert A. *The Gettysburg Campaign.* Conshohoken, Pa.: Combined Books, Inc., 1986.

O'Flaherty, Daniel. *General Jo Shelby: Undefeated Rebel.* Wilmington, N.C.: Broadfoot Publishing Co., 1987.

Parrish, William E. *A History of Missouri.* Vol. 3, *1860 to 1875.* Columbia: University of Missouri Press, 1973.

———. *Turbulent Partnership: Missouri and the Union, 1861–1865.* Columbia: University of Missouri Press, 1963.

Peterson, Richard C., et al. *Sterling Price's Lieutenants: A Guide to the Officers and Organization of the Missouri State Guard, 1861–1865.* Shawnee Mission, Kans.: Two Trails Publishing, 1995.

Phillips, Christopher. *Damned Yankee: The Life of General Nathaniel Lyon.* Columbia: University of Missouri Press, 1990.

Pollard, Edward A. *The Lost Cause: A New Southern History of the War of the Confederates.* New York: E. B. Treat and Co., 1866.

Prentis, Noble L. *Kansas Miscellanies.* Topeka: Kansas Publishing House, 1889.

Price, Captain Richard Scott. *Nathaniel Lyon: Harbinger from Kansas.* Springfield: Wilson's Creek National Battlefield Foundation, 1990.

Quarles, Benjamin. *The Negro in the Civil War.* Boston; Little, Brown, 1953.

Rea, Ralph R. *Sterling Price: The Lee of the West.* Little Rock: Pioneer Press, 1959.

Reavis, Logan U. *The Life and Military Service of Gen. William Selby Harney.* St. Louis: Bryan, Brand and Co., 1878.

Report of the Adjutant General of the State of Kansas, 1861–'65. 2 vols. Topeka: J. K. Hudson, 1896.

Rippley, La Vern J. *The German-Americans.* Twayne Publishers, ca. 1976.

Roberts, Bobby, and Carl Moneyhon. *Portraits of Conflict: A Photographic History of Arkansas in the Civil War.* Fayetteville: University of Arkansas Press, 1987.

Robertson, James I., Jr. *Soldiers Blue and Gray.* Columbia: University of South Carolina Press, 1988.

Rombauer, Robert J. *The Union Cause in St. Louis in 1861.* St. Louis: St. Louis Municipal Centennial, 1909.

Rose, Victor. *The Life and Services of Gen. Ben McCulloch.* 1888. Reprint, Austin: Steck Co., 1958.

Roster and Record of Iowa Soldiers in the War of the Rebellion, Together with Historical Sketches of Volunteer Organizations, 1861–1866. Vol. 1, *1st–8th Regiments—Infantry.* Des Moines: Emory H. English, State Printer, 1908.

Scharf, J. Thomas. *History of St. Louis City and County, from the Earliest Periods to the Present Day: Including Biographical Sketches of Representative Men.* 2 vols. Philadelphia: Louis H. Everts and Co., 1883.

Schrantz, Ward L. *Jasper County, Missouri, in the Civil War.* Carthage, Mo.: Carthage Press, ca. 1923.

Sergent, Mary Elizabeth. *They Lie Forgotten: The United States Military Academy, 1856–1861, Together with a Class Album for the Class of May, 1861.* Middletown, N.Y.: Prior King Press, ca. 1986.

Shalhope, Robert E. *Sterling Price: Portrait of a Southerner.* Columbia: University of Missouri Press, 1971.

Speer, William S., ed. *The Encyclopedia of the New West*. Marshall, Tex.: U.S. Biographical Publishing Co., 1881.

Steele, Phillip W., and Steve Cotrell. *The Civil War in the Ozarks*. Gretna, La.: Pelican Publishing Co., 1993.

Stuart, A. A. *Iowa Colonels and Regiments: Being a History of Iowa Regiments in the War of the Rebellion*. Des Moines: Mills and Co., 1865.

Swisher, Jacob A. *Iowa in Times of War*. Iowa City: State Historical Society, 1943.

Thomas, Robert B., ed. *Old Farmer's Almanac, No. 69*. Boston: Crosby, Nichols, Lee, and Co., 1861.

Tucker, Philip Thomas. *The South's Finest: The First Missouri Confederate Brigade from Pea Ridge to Vicksburg*. Shippensburg, Pa.: White Mane Publishing Co., Inc., 1993.

Van Crevald, Martin. *Supplying War: Logistics from Wallenstein to Patton*. Cambridge: Cambridge University Press, ca. 1977.

War Department. Record and Pension Office. *Organization and Status of Missouri Troops (Union and Confederate) in Service during the Civil War*. Washington, D.C.: Government Printing Office, 1902.

Warner, Ezra J. *Generals in Blue: Lives of the Union Commanders*. Baton Rouge: Louisiana State University Press, 1964.

——. *Generals in Gray: Lives of the Confederate Commanders*. Baton Rouge: Louisiana State University Press, 1959.

Webb, W. L. *Battles and Biographies of Missourians; or, The Civil War Period in Our State*. Kansas City: Hudson-Kimberly Publishing Co., 1900.

——. *The Centennial History of Independence, Mo*. N.p., ca. 1927.

Wilder, D. W. *The Annals of Kansas*. Topeka: T. Dwight Thatcher, Kansas Publishing House, 1886.

Wiley, Bell I. *The Life of Billy Yank: The Common Soldier of the Union*. Baton Rouge: Louisiana State University Press, 1952.

——. *The Life of Johnny Reb: The Common Soldier of the Confederacy*. Baton Rouge: Louisiana State University Press, 1943.

Winsor, Bill. *Texas in the Confederacy: Military Installations, Economy and People*. Hillsboro: Hill Junior College Press, 1978.

Winter, William C. *The Civil War in St. Louis*. St. Louis: Missouri Historical Society Press, 1994.

Winters, John D. *The Civil War in Louisiana*. Baton Rouge: Louisiana State University Press, 1963.

Wooten, Dudley G., ed. *A Comprehensive History of Texas*. 2 vols. Dallas: William G. Scarff, 1898.

Wyatt-Brown, Bertram. *Honor and Violence in the Old South*. New York: Oxford University Press, 1986.

Zucker, A. E., ed. *The Forty-Eighters: Political Refugees of the German Revolution of 1848*. New York: Columbia University Press, 1950.

Articles

Anderson, Thomas F. "The Indian Territory." *Confederate Veteran* 4 (March 1896): 85–87.

Austin, Robert A. "Battle of Wilson's Creek." *Missouri Historical Review* 27 (October 1932): 46–49.

Bomar, Joe Lee. "The Audrain Country Flag." *Confederate Veteran* 36 (March 1928): 98–99.

Caldwell, Martha B. "The Stubbs." *Kansas Historical Quarterly* 6 (1937): 124–31.

Castel, Albert, ed. "The Diary of General Henry Little, C.S.A." *Civil War Times Illustrated* 9 (October 1972): 5–11, 41–47.

"Clayton, Powell." *Dictionary of American Biography.* 20 vols., supp. New York: Charles Scribner's Sons, 1928–81, 4:187–88.

Covington, James W. "The Camp Jackson Affair." *Missouri Historical Review* 55 (April 1961): 197–212.

Dirck, Brian. " 'We Have Whipped Them Beautifully': The Arkansas Press and Wilson's Creek." *Missouri Historical Review* 84 (April 1990): 270–92.

"Eagle, James P." In *The National Cyclopedia of American Biography.* 62 vols., supp., 10:191–92. New York: James T. White and Co., 1898–1984.

First, Paco E. "Personality." *America's Civil War* 5 (July 1992): 8, 69–71.

Fischer, LeRoy H., and Jerry Gill. "Confederate Indian Forces outside of the Indian Territory." *Chronicles of Oklahoma* 46 (Autumn 1968): 249–84.

Fischer, LeRoy H., and Larry C. Rampp. "Quantrill's Civil War Operations in Indian Territory." *Chronicles of Oklahoma* 46 (Summer 1968): 155–81.

"Gov. Thomas J. Churchill." In *The Encyclopedia of the New West,* edited by William S. Speer, 18–19. Marshall, Tex.: U.S. Biographical Publishing Co., 1881.

Gunn, Jack W. "Ben McCulloch: A Big Captain." *Southwestern Historical Quarterly* 62 (July 1954): 1–21.

"Halderman, John A." In *The National Cyclopedia of American Biography.* 62 vols., supp., 7:556. New York: James T. White and Co., 1898–1984.

Hess, Earl J. "Osterhaus in Missouri: A Study in German-American Loyalty." *Missouri Historical Review* 78 (January 1984): 144–66.

"Hon. Charles Mitchell." *The Encyclopedia of the New West.* Edited by William S. Speer, 58–60. Marshall, Tex.: U.S. Biographical Publishing Co., 1881.

Hyde, Mrs. Charles R. "A Confederate Soldier from Arkansas." *Confederate Veteran* 37 (February 1929): 61–62.

"Jones, Daniel Webster." In *The National Cyclopedia of American Biography.* 62 vols., supp., 10; 193–94. New York: James T. White and Co., 1898–84.

Kirkpatrick, Arthur Roy. "Missouri in the Early Months of the Civil War." *Missouri Historical Review* 15 (April 1961): 235–66.

Long, E. B. "Frémont, Lyon, and Wilson's Creek." *Westerner's Brand Book* 14 (January 1958): 81–83.

McNeil, My Kinneth. "Confederate Treaties with the Tribes of Indian Territory." *Chronicles of Oklahoma* 42 (Winter 1964–65): 408–20.

Madaus, Howard Michael, and Robert D. Needham. "Unit Colors of the Trans-Mississippi Confederacy." Part 1. *Military Collector and Historian* 41 (Fall 1989): 123–41.

Malin, James C. "The Burlington, Iowa, Apprenticeship of the Kansas Poet Eugene Fitch Ware, 'Ironquill.' " *Iowa Journal of History* 52 (July 1959): 193–230.

Martin, George W. "The George Smith Memorial Library." *Collection of the Kansas State Historical Society, 1913–14* 13 (1914): 399–406.

Martin, Richard D. "First Regiment Iowa Volunteers." *Palimpsest* 46 (January 1965): 1–63.

Meserve, John Bartlett. "The Mayes." *Chronicles of Oklahoma* 15 (March 1937): 56–65.

Miller, Robert E. "General Mosby M. Parsons: Missouri Secessionist." *Missouri Historical Review* 80 (October 1985): 33–57.

Montgomery, Don, ed. "Far from Home and Kindred: The History of Confederate Companies Raised in Hempstead County." *Hempstead County Historical Society* 12 (Spring 1988): 12–24.

Newberry, Farrar. "Harris Flanagin." In *Arkansas in the Civil War*, edited by John Ferguson, 57–77. Little Rock: Arkansas History Commission, n.d.

Oates, Stephen B. "Texas under the Secessionists." *Southwestern Historical Quarterly* 67 (October 1963): 167–212.

Odom, Van D. "The Political Career of Thomas Overton Moore: Secession Governor of Louisiana." *Louisiana Historical Quarterly* 26 (October 1943): 3–35.

Osbourne, Vincent J. "Vincent Osbourne's Civil War Experience." *Kansas Historical Quarterly* 20 (February 1952): 108–33.

"Payne, John W." *The Encyclopedia of the New West*. Edited by William S. Speer, 278. Marshall, Tex.: U.S. Biographical Publishing Co., 1881.

Peterson, Dawn. "Battling for Freedom." *Springfield News Leader*, February 2, 1994.

Piston, William Garrett. "The 1st Iowa Volunteers: Honor and Community in a Ninety-Day Regiment." *Civil War History* 44 (March 1998): 5–23.

"Professor Charles Charlton." *The Encyclopedia of the New West*. Edited by William S. Speer, 328–29. Marshall, Tex.: U.S. Biographical Publishing Co., 1881.

Rorvig, Paul. "The Significant Skirmish: The Battle of Boonville, June 17, 1861." *Missouri Historical Review* 86 (January 1992): 127–48.

Scott, Kim, and Robert Myers. "The Extinct 'Grass Eaters' of Benton County: A Reconstructed History of the Harmonial Vegetarian Society." *Arkansas Historical Quarterly* 50 (Summer 1991): 140–57.

Shrader, Charles R. "Field Logistics in the Civil War." In *The U.S. Army War College Guide to the Battle of Antietam: The Maryland Campaign of 1862*, edited by Jay Luvaas and Harold W. Nelson, 255–84. Carlisle, Pa.: South Mountain Press, 1987.

"Springfield in 1835." *Missouri Historical Review* 31 (July 1935): 479–80.

Stevenson, Charles G. "The Search for Sokalski." In *A Civil War Centennial Tribute to Lt. Col. George O. Sokalski*. Troy, N.Y.: N.p., 1964.

Strother, Fay O. "An Arkansas General." *Arkansas Democrat Magazine*, December 30, 1962.

Throne, Mildred. "The First Battle—Wilson's Creek." *Palimpsest* 40 (September 1959): 373–77.

"Totten, James." In *Appleton's Cyclopedia of American Biography*. 6 vols. New York: D. Appleton and Co., 1899.

Trickett, Dean. "The Civil War in the Indian Territory, 1861." *Chronicles of Oklahoma* 18 (June 1940): 142–53.

Turner, Mary Nell, ed. "Hempstead County's Men Beat Their Plowshares into Swords: Excerpts from Journals and Letters." *The Hempstead County Historical Society* 12 (Spring 1988): 12–24.

Vandiver, W. D. "Reminiscences of General John B. Clark." *Missouri Historical Review* 20 (January 1926): 223–35.

———."Two Forgotten Heroes—John Hanson McNeill and His Son Jesse." *Missouri Historical Review* 21 (April 1927): 404–19

Warner, Charles H., and A. A. McGinnis, comps. "Captain Gib's Company, C.S.A." *The Independence County Chronicle* 2:46–56.

Wooster, Ralph A., and Robert Wooster. " 'Rarin' for a Fight': Texans in the Confederate Army." *Southwestern Historical Quarterly* 84 (April 1981): 387–426.

Theses and Dissertations

Ashcraft, Allan Coleman. "Texas, 1860–1865: The Lone Star State in the Civil War." Ph.D. diss., Columbia University, 1960.

Avery, Orville Ellis. "Confederate Defense of Texas, 1861–1865." M.A. thesis, University of Oklahoma, 1940.

Boeck, George Albert. "An Early Iowa Community: Aspects of Economic, Social, and Political Development in Burlington, Iowa, 1833–1866." Ph.D. diss., University of Iowa, 1961.

Crawford, Golda. "The Organization of the Kansas Troops in the Civil War." M.A. thesis, Kansas State College, 1990.

Crow, James Burchell. "Confederate Military Operations in Texas, 1861–1865." M.A. thesis, North Texas State College, 1957.

Felgar, Robert Patterson. "Texas in the War for Southern Independence, 1861–1865." Ph.D. diss., University of Texas, 1935.

Geise, William Royston. "The Confederate Military Forces in the Trans-Mississippi West, 1861–1865: A Study in Command." Ph.D. diss., University of Texas at Austin, 1974.

Meeks, Walter A. "The Role of Fort Scott, Kansas, in the Civil War." M.S. thesis, Kansas State Teacher's College, 1952.

Miller, Robert E. "Missouri Secessionist: General Mosby M. Parsons." M.A. thesis, University of Missouri–St. Louis, n.d.

Simmons, Lucy. "The Life of Sterling Price." M.A. thesis, University of Chicago, 1922.

Snyder, Perry Anderson. "Shreveport, Louisiana, during the Civil War and Reconstruction." Ph.D. diss., Florida State University, 1979.

Sturdevant, Rick Willard. "Girding for War: Conditions Underlying the Response of Iowa Counties to Troop Calls, 1861–1862." M.A. thesis, University of Northern Iowa, 1974.

Westover, John Glendower. "The Evolution of the Missouri Militia." Ph.D. diss., University of Missouri, 1948.

Whitworth, Bonnye Ruth. "The Role of Texas in the Confederate Government." M.A. thesis, Texas State College, 1951.

Index

Steele, Frederick, 139–40, 169, 184–85,
200, 205, 219, 237, 263, 282–83, 331,
338
Steele, John, 191
Steen, Alexander E., 114, 115, 223, 252
Stein, Michael W., 71
Steuben Guards, 62, 64, 275
Stewartville Rifles, 90
Stirman, Ras, 113, 114, 281
Stockton, Job B., 64, 69, 168
Stone, G. Harry, 175–76
Streaper, George F., 72–73, 323
"Stubbs, the." *See* Oread Guards
Sturgis, Samuel D., 13–14, 59, 69, 70–71,
75, 105, 118, 145, 166–67, 169, 173–74,
181–83, 186, 232, 263, 270, 274, 276,
282–83, 286, 289, 302–3, 305–7, 321,
329, 331, 337
Sweeny, Thomas W., 35, 76, 79, 105,
118–33 passim, 145, 173, 178, 180, 245,
268, 330
Swift, Francis P., 68
Switzler, Theodore A., 185, 199, 215, 219

Tanner, Robert, 236
Texas Hunters, 21, 23, 67, 224, 271
Third Arkansas Infantry. *See* Third
Infantry, Arkansas State Troops
Third Infantry, Arkansas State Troops,
98, 113, 136, 154, 208–9, 275–77, 281,
335
Third Louisiana Volunteer Infantry, 7–11,
18, 92, 93, 94, 100, 110–11, 114, 136, 141,
149–50, 154, 157, 160, 163, 213–19, 250–
52, 254, 270, 282–83, 292, 312, 321, 330,
335
Third Missouri Volunteer Infantry, 31,
34–35, 41, 76–77, 103, 119, 188–90, 222,
230, 247–61 passim, 310, 337
Third U.S. Infantry, 114
Thirteenth Illinois Volunteer Infantry, 47,
79, 262, 283, 338
Tholen, William, 268
Thomas, B. L., 224
Thomas, W. H. H., 87
Thompson, Edward F., 299
Thompson, Gideon W., 206
Thompson, M. Jeff, 165
Thornton, John C. C., 155, 206
Titsworth, John R., 17

Tod, Corporal. *See* Todt, Charles
Todt, Charles, 253
Toomer, John, 163
Topeka Rifles, 62
Totten, James, 12–13, 44, 73, 99, 112,
142–43, 145, 170, 181, 183, 197, 201,
203–5, 218, 232, 237–39, 263–65, 272,
275–77, 282–83, 337
Totten, William, 12
Totten Light Battery, 13–14, 17, 95, 98,
112. *See also* Pulaski Light Battery
Totten's Battery. *See* Second U.S.
Artillery: Company F
Tracy, Elisah L., 7, 10–11
Trask, Edward, 61
Tunnard, William F., 4–6, 218
Tunnard, William H. (Willie), 5, 93, 95,
100, 149–50, 163, 214–16, 218, 251,
253–54
Turners. *See* Turnverein
Turner Society. *See* Turnverein
Turnverein, 24–37 passim, 188

Uniforms, 11, 16–17, 21, 41–42, 52–53, 63,
65, 79, 82–83, 117, 133, 179, 205, 213,
243, 255, 274, 324
Union Rifles, 61, 62, 67, 326
U.S. Reserve Corps, 33–34

Van Dorn, Earl, 329
Vaughn, George, 82
Vernon Guards, 196
Vernon Rangers, 196
Vigilini, John P., 11, 251, 253–54, 322
Voerster, John D., 74, 337
Volunteer Militia of Missouri, 32, 88

Walcott, T. G., 251
Waldron,, George W., 55
Walker, John J., 134–35
Walker, Jonathan D., 98, 155, 208, 275,
336
Walker, Samuel, 68, 70, 275
Wallace, James, 264
Walling, Nelson, 22
Ware, Eugene F., 51, 72–73, 104, 125–27,
130–31, 138, 168, 171, 180–81, 187, 263,
280, 306
Washington Blues, 26, 32–33, 82, 87–88,
155, 207, 233, 241, 287

Washington Guards (Muscatine, Iowa),
47, 49, 51, 318, 325
Washington Guards (St. Louis, Mo.), 26,
87, 155
Watie, Stand, 92
Watkins, Nathaniel W., 37
Watson, William, 3–5, 8–11, 92, 154, 157,
159, 163, 214–15, 217–19, 252, 282–83,
292, 301
Weapons, 11, 17–31 passim, 44, 54, 63, 69,
86–88, 94, 122–23, 128, 130, 136, 143,
167, 189, 229, 239
Weaver, Mary E., 111–13
Weaver, Omer R., 111–13, 204, 213, 298,
302
Weaver, Samuel M., 112
Weigel, Josephine, 35
Weightman, Richard H., 155, 157, 208,
242–43, 270, 275, 336
Weightman's Brigade, 155, 275, 332, 336
Wells, O. J., 214
Wentz, Augustus, 49, 56, 325
Western Army, 135–37, 140, 148–63 pas-
sim, 192, 208, 213, 223, 246, 257, 260,
286–87, 300–301, 308, 311, 313, 317,
323, 335–37
Wherry, William M., 265, 331–32
Whetstone, E. A., 256
White, Matson K., 98
White, W. H., 288
Wide-Awakes, 26, 34, 37
Wigfall Cavalry, 22, 224
Wilkie, Franc B., 50, 57–58, 72, 120, 129,
130, 281, 294–95, 298, 317, 323
Wilson, James, 151
Wilson, T. B., 21
Wilson Creek: correct name of, 138;
described, 151–52

Wilson Guards, 49, 52–53, 325
Windsor Guards, 227
Wingo, Edmund T., 155, 207, 239, 276,
336
Wingo's Regiment, 81, 207, 239, 276,
336
Winn, Larkin, 153–54
Winn, Sofronia, 153
Winn farm, 153, 192, 201, 203, 208, 213,
233, 250, 275
Winn Rifles, 5–6, 251
Winston, Thomas W., 21, 224
Wiswell, James H., 70, 216, 218
Wood, Henry C., 182, 331–32, 337
Wood, John W., 299
Wood, Samuel N., 68, 126–27, 129,
160, 175, 181, 183–84, 187, 200, 272,
337–38
Woodruff, William E., Jr., 12, 95, 98–100,
149–50, 156, 160, 201, 203–4, 208–9,
212, 215, 233, 238, 255, 275, 286, 298,
336
Woodruff, William E., Sr., 12
Worsham, T. A., 332
Wright, Clark, 185, 199, 215, 219
Wyandotte Guards, 198, 275
Wyandotte Volunteers, 62, 64
Wyatt, John, 146–47, 150, 160, 291, 294,
296, 329
Wyman, John B., 79

Yates, Theodore, 198, 241, 274
Yeakly, Fannie, 66
Yell County Rifles, 93
Young, Cyrus M., 264

Zesch, Gustavus, 64, 275
Zublin, Ralph D., 104